Street by Street

GW00402886

PORTSMOUTH SOUTHAMPTON

EASTLEIGH, FAREHAM, GOSPORT, HAVANT, WINCHESTER

Chandler's Ford, Hayling Island, Hedge End, Horndean, Hythe, Lyndhurst, Portchester, Romsey, Southsea, Waterlooville

Ist edition May 2001

Published by AA Publishing (a trading name of Automobile Association Developments Limited, whose registered office is Norfolk House, Priestley Road, Basingstoke, Hampshire, RG24 9NY.
Registered number 1878835).

Mapping produced by the Cartographic Department of The Automobile Association.

ISBN 0 7495 2360 3

A CIP Catalogue record for this book is available from the British Library.

Printed by G. Canale & C. S.P.A., Torino, Italy

Ref: MX005

Key to map pages ii-iii

Key to map symbols iv-1

Enlarged scale pages 2-19

Street by Street 20-139

Index – towns & villages 140-141

Index – streets 141-159

Index – featured places 159-162

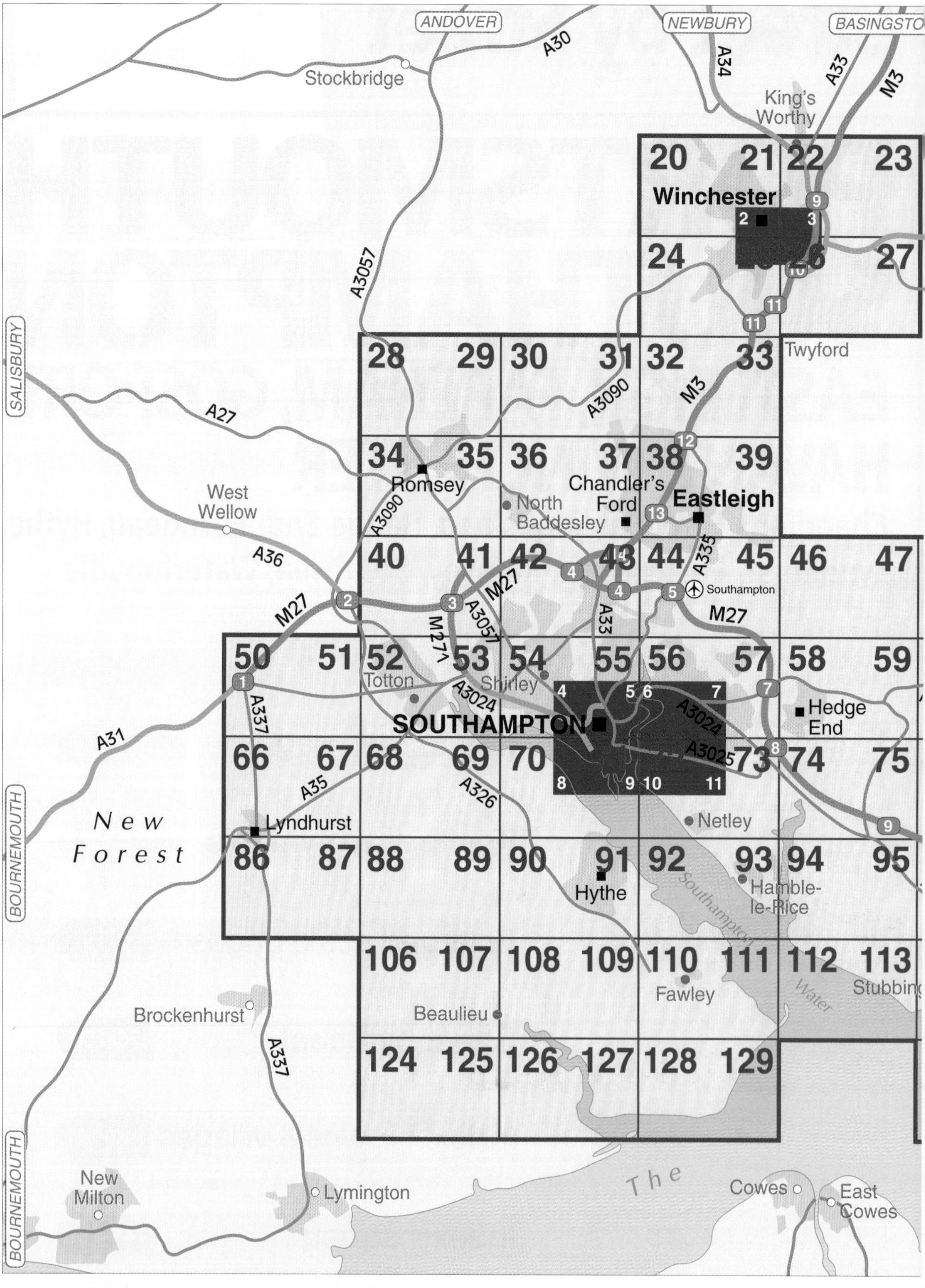

Enlarged scale pages **1:10,000** **6.3 inches to 1 mile**

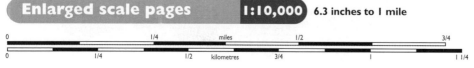

miles	0, 1/4, 1/2, 3/4
kilometres	0, 1/4, 1/2, 3/4, 1, 1 1/4

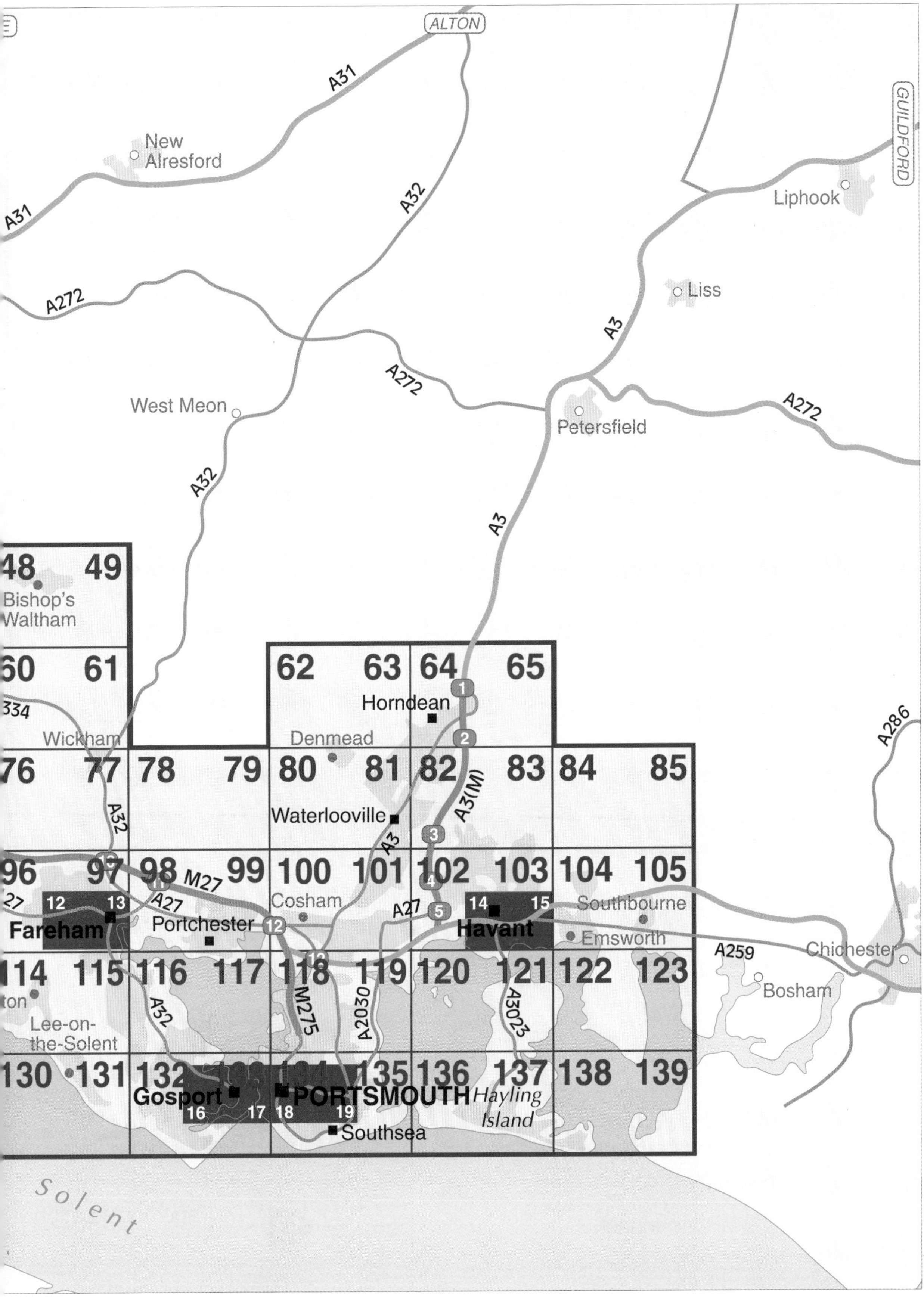

4.2 inches to 1 mile

Scale of main map pages 1:15,000

miles: 0 — 1/4 — 1/2 — 3/4 — 1

kilometres: 0 — 1/4 — 1/2 — 3/4 — 1 — 1 1/4 — 1 1/2 — 1 3/4

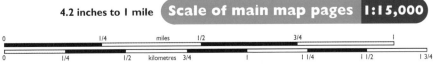

Junction 9	Motorway & junction
Services	Motorway service area
	Primary road single/dual carriageway
Services	Primary road service area
	A road single/dual carriageway
	B road single/dual carriageway
	Other road single/dual carriageway
	Restricted road
	Private road
	One way street
	Pedestrian street
	Track/ footpath
	Road under construction
	Road tunnel
P	Parking
P+	Park & Ride
	Bus/coach station
	Railway & main railway station
	Railway & minor railway station
	Underground station
	Light railway & station
	Preserved private railway
LC	Level crossing
	Tramway
	Ferry route
	Airport runway
	Boundaries- borough/ district
	Mounds
93	Page continuation 1:15,000
7	Page continuation to enlarged scale 1:10,000

	River/canal lake, pier		Toilet with disabled facilities
	Aqueduct lock, weir		Petrol station
465 Winter Hill	Peak (with height in metres)	PH	Public house
	Beach	PO	Post Office
	Coniferous woodland		Public library
	Broadleaved woodland		Tourist Information Centre
	Mixed woodland		Castle
	Park		Historic house/ building
	Cemetery	Wakehurst Place NT	National Trust property
	Built-up area		Museum/ art gallery
	Featured building		Church/chapel
	City wall		Country park
A&E	Accident & Emergency hospital		Theatre/ performing arts
	Toilet		Cinema

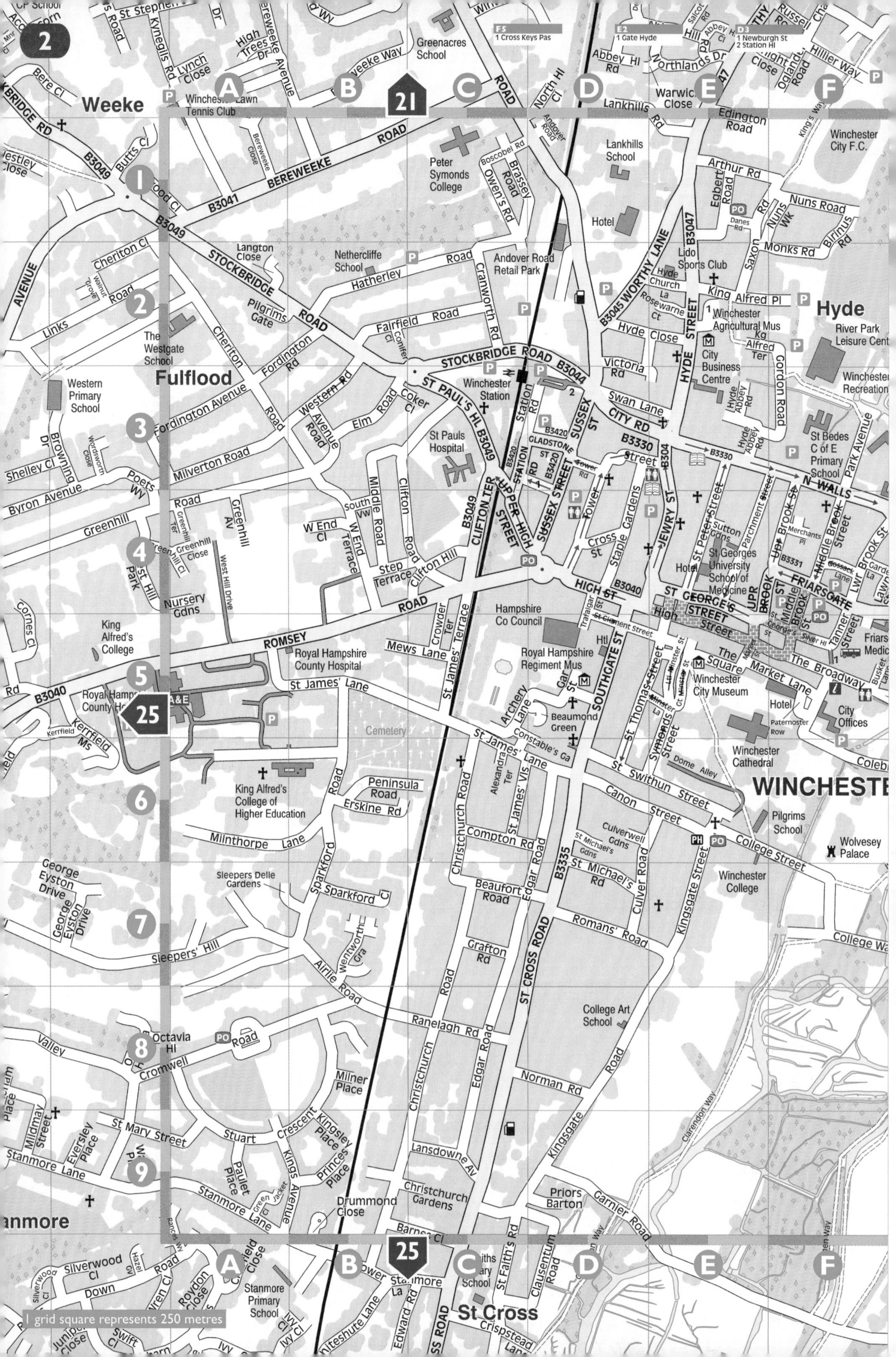
2
Weeke
Fulflood
Hyde
WINCHESTER
St Cross
Stanmore
21
25
A
B
C
D
E
F
1
2
3
4
5
6
7
8
9
F5 1 Cross Keys Pas
E2 1 Gate Hyde
D3 1 Newburgh St 2 Station Hl
Greenacres School
Winchester Lawn Tennis Club
Peter Symonds College
Lankhills School
Winchester City F.C.
Nethercliffe School
Andover Road Retail Park
Lido Sports Club
Winchester Agricultural Mus
City Business Centre
River Park Leisure Centre
The Westgate School
Western Primary School
Winchester Station
St Pauls Hospital
St Bedes C of E Primary School
Hampshire Co Council
Royal Hampshire Regiment Mus
Royal Hampshire County Hospital
King Alfred's College
King Alfred's College of Higher Education
Cemetery
Winchester City Museum
Winchester Cathedral
City Offices
Pilgrims School
Wolvesey Palace
Winchester College
College Art School
Sleepers Delle Gardens
Stanmore Primary School
University School of Medicine
Beaumond Green
Hotel
STOCKBRIDGE ROAD
BEREWEEKE ROAD
ROMSEY ROAD
ST CROSS ROAD
WORTHY LANE
HYDE STREET
HIGH ST
ST GEORGE'S STREET
SOUTHGATE ST
FRIARSGATE
N WALLS
CITY RD
UPPER HIGH STREET
CLIFTON TER
Christchurch Road
Kingsgate Road
Canon Street
St Swithun Street
College Street
Romans' Road
Airlie Road
Sleepers' Hill
Milnthorpe Lane
St James' Lane
Stanmore Lane
St Mary Street
Cromwell Road
Garnier Road
1 grid square represents 250 metres

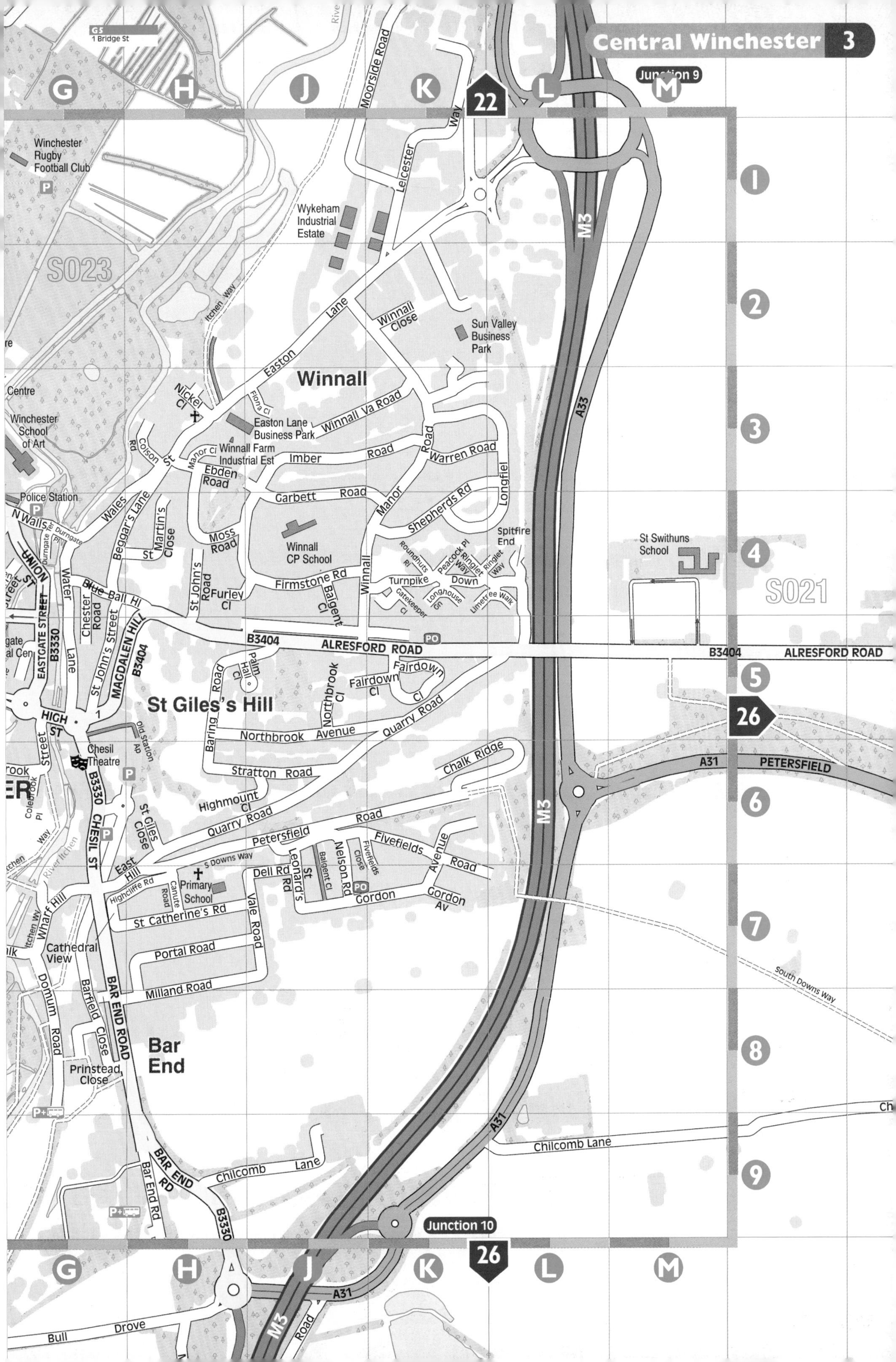
G5
1 Bridge St
G
H
J
K
22
L
M
Junction 9
Moorside Road
Winchester
Rugby
Football Club
P
Wykeham
Industrial
Estate
Leicester
Way
M3
S023
Itchen Way
Lane
Easton
Winnall
Close
Sun Valley
Business
Park
Winnall
Nickel
Cl
Flona Cl
Easton Lane
Business Park
Winnall Va Road
Winnall Farm
Industrial Est
Centre
Winchester
School
of Art
Colson
Rd
St
Manor Cl
Ebden
Road
Imber
Road
Road
Warren Road
Carbett
Road
Manor
Shepherds Rd
Longfiel
A33
Police Station
P
N Walls
Ter Durngate
Durngate Pl
Wales
Beggar's Lane
St Martin's
Close
St
Moss
Road
Winnall
CP School
Spitfire
End
St Swithuns
School
UNION ST
Water
Lane
Chester
Road
Blue Ball Hi
St John's
Road
Furley
Cl
Firmstone Rd
Balgent
Cl
Winnall
Roundhuts
Rl
Peacock Pl
Ringlet
Way
Ringlet
Way
Turnpike
Down
Gatekeeper
Cl
Longhouse
Gn
Limetree Walk
S021
EASTGATE STREET
B3330
St John's Street
MAGDALEN HILL
B3404
B3404
ALRESFORD ROAD
PO
B3404
ALRESFORD ROAD
Palm
Hall
Cl
Baring
Road
Northbrook
Cl
Fairdown
Cl
Fairdown
Cl
5
26
HIGH
ST
1
St Giles's Hill
Old Station
Rd
Northbrook
Avenue
Quarry Road
Chesil
Theatre
P
Street
B3330
Stratton
Road
Chalk Ridge
A31
PETERSFIELD
Highmount
Cl
Quarry Road
Road
St Giles
Close
Petersfield
P
CHESIL ST
Way
S Downs Way
Fivefields
Avenue
Road
Leonard's
Rd
St
Balgent Cl
Nelson Rd
Close
Fivefields
East
Hill
Highcliffe Rd
Canute
Road
Primary
School
Dell Rd
Gordon
PO
Gordon
Av
M3
St Catherine's Rd
Vale Road
Wharf Hill
Itchen Wy
Cathedral
View
Portal Road
South Downs Way
Domum
Road
Barfield
Close
BAR END ROAD
Milland Road
Bar
End
Printstead
Close
P+
A31
Chilcomb Lane
Ch
BAR END
RD
Bar End Rd
Chilcomb
Lane
B3330
P+
Junction 10
G
H
J
K
26
L
M
A31
Bull
Drove
M3
Road
I
2
3
4
5
6
7
8
9

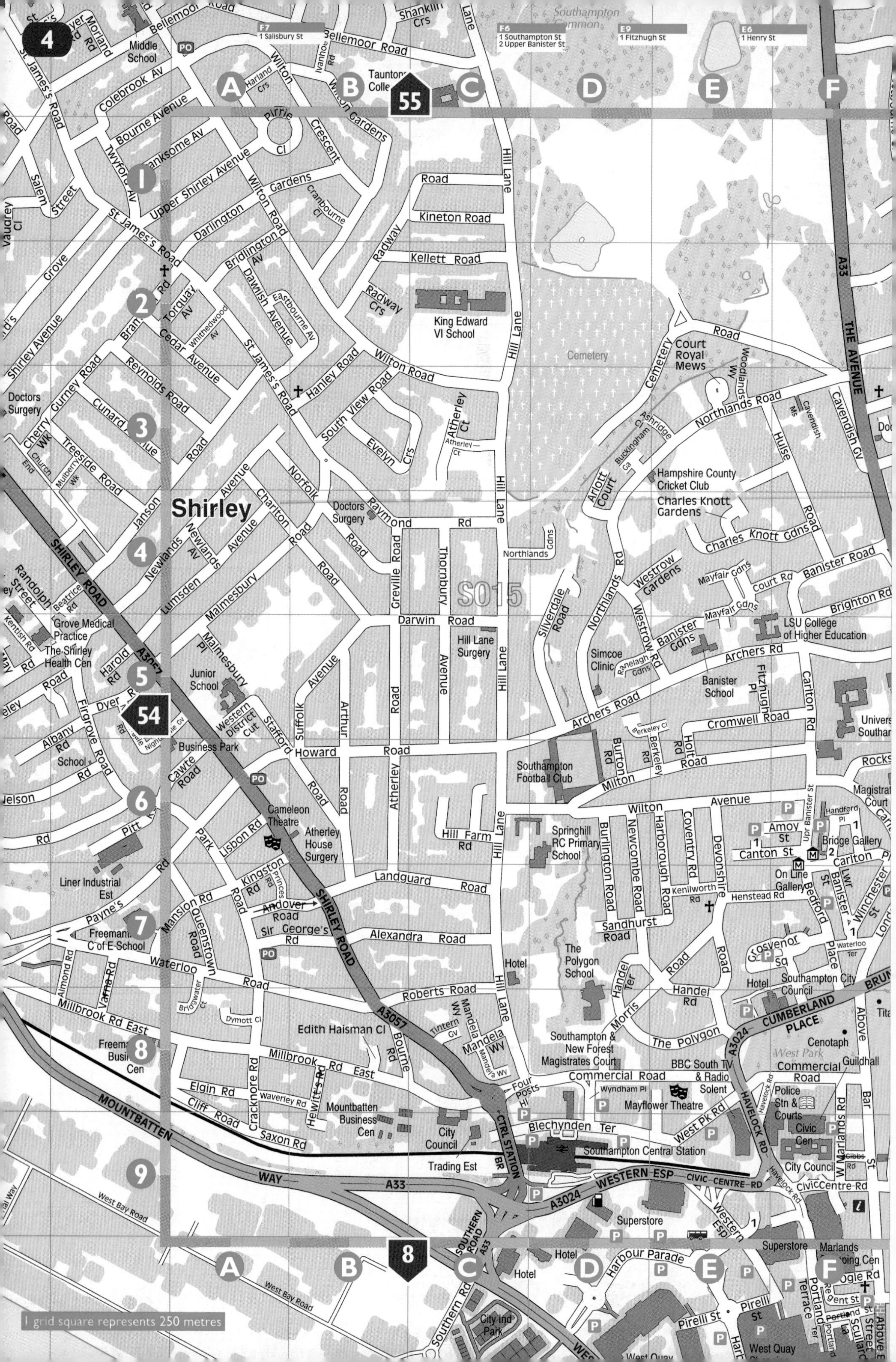
4
F7 1 Salisbury St
F6 1 Southampton St 2 Upper Banister St
E9 1 Fitzhugh St
E6 1 Henry St
55
54
8
A
B
C
D
E
F
1
2
3
4
5
6
7
8
9
Shirley
SO15
Southampton Common
Middle School
Taunton's College
King Edward VI School
Cemetery
Court Royal Mews
Hampshire County Cricket Club
Charles Knott Gardens
Doctors Surgery
Grove Medical Practice
The Shirley Health Cen
Junior School
Business Park
Hill Lane Surgery
Simcoe Clinic
LSU College of Higher Education
Banister School
Southampton Football Club
Cameleon Theatre
Atherley House Surgery
Springhill RC Primary School
The Polygon School
Liner Industrial Est
Freemantle C of E School
Freemantle Business Cen
Edith Haisman Cl
Mountbatten Business Cen
City Council
Trading Est
Southampton & New Forest Magistrates Court
BBC South TV & Radio Solent
Mayflower Theatre
Southampton Central Station
Hotel
Superstore
Southampton City Council
Cenotaph
West Park
Guildhall
Police Stn & Courts
Civic Cen
City Council
Bridge Gallery
On Line Gallery
Magistrates Court
Marlands Shopping Cen
City Ind Park
West Quay
Shirley Road
A3057
The Avenue
A33
Hill Lane
Wilton Road
Bellemoor Road
St James's Road
Upper Shirley Avenue
Howard Road
Archers Road
Northlands Road
Banister Road
Brighton Rd
Commercial Road
Cumberland Place
A3024
Western Esp
Civic Centre Rd
Havelock Rd
Mountbatten Way
West Bay Road
Millbrook Rd East
Waterloo Road
Roberts Road
Landguard Road
Alexandra Road
Harbour Parade
Blechynden Ter
Southern Road
Pirelli St
1 grid square represents 250 metres

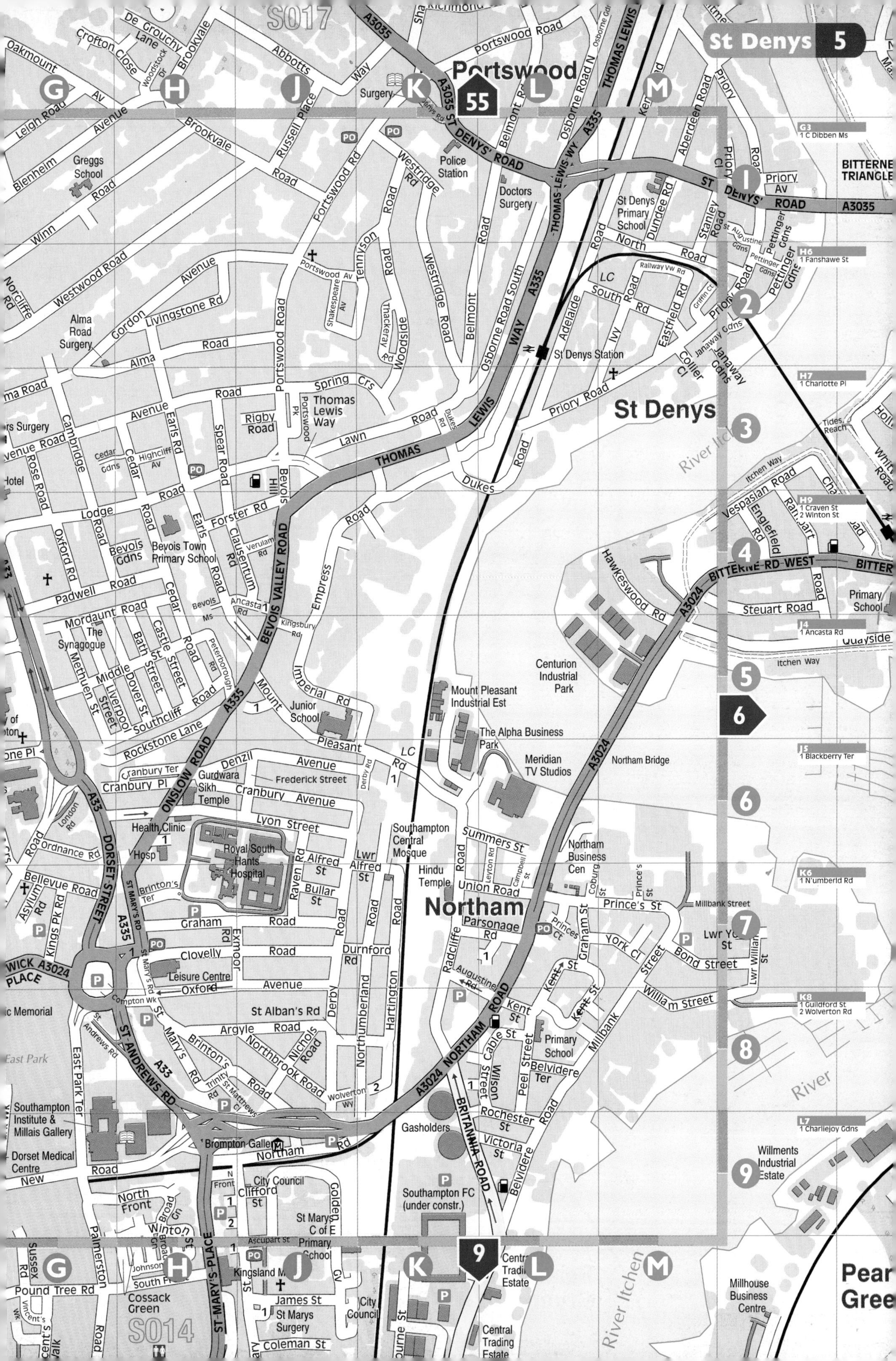

Portswood
55
St Denys
Northam
9
6
SO17
SO14
G
H
J
K
L
M
I
2
3
4
5
6
7
8
9
G3 1 C Dibben Ms
H6 1 Fanshawe St
H7 1 Charlotte Pl
H9 1 Craven St 2 Winton St
J4 1 Ancasta Rd
J5 1 Blackberry Ter
K6 1 N'umberld Rd
K8 1 Guildford St 2 Wolverton Rd
L7 1 Charliejoy Gdns
BITTERNE TRIANGLE
Portswood Road
St Denys' Road
A3035
Thomas Lewis Way
A335
Police Station
Doctors Surgery
St Denys Primary School
St Denys Station
Osborne Road South
Belmont Road
Westridge Road
Woodside Road
Thackeray Rd
Tennyson Road
Shakespeare Av
Portswood Av
Spring Crs
Thomas Lewis Way
Lawn Road
Dukes Road
Priory Road
Janaway Gdns
Collier Cl
Adelaide Road
South Rd
Ivy Rd
Eastfield Rd
Railway Vw Rd
Griffin Ct
North Road
Dundee Rd
Stanley Road
Aberdeen Road
Priory Av
Pettinger Gdns
St Augustine Gdns
River Itchen
Itchen Way
Vespasian Road
Englefield Rd
Bitterne Rd West
A3024
Steuart Road
Primary School
Quayside
Hawkeswood Rd
Centurion Industrial Park
Mount Pleasant Industrial Est
The Alpha Business Park
Meridian TV Studios
Northam Bridge
Empress Road
Imperial Rd
Junior School
Kingsbury Rd
Mount Pleasant Rd
Bevois Valley Road
Onslow Road
Bevois Hill
Bevois Town Primary School
Bevois Gdns
Bevois Ms
Ancasta Rd
Clausentum Rd
Verulam Rd
Forster Rd
Earls Road
Spear Road
Rigby Road
Cedar Road
Highcliff Av
Cedar Gdns
Lodge Road
Oxford Rd
Padwell Road
Mordaunt Road
The Synagogue
Methuen St
Middle Street
Liverpool Street
Dover St
Bath Street
Castle Street
Peterborough Rd
Southcliff Road
Rockstone Lane
Cranbury Ter
Cranbury Pl
Cranbury Avenue
Denzil Avenue
Frederick Street
Gurdwara Sikh Temple
Derby Rd
Lyon Street
Health Clinic
Hosp
Royal South Hants Hospital
Alfred St
Lwr Alfred St
Bullar St
Raven Rd
Brinton's Ter
Graham Road
Clovelly Road
Exmoor Rd
Leisure Centre
Oxford Avenue
St Alban's Rd
Argyle Road
Northbrook Road
Nichols Road
Brinton's Road
Trinity Rd
St Matthews Cl
Durnford Rd
Northumberland Road
Hartington Road
Wolverton Wy
Southampton Central Mosque
Hindu Temple
Summers St
Leyton Rd
Campbell St
Union Road
Parsonage Rd
Radcliffe Road
Augustine Rd
Northam Road
Kent St
Cable St
Wilson Street
Britannia Road
Peel Street
Belvidere Ter
Belvidere Road
Rochester St
Victoria St
Primary School
Gasholders
Southampton FC (under constr.)
Northam Business Cen
Coburg St
Prince's St
Princes Ct
Graham St
York Cl
Kent St
Millbank Street
Bond Street
Lwr York St
Lwr William St
William Street
Willments Industrial Estate
Millhouse Business Centre
Central Trading Estate
Dorset Street
A33
St Mary's Rd
St Andrews Rd
Compton Wk
St Mary's Place
St Andrews Rd
Wick A3024 Place
Ordnance Rd
London Rd
Bellevue Road
Asylum Rd
Kings Pk Rd
East Park
East Park Ter
Southampton Institute & Millais Gallery
Dorset Medical Centre
New Road
North Front
Brompton Gallery
Northam Rd
City Council
Clifford St
Golden Gv
St Marys C of E Primary School
Ascupart St
Broad Gn
Winton St
Johnson St
South Front
Kingsland Mkt
James St
St Marys Surgery
Coleman St
City Council
Cossack Green
Pound Tree Rd
Sussex Rd
Palmerston Road
Vincent's Wk
Alma Road Surgery
Alma Road
Gordon Avenue
Livingstone Rd
Cambridge Road
Avenue Road
Rose Road
Westwood Road
Winn Road
Greggs School
Blenheim Avenue
Brookvale Road
Leigh Road
Oakmount Av
Crofton Close
De Grouchy Lane
Woodstock Dr
Abbotts Way
Russell Place
Portswood Rd
Westridge Rd
Portswood Road N
Osborne Gdns
Kent Rd
Surgery
Norcliffe Rd
Hotel
Pear Green

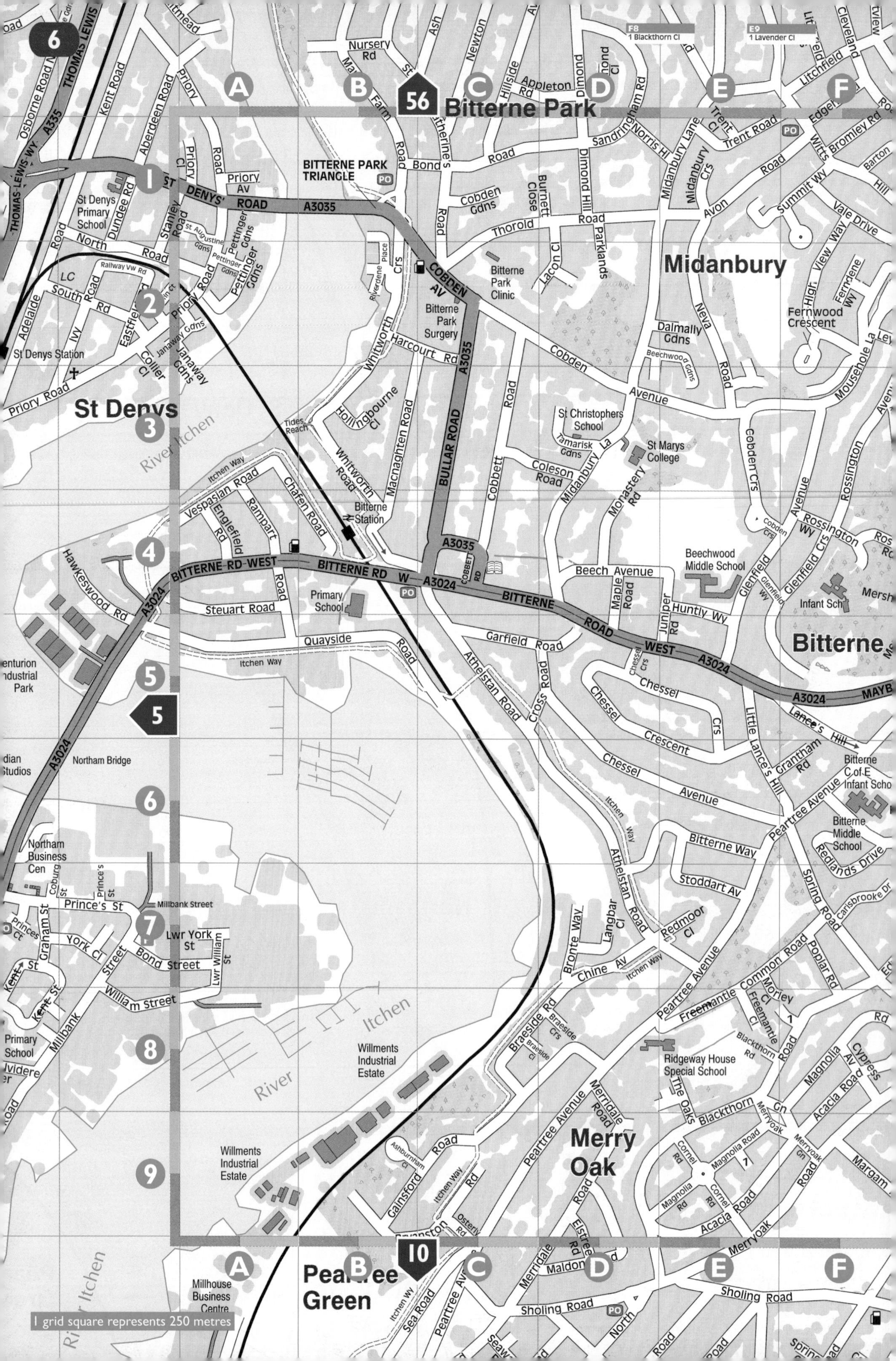

Bitterne Park
56
10
5
A
B
C
D
E
F
1
2
3
4
5
6
7
8
9
F8 1 Blackthorn Cl
E9 1 Lavender Cl
St Denys
Midanbury
Bitterne
Merry Oak
Peartree Green
BITTERNE PARK TRIANGLE
ST DENYS' ROAD
A3035
A3024
A335
THOMAS LEWIS WY
THOMAS LEWIS
Osborne Road
Kent Road
Aberdeen Road
Priory Road
Priory Cl
Priory Av
St Denys Primary School
Dundee Rd
North Road
Stanley Road
St Augustine Gdns
Pettinger Gdns
Railway Vw Rd
LC
South Rd
Adelaide Road
Ivy Road
Eastfield
Janaway Gdns
Collier Cl
St Denys Station
Priory Road
River Itchen
Itchen Way
Vespasian Road
Englefield Rd
Rampart Road
Chafen Road
Tides Reach
Whitworth Road
Whitworth Crs
Hollingbourne Cl
Macnaghten Road
Harcourt Rd
Riverdene Place
Bitterne Station
Bitterne Park Surgery
COBDEN AV
BULLAR ROAD
Bond Rd
Nursery Rd
Manor Farm Road
Ash
St Catherine's Road
Newton
Cobden Gdns
Thorold Road
Bitterne Park Clinic
Hillside Av
Appleton Rd
Dimond Hill
Dimond Cl
Burnett Close
Lacon Cl
Parklands
Sandringham Rd
Norris Hl
Midanbury Lane
Midanbury Crs
Trent Cl
Trent Road
Avon Road
Litchfield
Cleveland
Edge
Witts
Bromley Rd
Barton
Summit Wy
Vale Drive
High View Way
Ferndene Wy
Fernwood Crescent
Mousehole La
Dalmally Gdns
Beechwood Gdns
Neva Road
Cobden Avenue
Cobbett Road
St Christophers School
Tamarisk Gdns
Coleson Road
Midanbury La
St Marys College
Monastery Rd
Cobden Crs
Rossington Avenue
Rossington Wy
Glenfield Crs
Glenfield Wy
Beechwood Middle School
Infant Sch
Beech Avenue
Maple Road
Juniper Rd
Huntly Wy
BITTERNE RD WEST
BITTERNE RD W
BITTERNE ROAD WEST
COBBETT RD
Hawkeswood Rd
Steuart Road
Primary School
Quayside Road
Garfield Road
Athelstan Road
Cross Road
Chessel Crs
Chessel Crescent
Chessel Avenue
Little Lance's Hill
Lance's Hill
Grantham Rd
Peartree Avenue
Bitterne C of E Infant School
Bitterne Middle School
Redlands Drive
Spring Road
Carisbrooke Dr
Bitterne Way
Stoddart Av
Langbar Cl
Bronte Way
Redmoor Cl
Chine Av
Freemantle Common Road
Freemantle Cl
Poplar Rd
Morley Cl
Blackthorn Rd
Ridgeway House Special School
The Oaks
Blackthorn Gn
Magnolia Av
Cypress Av
Acacia Road
Merryoak Gn
Merryoak Road
Magnolia Road
Cornel Rd
Magnolia Rd
Margam
Braeside Rd
Braeside Crs
Braeside Cl
Merridale Road
Peartree Avenue
Elstree Rd
Maldon Road
Sholing Road
Ashburnham Cl
Gainsford Road
Osterly Rd
Swanston Rd
Itchen Wy
Sea Road
Peartree Av
North Road
Centurion Industrial Park
Northam Bridge
Meridian Studios
Northam Business Cen
Coburg St
Prince's St
Millbank Street
Princes Ct
Graham St
York Cl
Lwr York St
Lwr William St
Bond Street
Kent St
William Street
Millbank Street
Primary School
Belvidere
Willments Industrial Estate
Millhouse Business Centre
River Itchen
PO
1 grid square represents 250 metres

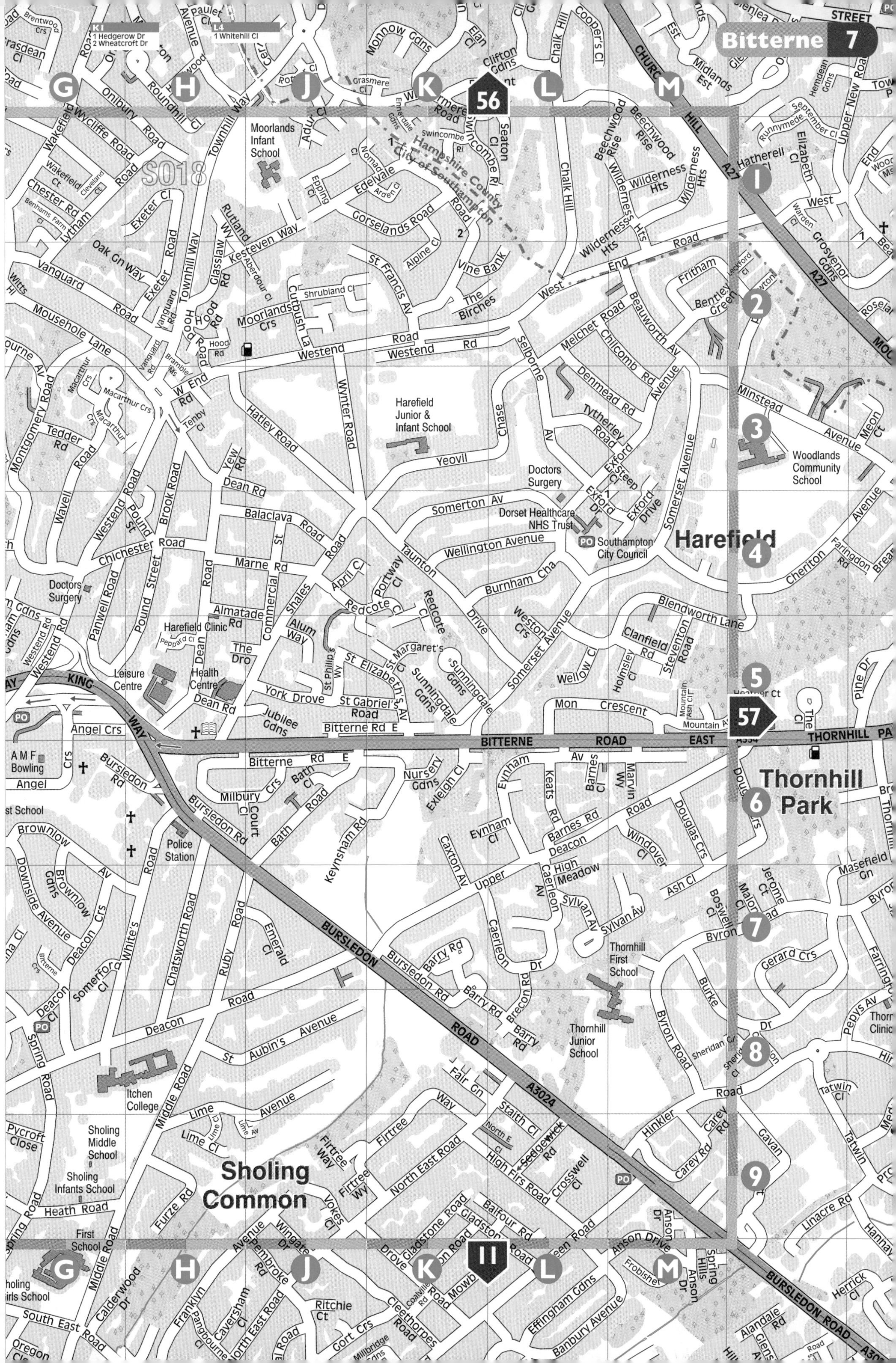
K1
1 Hedgerow Dr
2 Wheatcroft Dr
L4
1 Whitehill Cl
56
57
11
SO18
Hampshire County
City of Southampton
Moorlands Infant School
Harefield Junior & Infant School
Doctors Surgery
Dorset Healthcare NHS Trust
Southampton City Council
Woodlands Community School
Harefield
Harefield Clinic
Leisure Centre
Health Centre
A M F Bowling
Police Station
Thornhill Park
Thornhill First School
Thornhill Junior School
Itchen College
Sholing Middle School
Sholing Infants School
First School
Sholing Common
Wycliffe Road
Onibury Road
Roundhill Cl
Townhill Way
Wakefield Ct
Chester Rd
Lytham Road
Oak Gn Way
Exeter Road
Exeter Cl
Vanguard Road
Mousehole Lane
Rutland Wy
Glasslaw Rd
Kesteven Way
Aberdour Cl
Hood Road
Moorlands Crs
Westend Road
Westend Rd
Cutbush La
Shrubland Cl
Adur Cl
Epping Cl
Edelvale
Gorselands Road
Alpine Cl
St Francis Av
Vine Bank
The Birches
Monnow Gdns
Windermere Road
Swincombe Ri
Seaton Cl
Clifton Gdns
Chalk Hill
Cooper's Cl
Beechwood Rise
Wilderness Hts
West End Road
Fritham
Bentley Green
Melchet Road
Chilcomb Rd
Denmead Rd
Beauworth Av
Tytherley Road
Selborne Av
Chase
Yeovil
Hatley Road
Wynter Road
Minstead Avenue
Meon Ct
Church Hill
A27
Hatherell Cl
Elizabeth Cl
Upper New Road
September Cl
Runnymede
Grosvenor Gdns
Macarthur Crs
Montgomery Road
Tedder Rd
Wavell Road
Westend Road
Pound St
Brook Road
Yew Rd
Dean Rd
Balaclava Road
Chichester Road
Marne Rd
Commercial St
Shales Road
April Cl
Portway Cl
Taunton Drive
Redcote Cl
Somerton Av
Exford Cl
Exford Dr
Exford Drive
Steep Cl
Wellington Avenue
Burnham Cha
Somerset Avenue
Cheriton Avenue
Faringdon Rd
Blendworth Lane
Clanfield Rd
Steventon Road
Holmsley Cl
Wellow Cl
Weston Crs
Mon Crescent
Mountain Av
Heather Ct
Pine Dr
The Cl
Panwell Road
Pound Street
Almatade Rd
Peppard Cl
The Dro
Alum Way
St Phillip's Wy
St Elizabeth's Av
St Margaret's Cl
Sunningdale Gdns
York Drove
St Gabriel's Road
Jubilee Gdns
Bitterne Rd E
King Way
Angel Crs
Angel Crs
Bursledon Rd
BITTERNE ROAD EAST
A334
THORNHILL PARK
Bitterne Rd E
Bath Cl
Bath Road
Milbury Crs
Court Cl
Nursery Gdns
Exleigh Cl
Keynsham Rd
Eynham Av
Eynham Cl
Keats Rd
Barnes Cl
Marvin Wy
Barnes Rd
Deacon Road
Douglas Crs
Windover Cl
Caxton Av
Upper
High Meadow
Caerleon Av
Caerleon Dr
Sylvan Av
Ash Cl
Boswell Cl
Malory Cl
Jerome Ct
Byron Road
Masefield Gn
Gerard Crs
Burke
Byron Road
Sheridan Cl
Pepys Av
Tatwin Cl
Cavan
Linacre Rd
Carey Rd
Hinkler Road
Brownlow Av
Brownlow Gdns
Downside Avenue
Deacon Crs
Somerford Cl
White's Road
Chatsworth Road
Ruby Road
Emerald Cl
BURSLEDON ROAD A3024
Bursledon Rd
Barry Rd
Brecon Rd
Deacon Cl
Spring Road
Deacon Road
St Aubin's Avenue
Middle Road
Lime Avenue
Lime Cl
Pycroft Close
Firtree Way
Fair Gn
Staith Cl
North E Cl
Sedgewick Rd
High Firs Road
Crosswell Cl
North East Road
Furze Rd
Heath Road
Vokes Cl
Gladstone Road
Balfour Rd
Anson Drive
Anson Dr
Spring Hills
Wingate Dr
Pembroke Rd
Calderwood Dr
Franklyn Av
Caversham Cl
Pangbourne Cl
Ritchie Ct
Gort Crs
Cleethorpes Road
Coalville Rd
Mowbray Road
Effingham Gdns
Banbury Avenue
Frobisher
Alandale Rd
Herrick Cl
South East Road
Oregon Cl
Sholing Girls School
BURSLEDON ROAD A3024

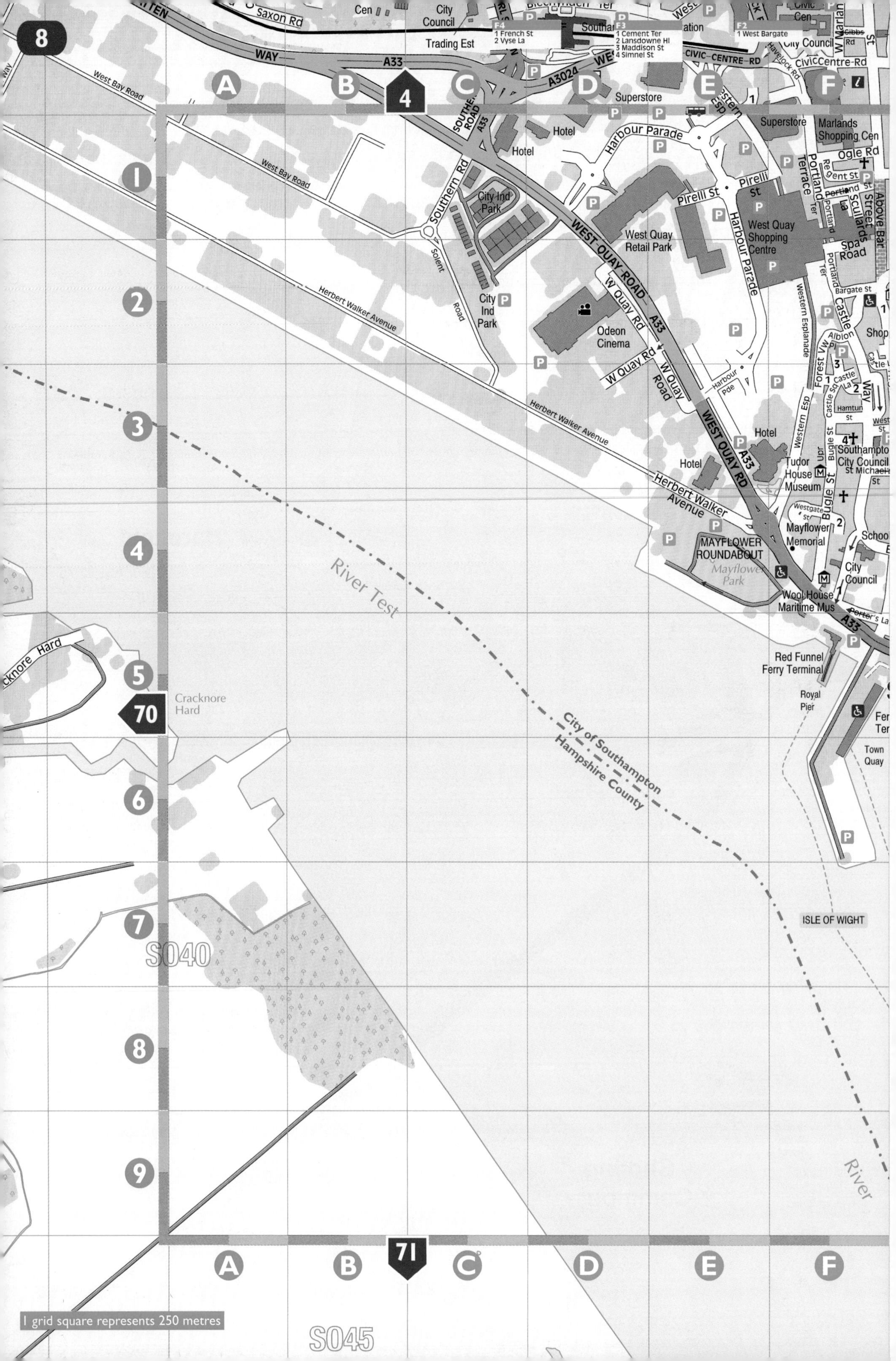

Saxon Rd
City Council
Trading Est
A33
WAY
A3024
CIVIC CENTRE RD
Civic Centre Rd
City Council
F4
1 French St
2 Vyse La
F3
1 Cement Ter
2 Lansdowne Hl
3 Maddison St
4 Simnel St
F2
1 West Bargate
Havelock Rd
W Marlands Rd
Gibbs Rd
West Bay Road
West Bay Road
Superstore
Hotel
Hotel
Harbour Parade
Superstore
Marlands Shopping Cen
Ogle Rd
Regent St
Portland Terrace
Portland Ter
Sculards La
Above Bar Street
Southern Road
A33
Southern Rd
City Ind Park
Solent Road
WEST QUAY ROAD
West Quay Retail Park
Pirelli St
Harbour Parade
West Quay Shopping Centre
Spa Road
Portland Ter
Western Esplanade
Bargate St
Castle Way
Albion Pl
Herbert Walker Avenue
City Ind Park
W Quay Rd
Odeon Cinema
W Quay Rd
W Quay Road
Harbour Pde
Forest Vw
Castle Sq
Castle La
Hamtun St
Western Esp
Hotel
Hotel
WEST QUAY RD
Herbert Walker Avenue
Tudor House Museum
Bugle St
Upr Bugle St
Southampton City Council
St Michael's St
Herbert Walker Avenue
Westgate St
Mayflower Memorial
School
MAYFLOWER ROUNDABOUT
Mayflower Park
City Council
Wool House Maritime Mus
Porter's La
River Test
cknore Hard
Cracknore Hard
70
Red Funnel Ferry Terminal
Royal Pier
Town Quay
City of Southampton
Hampshire County
ISLE OF WIGHT
SO40
River
71
SO45
A B C D E F
1 2 3 4 5 6 7 8 9
1 grid square represents 250 metres

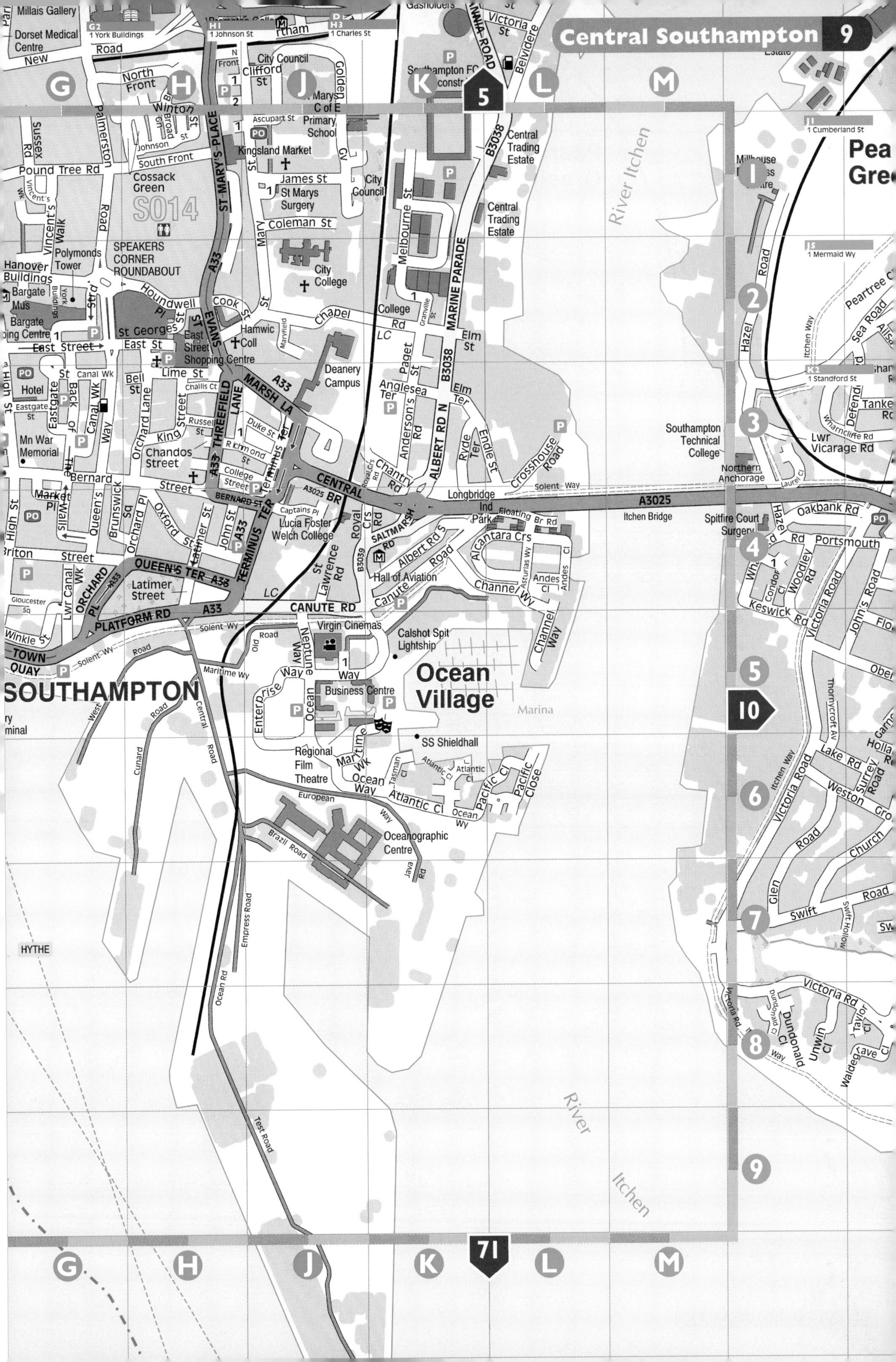
Millais Gallery
Dorset Medical Centre
New Road
G2 1 York Buildings
H1 1 Johnson St
H3 1 Charles St
North Front
Winton St
Broad Grn
Johnson St
South Front
City Council
Clifford St
St Marys C of E Primary School
Golden Gv
Ascupart St
Kingsland Market
James St
St Marys Surgery
Coleman St
Mary St
City Council
City College
Sussex Rd
Palmerston Road
Pound Tree Rd
Cossack Green
SO14
Vincent's Walk
Polymonds Tower
SPEAKERS CORNER ROUNDABOUT
Hanover Buildings
Bargate Mus
Bargate Shopping Centre
York Buildings
Houndwell Pl
Cook St
St Georges St
East Street
East Street Shopping Centre
Hamwic Coll
ST MARY'S PLACE
EVANS ST
A33
Canal Wk
Bell St
Lime St
Challis Ct
Hotel
Eastgate St
Back of Walls
Mn War Memorial
Orchard Lane
King Street
Russell St
Chandos Street
THREEFIELD LANE
MARSH LA
Duke St
Richmond St
College Street
Terminus Ter
Bernard Street
BERNARD ST
Market Pl
High St
Brunswick Sq
Queen's Way
Orchard Pl
Oxford St
Latimer St
John St
TERMINUS TER
Briton Street
Captains Pl
Lucia Foster Welch College
ORCHARD PL
QUEEN'S TER A33
Latimer Street
Gloucester Sq
Lwr Canal Wk
PLATFORM RD
Winkle St
TOWN QUAY
Solent Way
SOUTHAMPTON
CANUTE RD
Deanery Campus
Chapel Rd
MaryField
College Rd
LC
Paget St
Anglesea Ter
Anderson's Rd
Chantry Rd
Royal Crs Rd
Granville St
CENTRAL BR A3025
Southampton FC
Victoria St
Belvidere
5
Central Trading Estate
B3038
MARINE PARADE
Melbourne St
Elm St
Elm Ter
ALBERT RD N
Ryde Ter
Endle St
Crosshouse Road
Longbridge Ind Park
Floating Br Rd
Alcantara Crs
SALTMARSH RD
Albert Rd S
Hall of Aviation
Canute Road
Asturias Wy
Andes Cl
Channel Wy
Channel Way
B3039
St Lawrence Rd
Virgin Cinemas
Calshot Spit Lightship
Ocean Village
Marina
Old Road
Neptune Way
Enterprise Way
Business Centre
Ocean Way
Regional Film Theatre
Maritime Wk
SS Shieldhall
Tasman Cl
Atlantic Cl
Pacific Cl
Pacific Close
Ocean Way
European Way
Brazil Road
Oceanographic Centre
Java Rd
West Road
Cunard Road
Central Road
Maritime Wy
Empress Road
Ocean Rd
Test Road
HYTHE
River Itchen
Itchen Bridge
A3025
Solent Way
Millhouse Business Centre
Hazel Road
Itchen Way
J1 1 Cumberland St
J5 1 Mermaid Wy
K2 1 Standford St
Peartree Cl
Sea Road
Defender Rd
Tanker Rd
Wharncliffe Rd
Lwr Vicarage Rd
Southampton Technical College
Northern Anchorage
Laurel Cl
Spitfire Court Surgery
Oakbank Rd
Portsmouth Rd
Keswick Rd
Condor Cl
Woodley Rd
Victoria Road
John's Road
Thornycroft Av
Lake Rd
Surrey Road
Weston Gro
Glen Road
Church Road
Swift Road
Swift Hollow
Victoria Rd
Dundonald Cl
Unwin Cl
Taylor Cl
Waldegrave Cl
10
71
G H J K L M
1 2 3 4 5 6 7 8 9

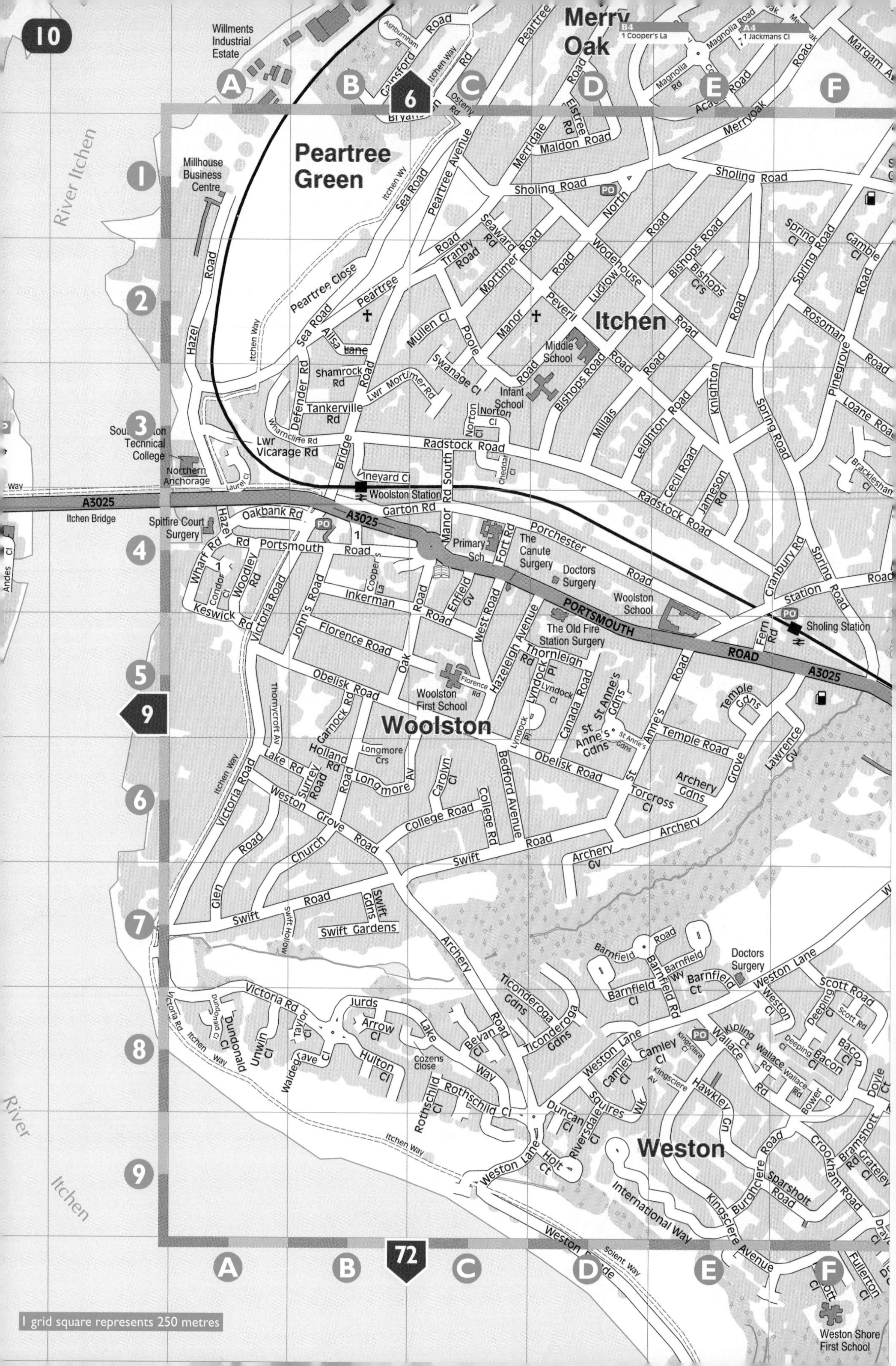

1 grid square represents 250 metres

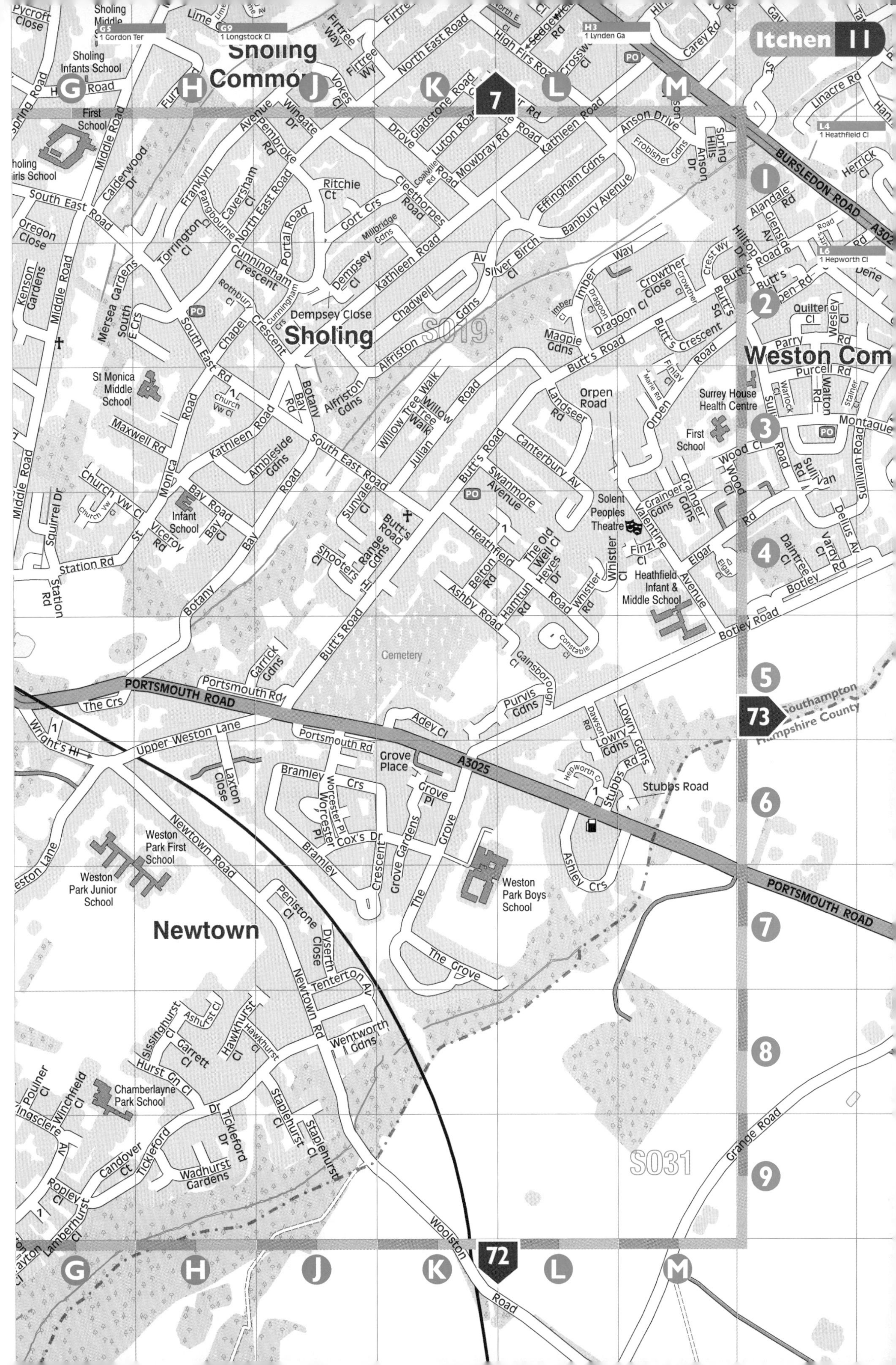

G5 1 Gordon Ter
G9 1 Longstock Cl
H3 1 Lynden Ga
L4 1 Heathfield Cl
L6 1 Hepworth Cl
Sholing Common
Sholing
Weston Com
Newtown
Pycroft Close
Sholing Middle
Sholing Infants School
First School
Sholing Girls School
Spring Road
Middle Road
South East Road
Oregon Close
Kenson Gardens
Calderwood Dr
Mersea Gardens
South E Crs
Franklyn Avenue
Pembroke Rd
Caversham Cl
Pangbourne Cl
North East Road
Torrington Cl
Wingate Dr
Cunningham Crescent
Rothbury Cl
Portal Road
Ritchie Ct
Gort Crs
Millbridge Gdns
Dempsey Cl
Kathleen Road
Cleethorpes Road
Coalville Rd
Gladstone Road
Luton Road
Drove Road
Mowbray Rd
Kathleen Road
Anson Drive
Frobisher Gdns
Spring Hills
Anson Dr
Effingham Gdns
Banbury Avenue
Silver Birch Av
Chadwell Av
Alfriston Gdns
Dempsey Close
Cunningham Crs
Chapel Crescent
South East Rd
St Monica Middle School
Church Vw Cl
Maxwell Rd
Monica Road
Kathleen Road
Ambleside Gdns
Bay Road
Botany Bay Rd
Infant School
Bay Cl
Viceroy Rd
Church Vw Cl
Squirrel Dr
Station Rd
Station Rd
St
Botany Bay Road
South East Road
Willow Tree Walk
Julian Road
Sunvale Cl
Butt's Road
Shooters Hill Cl
Range Gdns
Cemetery
Garrick Gdns
Portsmouth Rd
The Crs
PORTSMOUTH ROAD
A3025
Wright's Hl
Upper Weston Lane
Laxton Close
Portsmouth Rd
Bramley Crs
Worcester Pl
Cox's Dr
Bramley Crescent
Grove Place
Grove Pl
Grove Gardens
The Grove
Adey Cl
Weston Park First School
Weston Park Junior School
Newtown Road
Weston Park Boys School
Weston Lane
Penistone Cl
Dyserth Close
Tenterton Av
Newtown Rd
Wentworth Gdns
The Grove
Sissinghurst Cl
Ashurst Cl
Hawkhurst Cl
Garrett Cl
Hurst Gn Cl
Chamberlayne Park School
Poulner Cl
Winchfield Cl
Kingsclere Av
Tickleford Dr
Candover Ct
Wadhurst Gardens
Staplehurst Cl
Ropley Cl
Lamberhurst Cl
Layton Cl
Woolston Road
Grange Road
SO19
SO31
Imber Way
Imber Cl
Dragoon Cl
Crowther Close
Crest Wy
Hilltop Dr
Butt's Road
Butt's Sq
Butt's Crescent
Magpie Gdns
Butt's Road
Finlay Cl
Mabe Rd
Orpen Road
Landseer Rd
Canterbury Av
Swanmore Avenue
Heathfield Road
The Old Well Cl
Heyes Dr
Belton Rd
Hamtun Rd
Ashby Road
Whistler Rd
Whistler Cl
Constable Cl
Gainsborough Cl
Purvis Gdns
Solent Peoples Theatre
Valentine Avenue
Grainger Gdns
Finzi Cl
Heathfield Infant & Middle School
Elgar Rd
Wood Cl
Surrey House Health Centre
First School
Dawson Rd
Lowry Gdns
Hepworth Cl
Stubbs Rd
Stubbs Road
Ashley Crs
Botley Road
Southampton
Hampshire County
Alandale Rd
Glenside Av
BURSLEDON ROAD A3024
Herrick Cl
Linacre Rd
Quilter Cl
Wesley Rd
Parry Rd
Purcell Rd
Warlock Cl
Walton Rd
Stainer Cl
Montague
Sullivan Road
Sullivan Rd
Delius Av
Varda Cl
Daintree Cl
Botley Rd
PORTSMOUTH ROAD
Carey Rd
Firtree Way
Firtree Wy
Vokes Cl
North East Road
High Firs Road
Sedgewick Rd
Crosswell Cl
Lime Cl
PO
G H J K L M
1 2 3 4 5 6 7 8 9
7 72 73

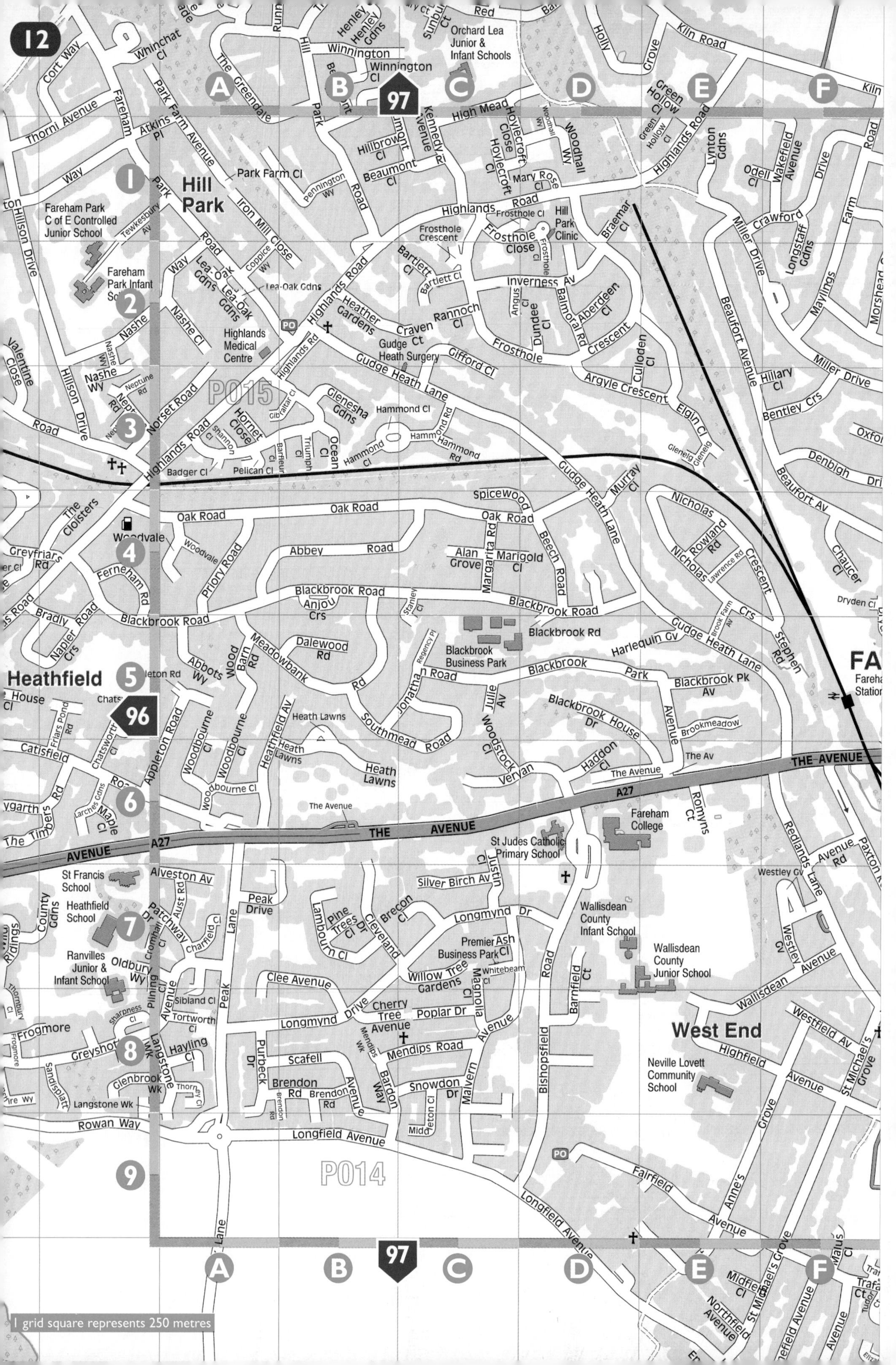

1 grid square represents 250 metres

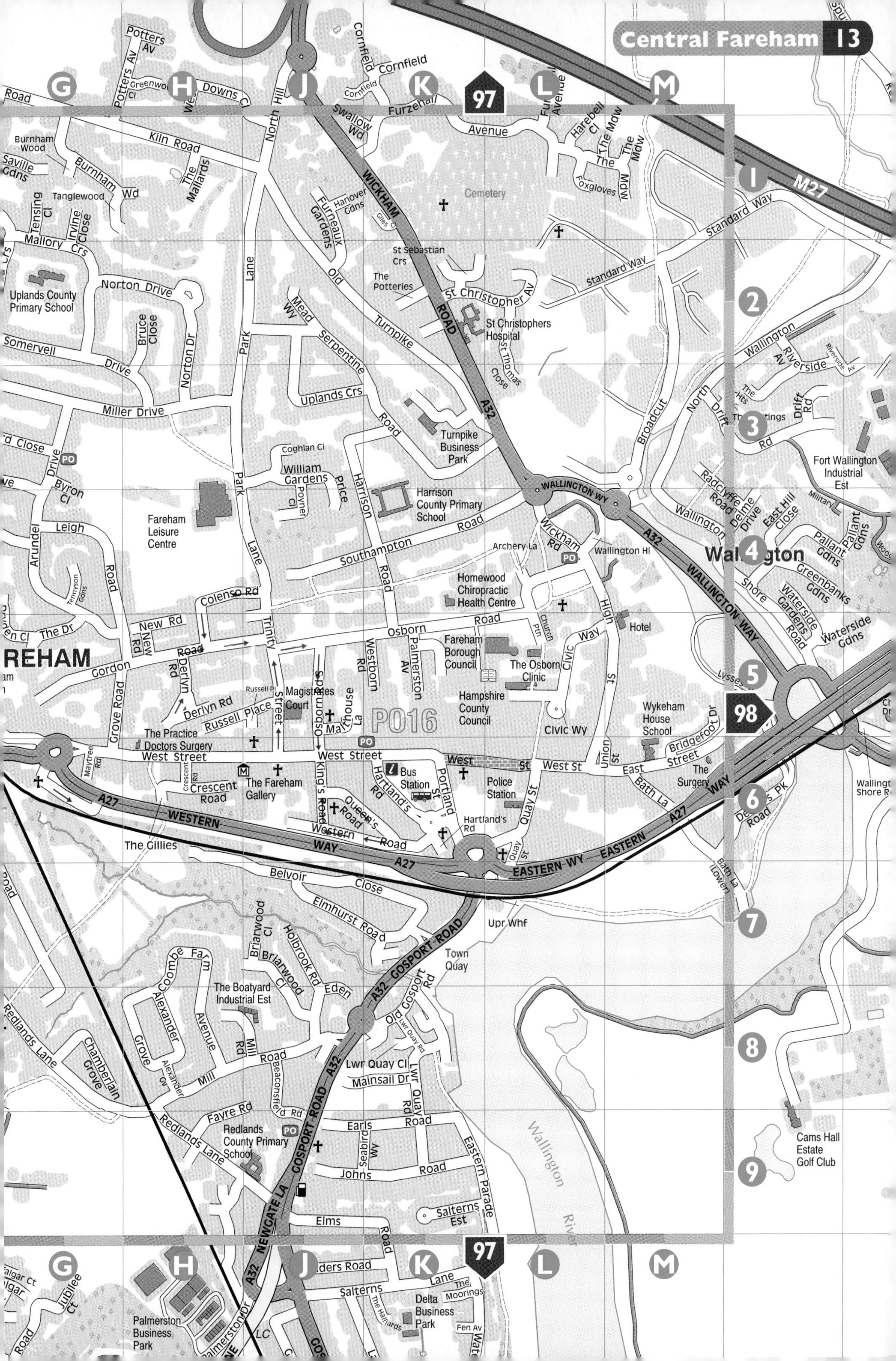
G
H
J
K
97
L
M
Potters Av
Potters Av
Greenwood Cl
Downs Cl
North Hill
Cornfield
Cornfield
Swallow Wd
Furzehall Avenue
Harebell Cl
The Mdw
The Mdw
The Mdw
Foxgloves
Road
Kiln Road
Burnham Wood
Saville Gdns
Burnham Wd
The Mallards
Tanglewood
Tensing Cl
Irvine Close
Mallory Crs
Uplands County Primary School
Norton Drive
Bruce Close
Somervell Drive
Norton Dr
Miller Drive
Park Lane
Furneaux Gardens
Hanover Gdns
Giles Cl
WICKHAM ROAD
Cemetery
St Sebastian Crs
The Potteries
St Christopher Av
St Christophers Hospital
St Thomas Close
Old Turnpike
Mead Wy
Serpentine Road
Uplands Crs
Turnpike Business Park
A32
Standard Way
Standard Way
M27
Wallington Riverside Av
Riverside Av
The Hts
The Bittings
North Drift
Drift Rd
Rd
Broadcut
Fort Wallington Industrial Est
Military
Radclyffe Road
Delme Drive
East Hill Close
Pallant Gdns
Pallant Gdns
Wallington
Wallington
Shore Road
Greenbanks Gdns
Waterside Gardens
Waterside Gdns
Lysses
Hotel
WALLINGTON WAY
Rd Close
Drive
PO
Byron Cl
Coghlan Cl
William Gardens
Poyner Cl
Price
Harrison Road
Harrison County Primary School
WALLINGTON WY
Wickham Rd
Archery La
Wallington Hl
Fareham Leisure Centre
Arundel
Leigh Road
Tennyson Gdns
Southampton Road
Homewood Chiropractic Health Centre
Colenso Rd
New Rd
New Rd
The Dr
Den Cl
REHAM
Osborn Road
Church Pth
High St
Civic Way
Fareham Borough Council
The Osborn Clinic
Gordon Road
Derlyn Rd
Derlyn Rd
Russell Pl
Russell Place
Trinity Street
Magistrates Court
Westborn Rd
Palmerston Av
Osborn Rd
Malthouse La
P016
Hampshire County Council
Civic Wy
Union St
Wykeham House School
Bridgefoot Dr
5
98
Grove Road
The Practice Doctors Surgery
Maytree Rd
West Street
West Street
West St
West St
East Street
The Surgery
Bath La
Crescent Rd
Crescent Road
The Fareham Gallery
King's Road
Queen's Road
Hartland's Rd
Bus Station
Portland St
Police Station
Quay St
Hartland's Rd
Western Road
A27
WESTERN WAY
A27
EASTERN WY
EASTERN
A27
WAY
Wallington Shore Rd
Delme Pk Road
Bath La (Lower)
The Gillies
Belvoir Close
Elmhurst Road
Upr Whf
Town Quay
Briarwood Cl
Holbrook Rd
Briarwood Cl
Coombe Farm Avenue
The Boatyard Industrial Est
Eden
A32 GOSPORT ROAD
Old Gosport Rd
Lwr Quay Rd
Redlands Lane
Alexander Grove
Mill Rd
Mill Road
Chamberlain Grove
Alexander Gv
Beaconsfield Rd
Lwr Quay Cl
Mainsail Dr
Lwr Quay Rd
Fayre Rd
Redlands County Primary School
PO
Redlands Lane
Earls Road
Seabird Wy
Johns Road
Eastern Parade
Wallington River
Salterns Est
Elms Road
A32 NEWGATE LA
Cams Hall Estate Golf Club
Jubilee Ct
Road
Palmerston Business Park
Palmerston Dr
Salterns Lane
Delta Business Park
The Moorings
The Halyards
Fen Av
1
2
3
4
6
7
8
9

HAVANT
Bedhampton
Brockhampton
Langstone
P09
103
102
121
A
B
C
D
E
F
1
2
3
4
5
6
7
8
9
Park Lane Medical Centre
Barncroft Infant School
St Thomas Mores RC Primary School
Havant Rugby Football Club
Bidbury Junior & Infant School
Havant College
Civic Offices
Havant Leisure Centre
Magistrates Court
Havant Station
Havant Sports Club
Havant War Memorial Hospital
Catherine Corbett Clinic
Bedhampton Station
Bosmere Junior School
Havant Business Cen
Havant Mus
The Parchment
The Mallards
The Saltings
B2149 BEDHAMPTON ROAD
B2149 NEW ROAD
B2149 PETERSFIELD ROAD
PARK ROAD NORTH B2149
PARK RD S B2149
A27(T)
A3023
LANGSTONE
Barncroft Way
Stockheath Lane
Stockheath
Hook's Lane
Hook's Farm Way
Fraser Road
James Rd
Staunton Rd
Wendover Road
Chidham Close
Cross Way
West Street
Park Way
Elm Lane
Solent Road
Brockhampton Road
Brockhampton Lane
Southmoor Lane
Penner Road
Brookside Rd
Harts Farm Way
Brookmead Wy
Langstone Avenue
Southbrook Road
Longmead Gdns
Woodbury Av
Hamilton Close
Langstone High St
Tower Gdns
Mill Lane
Solent Way
Wayfarer's Walk
King's Croft Lane
Bidbury Lane
Ingledene Cl
Meyrick Road
Knox Road
Ranelagh Road
Ridgway
Marples Wy
Juniper Sq
Orchard Road
Grove
East
North Street
South Street
Elm Park Road
Leigh Road
Mavis Crs
Fitzwygram Crs
The Drive
Fair Oak
Havant Farm Close
Russell Rd
Blendworth Crescent
Medstead Rd
Trosnant Road
Brookfield Close
Beaufort Road
Lester Aver
Brunswick Gardens
Jessie Road
Hazelholt
Ibsley Grove
Woodgreen Avenue
Timsbury Crs
Winkton Cl
Boundary Way
Homewell
Waterloo Road
Market Pde
The Pallant
St George's Street
Fairfield Rd
Regents Ct
Rectory Rd
1 grid square represents 250 metres

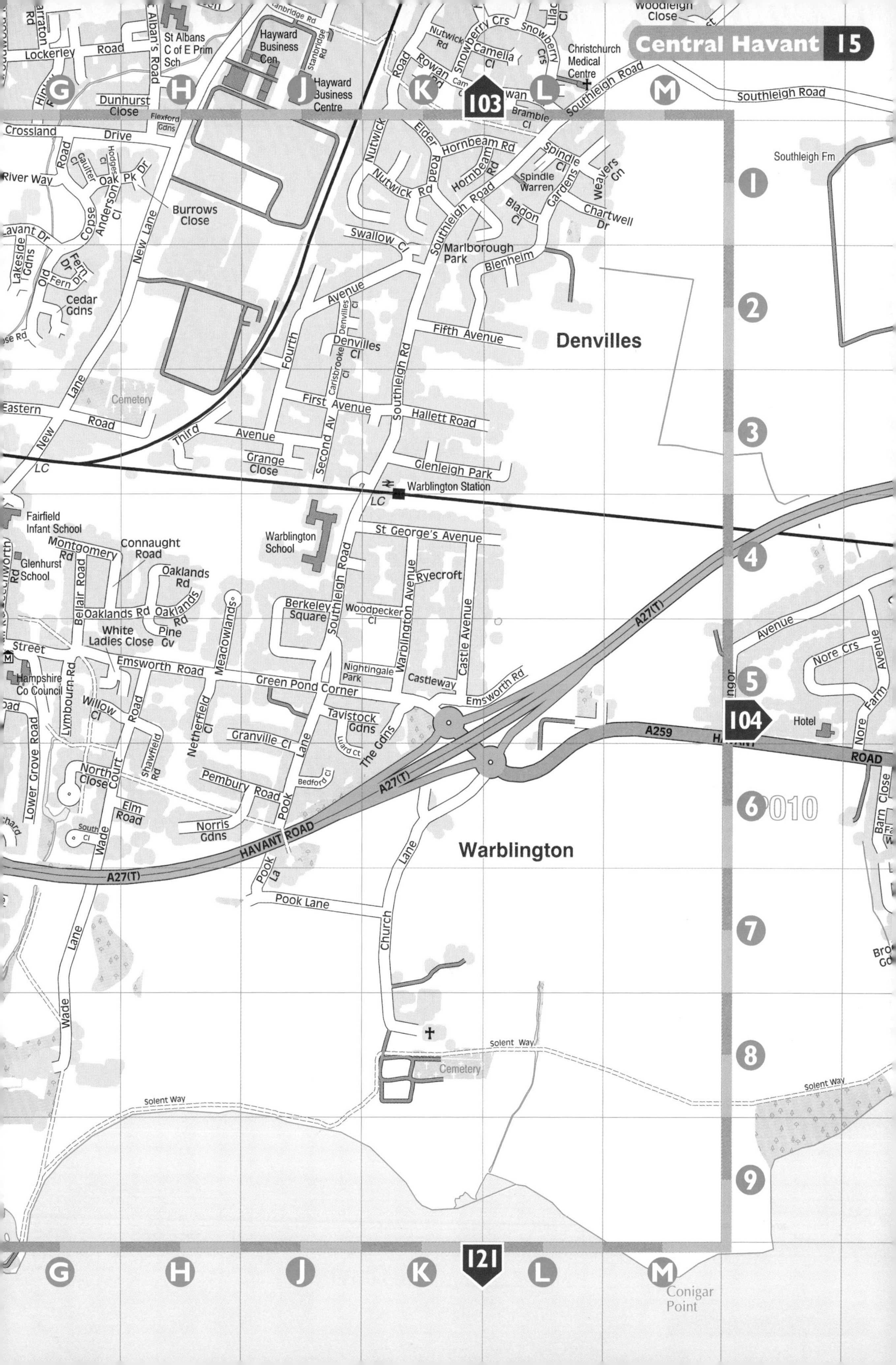
Lockerley Road
St Albans C of E Prim Sch
St Alban's Road
Hayward Business Cen
Hayward Business Centre
Stanbridge Rd
Nutwick Rd
Snowberry Crs
Camelia Cl
Rowan Rd
Lilac Cl
Christchurch Medical Centre
Woodleigh Close
Southleigh Road
Dunhurst Close
Flexford Gdns
Bramble Cl
103
Crossland Drive
River Way
Gaulter Cl
Hodges Cl
Oak Pk Dr
Anderson Cl
Copse
Burrows Close
New Lane
Nutwick Rd
Elder Road
Hornbeam Rd
Spindle Cl
Spindle Warren
Weavers Gn
Gardens
Chartwell Dr
Bladon Cl
Southleigh Road
Southleigh Fm
Lavant Dr
Lakeside Gdns
Fern Dr
Old Fern Dr
Cedar Gdns
Swallow Cl
Marlborough Park
Blenheim
Fourth Avenue
Denvilles Cl
Carisbrooke Cl
Fifth Avenue
Denvilles
Cemetery
Eastern Road
First Avenue
Southleigh Rd
Hallett Road
Third Avenue
Second Av
Grange Close
Glenleigh Park
LC
Warblington Station
Fairfield Infant School
Warblington School
St George's Avenue
Montgomery Rd
Connaught Road
Glenhurst School
Oaklands Rd
Bellair Road
Meadowlands
Berkeley Square
Woodpecker Cl
Warblington Avenue
Ryecroft
Castle Avenue
A27(T)
Avenue
Nore Crs
Nore Farm Avenue
White Ladies Close
Pine Gv
Street
Hampshire Co Council
Emsworth Road
Nightingale Park
Castleway
Green Pond Corner
Emsworth Rd
Lymbourn Rd
Willow Cl
Tavistock Gdns
Netherfield Cl
Granville Cl
Lane
Luard Ct
The Gdns
Shawfield Rd
A259
104
Hotel
ROAD
North Close
Court
Lower Grove Road
Pembury Road
Bedford Cl
Pook Lane
Elm Road
Norris Gdns
South Cl
Wade
HAVANT ROAD
Barn Close
Warblington
Pook La
Pook Lane
Church Lane
Wade Lane
Solent Way
Cemetery
Conigar Point
G H J K L M
1 2 3 4 5 6 7 8 9
121

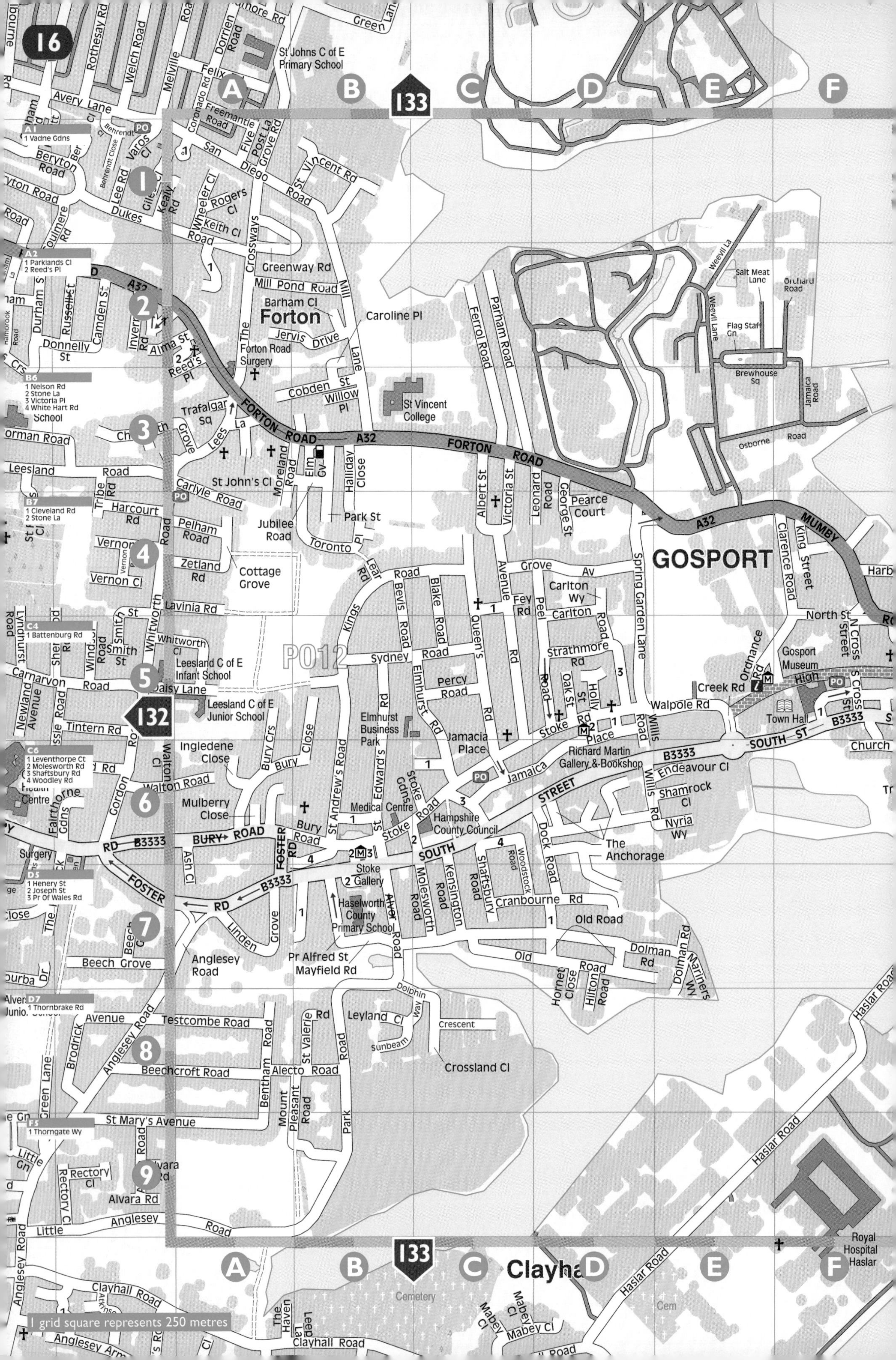
133
132
A
B
C
D
E
F
1
2
3
4
5
6
7
8
9
Forton
GOSPORT
Clayhall
PO12
A1
1 Vadne Gdns
A2
1 Parklands Cl
2 Reed's Pl
B6
1 Nelson Rd
2 Stone La
3 Victoria Pl
4 White Hart Rd
B7
1 Cleveland Rd
2 Stone La
C4
1 Battenburg Rd
C6
1 Leventhorpe Ct
2 Molesworth Rd
3 Shaftsbury Rd
4 Woodley Rd
D5
1 Henery St
2 Joseph St
3 Pr Of Wales Rd
D7
1 Thornbrake Rd
F5
1 Thorngate Wy
St Johns C of E Primary School
St Vincent College
Forton Road Surgery
Leesland C of E Infant School
Leesland C of E Junior School
Elmhurst Business Park
Medical Centre
Hampshire County Council
Stoke Gallery
Haselworth County Primary School
Richard Martin Gallery & Bookshop
Gosport Museum
Town Hall
Royal Hospital Haslar
Cemetery
Cem
Surgery
Health Centre
School
A32
B3333
FORTON ROAD
SOUTH STREET
SOUTH ST
MUMBY
BURY ROAD
FOSTER RD
Rothesay Rd
Welch Road
Melville Road
Dorrien Road
Felix Rd
Coronado Rd
Freemantle Road
Five Post La
Grove Rd
Green Lane
Avery Lane
Behrendt Cl
Behrendt Close
Varos Cl
Beryton Road
Lee Rd
Gilert Cl
Kealy Rd
Dukes Road
Bourne Road
Wheeler Cl
Rogers Cl
Keith Cl
San Diego Road
St Vincent Rd
Crossways
The Crossways
Greenway Rd
Mill Pond Road
Mill Lane
Barham Cl
Jervis Drive
Caroline Pl
Cobden St
Willow Pl
Durham St
Russell St
Camden St
Donnelly St
Inverness Rd
Alma St
Reed's Pl
Trafalgar Sq
Lees La
Grove
Norman Road
Leesland Road
Tribe Rd
Carlyle Road
Harcourt Rd
Pelham Road
Zetland Rd
Vernon Rd
Vernon Cl
Whitworth Road
Cottage Grove
Lavinia Rd
St John's Cl
Moreland Road
Elm Gv
Halliday Close
Jubilee Road
Park St
Toronto Pl
Lear Rd
Kings Road
Bevis Road
Blake Road
Sydney Road
Percy Road
Elmhurst Rd
Queen's Rd
Avenue
Jamacia Place
Jamaica Place
Ferrol Road
Parham Road
Albert St
Victoria St
Leonard Road
George St
Pearce Court
Grove Av
Fey Rd
Peel Road
Carlton Wy
Carlton Road
Strathmore Rd
Oak St
Holly St
Stoke Rd
Spring Garden Lane
Walpole Rd
Willis Road
Creek Rd
Ordnance Rd
High St
S Cross St
North St
N Cross Street
King Street
Clarence Road
Weevil La
Weevil Lane
Salt Meat Lane
Orchard Road
Flag Staff Gn
Brewhouse Sq
Jamaica Road
Osborne Road
Church
Harb
Endeavour Cl
Shamrock Cl
Nyria Wy
The Anchorage
Dock Road
Woodstock Road
Shaftsbury Road
Kensington Road
Molesworth Road
Alver Road
Cranbourne Rd
Old Road
Dolman Rd
Dolman Road
Mariners Wy
Hornet Close
Hilton Road
Carnarvon Road
Newland Avenue
Lyndhurst Road
Smith St
Windsor Road
Daisy Lane
Tintern Rd
Walton Cl
Walton Road
Ingledene Close
Bury Crs
Bury Close
Mulberry Close
Bury Road
Gordon Road
Fairthorne Gdns
Ash Cl
St Andrew's Road
St Edward's Rd
Stoke Gdns
Stoke Road
Linden Grove
Anglesey Road
Beech Grove
Pr Alfred St
Mayfield Rd
Dolphin Way
Leyland Cl
Sunbeam Way
Crescent
Crossland Cl
Testcombe Road
Brodrick Avenue
Anglesey Road
Beechcroft Road
Bentham Road
Alecto Road
St Valerie Rd
Mount Pleasant Road
Park Road
Green Lane
St Mary's Avenue
Rectory Cl
Alvara Rd
Little Anglesey Road
Little Gn
Clayhall Road
The Haven
Mabey Cl
Haslar Road
Haslar Rd
1 grid square represents 250 metres

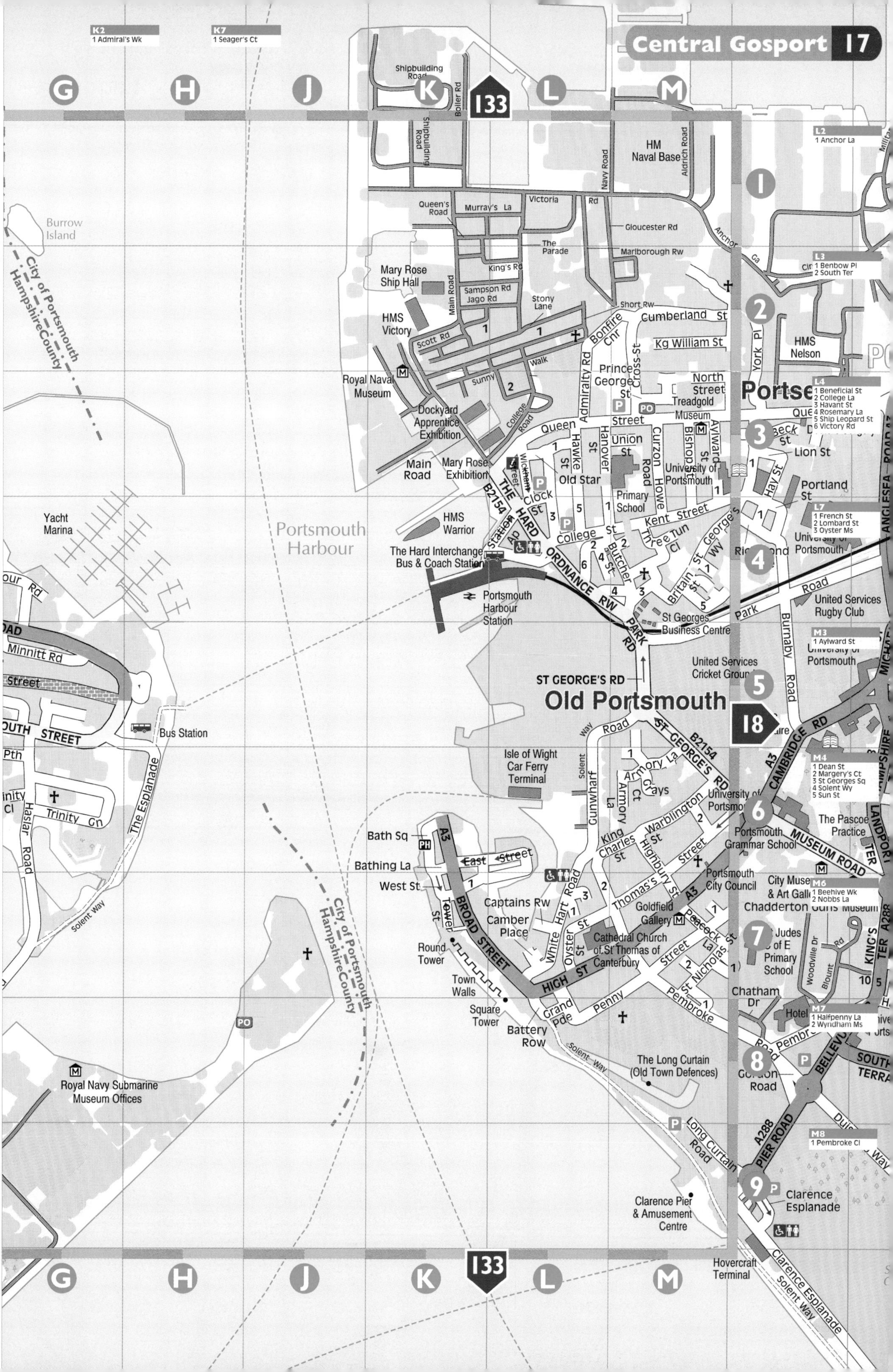
K2
1 Admiral's Wk
K7
1 Seager's Ct
G
H
J
K
L
M
133
18
L2
1 Anchor La
L3
1 Benbow Pl
2 South Ter
L4
1 Beneficial St
2 College La
3 Havant St
4 Rosemary La
5 Ship Leopard St
6 Victory Rd
L7
1 French St
2 Lombard St
3 Oyster Ms
M3
1 Aylward St
M4
1 Dean St
2 Margery's Ct
3 St Georges Sq
4 Solent Wy
5 Sun St
M6
1 Beehive Wk
2 Nobbs La
M7
1 Halfpenny La
2 Wyndham Ms
M8
1 Pembroke Cl
Shipbuilding Road
Boiler Rd
HM Naval Base
Navy Road
Aldrich Road
Queen's Road
Murray's La
Victoria Rd
Gloucester Rd
The Parade
Marlborough Rw
Anchor Ga
King's Rd
Mary Rose Ship Hall
Sampson Rd
Jago Rd
Main Road
Stony Lane
Short Rw
HMS Victory
Scott Rd
Bonfire Cnr
Cumberland St
Kg William St
York Pl
HMS Nelson
Royal Naval Museum
Sunny Walk
Admiralty Rd
Prince George St
Cross St
North Street
Treadgold Museum
Portse
Dockyard Apprentice Exhibition
College Road
Queen Street
Union St
Beck St
Lion St
Main Road
Mary Rose Exhibition
Wickham Street
Hawke St
Hanover St
Curzon Howe Road
Bishop St
Aylward St
University of Portsmouth
Old Star
Primary School
Hay St
Portland St
B2154
THE HARD
Clock St
Kent Street
College St
Three Tun Cl
St George's Wy
HMS Warrior
Station Ap
Butcher St
Britain St
Richmond
University of Portsmouth
ANGLESEA ROAD
The Hard Interchange Bus & Coach Station
ORDNANCE RW
Portsmouth Harbour Station
St Georges Business Centre
Park Road
United Services Rugby Club
PARK RD
Burrow Island
City of Portsmouth
Hampshire County
Yacht Marina
Portsmouth Harbour
Minnitt Rd
Street
SOUTH STREET
Bus Station
The Esplanade
Haslar Road
Trinity Gn
United Services Cricket Ground
Burnaby Road
ST GEORGE'S RD
Old Portsmouth
Solent Way
Road
B2154
ST GEORGE'S RD
A3
CAMBRIDGE RD
Isle of Wight Car Ferry Terminal
Gunwharf Rd
Armory La
Grays Ct
University of Portsmouth
MUSEUM ROAD
Portsmouth Grammar School
The Pascoe Practice
Bath Sq
PH
A3
Bathing La
East Street
West St
Tower St
King Charles St
Warblington St
Highbury St
White Hart Road
Thomas's St
Portsmouth City Council
City Museum & Art Gallery
Chadderton Gdns Museum
Captains Rw
Camber Place
Goldfield Gallery
Peacock La
St Jude's C of E Primary School
Woodville Dr
Blount Rd
KING'S TER
A288
BROAD STREET
Oyster St
Cathedral Church of St Thomas of Canterbury
Round Tower
HIGH ST
St Nicholas St
Town Walls
Square Tower
Grand Pde
Penny Street
Pembroke Road
Chatham Dr
Hotel
Battery Row
Solent Way
The Long Curtain (Old Town Defences)
Gordon Road
BELLEVUE TER
SOUTH TERRACE
Long Curtain Road
A288
PIER ROAD
Clarence Esplanade
Clarence Pier & Amusement Centre
Hovercraft Terminal
Clarence Esplanade
Solent Way
Royal Navy Submarine Museum Offices
PO
P

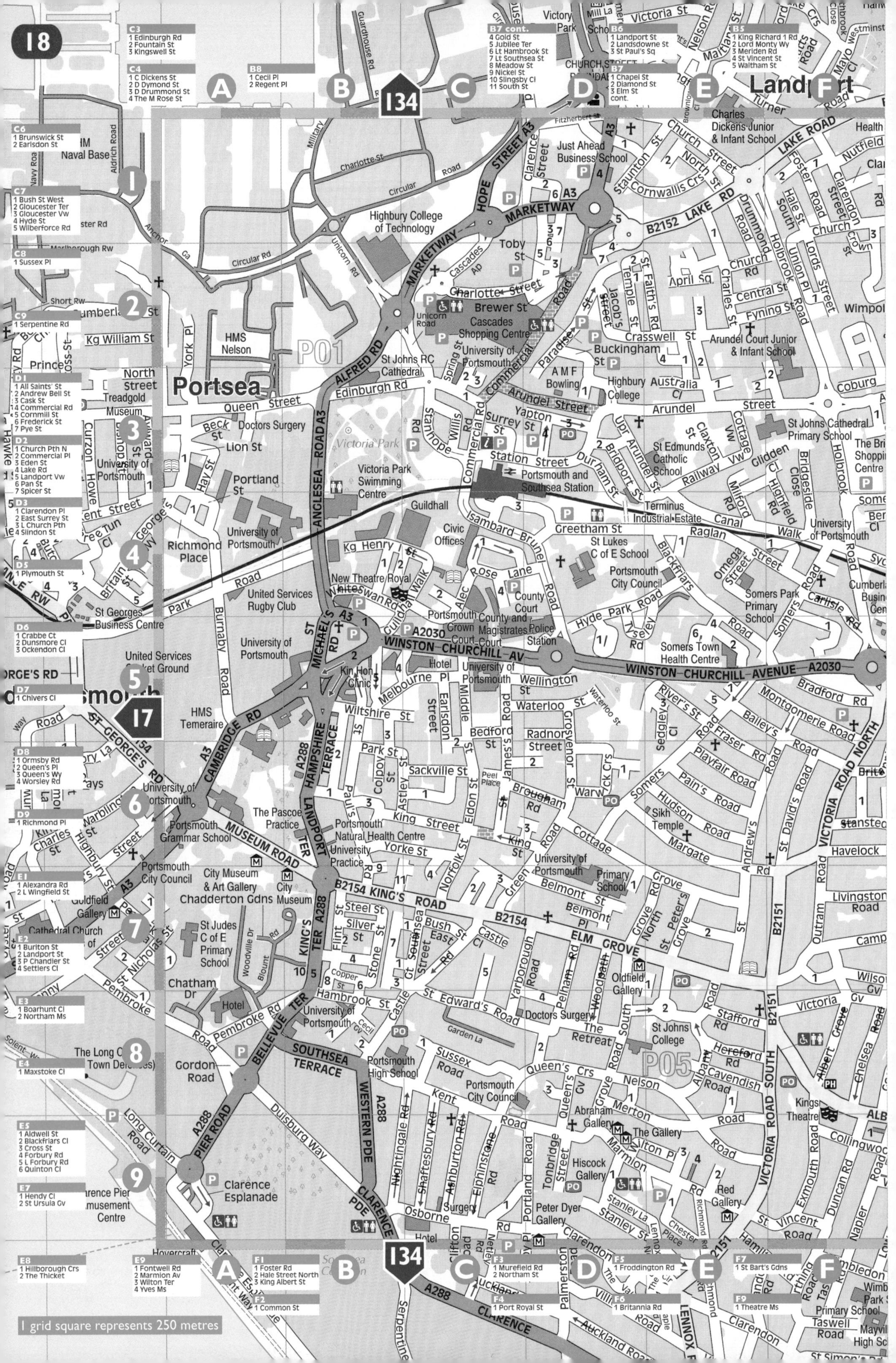
C3 1 Edinburgh Rd 2 Fountain St 3 Kingswell St
C4 1 C Dickens St 2 D Dymond St 3 D Drummond St 4 The M Rose St
B8 1 Cecil Pl 2 Regent Pl
B7 cont. 4 Gold St 5 Jubilee Ter 6 Lt Hambrook St 7 Lt Southsea St 8 Meadow St 9 Nickel St 10 Slingsby Cl 11 South St
B6 1 Landport St 2 Landsdowne St 3 St Paul's Sq
B7 1 Chapel St 2 Diamond St 3 Elm St cont.
B5 1 King Richard 1 Rd 2 Lord Monty Wy 3 Meriden Rd 4 St Vincent St 5 Waltham St
C6 1 Brunswick St 2 Earlsdon St
C7 1 Bush St West 2 Gloucester Ter 3 Gloucester Vw 4 Hyde St 5 Wilberforce Rd
C8 1 Sussex Pl
C9 1 Serpentine Rd
D1 1 All Saints' St 2 Andrew Bell St 3 Cask St 4 Commercial Rd 5 Cornmill St 6 Frederick St 7 Pye St
D2 1 Church Pth N 2 Commercial Pl 3 Eden St 4 Lake Rd 5 Landport Vw 6 Pan St 7 Spicer St
D3 1 Clarendon Pl 2 East Surrey St 3 L Church Pth 4 Slindon St
D5 1 Plymouth St
D6 1 Crabbe Ct 2 Dunsmore Cl 3 Ockendon Cl
D7 1 Chivers Cl
D8 1 Ormsby Rd 2 Queen's Pl 3 Queen's Wy 4 Worsley Rd
D9 1 Richmond Pl
E1 1 Alexandra Rd 2 L Wingfield St
E2 1 Burlton St 2 Landport St 3 P Chandler St 4 Settlers Cl
E3 1 Boarhunt Cl 2 Northam Ms
E4 1 Maxstoke Cl
E5 1 Aldwell St 2 Blackfriars Cl 3 Cross St 4 Forbury Rd 5 L Forbury Rd 6 Quinton Cl
E7 1 Hendy Cl 2 St Ursula Gv
E8 1 Hillborough Crs 2 The Thicket
E9 1 Fontwell Rd 2 Marmion Av 3 Wilton Ter 4 Yves Ms
F1 1 Foster Rd 2 Hale Street North 3 King Albert St
F2 1 Common St
F3 1 Murefield Rd 2 Northam St
F4 1 Port Royal St
F5 1 Froddington Rd
F6 1 Britannia Rd
F7 1 St Bart's Gdns
F9 1 Theatre Ms
A B C D E F
1 2 3 4 5 6 7 8 9
134
17
Portsea
Landport
P01
P05
HM Naval Base
HMS Nelson
Highbury College of Technology
Cascades Shopping Centre
St Johns RC Cathedral
Victoria Park
Victoria Park Swimming Centre
Portsmouth and Southsea Station
Guildhall
Civic Offices
New Theatre Royal
United Services Rugby Club
United Services Cricket Ground
University of Portsmouth
HMS Temeraire
Portsmouth Grammar School
City Museum & Art Gallery
Chadderton Gdns
St Judes C of E Primary School
Portsmouth High School
Clarence Esplanade
Clarence Pier Amusement Centre
Hovercraft
Southsea Common
The Long Curtain Town Defences
Gordon Road
Portsmouth City Council
Portsmouth Natural Health Centre
Portsmouth County and Magistrates Court
Police Station
Somers Town Health Centre
Somers Park Primary School
St Lukes C of E School
Terminus Industrial Estate
St Edmunds Catholic School
St Johns Cathedral Primary School
Arundel Court Junior & Infant School
Charles Dickens Junior & Infant School
Just Ahead Business School
AMF Bowling
Highbury College
Sikh Temple
Oldfield Gallery
St Johns College
Kings Theatre
Abraham Gallery
The Gallery
Hiscock Gallery
Red Gallery
Peter Dyer Gallery
Doctors Surgery
The Pascoe Practice
University Practice
Treadgold Museum
Richmond Place
St Georges Business Centre
Cathedral Church of
Goldfield Gallery
WINSTON CHURCHILL AVENUE A2030
MARKETWAY
ANGLESEA ROAD A3
ALFRED RD
HOPE STREET A3
CAMBRIDGE RD
MUSEUM ROAD
B2154 KING'S ROAD
ELM GROVE
PIER ROAD
BELLEVUE TER
SOUTHSEA TERRACE
WESTERN PDE
CLARENCE PDE
CLARENCE
VICTORIA ROAD SOUTH
VICTORIA ROAD NORTH
B2152 LAKE RD
LAKE ROAD
Commercial Rd
Arundel Street
Edinburgh Rd
Queen Street
Park Road
Burnaby Road
Isambard Brunel Rd
Greetham St
Canal Walk
Hyde Park Road
Bradford Rd
Montgomerie Road
Fawcett Rd
St Edward's Road
Castle Rd
Kent Road
Nelson Rd
Sussex Road
Osborne Rd
Clarendon Rd
Duisburg Way
Long Curtain Road
1 grid square represents 250 metres

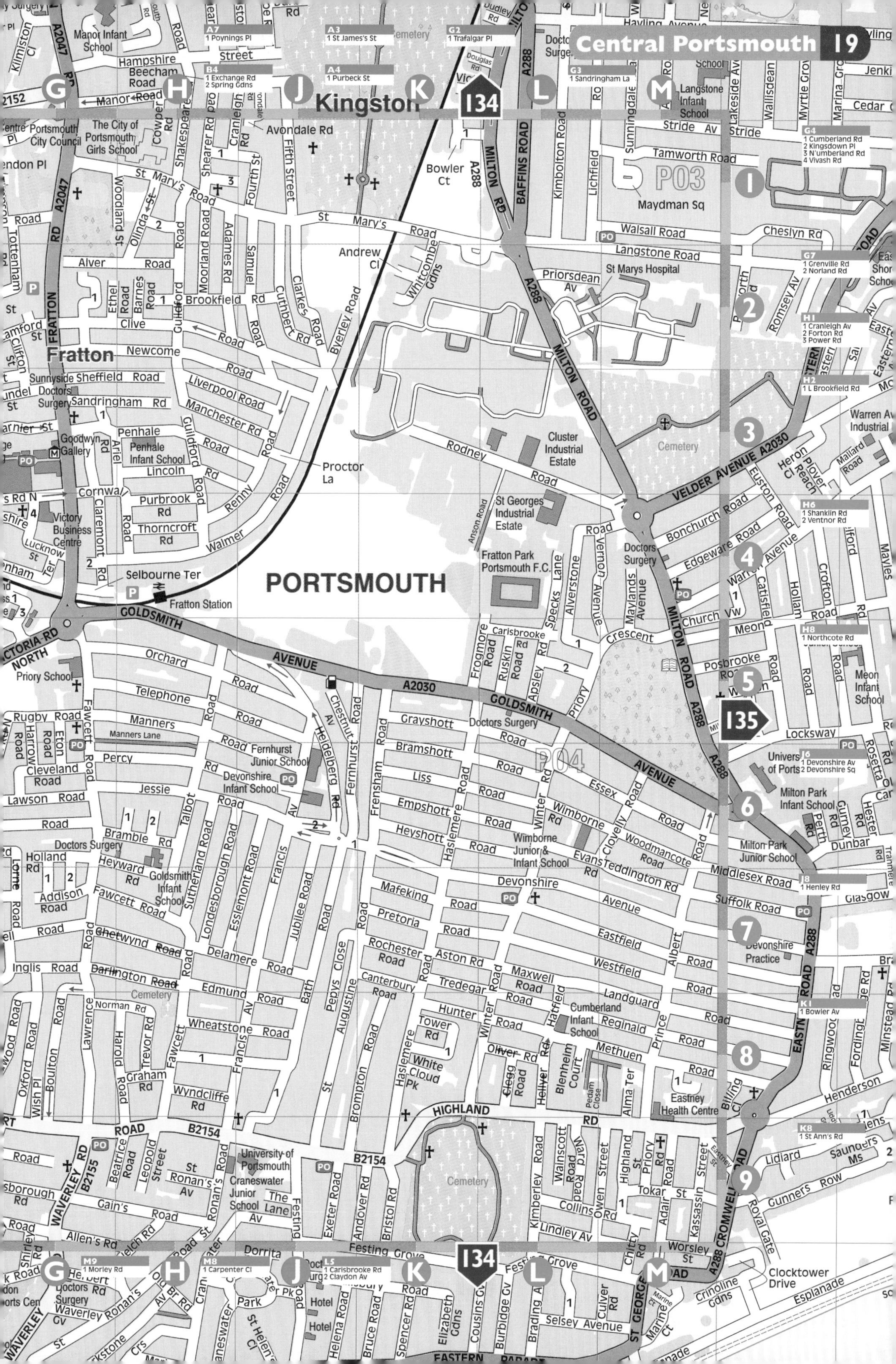
Kingston
Fratton
PORTSMOUTH
P03
P04
134
135
A7 1 Poynings Pl
A3 1 St James's St
G2 1 Trafalgar Pl
B4 1 Exchange Rd 2 Spring Gdns
A4 1 Purbeck St
G3 1 Sandringham La
G4 1 Cumberland Rd 2 Kingsdown Pl 3 N'umberland Rd 4 Vivash Rd
G7 1 Grenville Rd 2 Norland Rd
H1 1 Cranleigh Av 2 Forton Rd 3 Power Rd
H2 1 L Brookfield Rd
H6 1 Shanklin Rd 2 Ventnor Rd
H8 1 Northcote Rd
J6 1 Devonshire Av 2 Devonshire Sq
J8 1 Henley Rd
K1 1 Bowler Av
K8 1 St Ann's Rd
M9 1 Morley Rd
M8 1 Carpenter Cl
L5 1 Carisbrooke Rd 2 Claydon Av
Manor Infant School
Hampshire Street
Beecham Road
Manor Road
The City of Portsmouth Girls School
Portsmouth City Council
Avondale Rd
Fifth Street
Bowler Ct
MILTON RD
BAFFINS ROAD
Kimbolton Road
Lichfield
Tamworth Road
Maydman Sq
Stride Av
Langstone Infant School
Walsall Road
Langstone Road
Cheslyn Rd
St Mary's Road
Andrew Cl
Whitcombe Gdns
St Marys Hospital
Priorsdean Av
Brookfield Rd
Clive Road
Newcome Road
Sheffield Road
Sandringham Rd
Liverpool Road
Manchester Rd
Penhale Infant School
Goodwyn Gallery
Lincoln Rd
Cornwall Rd N
Purbrook Rd
Thorncroft Rd
Victory Business Centre
Walmer Road
Selbourne Ter
Fratton Station
Byerley Road
Proctor La
Rodney Road
Cluster Industrial Estate
St Georges Industrial Estate
Anson Road
Fratton Park Portsmouth F.C.
MILTON ROAD
Cemetery
VELDER AVENUE A2030
Bonchurch Road
Edgeware Road
Warren Avenue
Doctors Surgery
Church Vw
Meon Rd
Posbrooke Road
Locksway
Milton Park Infant School
Milton Park Junior School
Meon Infant School
GOLDSMITH AVENUE A2030
Orchard Road
Telephone Road
Manners Road
Manners Lane
Percy Road
Jessie Road
Priory School
Fernhurst Junior School
Devonshire Infant School
Heidelberg Rd
Chestnut Av
Grayshott Road
Bramshott Road
Liss Road
Empshott Road
Heyshott Road
Essex Road
Wimborne Rd
Wimborne Junior & Infant School
Woodmancote Road
Teddington Rd
Middlesex Road
Suffolk Road
Devonshire Avenue
Eastfield Road
Westfield Road
Landguard Road
Reginald Road
Methuen Road
Cumberland Infant School
Eastney Health Centre
Devonshire Practice
EASTNEY ROAD A288
Henderson Road
Mafeking Road
Pretoria Road
Rochester Road
Aston Rd
Canterbury Road
Tredegar Road
Maxwell Road
Hunter Road
Tower Rd
White Cloud Pk
Oliver Rd
HIGHLAND ROAD B2154
Delamere Road
Edmund Road
Wheatstone Road
Wyndcliffe Rd
Goldsmith Infant School
Addison Road
Fawcett Road
Chetwynd Road
Darlington Road
Inglis Road
Norman Rd
Graham Rd
WAVERLEY RD B2155
University of Portsmouth
Craneswater Junior School
St Ronan's Av
Gain's Road
Allen's Rd
Festing Grove
Festing Road
Collins Rd
Lindley Av
Tokar St
Worsley St
CROMWELL ROAD A288
Lidiard Gdns
Gunners Row
Royal Gate
Clocktower Drive
Esplanade
Crinoline Gdns
ST GEORGES ROAD
Marine Ct
Selsey Avenue
EASTERN PARADE
Hotel
Cousins Gv
Elizabeth Gdns
Spencer Rd
Bruce Road
Helena Road
St Helen's Cl
Doctors Surgery
Herbert Rd

A
B
C
D
E
1
2
3
4
5
6
7
Church Lane
Main Road
New Road
Northwood Park
Littleton
Rozelle Close
Holm Oak Cl
Fairclose Drive
The Hall Way
Pitter Cl
Fyfield Way
Hilden Way
Dale Close
Valley Road
North Drive
Bercote Close
South Drive
PO
Deane Down Drove
B3049
STOCKBRIDGE ROAD
Watley Lane
Lainston House Hotel
Lock's Lane
Home Lane
Church Lane
PH
Woodman Lane
Lambourne Close
Sparsholt Primary School
Bostock Close
Woodman Close
Dean Lane
Dean
Littleton Lane
Westview Road
Burrow Road
Downside Road
Sawyer Cl
Grovelands Road
Beech Copse
Teg
Lanham Lane
SO22
Teg Down
Lanham Lane
Crabwood Farm House
Clarendon Way
Crab Wood
24
Royal Winchester Golf Club
1 grid square represents 500 metres
Sarum Road

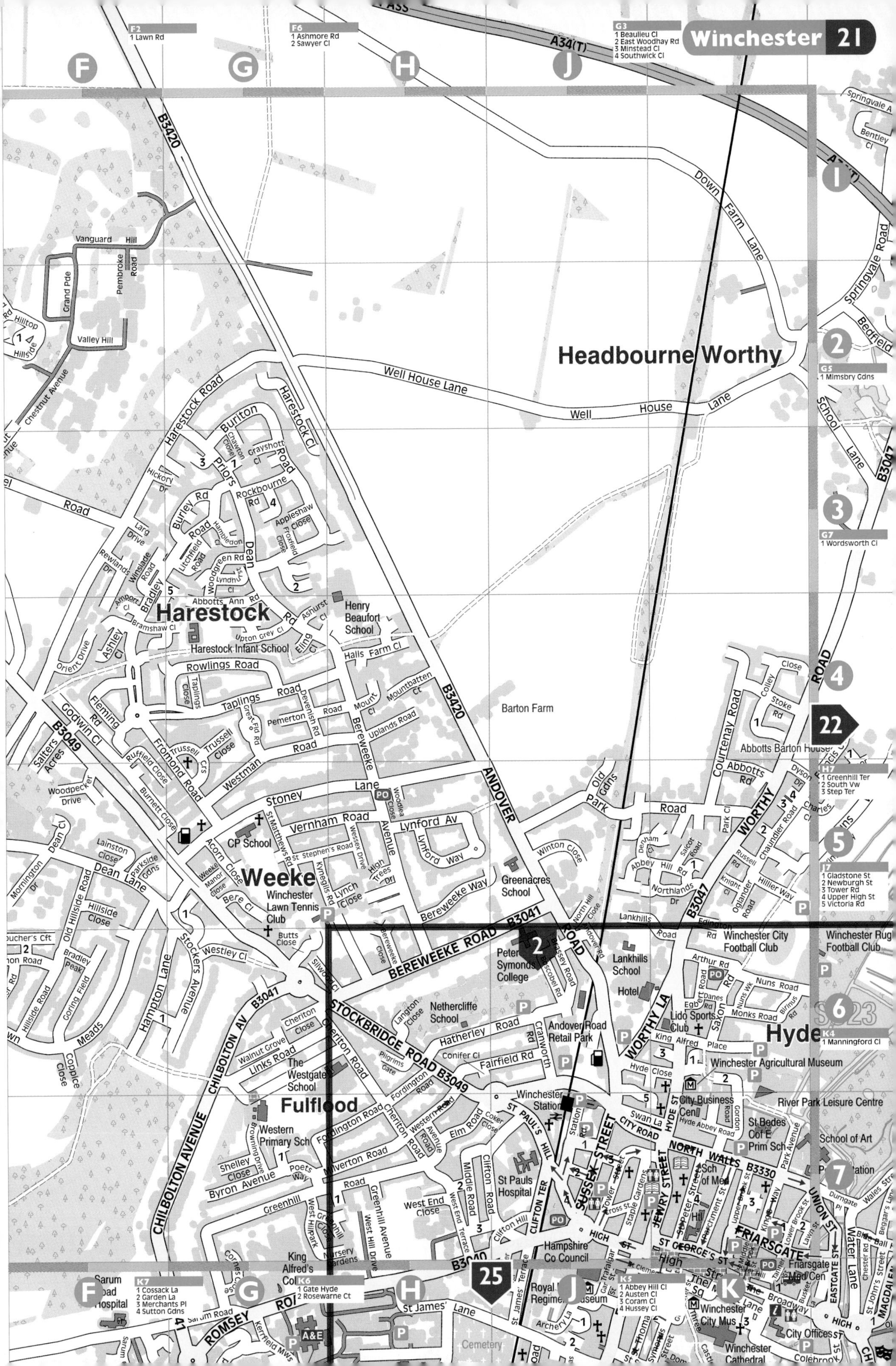
F2
1 Lawn Rd
F6
1 Ashmore Rd
2 Sawyer Cl
G3
1 Beaulieu Cl
2 East Woodhay Rd
3 Minstead Cl
4 Southwick Cl
F
G
H
J
I
A34(T)
B3420
Vanguard Hill
Pembroke Road
Grand Pde
Valley Hill
Hilltop
Hillside
Chestnut Avenue
Down Farm Lane
Springvale Road
Springvale A
Bentley Cl
Bedfield
Headbourne Worthy
Well House Lane
G5
1 Mimsbry Gdns
School Lane
B3047
G7
1 Wordsworth Cl
Harestock Road
Harestock Cl
Buriton
Chawton Close
Grayshott Cl
Priors Dean Road
Hickory Dr
Road
Rockbourne Rd
Burley Rd
Appleshaw Close
Froxfield Close
Larg Drive
Litchfield Road
Hambledon Cl
Woodgreen Rd
Lyndhurst Cl
Rewlands Dr
Winslade Road
Bradley Road
Amport Cl
Abbotts Ann Rd
Harestock
Ashurst Cl
Henry Beaufort School
Bramshaw Cl
Upton Grey Cl
Ashley Cl
Harestock Infant School
Eling Cl
Halls Farm Cl
Orient Drive
Rowlings Road
Taplings Close
Taplings Road
Devenish Rd
Mount Cl
Mountbatten Ct
Barton Farm
Fleming Rd
Godwin Cl
B3049
Pemerton Road
Great Fld Rd
Uplands Road
Bereweeke Road
Salters Acres
Trussell Crs
Trussell Close
Westman Road
Ruffield Close
Fromond Road
Woodpecker Drive
Burnett Close
Stoney Lane
Woodlea Close
ANDOVER ROAD
Vernham Road
St Matthews Rd
Lynford Av
Lynford Way
CP School
St Stephen's Road
Wessex Drive
Avenue
Dean Cl
Lainston Close
Parkside Gdns
Dean Lane
Mornington Dr
Old Hillside Road
Hillside Close
Weeke Manor Close
Acorn Close
Weeke
Winchester Lawn Tennis Club
Kynegils Rd
Lynch Close
High Trees Dr
Bereweeke Way
Greenacres School
Winton Close
Bere Cl
Butts Close
Bereweeke Close
BEREWEEKE ROAD B3041
Peter Symonds College
Bassett Road
Bascobel Rd
North Hill Close
Hyde Close
Westley Cl
Stockers Avenue
Hampton Lane
Bradley Peak
Goring Field
Hillside Road
Meads
Coppice Close
Boucher's Cft
Silwood Cl
Cheriton Close
Cheriton Road
B3041
CHILBOLTON AV
CHILBOLTON AVENUE
Walnut Grove
Links Road
The Westgate School
STOCKBRIDGE ROAD B3049
Langton Close
Nethercliffe School
Hatherley Road
Cranworth Rd
Andover Road Retail Park
Conifer Cl
Pilgrims Gate
Fairfield Rd
Fordington Road
Fulflood
Western Primary Sch
Browning Drive
Shelley Close
Byron Avenue
Poets Way
Milverton Road
Western Road
Avenue Road
Elm Road
Coker Close
Winchester Station
ST PAUL'S HILL
Station Rd
Greenhill Road
West Hill Park
Greenhill Close
Greenhill Avenue
West Hill Drive
Nursery Gardens
Middle Road
Clifton Road
West End Close
West End Terrace
St Pauls Hospital
Clifton Ter
Clifton Hill
Hampshire Co Council
King Alfred's Col
B3040
Old Gdns
Park Road
Courtenay Road
Colley Close
Stoke Rd
Abbotts Barton House
Abbotts Rd
WORTHY ROAD
Chaundler Road
Dyson Dr
Charles Cl
H7
1 Greenhill Ter
2 South Vw
3 Step Ter
J7
1 Gladstone St
2 Newburgh St
3 Tower Rd
4 Upper High St
5 Victoria Rd
Denham Cl
Abbey Hill Rd
Salcot Road
Park Cl
Russell Rd
Knight Cl
Oglander Road
Hillier Way
Northlands Dr
Lankhills Road
Edington Rd
Winchester City Football Club
Winchester Rugby Football Club
Lankhills School
Hotel
Arthur Rd
Egbert Road
Danes Rd
Saxon Rd
Nuns Wk
Nuns Road
Birinus Rd
WORTHY LA
Lido Sports Club
Monks Road
Hyde
K4
1 Manningford Cl
King Alfred Place
Winchester Agricultural Museum
Hyde Close
River Park Leisure Centre
City Business Cen
Hyde Abbey Road
Gordon Road
St Bedes C of E Prim Sch
Park Avenue
School of Art
Swan La
CITY ROAD
HYDE ST
SUSSEX STREET
NORTH WALLS B3330
Tower Street
Cross St
Staple Gardens
JEWRY STREET
St Peter Street
Sch of Med
Parchment St
Upper Brook St
Kings Way
Lower Brook St
UNION ST
Durngate Pl
Wales Street
Water Lane
Beggar's Lane
HIGH ST
ST GEORGE'S ST
FRIARSGATE
Friarsgate Med Cen
EASTGATE ST
Chester Rd
St John's Street
MAGDALEN HILL
The Square
The Broadway
Winchester City Mus
Winchester Cathedral
City Offices
Colebrook St
Royal Hampshire Regiment Museum
Archery La
St James' Terrace
St James' Lane
Cemetery
K5
1 Abbey Hill Cl
2 Austen Cl
3 Coram Cl
4 Hussey Cl
K6
1 Gate Hyde
2 Rosewarne Ct
K7
1 Cossack La
2 Garden La
3 Merchants Pl
4 Sutton Gdns
Sarum Road Hospital
Sarum Road
ROMSEY ROAD
Kerrfield Mws
A&E
K
2
3
4
5
6
7
22
25
SO23

A
B
C
D
E
1
2
3
4
5
6
7
B7
1 Baigent Cl
2 Gatekeeper Cl
3 Longhouse Gn
4 Peacock Pl
5 Ringlet Wy
6 Roundhuts Rl
C1
1 Old Rectory Gdns
C7
1 Limetree Wk
2 Spitfire End
A5
1 Green Park Cl
A4
1 Cavendish Gv
KINGS WORTHY
Abbots Worthy
Kingsworthy Primary School
Hinton House
Princes Mead School
Worthy Park
Springvale
Meadowlands
Boyne Mead Road
Frampton Wy
Loader Cl
Campion Way
Nations Hill
Springvale Av
Bentley Cl
St Nicholas
Mortimer Close
Hinton Fields
Mt. Pleasant
Church Lane
Willis Wave
The Woodlands
The Paddock
Court Road
Springvale Road
Bedfield Lane
LONDON ROAD
St Marys Cl
King's Way
BASINGSTOKE ROAD
A33
B3047
Park Lane
WINCHESTER BY-PASS
A34(T)
Itchen Way
Three Castles Path
Church Lane
Malthouse Cl
Pudding La
School Lane
Long Walk
Easton Lane
Lone Barn
Easton Down
M3
ROAD
21
Abbotts Barton House
Abbotts Rd
WORTHY
Dyson Dr
Francis Gdns
Grosvenor Dr
Charles Cl
Nuns Walk
King's Way
Russell Rd
Hillier Way
Oglander Road
River Itchen
Moorside Road
Junction 9
Leicester Way
3
Winchester City Football Club
Winchester Rugby Football Club
Nuns Road
Nuns Wk
Monks Road
SO23
Hyde
Wykeham Industrial Estate
Easton Lane
A272
Winchester Agricultural Museum
Winnall
Winnall Close
Winnall Mnr Rd
Sun Valley Business Park
River Park Leisure Centre
Easton Lane Business Park
Fiona Cl
Winnall Valley Road
Nickel Close
Colson Road
St Bedes CofE Prim Sch
School of Art
Park Avenue
Manor Cl
Ebden Road
Winnall Fm Industrial Est
Imber Road
Warren Road
Longfield Road
B3330
Police Station
Garbett Road
Durngate Pl
Wales Street
Beggar's Lane
Moss Road
St Martin's Close
Winnall CP School
Winnall Manor Road
Shepherds Road
St Swithuns School
UNION ST
FRIARSGATE
St John's Road
Firmstone Road
Furley Cl
Turnpike Down
Water Lane
Blue Ball Hill
Friarsgate Med Cen
EASTGATE ST
Chester Rd
ALRESFORD
A31
26
St Giles's Hill
Fairdown Close
Magdalen Hill
Winnall Down Farm
ALRESFORD
The Broadway
City Offices
Chesil Theatre
Baring Road
Northbrook Avenue
Chalk Ridge
Colebrook St
Winchester Cathedral
1 grid square represents 500 metres

F
G
Couch Green
J
B3047
Church Lane
Three Castles Path
Martyr Worthy
Chilland Lane
Chilland
Easton Lane
Station Cl
STATION HILL
Shelley Cl
School La
Itchen Abbas CP School
King's Way
Itchen Abbas
River Itchen
1
2
Avington Park
Avington
PH
PH
Easton
3
4
Mud Farm
Harfield
Chapel Lane
5
6
Larkwhistle Farm
Fair Lane
Pits Farm
7
o Man's and
R
B3404
H
27
A31
K
Cemetery

Wood
E2
1 Monmouth Sq
A
B
C
D
E
20
32
1
2
3
4
5
6
7
Sarum Road
Clarendon Way
Royal Winchester Golf Club
Sarum View
Kings School
Kilham Lane
Woodfield Drive
Branksome Close
B3040
St Peters School
Fairfax Close
Oliver's Battery Road
BADGER FAR
Enmill Farm
Enmill Lane
Pitt
A3090
Seldon Close
South Road
Downlands
Oliver's Battery Crs
PO
Braeside Close
Treble Close
Farley Close
Shepherds Close
Momford Road
South View Road
Compton Close
Oliver's Battery
Millers Lane
Sunnydown Road
Beyne Road
Pine Close
Broad View Lane
Beech Cl
Partridge Down
Compton Way
Priors Way
Plovers Down
Texas Drive
Old Kennels Close
Wedmore Close
Lisle Cl
Down Farm
Old Kennels Lane
Lane

1 grid square represents 500 metres

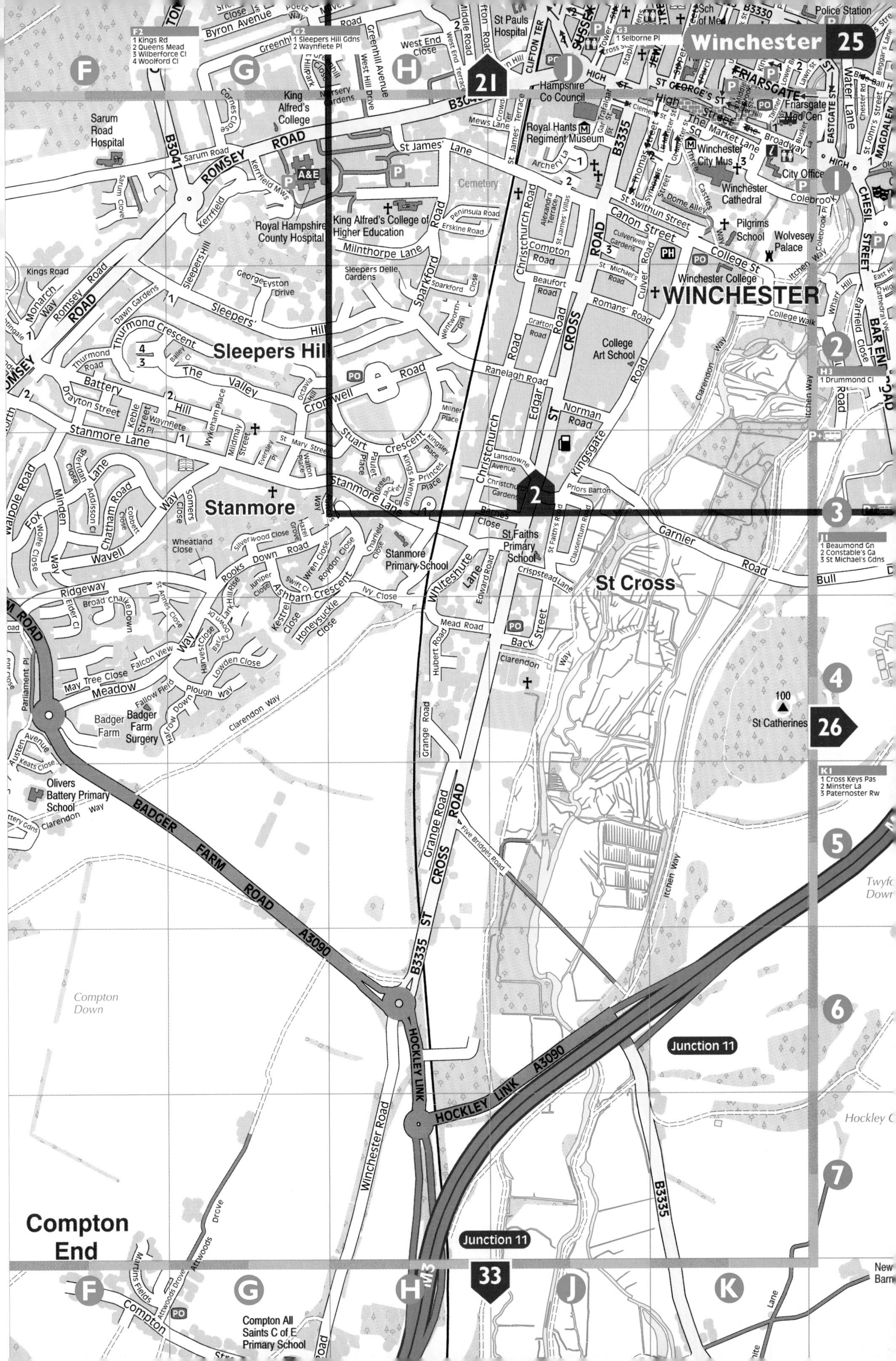
F2
1 Kings Rd
2 Queens Mead
3 Wilberforce Cl
4 Woolford Cl
G2
1 Sleepers Hill Gdns
2 Waynflete Pl
G3
1 Selborne Pl
H3
1 Drummond Cl
J1
1 Beaumond Gn
2 Constable's Ga
3 St Michael's Gdns
K1
1 Cross Keys Pas
2 Minster La
3 Paternoster Rw
21
26
33
2
Police Station
St Pauls Hospital
Byron Avenue
West End Close
Greenhill Avenue
West Hill Drive
King Alfred's College
Sarum Road Hospital
Sarum Road
ROMSEY ROAD
B3041
Hampshire Co Council
Royal Hants Regiment Museum
St James' Lane
Cemetery
Royal Hampshire County Hospital
King Alfred's College of Higher Education
Milnthorpe Lane
Peninsula Road
Erskine Road
Sparkford Road
Christchurch Road
Compton Road
Beaufort Road
Grafton Road
Canon Street
St Swithun Street
Culverwell Gardens
College St
Winchester College
Pilgrims School
Wolvesey Palace
Winchester Cathedral
Winchester City Mus
City Offices
Friarsgate Med Cen
FRIARSGATE
ST GEORGE'S ST
High Street
The Square
The Broadway
Market Lane
Colebrook St
CHESIL STREET
EASTGATE ST
Water Lane
WINCHESTER
College Walk
College Art School
Romans' Road
Kingsgate Road
ST CROSS ROAD
Edgar Road
Ranelagh Road
Norman Road
Milner Place
Cromwell Road
Stuart Crescent
Kingsley Place
Princes Place
Kings Avenue
Paulet Place
Sleepers Hill
Sleepers Delle Gardens
George Eyston Drive
Kings Road
Monarch Way
Thurmond Crescent
Dawn Gardens
Battery Hill
The Valley
Drayton Street
Stanmore Lane
Stanmore
Keble Street
Waynflete Pl
Wykeham Place
Mildmay Street
Eversley Pl
St Mary Street
Walton Place
Sheridan Close
Addisson Cl
Chatham Road
Cobbett Close
Walpole Road
Fox Lane
Minden Way
Wolfe Close
Wavell Way
Somers Close
Wheatland Close
Silverwood Close
Hazel Grove
Rooks Down Road
Wren Close
Roydon Close
Charfield Close
Stanmore Primary School
Ashbarn Crescent
Ivy Close
Kestrel Close
Honeysuckle Close
Juniper Close
Swift Cl
Ridgeway
Elder Cl
Broad Chalke Down
St Annes Close
Falcon View Way
Harvest Close
Lowden Close
May Tree Close
Meadow Way
Plough Way
Harrow Down
Fallow Field
Badger Farm
Badger Farm Surgery
Clarendon Way
Parliament Pl
Austen Avenue
Keats Close
Olivers Battery Primary School
BADGER FARM ROAD
A3090
Compton Down
Compton End
Martins Fields
Attwoods Drove
Compton
Compton All Saints C of E Primary School
Lansdowne Avenue
Christchurch Gardens
Priors Barton
Barnes Close
St Faiths Primary School
St Faith's Road
Clausentum Road
Garnier Road
Bull Dr
Crispstead Lane
St Cross
Whiteshute Lane
Edward Road
Mead Road
Back Street
Hubert Road
Clarendon Way
Grange Road
Five Bridges Road
Itchen Way
B3335
HOCKLEY LINK
Junction 11
Winchester Road
M3
St Catherines
100
Twyford Down
Hockley
Barfield Close
Wharf Hill
Drove
Lane

26
22
25
3
Junction 10
Police Station
Garbett Road
Manor Road
Shepherds Road
Winnall CP School
Firmstone Road
Turnpike
St Swithun's School
1 Palm Hall Cl
1 Prinstead Cl
1 Bridge St
FRIARSCATE
Friarsgate Med Cen
UNION ST
EASTGATE ST
Water Lane
MAGDALEN HILL
ALRESFORD ROAD
B3404
ALRESFORD
St Giles's Hill
Fairdown Close
Northbrook Avenue
Baring Road
Stratton Road
Highmount Cl
Quarry Road
Chalk Ridge
Old Station Approach
Chesil Theatre
CHESIL STREET
Petersfield Road
Fivefields Road
Gordon Avenue
Primary School
Winchester Cathedral
City Offices
Colebrook St
Pilgrims School
Wolvesey Palace
College St
College Walk
Itchen Way
Wharf Hill
Domum Road
Barfield Close
BAR END ROAD
St Catherine's Road
Portal Road
Vale Road
Milland Road
Bar End
Chilcomb Lane
B3330
Bar End Road
Bull Drove
Morestead Road
M3
A33
A31
Magdalen Hill Down
South Downs Way
Kings Lane
Chilcomb Lane
Chi
Twyford Down
Morestead Road
Hockley Golf Club
Morestead Down
Morestead Farm
New Farm
Hazeley Down
A
B
C
D
E
1
2
3
4
5
6
7
1 grid square represents 500 metres

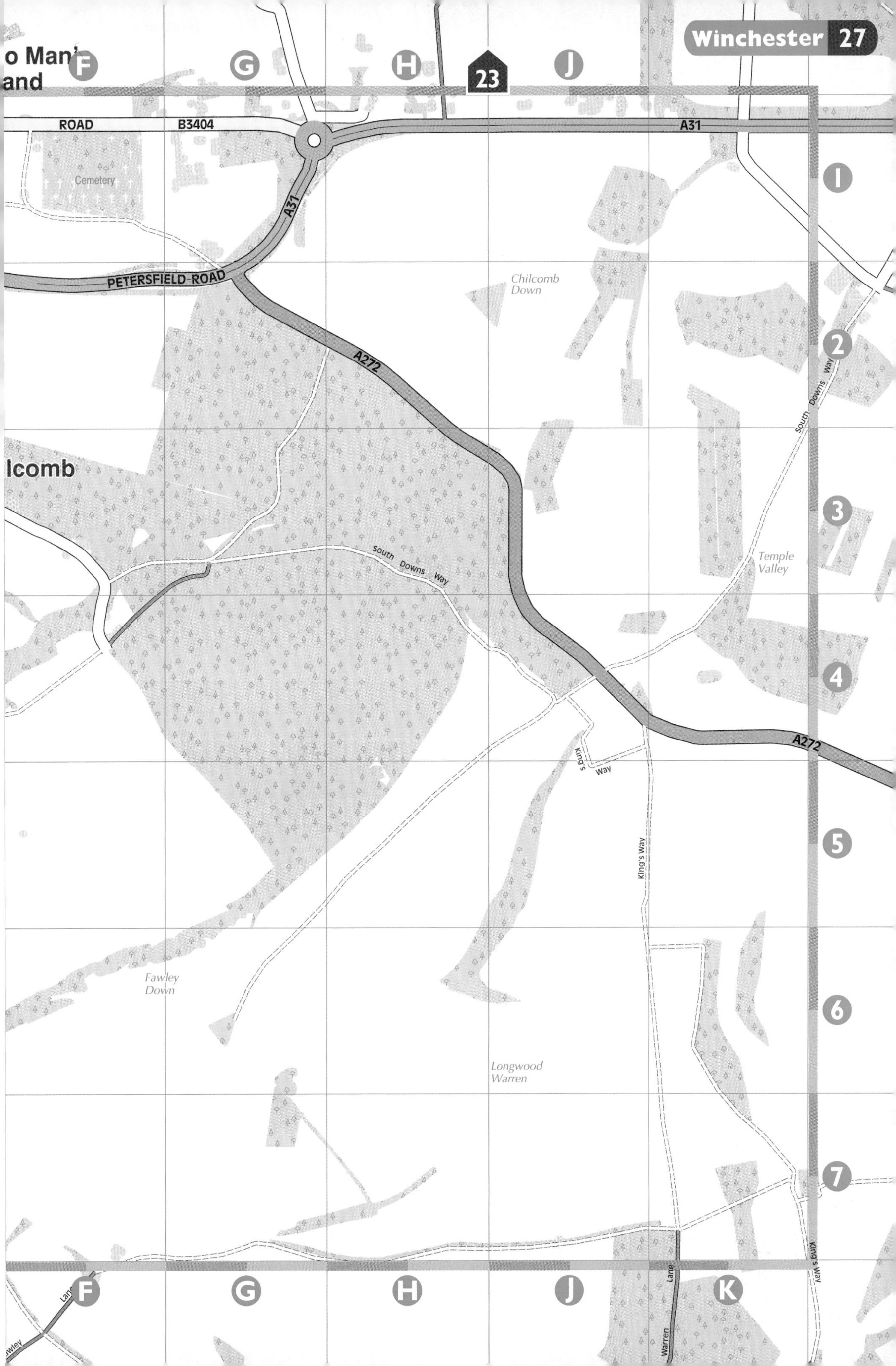
o Man'
and
F
G
H
J
23
ROAD
B3404
A31
Cemetery
A31
PETERSFIELD ROAD
Chilcomb
Down
A272
lcomb
South Downs Way
South Downs Way
Temple
Valley
A272
King's Way
King's Way
Fawley
Down
Longwood
Warren
Lane
Warren
Lane
King's Way
F
G
H
J
K
1
2
3
4
5
6
7

C2
1 The Milburns
Michelmersh
Monarch's Way
Staff Rd
Manor Farm Lane
Lane
Rudd Lane
Hill View Road
PO
New Road
Chapel La
Hunts Fm
STOCKBRIDGE ROAD
Mannyngham Way
Linhay Meads
Timsbury
A3057
Casbrook Common
Heron Lane
St Andrews Cl
Timsbury Manor
Jinny Lane
Yokesford Hill
Brook Fm
Belbins
Cooks Lane
STANBRIDGE LANE
B3084
GREATBRIDGE ROAD
Stanbridge Earls School
South Drive
Greatbridge Ho
Great Bridge
Roke Manor Fm
SO51
Greatbridge Business Park
A B C D E
1 2 3 4 5 6 7

34

G7
1 Cavendish Cl
H7
1 Anderson Cl
2 Ganger Rd
3 The Green
4 Norris Cl
5 Woodley Wy
F
G
H
J
K
Farley Lane
Paynes Hay Road
Paynes Hay Farm
Braishfield Road
Monarch's Way
Fern Hill Lane
Church Lane
Braishfield
Sharpes Fm
Lower St
Rudd Lane
Dummers Rd
Newport Lane
Common Hill Road
Hill Vw Rd
PO
Braishfield CP School
Kiln Lane
Megana Wy
Fairbornes Fm
Pucki
30
Abbotswood Fm
Jermyns Ho
Jermyns Lane
Sandy Lane
Belbins Business Park
Abbotswood
Cemetery
Cupernham Lane
Ganger Fm
A3090
THE STRAIGHT MILE
Woodley Cl
Woodley Close
Woodley Lane
Ganger Farm Lane
Foxcotte Cl
Horseshoe Dr
Stapleford Cl
Cavendish Cl
Brook Way
Brook Wy
Hunters Cres
Short Hl
School Road
Anstey Road
Halden Cl
Oakwood Cl
Pinewood Cl
Cedar Lawn
Peel Cl
Kinver Cl
Bransley Cl
Winterbourne
Richmond Lane
Woodley Lane
Carisbrooke Ct
Oxlease Cl
Junior & Infant
Cupernham
35
Woodley
Grovely Wy
Lane
1
2
3
4
5
6
7

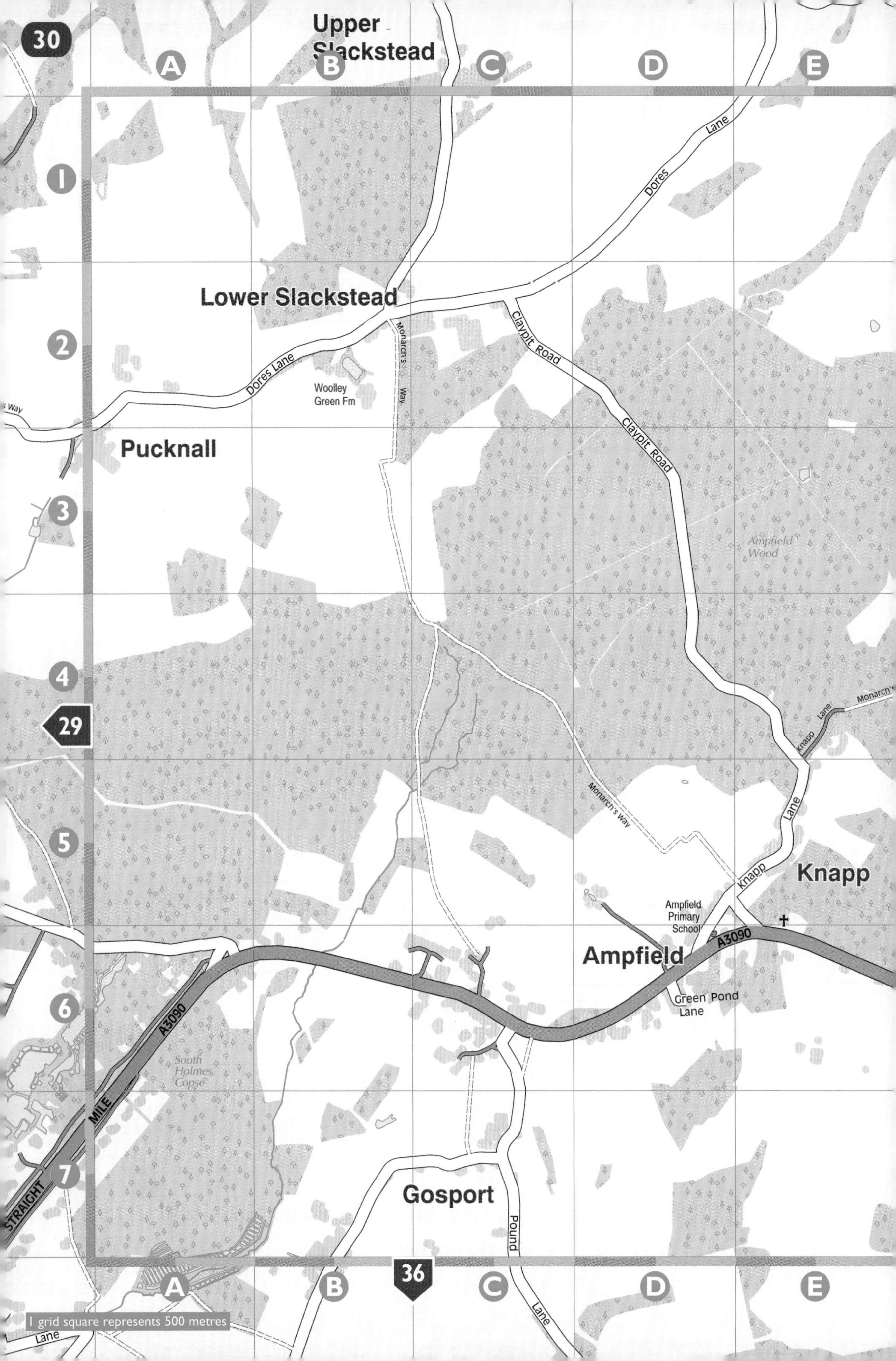
Upper Slackstead
A
B
C
D
E
1
2
3
4
5
6
7
Dores Lane
Lower Slackstead
Claypit Road
Monarch's Way
Woolley Green Fm
Pucknall
Ampfield Wood
29
Knapp Lane
Monarch's Way
Knapp
Ampfield Primary School
A3090
Ampfield
Green Pond Lane
South Holmes Copse
STRAIGHT MILE
Gosport
Pound Lane
36
Lane
1 grid square represents 500 metres

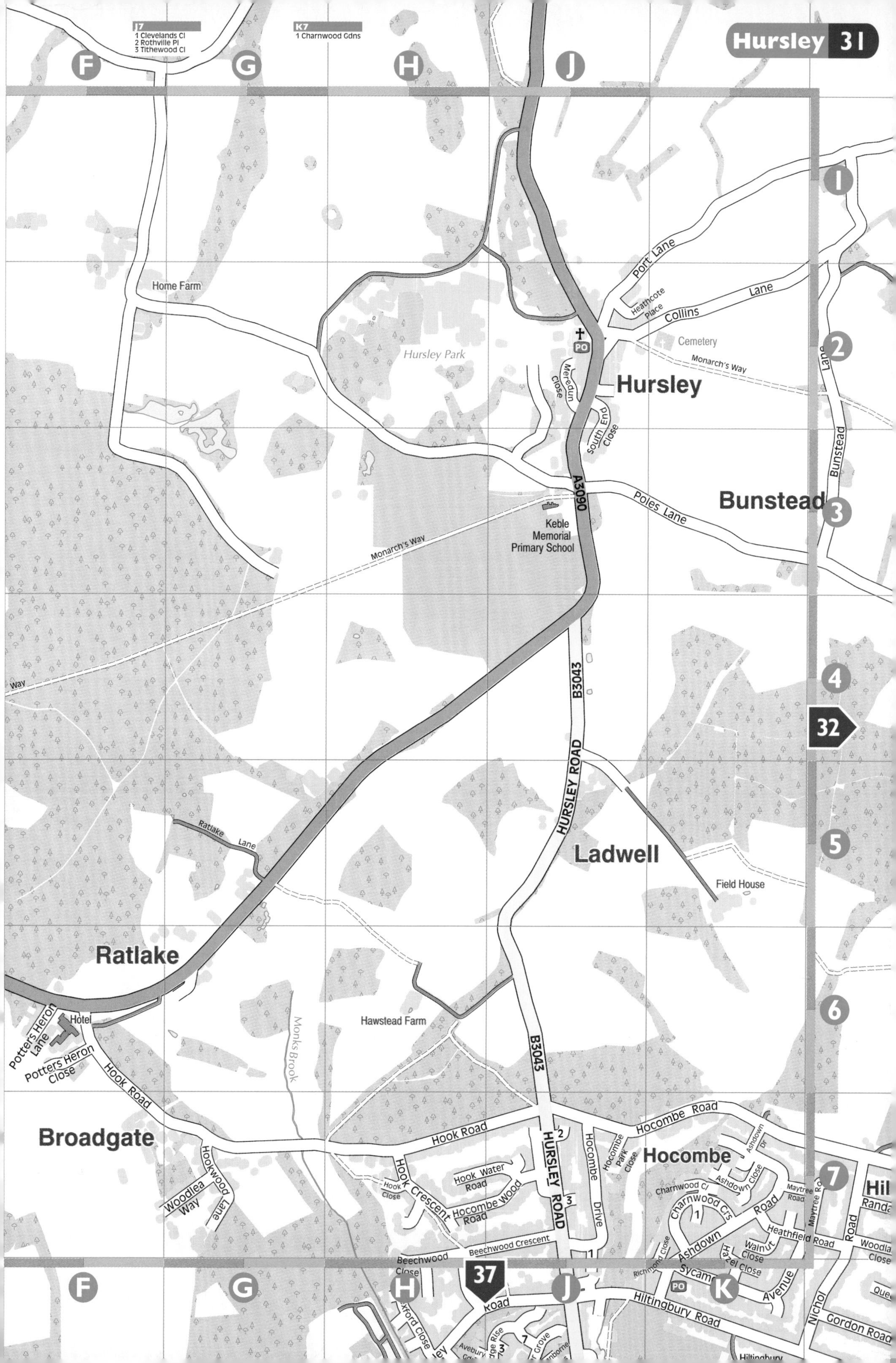
J7
1 Clevelands Cl
2 Rothville Pl
3 Tithewood Cl
K7
1 Charnwood Gdns
F
G
H
J
K
1
2
3
4
5
6
7
32
37
Home Farm
Hursley Park
Port Lane
Heathcote Place
Collins Lane
Cemetery
Monarch's Way
Meredun Close
PO
Hursley
South End Close
Bunstead Lane
Bunstead
A3090
Poles Lane
Keble Memorial Primary School
Way
B3043
HURSLEY ROAD
Ratlake Lane
Ladwell
Field House
Ratlake
Hotel
Potters Heron Lane
Potters Heron Close
Hawstead Farm
Monks Brook
Hook Road
Broadgate
Hookwood Lane
Woodlea Way
Hook Crescent
Hook Close
Hook Water Road
Hocombe Wood Road
Beechwood Crescent
Beechwood Close
Hocombe Road
Hocombe Drive
Hocombe Park Close
Hocombe
Ashdown Dr
Ashdown Close
Charnwood Cl
Charnwood Crs
Ashdown Road
Maytree Road
Maytree Rd
Heathfield Road
Walnut Close
Hazel Close
Richmond Close
Sycamore Avenue
Hiltingbury Road
Nichol Road
Gordon Road
Randall
Woodlea Close
Oxford Close
Avebury Gdns
Road

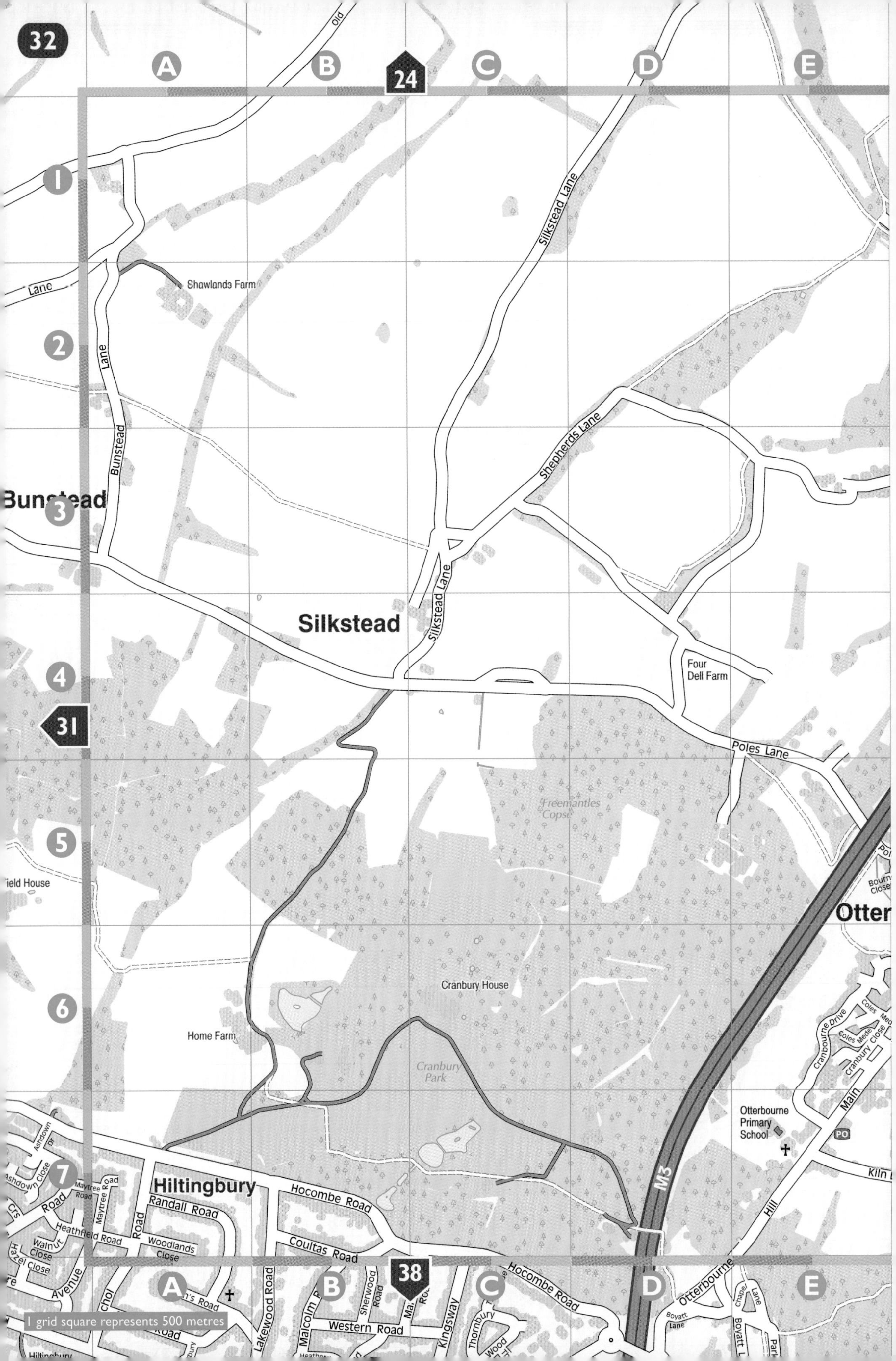

24
38
31
A
B
C
D
E
1
2
3
4
5
6
7
Old
Lane
Shawlands Farm
Bunstead Lane
Bunstead
Silkstead Lane
Shepherds Lane
Silkstead
Four Dell Farm
Poles Lane
Freemantles Copse
Field House
Otter
Bourne Close
Cranbury House
Home Farm
Cranbury Park
Hiltingbury
Ashdown Dr
Ashdown Close
Maytree Road
Road
Crs
Heathfield Road
Walnut Close
Hazel Close
Avenue
Randall Road
Woodlands Close
Hocombe Road
Coultas Road
Lakewood Road
Malcolm
Sherwood Road
Western Road
Kingsway
Thornbury
Wood
M3
Otterbourne
Boyatt Lane
Chapel Lane
Otterbourne Primary School
PO
Main
Hill
Kiln
Cranbourne Drive
Coles Mede
Cranbury Close
1 grid square represents 500 metres

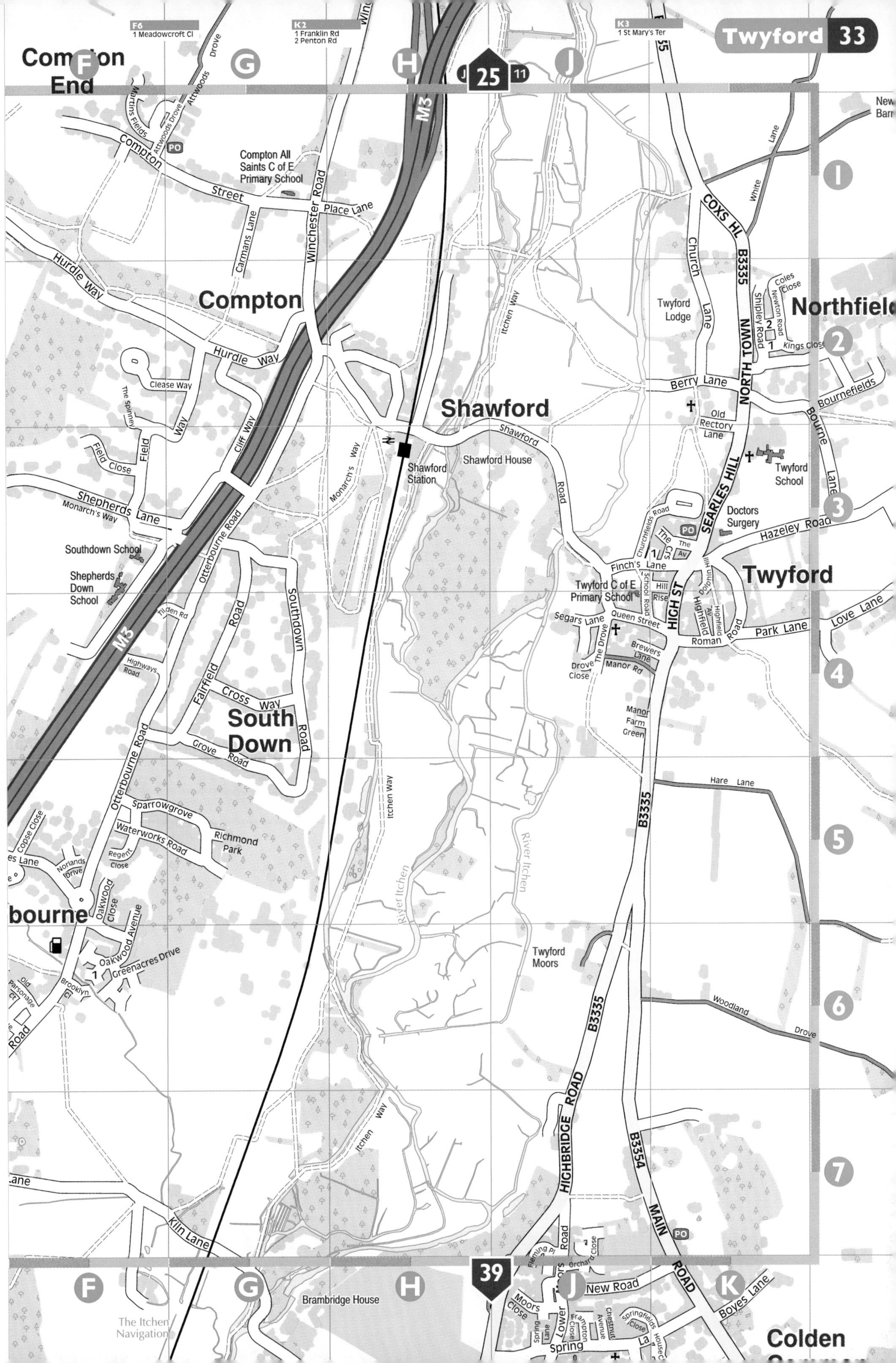
F6
1 Meadowcroft Cl
K2
1 Franklin Rd
2 Penton Rd
K3
1 St Mary's Ter
Compton End
F
G
H
J
25
11
M3
Drove
Attwoods
Martins Fields
Attwoods Drove
PO
Compton
Street
Compton All Saints C of E Primary School
Carmans Lane
Winchester Road
Place Lane
Hurdle Way
Compton
Hurdle Way
Clease Way
The Spinney
Field
Way
Field Close
Cliff Way
Shepherds Lane
Monarch's Way
Southdown School
Shepherds Down School
Otterbourne Road
Tilden Rd
Highways Road
Fairfield
Road
Southdown
Road
Cross Way
South Down
Grove Road
Otterbourne Road
Sparrowgrove
Waterworks Road
Richmond Park
Regent Close
Copse Close
Norlands Drive
Oakwood Close
Oakwood Avenue
Greenacres Drive
Brooklyn Cl
Old Parsonage Ct
Road
bourne
Lane
Kiln Lane
Shawford
Shawford
Road
Shawford House
Shawford Station
Monarch's Way
Itchen Way
Itchen Way
River Itchen
River Itchen
Itchen Way
Twyford Moors
New Barn
Lane
White
COXS HL
B3335
Church Lane
Twyford Lodge
NORTH TOWN
Shipley Road
Newton Road
Coles Close
Kings Close
Northfield
2
Berry Lane
Bournefields
Bourne Lane
Old Rectory Lane
SEARLES HILL
Twyford School
Doctors Surgery
Hazeley Road
3
Churchfields Road
The Crs
The Av
PO
Finch's Lane
Twyford C of E Primary School
School Road
Hill Rise
HIGH ST
Dolphin Hill
Highfield Av
Highfield
Twyford
Love Lane
Park Lane
Roman Road
Segars Lane
Queen Street
The Drove
Brewers Lane
Drove Close
Manor Rd
4
Manor Farm Green
Hare Lane
B3335
5
B3335
6
Woodland Drove
HIGHBRIDGE ROAD
B3354
MAIN ROAD
7
PO
Fleming Pl
Road
Orchard Close
39
Moors Close
Lower Moors
Spring Lane
Frampton Close
Chestnut Avenue
Springfields Close
New Road
Boyes Lane
K
Brambridge House
The Itchen Navigation
Colden
Spring

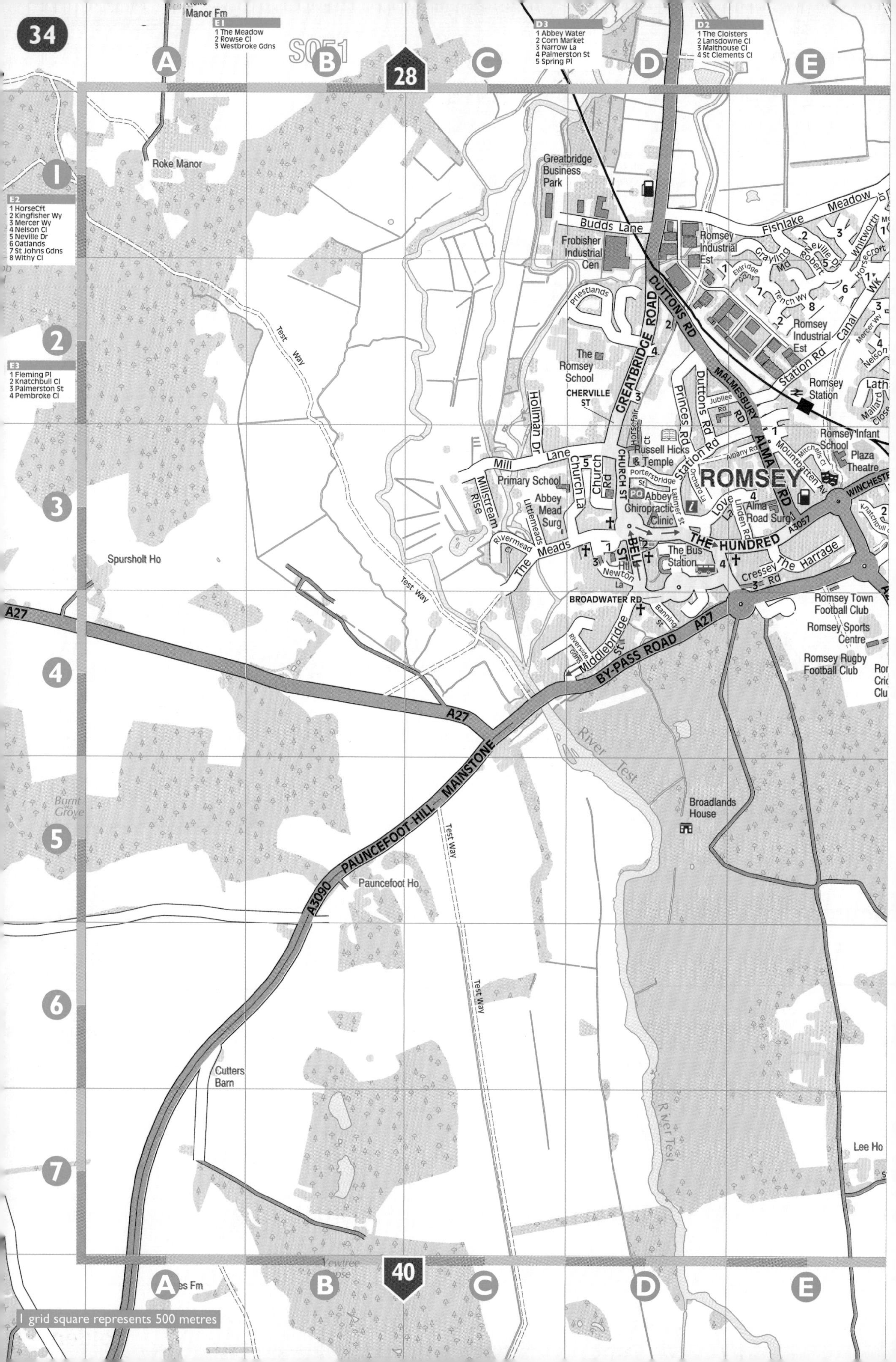
Manor Fm
E1
1 The Meadow
2 Rowse Cl
3 Westbroke Gdns
SO51
28
D3
1 Abbey Water
2 Corn Market
3 Narrow La
4 Palmerston St
5 Spring Pl
D2
1 The Cloisters
2 Lansdowne Cl
3 Malthouse Cl
4 St Clements Cl
A
B
C
D
E
E2
1 HorseCft
2 Kingfisher Wy
3 Mercer Wy
4 Nelson Cl
5 Neville Dr
6 Oatlands
7 St Johns Gdns
8 Withy Cl
E3
1 Fleming Pl
2 Knatchbull Cl
3 Palmerston St
4 Pembroke Cl
1
2
3
4
5
6
7
Roke Manor
Greatbridge Business Park
Budds Lane
Frobisher Industrial Cen
Romsey Industrial Est
Fishlake Meadow
Grayling Md
Eldridge Gdns
Tench Wy
Neville Dr
Robert
Whitworth
Horsecroft
Wk
Mercer Wy
Nelson
Priestlands
DUTTONS RD
GREATBRIDGE ROAD
Romsey Industrial Est
Station Rd
Canal
Romsey Station
The Romsey School
CHERVILLE ST
MALMESBURY RD
Jubilee Rd
Duttons Rd
Princes Rd
Mallard Close
Test Way
Holliman Dr
Horsefair Ct
Russell Hicks & Temple
Station Rd
Albany Rd
ALMA RD
Romsey Infant School
Plaza Theatre
Mill Lane
Primary School
Church La
Church Rd
CHURCH ST
Portersbridge St
Abbey Chiropractic Clinic
Orchard La
Latimer St
ROMSEY
Mountbatten Av
Mitchells Cl
WINCHESTER
Millstream Rise
Littlemeads
Abbey Mead Surg
Love La
Linden Rd
Alma Road Surg
A3057
Knatchbull Cl
Rivermead Cl
The Meads
BELL ST
THE HUNDRED
The Bus Station
Cressey Rd
The Harrage
Spursholt Ho
Hill
Newton La
BROADWATER RD
Banning St
Romsey Town Football Club
Romsey Sports Centre
A27
Riverside Gdns
Middlebridge St
BY-PASS ROAD
A27
Romsey Rugby Football Club
A27
River Test
Burnt Grove
PAUNCEFOOT HILL
MAINSTONE
Broadlands House
Test Way
A3090
Pauncefoot Ho
Test Way
Cutters Barn
River Test
Lee Ho
Yewtree
40
es Fm
1 grid square represents 500 metres

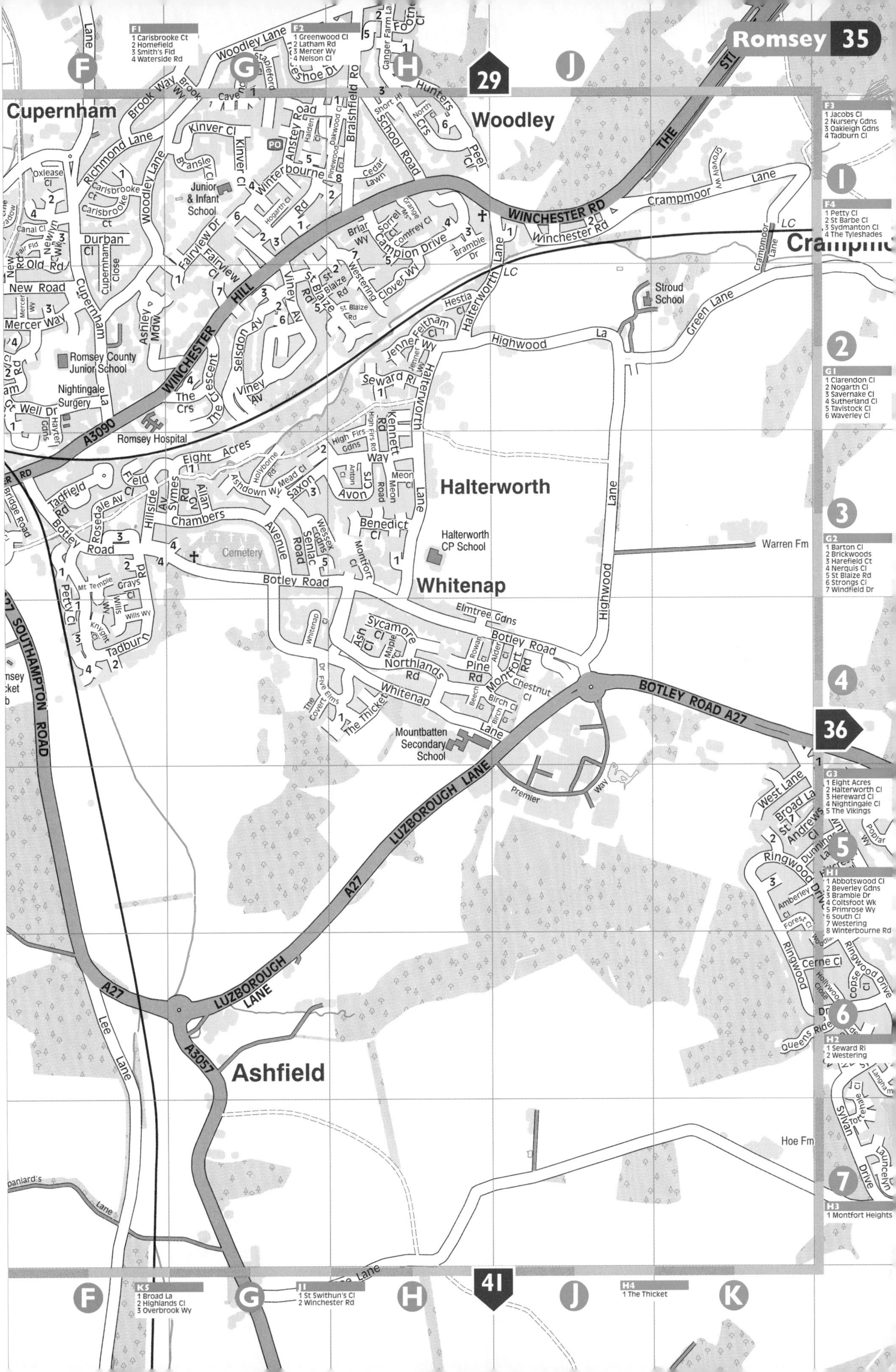
F1
1 Carisbrooke Ct
2 Homefield
3 Smith's Fld
4 Waterside Rd
F2
1 Greenwood Cl
2 Latham Rd
3 Mercer Wy
4 Nelson Cl
F3
1 Jacobs Cl
2 Nursery Gdns
3 Oakleigh Gdns
4 Tadburn Cl
F4
1 Petty Cl
2 St Barbe Cl
3 Sydmanton Cl
4 The Tyleshades
G1
1 Clarendon Cl
2 Nogarth Cl
3 Savernake Cl
4 Sutherland Cl
5 Tavistock Cl
6 Waverley Cl
G2
1 Barton Cl
2 Brickwoods
3 Harefield Ct
4 Nerquis Cl
5 St Blaize Rd
6 Strongs Cl
7 Windfield Dr
G3
1 Eight Acres
2 Halterworth Cl
3 Hereward Cl
4 Nightingale Cl
5 The Vikings
H1
1 Abbotswood Cl
2 Beverley Gdns
3 Bramble Dr
4 Coltsfoot Wk
5 Primrose Wy
6 South Cl
7 Westering
8 Winterbourne Rd
H2
1 Seward Ri
2 Westering
H3
1 Montfort Heights
K5
1 Broad La
2 Highlands Cl
3 Overbrook Wy
J1
1 St Swithun's Cl
2 Winchester Rd
H4
1 The Thicket
29
36
41
Cupernham
Woodley
Crampmoor
Halterworth
Whitenap
Ashfield
Romsey County Junior School
Nightingale Surgery
Romsey Hospital
Junior & Infant School
Stroud School
Halterworth CP School
Mountbatten Secondary School
Cemetery
Warren Fm
Hoe Fm
WINCHESTER RD
WINCHESTER HILL
A3090
BOTLEY ROAD A27
LUZBOROUGH LANE
A27
A3057
SOUTHAMPTON ROAD
Highwood Lane
Green Lane
Crampmoor Lane
Botley Road
Halterworth Lane
Lee Lane

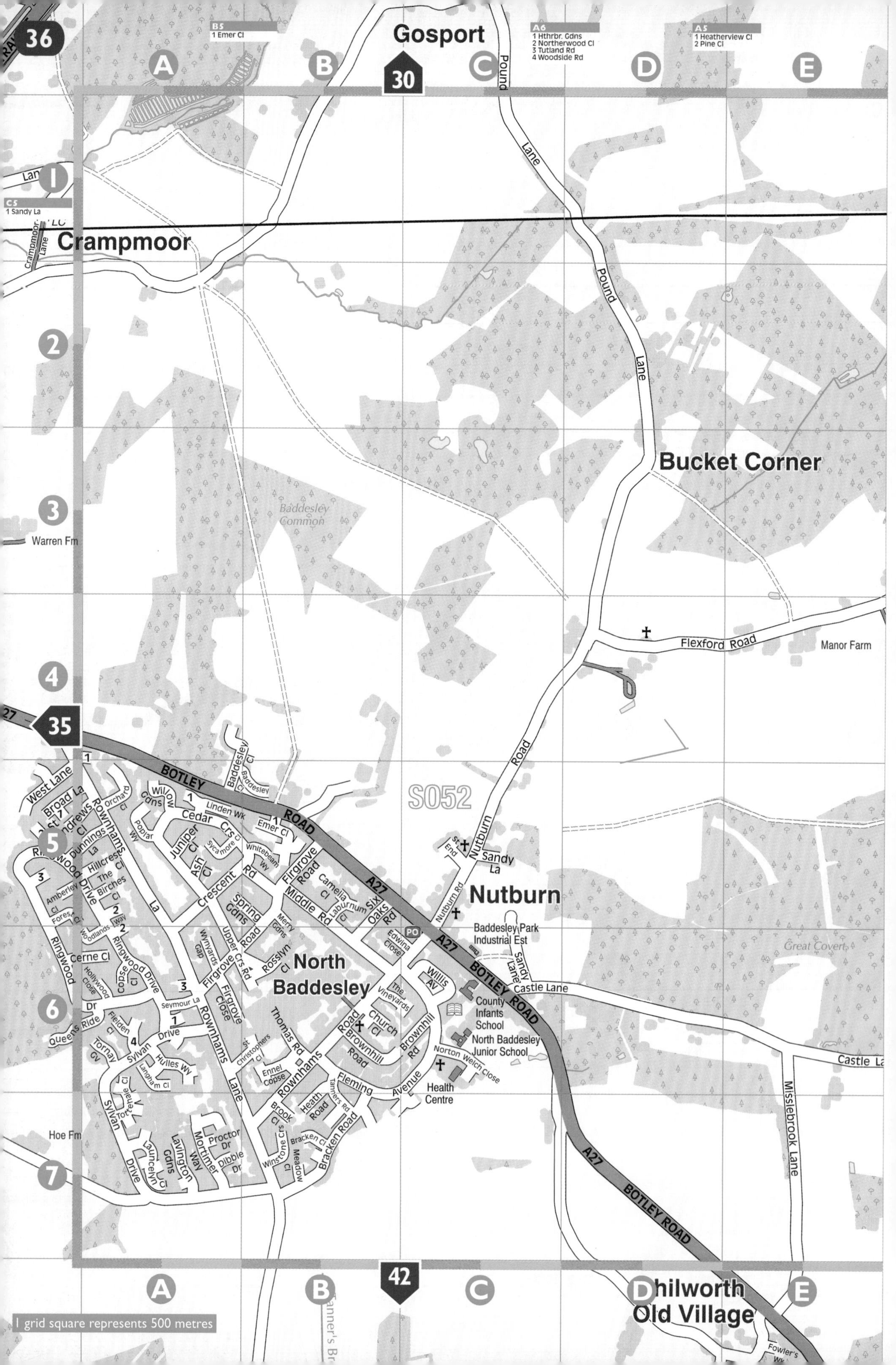
Gosport
30
B5
1 Emer Cl
A6
1 Hthrbr. Gdns
2 Northerwood Cl
3 Tutland Rd
4 Woodside Rd
A5
1 Heatherview Cl
2 Pine Cl
A
B
C
D
E
1
2
3
4
5
6
7
C5
1 Sandy La
Crampmoor
Crampmoor Lane
Pound Lane
Pound Lane
Baddesley Common
Bucket Corner
Warren Fm
Flexford Road
Manor Farm
35
A27
BOTLEY ROAD
Pound Road
SO52
Nutburn Road
Sandy La
Nutburn
Nutburn Rd
Baddesley Park Industrial Est
Great Covert
Sandy Lane
Castle Lane
Castle Lane
North Baddesley
County Infants School
North Baddesley Junior School
Norton Welch Close
Health Centre
West Lane
Broad La
St Andrews Cl
Rownhams La
Orchard
Willow Gdns
Cedar Crs
Linden Wk
Baddesley Cl
Emer Cl
Poplar Wy
Juniper Cl
Ash Cl
Sycamore Cl
Whitebeam Wy
Crescent Rd
Firgrove Road
Camelia Cl
Laburnum Cl
Six Oaks Rd
Middle Rd
Spring Gdns
Merry Gdns
Upper Crs Rd
Wynyards Gap
Dunnings La
Hillcrest
The Birches Cl
Ringwood Drive
Amberley Cl
Forest Cl
Woodlands Way
Ringwood Drive
Ringwood Dr
Cerne Cl
Hollywood Close
Copse Cl
Firgrove Rd
Firgrove Close
Rosslyn Cl
Road
Edwina Close
Willis Av
The Vineyards
Church Cl
Brownhill Road
Brownhill Rd
Seymour La
Rownhams Lane
Thomas Rd
St Christophers Cl
Queens Ride
Fielden Cl
Tornay Gv
Sylvan Drive
Hulles Wy
Langham Cl
Sylvan Drive
Tottehale Cl
Ennel Copse
Rownhams Rd
Fleming Avenue
Tanners Rd
Heath Road
Brook Cl
Winstone Crs
Bracken Cl
Bracken Road
Meadow Cl
Hoe Fm
Lavington Gdns
Mortimer Way
Proctor Dr
Dibble Dr
Launcelyn Cl
Misslebrook Lane
PO
A27 BOTLEY ROAD
42
Chilworth Old Village
Fowler's Wk
Tanner's Br
1 grid square represents 500 metres

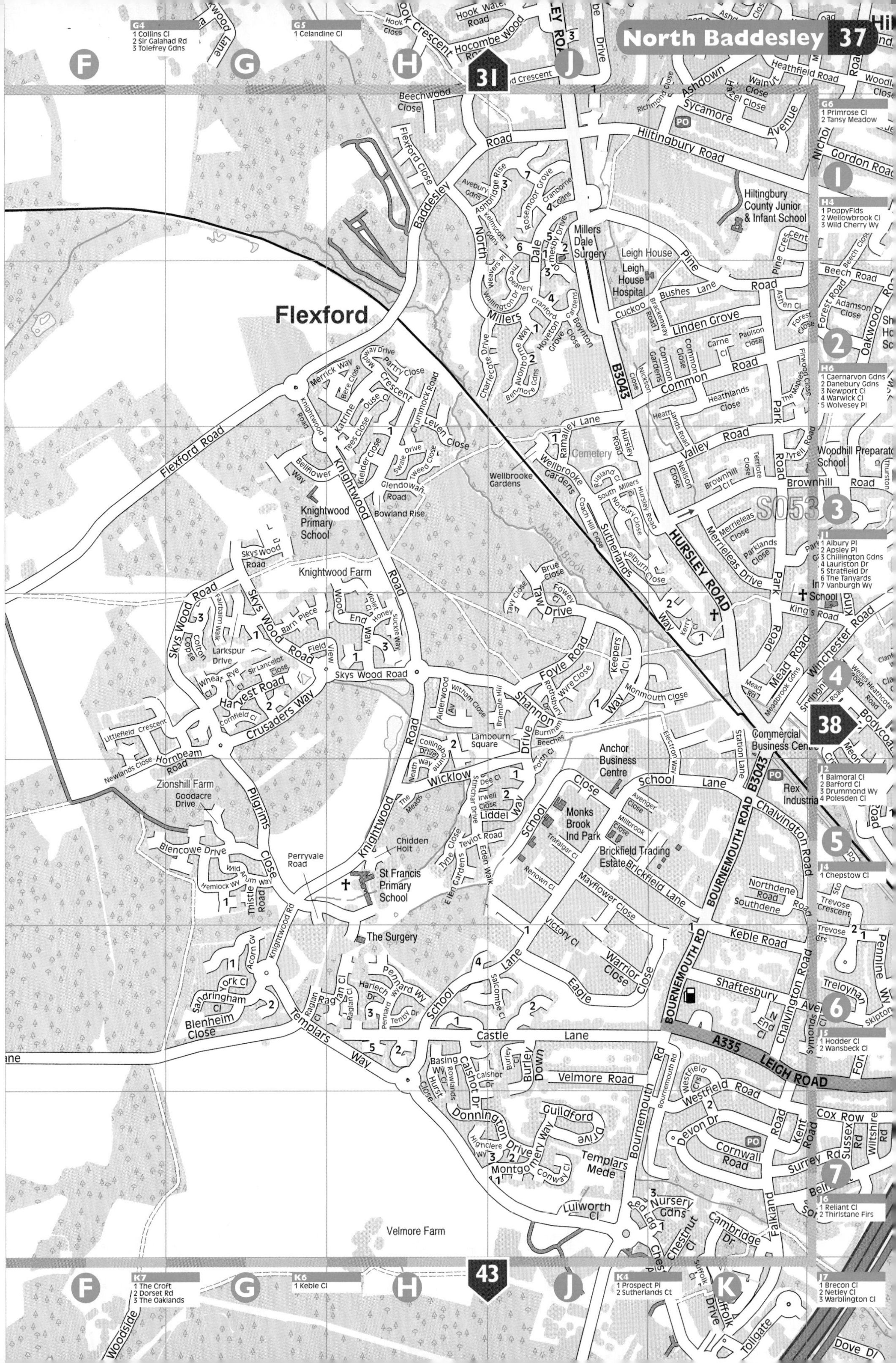
G4
1 Collins Cl
2 Sir Galahad Rd
3 Tolefrey Gdns
G5
1 Celandine Cl
G6
1 Primrose Cl
2 Tansy Meadow
H4
1 PoppyFlds
2 Wellowbrook Cl
3 Wild Cherry Wy
H6
1 Caernarvon Gdns
2 Danebury Gdns
3 Newport Cl
4 Warwick Cl
5 Wolvesey Pl
J1
1 Albury Pl
2 Apsley Pl
3 Chillington Gdns
4 Lauriston Dr
5 Stratfield Dr
6 The Tanyards
7 Vanburgh Wy
J2
1 Balmoral Cl
2 Barford Cl
3 Drummond Wy
4 Polesden Cl
J4
1 Chepstow Cl
J5
1 Hodder Cl
2 Wansbeck Cl
J6
1 Reliant Cl
2 Thirlstane Firs
J7
1 Brecon Cl
2 Netley Cl
3 Warblington Cl
K7
1 The Croft
2 Dorset Rd
3 The Oaklands
K6
1 Keble Cl
K4
1 Prospect Pl
2 Sutherlands Ct
F
G
H
J
K
31
38
43
Flexford
Flexford Road
Flexford Close
Baddesley Road
North Millers Dale
Hook Crescent
Hook Water Road
Hocombe Wood Road
Beechwood Close
Ashdown
Sycamore Avenue
Hiltingbury Road
Heathfield Road
Gordon Road
Hiltingbury County Junior & Infant School
Millers Dale Surgery
Leigh House
Leigh House Hospital
Pine Road
Cuckoo Bushes Lane
Linden Grove
Common Road
Heathlands Close
Valley Road
Brownhill Road
Woodhill Preparatory School
Ramalley Lane
Cemetery
Wellbrooke Gardens
Sutherlands Way
Merrieleas Drive
Parklands Close
Park Road
King's Road
Winchester Road
HURSLEY ROAD
B3043
Merrick Way
Partry Close
Crescent
Crummock Road
Leven Close
Knightwood Road
Knightwood Primary School
Bellflower Way
Glendowan Road
Bowland Rise
Knightwood Farm
Skys Wood Road
Barn Piece
Larkspur Drive
Harvest Road
Crusaders Way
Littlefield Crescent
Hornbeam Road
Newlands Close
Zionshill Farm
Goodacre Drive
Pilgrims Close
Blencowe Drive
Thistle Road
Taw Drive
Foyle Road
Shannon Way
Monmouth Close
Keepers Cl
Lambourn Square
Wicklow Drive
Liddel Way
Anchor Business Centre
School Lane
Monks Brook Ind Park
Brickfield Trading Estate
Brickfield Lane
Commercial Business Centre
Rex Industrial
BOURNEMOUTH ROAD
Chalvington Road
Northdene Road
Southdene Road
Keble Road
Shaftesbury Avenue
Trevose Crescent
Pennine Way
Treloyhan
Chidden Holt
Perryvale Road
St Francis Primary School
The Surgery
Victory Cl
Mayflower Close
Warrior Close
Eagle Close
Castle Lane
Templars Way
Blenheim Close
Sandringham Cl
York Cl
Acorn Gv
Velmore Road
Donnington Drive
Guildford Drive
Templars Mede
Lulworth Cl
Nursery Gdns
Cambridge Dr
Chestnut Cl
Velmore Farm
A335 LEIGH ROAD
Westfield Road
Devon Dr
Cornwall Road
Kent Road
Cox Row
Surrey Rd
Sussex Rd
Wiltshire Rd
Suffolk Drive
Tollgate
Dove Dr
Woodside
Monks Brook
SO53

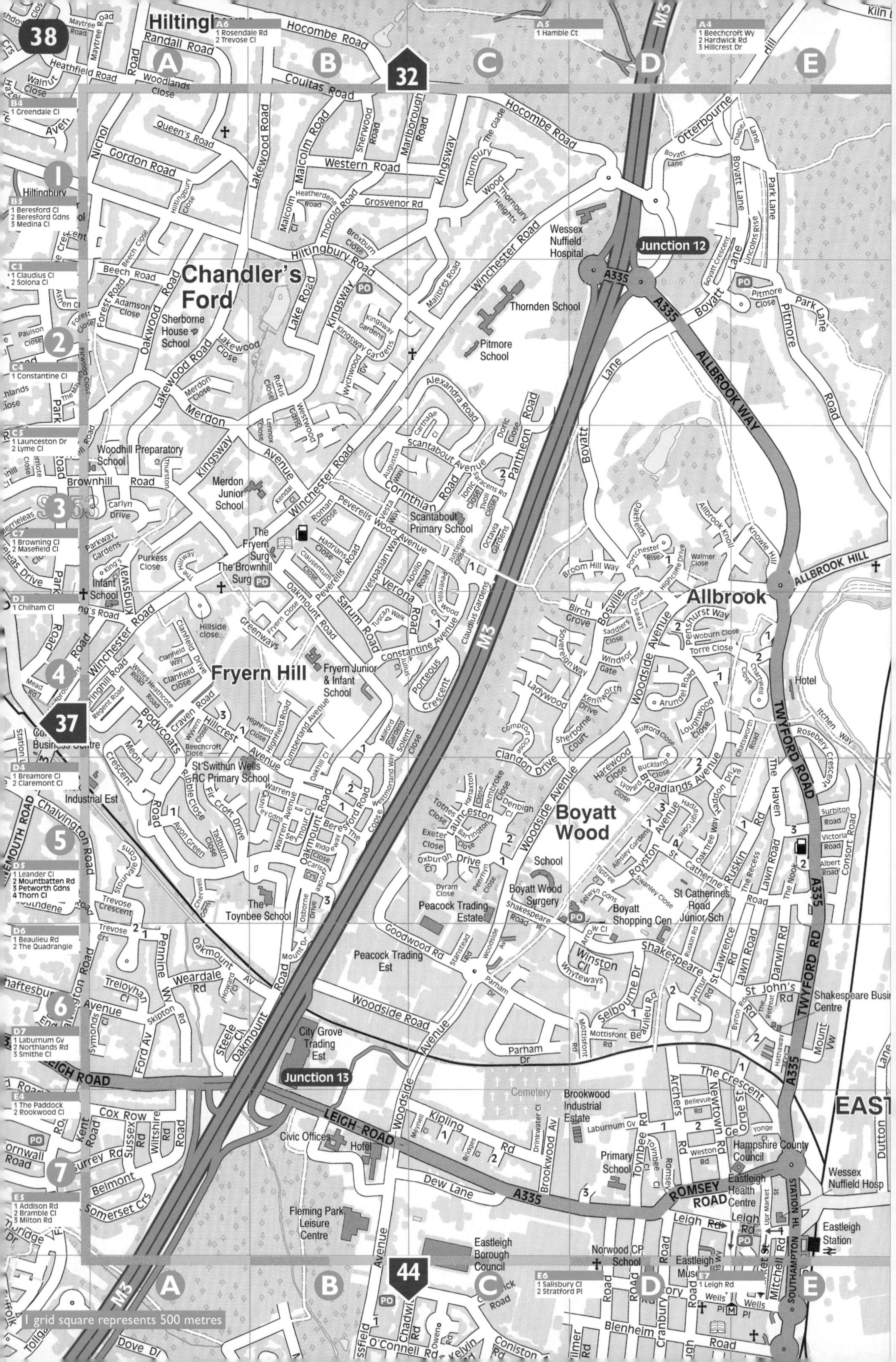
A6
1 Rosendale Rd
2 Trevose Cl
A5
1 Hamble Ct
A4
1 Beechcroft Wy
2 Hardwick Rd
3 Hillcrest Dr
B4
1 Greendale Cl
B5
1 Beresford Cl
2 Beresford Gdns
3 Medina Cl
C3
1 Claudius Cl
2 Solona Cl
C4
1 Constantine Cl
C5
1 Launceston Dr
2 Lyme Cl
C7
1 Browning Cl
2 Masefield Cl
D3
1 Chilham Cl
D4
1 Breamore Cl
2 Claremont Cl
D5
1 Leander Cl
2 Mountbatten Rd
3 Petworth Gdns
4 Thorn Cl
D6
1 Beaulieu Rd
2 The Quadrangle
D7
1 Laburnum Gv
2 Northlands Rd
3 Smithe Cl
E4
1 The Paddock
2 Rookwood Cl
E5
1 Addison Rd
2 Bramble Cl
3 Milton Rd
E6
1 Salisbury Cl
2 Stratford Pl
E7
1 Leigh Rd
32
37
44
A
B
C
D
E
1
2
3
4
5
6
7
Hiltingbury
Chandler's Ford
Fryern Hill
Allbrook
Boyatt Wood
Junction 12
Junction 13
M3
A335
ALLBROOK WAY
ALLBROOK HILL
TWYFORD ROAD
TWYFORD RD
LEIGH ROAD
ROMSEY ROAD
Hocombe Road
Coultas Road
Randall Road
Heathfield Road
Woodlands Close
Winchester Road
Hiltingbury Road
Kingsway
Lakewood Road
Merdon Avenue
Brownhill Road
Oakmount Road
Woodside Avenue
Boyatt Lane
Otterbourne Hill
Pitmore Road
Park Lane
Shakespeare Road
Goodwood Rd
Parham Dr
Woodside Road
Kipling Rd
Dew Lane
Chalvington Road
Leigh Road
Southampton Rd
Station Hill
Wessex Nuffield Hospital
Thornden School
Pitmore School
Sherborne House School
Woodhill Preparatory School
Merdon Junior School
The Fryern Surg
The Brownhill Surg
King's Infant School
Scantabout Primary School
Fryern Junior & Infant School
St Swithun Wells RC Primary School
The Toynbee School
Peacock Trading Estate
Peacock Trading Est
City Grove Trading Est
Boyatt Wood Surgery
Boyatt Shopping Cen
St Catherines Road Junior Sch
Cemetery
Brookwood Industrial Estate
Primary School
Civic Offices
Hotel
Fleming Park Leisure Centre
Eastleigh Borough Council
Norwood CP School
Eastleigh Museum
Hampshire County Council
Eastleigh Health Centre
Wessex Nuffield Hosp
Eastleigh Station
Shakespeare Business Centre
Industrial Est
Business Centre
EAST
1 grid square represents 500 metres

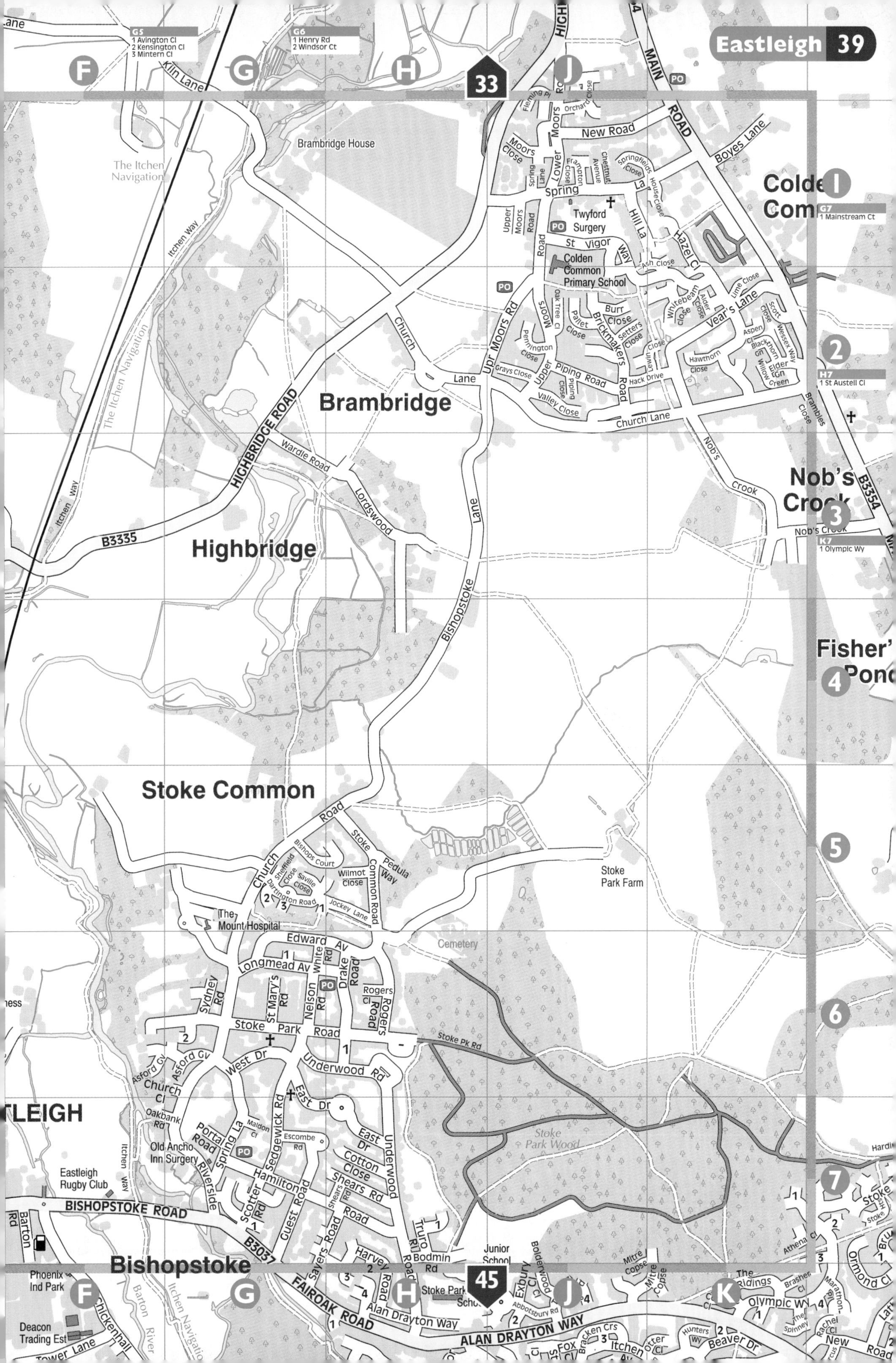
G5
1 Avington Cl
2 Kensington Cl
3 Mintern Cl
G6
1 Henry Rd
2 Windsor Ct
F
G
H
J
33
Kiln Lane
Main Road
PO
Brambridge House
The Itchen Navigation
Itchen Way
Fleming Pl
Orchard Close
New Road
Boyes Lane
Moors Close
Lower Moors Road
Spring Lane
Frampton Close
Chestnut Avenue
Springfields Close
Spring La
House Close
Colden Common
G7
1 Mainstream Ct
Upper Moors Road
Twyford Surgery
Hill La
Hazel Cl
St Vigor Way
Colden Common Primary School
Ash Close
Church Lane
Upr Moors Rd
Moors Oak Tree Cl
Pallet Close
Brickmakers Road
Burr Close
Setters Close
Whitebeam Close
Alder Close
Year's Lane
Lime Close
Scott Close
Wessex Way
Pennington Close
Grays Close
Upper Piping Road
Piping Close
Valley Close
Hack Drive
Linnet Close
Hawthorn Close
Aspen Cl
Blackthorn Gn
Willow Green
Elder Gn
H7
1 St Austell Cl
Brambles Close
Brambridge
Highbridge Road
Wardle Road
Lordswood
Nob's Crook
Nob's Crook
B3354
K7
1 Olympic Wy
B3335
Highbridge
Bishopstoke Lane
Fisher's Pond
Stoke Common
Church Road
Bishops Court
Sheffield Close
Saville Close
Dartington Road
Wilmot Close
Stoke Common Road
Pedula Way
Jockey Lane
Stoke Park Farm
The Mount Hospital
Cemetery
Edward Av
Longmead Av
White Rd
Drake Road
Sydney Rd
St Mary's Rd
Nelson Rd
Rogers Cl
Rogers Road
Stoke Park Road
Stoke Pk Rd
West Dr
Underwood Rd
Asford Gv
Church Cl
East Dr
TLEIGH
Oakbank Rd
Maldon Cl
Sedgewick Rd
Escombe Rd
East Dr
Stoke Park Wood
Portal Road
Spring La
Old Anchor Inn Surgery
Cotton Close
Underwood Road
Hardi
Eastleigh Rugby Club
Itchen Way
Riverside
Hamilton Road
Shears Rd
Stoke
BISHOPSTOKE ROAD
Scotter Rd
Guest Road
Shears Road
Barton Rd
B3037
Sayers Road
Truro Rise
Road
Bodmin Rd
Junior School
Bolderwood Cl
Mitre Copse
Athena Cl
Ormond Cl
Bishopstoke
Harvey Road
Stoke Park Schools
45
Exbury Cl
Abbotsbury Rd
The Ridings
Brasher Cl
Phoenix Ind Park
Barton River
Itchen Navigation
Chickenhall
FAIROAK ROAD
Alan Drayton Way
ALAN DRAYTON WAY
Olympic Wy
Marathon Pl
The Spinney
Rachel Cl
Deacon Trading Est
Tower Lane
Bracken Crs
Fox
Itchen Av
Otter Cl
Hunters Wy
Beaver Dr
New Road
K

34
A
B
C
D
E
1
2
3
4
5
6
7
Yewtree Copse
Ranvilles Fm
A3090
Ridge Lane
Ridge
Lee Park Fm
Lee Church L
Moorcourt Copse
Test Way
Moorcourt
Test Way
River Blackwater
Wade Hill Fm
River Test
Hill Street
Nursling Ho
Hillstreet
Colbury Ho
Broadlands Lake
Test Way
Brooke's Hill
Nursling Mill
Mill Lane
Green La
Brookes Hill Industrial Estate
SALISBURY ROAD
Manor Ho Fm
Lane
52
Testwood Lakes
Little Testwood Fm
1 grid square represents 500 metres

H6
1 Blake Cl
2 Blann Cl
3 Tuffin Cl
J6
1 Westways Cl
K5
1 Laverstoke Cl
K6
1 Bossington Cl
2 Fastnet Cl
3 Michelmersh Cl
F
G
H
J
K
35
42
53
Hoe Lane
Telegraph Wood
Toothill
Toothill Road
Lee Drove
Lee Lane
A3057
Upper Toothill Road
Greenhill Lane
Nightingale Wood
Lee
Coldharbour Lane
Upton
Upton Cr
Upton Lane
Lymer La
M271
The Atherley School
Upton La
Lane
Junction 3
Station Rd
Nursling Street
Nursling
C of E Primary School
Dairy Lane
Nursling Industrial Estate
Oriana
Canberra Rd
Mauretania Rd
Majestic Rd
Station Road
Weston La
Hillyfields
Yewtree Lane
Frogmore Lane
Redbridge Lane
ROMSEY ROAD
The Cedar School
Rowmans House Industrial Estate
Horns Drove
Rownhams Way
Rownhams Close
Oaklands Community School
Fairisle Junior & Infant School
Fairisle Road
Lord's Hill Way
Brownhill Rd
Millbrook Community
Testlands Av
Broadmead Rd
Winfrith Wy
Paulet Lacave Av
Rufus Cl
Betteridge Drive
Balmoral Way
Nutfield Rd
Hedgerow Cl
Hurricane Dr
Nutshalling Av
Cranmer Drive
Chambers Close
Watley Close
Wilks Cl
Crawford Cl
Lukin Dr
Standen Rd
Home Fld Dr
Mill Cl
Toogoods Wy
Cromarty Rd
Rockall Cl
Lundy Cl
Orkney Cl
Viking Cl
Malin Cl
Bakers Drove
Rosebank Cl
Jupiter Cl
Saturn Cl
Orion Cl
Mercury Cl
Pegasus Cl
Boniface Crs
Alderney Cl
Sarnia Ct
Jersey Cl
Guernsey Cl
Brownhill Wy
Kennedy
Link Rd
Roseway
Upr Brown
St Johns Glebe
St Johns Cl
Routs Way
Acorn Dr
Corts Rd
Armada
Hann Rd
Prince Rd
Loreille Cl
Normandy Cl
Barker Mill Cl
Broadbent Cl
Phillips Cl
Horsebridge Way
Jeffries Cl
Fairway Gdns
Hazeldown
Trowbridge Cl
Lakeside Av
Bridgers Cl
Evox
Bedwell Cl
Mossleigh Av
Menzies Cl
Fairlawn Cl
The Mews
Bakers Dro
Rown
Pack
PO

D7
1 Bransbury Cl
2 Lyburn Cl
3 Purbrook Cl
C5
1 Brambling Cl
A6
1 Armstrong Ct
2 Blackbushe Cl
3 Colt Cl
4 Lucas Cl
E1
1 Woodside Crs
36
41
54
BOTLEY ROAD
Chilworth
Old Village
Fowler's Wk
A27
Tanner's Brook
Lane
Packridge
Rownhams Lane
Parkway
Chilworth Cl
Manor Rd
University
Enterprise Rdo
Venture Road
Chilworth Drove
Southampton University
M27
Rownhams Service Area
Rownhams Service Area
Greenhill Lane
Road
Drove
Chilworth
Routs Way
Acorn Dr
Armada
Rownhams
Lord's Wood
Bakers Drove
The Mews
Glebe
St Johns
Hann Rd
Barker Mill Cl
Rownhams Close
Rownhams Way
Hampshire County
City of Southampton
Fairlawn Cl
Fyeford
Bedwell Cl
Forbes
Fraser
Buchanan
Matheson Rd
Matheson Rd
Chisholm Cl
Sinclair Rd
Sutherland Road
Sutherland Rd
Sinclair First & Junior School
Logan Cl
Lennox
Evox
Redward Rd
Bridgers Cl
Lakeside Av
Rosebank Cl
Bakers
Trowbridge
Welch Wy
Emmett Rd
Dunbar Cl
Menzies Cl
Rockall Cl
Cromarty
Lundy Cl
Orkney Cl
Malin Cl
Fairisle Road
Fairisle Junior & Infant School
Oaklands Community School
Rownhams Rd N
Lord's Hill Way
Lord's Hill Centre E
Lordshill Health Cen
Pembrey Cl
Hornchurch Rd
Wittering Rd
Northolt Gdns
Tangmere Drive
Calshot Cl
Croydon Cl
Gatwick Cl
Lewis Silkin Way
Abercrombie Gdns
Lord's Hill
S016
Aldermoor Road
Chevelston Crs
Andromeda Road
Pegasus Cl
Saturn Cl
Gemini Cl
Mercury Cl
Orion Cl
Eastchurch Cl
Odiham Cl
Olive
Conifer Road
Peach Rd
Linden Rd
Outer Circle
Aldermoor Av
Myrtle Rd
Brownhill Road
Upr
Jupiter Cl
Holly Oak Rd
Siskin Cl
Goldcrest Gdns
Sandpiper
Wryneck Cl
Whinchat Cl
Hawfinch Cl
Harrier Cl
Firecrest
Kestrel Cl
Gannet Cl
Plover Cl
Osprey Cl
Fulmar
Turnstone Gdns
Widgeon Cl
Warbler Cl
Sheldrake Gdns
Puffin Cl
First School
Junior School
Curlew Cl
Woburn Rd
Woburn Road
Dunvegan Drive
Balmoral Cl
Dunster Cl
Melville Close
Oakwood Dr
Oakwood Drive
Prunus Cl
Robinia Grn
Grafton Gdns
Abbotsfield Cl
Southampton City Council
Lord's Hill Way
Beaulieu Cl
Petworth Gdns
Longleat Gdns
Cowdray Close
Waltham Crs
Salerno Road
Taranto Rd
Aldermoor Rd
Aldermoor Cl
Aldermoor Health Centre
Springford Cl
Langrish Rd
Bradley Gn
Shaldon Cl
Wonston Rd
Greywell Av
Preshaw Cl
Jex Blake Cl
Springford Gdns
Springford
Coxford Road
Lordswood Rd
Dunkirk Rd
Falaise Cl
Arnheim Cl
Arnheim Rd
Lordswood
Lordswood Gdns
Southampton Sports Centre
Holly Brook Cemetery
Springford Crs
Valley Road
Highclere Road
Hill La
Seagarth La
School
A
B
C
D
E
Alder Road
Coxford Dro
Larch Road
Palm Road
Palm Rd
Willow Ct
Aldermoor
Princess Anne Hospital
Arcadia
Dolton Rd
Kennedy Road
Millbrook Community
Crs
St Martin's
1 grid square represents 500 metres

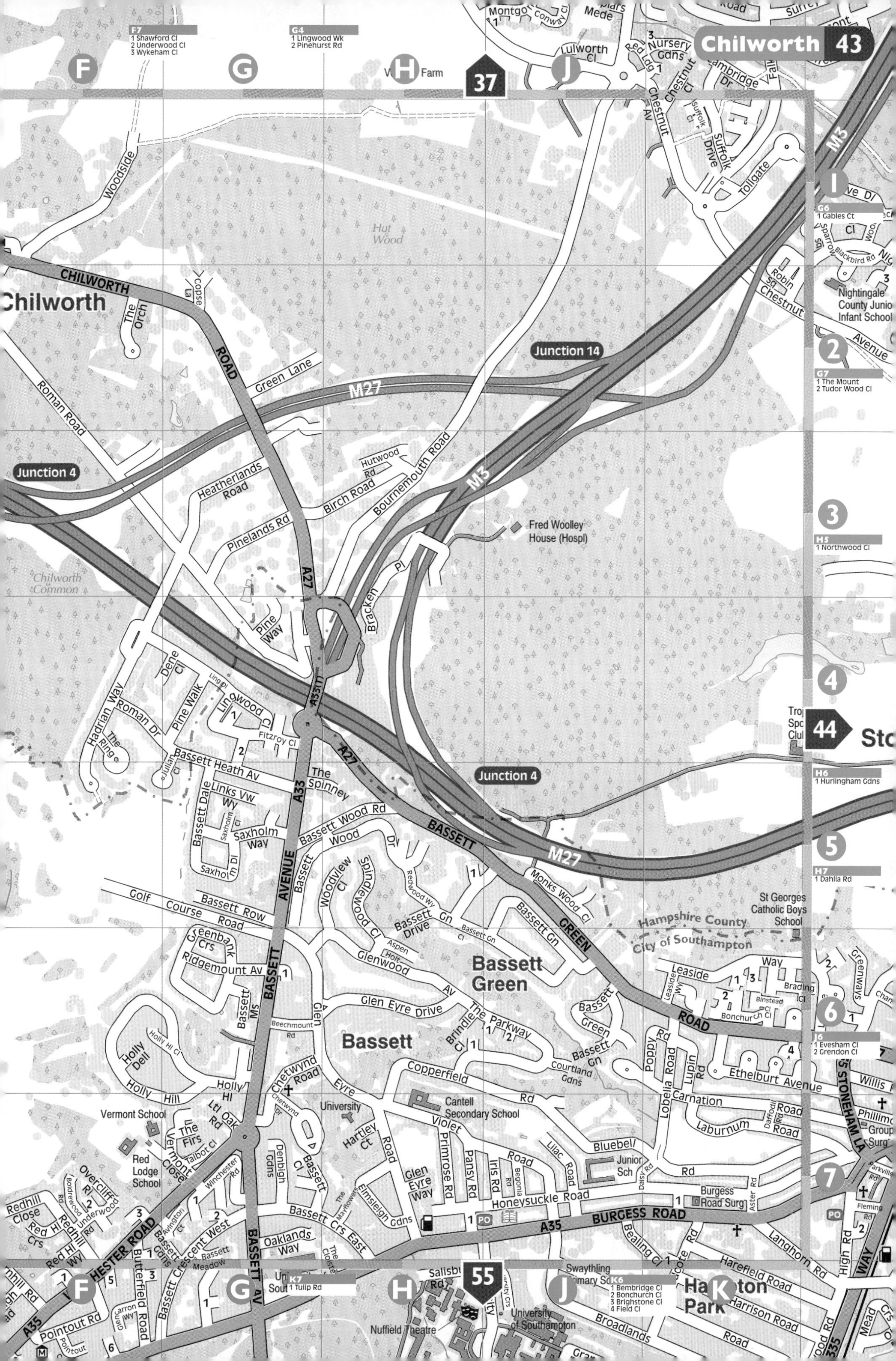
F7
1 Shawford Cl
2 Underwood Cl
3 Wykeham Cl
G4
1 Lingwood Wk
2 Pinehurst Rd
37
Lulworth Cl
Nursery Gdns
Chestnut Av
Chestnut Cl
Cambridge Dr
Suffolk Cl
Suffolk Drive
Tollgate
M3
Woodside
Hut Wood
CHILWORTH ROAD
Chilworth
The Orch
Copse La
G6
1 Gables Ct
Blackbird Rd
Robin Sq
Chestnut
Nightingale County Junior Infant School
Avenue
Junction 14
Green Lane
M27
Roman Road
G7
1 The Mount
2 Tudor Wood Cl
Junction 4
Heatherlands Road
Hutwood Rd
Birch Road
Bournemouth Road
Fred Woolley House (Hospl)
H5
1 Northwood Cl
Pinelands Rd
A27
Chilworth Common
Bracken Pl
Pine Way
A33(T)
Dene Cl
Hadrian Way
Roman Dr
Pine Walk
Ling Pl
Lingwood Cl
Fitzroy Cl
The Ring
Julian Cl
Bassett Heath Av
The Spinney
Junction 4
44
H6
1 Hurlingham Gdns
Bassett Dale
Links Vw Wy
Saxholm Cl
Saxholm Way
Saxholm Dl
Bassett Wood Rd
Bassett Wood Dr
BASSETT GREEN ROAD
M27
H7
1 Dahlia Rd
A33
BASSETT AVENUE
Woodview Cl
Spindlewood Cl
Redwood Wy
Golf Course Road
Bassett Row
Monks Wood Cl
Bassett Drive
Bassett Gn Cl
Bassett Gn
St Georges Catholic Boys School
Hampshire County
City of Southampton
Greenbank Crs
Ridgemount Av
Aspen Holt
Glenwood Av
Bassett Green
Leaside Way
Brading Cl
Binstead Cl
Bonchurch Cl
Greenways
Glen Eyre Drive
The Parkway
Bassett Ms
Beechmount Rd
Holly Hl Cl
Holly Dell
Holly Hill
Bassett
Brindle Cl
Bassett Green
Bassett Gn
Courtland Gdns
Poppy Rd
Lobelia Road
Lupin Rd
Ethelburt Avenue
J6
1 Evesham Cl
2 Grendon Cl
Willis
Chetwynd Road
Chetwynd Dr
Copperfield Rd
Carnation Road
Daffodil Road
Laburnum Rd
STONEHAM LA
Vermont School
University
Cantell Secondary School
Hartley Ct
Eyre Road
Violet Rd
Lilac Road
Red Lodge School
Lt Oak Rd
The Firs
Talbot Cl
Vermont Close
Winchester Rd
Overcliff Ri
Redhill Close
Boldrewood Rd
Denbigh Gdns
Bassett Cl
Primrose Rd
Pansy Rd
Iris Rd
Begonia Rd
Road
Bluebell Rd
Junior Sch
Daisy Rd
Aster Rd
Burgess Road Surg
Glen Eyre Way
Honeysuckle Road
PO
Underwood Rd
Red Hl Crs
Redhill
Red Hl Wy
CHESTER ROAD
Avington Ct
Bassett Crescent West
Bassett Gdns
Bassett Meadow
The Marlowes
Elmsleigh Gdns
Bassett Crs East
Oaklands Way
The Closes
A35 BURGESS ROAD
Bealing Cl
Langhorn Rd
Harefield Road
High Rd
Fleming
Parkville Rd
WAY
Butterfield Road
BASSETT AV
K7
1 Tulip Rd
Salisbury Rd
55
University Crs
K6
1 Bembridge Cl
2 Bonchurch Cl
3 Brighstone Cl
4 Field Cl
Swaythling Primary Sch
Harrison Road
Broadlands Road
Nuffield Theatre
University of Southampton
Pointout Rd
Pointout
Glencarron Wy
A35
A335

44
38
43
56
A
B
C
D
E
1
2
3
4
5
6
7
A6
1 Stoneham Cl
2 Summrfld Gdns
A2
1 Chestnut Ri
2 Greenfinch Cl
3 Jackdaw Ri
A1
1 Raven Sq
2 Starling Sq
3 Swallow Sq
A7
1 Havenstone Wy
2 Rayners Gdns
B1
1 Passfield Cl
B2
1 The Hawthorns
2 Maple Sq
B7
1 Alfred Rose Ct
2 Gilbury Cl
3 Grange Cl
4 Howard Cl
5 Lord Mountbatten Cl
6 Meadowside Cl
7 Pilgrim Pl
8 Westbrook Wy
C1
1 Grasmere
2 Thirlmere
C2
1 Jubilee Cl
C5
1 George Curl Wy
Belmont
Somerset Crs
Tollgate
M3
Dew Lane
A335
Fleming Park Leisure Centre
Eastleigh Borough Council
Norwood CP School
Eastleigh Museum
Wessex Nuffield Hosp
Eastleigh Station
Leigh Rd
Factory Road
Chadwick Road
Blenheim Road
Coniston
Grantham
Avenue
Passfield
O'Connell Rd
Chadwick Rd
Kelvin Rd
Scott Rd
Tennyson Rd
Spencer Rd
Elm Gv
Derby Road
Dove Dl
Swift Cl
Woodpecker Wy
Kestrel Road
Magpie Lane
Heron Sq
Nightingale Avenue
Blackbird Rd
Sparrow Sq
Robin Sq
Nightingale County Junior & Infant School
Linnet Sq
Falcon Square
Wren Rd
Locksley Road
Burns Cl
Cedar Rd
Cherbourg Road
Barton Peveril College
Alderman Quilley Secondary School
Hardy Rd
Goldsmith Road
Shelley Rd
Parnell Rd
Wilmer Rd
Nutbeem Rd
Chamberlayne Rd
Eastleigh College of Further Education
Desborough Road
Cranbury Road
Grantham Rd
High St
High Street
Market St
St Andrews Surgery
Mitchell Rd
Station Hill
Southampton Road
Wells Pl
Chestnut Avenue
Chestnut Av
Monks Brook Close
Abbotts Rd
Priory Rd
Friars Rd
Monks Way
Mansbridge Rd
Cheriton Rd
York Rd
Tichborne Rd
Arnold Road
Doncaster Road
South St
Campbell Road
Stoneham Lane
Monks Brook
Lakeside
Wide Lane
Mitchell Way
Wellington Sports Club
Eastleigh Football Club
North Stoneham
Tinker Aly
Spitfire Loop
Southampton Airport Parkway Station
Southampton International Airport
Wide La
Junction 5
Decoy Covert
Itchen Way
M27
St Georges Catholic Boys School
County
Stoneham Way
Greenways
Brading Cl
Leaside Wy
Channels Farm Rd
Dawnay Cl
Greenlea Crs
Bonchurch Cl
Orion Business Centre
Claudeen Cl
Mardon Cl
Walnut Av
Stoneham Cemetery Road
Cemetery
A27
Ethelburt Avenue
Willis Road
Phillimore Rd
Group Surg
Swaythling Station
A35 Stoneham La
Daffodil Rd
High Rd
Brookside Wy
Octavia Rd
Primary School
Farmery Cl
Bank Side
Friars Way
Wessex La
Monks Way
Claude Ashby Cl
Robert Cecil Av
Itchenside Cl
Mans Bridge
Mansbridge Road
Parkville Rd
Fleming Rd
Aster Rd
Langhorn Rd
Harefield Road
Harrison Rd
High Rd
Swaythling
Itchen Way
Moat Hl
St Helena Gdns
Maryland Cl
Romill Cl
1 grid square represents 500 metres

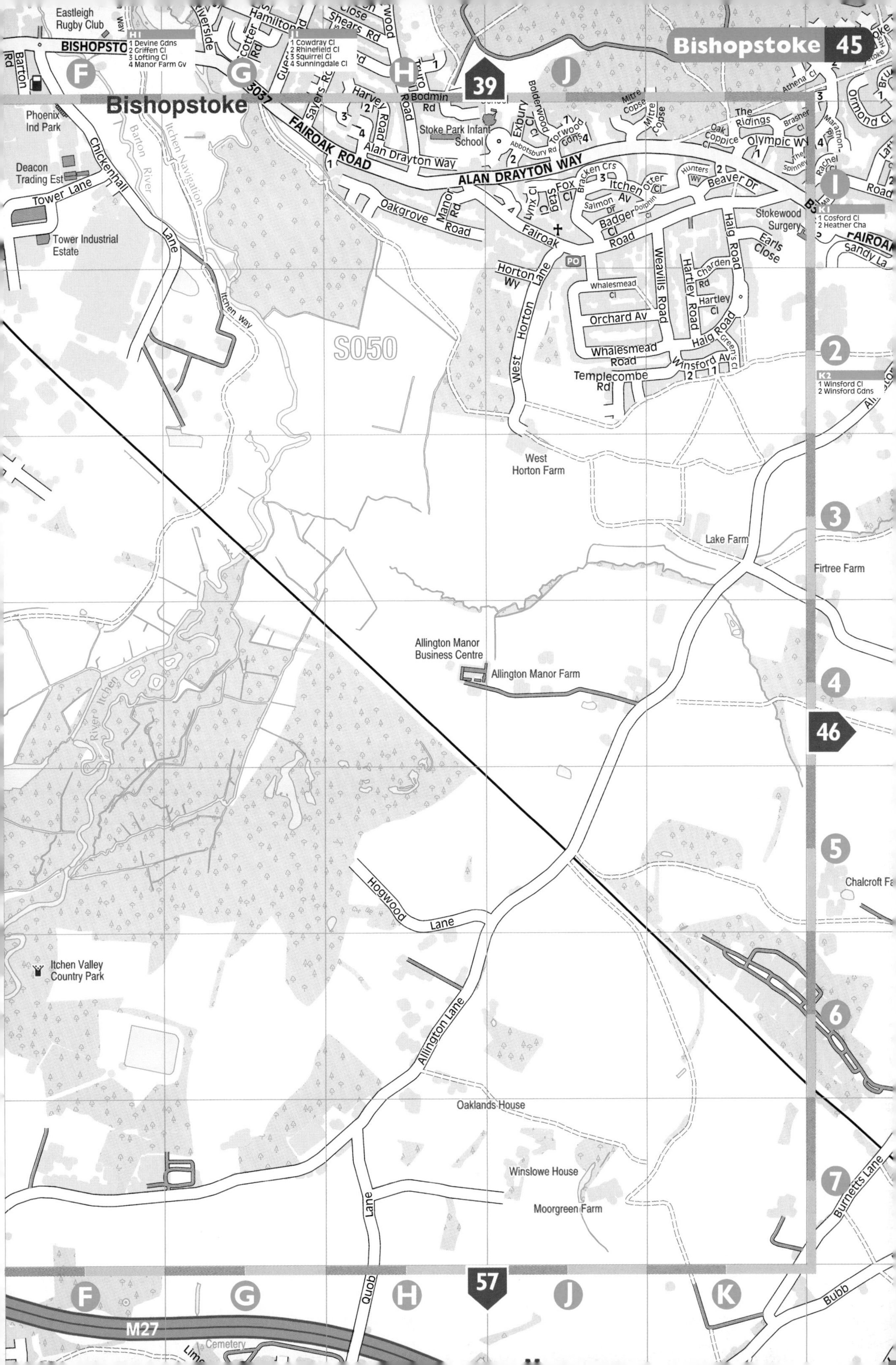
Eastleigh Rugby Club
BISHOPSTOKE
H1
1 Devine Gdns
2 Griffen Cl
3 Lofting Cl
4 Manor Farm Gv
I1
1 Cowdray Cl
2 Rhinefield Cl
3 Squirrel Cl
4 Sunningdale Cl
Hamilton Rd
Shears Rd
Barton Rd
Bishopstoke
39
B3037
FAIROAK ROAD
Phoenix Ind Park
Deacon Trading Est
Tower Lane
Tower Industrial Estate
Chickenhall Lane
Barton River
Itchen Navigation
Itchen Way
Harvey Road
Sayers Rd
Truro Road
Bodmin Rd
Alan Drayton Way
ALAN DRAYTON WAY
Stoke Park Infant School
Exbury Cl
Bolderwood Cl
Abbotsbury Rd
Torwood Gdns
Mitre Copse
Oak Coppice Cl
The Ridings
Brasher Cl
Olympic Wy
Athena Cl
Ormond Cl
Marathon Pl
The Spinney
Rachel Cl
Oakgrove Road
Manor Rd
Lynx Cl
Stag Cl
Fox Cl
Bracken Crs
Itchen Av
Otter Cl
Salmon Dr
Dolphin Cl
Badger Cl
Hunters Wy
Beaver Dr
Road
Stokewood Surgery
Earls Close
K1
1 Cosford Cl
2 Heather Cha
FAIROAK
Sandy La
Fairoak Road
PO
Horton Wy
West Horton Lane
Whalesmead Cl
Weavills Road
Hartley Road
Charden Rd
Haig Road
Hartley Cl
Orchard Av
Whalesmead Road
Green's Cl
Winsford Av
Templecombe Rd
K2
1 Winsford Cl
2 Winsford Gdns
SO50
West Horton Farm
Lake Farm
Firtree Farm
Allington Manor Business Centre
Allington Manor Farm
River Itchen
46
Hogwood Lane
Chalcroft Fa
Allington Lane
Itchen Valley Country Park
Oaklands House
Winslowe House
Moorgreen Farm
Lane
Burnetts Lane
Quob
57
M27
Cemetery
Bubb
F
G
H
J
K
I
2
3
4
5
6
7

1 grid square represents 500 metres

Dairy Farm
LANE
F
G
H
J
Woolstreet Farm
WINCHESTER ROAD
King's Way
Stakes La
The Crescent
Scivier's Lane
Alma Lane
Durley Hall Lane
Durley Hall Farm
Wintershill Hall
Wintershill
Greenwood Lane
Scivier's Lane
Winters Hill
Durley Street
Durley Street
The Drove
King's Way
PO
Manor Road
Durley Manor Farm
48
Brook Road
Durley Primary School
Durley
Parsonage Lane
Kytes Lane
Mincingfield Farm
Lower Farm
Brown Heath
White Gates
Mincingfield Lane
Heathen Street
Gregory Lane
Stapleford Farm
River Hamb
59
F
G
H
J
K
Calcot H
Hill Farm
Durley Mill
Mill Lane
Calcot
I
2
3
4
5
6
7

D3
1 Denewulf Cl
2 Middlebrook
3 St Bonnet Dr
Ashton
C3
1 Claylands Rd
2 Edington Cl
3 Princes Cl
4 St Swithun Cl
B3
1 Cunningham Av
2 Hermitage Cl
E4
1 Cricklewood Cl
2 Godfrey Pink Wy
3 Penfords Pdck
4 Shore Crs
E7
1 Clayhill Cl
Stakes Lane
Stakes La
Cross Lanes Farm
Ashton Lane
Shipcote Lane
New Rd
Beeches Hill
Vernon Hill House
Vernon Hill
THE HA
Roke Farm
Pondside Lane
Northbrook
Winters Hill
Ashton Close
Churchill Av
Northfield Cl
Marlow Rd
The Coach Station
BISHOP'S WALTHAM
Chalky Lane
Butts La
Albany Court
Albany Road
Albany Drive
Gravatom Business Centre
Battery Hill
Claylands Rd
Merlin Cl
Wayneflete Cl
Beaufort Drive
Andrewes Cl
Garfield Rd
Garfield Close
Brooklands Road
LOWER LANE
Free Street
Colville Dr
Infant School
Ridgemede Junior Scho
Hall Close
Oak Road
Kestrel Cl
Siskin Close
Newtown
Claylands Ct
Blanchard Rd
PH
Greens Cl
Langton Road
Pondside Lane
Morley Dr
B3035
Lower Lane
The Surg
St Peter's Street
Meon Valley Police Station
Pine Rd
King's Way
Park Road
Mallard Close
The Avenue
PO
Priory Cl
Southfields Cl
Malt Lane
Brook Street
Cross St
High Street
Houchin St
Basingwell St
Malvern Cl
Bank Street
Leopold Dr
Elizabeth Wy
Albert Rd
The Priory
Victoria Rd
Martin Street
Station Road
Ltl Shore La
Shore La
Cherry Gardens
Lane
Tangier
Bishop's Palace (remains of)
Eastways
Folly Field
Cricklemede
Bishop's Lane
COPPICE HILL B2177
Tangier Farm
47
Thickets House
Brooklands Farm
Locks Farm
B3035
BOTLEY ROAD
River Hamble
Clewers
Provene
60
Glide
ge Lane
House
1 grid square represents 500 metres
A
B
C
D
E
1
2
3
4
5
6
7

F7
1 Meadow Cl
J6
1 Beverley Gdns
2 Coronation Rd
J7
1 Rowan Cl
2 Russett Cl
Galley Down
The Hanger
B3035
B3032
B2177
Bishopsdown Stud Farm
Duncombe
Dundridge Lane
Dundridge
Damson Hill
Hill Top
Park La
Park Lane
Swanmore Park House
Upper Swanmore
Green Lane
Mayhill Farm
Tennyson Cl
Wordsworth Cl
Byron Close
Rareridge Lane
Elm Rd
Willow Rd
Sycamore Rd
Gunners Pk
Hoe Road
Hoe
Cemetery
West Hoe Lane
Jervis Court Lane
Suetts Lane
Swanmore Road
Moorlands Road
Donigers Dell
Hampton Hill
Well Lane
Cut Throat Lane
Vicarage Lane
Church Lane
Paradise Lane
Swanmore Business Park
Foxcombe Close
Church Road
Swanmore Church of England School
Bucketts Farm Cl
PO
Lower Chase Road
Broad Lane
The Drove
Chapel Road
Greenways
Larkspur Cl
Crofton Way
New Road
Myers Cl
Spring Lane
Spring Vale
Leacock Cl
Spring La
Swanmore
Dodds Lane
Swanmore County Secondary School
King's Way
Ludwell's La
Martin Cl
Medlicott Wy
Glendale
Droxford Road
Hillpound
The Lakes
Brewers Lane
Evelyn Cl
Meadow Gdns
Provene Gardens
Provene Close
The Ridings
Hill Crest
Waltham Business Park
Brickyard Road
Orchardlea
Forest Road
Linden Close
Chase Grove
Forest Close
Forest Farm
Gravel Hill
Mislingford Road
Dirty Copse
Shep

61

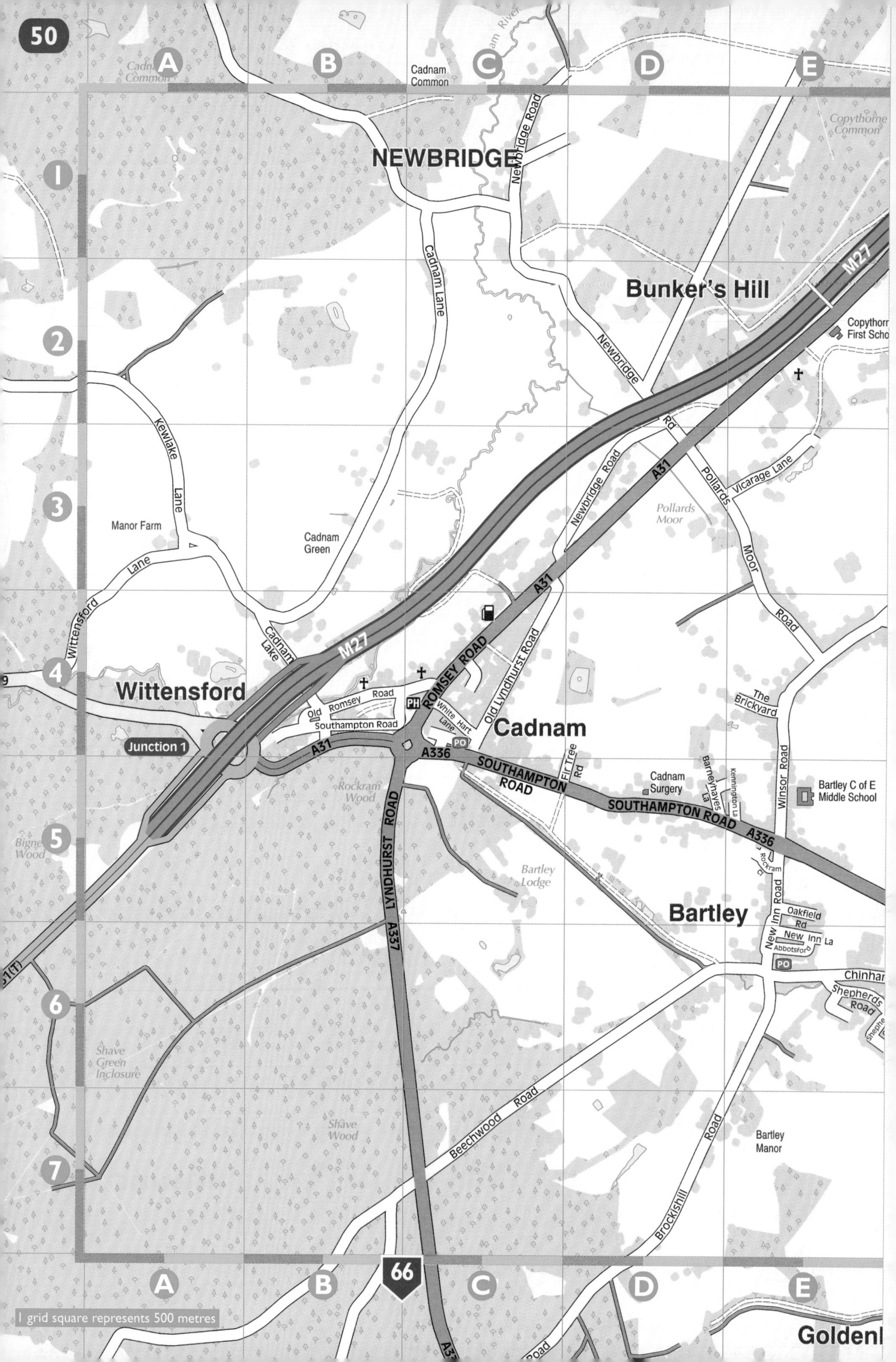
A
B
C
D
E
1
2
3
4
5
6
7
Cadnam Common
NEWBRIDGE
Newbridge Road
Copythorne Common
Cadnam Lane
Bunker's Hill
M27
Copythorne First School
Newbridge Rd
Kewlake Lane
Newbridge Road
A31
Pollards
Vicarage Lane
Pollards Moor
Manor Farm
Cadnam Green
Lane
Moor Road
Wittensford
Cadnam Lake
ROMSEY ROAD
Old Lyndhurst Road
Wittensford
Old Romsey Road
PH
White Hart Lane
Southampton Road
Cadnam
The Brickyard
Junction 1
PO
A336
SOUTHAMPTON ROAD
Fir Tree Rd
Cadnam Surgery
Barneyhayes La
Kennington La
Winsor Road
Bartley C of E Middle School
Rockram Wood
LYNDHURST ROAD
SOUTHAMPTON ROAD
A336
Bigne Wood
Rockram Cl
Bartley Lodge
Bartley
Oakfield Rd
A337
New Inn Road
New Inn La
Abbotsford
PO
Chinhar
Shepherds Road
Shave Green Inclosure
Beechwood Road
Shave Wood
Road
Bartley Manor
Brockishill
66
1 grid square represents 500 metres
Goldenl

Stonyford
F
G
H
J
ROMSEY ROAD
Whitemoor Lane
Brookes Industrial Estate
Loperwood Lane
1
Shorn Hill
Barrow Hill Road
Copythorne Crs
Copythorne
Barrow Hill
Barrow Hill Road
Pound Lane
Calmore Sports Club
Loperwood
Forest Way
Horseshoe Dr
Tatchbury Mount Hospital
2
Loperwood Lane
Calmore Crs
PO
Winsor
Winsor Road
Tatchbury Lane
Copied Hall Fm
Tatchbury Manor House
3
Spruce Drive
Michigan
Buckthorn Cl
4
52
Winsor Lane
A326
Bartley Grange
Eadens Lane
5
Crabb
Wellers
Olivers
Dickens Dell
Netley Marsh C of E Controlled Infant School
RINGWOOD ROAD
A336
Carlton Ho
Priestlands Cl
Road
Riverside Cl
Bourne Road
Paradise Lane
Woodlands Road
6
NETLEY MARSH
Bourne Lane
Willswood Fm
7
Purkiss Cl
Bartley Road
Lanesbridge Cl
67
Green Cl
Milvina Cl
F
G
H
J
K
Ashurst Bridge / hayes

B3
1 Gregory Gdns
2 Treagore Rd
B2
1 Snellgrove Pl
A5
1 Nickleby Gdns
2 Shawford Cl
A4
1 Clydesdale Dr
2 Enderwood Cl
3 Perrywood Gdns
B4
1 Alfred Cl
2 The Bramblings
3 Cedar Wood Cl
4 Chaffinch Cl
5 Chepstow Cl
6 The Linnets
7 Redwing Gdns
8 Sandlewood Cl
B5
1 Alfred Cl
2 Bullfinch Cl
3 Cherrywood Gdns
4 Crabapple Cl
5 Cypress Gdns
6 Milkwood Ct
7 Teal Cl
8 Watson Wk
9 Winchester Wy
B6
1 Ashwood Gdns
2 Chillenden Ct
3 Copinger Cl
4 Driftwood Gdns
5 Maple Gdns
6 Peregrine Cl
7 Timson Cl
C4
1 Boniface Cl
2 Selbourne Rd
C5
1 Drayton Pl
2 Goldsmith Cl
3 Lydgate
4 Priestley Cl
5 Shaw Cl
6 Wilde Cl
C6
1 Chillenden Ct
2 Hudson Ct
3 Thomas Cl
C7
1 Chiltern Cl
2 Highgrove Cl
D3
1 Hamtun Crs
D4
1 Meacher Cl
D5
1 Briardene Ct
2 Whitcombe Cl
D6
1 Springfield Dr
D7
1 Elldene Ct
2 Falstaff Wy
3 Hambert Wy
4 Trevone Cl
E4
1 Warwick Rd
E5
1 Sunny Wy
40
51
68
A B C D E
1 2 3 4 5 6 7
Mill
Mill Lane
Ho Fm
Industrial Estate
SALISBURY ROAD
Testwood Ho
Testwood Lakes
Little Testwood Fm
Pauletts Lane
Brunel Road
Eddystone Road
Stephenson Rd
Calmore Industrial Estate
Nutsey Av
Nutsey Lane
Trinity Business Centre
Lulworth Business Centre
Westwood Business Park
Nutwood Way
Testwood
Cooks Lane
Calmore Drive
Testwood Crs
Shakespeare Drive
Tennyson Road
Ewell Way
Stanley Road
Sutton Rd
Testwood Av
Huntingdon Cl
Junior & Infant School
Calmore
Calmore Crs
Loperwood Lane
Michigan Way
Spruce Drive
Calmore Road
Blackwater Dr
Mortimer Cl
Cheam Wy
Sylvia Crs
The Redfords
Oakfield Primary School
Hamtun Crs
Greenfields Av
Testwood School
Testwood Lane
St Michaels Road
Stannington Crs
Morpeth Avenue
Hammond's Green
Brackley Way
Northlands Road
Hammonds Way
Hammonds Cl
Totton Recreation Centre
Totton College
Water Lane
Sunset Road
Windermere Gdns
Mayfield Av
Westfield Road
Dr Munro & Partners Test Vale Surg
Forest Edge School
Abbotswood Junior School
Lydlynch County First School
Lydlynch Rd
Tedder Wy
Portal Rd
Barnsfield Crescent
Fritham Cl
Calmore Gdns
Andrew Cl
Coblands Av
First School
Forest Gate Surg
Hazel Farm Rd
Crabbs Way
Netley Marsh C of E Controlled Infant School
RINGWOOD ROAD
Maynard
Kinross Rd
Lackford Avenue
Culford Avenue
Rushington Av
Bartley Water
Frampton Wy
Lane
Rushington
SPICER'S HILL
A326
Roberts Rd
The Drive
Hounsdown Av
Brookside
Valley Rd
Riverview
Gutter
Hampshire Co Council
Hounsdown School
Hounsdown
Briarwood Road
Larchwood Rd
Harold Cl
Deerhurst Cl
Dorland Gdns
Rowan Cl
Serle Gardens
Long Beech Dr
Fletchwood Lane
Fletchwood Rd
Roundhouse Dr
Hunters Crs
Ashurst Bridge Road
Villswood Fm
Ashurst Bridge
A326
Totton Coll
Rushington Business Park
Cocklydown Lane
Chapel Lane
MAIN ROAD
Jacobs Wk
Foxhill
Knellers
Ibbotson Way
Birchlands
Denbigh Cl
Reynolds Dr
Roselei Dr
Surrey Cl
1 grid square represents 500 metres

F5
1 Rumbridge Gdns
2 Station Rd N
F6
1 Boothby Cl
G5
1 Station Rd S
Hillyfield
41
Station Road
Weston La
Majestic Rd
Nursling Industrial Est
Andes Road
Test Way
Test Lane
Yewtree Lane
Redbridge Lane
Frogmore Lane
Jerrett's Lane
Danebury Wy
Brownhill Way
Brownhill Wy
Boniface Crs
Alderney Cl
St Martin's Cl
Jersey Cl
Guernsey Cl
Sarnia Ct
Jupiter Cl
Orion Cl
Mercury Cl
Kennedy Rd
Link Rd
Millbrook Community School
Millbrook Secondary School
J2
1 Goodwin Cl
Lwr Brownhill Rd
Barons Md
Corbiere Cl
Nutfield Ct
Court
Atherfield Rd
Brownhill Ct
Flamborough Cl
Colne Ct
Oldbury Ct
Colburn Cl
Seafield Rd
Bream Cl
Windbury Rd
Tetney Cl
Selsey Cl
Lulworth Gn
Lulworth Cl
Green Lane
Watts Cl
Cowley Cl
Kern Cl
Redbridge La
Brownhill Rd
LC
Mansel Road West
Hayburn Rd
Blakeney Rd
Anderby Rd
Maplin Rd
Blyth Cl
Windermere Av
Buttermere Cl
Thirlmere Road
Ordnance Survey Office
Maybush
K1
1 Holkham Cl
Ennerdale Rd
Tindale Road
Crabwood Road
Crabwood Cl
Glencoyne Gdns
Winston Cl
Holy Family RC Primary School
Southampton City Council
Mansel Infant & Junior Schools
Canford Cl
Culver Close
Kendal Avenue
Test Valley Business Centre
Yeoman Industrial Park
Redbridge Lane
Southampton Sports Club
Thorness Cl
Porlock Road
Seacombe Gn
Vellan Ct
Durlston Rd
M271
Mansel Ct
Mansel Rd
Ullswater Rd
Avenue
Wimpson Gdns
Wimpson La
Newlands Infant & Middle School
PO
Wimpson
Derwent Rd
Evenlode Road
Bideford Close
Pevensey Cl
Ingleton Rd
Copeland Rd
Cromer Rd
Perran Rd
Studland Road
Studland Cl
Ballard Cl
Sedbergh Rd
Colwell Cl
Totland Cl
Waveney Gn
Cherwell Crs
Welland Gn
Windrush Rd
Teme Crs
Severn Rd
Isis Cl
Borrowdale Rd
East Rd
Ribble Ct
Wimpson
Paignton Rd
Mason Manor Primary School
Crigdon Cl
K3
1 Orwell Cl
Test Way
Stirling Cl
Stirling Crs
Pembroke Close
York Cl
Arundel Rd
Associated Football Club
Testwood Pl
Gover Road
Westover Rd
Coniston Road
Cuckmere Lane
Kendal Av
Brookwood Av
Mardale Rd
Road
Calder Cl
Cheviot Rd
Binsey Cl
Community School
Millbrook Clinic
Cumbrian Way
Civic Cen
Jennings Rd
Compton Road
TOTTON
A35
REDBRIDGE CSWY
Old Redbridge Road
Tate Rd
Pat Bear Cl
Station Rd
Redbridge
Redbridge Primary School
Parkside Av
Brunel Rd
Oak Cl
Oakridge Rd
Lebanon Rd
Allington Road
REDBRIDGE RD
Green Park Rd
Kendal Av
Quantock Rd
Chiltern
Pennine
54
K4
1 Teme Rd
2 Tosson Cl
Tanners Brook Junior School
Causeway Crs
Police Station
Salterns School
Beaumont Rd
Library Rd
Redbridge Station
COMMERCIAL ROAD
Junction Road
Mill Rd
Totton Station
Road
LC
Treeside Av
HIGH STREET
BY-PASS
River Test
Second Av
Millbrook Trading Estate
First Avenue
Cleasby Cl
Millbrook
Super Bow
Cemetery
Millbrook Rd W
Trinity Ind Est
Boundary Cl
MILLBROOK
Wigg Gdns
Osborne Rd
Brokenford
RUMBRIDGE STREET
Winsor Rd
TOTTON
Rose Rd
Eling Lane
Eling County Infant School
School Road
Fisher's Rd
Bartram Rd
Manor House Av
Tanners Brook Wy
Western Avenue
Down's Park Avenue
Milverton Rd
Down's Pk Rd
Down's Pk Crs
Lexby Rd
The Heritage Centre & Museum
Tide Mill
Eling Hill
Cemetery
Eling
MARCHWOOD
The Retreat
Bury Lane
Lane
BY-PASS
Marchwood
69
City of Southampton
Hampshire Co
F
G
H
J
K
I
2
3
4
5
6
7

54
42
53
70
A5
1 Castleshaw Cl
2 Hameldon Cl
G1
1 Meadowhead Rd
A4
1 Cateran Cl
2 Langdale Cl
3 Whernside Cl
4 Whitestone Cl
A3
1 Crabtree
2 Hawswater Cl
A6
1 Marianne Cl
B3
1 The Mount
B6
1 Mottisfont Cl
C4
1 Ashdene
2 Church St
3 Newman St
4 Regent's Gv
5 Settle Cl
C5
1 Endeavour Cl
2 Rgnt's Pk Gdns
C6
1 Victory Crs
2 Victory Sq
3 Waterhouse La
D2
1 Vinery Rd
D3
1 Didcot Rd
2 Newbury Rd
3 Vaudrey Cl
D4
1 Mayflower Rd
2 Victor St
3 Vincent's Gv
D5
1 Beatrice Rd
2 May Rd
D6
1 Lakelands Dr
E1
1 Lordswood Cl
2 Wolverley Ct
E2
1 Fushsia Gdns
2 Lincoln Ct
E3
1 Cranbourne Cl
E5
1 W District Cut
E6
1 Princes Rd
2 Queenstown Rd
E7
1 Bridgwater Ct
2 Dymott Cl
3 Edith Haisman Cl
A
B
C
D
E
1
2
3
4
5
6
7
Hill
Lordswood
Aldermoor
Coxford
Shirley Warren
Maybush
Old Shirley
Wimpson
Millbrook
Shirley
Freemantle
SO15
Health Centre
Hollybrook Cemetery
Princess Anne Hospital
Southampton General Hosp
A&E
Millbrook Community School
Secondary School
Ordnance Survey Office
Newlands Infant & Middle School
Western Community Hospital
Mason Manor Primary School
Millbrook Clinic
Tanners Brook Junior School
Tanners Brook Infant School
Super Bowl
Cemetery
Trinity Ind Est
Primary School
Regents Park Girls School
Southampton City Council
Regents Park Surg
Middle & Primary School
Police Stn
Swimming Pool
The Shirley Health Cen
Doctors Surgery
Victor Street Surg
Infant School
Oatlands House Health Clinic
Middle School
Northbrook Industrial Est
Malvern Business Centre
Bellemoor Secondary School
School
Middle School
Junior School
Shirley Bus Park
Atherley House Surg
Cameleon Theatre
Solent Industrial Cen
Solent Business Cen
Liner Industrial Est
Freemantle Business Cen
Mountbatten Bus Cen
Stanton Ind Est
ROMSEY ROAD
WINCHESTER ROAD
A35
TEBOURBA WAY
SHIRLEY HIGH ST
SHIRLEY ROAD
MILLBROOK ROAD WEST
A33
MOUNTBATTEN
A3057
Coxford Road
Lordswood Rd
Dale Valley Road
Tremona Rd
Brownhill
Palm Rd
Vine Road
Kennedy Road
Rosewall Road
Lancaster Road
Ashmead Rd
Rownhams Road
Warren Avenue
Sycamore Rd
Chestnut Road
Jessamine Rd
Irving Road
Redbridge Hill
Oakley Road
Clifton Road
Tilbrook Rd
Stanton Road
Mill Road
South Mill Road
Westbury Road
Creighton Road
Third Avenue
Western Avenue
Western Av
Imperial Way
Paynes Rd
Waterloo Road
Millbrook Road
Cliff Rd
Bellemoor Road
Darlington Gardens
Wilton Road
Norfolk Road
Malmesbury Rd
Howard's Grove
Shirley Avenue
Church St
Park Road
Waterhouse Lane
Nelson Rd
Richmond Rd
Norham Av
Seymour Rd
Burgess Rd
Warwick Rd
Luccombe Rd
Shanklin Road
Millbrook Point Rd
Herbert Walker Av
1 grid square represents 500 metres

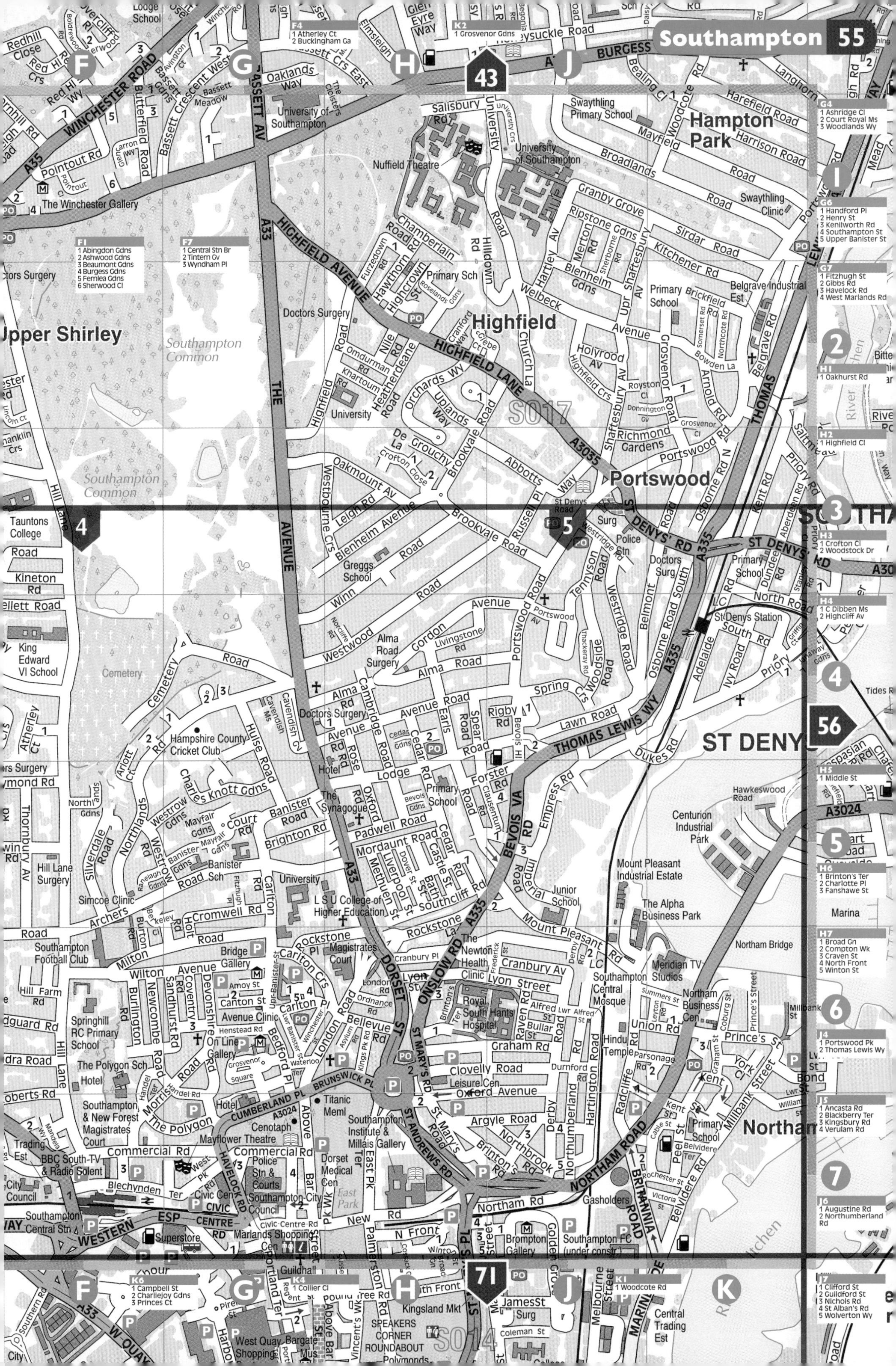
F
G
H
J
I
K
43
4
5
56
71
2
3
4
5
6
7
F4
1 Atherley Ct
2 Buckingham Ga
K2
1 Grosvenor Gdns
G4
1 Ashridge Cl
2 Court Royal Ms
3 Woodlands Wy
G6
1 Handford Pl
2 Henry St
3 Kenilworth Rd
4 Southampton St
5 Upper Banister St
G7
1 Fitzhugh St
2 Gibbs Rd
3 Havelock Rd
4 West Marlands Rd
H1
1 Oakhurst Rd
H2
1 Highfield Cl
H3
1 Crofton Cl
2 Woodstock Dr
H4
1 C Dibben Ms
2 Highcliff Av
H5
1 Middle St
H6
1 Brinton's Ter
2 Charlotte Pl
3 Fanshawe St
H7
1 Broad Gn
2 Compton Wk
3 Craven St
4 North Front
5 Winton St
J4
1 Portswood Pk
2 Thomas Lewis Wy
J5
1 Ancasta Rd
2 Blackberry Ter
3 Kingsbury Rd
4 Verulam Rd
J6
1 Augustine Rd
2 Northumberland Rd
J7
1 Clifford St
2 Guildford St
3 Nichols Rd
4 St Alban's Rd
5 Wolverton Wy
F1
1 Abingdon Gdns
2 Ashwood Gdns
3 Beaumont Gdns
4 Burgess Gdns
5 Fernlea Gdns
6 Sherwood Cl
F7
1 Central Stn Br
2 Tintern Gv
3 Wyndham Pl
K6
1 Campbell St
2 Charliejoy Gdns
3 Princes Ct
K4
1 Collier Cl
K1
1 Woodcote Rd
Upper Shirley
Southampton Common
Highfield
Hampton Park
Portswood
ST DENYS
Northam
S017
S014
WINCHESTER ROAD
A35
BASSETT AV
A33
THE AVENUE
HIGHFIELD AVENUE
HIGHFIELD LANE
A3035
BURGESS
THOMAS LEWIS WY
A335
ST DENYS' RD
BEVOIS VA RD
ONSLOW RD
DORSET ST
ST MARY'S RD
ST ANDREWS RD
NORTHAM ROAD
BRITANNIA ROAD
MARINE PDE
WESTERN ESP
CIVIC CENTRE RD
HAVELOCK RD
CUMBERLAND PL
BRUNSWICK PL
A3024
Redhill Close
Red Hill Crs
Red Hill Wy
Pointout Rd
Butterfield Road
Bassett Crescent West
Bassett Meadow
Bassett Gdns
Oaklands Way
The Cloisters
Elmsleigh
Glen Eyre Way
Honeysuckle Road
Bealing Cl
Woodcote Rd
Harefield Road
Harrison Road
Broadlands Road
Mayfield Road
Swaythling Primary School
Swaythling Clinic
Salisbury Rd
University Crs
University Road
University of Southampton
Nuffield Theatre
The Winchester Gallery
Chamberlain Road
Furzedown Rd
Hawthorn Rd
Highcrown St
Roselands Gdns
Primary Sch
Hilldown Rd
Church La
Granby Grove
Ripstone Gdns
Merton Rd
Sherborne Rd
Blenheim Gdns
Hartley Av
Upr Shaftesbury Av
Sirdar Road
Kitchener Rd
Welbeck Avenue
Primary School
Brickfield Rd
Somerset Rd
Northcote Rd
Bowden La
Belgrave Industrial Est
Belgrave Rd
Holyrood Av
Highfield Crs
Royston Cl
Donnington Gv
Grosvenor Road
Grosvenor Cl
Arnold Rd
Shaftesbury Av
Richmond Gardens
Portswood Rd
Osborne Rd N
Saltmead
Priory Rd
Kent Rd
Aberdeen Rd
Doctors Surgery
Nile Rd
Omdurman Rd
Khartoum Rd
Heatherdeane Road
Highfield Road
University
Cranford Wy
Glebe Ct
Orchards Wy
Uplands Way
Brookvale Road
De Grouchy La
Crofton Close
Oakmount Av
Abbotts Way
Russell Pl
St Denys Road
Westbourne Crs
Leigh Rd
Blenheim Avenue
Greggs School
Winn Road
Surg
Police Stn
Doctors Surg
Westridge Rd
Tennyson Road
Westridge Road
Belmont Rd
Osborne Road South
Primary School
Dundee Rd
North Road
St Denys Station
South Rd
Adelaide Rd
Ivy Road
Priory Rd
Griffin Ct
Tides R
Upper Shirley
Lester Rd
Lincoln Ct
Franklin Crs
Hill Lane
Tauntons College
Kineton Rd
Bellett Road
King Edward VI School
Cemetery
Cemetery Road
Westwood Road
Norcliffe Rd
Alma Road Surgery
Gordon Avenue
Livingstone Rd
Portswood Av
Thackeray Rd
Woodside Road
Alma Road
Spring Crs
Lawn Road
Dukes Rd
Atherley Ct
Doctors Surgery
Raymond Rd
Thornbury Av
Northlands Gdns
Arlott Ct
Hampshire County Cricket Club
Hulse Road
Cavendish Ms
Cavendish Gv
Doctors Surgery
Alma Rd
Cambridge Road
Avenue Road
Earls Road
Spear Road
Rigby Rd
Bevois Hl
Cedar Gdns
Cedar Rd
Rose Rd
Hotel
Lodge Road
Forster Rd
Empress Rd
Hawkeswood Road
Centurion Industrial Park
A3024
Charles Knott Gdns
Silverdale Road
Northlands Rd
Westrow Gdns
Mayfair Gdns
Court Rd
Banister Road
Brighton Rd
The Synagogue
Oxford Rd
Primary School
Bevois Gdns
Padwell Road
Clausentum Rd
Mordaunt Road
Cedar Rd
Liverpool St
Methuen St
Dover St
Castle St
Bath St
Southcliff Rd
Imperial Road
Junior School
Mount Pleasant Industrial Estate
The Alpha Business Park
Marina
Hill Lane Surgery
Banister Sch
Ranelagh Gdns
Westrow Rd
Fitzhugh St
Carlton Rd
University
L S U College of Higher Education
Simcoe Clinic
Archers Road
Bellevue Rd
Keeley Cl
Cromwell Rd
Holt Rd
Burton Rd
Milton Road
Southampton Football Club
Bridge Gallery
Rockstone Pl
Magistrates Court
Carlton Crs
Rockstone La
The Newton Health Clinic
Frederick St
Cranbury Pl
Cranbury Av
Mount Pleasant Rd
Derby Rd
Southampton Central Mosque
Meridian TV Studios
Northam Bridge
Northam Business Cen
Wilton Avenue
Hill Farm Rd
Burlington Rd
Newcombe Road
Sandhurst Rd
Coventry Rd
Devonshire Rd
Amoy St
Canton St
Upr Banister St
Carlton Pl
London Road
Ordnance Rd
Lyon St
Lyon Street
Royal South Hants Hospital
Alfred St
Lwr Alfred St
Raven Rd
Bullar St
Summers St
Leyton Rd
Union Rd
Coburg St
Prince's Street
Millbank St
Springhill RC Primary School
Avenue Clinic
Henstead Rd
Winchester St
Lwr Banister St
Asylum Rd
Kings Pk Rd
Bellevue Rd
On Line Gallery
Bedford Pl
Graham Rd
Graham Road
Hartington Road
Durnford Rd
Hindu Temple
Parsonage Rd
Prince's St
York Cl
Millbank Street
Bond St
Lwr Bond St
Guard Rd
Andra Road
The Polygon Sch
Hotel
Roberts Rd
Morris Road
Handel Ter
Handel Rd
Grosvenor Square
Waterloo Ter
Clovelly Road
Leisure Cen
Oxford Avenue
Radcliffe Rd
Kent St
William St
Southampton & New Forest Magistrates Court
The Polygon
Hotel
Titanic Meml
Argyle Road
Derby Rd
Northumberland Rd
Primary School
Belvidere Ter
Cable St
Peel St
Trading Est
BBC South TV & Radio Solent
Commercial Rd
Mayflower Theatre
Cenotaph
Commercial Rd
Police Stn & Courts
Southampton Institute & Millais Gallery
East Pk Ter
Dorset Medical Cen
St Mary's Road
Northbrook Rd
Brinton's Rd
Rochester St
Victoria St
Belvidere Rd
Gasholders
Itchen
City Council
Blechynden Ter
West Pk Rd
Civic Cen
Southampton City Council
East Park
Pk Wk
Above Bar
Northam Rd
Southampton Central Stn
Superstore
Civic Centre Rd
Marlands Shopping Cen
New Rd
Palmerston Rd
N Front
Winton St
St Mary's Pl
Brompton Gallery
Golden Gro
Southampton FC (under constr.)
Portland Ter
Guildhall
Southern Rd
W Quay Rd
Regent St
Pound Tree Rd
North Front
Kingsland Mkt
Speakers Corner Roundabout
St Mary Street
JamesSt
Surg
Coleman St
Melbourne Street
Central Trading Est
West Quay Shopping
Bargate Mus
Polygon
City
Harbour Pde
Vincent's Wk
Above Bar St
Langhorn Rd
Portswood Rd
Bitterne
River Itchen
Vespasian Rd
Chapel
Marine Pde

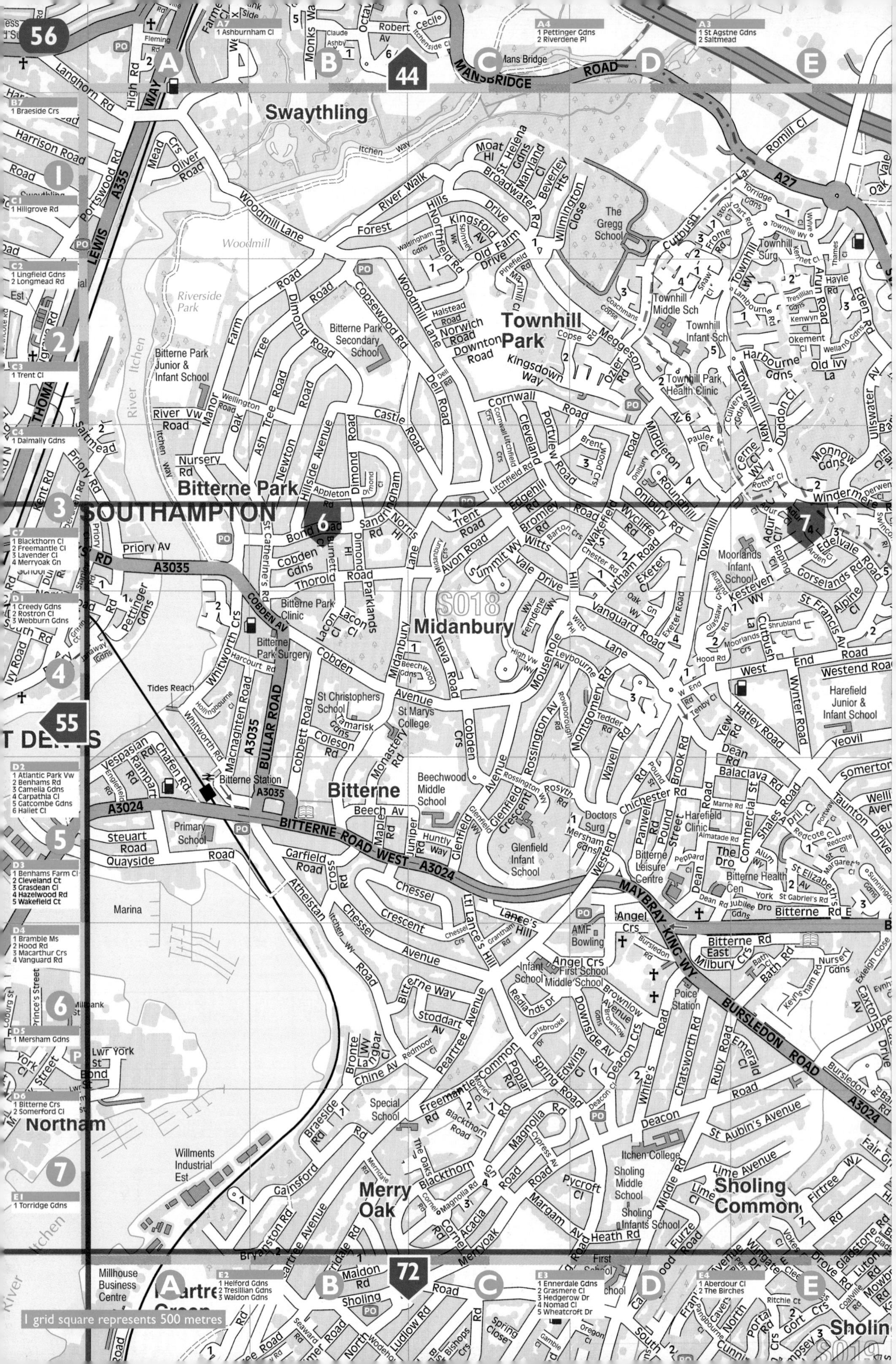
56
44
55
72
6
7
A
B
C
D
E
1
2
3
4
5
6
7
A7
1 Ashburnham Cl
A4
1 Pettinger Gdns
2 Riverdene Pl
A3
1 St Agstne Gdns
2 Saltmead
B7
1 Braeside Crs
C1
1 Hillgrove Rd
C2
1 Lingfield Gdns
2 Longmead Rd
C3
1 Trent Cl
C4
1 Dalmally Gdns
C7
1 Blackthorn Cl
2 Freemantle Cl
3 Lavender Cl
4 Merryoak Gn
D1
1 Creedy Gdns
2 Rostron Cl
3 Webburn Gdns
D2
1 Atlantic Park Vw
2 Benhams Rd
3 Camelia Gdns
4 Carpathia Cl
5 Gatcombe Gdns
6 Hallet Cl
D3
1 Benhams Farm Cl
2 Cleveland Ct
3 Grasdean Cl
4 Hazelwood Rd
5 Wakefield Ct
D4
1 Bramble Ms
2 Hood Rd
3 Macarthur Crs
4 Vanguard Rd
D5
1 Mersham Gdns
D6
1 Bitterne Crs
2 Somerford Cl
E1
1 Torridge Gdns
E2
1 Helford Gdns
2 Tresillian Gdns
3 Waldon Gdns
E3
1 Ennerdale Gdns
2 Grasmere Ct
3 Hedgerow Dr
4 Nomad Cl
5 Wheatcroft Dr
E4
1 Aberdour Cl
2 The Birches
Swaythling
Townhill Park
Bitterne Park
SOUTHAMPTON
Midanbury
SO18
Bitterne
Merry Oak
Sholing Common
Northam
MANSBRIDGE ROAD
Mans Bridge
A27
A335
LEWIS WAY
A3035
COBDEN AV
BULLAR ROAD
A3024
BITTERNE ROAD WEST
MAYBRAY KING WY
BURSLEDON ROAD
Woodmill
Woodmill Lane
Riverside Park
River Itchen
Itchen Way
Bitterne Park Junior & Infant School
Bitterne Park Secondary School
The Gregg School
Townhill Middle Sch
Townhill Infant Sch
Townhill Park Health Clinic
Moorlands Infant School
Harefield Junior & Infant School
Bitterne Park Clinic
Bitterne Park Surgery
St Christophers School
St Marys College
Beechwood Middle School
Glenfield Infant School
Bitterne Leisure Centre
Harefield Clinic
Bitterne Health Cen
AMF Bowling
Infant School
First School
Middle School
Poice Station
Doctors Surg
Townhill Surg
Special School
Itchen College
Sholing Middle School
Sholing Infants School
Primary School
Bitterne Station
Tides Reach
Marina
Willments Industrial Est
Millhouse Business Centre
Harrison Road
Portswood Rd
High Rd
Langhorn Rd
Mead Crs
Oliver Road
River Walk
Forest Hills
Northfield Rd
Kingsfold Av
Old Farm Drive
Moat Hl
St Helena Gdns
Maryland Cl
Beverley Hts
Broadwater Rd
Wilmington Close
Meggeson Av
Ozier Rd
Kingsdown Way
Cornwall Road
Cornwall Crs
Litchfield Crs
Cleveland Rd
Portview Road
Brentwood Crs
Middleton Cl
Onibury Rd
Roundhill Cl
Townhill Way
Duddon Cl
Harbourne Gdns
Okement Cl
Arun Road
Eden Rd
Old Ivy La
Ullswater Av
Monnow Gdns
Windermere Av
Romill Cl
Oak Vale
Cutbush La
Frome Rd
Halstead Road
Norwich Road
Downton Road
Dell Road
Copsewood Rd
Dimond Road
Tree Road
Farm Road
Manor Road
Wellington Road
Oak Road
Ash Tree Road
Newton Road
River Vw Road
Nursery Rd
Saltmead
Priory Rd
Kent Rd
Priory Av
Castle Road
Hillside Avenue
Appleton Rd
Sandringham Rd
Norris Hl
Trent Road
Bond Road
Cobden Gdns
Thorold Road
Burnett Cl
Dimond Hl
Parklands
Lacon Cl
Midanbury Lane
Avon Road
Summit Wy
Vale Drive
Edgehill Rd
Bromley Rd
Witts Hill
Wakefield Road
Wycliffe Rd
Lytham Road
Exeter Cl
Exeter Road
Vanguard Road
Kesteven Wy
Epping Cl
Edelvale Road
Gorselands Rd
Alpine Cl
St Francis Av
Shrubland Cl
Moorlands Crs
Hood Rd
West End Road
Westend Road
Wynter Road
Hatley Road
Yeovil
Somerton Av
Taunton Dr
Dean Rd
Balaclava Rd
Shales Road
Commercial St
Pound Street
Brook Rd
Chichester Rd
Panwell Rd
Mousehole Lane
Leybourne Av
Montgomery Rd
Wavell Rd
Tedder Rd
Rossington Av
Rossington Wy
Rosyth Rd
Glenfield Crescent
Glenfield Av
Mersham Gdns
Westend Rd
Neva Road
Cobden Crs
Cobden Avenue
Whitworth Crs
Whitworth Rd
Harcourt Rd
Hollingbourne Cl
Macnaghten Road
Vespasian Rd
Rampart Rd
Chafen Rd
Englefield Rd
Cobbett Road
Tamarisk Gdns
Coleson Rd
Monastery Rd
Beech Av
Maple Rd
Juniper Rd
Huntly Way
Steuart Road
Quayside Road
Garfield Road
Cross Rd
Athelstan Road
Chessel Crescent
Chessel Avenue
Itchen Wy
Ltl Lance's Hill
Lances Hill
Grantham Rd
Angel Crs
Bursledon Rd
Bitterne Rd East
Bitterne Rd E
Milbury Crs
Bath Rd
Nursery Gdns
Keynsham Rd
Caxton Av
Exleigh Close
Bitterne Way
Stoddart Av
Peartree Avenue
Redlands Dr
Downside Av
Brownlow Avenue
Deacon Crs
White's Road
Chatsworth Rd
Ruby Road
Emerald Cl
Bronte Wy
Langbar Cl
Chine Av
Redmoor Cl
Common Rd
Poplar Rd
Freemantle Common Rd
Spring Road
Edwina Cl
Blackthorn Road
Magnolia Rd
Cypress Av
Merridale Rd
The Oaks
Braeside Rd
Gainsford Rd
Peartree Avenue
Blackthorn Gn
Acacia Rd
Cornel Rd
Merryoak Road
Margam Av
Pycroft Cl
Middle Rd
Deacon Road
St Aubin's Avenue
Lime Avenue
Lime Cl
Firtree Wy
Furze Rd
Heath Rd
Bryanston Rd
Maldon Rd
Sholing Rd
Ludlow Rd
Spring Close
Ritchie Ct
Gort Crs
Fair Gn
Fleming Rd
Claude Ashby Cl
Robert Cecil Av
Itchenside Cl
Monks Way
Lower York St
Bond St
York Street
Prince's Street
Millbank St
Brook Rd
Dean Rd
Jubilee Gdns
York Dro
St Gabriel's Rd
St Elizabeth's Av
Redcote Cl
Portway Cl
Alum Wy
April Cl
The Dro
Almatade Rd
Marne Rd
Peppard Cl
1 grid square represents 500 metres

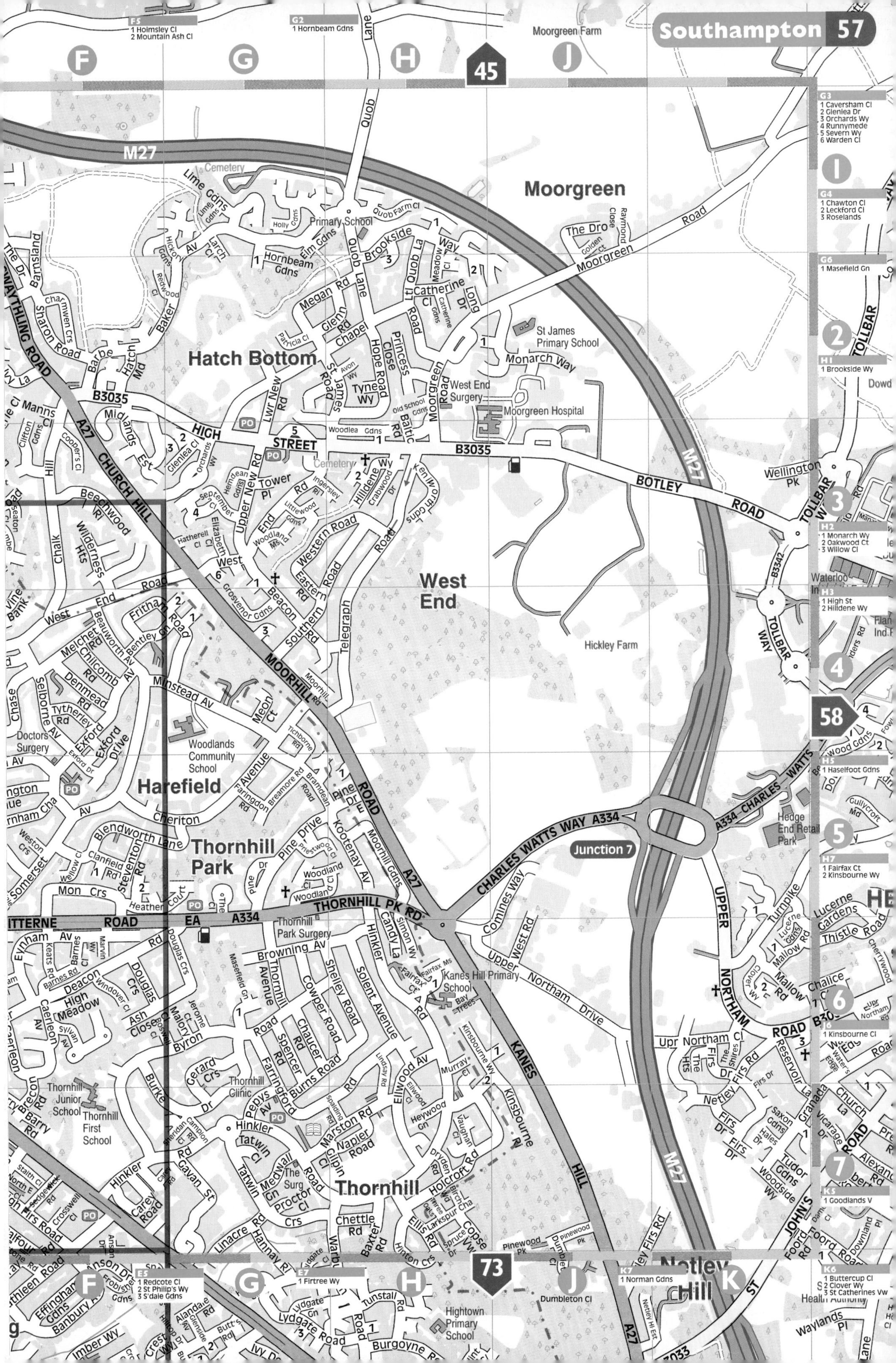
F5
1 Holmsley Cl
2 Mountain Ash Cl
G2
1 Hornbeam Gdns
Moorgreen Farm
45
G3
1 Caversham Cl
2 Glenlea Dr
3 Orchards Wy
4 Runnymede
5 Severn Wy
6 Warden Cl
G4
1 Chawton Cl
2 Leckford Cl
3 Roselands
G6
1 Masefield Gn
H1
1 Brookside Wy
H2
1 Monarch Wy
2 Oakwood Ct
3 Willow Cl
H3
1 High St
2 Hilldene Wy
H5
1 Haselfoot Gdns
H7
1 Fairfax Ct
2 Kinsbourne Wy
J6
1 Kinsbourne Cl
K5
1 Goodlands V
K6
1 Buttercup Cl
2 Clover Wy
3 St Catherines Vw
E5
1 Redcote Cl
2 St Philip's Wy
3 S'dale Gdns
E7
1 Firtree Wy
K7
1 Norman Gdns
58
73
M27
Moorgreen
Hatch Bottom
West End
Harefield
Thornhill Park
Thornhill
Netley Hill
Cemetery
Primary School
St James Primary School
West End Surgery
Moorgreen Hospital
Hickley Farm
Woodlands Community School
Doctors Surgery
Thornhill Park Surgery
Kanes Hill Primary School
Thornhill Clinic
Thornhill Junior School
Thornhill First School
The Surg
Hightown Primary School
Hedge End Retail Park
Junction 7
Wellington Pk
Waterloo Ind
B3035
HIGH STREET
BOTLEY ROAD
Moorgreen Road
CHARLES WATTS WAY A334
A334 CHARLES WATTS
THORNHILL PK RD
A27
MOORHILL ROAD
CHURCH HILL
KANES HILL
SWAYTHLING ROAD
UPPER NORTHAM ROAD
TOLLBAR WAY
B3342
Quob Lane
Upper Northam Drive
West End Road
Telegraph Road
Western Road
Eastern Road
Southern Rd
Beacon Rd
Chapel Rd
Hope Road
Monarch Way
Dumbleton Cl
Pinewood Pk
Netley Firs Rd
Reservoir La
Church La
Vicarage Rd
JOHN'S ST
Lucerne Gardens
Thistle Road
Chalice Ct
Mallow Rd
Turnpike Wy
Comines Way
Pine Dr
Kootenay Av
Thornhill Avenue
Shelley Road
Solent Avenue
Cowper Road
Chaucer Rd
Spencer Rd
Burns Road
Browning Av
Hinkler Rd
Ellwood Av
Kinsbourne Ri
Holcroft Rd
Copse Vw
Cheriton Av
Minstead Av
Avenue Rd
Exford Drive
Selborne Av
Chalk Hill
Beechwood Ri
Wilderness Hts
West End Road
Somerset Av
Mon Crs
Heather Ct
Deacon Rd
High Meadow
Caerleon Av
Douglas Crs
Ash Close
Byron Rd
Gerard Crs
Farringford Rd
Pepys Av
Marston Rd
Napier Road
Tatwin Cl
Medwall Gn
Proctor Cl
Carey Road
Linacre Rd
Hannay Ri
Chettle Rd
Baxter Rd
Ellis Rd
Lydgate Road
Tunstall Rd
Burgoyne Rd
Alandale Rd
Effingham Gdns
Banbury Av
Dumbleton Cl
Waylands Pl

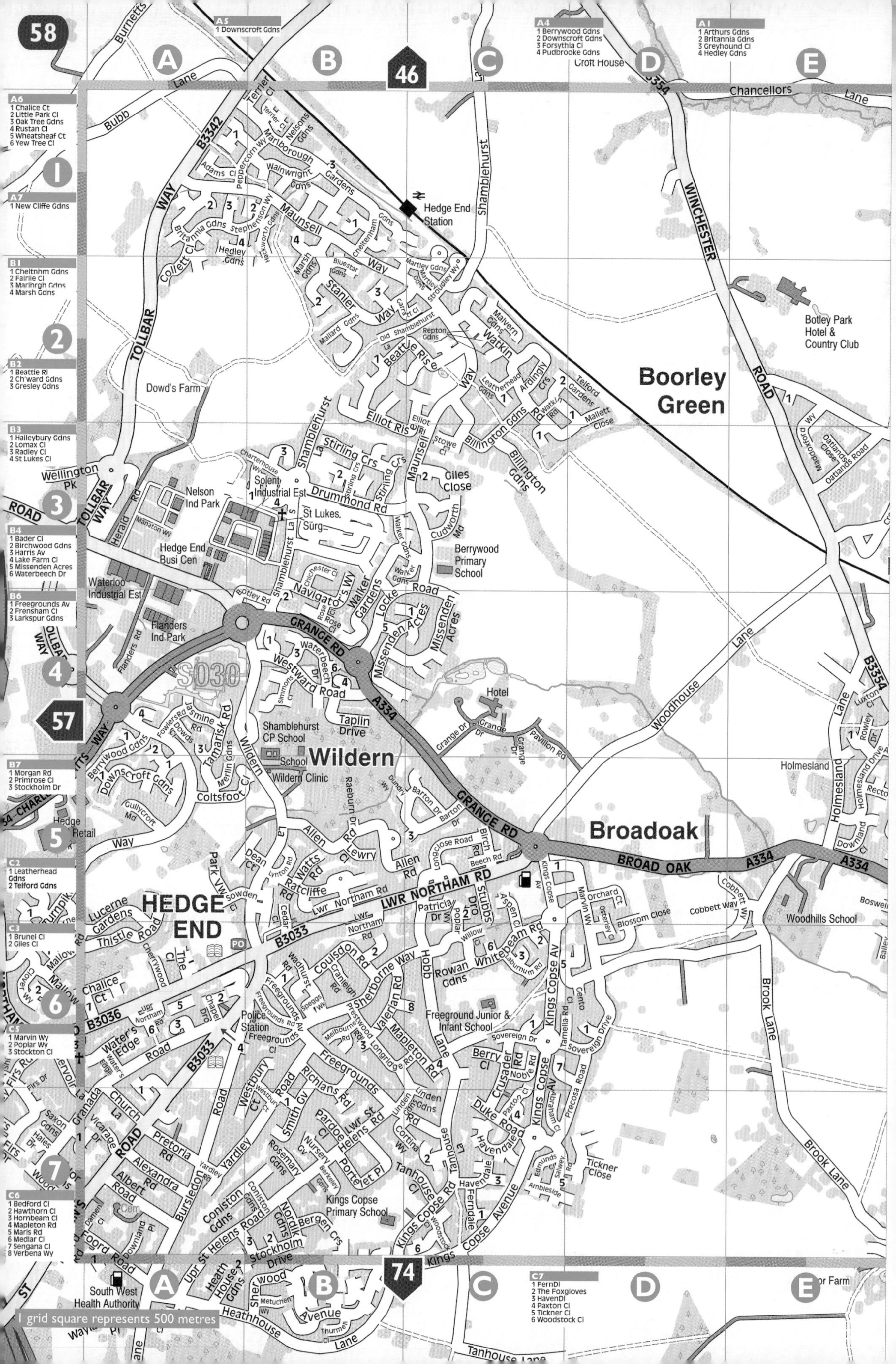
A5
1 Downscroft Gdns
A4
1 Berrywood Gdns
2 Downscroft Gdns
3 Forsythia Cl
4 Pudbrooke Gdns
A1
1 Arthurs Gdns
2 Britannia Gdns
3 Greyhound Cl
4 Hedley Gdns
A6
1 Chalice Ct
2 Little Park Cl
3 Oak Tree Gdns
4 Rustan Cl
5 Wheatsheaf Ct
6 Yew Tree Cl
A7
1 New Cliffe Gdns
B1
1 Cheltnhm Gdns
2 Fairlie Cl
3 Marlbrgh Gdns
4 Marsh Gdns
B2
1 Beattie Ri
2 Ch'ward Gdns
3 Gresley Gdns
B3
1 Haileybury Gdns
2 Lomax Cl
3 Radley Cl
4 St Lukes Cl
B4
1 Bader Cl
2 Birchwood Gdns
3 Harris Av
4 Lake Farm Cl
5 Missenden Acres
6 Waterbeech Dr
B6
1 Freegrounds Av
2 Frensham Cl
3 Larkspur Gdns
B7
1 Morgan Rd
2 Primrose Cl
3 Stockholm Dr
C2
1 Leatherhead Gdns
2 Telford Gdns
C3
1 Brunel Cl
2 Giles Cl
C5
1 Marvin Wy
2 Poplar Wy
3 Stockton Cl
C6
1 Bedford Cl
2 Hawthorn Cl
3 Hornbeam Cl
4 Mapleton Rd
5 Marls Rd
6 Medlar Cl
7 Sengana Cl
8 Verbena Wy
C7
1 FernDl
2 The Foxgloves
3 HavenDl
4 Paxton Cl
5 Tickner Cl
6 Woodstock Cl
46
57
74
A
B
C
D
E
1
2
3
4
5
6
7
Boorley Green
Broadoak
Wildern
HEDGE END
Hedge End Station
Botley Park Hotel & Country Club
Dowd's Farm
Nelson Ind Park
Solent Industrial Est
Hedge End Busi Cen
Waterloo Industrial Est
Flanders Ind Park
St Lukes Surg
Berrywood Primary School
Shamblehurst CP School
Wildern Clinic
Hotel
Holmesland
Woodhills School
Freeground Junior & Infant School
Police Station
Kings Copse Primary School
South West Health Authority
Croft House
Chancellors Lane
WINCHESTER ROAD
TOLLBAR WAY
GRANGE RD
BROAD OAK
LWR NORTHAM RD
Woodhouse Lane
Brook Lane
Kings Copse Avenue
Tanhouse Lane
Heathhouse Lane
B3342
B3354
B3033
B3036
A334
SO30
1 grid square represents 500 metres

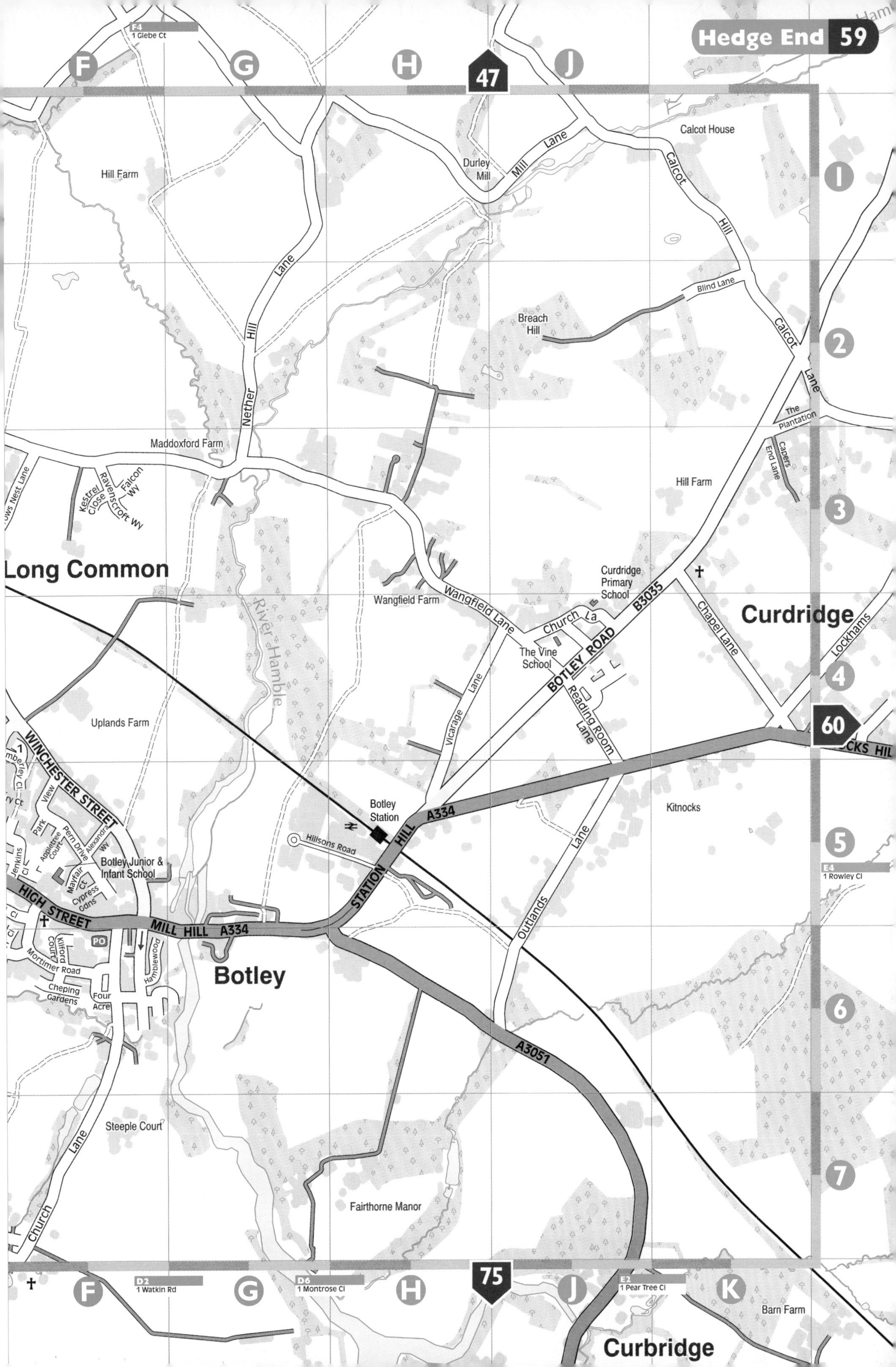
F4
1 Glebe Ct
F
G
H
47
J
Calcot House
Hill Farm
Durley Mill
Mill Lane
Calcot Hill
1
Lane
Nether Hill
Blind Lane
Breach Hill
Calcot Lane
2
The Plantation
Capers End Lane
Maddoxford Farm
Hill Farm
Kestrel Close
Ravenscroft Wy
Falcon Wy
3
Long Common
Curdridge Primary School
Wangfield Farm
Wangfield Lane
Church La
B3035
River Hamble
The Vine School
BOTLEY ROAD
Chapel Lane
Curdridge
Lockhams
4
Uplands Farm
Vicarage Lane
Reading Room Lane
60
WINCHESTER STREET
Kitnocks
Botley Station
A334
Hillsons Road
STATION HILL
Outlands Lane
5
E4
1 Rowley Cl
Park View
Appletree Court
Perm Drive
Alexandra Wy
Botley Junior & Infant School
Jenkins Cl
Mayfair Ct
Cypress Gdns
HIGH STREET
MILL HILL A334
PO
Kilford Court
Hamblewood
Mortimer Road
Cheping Gardens
Four Acre
Botley
6
A3051
Steeple Court
Church Lane
7
Fairthorne Manor
F
D2
1 Watkin Rd
G
D6
1 Montrose Cl
H
75
J
E2
1 Pear Tree Cl
K
Barn Farm
Curbridge

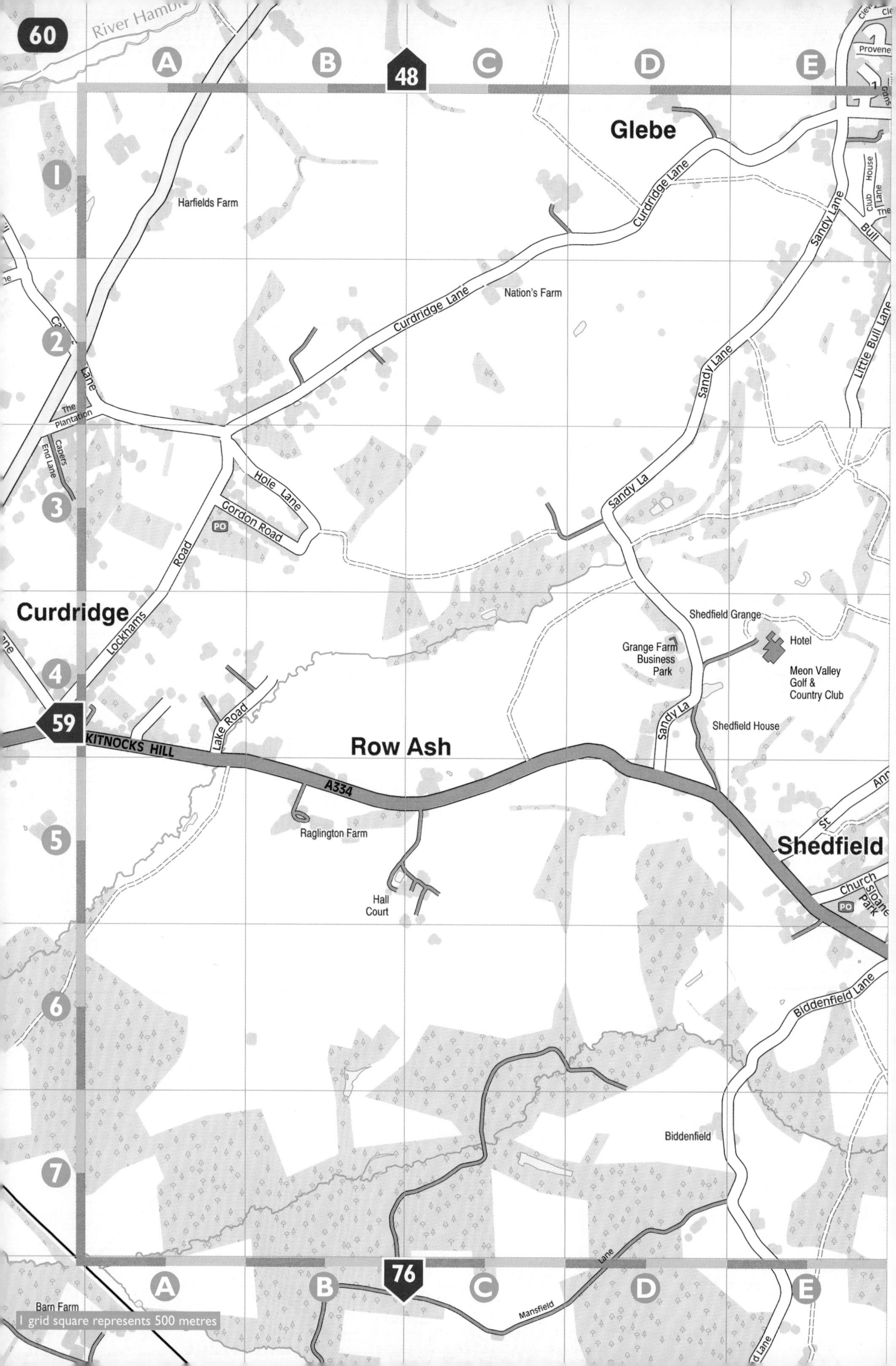

1 grid square represents 500 metres

Waltham Chase
Shirrell Heath
Turkey Island
Kingsmead
Hillpound
49
77
F
G
H
J
I
K
2
3
4
5
6
7
F1 1 Forest Gdns
K1 1 Hunters Cha
Waltham Business Park
New Road
The Lakes
Martin
Medicott
Glenda
Orchardlea
Brickyard Road
Forest Road
Forest Farm
Gravel Hill
Mislingford Road
Dirty Copse
Evelyn
The Ridings
Meadow
Gardens
Provene Close
B2177
Chase Grove
Linden Close
Forest Close
Poplars
Beaucroft Road
Chase Farm Cl
Ashley Gardens
PO
Lane
Red Leaves
Brooklynn Cl
St John the Baptist School
Bishop's Wood Road
Bishopsmore
Hawk's Nest
Solomons Lane
Lane
Hearne Gardens
Black Horse Lane
Shirrell Heath
High Street
Smiths Lane
Winters Road
Hospital Road
Bishops Lane
Twynhams Hill
Newmans Hill
River Meon
Camblins Lane
Nightingale Cl
WINCHESTER ROAD
Upper Church Rd
Road
Cemetery
Fairlands Montessori School
Canford Close
Frith Lane
Kingsmead
Close Wood
Pricketts Hill
Frith Farm
A334
Northfields Farm Lane
Northfields Farm
A32
Blind Lane
Mill Lane
Titchfield Lane
WINCHESTER
Wickham C of E Controlled Primary School
Cold Harbour Farm
The Spur
The Circle
Garnier Park
Dickson Place
River
Rookes

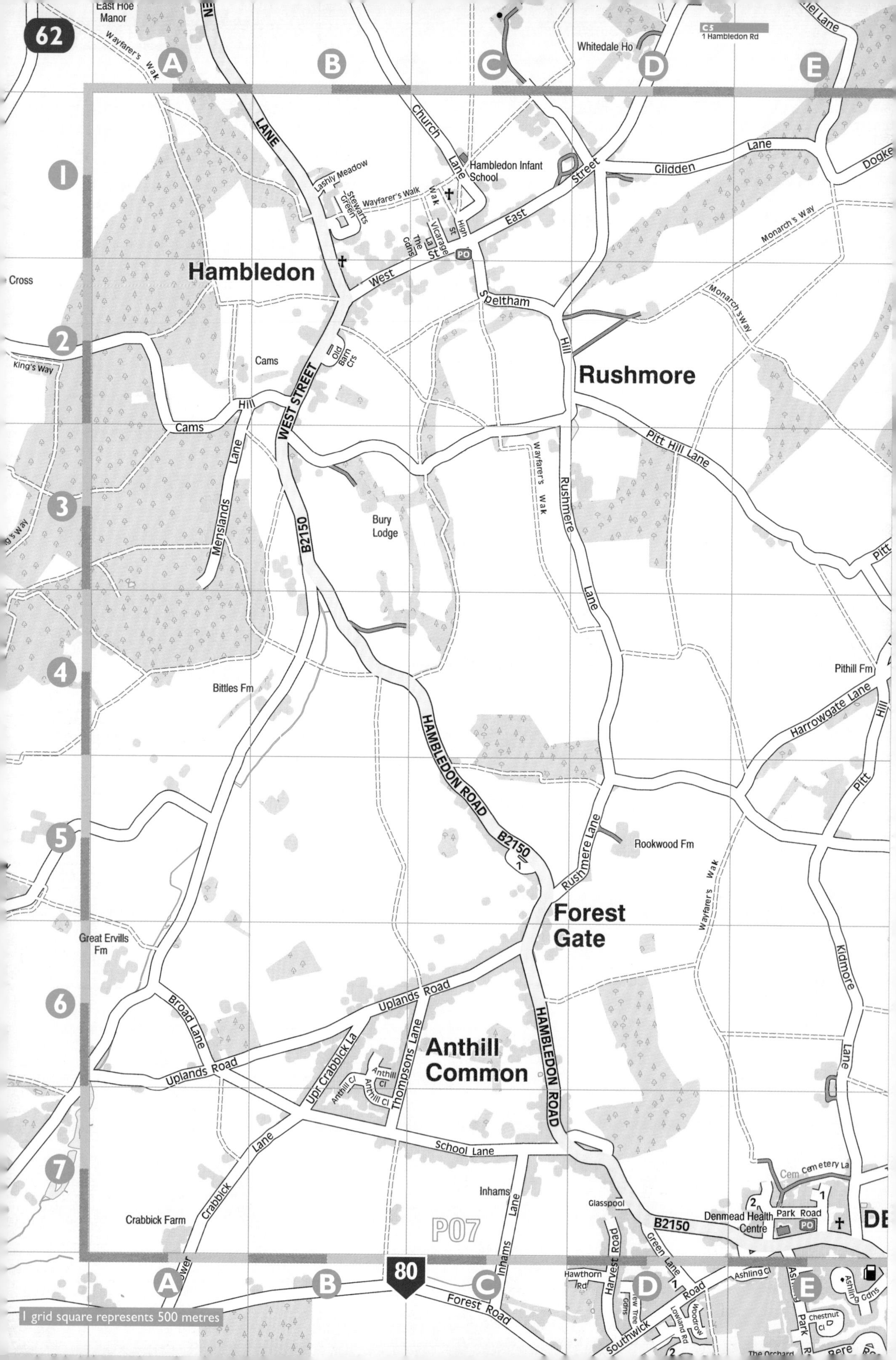

1 grid square represents 500 metres

F
G
H
J
Dockenn
Lane
nel Lane
Glidden Fm
Monarch's Way
Old Mill Lane
I
2
3
4
5
6
7
Lane
Horsepost
Pitt Hill Lane
Harrowgate Lane
Denmead Mill
Hill Lane
Monarch's Way
Monarch's Way
Hinton Manor Lane
Broadway Lane
Hinton Daubnay
Old Mill Lane
Tagdell
Lovedean Lane
64
Monarch's Way
Day Lane
Coldhill Lane
The Crossways
Broadway Fm
New Road
The Curve
Woodland View
Whitley Rd
Loxwood
White Horse Lane
Broadway Lane
Edneys Lane
Lovedean Lane
Lovedean
Eastland Gate
Ashley Cl
pse Road
Meadowlands Junior School
Woodcroft La
anner's Lane
ENMEAD
Lane
Shrover
Meadowlands Infant School
Woodcroft Lane
81
K
Anmore Road
Martin Avenue
The Heath
Denmead
Fulmer Walk
Partridge Gardens
Linnet Cl
Eagle Av
Kite Cl
Grebe Cl
Chaffinch Cl
Eagle Av
Curlew Gdns
Dove Cl
Blackbird Cl
Sparrow Cl
Coleridge

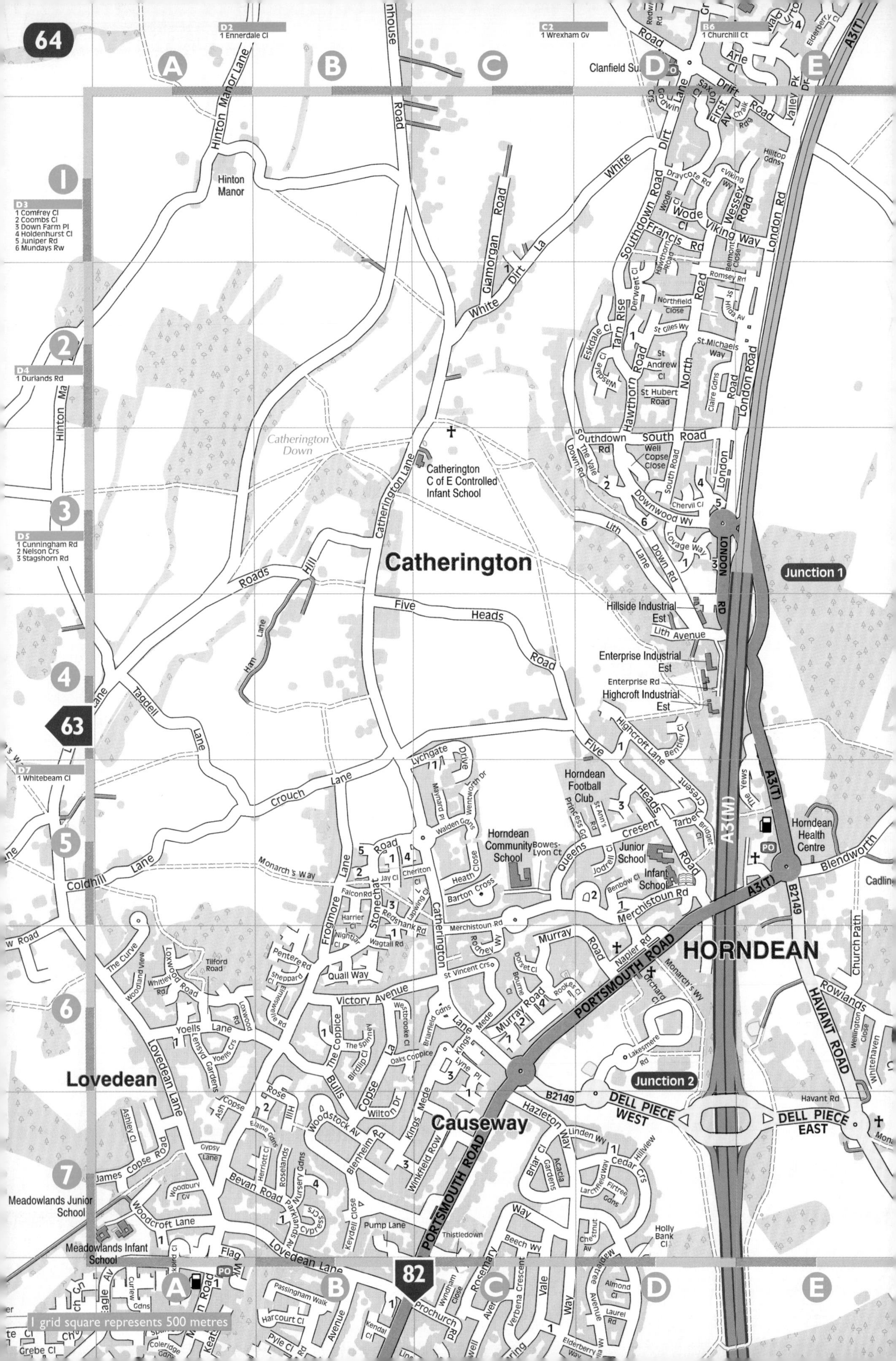
D2
1 Ennerdale Cl
C2
1 Wrexham Gv
B6
1 Churchill Ct
D3
1 Comfrey Cl
2 Coombs Cl
3 Down Farm Pl
4 Holdenhurst Cl
5 Juniper Rd
6 Mundays Rw
D4
1 Durlands Rd
D5
1 Cunningham Rd
2 Nelson Crs
3 Stagshorn Rd
D7
1 Whitebeam Cl
63
82
Hinton Manor Lane
Hinton Manor
Catherington Down
Catherington Lane
Catherington C of E Controlled Infant School
Catherington
Glamorgan Road
White Dirt La
Roads Hill
Ham Lane
Five Heads Road
Tagdell Lane
Crouch Lane
Coldhill Lane
Monarch's Way
Clanfield
Southdown Road
Francis Rd
Viking Way
Wessex Road
London Road
Hawthorn Road
North Road
Tarn Rise
Eskdale Cl
St Hubert Road
South Road
Downwood Wy
Lovage Way
Lith Lane
Down Rd
Lith Avenue
Hillside Industrial Est
Enterprise Industrial Est
Enterprise Rd
Highcroft Industrial Est
Highcroft Lane
Junction 1
Junction 2
A3(M)
A3(T)
LONDON RD
Horndean Football Club
Horndean Community School
Bowes-Lyon Ct
Queens Cresent
Junior School
Infant School
Merchistoun Rd
Horndean Health Centre
Blendworth
HORNDEAN
PORTSMOUTH ROAD
Napier Rd
Murray Road
Lakesmere Rd
B2149
DELL PIECE WEST
DELL PIECE EAST
HAVANT ROAD
Havant Rd
Rowlands
Church Path
Lovedean
Lovedean Lane
Causeway
Victory Avenue
Frogmore Lane
Stonechat
Quail Way
Bulls Copse La
Woodstock Av
Blenheim Rd
Kings Mede
Winkfield Row
Hazleton Way
Cedar Crs
Hillview
Yoells Lane
Loxwood Road
James Copse Road
Bevan Road
Woodcroft Lane
Meadowlands Junior School
Meadowlands Infant School
Pump Lane
Thistledown
Rosemary
Verbena Crescent
Vale
Holly Bank Cl
Almond Cl
Laurel Rd
Prochurch Rd
Passingham Walk
Harcourt Cl
Pyle Cl
Grebe Cl
Keats
Cadlington
1 grid square represents 500 metres

F
G
H
J
K
1
2
3
4
5
6
7
Horndean Down
South Lane
Netherley Fm
Sussex Border Path
New Barn Fm
PO8
Crabden Lane
Horndean Road
Woodhouse Road
Rowlands Castle Road
Blendworth
Woodhouse Lane
Wick Fm
Idsworth Ho
Castle Road
Treadwheel Road
Woodhouse
Pyle Fm
Monarch's Way
Magpie Road
Lane
The Holt
83

C7
1 Foldsgate Cl
2 Racecourse Vw
50
A
B
C
D
E
1
2
3
4
5
6
7
Brockishill
Goldenl
Brockishill Road
A337
Brockis Hill
Minstead Lodge
Bull Lane
Football Green
Brockishill Inclosure
Mill Lane
Furzy Lawn Inclosure
Bartley Water
The Kennels
The Mill House
Manor Park
Pikes Hill
Westwood Rd
Fenwick Hospital
Pikeshill
Police Station
Broughton Road
Calpe Av
Custards Rd
New Forest Golf Club
Emery Down
Northerwood House
Silver St
86
Forest Gdns
Queen's Pde
ROMSEY RD
Pemberton Rd
Wellands Rd
Princes Crsesent
Hotel
LYNDHURST
Custards
Sch
Htl
Garden Close
Northerwood Av
Knightwood Cl
PH
PO
1 grid square represents 500 metres

F
G
H
J
51
I
2
3
4
5
6
7
Purkiss Cl
Bartley Road
Green Cl
Milvina Cl
PH
hayes
Woodlands Road
Great Fletchwood Fm
Hotel
Woodlands
Foyers
Bartley Road
Woodlands Road
The Crs
Woodlands Drove
Alpine Road
Hazel Gv
Busketts Wood
Fletchwood Rd
Fletchwood Copse
Busketts Lawn Inclosure
Busketts Wy
Peterscroft Av
Ash Rd
Holly
PO
Ashur Hospi
Ironshill Lodge
A35
68
Ironshill Inclosure
Lodgehill Cottage
A35
Ashurst Wood
ROAD
Mallard Wood
Ashurst Lodge
SOUTHAMPTON
Dunces Arch
White Moor
Beaulieu River
87
F
G
H
J
K

1 grid square represents 500 metres

Eling
K4
1 Lakeland Gdns
2 Lloyd Av
The Retreat
MARCHWOOD
BY-PASS
Lane
Hill
Bury Lane
F
G
H
J
53
City of Southampton
Hampshire County
Marchwood Road
Trotts Lane
A326
Bury Fm
Bury Road
Trotts
Cork La
Normandy Way
Bury Rd
Cork La
Shorefield
The Gulls
LC
Marchwood
Main
Pooksgreen
Bilberry Dr
The Rushes
Reed Dr
The Tussocks
Alder Cl
Melick Cl
Tavell's Lane
Woodpecker Drive
Kingfisher Wy
The Rowans
Cranberry Cl
Marchwood Junior School
Park Lane
Pooksgreen
Bolhinton Av
Park Cl
Marshfield Cl
Tavells Cl
Sandpiper Cl
Langley Lodge
Poplar Dr
Kestrel Cl
Osprey Cl
Vicarage Rd
PO
Staplewood Lane
Long Lane
Woodside Cl
St Johns Dr
Main
Mulberry Rd
Staplewood La
The Crs
Plantation Dr
Burma Wy
70
Larkspur Dr
Willow Dr
Spindlewood Wy
Marchwood C of E Infant School
Hythe Road
MARCHWOOD
Staplewood Lane
Arters Lawn
Twiggs Lane
End
Lane
Twiggs
Beaulieu Road
89
F
G
H
J
K
Birchlands Farm
Foxhill Farm
2
3
4
5
6
7

B4
1 Acorn Cl
2 The Limes
3 Malcroft Ms
4 Ripplewood
5 Tanglewood
6 Woodmoor Cl
A4
1 Crooked Hays Cl
2 St Johns Ct
A3
1 Pebble Ct
D3
1 Cracknore H La
A
B
C
D
E
54
69
90
1
2
3
4
5
6
7
A33
Saxon Rd
Mountbatten Bus Cen
Imperial Wy
Herbert Walker Avenue
West Bay Road
City of Southampton
Hampshire County
River Test
Quayside Wk
Maritime Av
Ordnance Way
Magazine La
Admiralty Wy
Cork La
Normandy Way
Shorefield Rd
Tides Way
The Gulls
Bury Rd
Main Road
Old Magazine Cl
Gage Cl
Gardiner Cl
Drake Cl
Old Cracknore Cl
The Rushes
Reed Dr
The Tussocks
Moss Dr
Lichen Wy
Bilberry Dr
Alder Cl
Melick Cl
Pond Cl
Aaron Ct
Lane
The Rowans
Cranberry Cl
Marchwood Junior School
The Surg
Kingfisher Wy
Woodpecker Dr
Sandpiper
Osprey Cl
Vicarage Rd
PO
Main Rd
Mulberry Rd
Maryvale
Africa Dr
Burma Wy
Philpott Dr
Adams Wd Dr
Malthouse Gdns
Oakland Dr
Ferndale Rd
Evergreen Cl
Wood Glade Cl
Frome Cl
Elder Cl
The Hawthorns
Autumn Road
Rosewood Gdns
Kingswood
Dapple Pl
Cracknore Hard Lane
Cracknore Hard
Cracknore
Larkspur Dr
Willow Dr
Spindlewood Wy
Hythe Road
LC
Pumpfield Farm
Marchwood C of E Infant School
MARCHWOOD BY-PASS
A326
Main Road
Veal's Lane
Marchwood Priory Hospital
Church Farm Close
Gdn City
Church Farm
Lock's Farm
Dibden
The Old Manor
1 grid square represents 500 metres

G1
1 Albion Pl
2 Scullards La
G2
1 Vyse La
H1
1 Johnson St
2 St Georges St
3 York Buildings
H2
1 Charles St
2 Gloucester Sq
3 Market Pl
4 Russell St
J1
1 Maryfield
J2
1 Paget St
2 Richmond St
3 Royal Cres Rd
4 St Lawrence Rd
5 Saltmarsh Rd
J3
1 Atlantic Cl
2 Mermaid Wy
K2
1 Asturias Wy
K3
1 Ocean Wy
55
72
8
9
91
F
G
H
J
K
1
2
3
4
5
6
7
Southampton Central Sta
Civic Cen
Civic Centre Rd
Southampton Council
Superstore
Guildhall
Northam Rd
Gasholders
Brompton Gallery
Southampton FC (under constr.)
Golden Grove
Melbourne Street
Marine Pde
Britannia Road
North
Rochester St
Harbour Pde
Hotel
A33
W Quay Road
Southern Rd
Odeon Cinema
West Quay Retail Park
West Quay Shopping Centre
Portland Ter
Pirelli St
Bargate Mus
Pound Tree Rd
South Front
Kingsland Mkt
Speakers Corner Roundabout
SO14
St Mary St
Polymonds
Hanover Buildings
Bargate Shop Cen
East Street Shop Cen
Houndwell Pl
East St
Lime St
James St
Surg
Coleman St
College
Hamwic Coll
Chapel Rd
Elm Street
Central Trading Est
B3038
Deanery Campus
Albert Rd N
Evans St
Threefield La
Marsh La
Terminus Ter
Central Br
The Itchen Bridge
A3025
Southampton Technical College
Solent Rd
W Quay Rd
Castle Way
High St
Hamtun St
West St
Mn War Mem
Back of the Walls
Canal Wk
Orchard La
King St
Bernard St
College St
Captains Pl
College
Queen's Way
Oxford St
Briton St
Tudor House Mus
Mayflower Roundabout
Mayflower Mem
Herbert Walker Av
Bugle St
French St
Sch
Wool House Maritime Mus
Porter's La
Town Quay
Platform Rd
Queen's Ter
Canute Road
Hall of Aviation
Albert Rd S
Canute Rd
Floating Br Rd
Alcantara Crs
Channel Wy
Andes Close
Longbridge Ind Park
Spitfire Court Surgery
Red Funnel Ferry Terminal
Royal Pier
God's House Tower Museum
Maritime Wy
Virgin Cinemas
Calshot Spit Lightship
Ocean Way Business Cen
Regional Film Theatre
SS Shieldhall
Tasman Cl
Pacific Cl
Ocean Village
Ferry Terminal
Town Quay
West Road
Central Road
Cunard Rd
European Way
Brazil Road
Oceanographic Centre
Java Rd
Ocean Rd
Empress Road
Test Rd
River Test
River Itchen
Isle of Wight
Hythe
City of Southampton
Hampshire County
Endeavour Way
White Heather Ct
Astra Ct
Marina
Velsheda Court
Shamrock Way
Waterside
Jessop Cl
West St
Solent Way
PO
Victoria Road
Keswick Rd
Woodley
Swift
Unwin Cl
Glen Rd
Lake Rd

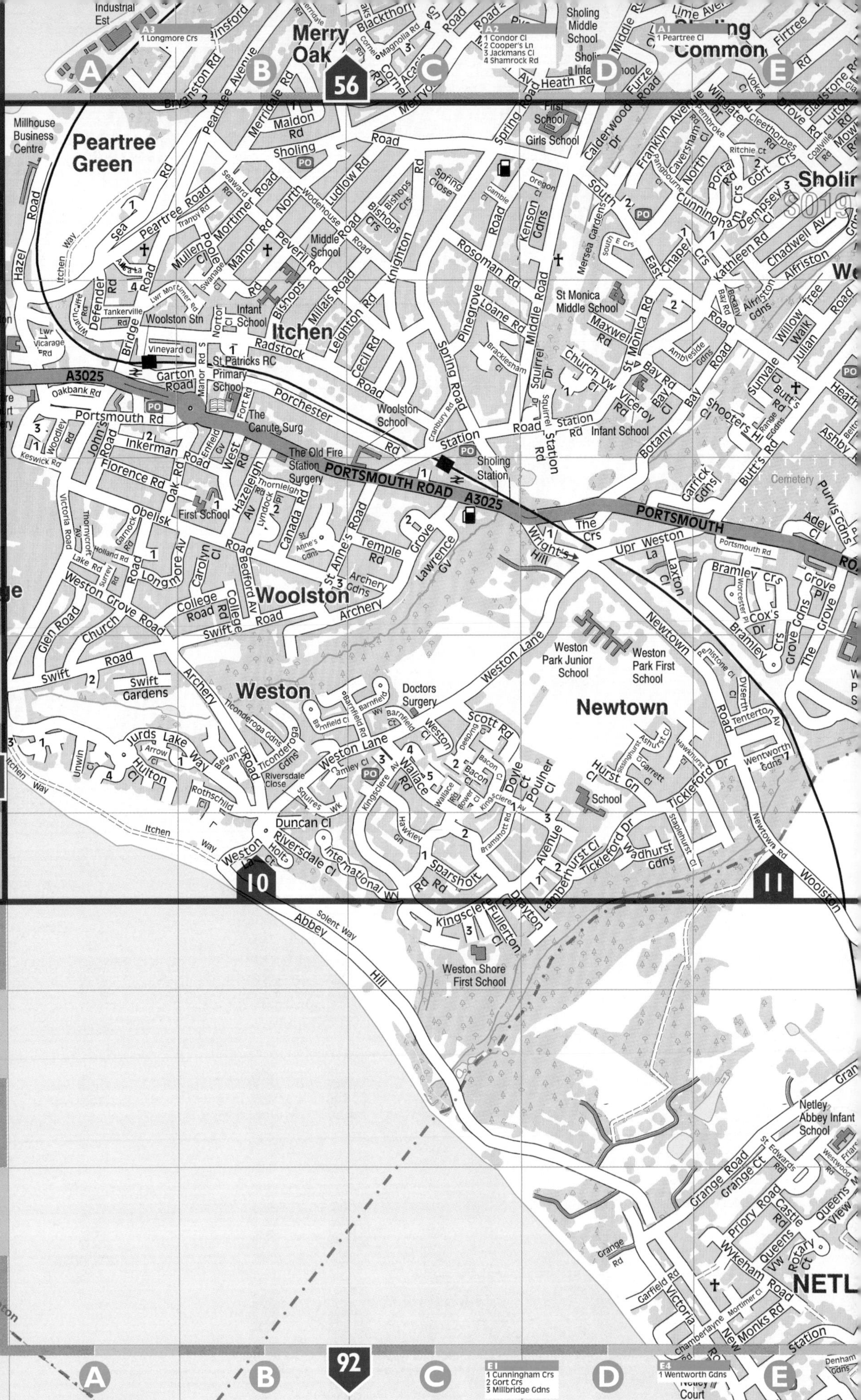

A4
1 Dundonald Cl
2 Swift Hollow
3 Victoria Rd
4 Waldegrave Cl

B1
1 Elstree Rd
2 Osterly Rd

B2
1 Cheddar Cl

B3
1 Florence Rd
2 Lyndock Cl
3 Torcross Cl

B4
1 Cozens Cl

C3
1 Fern Rd
2 Temple Gdns

C4
1 Bramshott Rd
2 Deeping Cl
3 Kingsclere Cl
4 Kipling Ct
5 Wallace Rd

C5
1 Burghclere Rd
2 Crookham Rd
3 Foxcott Cl

D1
1 Rothbury Cl
2 Torrington Cl

D2
1 Applewood Gdns
2 Lynden Ga

D3
1 Gordon Ter

D5
1 Longstock Cl
2 Ropley Cl
3 Winchfield Cl

E1
1 Cunningham Crs
2 Gort Crs
3 Millbridge Gdns

E4
1 Wentworth Gdns

1 grid square represents 500 metres

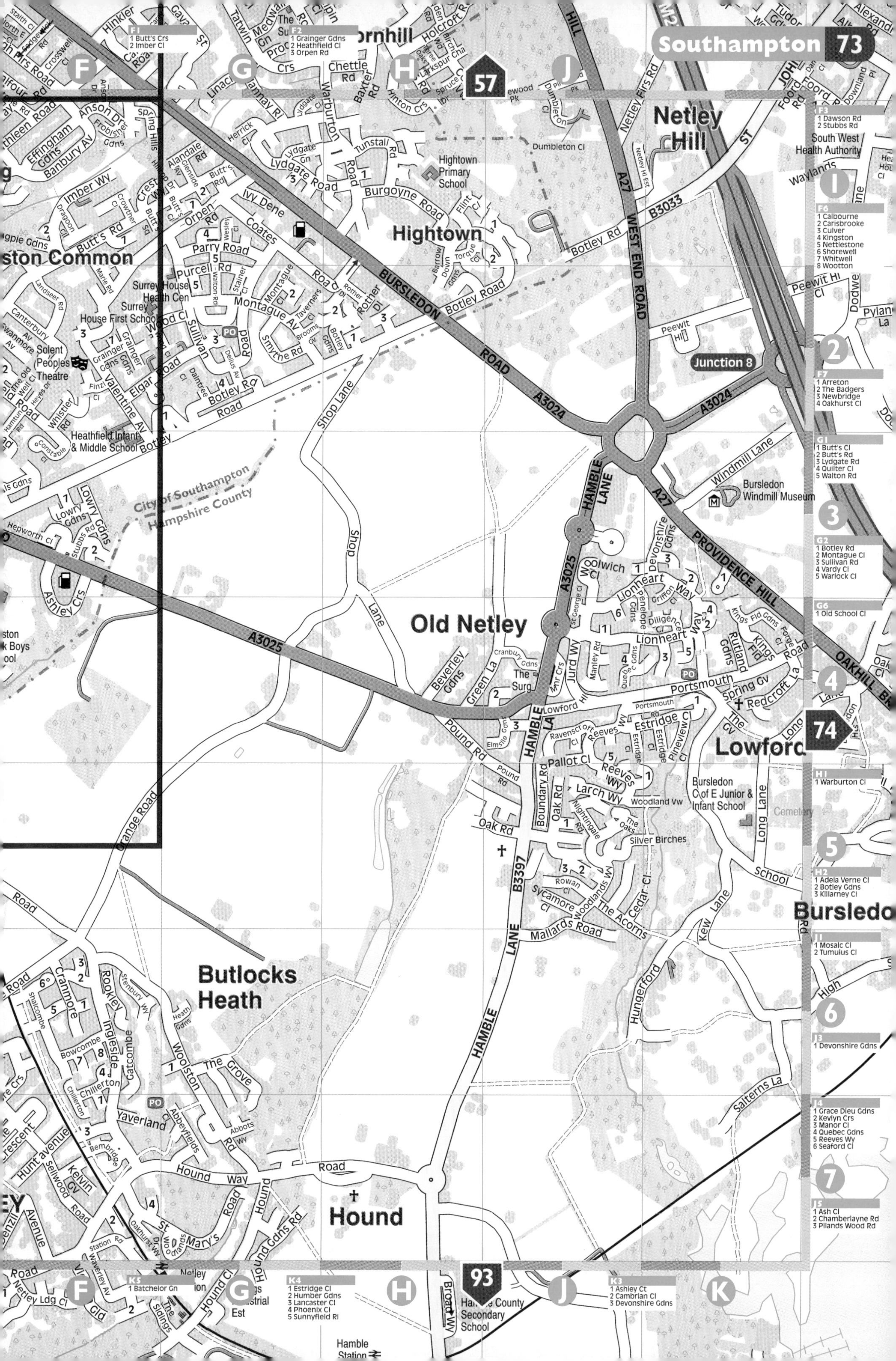
Netley Hill
Hightown
Hightown Primary School
Old Netley
Lowford
Bursledon
Butlocks Heath
Hound
Junction 8
Bursledon Windmill Museum
South West Health Authority
Surrey House Health Cen
Surrey House First School
Solent Peoples Theatre
Heathfield Infant & Middle School
Bursledon C of E Junior & Infant School
Cemetery
Hamble County Secondary School
Hamble Station
City of Southampton
Hampshire County
BURSLEDON ROAD
A3024
A3025
A27
B3033
B3397
WEST END ROAD
HAMBLE LANE
PROVIDENCE HILL
OAKHILL
Botley Road
Shop Lane
Grange Road
Hound Road
Hound Way
Woolston Rd
Windmill Lane
Portsmouth Rd
Mallards Road
Long Lane
Kew Lane
Hungerford
Salterns La
School Rd
Pound Rd
Lionheart Way
Peewit Hl
Parry Road
Montague Av
Lydgate Road
Burgoyne Road
Warburton Road
F1
1 Butt's Crs
2 Imber Cl
F2
1 Grainger Gdns
2 Heathfield Cl
3 Orpen Rd
F3
1 Dawson Rd
2 Stubbs Rd
F6
1 Calbourne
2 Carisbrooke
3 Culver
4 Kingston
5 Nettlestone
6 Shorewell
7 Whitwell
8 Wootton
F7
1 Arreton
2 The Badgers
3 Newbridge
4 Oakhurst Cl
G1
1 Butt's Cl
2 Butt's Rd
3 Lydgate Rd
4 Quilter Cl
5 Walton Rd
G2
1 Botley Rd
2 Montague Cl
3 Sullivan Rd
4 Vardy Cl
5 Warlock Cl
G6
1 Old School Cl
H1
1 Warburton Cl
H2
1 Adela Verne Cl
2 Botley Gdns
3 Killarney Cl
J1
1 Mosaic Cl
2 Tumulus Cl
J3
1 Devonshire Gdns
J4
1 Grace Dieu Gdns
2 Kevlyn Crs
3 Manor Cl
4 Quebec Gdns
5 Reeves Wy
6 Seaford Cl
J5
1 Ash Cl
2 Chamberlayne Rd
3 Pilands Wood Rd
K5
1 Batchelor Gn
K4
1 Estridge Cl
2 Humber Gdns
3 Lancaster Cl
4 Phoenix Cl
5 Sunnyfield Ri
K3
1 Ashley Ct
2 Cambrian Cl
3 Devonshire Gdns
57
74
93
F
G
H
J
K
I
2
3
4
5
6
7

C6
1 Sw'ick Shore Rd
C5
1 Lawson Cl
2 Lr Swanwick Rd
3 Querida Cl
A1
1 Foord Rd
58
Kings Copse Primary School
Alexandra Rd
Albert Road
Bursledon
Consort Gdns
Upr St Helens Road
Nordik Gdns
Stockholm Drive
Sherwood Avenue
Metuchen Wy
Thurmell Cl
Heathhouse Lane
Heath House Gdns
Heath House Cl
Foord Road
Foord Rd
Downland
Damen Cl
Cem
ST JOHN'S
South West Health Authority
Waylands Pl
Kings
Copse Rd
Havendale
Fernoy
Tanhouse Cl
Tanhouse Lane
Manor Farm
Peewit Hl Cl
Dodwell Lane
Pyland's La
Pyland's Lane
Manor Farm Country Park
River Hamble
Windmill Lane
Bursledon Windmill Museum
SO31
M27
Blundell Lane
Brixedone Farm
Kings Fld Gdns
Rutland Gdns
Kings Fld
Forge Road
Spring Gdns
Redcroft La
The Gv
73
Lowford
Oakhill Cl
OAKHILL BRIDGE ROAD
Bridge Cl
Bridge Rd
Bursledon Hts
Lane
Coal Pk La
Coal Park Lane
Coal Park La
Lower Swanwick
Hill Place
Old Br House Rd
Jarvis Flds
Cemetery
Long Lane
Church La
Station Rd
Northview Gallery
Embay Rd
Bentham Way
Green Lane
Swanwick Lane
Anglers Way
Wayside
Tollgate Rd
Quay Hvn
Bye Road
Sopwith Way
New Road
Swanwick La
Manor Fm
Glen Rd
Glen Ho
Walpole La
School
Bursledon
Bursledon Station
Station Hl
High Street
PH
Lands End Road
Swanwick Business Park
Oslands Dr
Swan Cl
Marina
Brooklands
Salterns La
River Hamble
Glen Road
Chapel Rd
Spring Road
Glenn Rd
Pond Road
Addison Road
Addison Rd
Painswick Cl
The Green
The Gn
A27
BRIDGE ROAD
St Paul's Rd
Glenn Road
Holly Hill La
Badgers Run
Allotment Road
Woodlands Close
Woodthorpe Gdns
Woodlands Cl
Sarisbury
Sarisbury Green C of E Primary School
Hawthorn La
Bramble La
Regents Gate
Crableck Lane
94
Coldeast Wy
A
B
C
D
E
1
2
3
4
5
6
7
1 grid square represents 500 metres

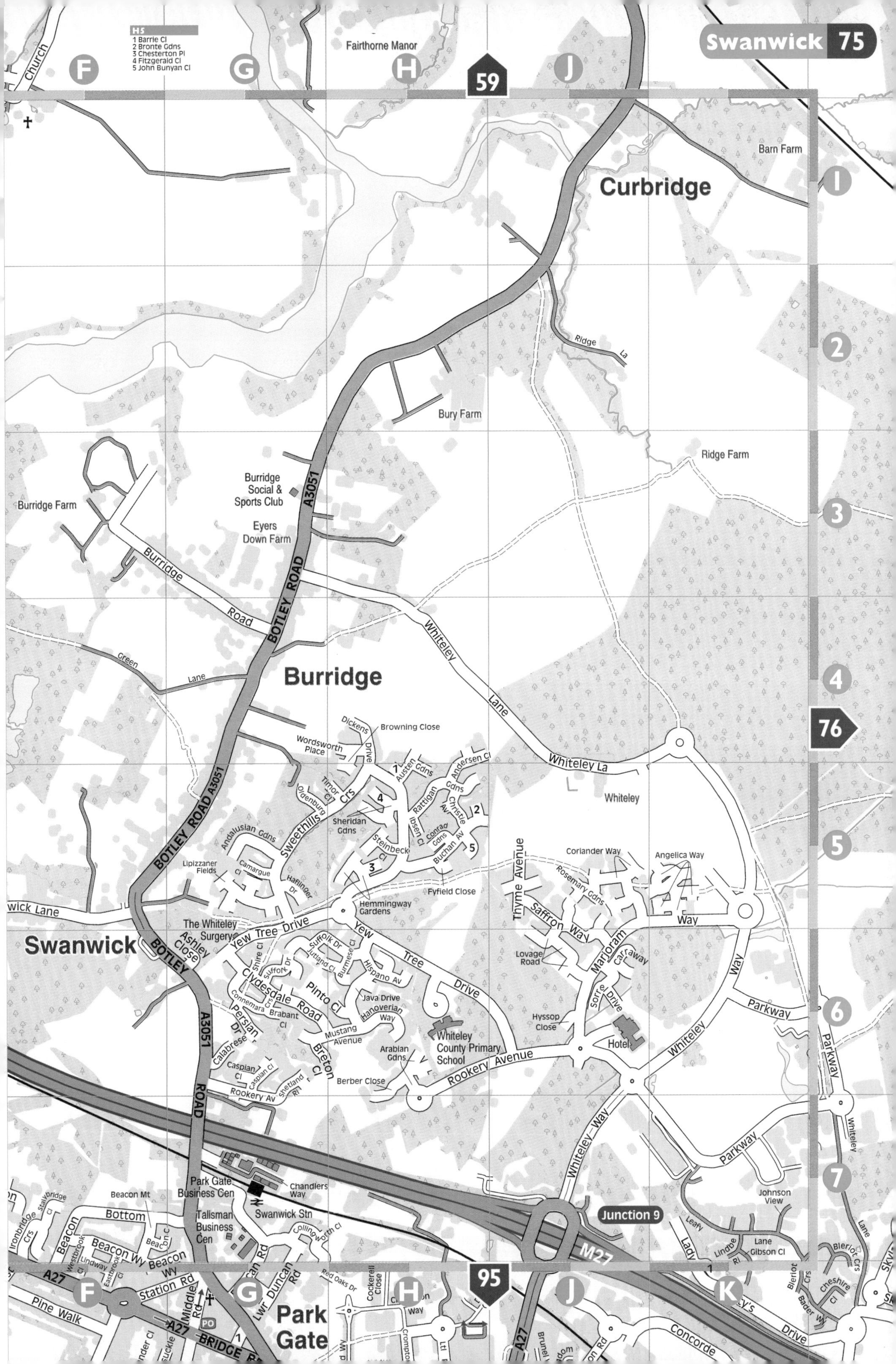
H5
1 Barrie Cl
2 Bronte Gdns
3 Chesterton Pl
4 Fitzgerald Cl
5 John Bunyan Cl
F
G
H
59
J
I
2
3
4
76
5
6
7
K
95
Church
Fairthorne Manor
Curbridge
Barn Farm
Ridge La
Bury Farm
Ridge Farm
Burridge Social & Sports Club
Eyers Down Farm
Burridge Farm
A3051
BOTLEY ROAD
Burridge Road
Green Lane
Burridge
Whiteley Lane
Whiteley La
Whiteley
Dickens Drive
Browning Close
Wordsworth Place
Austen Gdns
Andersen Cl
Timor Cl
Oldenburg Crs
Sweethills Crs
Sheridan Gdns
Rattigan Gdns
Christie Av
Ibsen Cl
Conrad Gdns
Steinbeck Cl
Buchan Av
Andalusian Gdns
Lipizzaner Fields
Camargue Cl
Haflinger Dr
Hemmingway Gardens
Fyfield Close
Thyme Avenue
Coriander Way
Angelica Way
Rosemary Gdns
Saffron Way
Way
Lovage Road
Marjoram
Carraway
Sorrel Drive
Hyssop Close
Hotel
wick Lane
Swanwick
The Whiteley Surgery
Ashley Close
Yew Tree Drive
Shire Cl
Suffolk Dr
Jutland Cl
Burmese Cl
Hispano Av
Clydesdale Road
Connemara Crs
Brabant Cl
Pinto Cl
Java Drive
Hanoverian Way
Persian Dr
Mustang Avenue
Breton Cl
Arabian Gdns
Whiteley County Primary School
Rookery Avenue
Calabrese
Caspian Cl
Berber Close
Rookery Av
Shetland Ri
Whiteley Way
Parkway
Junction 9
M27
Park Gate Business Cen
Chandlers Way
Swanwick Stn
Talisman Business Cen
Collingworth Cl
Beacon Mt
Beacon Bottom
Ironbridge Crs
Stanbridge Cl
Westbrook Cl
Lindway
Eastbrook Cl
Beacon Wy
A27
Station Rd
Middle Rd
PO
Pine Walk
BRIDGE
Lwr Duncan Rd
Red Oaks Dr
Cockerell Close
Park Gate
Crompton Way
Concorde
Johnson View
Leafy Lane
Lady
Lindbe Ri
Gibson Cl
Bleriot Crs
Cheshire Cl
Bader Wy
Drive
Skylark

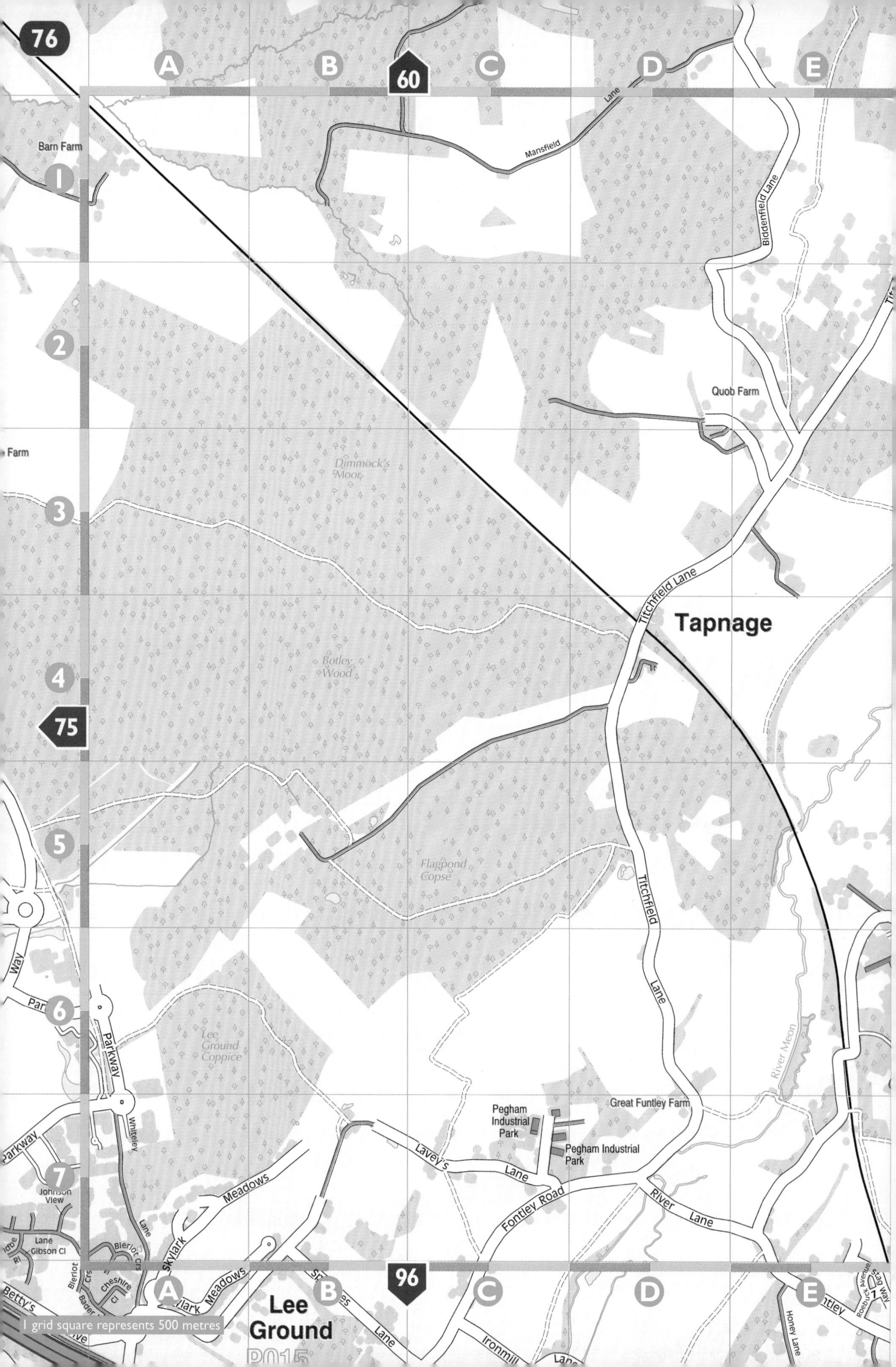

76
60
75
96
A
B
C
D
E
1
2
3
4
5
6
7
Barn Farm
Farm
Mansfield Lane
Biddenfield Lane
Quob Farm
Dimmock's Moor
Titchfield Lane
Tapnage
Botley Wood
Flagpond Copse
Titchfield Lane
River Meon
Lee Ground Coppice
Parkway
Way
Whiteley
Great Funtley Farm
Pegham Industrial Park
Pegham Industrial Park
Lavey's Lane
Fontley Road
River Lane
Meadows
Skylark Meadows
Lane
Johnson View
Lane
Gibson Cl
Bleriot Crs
Cheshire Cl
Bader
Betty's
Lee Ground
Lane
Ironmill
Honey Lane
Roebuck Avenue
Stag Way
1 grid square represents 500 metres

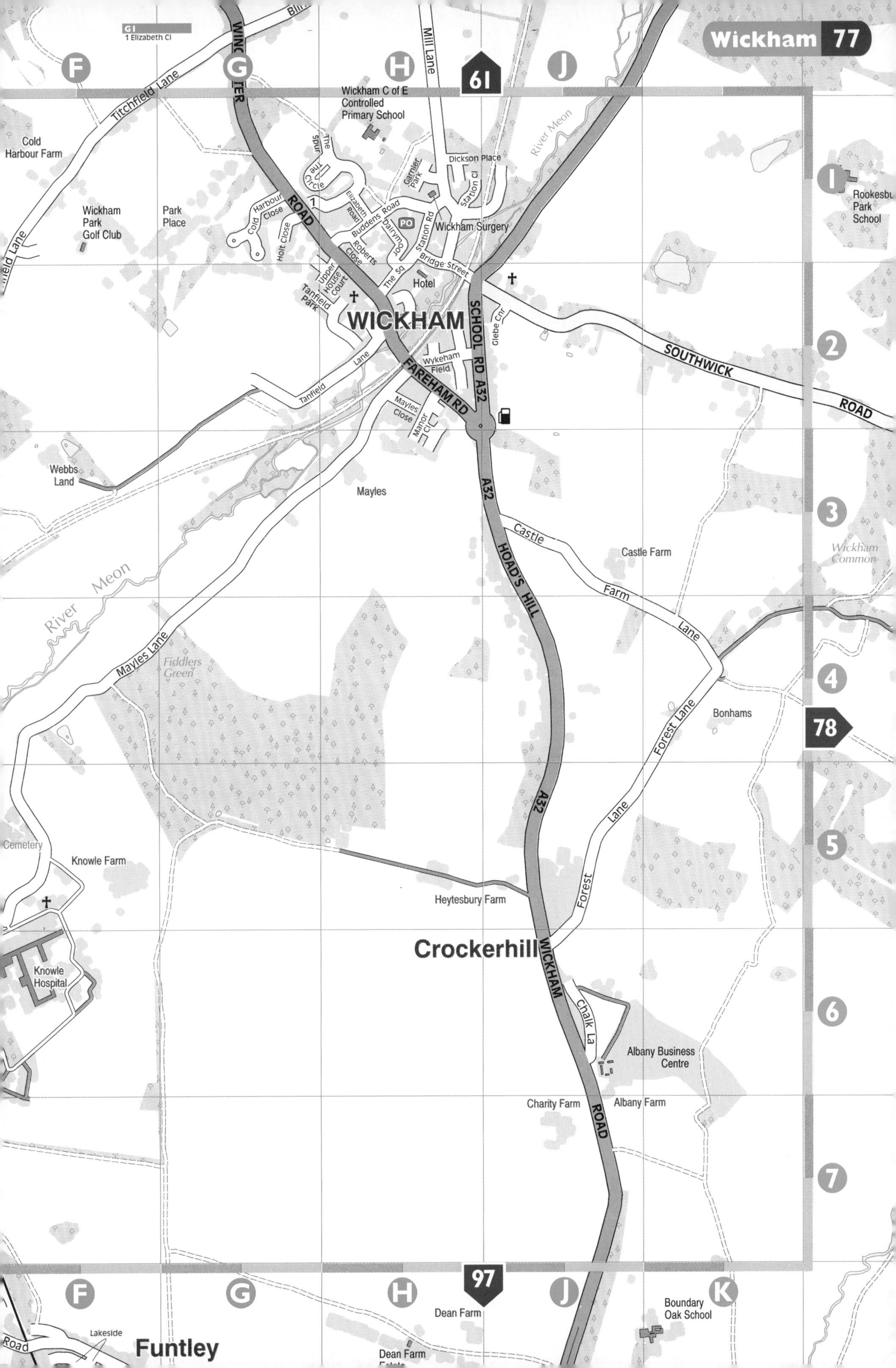
G1
1 Elizabeth Cl
F
G
H
J
61
Titchfield Lane
WINCHESTER ROAD
Mill Lane
Wickham C of E
Controlled
Primary School
River Meon
Cold
Harbour Farm
The Spur
The Circle
Garnier Park
Dickson Place
Station Cl
Rookesbury
Park
School
Wickham
Park
Golf Club
Park
Place
Cold Harbour Close
Holt Close
Elizabeth Road
Buddens Road
Dairymoor
PO
Station Rd
Wickham Surgery
Roberts Close
Bridge Street
Upper House Court
Tanfield Park
The Sq
Hotel
WICKHAM
SCHOOL RD A32
Glebe Cnr
SOUTHWICK ROAD
Wykeham Field
Tanfield Lane
FAREHAM RD
Mayles Close
Manor Cl
Webbs
Land
Mayles
A32
Castle Farm Lane
Castle Farm
HOAD'S HILL
Wickham
Common
Mayles Lane
Fiddlers
Green
Forest Lane
Bonhams
78
Cemetery
Knowle Farm
Heytesbury Farm
Crockerhill
WICKHAM ROAD
Knowle
Hospital
Chalk La
Albany Business
Centre
Charity Farm
Albany Farm
1
2
3
4
5
6
7
97
K
Dean Farm
Boundary
Oak School
Road
Lakeside
Funtley
Dean Farm
Estate

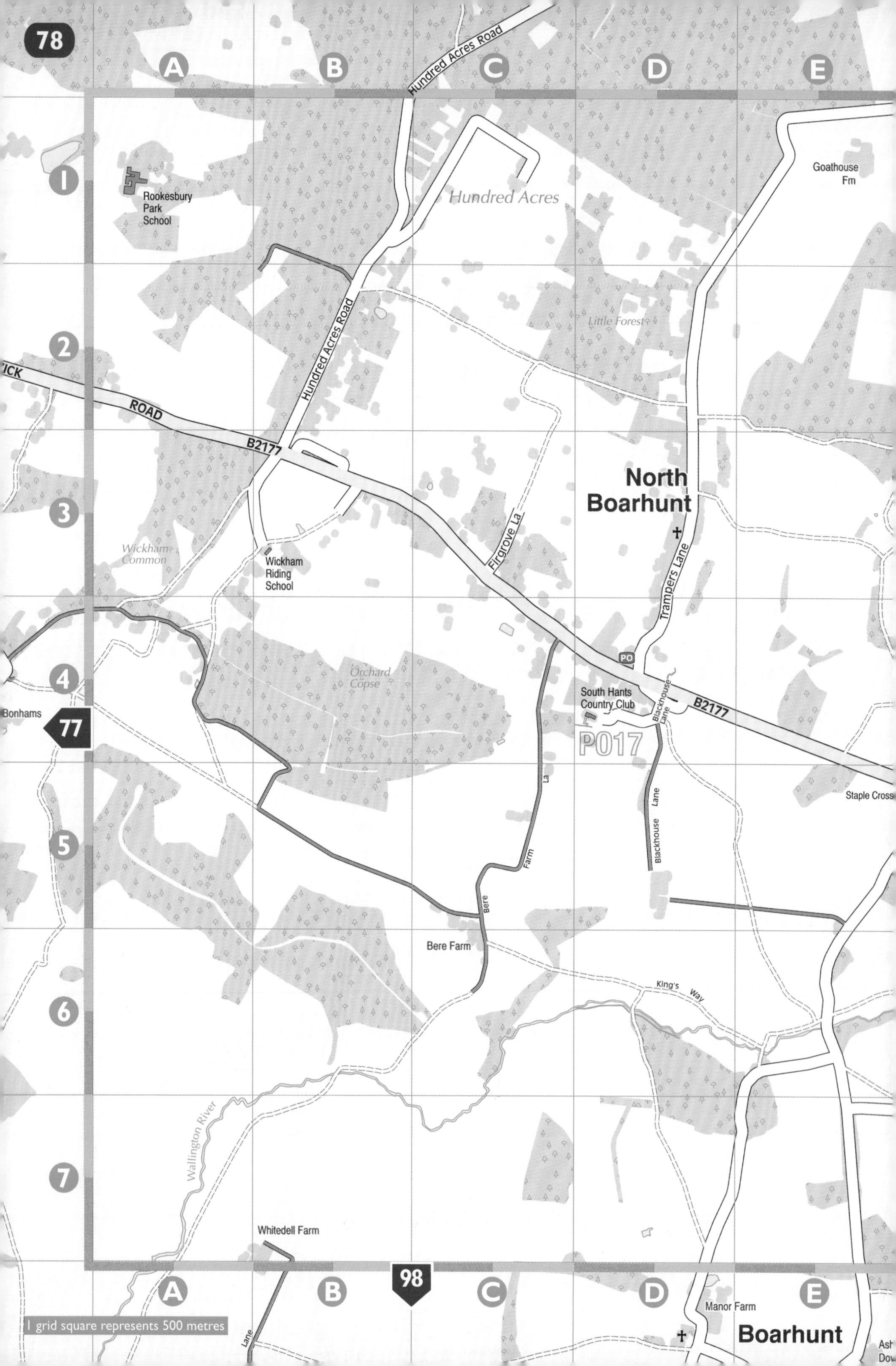
A
B
C
D
E
1
2
3
4
5
6
7
Hundred Acres Road
Rookesbury
Park
School
Hundred Acres
Goathouse
Fm
Little Forest
ICK
ROAD
B2177
Hundred Acres Road
North
Boarhunt
Firgrove La
Trampers Lane
Wickham
Common
Wickham
Riding
School
Orchard
Copse
PO
South Hants
Country Club
Blackhouse
Lane
B2177
PO17
Bonhams
Staple Cross
La
Farm
Bere
Blackhouse
Lane
Bere Farm
King's
Way
Wallington River
Whitedell Farm
Lane
Manor Farm
Boarhunt
Ash
Do
1 grid square represents 500 metres

77

98

Hoe Moor Farm
End
Crabbick Fa
Forest Fm
F
G
H
J
Trampers Lane
King's Way
Forest Road
Hipley
Kiln Lane
Apless Lane
I
2
3
4
5
6
7
80
Shoot Hill
Hipley Copse
Beckford Lane
Lower Beckford
Quagg Fm
Ashlands
Lovelocks
Common Lane
King's Way
B2177
Mitchelland
Lodge Farm
Walton Heath
Place Wo
Portchester Lane
Bridge
Boulter La
Wood Lane
Norton Rd
North
Castle Rd
Norton Cl
Road
West Rd
Main Drive
Road E
South Rd
East Road
Prior
Back Lane
St
Southwick
North
West Street
Doctors Surgery
PO
High St
Fareham Road
Pinsley
Drive
99
Southwick Park Naval Recreation Centre
K
Southwick Park Lake
m Farm

E2
1 The Tithe
D2
1 The Pastures
D1
1 Frenchies Vw
2 Furdies
3 Peakfield
Crabbick Lane
Lower
Inhams
Inhams Lane
Glasspool
B2150
Denmead Health Centre
Park Road
Cem
DE
62
PO7
Forest Road
Hawthorn Rd
Harvest Road
Yew Tree Gdns
Green Lane
Southwick Road
Lowland Rd
Woodrow
The Smithy
Ashling Cl
Ashling Park Road
Ashling Gdns
Chestnut Cl
The Orchard
Bere Road
Field Wy
Denm Ju Sch
The Willows
The Meadow
Home Mead
Brookside Cl
The Liberty
Pond Piece
Cottage Cl
The Spring
Old River
Forest Md
Kilnside
Bunkers Hill
Forest of Bere
Creech Woods
The Spinney
Paddock End
Parklands Business Park
Furzeley Road
Sheepwash Lane
Newlands
Lovelocks
Furzeley Corner
Creech Farm
79
Closewood
Belney Farm
Belney Lane
Wayfarer's Wk
Sheepwash Farm
Place Wood
Wanstead Farm
Wood Lane
North Road E
South Rd
East Road
Priory Rd
Drive
Pitymoor Lane
Wayfarer's Walk
Southwick Park Naval Recreation Centre
100
Comphouse Farm
Purbrook
A
B
C
D
E
1
2
3
4
5
6
7
1 grid square represents 500 metres

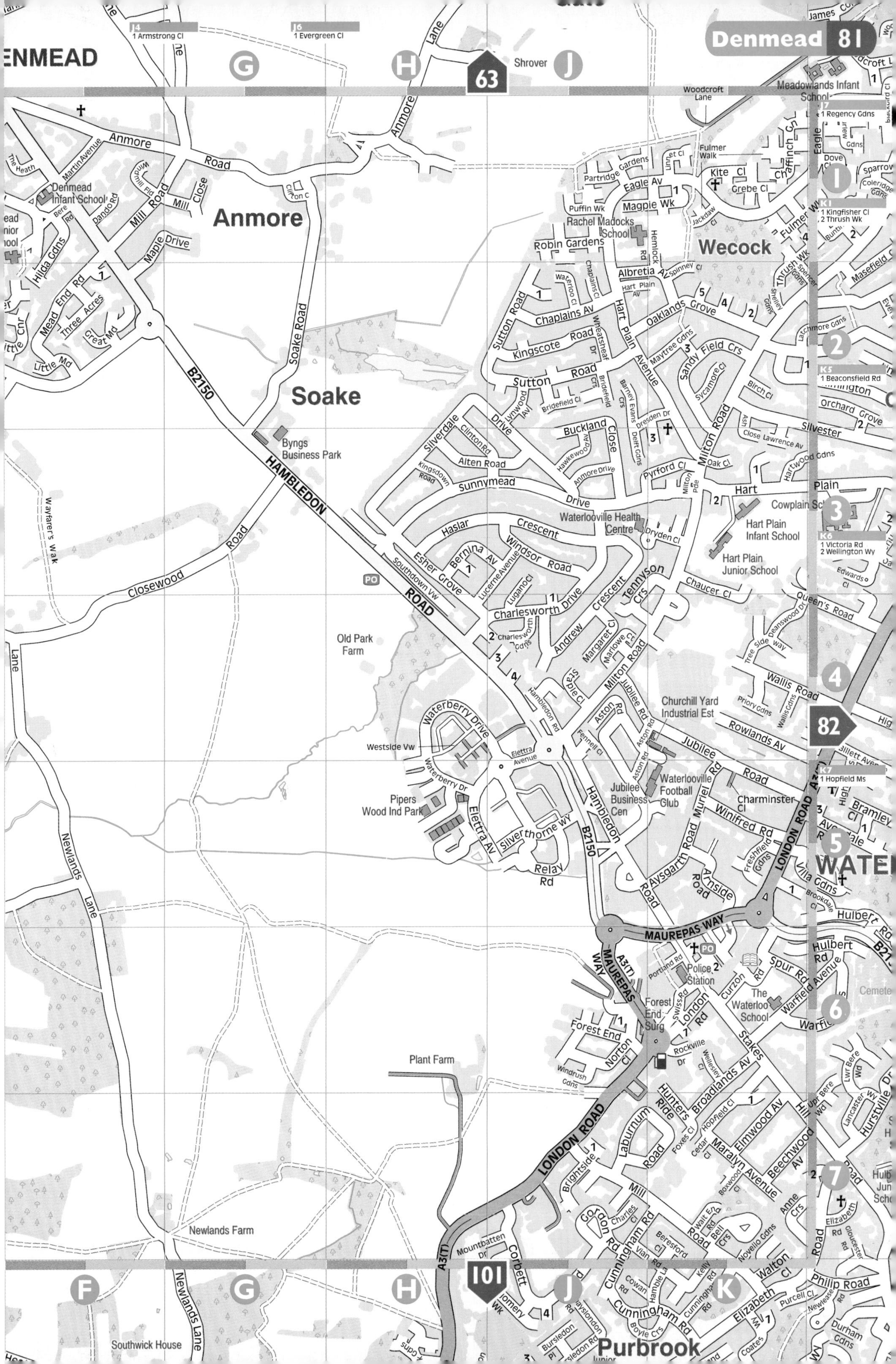

DENMEAD
J4 1 Armstrong Cl
J6 1 Evergreen Cl
G
H
63
Shrover
J
Woodcroft Lane
Meadowlands Infant School
J7 1 Regency Gdns
Anmore Road
Anmore Lane
Anmore
Soake
Soake Road
Denmead Infant School
Martin Avenue
Hilda Gdns
Mead End Rd
Three Acres
Great Md
Little Md
Dando Rd
Mill Road
Mill Close
Maple Drive
Windmill Fld
B2150
HAMBLEDON ROAD
Byngs Business Park
Closewood Road
Wayfarer's Walk
Old Park Farm
Westside Vw
Pipers Wood Ind Park
Waterberry Drive
Elettra Avenue
Elettra Av
Silverthorne Wy
Relay Rd
Lane
Newlands Lane
Plant Farm
Newlands Farm
Southwick House
Partridge Gardens
Eagle Av
Puffin Wk
Magpie Wk
Rachel Madocks School
Robin Gardens
Hemlock Rd
Kite Cl
Grebe Cl
Fulmer Walk
Chaffinch Gn
Wecock
Albretia Av
Spinney Cl
Hart Plain Av
Chaplains Av
Sutton Road
Kingscote Road
Wheatsheaf Dr
Hart Plain Avenue
Oaklands Grove
Maytree Gdns
Sandy Field Crs
Sycamore Cl
Milton Road
Birch Cl
Lawrence Av
Orchard Grove
Silvester
Hartwood Gdns
Bridefield Cl
Bridefield Crs
Barney Evans Crs
Delft Gdns
Dresden Dr
Buckland Close
Hawkewood Av
Anmore Drive
Pyrford Cl
Oak Cl
Lynwood Av
Drive
Silverdale
Clinton Rd
Alten Road
Kingsdown Road
Sunnymead Drive
Hart Plain
Cowplain School
Hart Plain Infant School
Hart Plain Junior School
Waterlooville Health Centre
Dryden Cl
Haslar Crescent
Windsor Road
Bernina Av
Esher Grove
Lucerne Avenue
Lugano Cl
Charlesworth Drive
Charlesworth Gdns
Southdown Vw
ROAD
PO
Andrew Crescent
Tennyson Crs
Chaucer Cl
Margaret Cl
Marlowe Ct
Milton Road
Jubilee Rd
Stable Cl
Hambledon Rd
Aston Rd
Fennell Cl
Churchill Yard Industrial Est
Jubilee Road
Rowlands Av
Queen's Road
Deanswood Dr
Tree Side Way
Wallis Road
Priory Gdns
Wallis Gdns
Edwards Cl
K6 1 Victoria Rd 2 Wellington Wy
K5 1 Beaconsfield Rd
K1 1 Kingfisher Cl 2 Thrush Wk
K7 1 Hopfield Ms
Jubilee Business Cen
Waterlooville Football Club
Muriel Rd
Charminster Cl
Winifred Rd
Aysgarth Road
Arnside Road
Freshfield Gdns
LONDON ROAD
Hambledon Road
B2150
MAUREPAS WAY
A3(T)
Portland Rd
Police Station
Forest End Surg
Swiss Rd
London Rd
Curzon Rd
The Waterloo School
Spur Rd
Warfield Avenue
Hulbert Rd
Villa Gdns
Brookdale Cl
Bramley Cl
Avondale
WATE
Cemete
Forest End
Norton Cl
Windrush Gdns
Rockville Dr
Wellesley Cl
Stakes Hill Road
Broadlands Av
Hunters Ride
Hopfield Cl
Elmwood Av
Beechwood Av
Upr Bere Wd
Lwr Bere Wd
Lancaster Wy
Hurstville Dr
Laburnum Road
Foxes Cl
Cedar Cl
Maralyn Avenue
Boxwood Cl
Brightside
Mill Road
Gordon Rd
Charles Cl
Cunningham Rd
Beresford Cl
Vian Rd
Walt Gn
Bell Crs
Novello Gdns
Anne Crs
Elizabeth Rd
Gloucester Rd
Mountbatten Dr
Corbett Rd
101
Cowan Rd
Hamble La
Kelly Rd
Walton Cl
Philip Road
Purcell Cl
Newlease Rd
Durham Gdns
Cunningham Rd
Elizabeth Rd
Coates Wy
Boyle Crs
Bursledon Pl
Purbrook
82
1
2
3
4
5
6
7
F
G
H
J
K

B5
1 Fabian Cl
2 Florentine Wy
3 Juliet Ct
4 Sebastian Gv
5 Valentine Ct
A7
1 Lantana Cl
2 Orsmond Cl
A5
1 Brooklyn Dr
2 Cavendish Cl
3 Hannah Gdns
B6
1 Broadmdws La
2 Danesbrook La
3 Dornmere La
4 Hampton Cl
5 Holyrood Cl
6 Monarch Cl
7 Osborne Cl
8 Prince of Wales Cl
9 Sapphire Cl
B7
1 Betula Cl
2 Campion Cl
3 Reedmace Cl
4 Salvia Cl
C5
1 Sonnet Wy
D4
1 Thresher Cl
E6
1 Crabwood Ct
2 Hannington Rd
E7
1 Durford Ct
2 Hurstbourne Cl
3 Locksheath Cl
64
81
102
Meadowlands Infant School
Lovedean Lane
Milton Road
Keats Cl
Prochurch Rd
Rosemary
Spring Vale
Greenfield Crescent
Hazleton Way
Padnell Road
Padnell Junior School
Padnell Infant School
Doctors Surgery
Cowplain
LONDON ROAD
A3(T)
A3(M)
Blendworth Common
The Queen's Inclosure
Queens Inclosure Primary School
Park Lane
Willow Tree Avenue
Cherry Tree Avenue
Idsworth Road
Hart Plain Avenue
Hart Plain Junior School
Queen's Road
Highfield Avenue
Bell's Copse
Dunsbury Hill Fm
Junction 3
WATERLOOVILLE
Hulbert Rd
B2150
Cemetery
HULBERT ROAD
Stakes Hill Infant School
Hulbert Junior School
Stakes Lodge Surgery
Springwood Av
Hockham Court
Primary School
Stacey Court
Bucklers Court
Swanmore Rd
Rowbury Rd
Woolston Rd
Park Community
Sparsholt Cl
Thruxton Rd
Yateley Cl
Warnford Crs
Brockenhurst
Nutley Rd
Philip Road
Frendstaple
Covert Gv
Lombardy Ri
Woodsedge
1 grid square represents 500 metres

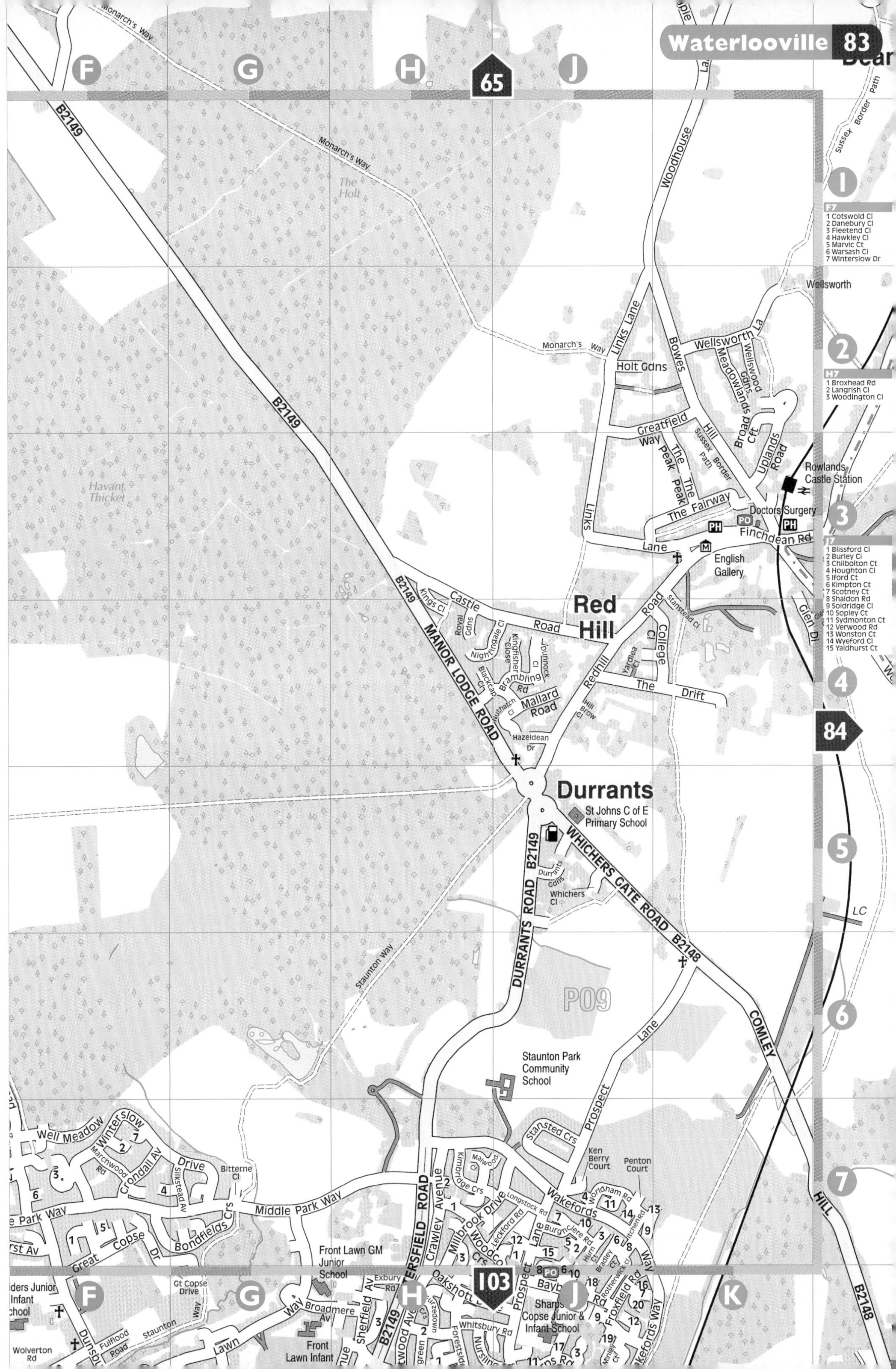
F
G
H
65
J
Monarch's Way
B2149
The Holt
Havant Thicket
Woodhouse
Sussex Border Path
1
F7
1 Cotswold Cl
2 Danebury Cl
3 Fleetend Cl
4 Hawkley Cl
5 Marvic Ct
6 Warsash Cl
7 Winterslow Dr
Wellsworth
2
H7
1 Broxhead Rd
2 Langrish Cl
3 Woodington Cl
Links Lane
Bowes
Wellsworth La
Holt Gdns
Wellswood Gdns
Meadowlands
Broad Cft
Uplands Road
Greatfield Way
The Peak
Hill
Rowlands Castle Station
The Fairway
Doctors Surgery
3
PH
PO
Finchdean Rd
J7
1 Blissford Cl
2 Burley Cl
3 Chilbolton Ct
4 Houghton Cl
5 Iford Ct
6 Kimpton Ct
7 Scotney Ct
8 Shaldon Rd
9 Soldridge Cl
10 Sopley Ct
11 Sydmonton Ct
12 Verwood Rd
13 Wonston Ct
14 Wyeford Cl
15 Yaldhurst Ct
Links
Lane
English Gallery
Kings Cl
Castle Road
Red Hill
Stanstead Cl
Glen Dl
Royal Gdns
Nightingale Cl
Kingfisher Close
Dunnock Cl
Road
College Cl
Blackcap Cl
Brambling Rd
Redhill
Yardlea Cl
The Drift
4
MANOR LODGE ROAD
Nuthatch Cl
Mallard Road
Hill Brow Cl
Hazeldean Dr
84
Durrants
St Johns C of E Primary School
5
DURRANTS ROAD
WHICHERS GATE ROAD
Durrants Gdns
Whichers Cl
LC
B2148
Staunton Way
PO9
6
COMLEY
Lane
Staunton Park Community School
Prospect
Stansted Crs
Well Meadow
Winterslow
Marchwood Rd
Crondall Av
Drive
Silkstead Av
Bitterne Cl
Ken Berry Court
Penton Court
7
Middle Park Way
Kimbridge Crs
Malwood Cl
Wakefords
Worldham Rd
HILL
Park Way
Crs
Bondfields
Millbrook Drive
Longstock Rd
Leckford Rd
Burghclere Rd
Copse
Great
Dr
Front Lawn GM Junior School
PETERSFIELD ROAD
Crawley Avenue
Woodcot Crs
Lane
Hurn Ct
Bradley Ct
Rotherwick Cl
Way
Froxfield Rd
103
Exbury Rd
Oakshott Dr
Prospect
Baybridge
Gt Copse Drive
Broadmere Av
Sherfield Av
Sharps Copse Junior & Infant School
Wakefords Way
K
Whitsbury Rd
Staunton
Road
Fulflood
Dunsbury
Lawn
Front Lawn Infant
Wolverton Rd
Nursling
B2149
B2148

1 grid square represents 500 metres

F
G
H
J
1
2
3
4
5
6
7
K
Watergate
Watergate Hanger
Broadreed Fm
B2146
Lumley Seat
Monarch's Way
Lane
Monarch's Way
Monarch's Wy
Woodlands
Woodlands Cotts
Stanstead House
Newbarn
Lane
Park Lane
Sindle's Fm
Monument
La
Racton Park Fm
B2147
Aldsworth
105
Ractonpark Wood
Common Road

C2
1 Clay La
2 Fir Cl
3 Great Mead
4 Oak Cl
5 Shrubbs Hill Gdns
C1
1 Clarence Rd
2 Empress Rd
3 Wellands Rd
B1
1 Haskells Cl
D2
1 The Meadows
Emery Down
Broughton Road
Station
Calpe Av
66
Golf Club
Silver St
PO
PH
Forest Gdns
Queen's Pde
LYNDHURST
King's Cl
ROMSEY RD
Pemberton Rd
Wellands Rd
Custards
Princes Crsesent
Hotel
Garden Close
Northerwood Av
Sch
Htl
Knightwood Cl
Elcombes Cl
Knightwood Avenue
HIGH ST
HIGH ST A35
Church Lane
Lyndhurst Surgery
New Forest Museum & Visitors Centre
Cemetery
BOURNEMOUTH ROAD
Dearing Cl
Shaggs Meadow
BEAULIEU
Sandy Lane
SHRUBBS HILL RD
The Meadows
GOSPORT LANE A35
Cedarmount
CHAPEL LANE
Goose Green
Cuffnell's Farm
Clayhill
Pondhead Inclosure
Hillary Close
Bank
Foxlease
Pinkney Lane
Beechen Lane
HILL
High Coxlease House
Brick Kiln Inclosure
Park Ground Inclosure
Gritnam
CLAY
Gritnam Wood
A337
Butts Lawn
Whitley Wood
Hursthill Inclosure
New Park Plantation
1 grid square represents 500 metres
Poundhill Heath
Hollands Wood

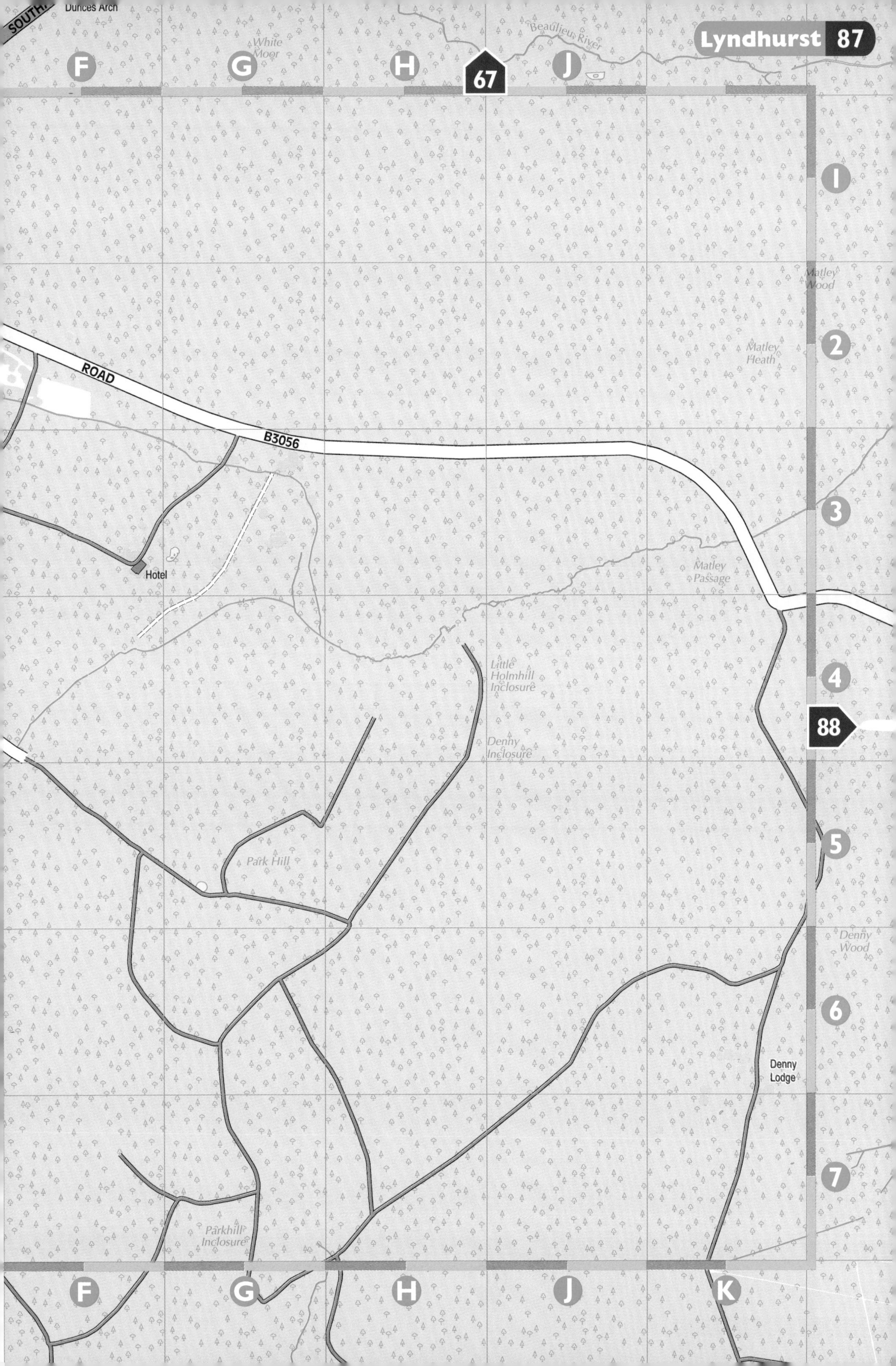
SOUTH
Dunces Arch
White Moor
Beaulieu River
67
F
G
H
J
1
Matley Wood
2
Matley Heath
ROAD
B3056
3
Hotel
Matley Passage
4
Little Holmhill Inclosure
Denny Inclosure
88
Park Hill
5
Denny Wood
6
Denny Lodge
7
Parkhill Inclosure
F
G
H
J
K

A
B
68
C
D
E
Longdown Inclosure
1
Matley Wood
2
Matley Heath
3
Decoy Pond Farm
4
Black Down
87
5
Beaulieu Road Station
Hotel
Denny Wood
6
Denny Lodge
BEAULIEU ROAD B30
New Forest
7
106
1 grid square represents 500 metres

F
G
H
69
J
Twiggs Lane End
Beaulieu Road
Birchlands Farm
Foxhill Farm
Carter's Lane
I
2
Ipley Inclosure
3
Ipley Manor
Yew Tree Heath
4
90
5
6
Beaulieu River
Ferny Crofts
7
F
Pig Bush
G
Culverley Farm
H
107
J
K

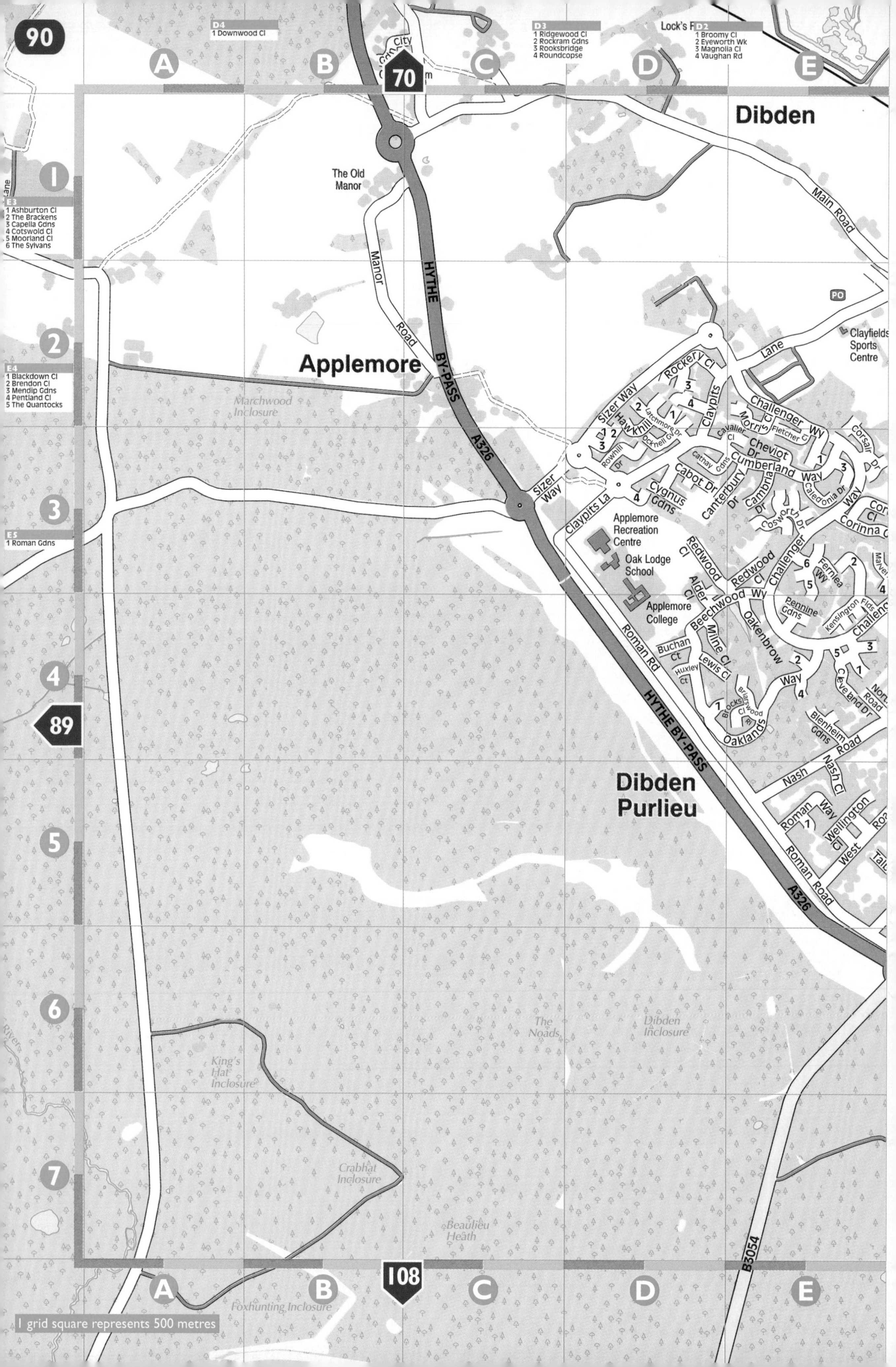
D4
1 Downwood Cl
D3
1 Ridgewood Cl
2 Rockram Gdns
3 Rooksbridge
4 Roundcopse
D2
1 Broomy Cl
2 Eyeworth Wk
3 Magnolia Cl
4 Vaughan Rd
E3
1 Ashburton Cl
2 The Brackens
3 Capella Gdns
4 Cotswold Cl
5 Moorland Cl
6 The Sylvans
E4
1 Blackdown Cl
2 Brendon Cl
3 Mendip Gdns
4 Pentland Cl
5 The Quantocks
E5
1 Roman Gdns
70
89
108
Dibden
Main Road
The Old Manor
Manor Road
HYTHE BY-PASS
A326
Applemore
Marchwood Inclosure
Clayfields Sports Centre
Lane
Sizer Way
Rockery Cl
Claypits
Challenger Wy
Morris
Fletcher Cl
Cheviot Dr
Cumberland Way
Cabot Dr
Cygnus Gdns
Canterbury Dr
Cambria Dr
Caledonia Dr
Claypits La
Applemore Recreation Centre
Oak Lodge School
Applemore College
Redwood Cl
Alder Cl
Beechwood Wy
Oakenbrow
Pennine Gdns
Fernlea Wy
Roman Rd
Buchan Ct
Milne Cl
Lewis Cl
Huxley Ct
Oaklands Way
Blenheim Gdns
Road
Nash
Nash Cl
Roman Way
Wellington Cl
West
Roman Road
Dibden Purlieu
The Noads
Dibden Inclosure
King's Hat Inclosure
Crabhat Inclosure
Beaulieu Heath
B3054
Foxhunting Inclosure
1 grid square represents 500 metres

F4
1 Marlborough Ct

F5
1 Haynes Wy
2 Woodlands Ct

H1
1 Mount House Cl

G3
1 Boundstone
2 Conifer Cl
3 Hawthorn Rd
4 Midway
5 Tormead

G4
1 Badgers Wk
2 Byeways
3 Drakes Cl
4 Forest Hill Wy
5 Heathfield
6 Noads Cl

G5
1 Chaveney Cl
2 Hartley Wk
3 Lambourne Cl
4 Ratcliffe Rd
5 Windmill Copse

G6
1 Corbould Rd

H2
1 Alexandra Cl
2 Carpenter Cl
3 Court House Cl
4 Drummond Rd
5 Fairfield Cl
6 Green Cl
7 Mariners Ms
8 Pylewell Rd

H3
1 Abbey Cl
2 Coat Gdns
3 Freedom Ct

H4
1 Frayslea
2 Greatwood Cl
3 Knightstone Gra
4 Langdwn Lwn Cl
5 Rose Cl

H5
1 Andrew Cl
2 Buttercup Cl
3 Butts Ash La
4 Chaloner Crs
5 Hartley Cl
6 Ingle Gln
7 Northbourne Cl
8 Silvers End

H6
1 Devonshire Gdns
2 Stokesay Cl

J2
1 Sir Christopher Cl

J6
1 Laburnum Crs
2 Maple Rd

J5
1 Furzedown Ms
2 Hamilton Ms

J4
1 Pinewood Crs
2 Spinney Gdns
3 Tates Rd

J3
1 Tates Rd

A
B
72
C
D
E
NETL
Wykeham Road
Victoria Road
Garfield
Rd
Grange
1 Sedgemead
Chamberlayne Rd
Mortimer Cl
New Road
Monks
Station
Denham Gdns
Netley Court School
PO
Road
1
2
3
4
5
6
7
91
Frostlane
Southampton
West Road
East Road
Charleston Road
Road
First Street
Second St
Av C
Av D
Avenue E
Av C
Cadland Road
Cadland Creek
110
J Av
H Av
Avenue
Foreshore
1 grid square represents 500 metres

F1
1 Latelle Cl
2 Waverley Ct
G4
1 Westfield Common
H3
1 Coronation Pde
2 Hardwicke Wy
J3
1 Acorn Ct
J4
1 College Cl
2 Pegasus Cl
K2
1 Kingfisher Cl
2 St Agatha's Rd
K3
1 Oakwood Wy
K4
1 Hamble Hse Gdns
73
94
111
F
G
H
J
K
1
2
3
4
5
6
7
HAMBLE-LE-RICE
Hound
Netley Station
Sidings Industrial Est
Hamble County Secondary School
Hamble Station
Royal Victoria Country Park
Hamble County Primary School
Hamblecliff House
Hamble Common
Solent Way
Hamble Lane
B3397
Satchell Lane
Mariner's Cl
Mercury Gdns
Cerdic Ms
Crowsport
The Bartletts
Meadow La
Well La
River Gn
Green Lane
Copse La
Old Priory Cl
Solent Mdw
Emmons Cl
Sylvan La
School Lane
Verdon Av
Tutor Cl
Sydney Avenue
Flowers Cl
Astral Gardens
Baron Rd
Barton Dr
Spitfire Wy
Cirrus Gdns
Aquila Wy
Deanfield Cl
Kings Av
Yorke Way
Chalmers Wy
Cliffe Av
Coach Road
Grantham Av
Norbury Gdns
South Ct
Westfield Cl
Beech Gdns
Beech Cl
Ensign Way
Albert Cl
Nightingale Wk
Victoria Gld
Netley Ldg Cl
Waverley Av
Station Rd
Oakhurst Wy
St Mary's Road
Woodlands Dr
Hound Way
Hound Road
Hound Gdns Rd
Hound Cl
The Sidings
Broad Wy
Fry Cl
Spit
River
Water
PO

D3
1 Littlewood Gdns
C6
1 Beechwood Cl
2 Birchdale Cl
3 Cheviot Gn
4 Glenda Cl
5 Larchdale Cl
6 ShellCft
7 Spenser Cl
C3
1 Brook Cl
A27
74
A
B
C
D
E
1
2
3
4
5
6
7
D5
1 Albacore Av
2 Enterprise Cl
3 Knights Cl
4 Trimaran Rd
5 Westerley Cl
E3
1 Rowe Ashe Wy
2 Wildern Cl
E4
1 Bryony Cl
2 Burgundy Cl
3 Elder Cl
4 Larkspur Cl
5 Shepherds P Cl
6 Snapdragon Cl
7 Speedwell Cl
E5
1 Galleon Cl
93
112
Sarisbury
Sarisbury Green C of E Primary School
Regents Gate
Sarisbury Infant School
Brookfield Secondary School
Cem
Crableck Lane
Holly Hill Lane
Holly Hill La
Hawthorn La
Bramble La
Barnes La
Barnes Lane
Allotment Road
St Paul's Rd
Glenn Road
Woodland Close
Painswick Cl
Addison Rd
Sherwood Gdns
Brookfield Gardens
Barnbrook Road
Norwich Cl
Valley Ri
Dene Cl
Brook Lane
Highnam Gdns
Barnes Cl
Winnards Pk
Holly Cl
Ambledale
Dormy Cl
Vine Cl
Brook Avenue
Twiggs End Cl
Strawberry Hl
Heath Rd N
Lockswood
Marken Cl
Delft Cl
Holland Park
Cumber Rd
Peters Road
Peters Close
Tulip Gdns
Chichester Close
Upr Brook Dr
Cornflower Cl
Peters Rd
St Georges Rd
St Davids Rd
Coltsfoot Drive
Upper Brook Dr
Bluebell Copse
Crescent Road
Lydney Road
Exeter Cl
Poppy Cl
Gorse Cl
Bilberry
Greenaway Lane
Greenaway La
Willow Cl
Herb
Yarrow Wy
Cowslip Cl
Celandine Av
Primrose Way
Harvey Crs
Saxon Cl
Warsash Road
Stone Crop Cl
Horseshoe Ldg
Marina
River Hamble
Hamble Common
Hamble Spit
Thornton Avenue
Crofton Way
Hamble Cl
Mariners Wy
Passage Lane
Brook Lane
Warsash
Whiteways Ms
Warsash Road
Cutter Av
Schooner
Wayfarer Cl
Corvette Av
Sampan Cl
Coracle Cl
Catamaran Cl
Canoe Cl
Brigantine Rd
Trimaran Cl
Clipper Cl
Dibles Road
Coleridge Cl
Fleet End Road
Green La
Green Lane
Havelock Road
Garden Ms
Foy Gdns
Newtown Road
Osborne Road
Bevis Cl
Sandycroft
Church Road
Aspen Av
Elmdale Close
Spruce Cl
New Rd
Hook with Warsash Primary School
Oakwood Cl
Queen's Rd
Meadcroft Cl
Hewetts Ri
Pitchponds Rd
Romford Rd
Howerts Cl
Hornby Cl
Lower Spinney
Jumar Close
Rossan Av
Newtown
Solent Way
Gilchrist Gdns
Hook Park Road
Hook
Hook Park Rd
Fleet End Bottom
Solent Court
Solent Drive
1 grid square represents 500 metres

Junction 9
M27
A27
75
96
113
F
G
H
J
K
I
2
3
4
5
6
7
G1
1 Dove Gdns
2 Northmore Cl
G2
1 Laurel Cl
2 St Cuthberts Cl
G3
1 Conference Dr
2 St Simon Cl
G4
1 CoombeDl
2 GlenDl
H2
1 Birchen Cl
2 Grassymead
3 The Pastures
H3
1 Font Cl
2 HolmGv
3 Montpelier Cl
4 Ravenswood
5 Verger Cl
6 W'minster Gdns
H4
1 Emmanuel Cl
2 Kensington Gdns
3 RyeCft
4 Sloe Tree Cl
H5
1 Churchill Cl
2 Huntingdon Cl
3 Sycamore Cl
4 The Tanners
J2
1 Barnes Wallis Rd
J3
1 Mere Cft
K3
1 Jacaranda Cl
K1
1 Ashwood
J4
1 Horseshoe Cl
Park Gate
Locks Heath
Titchfield Park
Titchfield Common
Titchfield
Abshot
Park Gate Business Cen
Talisman Business Cen
Chandlers Way
Swanwick
Bottom
Beacon Wy
Beacon Wy
Station Rd
Pine Walk
BRIDGE RD
SOUTHAMPTON RD
SOUTHAMPTON RD-A27
Park Gate Junior School
Northmore Road
Drake Cl
Hardy Cl
Admirals Road
Lyndale Rd
Hunts Pond Road
Beverley Close
Park Gln
Gillcrest
Nuttash
Merryfield
Longacres
Wheatlands
Hertsfield
Mayridge
Lichfield Rd
Lincoln Cl
Crompton Way
Red Oaks Dr
Cockerell Close
Dewar Close
Telford Wy
Whittle Av
Gloster Ct
Apple Industrial Est
Barratt Ind Park
Fareham Borough Council
Mitchell Cl
Brunel Wy
Kingdom Cl
Brabazon Rd
Concorde Way
Betty's Drive
Lady
Lindbergh Rl
Lane
Gibson Cl
Bleriot Cl
Bader Wy
Whiteley
Witherbed Lane
Brunel Way
Barnes Wallis Road
Segensworth Road
Segensworth Rd
Park Farm
Amaryllis Close
Grevillea Avenue
Hill Croft
Titchfield Park Road
Fern Wy
St Leonards Cl
Westway
Northway
Southway
Farm Road
Cartwright
Hotel
Warsash Road
St Margarets Lane
West Hill Park School
Common Lane
Coach
The Cl
Bellfield
Hewett Road
Cem
Brownwich Lane
Occupation Lane
Hookgate Coppice
Hook Lane
Hook La
Ltl Abshot Rd
Abshot Rd
Warsash Road
Brook Lane
Oleander Cl
Honeysuckle Cl
Hollybrook Gdns
The Glades
Dingle Way
Headland Dr
Fell Cl
Chine Cl
Meadow Av
Moorland Cl
Parklands
Downland Cl
Old Common Gdns
Locks Road
Brewer Cl
Cunningham Dr
Hood Cl
Topiary Gdns
Laurel Road
Laurel Gdns
St Cuthberts La
Crispin Cl
Home Rule Road
Richards Cl
Chancel Rd
Church Cl
Church Close
Lodge Rd
Malcolm Cl
Daisy Lane
Church Road
Centre Way
Lockswood Surgery
High Oaks Cl
Maytree Close
Laxton Cl
Kingfisher Copse
Woodpecker Copse
Cem
Lambourne Dr
Pershore Cl
Grieve Av
Grenadier Cl
St Tristan Cl
Cardinal Way
Deacon Rd
Deacon Rd
Ashwood
St Johns C of E Infant School
Lower Church Rd
The Chantry
Cleric Ct
Bishops Ga
Wellsmoor
Belfry Wk
Steeple Wy
The Chase
Course Pk Crs
Priestfields
Prelate Way
The Gallops
Goodwood Cl
The Hurdles
Ascot Close
Stable Cl
Primate Road
St Anthonys RC Primary School
Locks Road Surgery
The Chestnuts
Monarch Cl
James
The Vale
St John's Road
Hazel Gv
Park Gate
Old Gdn Cl
Orwell Crs
Field Cl
Lawn Dr
Montere
Monterey Dr
Glendale
Jesmond Gv
The Brackens
Locksheath Park Road
Huxley Cl
Milton Gv
Summerfields
Streamleaze
Cambridge Gn
Clare Cl
Magdalene Wy
Wellow Gdns
Girton Cl
Netley Road
Cyprus Road
Chartwell Cl
Balliol Cl
Trelose Wy
Kelsey
Penhale Gdns
Talland Rd
Clarendon Crs
Abshot Cl
St Edmund Cl
Brasenose
Oriel Dr
Oaklands Way
Chestnut
Sycamore Cl
Robins Meadow
Cox Dl
Kites Cft
Pound Ga Dr
Raley Road
Michaels Rd
Victoria Cl
Shorewood Cl
Locksheath County Infants & Primary School
Sovereign Crescent
Sixpenny Close
The Florins
Warsash Road
Hunts Pond Road
Jubilee
West
PO

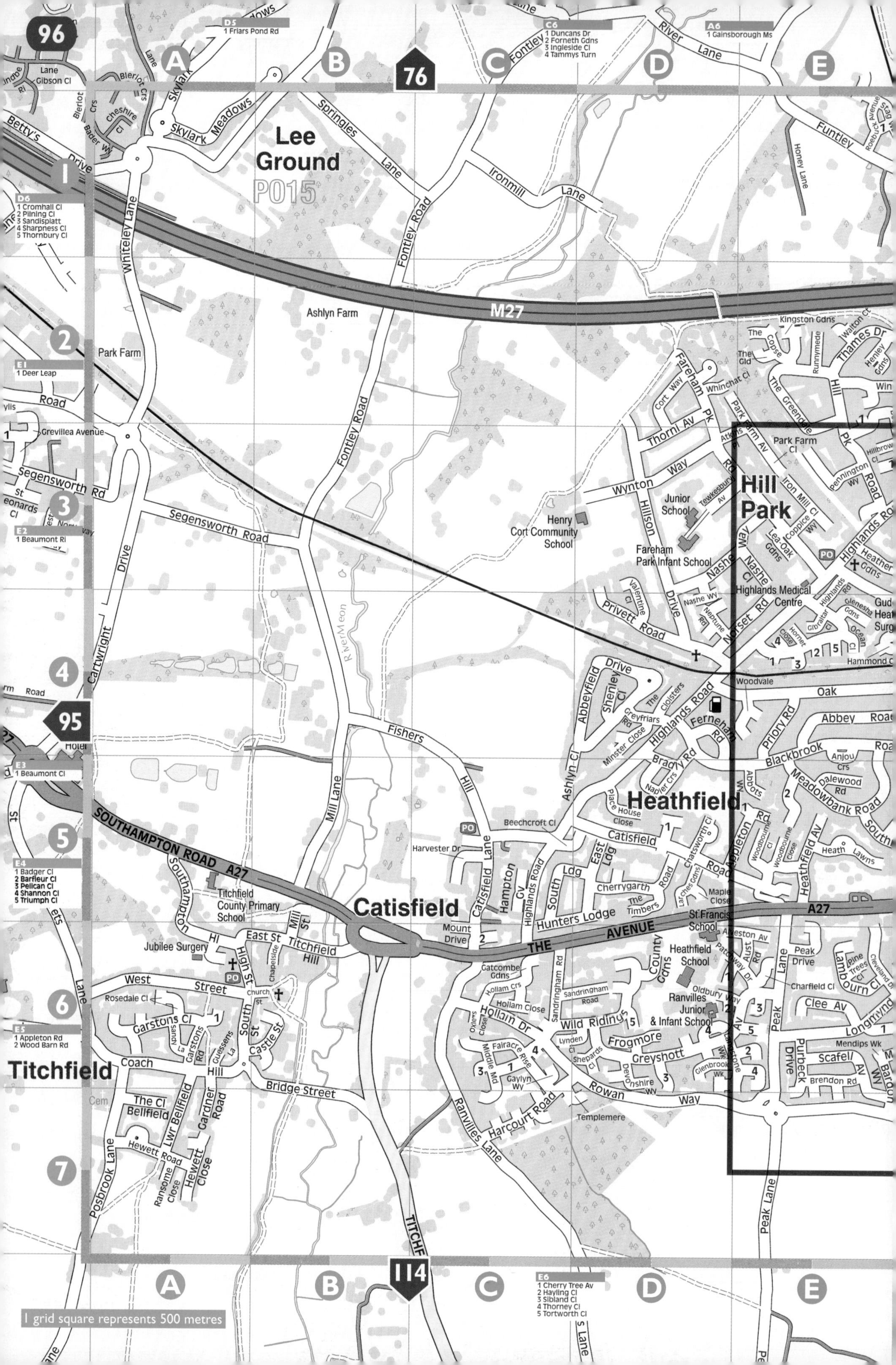

76
D5
1 Friars Pond Rd
C6
1 Duncans Dr
2 Forneth Gdns
3 Ingleside Cl
4 Tammys Turn
A6
1 Gainsborough Ms
A
B
C
D
E
Lee Ground
PO15
Skylark Meadows
Springles Lane
Ironmill Lane
Fontley Road
Fontley
River Lane
Funtley
Honey Lane
Roebuck Avenue
Lane
Gibson Cl
Bleriot Crs
Cheshire Cl
Bader Wy
Betty's Drive
1
D6
1 Cromhall Cl
2 Pilning Cl
3 Sandisplatt
4 Sharpness Cl
5 Thornbury Cl
Whiteley Lane
M27
Ashlyn Farm
2
Park Farm
E1
1 Deer Leap
Road
Grevillea Avenue
Segensworth Rd
3
E2
1 Beaumont Ri
Segensworth Road
Kingston Gdns
The Copse
The Gld
Thames Dr
Runnymede
Henley Gdns
Fareham Pk
Whinchat Cl
Cort Way
The Greendale
Hill Pk
Thorni Av
Park Farm Av
Park Farm Cl
Atkins Pl
Wynton Way
Pk Rd
Hillbrow Cl
Pennington Wy
Road
Highlands Rd
Junior School
Tewkesbury Av
Hill Park
Iron Mill Cl
Henry Cort Community School
Hillson Drive
Coppice Wy
Lea-Oak Gdns
Nashe Cl
Nashe Way
Fareham Park Infant School
PO
Heather Gdns
Highlands Medical Centre
Valentine Cl
Nashe Wy
Privett Road
Neptune Rd
Dorset Rd
Gibraltar Cl
Highlands Rd
Glenesha Gdns
Hornet Close
Ocean Cl
Hammond Cl
River Meon
Cartwright Drive
4
Road
95
Hotel
Abbeyfield Drive
Shenley Cl
The Cloisters
Greyfriars Rd
Minster Close
Highlands Road
Ferneham Rd
Woodvale
Oak
Priory Rd
Abbey Road
Blackbrook Road
Anjou Crs
Dalewood Rd
Meadowbank Road
E3
1 Beaumont Cl
Fishers Hill
Mill Lane
Ashlyn Cl
Bradly Rd
Napier Crs
Abbots Wy
Place House Close
Heathfield
Appleton Rd
Woodbourne Cl
Woodbourne Close
Heathfield Av
Heath Lawns
5
SOUTHAMPTON ROAD A27
E4
1 Badger Cl
2 Barfleur Cl
3 Pelican Cl
4 Shannon Cl
5 Triumph Cl
Southampton Hl
Titchfield County Primary School
Catisfield
Harvester Dr
Catisfield Lane
Beechcroft Cl
Hampton Gv
Highlands Road
South Ldg
East Ldg
Catisfield Road
Chatsworth Cl
Cherrygarth Road
The Timbers
Larches Gdns
Maple Close
Hunters Lodge
St Francis School
A27
Mount Drive
THE AVENUE
Jubilee Surgery
East St
Mill St
Titchfield Hill
Chapelside
High St
Catcombe Gdns
Sandringham Rd
County Gdns
Heathfield School
Allneston Av
Pattway Dr
Aust Rd
Peak Lane
Peak Drive
Lambourn Cl
Pine Trees Cl
Cleveland Dr
Charfield Cl
West Street
Church St
6
Rosedale Cl
Garstons Cl
Sandy La
Garstons Rd
Guessens La
South St
Castle St
E5
1 Appleton Rd
2 Wood Barn Rd
Hollam Crs
Hollam Close
Hollam Dr
Sandringham Road
Oldbury Way
Ranvilles Junior & Infant School
Clee Av
Longmynd
Wild Ridings
Frogmore
Lynden Cl
Shepards Cl
Greyshott
Devonshire Wy
Glenbrook Wk
Wk
Mendips Wk
Scafell Av
Purbeck Drive
Brendon Rd
Oxleys Close
Middle Md
Fairacre Rise
Gaylyn Wy
Titchfield
Coach Hill
Bridge Street
Cem
The Cl
Bellfield
Lwr Bellfield
Gardner Road
Hewett Road
Hewett Close
Ransome Close
Posbrook Lane
Ranvilles Lane
Harcourt Road
Rowan Way
Templemere
Peak Lane
7
TITCHF
114
E6
1 Cherry Tree Av
2 Hayling Cl
3 Sibland Cl
4 Thorney Cl
5 Tortworth Cl
1 grid square represents 500 metres

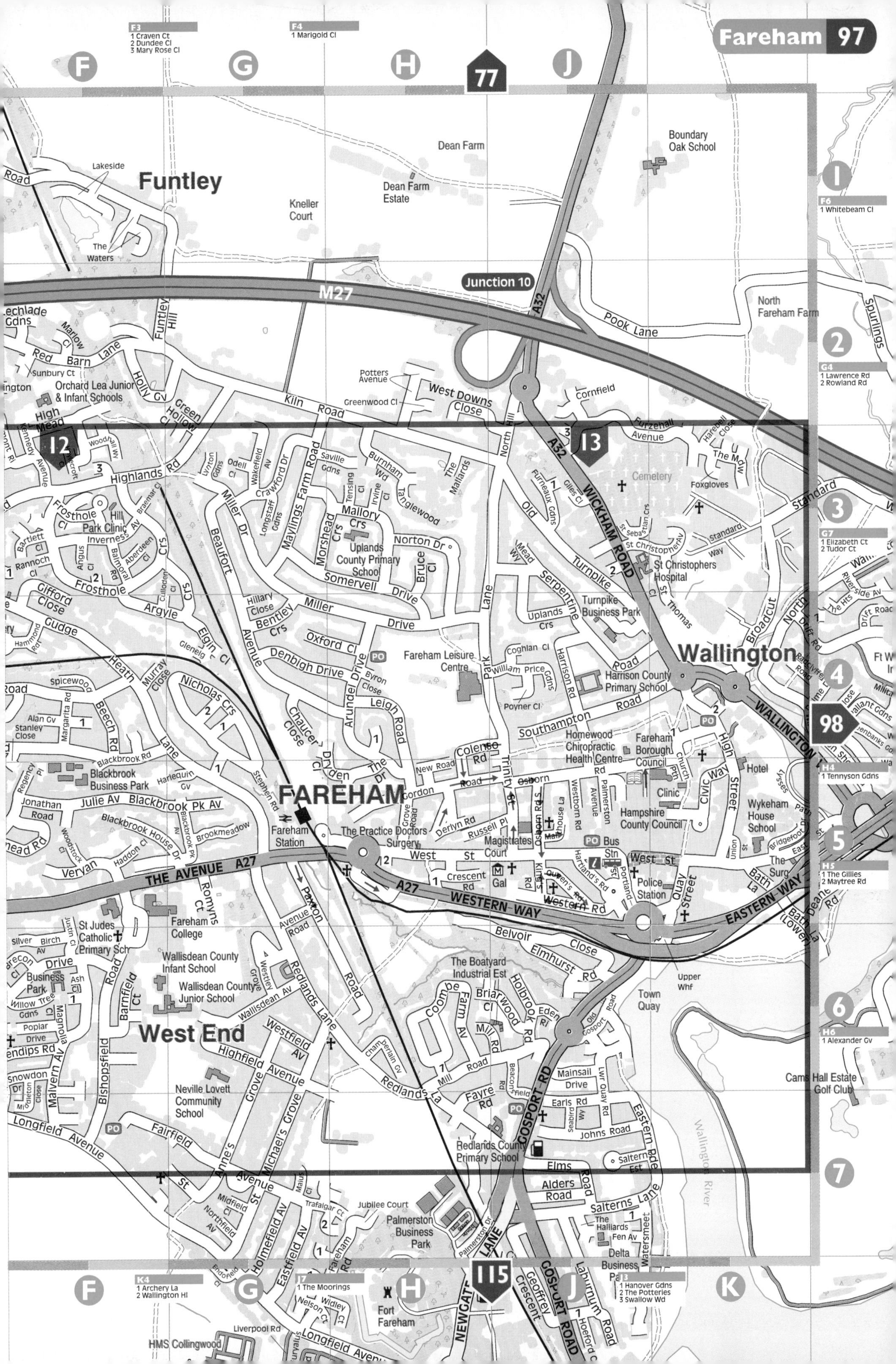
F3
1 Craven Ct
2 Dundee Cl
3 Mary Rose Cl
F4
1 Marigold Cl
F
G
H
J
77
Funtley
Lakeside
The Waters
Kneller Court
Dean Farm
Dean Farm Estate
Boundary Oak School
F6
1 Whitebeam Cl
Junction 10
M27
A32
Pook Lane
North Fareham Farm
Spurlings
G4
1 Lawrence Rd
2 Rowland Rd
Lechlade Gdns
Marlow Cl
Red Barn Lane
Sunbury Ct
Funtley Hill
Orchard Lea Junior & Infant Schools
High Mead
Holly Gv
Green Hollow Cl
Kiln Road
Potters Avenue
Greenwood Cl
West Downs Close
Cornfield
North Hill
12
13
Furzehall Avenue
Harebell Close
The Mdw
Cemetery
Foxgloves
Standard Way
Kennedy Avenue
Highlands Rd
Frostholé Cl
Hill Park Clinic
Inverness Av
Bartlett Cl
Rannoch Cl
Angus Cl
Balmoral Rd
Aberdeen Cl
Frostholé Crs
Argyle Crs
Culloden Cl
Gifford Close
Gudge Heath Lane
Hammond Rd
Glenelg
Elgin Cl
Lynton Gdns
Odell Cl
Wakefield Av
Crawford Dr
Longstaff Gdns
Miller Dr
Beaufort Avenue
Maylings Farm Road
Saville Gdns
Burnham Wd
Tensing Cl
Irvine Cl
Mallory Crs
Morshead Crs
Uplands County Primary School
Norton Dr
Bruce Cl
Somervell Drive
Tanglewood
The Mallards
Old Turnpike
Furneaux Gdns
Giles Cl
Wickham Road
St Sebastian Crs
St Christopher Av
St Christophers Hospital
St Thomas Cl
Mead Wy
Serpentine
Turnpike Business Park
Uplands Crs
G7
1 Elizabeth Ct
2 Tudor Ct
Riverside Av
The Hts
Drift Road
Broadcut
North Wallington
Radclyffe Rd
Wallington
Hillary Close
Bentley Crs
Miller Drive
Oxford Cl
Denbigh Drive
Arundel Drive
Byron Close
Fareham Leisure Centre
Park Lane
Coghlan Cl
William Price Gdns
Harrison Rd
Harrison Road
Harrison County Primary School
Poyner Cl
Southampton Road
Wallington Way
98
H4
1 Tennyson Gdns
Spicewood
Margarita Rd
Alan Gv
Stanley Close
Beech Rd
Murray Close
Nicholas Crs
Chaucer Close
Leigh Road
Dryden Cl
The Dr
Colenso Rd
New Road
Homewood Chiropractic Health Centre
Fareham Borough Council
Church Path
Civic Way
High Street
Hotel
Blackbrook Rd
Blackbrook Business Park
Harlequin Gv
Stephen Rd
Regency Pl
Jonathan Road
Julie Av
Blackbrook Pk Av
Blackbrook House Dr
Brookmeadow
Woodstock Cl
Haddon Cl
Veryan
FAREHAM
Fareham Station
The Practice Doctors Surgery
Gordon Road
Grove Road
Derlyn Rd
Osborn Road
Trinity St
Russell Pl
Magistrates Court
Osborn Rd S
Westbury Rd
Palmerston Avenue
Clinic
Hampshire County Council
Wykeham House School
Lysses Path
Bus Stn
West St
Union St
Bridgefoot Dr
Bath La
The Surg
H5
1 The Gillies
2 Maytree Rd
THE AVENUE A27
Romyns Ct
Paxton Road
Avenue Road
Crescent Rd
Gal
Kings Rd
Queen's Rd
Hartland's Rd
Portland St
Police Station
Quay Street
A27 WESTERN WAY
Western Rd
EASTERN WAY
Bath La (Lower)
Deane Rd
St Judes Catholic Primary Sch
Fareham College
Justin Cl
Silver Birch Av
Wallisdean County Infant School
Wallisdean County Junior School
Westley Grove
Wallisdean Av
Redlands Lane
Belvoir Close
Elmhurst Rd
The Boatyard Industrial Est
Upper Whf
Town Quay
Business Park
Ash Cl
Willow Tree Gdns
Poplar Drive
Magnolia
Barnfield Ct
Bishopsfield Road
West End
Westfield Av
Highfield Avenue
Chamberlain Gv
Coombe Farm Av
Briarwood Cl
Holbrook Rd
Eden Ri
Mill Rd
Old Gosport Road
6
H6
1 Alexander Gv
Endips Rd
Snowdon Dr
Middleton Close
Malvern Av
Neville Lovett Community School
Grove
Michael's Grove
Redlands La
Mill Road
Fayre Rd
Beacons Field
Mainsail Drive
Lwr Quay Rd
Earls Rd
Seabird Wy
Johns Road
Eastern Pde
GOSPORT RD
Cams Hall Estate Golf Club
Wallington River
Longfield Avenue
Fairfield
Redlands County Primary School
Saltern Est
Elms Road
7
Anne's Avenue
St Michael's
Malus Cl
Midfield Cl
Northfield Av
Trafalgar Ct
Jubilee Court
Palmerston Business Park
Alders Road
Salterns Lane
The Halliards
Fen Av
Delta Business Pk
Watersmeet
Holmefield Av
Eastfield Av
Fareham Rd
Palmerston Dr
Newgate LANE
115
Geoffrey Crescent
GOSPORT ROAD
Laburnum Road
K4
1 Archery La
2 Wallington Hl
J7
1 The Moorings
J3
1 Hanover Gdns
2 The Potteries
3 Swallow Wd
K
Fort Fareham
Nelson Ct
Widley Ct
Liverpool Rd
HMS Collingwood
Longfield Avenue
Hoeford Cl

B6
1 Goldcrest Cl
2 Partridge Cl
A5
1 Waterside Gdns
A4
1 The Maltings
A
B
C
D
E
78
Whitedell Farm
Manor Farm
Boarhunt
1
C5
1 Cams Bay Cl
2 East Cams Cl
Lane
Whitedell
Road
Boarhunt
North Fareham Farm
Spurlings
Nine Elms Lane
2
C6
1 Cormorant Cl
2 Cygnet Ct
3 Eagle Cl
4 Falcon Cl
5 Grebe Cl
6 Lapwing Gv
7 The Linnets
8 Wren Wy
Road
Boarhunt Road
Monument
Down Barn Farm
Boarhunt Road
Swivelton Lane
King's Way
3
Standard
Way
M27
Junction 11
Fort Nelson
National Museum of Artillery
D6
1 Severn Cl
Wallington
Riverside Av
The Hts
Drift Road
Military Rd
King's Way
Portsdown Hill Road
Broadcut
North
Drift Rd
Military Road
King's Way
Downend Road
Radclyffe Rd
Ft Wallington Industrial Estate
King's Way
4
Pallant Gdns
Military
Rd
East Hl Close
Greenbanks Gdns
Woodlands
Pinks Hill
97
Wallington Shore Rd
A27
Paradise La
Paradise Lane
Road
E5
1 Boxwood Cl
2 Tudor Cl
Waterside Gdns
King's Way
Danes Rd
Saxon Cl
Wykeham House School
Crest Cl
The Tor Cl
Causeway
Downend
Lancaster Cl
Merlin Gdns
Ventnor Way
St Catherines Way
Alum Way
The Ridgeway
Jute Cl
5
Cams Hill
PO16
The Thicket
The Spinney
Camelot Crs
Solent Vw
Hawthorn
E6
1 Hatherley Dr
2 Rudgwick Cl
3 Stoneleigh Cl
The Dell
Paradise Lane
CAMS HILL A27
The Pines
Tamar Cl
Winnham Drive
Deane's Pk Rd
Bath La (Lower)
EASTERN
Cams Hill School
Shearwater
Rooksway Grove
Birdwood Grove
Hawkwell
Swancote
Curlew Dr
The Thicket
Winnham Dr
Upr Cornaway La
Dore Avenue
Redwood Dr
Red B
Primar
Rockingham Wy
Cams Hall
A27 PORTCHESTER RD
6
Chaffinch Wy
Teal Cl
Wagtail Wy
Beaulieu Av
Ashtead Cl
Romsey Avenue
The Queensway
Kingfishers
King's Way
The Peregrines
Quintrell Av
E7
1 Sissinghurst Rd
Peacock Close
Av
Flamingo Ct
Condor Avenue
Wicor County Primary School
PORTC
Cams Hall Estate Golf Club
Cornaway La
Nelson Av
Wessex
Brenchley Cl
Hatherley Crescent
Central Road
Road
Kenya Rd
Kg John Av
Whitehaven
PO
Fareham Borough Council
Cranleigh
Gate House Rd
Sandport Gv
7
Orchard Grove
Way
Cranleigh Rd
Sissinghurst Rd
Tattershall Crs
Seafield Road
Wicor Mill Lane
Foxbury Gv
Norgett
116
Moraunt Dr
Cador Dr
Albion Cl
Audret Cl
Kilwich Way
Windr
King's Way
1 grid square represents 500 metres
Foxbury

F5
1 Canon's Barn Cl
2 Steep Cl
F7
1 Gladstone Gdns
Southwick
Back Lane
West Street
North
Doctors Surgery
High St
79
B2177
Fareham Road
Southwick Park
Naval Recreation Centre
Southwick Park Lake
G5
1 Conifer Ms
H5
1 Rowland Rd
H6
1 Elgar Cl
2 Hopkins Cl
Offwell Farm
Drove Road
New Barns
Porchester Lane
Crooked Walk Lane
Portchester Lane
Nelson Lane
Portsdown Hill Road
Skew Road
Fort Southwick
Workshop Rd
North Rd
The Circus Road
Hilltop
Link Road
South
James Callaghan
Ports Down
M27
100
Hillsley
Kingscote Rd
Almondsbury Road
Tintern Cl
Butterfly Drive
Rockrose Wy
J5
1 Ridgeway Cl
2 Winterbourne Rd
K5
1 Dellfield Cl
2 Desborough Cl
3 Rothwell Cl
Waltham Cl
Kilmiston Dr
Weyhill Cl
Rogate Gdns
Dore Avenue
High Vw
Harting Gdns
Froxfield Gdns
Nyewood Av
Hill Road
Junior & Infant School
Laverock Lea
Burrton Close
Dore Avenue
Red Barn
Hill View Rd
Richmond Rise
Linden Lea
Simpson Cl
The Hillway
Anson Grove
Carlton Road
Pentland Rise
Benedict Wy
Browning Avenue
Keats Av
Chaucer Av
Shelley Av
Dryden Av
Coleridge Rd
Masefield Av
Macaulay Av
Coleridge Rd
Wordsworth Av
Southwick Av
Edward Gv
Seaview Av
Montrose Av
Portobello Gv
Leith Avenue
Portsview Gdns
Colinton Av
Morningside Av
Mountview Av
Raymond Rd
Newbolt Rd
Bude Cl
Falmouth Road
Hillside Crs
Mousehole Rd
Truro Rd
Pamela Av
Pendennis Rd
Helston Rd
Portsview Avenue
Jubilee Avenue
Sedgefield Close
Allaway Avenue
Longdean Cl
Chedworth Crs
Deerhurst Crescent
Beverston Road
Woofferton Road
Doctors Surgery
Birdlip Rd
Allaway Av
Paulsgrove
Kelvin Grove
Junior School
Saxon Shore Infant Sch
King Richard School
St Pauls RC Primary School
Bourne Rd
The Crossway
Portchester Station
The Kingsway
The Fairway
The Downsway
The Close
Helena Wy
The Leaway
St James Wy
Station Rd
New Town
Portsdown Rd
Neelands Gv
Parry Cl
Sullivan Cl
Coltsmead
Beach Dr
Shorehaven
Farmlea Rd
Port Wy
A27 SOUTHAMPTON ROAD
K6
1 Bodmin Rd
2 Watersedge Rd
CHESTER
Portchester Health Centre
West St
PO
Kg George Road
Jubilee Rd
Qu Mary Rd
Postern Cl
The Keep
Castle Street
Hampshire County
City of Portsmouth
Hamilton Road
Lock View
Port Wy
Newlyn Wy
Sennen Pl
Carbis Cl
Westlands Medical Centre
Westlands Gv
Allenby Gv
Vincent Gv
Frobisher Gv
Marlborough Gv
Clive Grove
Wellington Gv
Shrubbery Cl
Portchester Community School
Sunningdale Rd
Castle Grove
Myrtle Avenue
Castle County Primary School
Cow Lane
Lock Approach
Hart Lane
White Hart La
Neville Av
Olive Crs
Edgar Crs
Marina Gv
Seaway Gv
Coral Cl
Kent Gv
Grove Avenue
Merton Avenue
Westbrook Rd
Merton Crs
Denville Av
Bayly Avenue
Windsor Rd
York Gdns
Benham Gv
Norman Cl
Castle View Rd
Castle St
Roman Gv
Harbour Vw
Wicor Pth
Waterside
117
Marina Keep
Mullion Cl
Bryher Island
Port Way
F
G
H
J
K
I
2
3
4
5
6
7

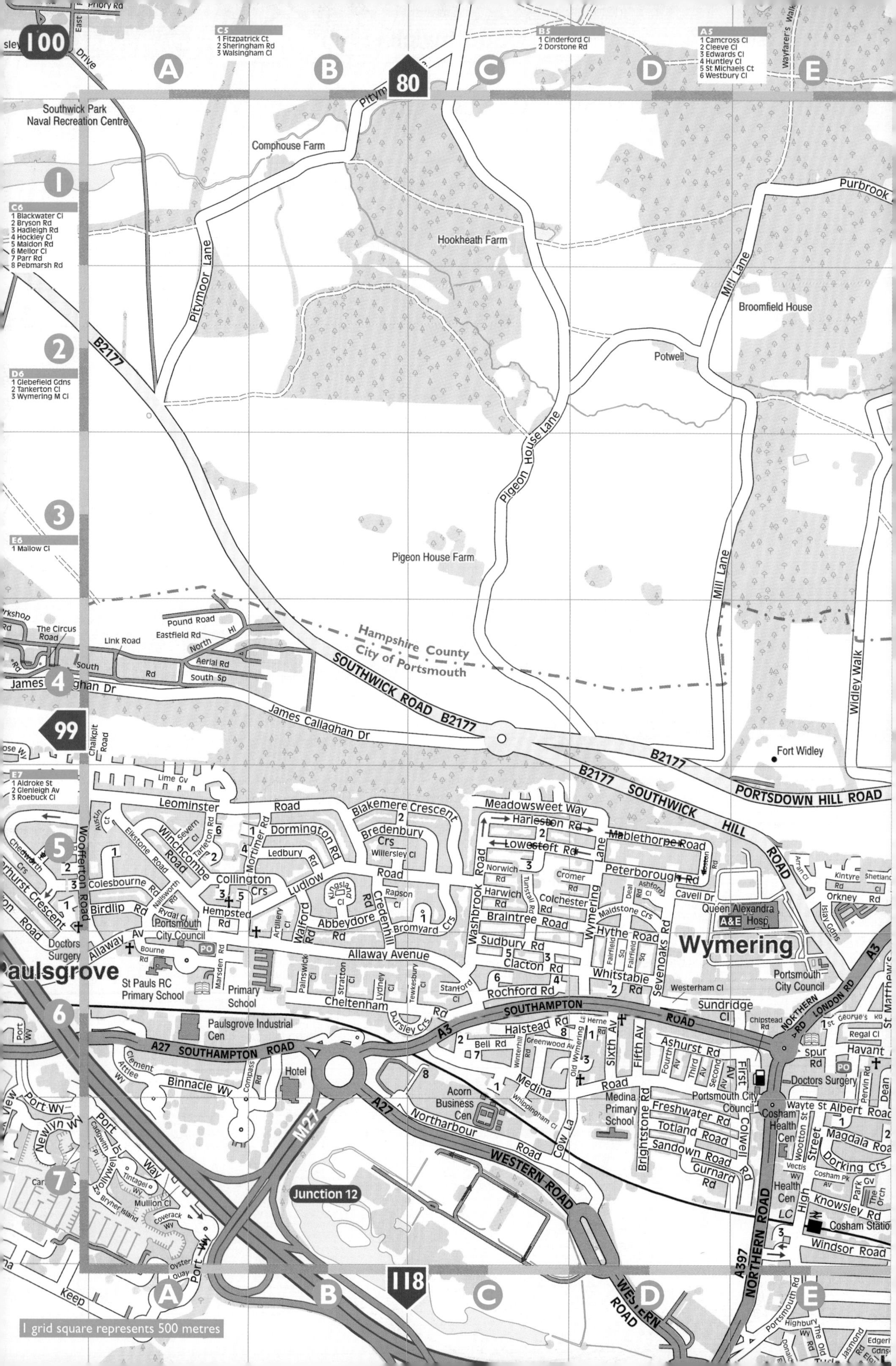

1 grid square represents 500 metres

F7
1 The Close
G4
1 C'church Gdns
2 Thornton Cl
F
G
H
J
I
K
Newlands
81
Southwick House
Newlands Lane
Purbrook Heath Road
Purbrook Cricket Club
Widley Walk
Wayfarer's Wk
Widley Farm
Meadow Edge
Wayfarer's Walk
New Down La
Boundary Way
Dell Crest Pth
Hilltop Crs
Greenlea Cl
Oakhurst Gdns
Dell Cl
Hillside Av
Lily Av
Geoffrey Avenue
Lansdowne Av
Victoria Av
Highbank Av
LONDON ROAD
A3(T)
Marrels Wd
Purbrook Gdns
Crofton Cl
Corbett Road
Montgomery Wk
Purbrook
Junior & Infant School
Woodlands Gv
Aldermoor Rd
Stakes Road
Westbrook Gv
Queens Gv
Shaftesbury Av
Bursledon Pl
Bursledon Rd
Dayslondon Rd
Newlands Rd
Alsford Rd
Cunningham Rd
Gordon Rd
Charles Cl
Mill Road
Beresford Cl
Vian Rd
Hamble La
Cowan Rd
Boyle Crs
Kelly Rd
Walt Rd
Bell Crs
Novello Gdns
Walton Cl
Elizabeth Wy
Coates Wy
Purcell Cl
Ireland Wy
Sullivan Way
Bliss Cl
Lambert Cl
Britten Wy
Vine Coppice
Chilsdown Wy
Elgar Cl
Holst Wy
Kennedy Close
Jacqueline Av
Park Farm Rd
Ladybridge Road
Penjar Av
Balmoral Dr
Elstead Gdns
Park Avenue
Park Road
Greenacre Gdns
Alameda Wy
Alameda Road
Stakes Road
Claremont Gdns
Craigwell Rd
Morelands Road
Timberlane
Sandy Brow
Fir Copse Rd
St John's Av
Ley Capel
Shillinglee
Crown Cl
Portsdown Group Practice
Frances Road
Privett Road
Serpentine Rd
Lone Valley
Deverell Pl
Bushy Mead
Valley Cl
Applewood Gv
Widley
Purbrook Park School
Widley Gdns
The Thicket
Copse Cl
The Dale
The Rise
Underdown Av
Parker Gardens
The Crest
The Brow
Sovereign La
Farthings Ga
Minters Lepe
Tanner's Rge
Ardington Rl
Liddiards Way
Crookhorn Lane
Oracle Dr
Mercury Pl
Hector Cl
Jason Pl
College Rd
Morelands Primary School
102
Hampshire County
City of Portsmouth
B2177
Hoylake Rd
Peter Ashley Rd
Troon Crs
PORTSDOWN HILL ROAD
Birkdale Av
Farlington
Burnham Road
Ainsdale Rd
Gillman Road
LONDON ROAD
Chalkridge Road
Chidham Rd
Cranborne Road
Widley Road
Courtmount Gv
Colville Rd
St John's Road
Southdown Rd
Carmarthen Avenue
Brecon Avenue
Merthyr Avenue
Aberdare Av
Drayton Lane
Down End Road
Down End
Augustine Rd
Uplands Road
Portsdown Avenue
Moortown Av
Sea View Road
St Helen's Rd
Highlands Rd
Blake Road
Grant Road
Galt Road
Woodfield Avenue
Gillman Rd
Old Rd
Solent Infant School
Eveleigh Road
Lampeter Av
Penarth Av
Solent Road
School
Drayton
Dene Hollow
Solent Junior School
HAVANT ROAD
Farlington
Broad Gdns
Walberton Av
St Colman's Av
Padwick Avenue
Burrill Av
Bernard Avenue
Lodge Av
East Cosham Rd
Cosham
Havant Road
Medical Cen
Doctors Surgery
Aldsworth Cl
Manor Ms
Waverley Rd
Laburnum Av
Lindisfarne Cl
Mulberry Lane
Woolner Av
Lendorber Av
East Ct
Court Cl
Tregaron Av
Carshalton Av
Racton Av
Southbourne Av
Chilgrove Rd
Park
Mulberry Av
Junior & Infant School
Hilary Av
Mansvid Av
Dysart Avenue
Salisbury Road
Widley Ct Dr
Beaconsfield Avenue
Gofton Av
Braemar Av
Invergordon Av
Manor Crs
Lower Drayton Lane
Central Road
Scholars' Wk
Springfield School
Homefield Rd
Station Road
South Road
Lealand Road
Lealand Gv
Copsey Gv
Copsey Cl
Grove Road
A2030
EASTERN ROAD
Waterworks Road
Nutbourne Rd
Prinsted Crs
Zetland Rd
First Avenue
Second Avenue
Lwr Farlington Rd
Hardy Rd
Fitzherbert Spur
Fitzherbert Road
Warrior Business Centre
The Saltings
Binness Way
Farm Way
Old Farm Way
Shearwater Dr
Cygnet Rd
Kestrel Pl
Lonsdale Avenue
Court Lane
Old Manor Way
Kirton Rd
Rosebery Av
Knowsley Crs
Langdale Av
Pangbourne Av
Kinross Crs
Grove Road
Fitzherbert Rd
Old Reservoir Rd
Marshlands Rd
Fishers Gv
119
East Industrial Cen
Hawthorn
Chatsworth
Pitreavie Road
Highbury
Overcourt Rd
Crescent Avenue
Station Rd
Wainwright Cl
K7
1 Watermead Rd
K6
1 Acorn Cl
2 Copper Beech Dr
3 Elmtree Rd
4 Oakapple Gdns
A27
G6
1 Lordington Cl
G7
1 Court Mead
H1
1 Post Office Rd
H2
1 Abbots Cl
2 The Crescent
3 Tanglewood Cl
H3
1 Downside Rd
2 Gitsham Gdns
H6
1 Aldsworth Gdns
J1
1 Aldermoor Rd E
2 Alexander Cl
3 Kentidge Rd
4 Marlborough Cl
J2
1 Ivy Ct
J6
1 King Arthur's Ct
K1
1 Gilbert Wy
K3
1 The Boltons
2 The Florins
3 Ha'penny Dell
4 Penny Pl
K4
1 Minerva Cl
2
3
4
5
6
7
PORTSD

102
82
101
120
A
B
C
D
E
1
2
3
4
5
6
7
B1
1 Tamarisk Cl
A2
1 Elgar Wk
2 Khandala Gdns
A1
1 Dogwood Dell
2 Honeysuckle Ct
3 Rosebay Ct
4 Sweetbriar Gdns
C2
1 Ampfield Cl
C3
1 Bedhmptn H Rd
D2
1 Boldre Cl
2 Crookham Cl
3 Dibden Cl
4 Dockenfield Cl
5 Rhinefield Cl
6 Rockbourne Cl
D3
1 Gwatkin Cl
2 St Nicholas' Rd
D4
1 Belmont Gv
E1
1 Farleigh Cl
2 Monkwood Cl
3 Testwood Rd
4 Tichborne Gv
5 Weyhill Cl
6 Winslade Rd
E2
1 Cheriton Cl
E3
1 Milford Cl
2 Wellow Cl
Hulbert Junior School
Surgery
Springwood
Philip Road
Frendstaple
Covert Gv
Woodsedge
Lombardy Ri
Oaklands RC School
HULBERT ROAD
B2150
Primary School
Park Community School
Park House Farm Way
Keyhaven Drive
Linkenholt Way
Hordle Road
Purbrook Way
Leigh Park
Chalton Crescent
Selborne Av
Middle Park Way
Middle Park Medical Centre
Barncroft Junior School
Barncroft Infant School
Medical Centre
Priorsdean Crescent
Finchdean Road
Junction 4
The Crookhorn Community School
Stakes Hill Road
Riverside School
Portsdown Group Practice
The South Downs College
College Road
Apollo Dr
Atlantis Av
Perseus Place
Zeus La
Chestnut Av
Pinewood Av
Oakwood Av
Littlepark Av
Mitchell Rd
Newbarn Road
Matthews Close
Jessie Road
Ernest Road
St Michael's Rd
Hook's Lane
St Thomas Mores RC Primary School
Havant Rugby Football Club
Bidbury Junior & Infant School
BEDHAMPTON RD B2149
Scratchface Lane
A3(M)
Penhurst Road
Maylands Road
Brooklands Road
Roman Way
Qu Anne's Dr
Lester Av
Beaufort Rd
Wessex Superbowl
B2177
Havant Retail Park
BEDHAMPTON HL RD
PORTSDOWN HILL ROAD
Hampshire County
City of Portsmouth
Bedhampton
Bedhampton Station
Junction 5
Lower Road
Meyrick Road
Ranelagh Rd
Woodfield Avenue
Fortunes Way
Penk Ridge
Auriol
A2030
HAVANT ROAD
Rectory Road
Rectory Av
A27(T)
Harts Farm Way
Havant Business Center
Brockhampton Rd
Solent Way
Southmoor Lane
Warrior Business Centre
A27
Sullivan Way
Walton Cl
Elizabeth Rd
1 grid square represents 500 metres

F4
1 Brookfield Cl
2 Chidham Sq

F5
1 Clarendon Rd
2 Selbourne Rd

G2
1 Colemore Sq
2 Woodlands Wy

G3
1 Compton Cl
2 Havant Farm Cl
3 Linden Wy

G5
1 The Parchment

H1
1 Curdridge Cl
2 Hiltingbury Av
3 Rooksbury Cft
4 Witchampton Cl

H2
1 Douglas Gdns
2 Muccleshell Cl

H3
1 Anderson Cl
2 Flexford Gdns
3 Hodges Cl

H5
1 White Ladies Cl

J1
1 Ashe Rd
2 Bentley Ct
3 Bramshaw Ct
4 Deane Ct
5 Fawley Ct
6 Fullerton Cl
7 Heckfield Cl
8 Holbury Ct
9 Meadend Cl
10 Muscliffe Ct
11 Newnham Ct
12 Oakfield Ct
13 Stanford Ct
14 Stockbridge Cl
15 Sway Ct
cont.

J1 cont.
16 Tisted Ct
17 Tunworth Ct
18 Warbrook Ct
19 Wherwell Ct
20 Woolmer Ct
21 Worthy Ct

104
84
103
122
A
B
C
D
E
1
2
3
4
5
6
7
C4
1 Emsbrook Dr
C2
1 Winfield Wy
B3
1 Barwell Gv
2 Panton Cl
C6
1 Frobisher Gdns
2 King's Ter
3 Orange Rw
D4
1 Westbourne Cl
D6
1 The Fishermans
2 Frankland Ter
3 Harbour Wy
4 Marina Cl
5 Pelham Ter
E1
1 Byerley Cl
E3
1 Church Vw
2 Old Rectory Cl
3 The Square
Emsworth Common Road
Bartons Road
Southleigh Park
Hollybank
Monk's Fm
West Sussex County
Hampshire County
Commonside
Long Copse Lane
HORNDEAN ROAD
B2148
East Leigh Road
Southleigh Road
Southleigh Fm
Spencer Road
Woolmer Street
Tudor Av
Hollybank Lane
Birch Tree Close
Birch Tree Drive
Redlands Lane
Wraysbury Pk Dr
Nursery Cl
Cumberland Av
Greville Green
Adderbury Av
Longfield Rd
Helston Drive
Hedgerow Gardens
Cobblewood
Woodlands Avenue
Fairlea Road
Garland Av
Bellevue La
Christopher Way
NEW BRIGHTON ROAD
B2147
WESTBOURNE ROAD
Sussex Border Path
New Brighton
Lewis Road
Ward Crs
Oakmeadow Cl
Wickor Wy
Wickor Close
Westbourne Avenue
Danbury Court
St James C of E Primary School
Hotel
A27(T)
Coldharbour Farm Rd
Lumley Road
Lumley
Hermitage
The Rookery
Sadlers Walk
PO10
Mill Lane
River Ems
North St
The Art Gallery
George & Dragon Surg
EAST ST
New Rd
Whitechimney RW
Westbourne
Emsworth Primary School
Glenwood School
Washington Rd
Emsworth Station
Sultan Road
Seagull La
Malvern Ms
Victoria Road
Selangor Avenue
Nore Crs
Park Crs
Record Road
Bosmere Gardens
Bridge Road
NORTH ST
Palmer's Rd
Emsworth Mus
Victoria Cottage Hosp
A259
HAVANT ROAD
Emsworth Surg
Beach Road
Kingsey Av
Clovelly Road
Valetta Park
Warblington Road
Western Parade
Beacon Sq
Bath Road
Creek End
The Promenade
Queen St
King St
South St
Slipper Road
Pagham Cl
Woodfield Pk Rd
Gordon Road
Thorney Road
Southbourne Av
Penny Lane
Apple Grove
Roundhouse Meadow
Heron Quay
Osprey Quay
Mill Quay
Solent Way
Wayfarer's Walk
Sussex Border
EMSWORTH
Conigar
Thornham
1 grid square represents 500 metres

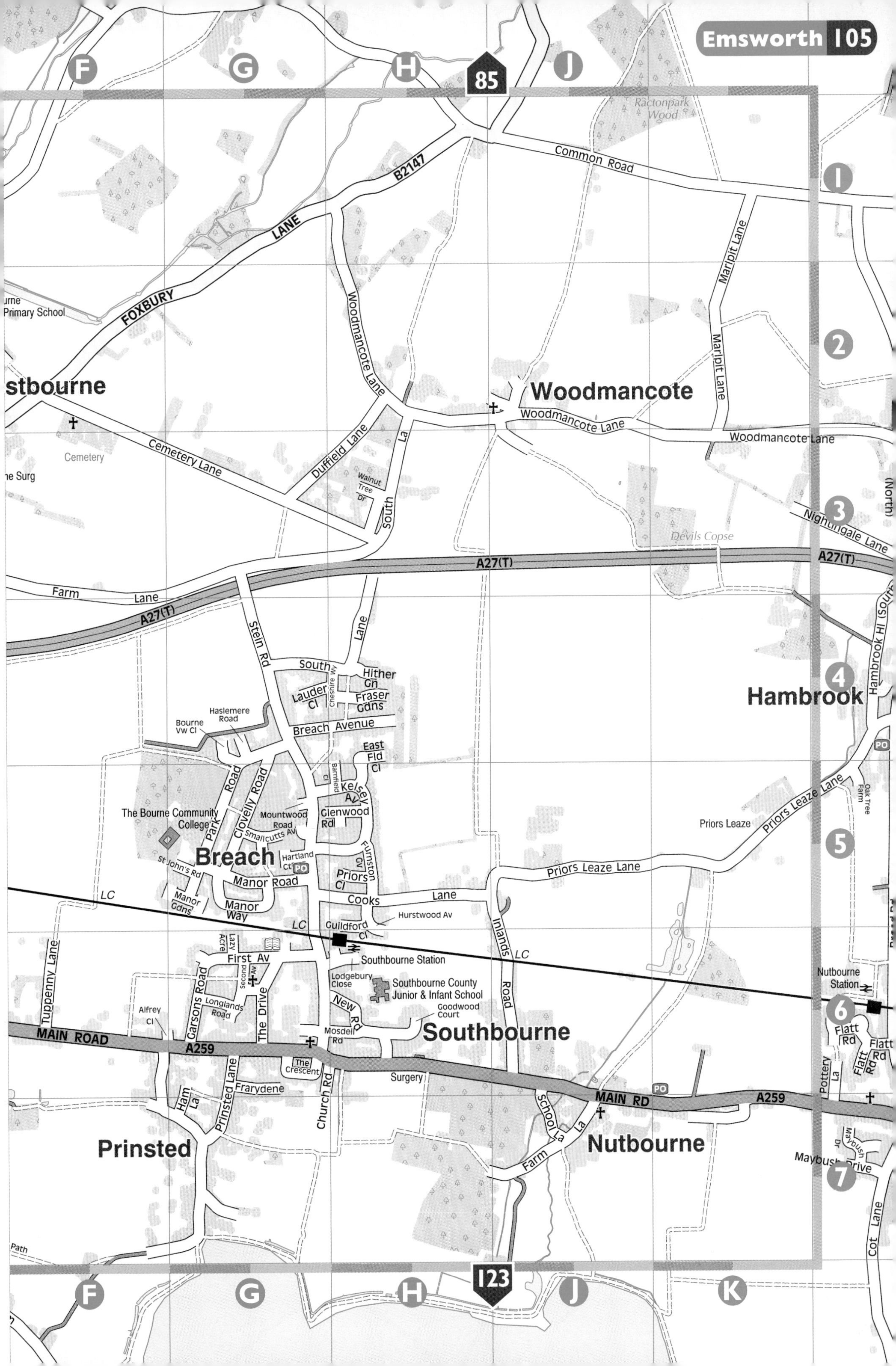

F
G
H
85
J
Ractonpark Wood
Common Road
B2147
FOXBURY LANE
Woodmancote Lane
Marlpit Lane
urne Primary School
stbourne
Woodmancote
Woodmancote Lane
Cemetery
Cemetery Lane
Duffield Lane
South La
Walnut Tree Dr
ne Surg
Nightingale Lane
(North)
Devils Copse
A27(T)
Farm Lane
Stein Rd
Lane
South
Hither Gn
Lauder Cl
Cheshire Wy
Fraser Gdns
Hambrook
Hambrook Hl (South)
Bourne Vw Cl
Haslemere Road
Breach Avenue
East Fld Cl
Barnfield Cl
Kelsey Av
Park Road
Clovelly Road
The Bourne Community College
Mountwood Road
Smallcutts Av
Glenwood Rd
Oak Tree Farm
Priors Leaze Lane
Priors Leaze
Breach
Hartland Ct
PO
Furnston Gv
Priors Cl
St John's Rd
Manor Road
Priors Leaze Lane
Manor Gdns
Manor Way
Cooks Lane
Hurstwood Av
LC
Guildford Cl
Inlands Road
Lazy Acre
First Av
Southbourne Station
Tuppenny Lane
Garsons Road
Second Av
Lodgebury Close
Southbourne County Junior & Infant School
Nutbourne Station
Longlands Road
New Rd
Goodwood Court
Alfrey Cl
The Drive
Mosdell Rd
Southbourne
Flatt Rd
MAIN ROAD
A259
The Crescent
Surgery
Pottery La
Frarydene
Prinsted Lane
Church Rd
School La
MAIN RD
Ham La
Farm La
Nutbourne
Maybush Dr
Maybush Drive
Prinsted
Cot Lane
Path
123
K
1
2
3
4
5
6
7

1 grid square represents 500 metres

F
G
H
89
J
Pig Bush
Culverley Farm
1
North Gate
North Lane
Shepton Bridge
2
Tantany Wood
Penerley Lodge
3
Stubbs Wood
Leygreen Farm
4
108
National Motor Museum
5
Palace House
Furzey Lodge
6
Furzey Lane
Beaulieu
HIGH ST B3054
Hatchet Gate
B3055
HATCHET LANE B3054
7
F
G
H
125
J
K
Swinesleys Farm
Masseys La

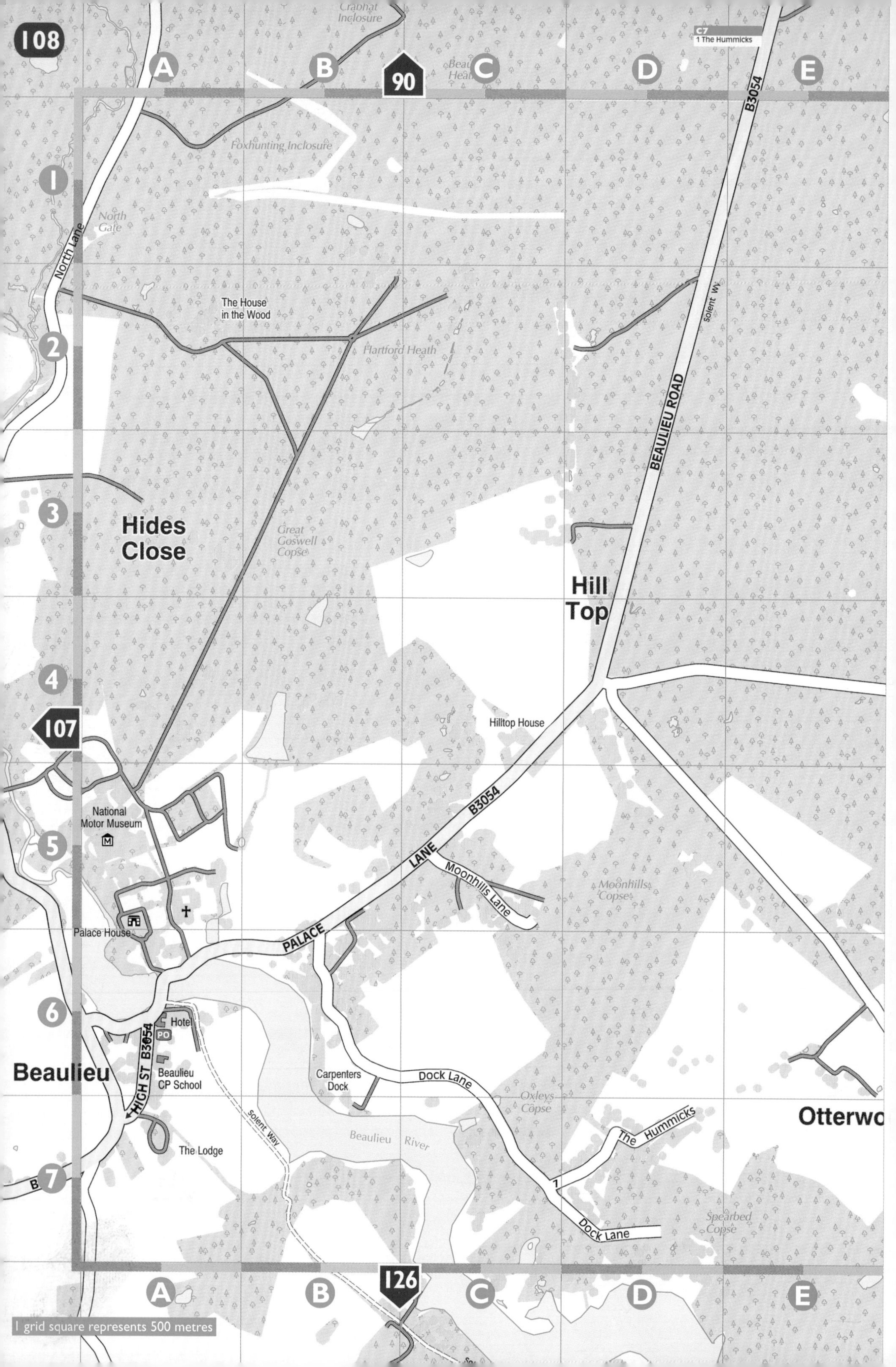

1 grid square represents 500 metres

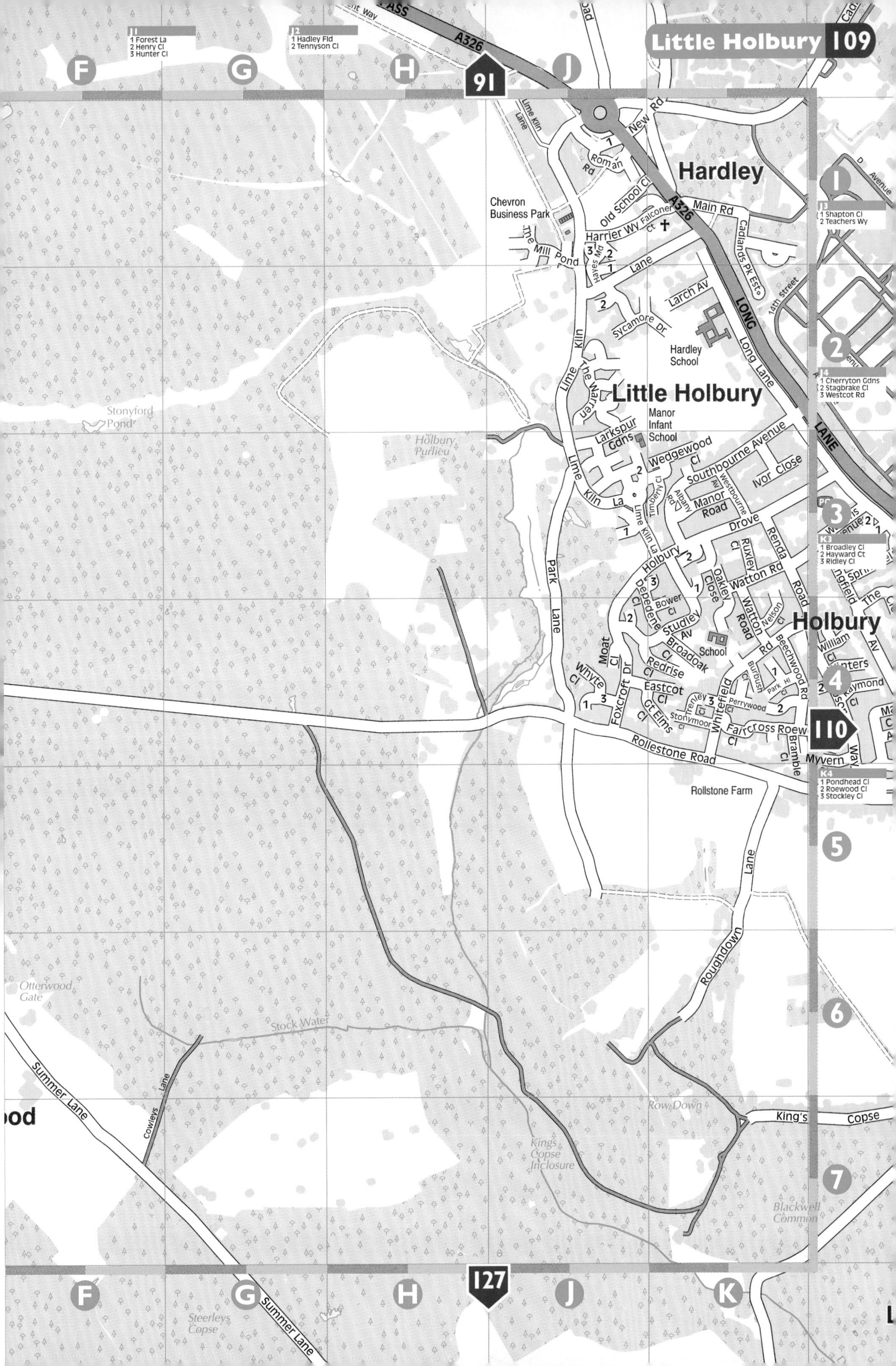
J1
1 Forest La
2 Henry Cl
3 Hunter Cl
J2
1 Hadley Fld
2 Tennyson Cl
A326
91
Hardley
New Rd
Roman Rd
Lime Kiln Lane
Chevron Business Park
The Mill Pond
Old School Cl
Harrier Wy
Falconer Ct
Main Rd
Hayes Md
Lane
Cadlands Pk Est
14th Street
Larch Av
Sycamore Dr
Hardley School
LONG LANE
Long Lane
J3
1 Shapton Cl
2 Teachers Wy
J4
1 Cherryton Gdns
2 Stagbrake Cl
3 Westcot Rd
Stonyford Pond
Holbury Purlieu
Lime Kiln
The Warren
Little Holbury
Manor Infant School
Larkspur Gdns
Wedgewood Cl
Southbourne Avenue
Ivor Close
Lime Kiln La
Timberly Cl
Albany Rd
Westbourne Av
Manor Road
Drove
Renda Road
K3
1 Broadley Cl
2 Hayward Ct
3 Ridley Cl
Holbury
Park Lane
Depedene Cl
Bower Cl
Oakley Close
Ruxley Cl
Watton Rd
Watton Road
Nelson Cl
Studley Av
School
Moat Cl
Broadoak Cl
Redrise Cl
Whyte Cl
Foxcroft Dr
Eastcot Cl
Gt Elms Cl
Trenley Cl
Stonymoor Cl
Whitefield
Burbush Cl
Park Hl
Perrywood
Beechwood Rd
Faircross Cl
Roewood
Bramble Cl
Rollestone Road
Myvern
110
K4
1 Pondhead Cl
2 Roewood Cl
3 Stockley Cl
Rollstone Farm
Roughdown Lane
Otterwood Gate
Stock Water
Summer Lane
Cowleys Lane
Row Down
King's Copse
Kings Copse Inclosure
Blackwell Common
F
G
H
J
K
127
Steerleys Copse

A5
1 Wentworth Gdns
A4
1 Ashleycross Cl
2 Hobson Wy
A3
1 Sloane Av
2 Sloane Ct
92
B5
1 The Greenwich
2 Harvey Ct
B6
1 Edward Cl
2 Fields Cl
3 Pendleton Gdns
C5
1 Fourshells Cl
2 Thornhill Cl
C6
1 Valley Cl
E4
1 Admirals Cl
2 ChurchFlds
3 Denny Cl
4 The Lane
5 Linda Rd
6 Meadow Wy
7 The Paddocks
8 Rhyme Hall Ms
9 The Square
10 Whites La
109
128
Oil Refinery
Holbury
Fawley
Blackfield
Langley
SO45
FAWLEY ROAD
B3053
LONG LANE
Long Copse
Rollestone Rd
Newlands Road
South Avenue
E Avenue
J Av
H Avenue
D Avenue
13th Street
12th Street
11th Street
10th Street
9th Street
8th Street
7th Street
6th Street
5th Street
4th Street
3rd Street
2nd St
1st Street
Foreshore
Burmah Road South
Cadland Road
P.L.P.H. Rd
Marsh Lane
Church Lane
School Rd
Fawley County First School
Fawley Business Centre
Ashdown Road
Slades Hill
Blackfield Rd
The Pentagon
Chapel La
Blackfield Health Centre
Blackfield Junior & Infant School
Hampton Lane
Blackfield Road
Dark Lane
Exbury Rd
King's Copse Road
Thornbury Avenue
Walker's Lane South
Green Lane
Fields Heath
Fields Farm
Tom's Down
Mopley Pond
Badminston Common
Blackwell Common
Cem
PO
1 grid square represents 500 metres

F
G
H
93
J
1
2
3
ISLE OF
4
112
5
6
7
North Trestle Road
Burmah
Road N
South
Trestle
Road
Agwi
Road
Old
Agitor Road
Road
Flume Rd
Lane
Copthorne Lane
Ashlett Cl
Ashlett
Ashlett Road
Clinic
Ashlett Creek
Stonehills
LEY BY-PASS
Stonehills
B3053
Northern Access Road
Northern Access Rd
Badminston Farm
Badminston Lane
Drove
Badminston
Ower
B3053
Stanswood Road
Calshot
PO
Calshot Cl
129
Sprat's Down
F
G
H
J
K
B3053
Castle Lane

Gilchrist Gdns
Hook Pk Road
94
Solent Court
Solent Drive
Hook Park Road
Workman's Lane
Cowes Lane
Hook Park
Hook Lane
Solent Way
Chilling Lane
Chilling
Workman's La
ISLE OF WIGHT
111
Calshot Castle
A
B
C
D
E
1
2
3
4
5
6
7

F
G
H
95
J
Brownwich Lane
Posbrook Lane
Singledge
Little Posbrook
Triangle Lane
Brownwich Lane
Brownwich Farm
Solent Way
Solent Way
Meon
114
Titchfield Haven
Cliff
1
2
3
4
5
6
7
F
G
H
J
K

96
130
113
C3
1 Dolphin Ct
2 Forties Cl
3 Shannon Rd
4 Tawny Owl Cl
C2
1 Hazelwood
B5
1 Fitzwilliam Av
C4
1 Biscay Cl
2 Crabth. Fm La
3 Faroes Cl
4 Fastnet Wy
5 Fisher Cl
6 Forth Cl
7 Hebrides Cl
8 Humber Cl
9 The Scimitars
C5
1 Blankney Cl
2 Bramham Moor
3 Goodsell Cl
4 Sea Kings
C6
1 Boyd Cl
D2
1 Discovery Cl
D3
1 The Paddock
D5
1 Wedgewood Cl
D6
1 Dallington Cl
2 Ferncroft Cl
3 Mayflower Cl
4 Tamarisk Cl
E2
1 Summerleigh Wk
E3
1 Derwent Cl
2 Pinewood Cl
3 Thirlmere Cl
E4
1 Belmont Cl
2 Peartree Cl
E5
1 Orion Cl
E6
1 Tonnant Cl
A
B
C
D
E
1
2
3
4
5
6
7
Little Posbrook
Posbrook La
Ransome Close
PO14
River Meon
Meon View Farm
Titchfield Haven
Hill Head
STUBBINGTON
Titchfield Road B3334
Ranvilles Lane
Peak Lane
Oakcroft Lane
Cemetery
Sumar Close
Stroud Green Lane
Spartan Cl
Lychgate Gn
Marks Rd
Morgans Dr
Newton Cl
Garnett Close
St Mary's Road
Pembury Rd
Grasmere Way
Meoncross School
Windermere Av
Foster Cl
Herons Close
Green Rd
Ennerdale Rd
Scott Cl
Anzac Cl
The Croft
Darren Cl
Burnt House Lane
Tangyes Close
Ditton Cl
Cains Cl
Longs La
Deal Close
Canterbury Rd
Rectory Cl
Cutlers La
Halletts Cl
Vicarage La
Anker Lane
Mays Lane
Cuckoo Lane
Jay Cl
Tawny Owl Cl
Country Vw
The Oakes
Puffin Crs
Turtle Close
Finisterre Cl
Old St
Kestrel Cl
Upr Old St
Cuckoo La
Cromarty Close
Old Street
Malin Cl
Shannon Road
Fair Isle Cl
Dover Cl
Fury Way
Drive
Viking Cl
The Gannets
Robins Close
Park Lane
Croftlands Avenue
Stubbington Green
Stubbington Gn
Anne Dale County Junior & Infant School
Village Close
Mayfield Cl
Dale Rd
Queens Rd
Oakdown Rd
Beresford Rd
Alfred Rd
Crescent
Ravens Cl
Harold Road
B3334
Berry Lane
Vixen Cl
Plymouth
Hawk Cl
Plover Cl
The Grove
Andrew Place
Bells Lane
La End
Angelus Close
Glyn Dr
Glyn Way
Eric Road
Fay Close
Martin Av
Martin Road
Elizabeth Rd
Francis Pl
Leviathan Cl
Westways
Northways
Southways
Cowdray Park
Pytchley Close
Barlow Close
Whaddon Cha
Fernie Cl
Violet Av
Harriet Cl
Carisbrooke Avenue
Pembroke Crescent
Corfe Close
Berkeley Close
Denham Close
Mancroft Avenue
Hammond County Junior & Infant School
Seaton Close
Cremyll Cl
Stuart Cl
Stubbington Lane
Victory Rd
E House Av
Conqueror Wy
Ajax Cl
William Close
Kingsmead Avenue
Jersey Close
Glenthorne Cl
Hammond Industrial Est
Ashton Wy
Knights Bank Road
Short Road
Old Street
Ltl Gays
Gays Gt
Haven Crs
Cliff Road
Solent Road
Elsfred Rd
Sanross Cl
Way
Crofton Lane
Walnut Drive
Moody Road
Old Farm Lane
Midways
Nursery Lane
The Glebe
Westgate
Deans Gate
Bell Davies Road
Robinson Road
Caspar John Close
Cottesway East
Cottes Way
Bramble Cl
Osborne Vw Rd
Hurst Close
Ellerslie Close
Valsheba Drive
Pilgrims Way
Farm Edge Road
Beverley Road
Springfield Way
Linkway
Mulberry Av
Hill Head Road
Solent Way
Seafield Park Road
Monks Way
Seamead
Salterns Road
Crofton Avenue
Sea La
HMS Daedalus
Implacable Rd
Unicorn Rd
Drake Rd
The Solent
PO

G1
1 Wallington Ct
H1
1 Southwick Ct
Jubilee Court
H5
1 Keyhaven Cl
I1
1 Farrier Wy
J4
1 Honeysuckle Cl
2 The Mead
3 Myrtle Cl
4 Nesbitt Cl
5 Puffin Gdns
J5
1 Dandelion Cl
2 Mallard Gdns
J6
1 Ankerwyke
2 Calshot Wy
K2
1 Bridgemary Wy
K3
1 Harwood Cl
2 Mountbatten Cl
K4
1 Cameron Cl
K5
1 Beaulieu Pl
2 Birchmore Cl
3 Clover Cl
4 Nicholl Pl
5 Niton Cl
6 Ramsay Pl
7 Warsash Gv
K7
1 Davis Cl
2 Snape Cl
K6
1 Hoylake Cl
2 The Fairway
3 Sunningdale Cl
97
116
131
Fleetlands
Woodcot
Bridgemary
Peel Common
Rowner
Gosport Airfield
Chark Common
PO13
HMS Collingwood
Fort Fareham
Collingwood Business Park
Fareham Megabowl
Delta Business Park
Newlands Farm
Crofton School
Spencer Court
Holbrook County Junior & Infant School
Bridgemary Community School
Bedenham County Junior & Infant School
Junior & Infant School
Rowner Health Centre
Grange County Junior & Infant School
Junior School
Newgate Lane
B3385
Gosport Road
A32
Fareham Road
Rowner Road
B3334
Broom Way
Brune Lane
Shoot Lane
Chark La
Woodcote Lane
Tanners Lane
Longfield Avenue
Alders Road
Salterns Lane
Laburnum Road
Geoffrey Crescent
Wych Lane
Tukes Avenue
Kent Road
Osborn Crs
James Road
Chatfield Rd
Gregson Avenue
Keyes Road
Montgomery Rd
Prideaux-Brune Av
Birch Dr
Bridgemary Road
Bridgemary Avenue
Lederle Lane
Heron Way
Brookers Lane
Carisbrooke Rd
Heather Cl
The Curve
The Parkway
Brewers Lane
Beauchamp Av
Corran Avenue
Rowner Close
Green Crescent
Pump La
Long Drive
Dormy Way
Rowallan Av
Mansfield Road
Franklin Rd
Highwood Road
St Nicholas Av
Samson Close
Cornwall Close
Charden Rd
Camp Rd
Albert Road
Avocet Walk
Dell Quay Close
Chichester Close
Bosham Walk
Meon Close
Stradbrook
Fairwater Close
Hamilton Grove
Staplers Reach
Edgecombe Crs
Sedgewick Close
Brune La
Bucksey Rd
Biddlecombe Cl
Grange Lane
Cherque Lane
Homer Close
Fieldhouse Dr
Fell Drive
Manor Way
Norwich Place
Ark Royal Crs
Triumph Road
Royal Sovereign Av
Neptune Road
Pelican Rd
Dreadnought Rd
Ocean Road
Mermaid Road
Excellent Rd
Shannon Rd
Venerable Rd
Barfleur Road
Ville De Paris Rd
Culloden Rd
Gibraltar Rd
Prince Rd
Hornet Road
Sampson Road
Liverpool Rd
Queen Rd
Hector Rd
Eurvalus Rd
Holmefield Av
Eastfield Av
Fort Fareham Rd
Nelson Cr
Widley Ct
Midfield Cl
Northfield Av
Endofield Cl
Stroud Green Lane
Field Close
Woodside
Meadow Wk
Burnside
Springcroft
Brookside
Primrose Close
Bridgemary Gv
Morris Cl
Conifer Gv
Vian Cl
Lapthorn Close
Ferndale Ms
Wycote Rd
Nursery Cl
Gregson Close
Pettycot Crs
Dayshes Cl
Stoners Cl
Ventnor Rd
Guillemot Gdns
Cavanna Cl
Petrel Walk
Kittiwake Close
Albatross Wk
Bramble Way
Shearwater Close
Gull Cl
Cowslip Cl
Totland Rd
Merstone Rd
Chale Close
Brading Av
Trevose Close
Glebe Dr
Nobes Av
Agnew Road
Layton Road
Fisher Road
Horton Rd
Harris Rd
Cunningham Dr
Foxbury

116
98
115
132
A
B
C
D
E
1
2
3
4
5
6
7
A7
1 Gilbert Cl
2 Tudor Cl
A6
1 Lawn Cl
2 Orange Gv
3 The Spinney
4 Walker Pl
A5
1 The Coppice
2 Holland Pl
3 Jacomb Pl
4 Kielder Gv
5 Savernake Cl
6 Stocker Pl
B5
1 Lombardy Cl
B6
1 The Chine
2 The Glen
3 The Hoe
4 The Mount
5 Sycamore Cl
6 The Thicket
7 Yewside
B7
1 Madison Cl
2 Newbroke Rd
C7
1 Eastbrook Cl
2 Jason Wy
3 Tynedale Cl
D7
1 Beaumont Ct
E7
1 Moraunt Cl
Council
Orchard Grove
Wicor Mill Lane
Foxbury Gv
Moraunt Dr
Capper Dr
Albion Cl
Audret Cl
Kilwich Way
King's Way
Foxbury Point
Fleetlands
Main Road
Foxbury Lane
Foxbury La
Aerodrome Road
Bedenham Lane
Venture Ind Park
Pewit Island
FAREHAM ROAD
A32
Aerodrome Rd
Prideaux-Brune
Maynard
Hanbidge Crs
Horton Rd
Montgomery Rd
Keyes Road
Keyes Cl
Harris Rd
Cunningham Dr
Bridgemary Avenue
Tedder Rd
Wavell Rd
Bedenham County Junior & Infant School
Agnew Road
Nobes
Perth Rd
Camp Rd
Tarius Cl
Braemar Road
Balmoral Close
Braemar Cl
Lerryn Rd
Beverly Cl
Nobes Cl
Lane
Hawkins Rd
Founders Wy
Downside
Beauchamp
Rowner Close
Avenue
Tichborne Way
Forest
Charnwood
Rosewood
Aspengrove
Vineside
The Limes
The Firs
Pinewood Wy
Almondside
The Nook
Oakdene
Ashdown
Acorn Close
Junior School
Rowner County Infant School
Holbrook Recreation Centre
Gosport Ice Rink
Turner Av
Green Crescent
Copse La
Phoenix Way
Trevose Close
Rowner Health Centre
Gorselands
Alliance Cl
Fleet Cl
Withies Rd
Landon Rd
Bracklesham Rd
Lawn Cl
Austerberry Wy
Tudor Cl
Pound Cl
Charden Rd
ROWNER ROAD
B3334
Doctors Surg
Henville Close
Masten Crs
Shackleton Road
Vanstone
Marles Cl
Aldermoor Road
Grange Lane
Grange County Junior & Infant School
St Nic
Halyard Close
Cornwell Close
Brune Park Community School
Beryl Av
Battery Close
Brockhurst Medical Cen
Norfolk Rd
Fort Brockhurst
Wingate Road
Alphage Rd
Gunners
School Rd
Anthony Gv
Cedar Cl
Hamlet Way
Blackthorn Dr
Wandesford Pl
Richard Gv
Frater Lane
Frater La
Parker Close
Stanley Cl
Orchard Cl
Ham La
Naish Dr
Chestnut Wk
Quay Lane
Elson Road
Elson Rd
Brighton Av
Hastings Avenue
Worthing Avenue
Selsey Avenue
Elson Lane
Elson County Infant School
Elson County Junior School
Goodway Sea School
Castle Vw
St Thomas's Road
Chapel St
Blenheim Gdns
Thornton Rd
Goodwood Cl
Elson
Exmouth Rd
Rydal Rd
Amberley Rd
Findon Road
Eastbourne Av
Weymouth Av
Bournemouth Av
Torquay Av
Dunkeld
Sedgeley Gv
Bramber Rd
Albemarle Avenue
Fairhome Cl
Reeds Rd
Tewkesbury Av
Mergans Cl
Widgeon Cl
Bittern Cl
Coombe Rd
Fieldmore
Chantry Road
Palmyra Rd
Heaton Rd
The Shrubbery
Kingsley Rd
Holmdale Rd
Shalbourne
1 grid square represents 500 metres

Portchester Community
Castle Grove
Castle County Primary School
Cow Lane
Marlborough Gv
F7
1 Alencon Cl
2 Kynon Cl
Hart Lane
White Hart La
PO
Coral Cl
Seaway Gv
Coppins Gv
Marina Gv
Kent Gv
Grove
Harbour Vw
Grove Avenue
Merton Avenue
Olive Crs
Neville Av
Edgar Crs
Windsor Rd
York Gdns
Castle St
Cooper Gv
Benham Gv
Westbrook Rd
Denville Av
Bayly Avenue
Norman Cl
Castle View Rd
Merton Crs
Roman Gv
Wicor Pth
Waterside La
Alton Gv
Lansdown Av
Lonsdale Av
Kenwood Rd
Webb Rd
Beachway
Cemetery
Hospital Lane
Church Rd
Portchester Castle
King's Way
Carbis Cl
Lock Approach
Marina Keep
Whale Island
N Battery
Whale
Wardroom Road
Quarterdeck
Guardroom
Chatfield Av
Pier
Portsmouth Harbour
Bucklers Road
Lane
F
G
H
J
K
I
2
3
4
5
6
7
99
118
133

118
100
117
134
Junction 12
A
B
C
D
E
1
2
3
4
5
6
7
C5
1 Connaught Rd
2 Kg Edwd's Crs
3 Penrose Cl
B5
1 Tipner Gn
2 Victory Gn
A5
1 Fraser Rd
C6
1 Bucklers Ct
2 Croft Rd
3 St Mark's Rd
C7
1 Chapel St
2 Dumbarton Cl
3 Hercules St
4 Kilpatrick Cl
5 Silverlock Cl
6 Spenlow Cl
D2
1 Midway Rd
2 Portswood Rd
D3
1 Eastwood Rd
2 Falklands Rd
3 St Francis Ct
D4
1 Kearsney Av
2 Templeton Cl
D7
1 Pink Rd
2 St Stephen's Rd
E3
1 Balderton Cl
2 Benham Dr
3 Breech Cl
4 Escur Cl
5 Newney Cl
6 Oldgate Gdns
7 Padbury Cl
8 St Barbara Wy
9 Thorncliffe Cl
E7
1 Northcote Av
Carbis Cl
Mullion Cl
Coverack
Bryher Island
Oyster Quay
Port Wy
Keep
Horsea Island
M27
M275
A27 WESTERN ROAD
A397 NORTHERN ROAD
Health Cen
Cosham Station
Knowsley Rd
Windsor Road
Portsmouth Rd
Highbury Wy
Tudor
LONDON RD
A3
Military Road
Firgrove Crs
Rampart Gdns
Scott
Peronne Rd
Bapaume Rd
Feltons Pl
Parsons Cl
Farmside Gardens
Hilsea Crs
North Av
Horsea Road
South Av
Horsea Lane
Northwood Rd
Fawley Rd
The City of Portsmouth Boys School
Oakwood Road
Elmwood
Barham Wy
Valiant Gdns
Matapan Rd
Howard Rd
Salerno Road
Narvik Road
Normandy
Dieppe Crs
NORTHERN PARADE
Phoenix Sq
Westwood Road
Beechwood Rd
Wyllie Rd
Conan Rd
Southwood Rd
Curtis Md
De Lisle Cl
Hilsea
Infant School
The Ridings
Egan Cl
Whitecross Gdns
Gatcombe Dr
COPNOR ROAD
Northern Parade Clinic
Doyle Avenue
Doyle Cl
Northern Parade Junior School
Infant School
Kipling Road
Meredith Road
Vita Rd
Telford Rd
Brunel Rd
Amberley Road
Merrivale Road
Torrington Road
Madeira Road
Windermere Rd
Compton Road
A288
City of Portsmouth Sports Club
Waterside School
Tipner Lane
Tipner
Range Gn
Osier Cl
Target
Hilldowns Av
Harbour Wy
Stamshaw Junior School
Tipner Road
Walker Rd
Twyford Av
North End Gv
Nelson Av
Magdalen Road
Hartley Road
Ophir Road
Shadwell Rd
Doctors Surgery
St Chad's Av
Randolph Rd
Battenburg Avenue
Cliffdale Primary School
St Swithun's Rd
Childe Square
Walden Rd
Jervis Road
Widley Rd
Strode Road
Gruneisen Rd
Oriel Road
Hewett Road
Wadham Road
Inhurst Rd
Domum Road
North End Av
Mayfield Road
PO2
North End
Wilson Rd
Stamshaw & Tipner Leisure Centre
Infant School
London Av
Munster Rd
Thurbern Road
Kirby Road
Newcomen Rd
Winstanley Rd
Meyrick Road
Knox Road
Ranelagh Rd
Lwr Derby Rd
Stanley Rd
Simpson Rd
Cardiff Rd
Monmouth Rd
Primary School
Gladys Avenue
A2047
Montague Rd
Stubbington Avenue
Beresford Rd
Fearon Rd
Balfour Road
Crofton Rd
Lyndhurst Rd
Hanway Group Practice
Infant School
Junior School
Kenyon Rd
Chelmsford Rd
Kensington Rd
Winton Rd
Heathcote Rd
Stamshaw
Whale Island
N Battery Rd
Evans Cl
Cornwell Cl
Mantle Sq
Whaley Rd
Eastern Rd
Wardroom Road
W Battery Rd
Quarterdeck Av
Domvilles Ap
Guardroom Rd
Shed Rd
Drill
Head
Pier
Chatfield
Whale Island Wy
Island View Terrace
TWYFORD AV
STAMSHAW RD
Angerstein Rd
Odeon Cinema
Wykeham Road
Copythorn Road
Grove Road
Emsworth Rd
Drayton Rd
Laburnum Rd
Beaulieu Rd
Burlington Rd
Derby Rd
Derby Road
Grange Rd
Pitcroft Rd
Surg
Seagrove Rd
Bevis Road
Heathfield Rd
Police Station
KINGSTON CRS
LONDON RD
Ashling La
Havant Rd
Doctors Surg
Chichester Road
Farlington Rd
Paddington Rd
Belgravia Rd
Epworth Rd
Junior Sc
Wallington Rd
Rudmore Sq
Mile End Rd
Kingston Crs
Garfield Rd
Basin St
Isambard Brunel Junior School
Portchester Rd
Wymering Rd
Meredith Infant School
Paulsgrove Rd
Preston Rd
Bedhampton Rd
Wallace Rd
Westbourne Rd
Funtington Rd
Bosham Rd
Doctors Surgery
Road Vw
George Byng Wy
Continental Ferry Port
Wharf Road
Kettering Ter
Buckland Medical Cen
Junior & Infant Sch
Nessus St
Malthouse Rd
Clydebank Rd
Queens Road
Surgery
Powerscourt Road
Queen's Road
Lomond Cl
Stirling St
Washington Rd
Winchester Road
Jersey Rd
Malta Rd
Lynn Road
Aylesbury Rd
Carnarvon Rd
Byron Rd
Tennyson Rd
Percival Rd
Whitworth Rd
Estella Rd
Steerforth Cl
Malins Rd
Binsteed Road
Cyprus Rd
New Road East
KINGSTON RD
Hanway Road
Arnaud Cl
Toronto Road
Junior School
Inverness Rd
Seymour Cl
Cressy Road
Agincourt Rd
Emanuel St
Baker St
Cairo St
Sultan Rd
Prince's St
Regent St
Herbert St
Victory
Flathouse
MILE END RD
Duke Cr
Hanway Surgery
A2047
Bettesworth Rd
Belmore Cl
Ernest Rd
Shearer Rd
George St
Durban Rd
South Rd
Victoria St
Lodge Street School Branch Clinic
Cemetery
1 grid square represents 500 metres

Beaconsfield Avenue
Lonsdale Ave
F1
1 Wembley Gv
Braemar Av
F7
1 Eastbourne Rd
2 Moneyfield La
3 Stapleton Rd
Springfield School
Fitzherbert
Warrior Business Cen
Knowsley Crs
Road
Rosebery Av
Langdale Av
Old Manor Way
Pangbourne Av
Kinross Crs
Grove
Road
101
Reservoir Rd
Old Rd
Marshlands Rd
Fishers Gv
Hawthorn
Chatsworth
Crescent
Avenue
Highbury
Grove
Highbury
Dovercourt Rd
Wembley Gv
Primary School
Redwood Park School
Highbury College
A27
Lwr Drayton La
Karen Av
Stroudley Av
Wainwright Cl
Station Rd
Kirtley Cl
Eastern Industrial Cen
EASTERN ROAD
Walton Road
Road
Walton
A27
I
G3
1 Hartwell Rd
Farlington Marshes
2
G4
1 Latimer Ct
2 Plumpton Gdns
Shawcross Ind Park
Ackworth Road
Limberline Road
Gunstore Road
Airport Service Rd
Holdenbury Ct
Buckby La
Daventry La
Althorpe Dr
Blakesley La
Foxley Dr
Tiffield Cl
Holcot Lane
Burcote Dr
Corby Crs
Sywell Crs
Sutton Cl
Marston La
Yardley Cl
Brampton La
Ecton La
Solent Way
EASTERN RD
RSPB Reserve
3
H3
1 Adstone La
2 Broughton Ct
3 Everdon La
4 Maidford Gv
Hobby Cl
Merlin Dr
Norway Road
Portsmouth Rugby Football Club
Hilsea Station
Williams Rd
Sharps Cl
Anchorage Road
Anchorage Park
Civil Service Sports Ground
Mitchell Wy
Painter Cl
4
Neville Shute Road
Wesley Grove
Lovett Road
Green Lane
Devon Rd
Highgrove Ind Park
Bolde Close
Quartremaine Road
Airport Service Road
Robinson Wy
Keel Close
Fairway Business Cen
A2030
120
Broom Channel
Whitcombe Av
Kilcot Road
Doctors Surgery
Locarno Rd
Aylen Road
Blueprint
Portfield Rd
Dundas Cl
Dundas Lane
Bilton Wy
Road
Solent Way
5
Monckton Road
Dartmouth Road
Vernon Road
Ninian Pk Rd
Glenthorne Rd
Dundas Spur
Dundas Spur
Dundas Sp
PO3
O Jays Industrial Park
Claybank Sp
Kiln Rd
Victory Trading Est
Dundas La
Admiral Lord Nelson School
Copnor
Burrfields Road
Tokio Rd
Mayhall Rd
Highgate Rd
PO
Seafield Rd
Copnor Infant School
Salcombe Avenue
Redcar Av
Moneyfield Av
Burrfields Road
Burrfields Retail Park
Hotel
EASTERN RD
6
Kendal Av
Keswick Av
Coniston Av
Collis Rd
Manor Pk Av
Station Road
Martin Rd
Paignton Av
Sidmouth Av
Seaton Avenue
Teignmouth Rd
Portsea Island
A2030
Solent Way
7
Folkestone Road
Chesterfield Road
Cobden Av
Tynton Grove
Ripley Grove
Idsworth Rd
Westover Road
Northover Rd
Primary School
Highgrove Rd
Stanley Avenue
Algiers Rd
Cooper Rd
Colebrook Av
Tangier Road
135
Dover Rd
St Piran's Av
Chaseway Av
Whitecliffe Av
Chilcote Rd
Neville Rd
F
G
Baffins
H
J
K
Sword Sands Rd
A2030
Ru

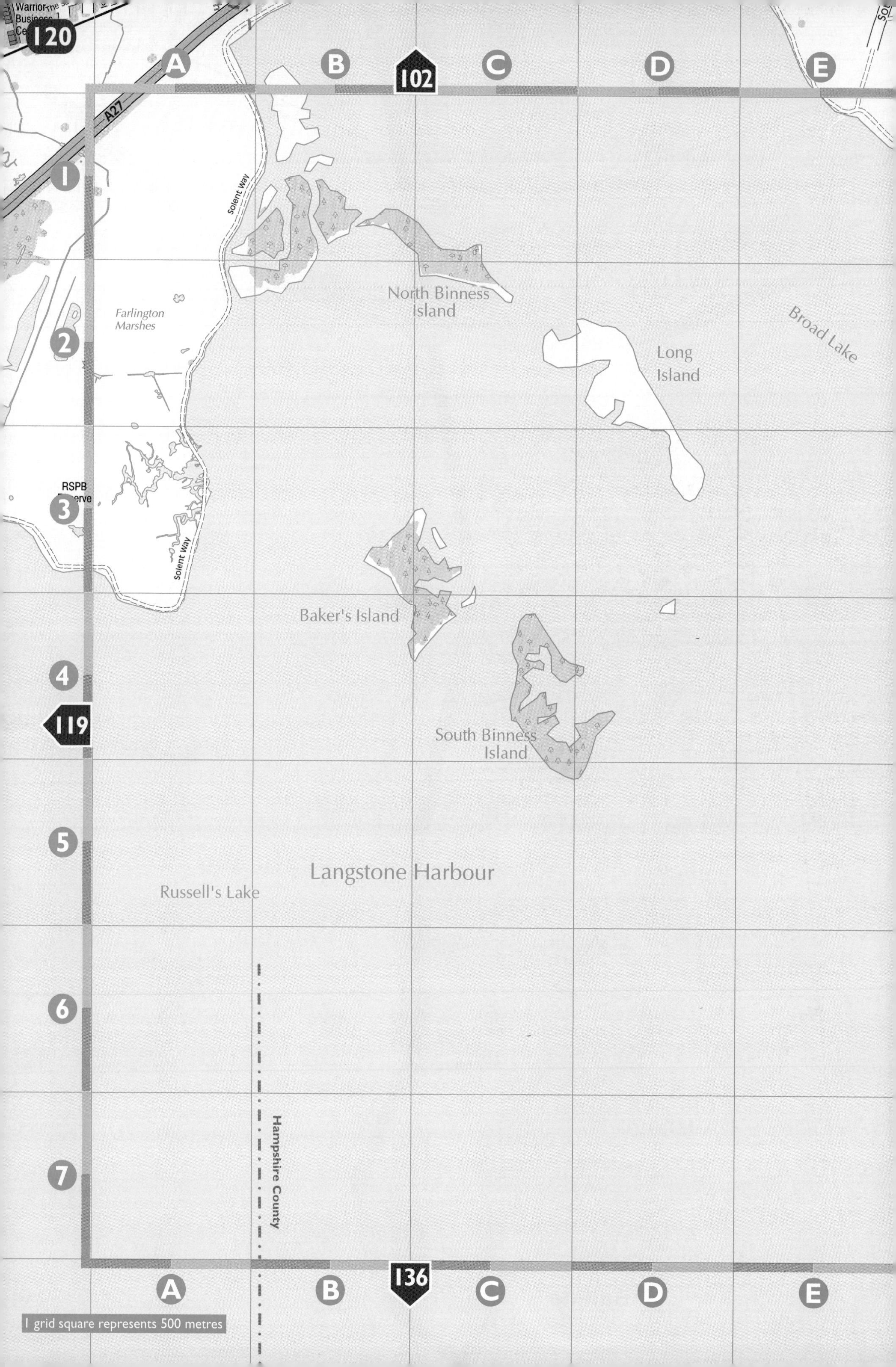
120
A
B
102
C
D
E
A27
1
Solent Way
Farlington Marshes
North Binness Island
Broad Lake
Long Island
2
RSPB
3
Solent Way
Baker's Island
4
119
South Binness Island
5
Langstone Harbour
Russell's Lake
6
7
Hampshire County
A
B
136
C
D
E
1 grid square represents 500 metres

F
G
H
J
K
103
137
122
1
2
3
4
5
6
7
Langstone
LANGSTONE ROAD
Langstone
Mill
Lane
Harbourside
Langstone High
PH
St
Gdns
Tower
The Saltings
Solent Way
Conigar
Point
Swear
Dee
A3023
Langstone Bridge
Northney Road
Hotel
Spinnaker Grange
Northney La
Northney
Northney Road
St Peter's Rd
Clovelly Rd
Pycroft Close
Church Lane
North
St Peter's Av
St Peter's Road
New Cut
Island Cl
Kingsway
Queensway
Avenue Road
HAVANT ROAD
Meadow Cl
Rogers Md
Victoria Road
Mill Close
HAYLING ISLAND
Stoke
Croft Lane
Northwood Lane
Castlemans Lane
Chichester Road
Tye
Gutner Lane
Woodgason Lane
West Lane
PO
Copse Lane
Fleet
Yew Tree Rd
Daw Lane
HAVANT ROAD

1 grid square represents 500 metres

F
G
H
105
J
Cot La
Path
Lane
I
2
3
4
5
6
7
Chidham Point
Printsted Point
Sussex Border Path
PH
Marsh Lane
Marsh La
Stanbury Point
Thorney Island
New Barn
West Thorney
Thorney Island Airfield
Smith Lane
Thorney Old Pk
Church Road
Vulcan Road
Victor Rd
Varsity Road
Valiant Road
Pleasant Lane
Valetta Road
Thorney Channel
139
K
Sussex Border

106
A
B
C
D
E
1
2
3
4
5
6
7
Hatchet Moor
Beaulieu Heath
Greenmoor
B3054
Crockford Bridge
Crockford Stream
Pilley
Wooden House La
Pilley St
Pilley Bailey
Norley Inclosure
Holly Lane
Jordans
Lane
Bull Hill
Bull Hill
PO
Lucky La
Norleywood Road
Norley Farm
Norleyw
Thatchers La
Joys
on Farm
1 grid square represents 500 metres

B3054
F
G
H
107
J
Hatchet Pond
Masseys La
East Boldre Road
Heath La
Whithers La
Pages Lane
Gaza Av
Matthews Lane
Sweyns Lease
PO
Chapel Lane
Wallace La
Warton Cl
B3054
HATCHET LANE
Swinesleys Farm
Beufre Farm
Lodge Lane
Knights Copse
New Inn La
Cripple Gate Lane
Church La
East Boldre
1
2
3
4
126
Newhouse Copse
5
Newlands
6
Horsemoor Copse
Newlands Plantation
7
F
G
H
J
K
Main Road
St Leonards Road
Beck Farm
ood

B3054
108
Dock Lane
Spearbed Copse
Solent Way
Keeping Copse
Beaulieu River
Beufre Farm
Lane
Lodge
Keeping
Bucklers Hard
Ashen Wood
PH
Hotel
Little Purnel
125
Lodge Farm
Tylers Copse
Clobb
Salt
Drokes
Coopers Wood
St Leonards Grange
Gins
Bergerie
Solent Way
1 grid square represents 500 metres

F
G
H
109
J
Summer Lane
Steerleys Copse
Dark Water
1
Yard Wood
2
Main Drive
Summer Lane
Gilbury Hard
3
Exbury House
Exbury
4
128
Salternshill Copse
Haxland Pits
5
Lower Exbury
6
Gins
Lane
Beaulieu River
7
Gins House
F
G
H
J
K
Needs

1 grid square represents 500 metres

Sprat's Down
Stanswood Road
Tristan Close
Calshot Cl
Castle Lane
B3053
Hillhead
Eaglehurst
Stanswood Road
Stanswood Farm
Nelson's Place
Stanswood Bay
Stanswood Road
Cadland House
Stansore Point
F
G
H
J
K
1
2
3
4
5
6
7

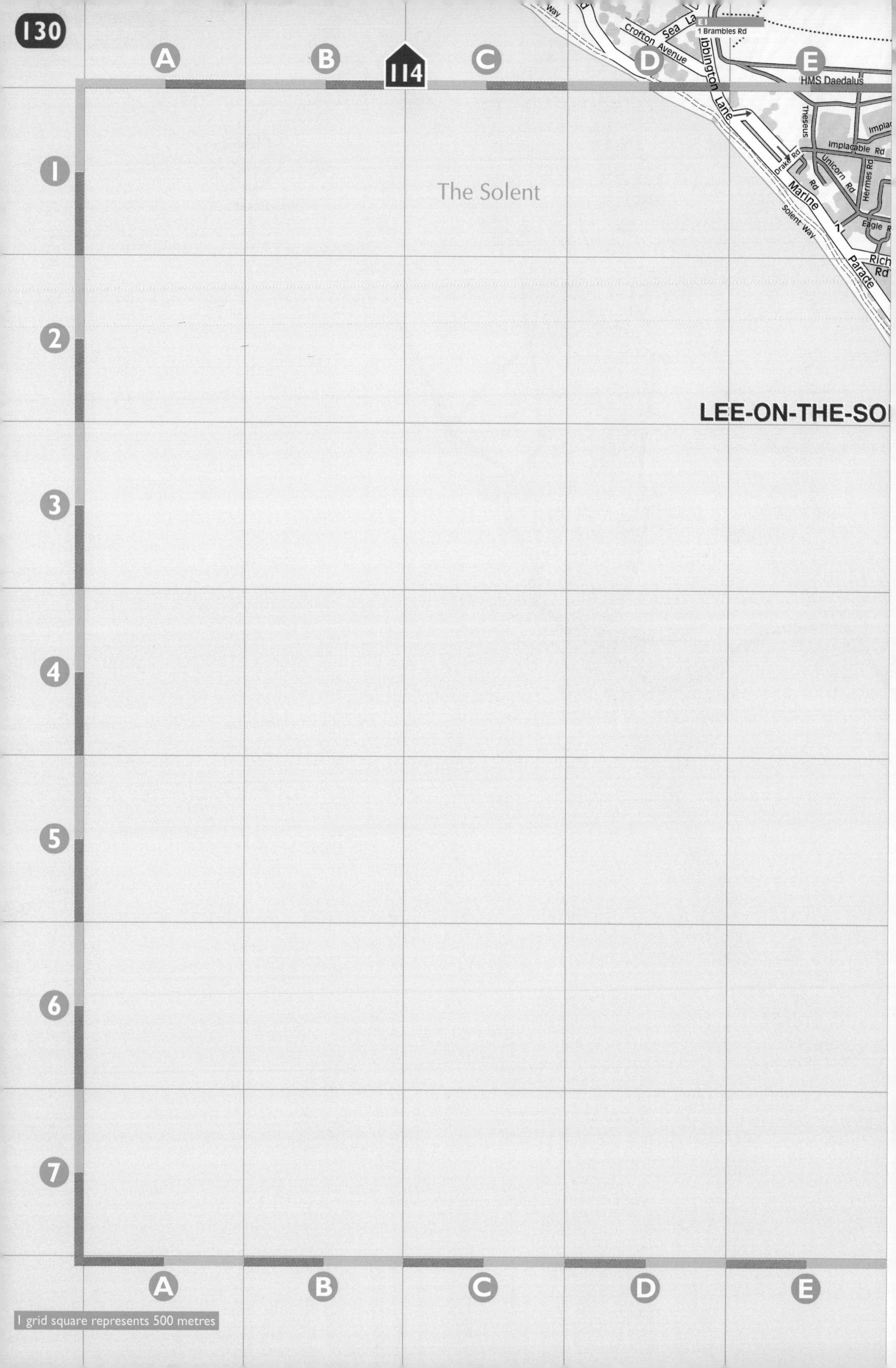
114
A
B
C
D
E
1
2
3
4
5
6
7
The Solent
Crofton Avenue
Sea La
E1
1 Brambles Rd
Lane
HMS Daedalus
Theseus
Implacable Rd
Drake Rd
Unicorn Rd
Hermes Rd
Rd
Marine Parade
Solent Way
Way
Eagle
Rd
LEE-ON-THE-SO
1 grid square represents 500 metres

F1
1 Inverkip Cl
2 Nottingham Pl
3 Southcliff
F2
1 Olave Cl
2 Osborne Rd
3 Queens Cl
115
132
Rowner
Franklin Rd
Grange County Junior & Infant School
Owen Close
Highwood Road
St Nicholas Av
Broomfield Crs
Biddlecombe Cl
Grange Lane
Sandhill Lane
Chark La
Argus Road
Ark Royal Crs
Manor
Norwich Place
Vengeance Rd
King's Road
Newton Pl
St Annes School
Court Road
Victoria
Milvil Road
Swanage Road
Britten Rd
Grove Road
B3385 MANOR WAY
BROOM WAY
Eastcliff Cl
Westcliff Cl
Court Barn Lane
Ross Way
Fieldhouse Dr
Falklands Close
Blackbird Way
Fell Drive
Goldfinch La
Cheltenham Crescent
Leamington Crescent
Smeeton Rd
Cornfield Rd
Wheatcroft Road
Russell Close
Petrie Road
Studland Road
Clanwilliam Road
Lulworth Rd
Russell Road
Derwent Rd
Compton Close
Francis Close
Sea Crest Rd
Skipper Way
Spencer Drive
Cherry Cl
Elmore Close
Elmore Road
Avon Close
Lee-on-the-Solent Infant School
Junior School
Rowan Close
Elmore Avenue
Gosport Road
Seymour Rd
Cross Rd
Anglesea Rd
Wootton Road
Raynes Rd
Portsmouth Road
Queens Rd
Lakeside
South Pl
Clifton Rd
Ryde Place
Montserrat Road
West
Lee-on-the-Solent Health Cen.
PIER ST
High Street
Beach Rd
Marine Parade East
MILVIL RD B3333
Solent Way
Hotel
Hollybank
Salisbury Terrace
Cambridge Road
MARINE PDE EAST
LENT
Pennine Way
Warwick Close
Lancaster Close
York Crs
Chester Crs
Canterbury Close
PORTSMOUTH ROAD B3333
PRIVETT ROAD
Browndown
Browndown Point
The Solent
River Alver
Woodlands Close
Frobisher Close
Rodney Close
Howe Rd
Oakthorn Cl
Rambler Dr
Raven Close
Griffin Wk
Stares Cl
Paffard Close
Ayling Close
Dampier Close
Lanyard Dr
Marlin Cl
Nimrod Dr
Infant School
Howe
Anson Cl
Little Woodham
Browndown Road
G1
1 Chaffinch Wy
2 Common Barn La
3 Empson Wk
4 Kenilworth Cl
5 Magpie La
6 Martin Cl
7 Sparrow Ct
8 Swallow Ct
9 Swift Cl
G2
1 Chilcomb Cl
2 Esmonde Cl
3 Gibson Cl
4 Harrier Cl
5 Headley Cl
6 Kimpton Cl
7 Osprey Gdns
8 Trent Wy
9 Waveney Cl
G3
1 Cheyne Wy
2 Maple Cl
H3
1 Larch Cl
H4
1 The Seagulls
K1
1 Connigar Cl
K2
1 Davenport Cl
2 Hudson Cl
F G H J K
1 2 3 4 5 6 7

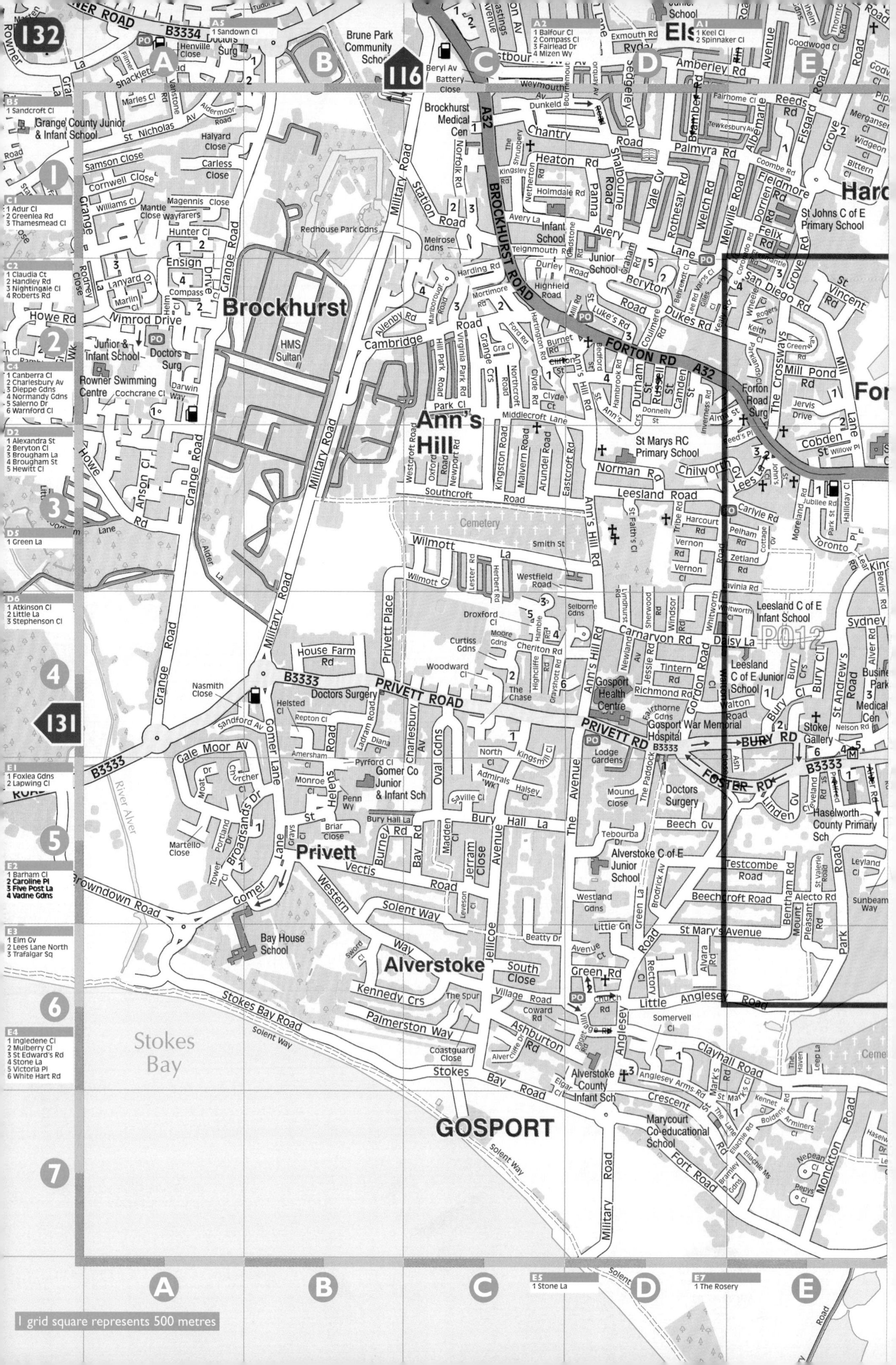
A5
1 Sandown Cl
A2
1 Balfour Cl
2 Compass Cl
3 Fairlead Dr
4 Mizen Wy
A1
1 Keel Cl
2 Spinnaker Cl
B5
1 Sandcroft Cl
C1
1 Adur Cl
2 Greenlea Rd
3 Thamesmead Cl
C2
1 Claudia Ct
2 Handley Rd
3 Nightingale Cl
4 Roberts Rd
C4
1 Canberra Cl
2 Charlesbury Av
3 Dieppe Gdns
4 Normandy Gdns
5 Salerno Dr
6 Warnford Cl
D2
1 Alexandra St
2 Beryton Cl
3 Brougham La
4 Brougham St
5 Hewitt Cl
D5
1 Green La
D6
1 Atkinson Cl
2 Little La
3 Stephenson Cl
E1
1 Foxlea Gdns
2 Lapwing Cl
E2
1 Barham Cl
2 Caroline Pl
3 Five Post La
4 Vadne Gdns
E3
1 Elm Gv
2 Lees Lane North
3 Trafalgar Sq
E4
1 Ingledene Cl
2 Mulberry Cl
3 St Edward's Rd
4 Stone La
5 Victoria Pl
6 White Hart Rd
E5
1 Stone La
E7
1 The Rosery
116
131
A
B
C
D
E
1
2
3
4
5
6
7
Brockhurst
Ann's Hill
Privett
Alverstoke
GOSPORT
Stokes Bay
Brune Park Community School
Grange County Junior & Infant School
Brockhurst Medical Cen
HMS Sultan
Redhouse Park Gdns
Rowner Swimming Centre
Junior & Infant School
Doctors Surg
Infant School
Junior School
St Marys RC Primary School
St Johns C of E Primary School
Forton Road Surg
Cemetery
Leesland C of E Infant School
Leesland C of E Junior School
Gosport Health Centre
Gosport War Memorial Hospital
Doctors Surgery
Gomer Co Junior & Infant Sch
Haselworth County Primary Sch
Alverstoke C of E Junior School
Bay House School
Alverstoke County Infant Sch
Marycourt Co-educational School
Stoke Gallery
Lodge Gardens
A32
B3333
B3334
BROCKHURST ROAD
FORTON RD
PRIVETT ROAD
PRIVETT RD
BURY RD
FOSTER RD
Military Road
Grange Road
Station Road
Brockhurst Medical Cen
Cambridge Road
Southcroft Road
Leesland Road
Norman Rd
Carnarvon Rd
Ann's Hill Rd
The Avenue
Bury Hall La
Vectis Road
Solent Way
Stokes Bay Road
Palmerston Way
Kennedy Crs
Village Road
Little Anglesey Road
Anglesey Arms Rd
Clayhall Road
Crescent Rd
Fort Road
Gomer Lane
Browndown Road
River Alver
P012
1 grid square represents 500 metres

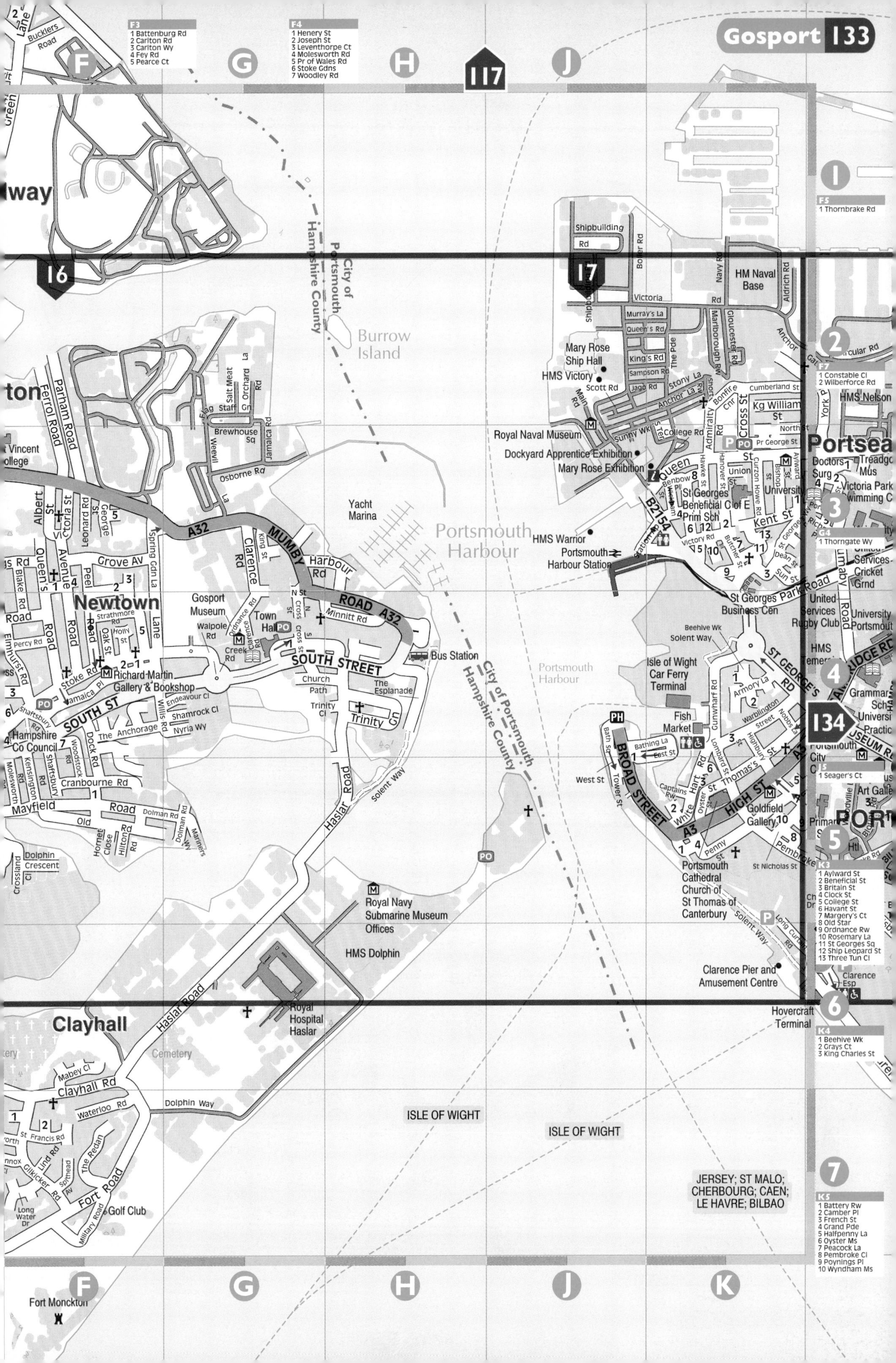
117
16
17
134
F3
1 Battenburg Rd
2 Carlton Rd
3 Carlton Wy
4 Fey Rd
5 Pearce Ct
F4
1 Henery St
2 Joseph St
3 Leventhorpe Ct
4 Molesworth Rd
5 Pr of Wales Rd
6 Stoke Gdns
7 Woodley Rd
F5
1 Thornbrake Rd
F7
1 Constable Cl
2 Wilberforce Rd
G4
1 Thorngate Wy
J5
1 Seager's Ct
K3
1 Aylward St
2 Beneficial St
3 Britain St
4 Clock St
5 College St
6 Havant St
7 Margery's Ct
8 Old Star
9 Ordnance Rw
10 Rosemary La
11 St Georges Sq
12 Ship Leopard St
13 Three Tun Cl
K4
1 Beehive Wk
2 Grays Ct
3 King Charles St
K5
1 Battery Rw
2 Camber Pl
3 French St
4 Grand Pde
5 Halfpenny La
6 Oyster Ms
7 Peacock La
8 Pembroke Cl
9 Poynings Pl
10 Wyndham Ms
Bucklers Road
City of Portsmouth
Hampshire County
Burrow Island
Portsmouth Harbour
Yacht Marina
Newtown
Parham Road
Ferrol Road
Salt Meat
Orchard La
Flag Staff Gn
Brewhouse Sq
Weevil La
Jamaica Rd
Osborne Rd
A32
MUMBY ROAD A32
Harbour Rd
Clarence Rd
King St
Albert St
Victoria St
Leonard Rd
George St
Spring Gdn La
Grove Av
Queen's Rd
Avenue Road
Peel Rd
Blake Rd
Newtown Lane
Gosport Museum
Walpole Rd
Ordnance Rd
Town Hall
Minnitt Rd
N St
Cross St
SOUTH STREET
Bus Station
Richard Martin Gallery & Bookshop
Strathmore Rd
Holly St
Oak St
Percy Rd
Elmhurst Rd
Stoke Rd
Jamaica Pl
SOUTH ST
Endeavour Cl
Shamrock Cl
Nyria Wy
The Anchorage
Willis Rd
Church Path
Trinity Cl
Trinity Gn
The Esplanade
Hampshire Co Council
Shaftsbury Rd
Dock Rd
Woodstock Rd
Kensington Rd
Molesworth Rd
Cranbourne Rd
Mayfield Road
Old Road
Dolman Rd
Hornet Close
Hilton Rd
Mariners Wy
Dolphin Crescent
Crossland Cl
Haslar Road
Solent Way
Royal Navy Submarine Museum Offices
HMS Dolphin
Royal Hospital Haslar
Clayhall
Cemetery
Mabey Cl
Clayhall Rd
Dolphin Way
Waterloo Rd
St Francis Rd
The Redan
Lind Rd
Gilkicker Rd
Spithead Av
Long Water Dr
Fort Road
Military Road
Golf Club
Fort Monckton
ISLE OF WIGHT
Portsmouth Harbour
Shipbuilding Rd
Boiler Rd
Navy Rd
Aldrich Rd
HM Naval Base
Victoria Rd
Murray's La
Queen's Rd
King's Rd
Sampson Rd
Jago Rd
The Pde
Marlborough Rw
Gloucester Rd
Mary Rose Ship Hall
HMS Victory
Scott Rd
Main Rd
Stony La
Anchor La
Cumberland St
Kg William St
HMS Nelson
North St
Pr George St
Royal Naval Museum
Dockyard Apprentice Exhibition
Mary Rose Exhibition
Sunny Wk
College Rd
Admiralty Rd
Cross St
Queen St
Union St
St Georges Beneficial C of E Prim Sch
B2154
Kent St
HMS Warrior
Portsmouth Harbour Station
Victoria Rd
Butcher St
Dean St
Sun St
St Georges Park Road
St Georges Business Cen
Beehive Wk
Solent Way
ST GEORGE'S RD
Isle of Wight Car Ferry Terminal
Armory La
Warblington Street
Gunwharf Rd
Fish Market
Bathing La
East St
Bath Sq
Tower St
West St
BROAD STREET
Captains Rw
Hart Rd
Lombard St
St Thomas's St
Highbury St
HIGH ST
A3
Goldfield Gallery
Penny St
White Hart Rd
Oyster St
Portsmouth Cathedral Church of St Thomas of Canterbury
St Nicholas St
Pembroke Rd
Long Curtain Rd
Clarence Pier and Amusement Centre
Hovercraft Terminal
Clarence Esp
JERSEY; ST MALO; CHERBOURG; CAEN; LE HAVRE; BILBAO
Portsea
Doctors Surg
Mus
Victoria Park
University
United Services Cricket Grnd
United Services Rugby Club
University Portsmouth
HMS Temeraire
Grammar Sch
Portsmouth City C
Art Galle
Primary S
Htl
Circular Rd
York Pl
F
G
H
J
K
I
2
3
4
5
6
7

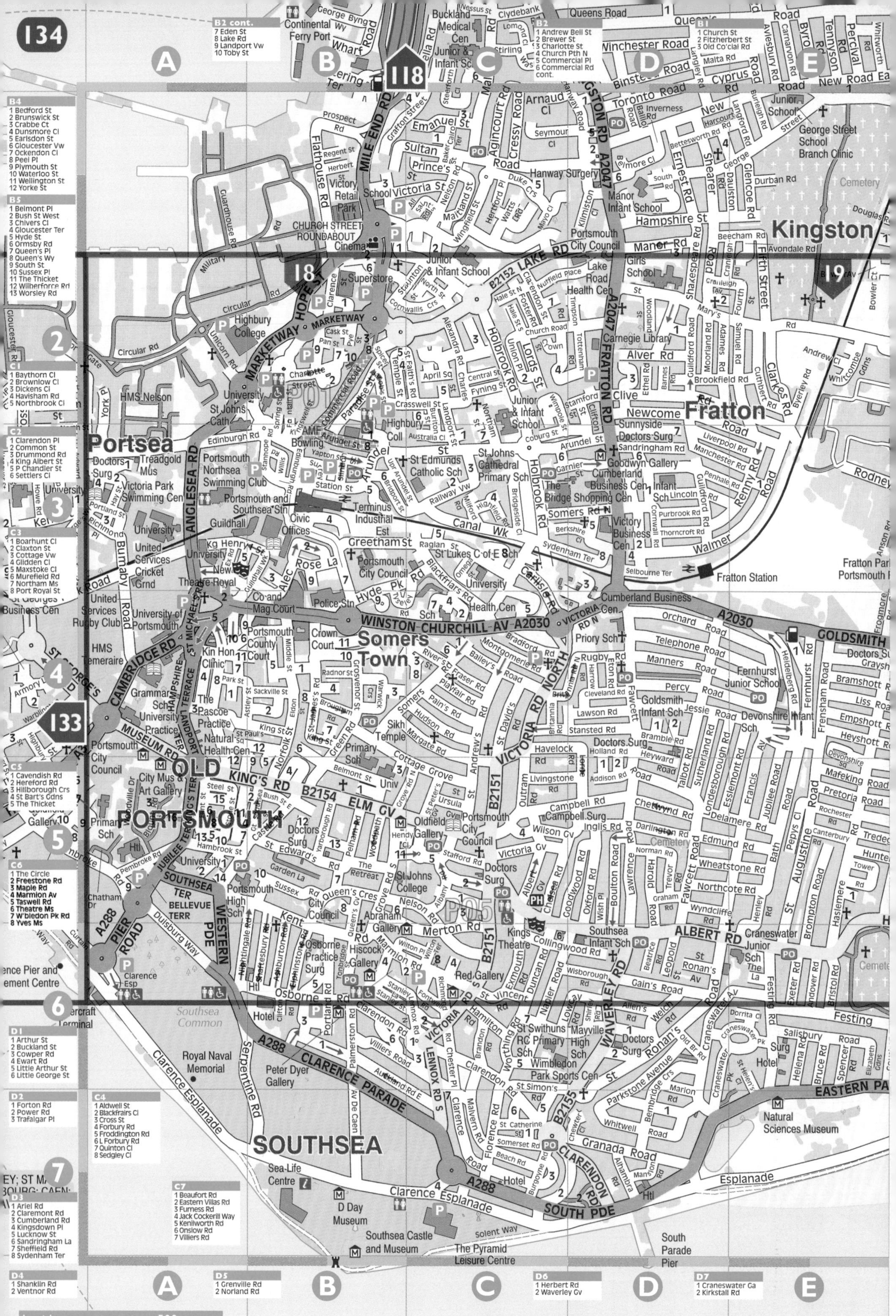

1 grid square represents 500 metres

A3
1 Beck St
2 Lion St
3 Purbeck St
4 St James's St
5 Spring Gdns

A4
1 Colpoy St
2 King Richard 1 Rd
3 Landport St
4 Landsdowne St
5 Lord Monty Wy
6 Melbourne Pl
7 Meriden Rd
8 St Paul's Rd
9 St Vincent St
10 Waltham St
11 Wiltshire St

B3
1 Buckingham St
2 C Dickens St
3 D Dymond St
4 D Drummond St
5 Durham St
6 E Surrey St
7 I Brunel Rd
8 Lwr Church Pth
9 The M Rose St

A5
1 Cecil Gv
2 Cecil Pl
3 Chadderton Gdns
4 Chapel St
5 Copper St
6 Diamond St
7 Elm St
8 Cold St
9 Gordon Rd
10 Lt Hambrook St
11 Lt Southsea St
12 Meadow St
13 Nickel St
14 Regent Pl
15 Silver St
16 Slingsby St

B6
1 Auckland Rd W
2 Lennox Rd N
3 Netley Rd
4 Netley Ter
5 Richmond Pl
6 Serpentine Rd
7 The Vale

F1
1 Dudley Rd

F4
1 Carisbrooke Rd

F5
1 Blenheim Ct
2 Carpenter Cl
3 Pedam Cl

F6
1 Nettlestone Rd
2 Worsley St

G3
1 Blendworth Rd
2 Chevening Ct
3 Oxted Ct
4 Plover Reach

G4
1 Hester Rd
2 Melrose Cl
3 Milton Park Av
4 Old Canal

G5
1 Billing Cl
2 Tranmere Rd

G6
1 Drysdale Ms
2 Eastney St
3 Mountbatten Sq
4 Pitcairn Ms
5 Saunders Ms

H2
1 Godwit Rd
2 Revenge Cl
3 Seagull Cl

H3
1 Brasted Ct
2 Longfield Cl
3 Redwing Ct
4 Wayfarer Cl

H4
1 Towpath Mead

H5
1 Eastney Farm Rd

J3
1 Sovereign Dr

E1
1 Victor Rd

E4
1 Chestnut Av

E5
1 White Cloud Pk

1 grid square represents 500 metres

F4
1 Aubrey Cl
2 Grayland Cl
3 Lexden Gdns
4 Newtown La
5 Spinnaker Cl
G5
1 Walnut Tree Cl
Fleet
Daw
Yew Tree Rd
HAVANT ROAD
121
H5
1 Spencer Cl
2 Willow Wood Rd
H6
1 The Sanderlings
J5
1 Whitethorn Rd
J6
1 Pebble Cl
2 Sunshine Av
K6
1 Chandlers Cl
138
A3023
Mill Rythe La
PO11
Manor Ho
Lane
Rest-A-Wyle Av
Pound Lea
Kings Road
Road
Woodlands La
Dennhill Cl
Brights La
Higworth La
Saltmarsh La
West
Dover Court
Lulworth Cl
Wardens Cl
ROAD
Glebe Cl
Atherley Road
Katrina Gdns
Dundonald Cl
Eastwood Cl
Ithica Cl
Burwood Grove
Charleston Cl
Mead
Gilbert
Sycamore Dr
Church
Tournerbury Lane
Poplar Grove
Beech Grove
Laburnum Grove
Dances Wy
West Lane
Legion Rd
Hawthorne Gv
MANOR
Aubrey Cl
Hamfield Drive
Fathoms Reach
St Mary's Road
Mengham Infant School
Station Road
Southleigh Gv
Palmerston Rd
Mengham Junior School
James Cl
Cherrywood Gdns
Gv
St Leonard's Avenue
Fir Tree Rd
Linden Gv
St Margarets Rd
Goldring Cl
My Lords La
Teal Cl
St Mary's Road
West Town
Garden Cl
South Road
Elwell Gn
Brairwood Gdns
Oakwood Rd
Ashwood Cl
Elm Gv
Hayling Island Health Centre
Fernhurst Close
Bathurst Cl
BEACH ROAD
Lane
Stamford Av
Winston Cl
Magdala Rd
Green Lane
Hollow Lane
Old Timbers
Westfield Avenue
Victoria Av
Alexandra Avenue
Tudor Cl
Elm Cl
Mengham Rd
Selsmore Road
Mengham La
Mengham
Stead Close
Osprey Dr
Mengham
Simmons Gn
Salterns Cl
Salterns Lane
Seaview
Astra Dr
Burdale Dr
Sea Front
St Johns
Solent Dr
Ramsey Rd
Lyndhurst Cl
Chichester Avenue
Sea Grove Av
Webb Lane
Mengham Avenue
Bound Lane
North Crs
Rails Lane
Blackthorn Dr
Blackthorn Rd
Ilex Walk
Kingfisher Cl
Selsmore Avenue
Beach Rd
Sea Front
Manor Wy
Grand Pde
Orchard Rd
Norman Rd
Silversands Gdns
Fishery Lane
Webb Cl
Wyborn Cl
St Andrew's Road
Harold Road
Foreland Ct
Marshall Rd
Westfield
Old School Dr
St Hermans Rd
Eastoke
SOUTH HAYLING
Sea Front
Old School Dr
Sea Front
Southwood Road
The Glade
Culver Dr
Bembridge Drive
Meath Cl
The Strand
West
Hayling Bay
F
G
H
J
K
1
2
3
4
5
6
7

1 grid square represents 500 metres

F
G
H
123
J
I
2
3
4
5
6
7
K
Sussex Border Path
Longmere Point
Pilsey Island
Chichester Harbour
East Head
Rookwood Lane
Rookwood Lane
Rookwood Road
ROOKWOOD RD
Ellanore Lane
Summerfield Rd
Summerfield Road
PO
Elmstead Park Road
Cunliffe Close
Locksash Cl
Elmstead Gdns
Elmstead Pk Rd
Meadow La
Elms Wy
Elms Lane
Roman Landing
Roman Landing
Roman Landing
Roman Landing
B2179
Pound Rd
West Wittering Parochial School
Coastguard Lane
The Wad
Royce Close
Royce Way
Elms Ride
Elms Ride
Middlefield
The Byeway
Seaward Dr
Wellsfield
West Witteri
West Strand
Berrybarn Lane
CAKEHAM

Abbotswood 29 F6
Abbots Worthy 22 C1
Abshot 95 F6
Aldermoor 54 B1
Allbrook 38 D4
Alverstoke 132 B6
Ampfield 30 D6
Anchorage Park 119 H4
Anmore 81 G1
Ann's Hill 132 C3
Anthill Common 62 C6
Applemore 90 B2
Ashfield 35 G6
Ashlett 111 F4
Ashurst 68 B3
Ashurst Bridge 52 B7
Avington 23 K2
Baffins 135 G1
Bank 86 A3
Bar End 3 H8
Barrow Hill 51 G2
Bartley 50 D5
Bassett 43 H6
Bassett Green 43 H6
Beaulieu 107 K6
Bedhampton 102 D5
Bishopstoke 45 F1
Bishop's Waltham 48 C2
Bitterne 6 F5
Bitterne Park 56 A3
Blackfield 110 D7
Blendworth 64 E5
Boarhunt 98 E1
Boorley Green 58 D2
Botley 59 G6
Boyatt Wood 38 C5
Braishfield 29 H2
Brambridge 39 G2
Breach 105 G5
Bridgemary 115 J4
Broadgate 31 F7
Broadoak 58 D5
Brockhampton 14 A7
Brockhurst 132 A2
Brooke's Hill 40 A7
Brown Heath 47 H6
Bucket Corner 36 D3
Bucklers Hard 126 D3
Bull Hill 124 A7
Bunker's Hill 50 D2
Bunstead 31 K3
Burridge 75 G4
Bursledon 73 K5
Butlocks Heath 73 G6
Buttsash 91 J6
Cadnam 50 C4
Calmore 52 B3
Calshot 111 J7
Catherington 64 B3
Catisfield 96 B5
Causeway 64 C7
Chandler's Ford 38 A2
Chilcomb 26 E3
Chilworth 42 E2
Chilworth Old Village 42 D1
Clayhall 133 F6
Clayhill 86 D3
Colbury 68 C3
Colden Common 39 K1
Compton 33 G2
Compton End 25 F7
Copnor 119 F6
Copythorne 51 F2
Cosham 101 F6
Cowplain 82 A2
Coxford 54 B2
Crampmoor 35 K1
Crockerhill 77 H6
Cupernham 35 F1
Curbridge 75 J1
Curdridge 59 K4
Custards 86 D1
Dean 20 B4
Denmead 62 E7
Denvilles 15 L2
Dibden 90 E1
Dibden Purlieu 90 D5
Drayton 101 H6
Dundridge 49 J2
Durley 47 G5
Durley Street 47 H3
Durrants 03 J5
East Boldre 125 J3
Eastland Gate 63 J7
Eastleigh 38 E7
Eastney 135 H5
Easton 23 F2
Eling 53 G7
Elson 116 D7
Emery Down 66 A7
Emsworth 104 B7
Exbury 127 J3
Fair Oak 46 B1
Fareham 12 F5
Farlington 101 J6
Fawley 110 E5
Fleet 121 G7
Fleetend 94 E5
Fleetlands 115 K2
Flexford 37 G2
Forest Gate 62 C5
Forton 16 A2
Foxhills 68 C2
Foyers 67 F2
Fratton 19 G2
Freemantle 54 D6
Frostlane 91 K4
Fryern Hill 38 A4
Fulflood 21 G7
Funtley 97 F1
Furzeley Corner 80 E4
Furzey Lodge 107 G6
Glebe 60 D1
Goldenhayes 66 E1
Goose Green 86 D2
Gosport 30 B7
Gosport 16 D4
Halterworth 35 H3
Hambledon 62 B2
Hamble-le-Rice 93 J3
Hambrook 105 K4
Hampton Park 55 K1
Hardley 109 K1
Hardway 132 E1
Harefield 7 M4
Harestock 21 F4
Hatch Bottom 57 G2
Hatchet Gate 107 G7
Havant 14 E1
Hayling Island 121 H5
Headbourne Worthy 21 J2
Heathfield 96 D5
Hedge End 58 A5
Hermitage 104 D5
Hides Close 108 A3
Highbridge 39 G3
Highbury 118 E1
Highfield 55 H2
Hightown 73 H1
Hill Head 114 A6
Hill Park 12 A1
Hillpound 49 K7
Hillstreet 40 A6
Hill Top 108 D3
Hillyfields 41 H7
Hilsea 118 E3
Hiltingbury 32 A7
Hocombe 31 K6
Hoe 49 G4
Holbury 109 K4
Hook 94 D7
Hook Park 112 C1
Horndean 64 D6
Horton Heath 46 C4
Hound 73 H7
Hounsdown 68 D1
Hursley 31 J2
Hyde 2 F2
Hythe 91 J2
Itchen 10 D2
Itchen Abbas 23 K1
Kingsmead 61 K4
Kingston 134 E1
Kings Worthy 22 B1
Knapp 30 E5
Ladwell 31 J5
Langdown 91 J3
Langley 128 A1
Langstone 121 F1
Lee 41 F3
Lee Ground 96 B1
Lee-on-the-Solent 130 D2
Leigh Park 102 E2
Lepe 128 D6
Little Holbury 109 J2
Little Posbrook 113 K2
Littleton 20 E2
Locks Heath 95 G2
Long Common 58 E3
Lord's Hill 42 B7
Lordswood 42 E7
Lovedean 63 K6
Lower Slackstead 30 A2
Lower Swanwick 74 B5
Lowford 73 K4
Lumley 104 D5
Lyndhurst 86 B1
Marchwood 69 K3
Martyr Worthy 23 G1
Maybush 53 K2
Mead End 81 F2
Meon 113 K4
Merry Oak 6 D9
Midanbury 6 E2
Millbrook 53 K5
Milton 135 H4
Moorcourt 40 B4
Moorgreen 57 J1
Netley 72 E7
Netley Hill 73 K1
Netley Marsh 51 K6
New Brighton 104 D3
New Town 11 H7
Newbridge 50 B1
Newtown 48 A3
Newtown 94 C7
No Man's Land 22 E7
Nob's Crook 39 K3
North Baddesley 36 B6
North Boarhunt 78 D3
North End 118 E5
North Hayling 121 J4
North Stoneham 44 A4
Northam 5 K7
Northbrook 48 D2
Northfields 33 K2
Northney 121 K3
Nursling 41 H6
Nutbourne 105 J7
Nutburn 36 C5
Ocean Village 9 K5
Old Netley 73 H4
Old Portsmouth 17 L5
Old Shirley 54 B3
Oliver's Battery 24 D5
Otterbourne 32 E5
Otterwood 108 E7
Park Gate 95 G1
Paulsgrove 99 K6
Peartree Green 10 B1
Peel Common 115 G5
Pikeshill 66 B7
Pilley 124 A6
Pitt 24 D3
Pooksgreen 69 J3
Portchester 98 E6
Portsea 18 A3
Portsea Island 119 G7
Portsmouth 19 J4
Portswood 55 J3
Prinsted 105 F7
Privett 132 B5
Pucknall 30 A3
Purbrook 101 J1
Ratlake 31 F6
Red Hill 83 J4
Redbridge 53 H4
Ridge 40 B2
Romsey 34 D3
Row Ash 60 B4
Rowland's Castle 83 K3
Rowner 115 K7
Rownhams 42 A4
Rushington 52 E6
Rushmore 62 D2
St Cross 25 J3
St Denys 5 M3
St Giles's Hill 3 H5
Sarisbury 94 D1
Shawford 33 H2
Shedfield 60 E5
Shirley 4 A4
Shirley Warren 54 C2
Shirrell Heath 61 H3
Sholing 11 J2
Sholing Common 7 H9
Shorn Hill 51 K1
Silkstead 32 B4
Sleepers Hill 25 G2
Soake 81 G2
Southampton 8 F5
Southbourne 105 H6
South Down 33 G4
South Hayling 137 F6
Southwick 79 H7
Stamshaw 118 A6
Stanmore 25 G3
Stockheath 103 F3
Stoke 121 H6
Stoke Common 39 F5
Stonehills 111 F5
Stubbermere 84 D5
Stubbington 114 E4
Swanmore 49 J6
Swanwick 75 F6
Swaythling 56 B1
Tapnage 76 D4
Testwood 52 D2
Thorney Island 123 F4
Thornhill 57 H7
Thornhill Park 57 G5
Timsbury 20 D2
Tipner 118 A4
Titchfield 95 K6
Titchfield Common 95 F5
Titchfield Park 95 J3
Toothill 41 K2
Totton 53 F4
Townhill Park 56 C2
Trotts 69 H2
Turkey Island 61 G5
Twyford 33 K3
Tye 121 K6
Upper Shirley 54 E2
Upper Swanmore 49 K3
Upton 41 J4
Wallington 13 M4
Waltham Chase 61 F1
Walton Heath 79 F6
Warblington 15 L6
Warsash 94 C5
Waterlooville 82 A5
Wecock 81 K1
Weeke 21 G5
West Common 128 B2
West End 57 H4
West End 12 E8
West Leigh 103 H1
West Thorney 123 G5
Westbourne 104 E2
Weston 10 E9
Whitenap 35 H3
Wickham 77 H2
Widley 101 H4
Wildern 58 B5
Wimpson 53 K3
Winchester 2 E6
Winnall 3 J3
Winsor 51 G3
Wintershill 47 J2
Wittensford 50 A4
Woodcot 115 H4
Woodlands 67 H2
Woodley 35 H1
Woodmancote 105 J2
Woolston 10 B6
Wymering 100 D6

USING THE STREET INDEX

Street names are listed alphabetically. Each street name is followed by its postal town or area locality, the Postcode District, the page number, and the reference to the square in which the name is found.

Example: **Abbey Cl** *FAWY* SO45 .... **91** H3 1

Some entries are followed by a number in a blue box. This number indicates the location of the street within the referenced grid square. The full street name is listed at the side of the map page.

GENERAL ABBREVIATIONS

ACC ACCESS
ALY ALLEY
AP APPROACH
AR ARCADE
ASS ASSOCIATION
AV AVENUE
BCH BEACH
BLDS BUILDINGS
BND BEND
BNK BANK
BR BRIDGE
BRK BROOK
BTM BOTTOM
BUS BUSINESS
BVD BOULEVARD
BY BYPASS
CATH CATHEDRAL
CEM CEMETERY
CEN CENTRE
CFT CROFT
CH CHURCH
CHA CHASE
CHYD CHURCHYARD
CIR CIRCLE
CIRC CIRCUS
CL CLOSE
CLFS CLIFFS
CMP CAMP
CNR CORNER
CO COUNTY
COLL COLLEGE
COM COMMON
COMM COMMISSION
CON CONVENT
COT COTTAGE
COTS COTTAGES
CP CAPE
CPS COPSE
CR CREEK
CREM CREMATORIUM
CRS CRESCENT
CSWY CAUSEWAY
CT COURT
CTRL CENTRAL
CTS COURTS
CTYD COURTYARD
CUTT CUTTINGS
CV COVE
CYN CANYON
DEPT DEPARTMENT
DL DALE
DM DAM
DR DRIVE
DRO DROVE
DRY DRIVEWAY
DWGS DWELLINGS
E EAST
EMB EMBANKMENT
EMBY EMBASSY
ESP ESPLANADE
EST ESTATE
EX EXCHANGE
EXPY EXPRESSWAY
EXT EXTENSION
F/O FLYOVER
FC FOOTBALL CLUB
FK FORK
FLD FIELD
FLDS FIELDS
FLS FALLS
FLS FLATS
FM FARM
FT FORT
FWY FREEWAY
FY FERRY
GA GATE
GAL GALLERY
GDN GARDEN
GDNS GARDENS
GLD GLADE
GLN GLEN
GN GREEN
GND GROUND
GRA GRANGE
GRG GARAGE
GT GREAT
GTWY GATEWAY
GV GROVE
HGR HIGHER
HL HILL
HLS HILLS
HO HOUSE
HOL HOLLOW
HOSP HOSPITAL
HRB HARBOUR
HTH HEATH
HTS HEIGHTS
HVN HAVEN
HWY HIGHWAY
IMP IMPERIAL
IN INLET
IND EST INDUSTRIAL ESTATE
INF INFIRMARY
INFO INFORMATION
INT INTERCHANGE
IS ISLAND
JCT JUNCTION
JTY JETTY
KG KING
KNL KNOLL
L LAKE
LA LANE
LDG LODGE
LGT LIGHT
LK LOCK
LKS LAKES
LNDG LANDING
LTL LITTLE
LWR LOWER
MAG MAGISTRATE
MAN MANSIONS
MD MEAD
MDW MEADOWS
MEM MEMORIAL
MKT MARKET
MKTS MARKETS
ML MALL
ML MILL
MNR MANOR
MS MEWS
MSN MISSION
MT MOUNT
MTN MOUNTAIN
MTS MOUNTAINS
MUS MUSEUM
MWY MOTORWAY
N NORTH
NE NORTH EAST
NW NORTH WEST
O/P OVERPASS
OFF OFFICE
ORCH ORCHARD
OV OVAL
PAL PALACE
PAS PASSAGE
PAV PAVILION
PDE PARADE
PH PUBLIC HOUSE
PK PARK
PKWY PARKWAY
PL PLACE
PLN PLAIN
PLNS PLAINS
PLZ PLAZA
POL POLICE STATION
PR PRINCE
PREC PRECINCT
PREP PREPARATORY
PRIM PRIMARY
PROM PROMENADE
PRS PRINCESS
PRT PORT
PT POINT
PTH PATH
PZ PIAZZA
QD QUADRANT
QU QUEEN
QY QUAY
R RIVER
RBT ROUNDABOUT
RD ROAD
RDG RIDGE
REP REPUBLIC
RES RESERVOIR
RFC RUGBY FOOTBALL CLUB
RI RISE
RP RAMP
RW ROW
S SOUTH
SCH SCHOOL
SE SOUTH EAST
SER SERVICE AREA
SH SHORE
SHOP SHOPPING
SKWY SKYWAY
SMT SUMMIT
SOC SOCIETY
SP SPUR
SPR SPRING
SQ SQUARE
ST STREET
STN STATION
STR STREAM
STRD STRAND
SW SOUTH WEST
TDG TRADING
TER TERRACE
THWY THROUGHWAY
TNL TUNNEL
TOLL TOLLWAY
TPK TURNPIKE
TR TRACK
TRL TRAIL
TWR TOWER
U/P UNDERPASS
UNI UNIVERSITY
UPR UPPER
V VALE
VA VALLEY
VIAD VIADUCT
VIL VILLA
VIS VISTA
VLG VILLAGE
VLS VILLAS
VW VIEW
W WEST
WD WOOD
WHF WHARF
WK WALK
WKS WALKS
WLS WELLS
WY WAY
YD YARD
YHA YOUTH HOSTEL

POSTCODE TOWNS AND AREA ABBREVIATIONS

BPWT Bishop's Waltham
BROC Brockenhurst
CHAM Cosham
CHFD Chandler's Ford
ELGH Eastleigh
EMRTH Emsworth/Southbourne
ENEY Eastney
FAWY Fawley/Hythe
FHAM Fareham
FHAM/PORC Fareham/Portchester
FHAM/STUB Fareham/Stubbington
GPORT Gosport
HAV Havant
HEND Hedge End
HISD Hayling Island
HLER Hamble-le-Rice
HORN Horndean
HSEA Hilsea
ITCH Itchen
LSOL/BMARY Lee-on-the-Solent/Bridgemary
LYMN Lymington
LYND Lyndhurst
NBAD North Baddesley
NEND North End
PSEA Portsea
PTSW Portswood
RCCH Rural Chichester
ROMY Romsey
ROWN Rownhams
RWIN Rural Winchester
SELS Selsey
SHAM Southampton
SSEA Southsea
TOTT Totton
WEND West End
WHAM Wickham
WINC Winchester
WINW Winchester west
WSHM Southampton west
WVILLE Waterlooville/Denmead

10th St *FAWY* SO45 110 A3
11th St *FAWY* SO45 110 A2
12th St *FAWY* SO45 110 A2
13th St *FAWY* SO45 110 A1
14th St *FAWY* SO45 109 K2
1st St *FAWY* SO45 110 D4
2nd St *FAWY* SO45 110 D2
3rd St *FAWY* SO45 110 C3
4th St *FAWY* SO45 110 C3
5th St *FAWY* SO45 110 C2
6th St *FAWY* SO45 110 B3
7th St *FAWY* SO45 110 B2
8th St *FAWY* SO45 110 B3
9th St *FAWY* SO45 110 A3

A

Aaron Ct *TOTT* SO40 70 A3
A Av *FAWY* SO45 110 A2
Abbey Cl *FAWY* SO45 91 H3 1
Abbeydore Rd *CHAM* PO6 100 B5
Abbeyfield Dr *FHAM* PO15 96 D4
Abbeyfields Cl *HLER* SO31 73 G7
Abbey Hl *ITCH* SO19 72 B5
Abbey Hill Cl *WINC* SO23 21 K5 1
Abbey Hill Rd *WINC* SO23 21 J5
Abbey Rd *FHAM* PO15 12 B4
Abbey Water *ROMY* SO51 34 D3 1
Abbotsbury Rd *ELGH* SO50 45 J1
Abbots Cl *WVILLE* PO7 101 H2 1
Abbotsfield *TOTT* SO40 52 D5
Abbotsfield Cl *ROWN* SO16 42 D6
Abbotsford *TOTT* SO40 50 E6
Abbotstone Av *HAV* PO9 103 H2
Abbots Wy *FHAM* PO15 12 A5
HLER SO31 73 G7
Abbotswood Cl *ROMY* SO51 35 H1 1
Abbotts Ann Rd *WINW* SO22 21 G4
Abbotts Rd *ELGH* SO50 44 B2
WINC SO23 21 K5
Abbotts Wy *PTSW* SO17 55 J3
Abercrombie Gdns *ROWN* SO16 42 B7
Aberdare Av *CHAM* PO6 101 G5
Aberdeen Cl *FHAM* PO15 12 D2
Aberdour Cl *WEND* SO18 7 H2
Abingdon Gdns *ROWN* SO16 55 F1 1
Above Bar St *SHAM* SO14 4 F8
Abraham Cl *HEND* SO30 58 C7
Abshot Cl *FHAM/STUB* PO14 95 G5
Abshot Rd *FHAM/STUB* PO14 95 G5
Acacia Gdns *HORN* PO8 64 C7
Acacia Rd *ITCH* SO19 6 E9
Acer Wy *HAV* PO9 103 J2
Ackworth Rd *HSEA* PO3 119 F2
Acorn Cl *CHAM* PO6 101 K6 1
WINW SO22 21 G5
LSOL/BMARY PO13 116 A6
TOTT SO40 70 B4 1
Acorn Ct *HLER* SO31 93 J3 1
Acorn Dr *ROWN* SO16 41 K4
Acorn Gv *NBAD* SO52 37 G6
The Acorns *HLER* SO31 73 J5
Acre La *HORN* PO8 82 D4
Adair Rd *ENEY* PO4 19 M9
Adames Rd *PSEA* PO1 19 H1
Adams Cl *HEND* SO30 58 A1
Adamson Cl *CHFD* SO53 38 A2
Adams Rd *FAWY* SO45 91 H4
Adams Wood Dr *TOTT* SO40 70 A4
Adderbury Av *EMRTH* PO10 104 C2
Addison Rd *ELGH* SO50 38 E5 1
ENEY PO4 19 G7
HLER SO31 74 E7
Addison Cl *WINW* SO22 25 F3
Adelaide Rd *PTSW* SO17 5 L2
Adela Verne Cl *ITCH* SO19 73 H2 1
Adey Cl *ITCH* SO19 11 K5
Adhurst Rd *HAV* PO9 103 H2
Admirals Cl *FAWY* SO45 110 E4 1
Admirals Rd *HLER* SO31 95 G2
Admirals Wk *GPORT* PO12 132 C5
PSEA PO1 17 K2 1
Admiralty Rd *PSEA* PO1 17 L3
Admiralty Wy *TOTT* SO40 70 A2
Adsdean Cl *HAV* PO9 103 F2 1
Adstone La *HSEA* PO3 119 H3 1
Adur Cl *GPORT* PO12 132 C1 1
WEND SO18 7 J1
Aerial Rd *CHAM* PO6 100 A4
Aerodrome Rd
LSOL/BMARY PO13 116 B5
Africa Dr *TOTT* SO40 70 A4
Agincourt Rd *NEND* PO2 134 C1
Agitor Rd *FAWY* SO45 111 F2
Agnew Rd *LSOL/BMARY* PO13 115 K4
Aikman La *TOTT* SO40 52 A5
Ailsa La *ITCH* SO19 10 B2
Ainsdale Rd *CHAM* PO6 101 J5
Ainsley Gdns *ELGH* SO50 38 D5
Aintree Cl *ELGH* SO50 46 C4 1
Aintree Dr *WVILLE* PO7 82 C4
Aintree Rd *TOTT* SO40 52 B3
Airlie Rd *WINW* SO22 2 B7
Airport Service Rd *HSEA* PO3 119 G4
Ajax Cl *FHAM/STUB* PO14 114 E6
Alameda Rd *WVILLE* PO7 101 J2
Alameda Wy *WVILLE* PO7 101 J2
Alandale Rd *ITCH* SO19 73 G1
Alan Drayton Wy *ELGH* SO50 45 H1
Alan Gv *FHAM* PO15 12 C4
Albacore Av *HLER* SO31 94 D5 1
Albany Ct *BPWT* SO32 48 B3
Albany Dr *BPWT* SO32 48 B3
Albany Rd *BPWT* SO32 48 B3
FAWY SO45 109 K3
ROMY SO51 34 D3
SSEA PO5 18 E8
WSHM SO15 54 D6
Albatross Wk
LSOL/BMARY PO13 115 J5
Albemarle Av *GPORT* PO12 132 E1
Albert Cl *HLER* SO31 93 F1
Albert Gv *SSEA* PO5 18 F8
Albert Rd *BPWT* SO32 48 C4
CHAM PO6 100 E7
ELGH SO50 38 E5
FHAM/STUB PO14 115 G5
HEND SO30 58 A7
SSEA PO5 18 F9
Albert Rd North *SHAM* SO14 9 K3
Albert Rd South *SHAM* SO14 9 K4
Albert St *GPORT* PO12 16 C4
Albion Cl *FHAM/PORC* PO16 116 E1
Albion Pl *SHAM* SO14 8 F2
Albretia Av *HORN* PO8 81 J2
Albury Pl *CHFD* SO53 37 J1 1
Alcantara Crs *SHAM* SO14 9 K4
Alder Cl *FAWY* SO45 90 D3
ROMY SO51 35 J4
RWIN SO21 39 K2
TOTT SO40 70 A3
Alder Hill Dr *TOTT* SO40 52 A4
Alder La *LSOL/BMARY* PO13 132 A3
Aldermoor Av *ROWN* SO16 42 B7
Aldermoor Cl *ROWN* SO16 42 D7
Aldermoor Rd
LSOL/BMARY PO13 132 A1
ROWN SO16 42 C7
WVILLE PO7 101 J2
Aldermoor Rd East
WVILLE PO7 101 J1 1
Alderney Cl *ROWN* SO16 41 K7
Alder Rd *ROWN* SO16 54 A1
Alders Rd *FHAM/PORC* PO16 97 J7
Alderwood Av *CHFD* SO53 37 H4
Alderwood Cl *HAV* PO9 102 B3
Aldrich Rd *PSEA* PO1 17 M1
Aldroke St *CHAM* PO6 100 E7 1
Aldsworth Cl *CHAM* PO6 101 H6
Aldsworth Gdns *CHAM* PO6 101 H6 1
Aldwell St *SSEA* PO5 18 E5 1
Alec Rose La *PSEA* PO1 18 C4
Alecto Rd *GPORT* PO12 16 A8
Alencon Cl *GPORT* PO12 117 F7 1
Alexander Cl *TOTT* SO40 52 C4
WVILLE PO7 101 J1 2
Alexander Gv
FHAM/PORC PO16 13 H8
Alexandra Av *HISD* PO11 137 G6
Alexandra Cl *FAWY* SO45 91 H2 1
Alexandra Rd *CHFD* SO53 38 C2
FAWY SO45 91 H2
HEND SO30 58 A7
PSEA PO1 18 E1 1
WSHM SO15 4 B7
Alexandra St *GPORT* PO12 132 D2 1
Alexandra Ter *WINC* SO23 2 C6
Alexandra Wy *HEND* SO30 59 F5
Alfred Cl *TOTT* SO40 52 B4 1
TOTT SO40 52 B5 1
Alfred Rd *FHAM/STUB* PO14 114 E4
PSEA PO1 18 B3
Alfred Rose Ct *WEND* SO18 44 B7 1
Alfred St *SHAM* SO14 5 J6
Alfrey Cl *EMRTH* PO10 105 F6
Alfriston Gdns *ITCH* SO19 11 K3
Algiers Rd *HSEA* PO3 119 G7
Alhambra Rd *ENEY* PO4 134 D7
Allan Gv *ROMY* SO51 35 G3
Allaway Av *CHAM* PO6 99 J6
Allbrook Ct *HAV* PO9 82 E7
Allbrook Hl *ELGH* SO50 38 E3
Allbrook Knoll *ELGH* SO50 38 D3
Allbrook Wy *ELGH* SO50 38 D2
Allcot Rd *HSEA* PO3 118 E5
Allenby Gv *FHAM/PORC* PO16 99 F7
Allenby Rd *GPORT* PO12 132 B2
Allendale Av *EMRTH* PO10 104 B3
Allen Rd *HEND* SO30 58 B5
Allen's Rd *SSEA* PO5 19 G9
Allerton Cl *TOTT* SO40 52 C3
Alliance Cl *LSOL/BMARY* PO13 116 A7
Allington La *HEND* SO30 45 H6
Allington Rd *WSHM* SO15 53 J5
Allmara Dr *WVILLE* PO7 101 K1
Allotment Rd *HLER* SO31 94 D1
All Saint's Rd *PSEA* PO1 134 C1
All Saint's St *PSEA* PO1 18 D1 1
Alma La *BPWT* SO32 47 G1
Alma Rd *ROMY* SO51 34 E3
SHAM SO14 4 F3
Alma St *GPORT* PO12 132 D2
Almatade Rd *WEND* SO18 7 H4
Alma Ter *ENEY* PO4 19 M8
Almond Cl *CHAM* PO6 102 A6
HORN PO8 82 D1
Almond Rd *WSHM* SO15 54 D7
Almondsbury Rd *CHAM* PO6 99 J4
Almondside
LSOL/BMARY PO13 116 B6
Alpine Cl *WEND* SO18 7 K2
Alpine Rd *TOTT* SO40 67 J2
Alresford Rd *HAV* PO9 103 F2 2
RWIN SO21 26 E1
WINC SO23 3 J5
Alsford Rd *WVILLE* PO7 101 J1
Alten Rd *WVILLE* PO7 81 H3
Althorpe Dr *HSEA* PO3 119 H3
Alton Cl *ELGH* SO50 46 A1
Alton Gv *FHAM/PORC* PO16 117 F1
Alum Cl *FAWY* SO45 110 A4
Alum Wy *FHAM/PORC* PO16 98 B5
WEND SO18 7 J5
Alvara Rd *GPORT* PO12 132 D6
Alvercliffe Dr *GPORT* PO12 132 C6
Alver Rd *GPORT* PO12 16 B7
PSEA PO1 19 G2
Alverstone Rd *ENEY* PO4 19 L4
Alveston Av *FHAM/STUB* PO14 96 D6
Amarylis Cl *FHAM* PO15 95 K2
Amberley Cl *HEND* SO30 58 E4
NBAD SO52 35 K5
Amberley Ct *TOTT* SO40 52 D6
Amberley Rd *GPORT* PO12 116 D7
NEND PO2 118 E4
Amberslade Wk *FAWY* SO45 91 G5
Amberwood Cl *TOTT* SO40 52 B2
Ambledale *HLER* SO31 94 D2
Ambleside *HEND* SO30 58 C7
Ambleside Gdns *ITCH* SO19 11 H3
Amersham Cl *GPORT* PO12 132 B4
Amethyst Gv *WVILLE* PO7 82 C5
Amoy St *WSHM* SO15 4 E6
Ampfield Cl *HAV* PO9 102 C2 1
Amport Cl *WINW* SO22 21 F4
Amport Ct *HAV* PO9 82 E7
Ampthill Rd *WSHM* SO15 54 C5
Amyas Ct *ENEY* PO4 135 H4
Ancasta Rd *SHAM* SO14 5 J4 1
Anchorage Rd *HSEA* PO3 119 G4
The Anchorage *GPORT* PO12 16 D6
Anchor Ga *PSEA* PO1 17 M1
Anchor La *PSEA* PO1 17 L2 1
Andalusian Gdns *HLER* SO31 75 G5
Anderby Rd *ROWN* SO16 53 J2
Andersen Cl *HLER* SO31 75 H5
Anderson Cl *HAV* PO9 15 G1
ROMY SO51 29 H7 1
Anderson's Rd *SHAM* SO14 9 K3
Andes Cl *SHAM* SO14 9 L4
SHAM SO14 9 L4
Andes Rd *ROWN* SO16 53 G1
Andover Rd *ENEY* PO4 19 K9
WINW SO22 21 H5
WSHM SO15 4 A7
Andrew Bell St *PSEA* PO1 18 D1 2
Andrew Cl *FAWY* SO45 91 H5 1
PSEA PO1 19 J2
TOTT SO40 52 C5
Andrew Crs *WVILLE* PO7 81 J4
Andrewes Cl *BPWT* SO32 48 D3
Andrew Pl *FHAM/STUB* PO14 114 C5
Andromeda Rd *ROWN* SO16 41 K7
Anfield Cl *ELGH* SO50 46 B2
Angel Crs *ITCH* SO19 7 G6
Angelica Gdns *ELGH* SO50 46 B4
Angelica Wy *FHAM* PO15 75 K5
Angelo Cl *WVILLE* PO7 82 B5
Angelus Cl *FHAM/STUB* PO14 114 D5
Angerstein Rd *NEND* PO2 118 C6
Anglers Wy *HLER* SO31 74 C5
Anglesea Rd
LSOL/BMARY PO13 131 H4
PSEA PO1 18 B4
WSHM SO15 54 C3
Anglesea Ter *SHAM* SO14 9 K3
Anglesey Arms Rd
GPORT PO12 132 D6
Anglesey Rd *GPORT* PO12 16 A7
Angus Cl *FHAM* PO15 12 C2
Anjou Crs *FHAM* PO15 12 B4
Anker La *FHAM/STUB* PO14 114 D3
Ankerwycke
LSOL/BMARY PO13 115 J6 1
Anmore Dr *WVILLE* PO7 81 J3
Anmore La *WVILLE* PO7 81 H1
Anmore Rd *WVILLE* PO7 81 F1
Anne Crs *WVILLE* PO7 81 K7
Ann's Hill Rd *GPORT* PO12 132 D3
Anson Cl *LSOL/BMARY* PO13 132 A3
Anson Dr *ITCH* SO19 7 M9
Anson Gv *FHAM/PORC* PO16 99 G5
Anson Rd *ELGH* SO50 46 B4
ENEY PO4 19 K4
Anstey Rd *ROMY* SO51 35 G1
Anthill Cl *WVILLE* PO7 62 B6
Anthony Gv *GPORT* PO12 116 C6
LSOL/BMARY PO13 116 C6
Anton Cl *ROMY* SO51 35 H3
Anvil Cl *HORN* PO8 82 D4
Anzac Cl *FHAM/STUB* PO14 114 D3
Apless La *WVILLE* PO7 79 J1
Apollo Dr *WVILLE* PO7 102 A3
Apollo Rd *CHFD* SO53 38 C3
Apple Gv *EMRTH* PO10 104 E6
Appleshaw Cl *WINW* SO22 21 G3
Appleton Rd *FHAM* PO15 96 D5
WEND SO18 56 B3
Appletree Cl *TOTT* SO40 52 B4
Appletree Ct *HEND* SO30 59 F5
Applewood Gv *WVILLE* PO7 101 H4
Applewood Pl *TOTT* SO40 52 B6
Applewood Rd *HAV* PO9 102 D3
April Cl *WEND* SO18 7 J4
April Gv *HLER* SO31 94 D3
April Sq *PSEA* PO1 18 E2
Apsley Pl *CHFD* SO53 37 J1 2
Apsley Rd *ENEY* PO4 19 L5
Aquila Wy *HLER* SO31 93 J4
Arabian Gdns *FHAM* PO15 75 H6
Arcadia Cl *ROWN* SO16 54 C1
Archers Cl *TOTT* SO40 52 B2
Archers Rd *ELGH* SO50 38 D6
WSHM SO15 4 D5
Archery Gdns *ITCH* SO19 10 E6
Archery Gv *ITCH* SO19 10 D6
Archery La *FHAM/PORC* PO16 13 L4
WINC SO23 2 C5
Archery Rd *ITCH* SO19 10 C7
Arden Cl *WEND* SO18 7 K1
Ardingly Crs *HEND* SO30 58 C2
Ardington Ri *WVILLE* PO7 101 K3
Argosy Cl *HLER* SO31 94 E5
Argus Rd *LSOL/BMARY* PO13 131 G1
Argyle Crs *FHAM* PO15 12 D3
Argyle Rd *SHAM* SO14 5 H8
Ariel Rd *PSEA* PO1 19 G3
Ark Royal Crs
LSOL/BMARY PO13 131 F1
Arliss Rd *ROWN* SO16 54 B3
Arlott Ct *WSHM* SO15 4 D4
Armada Cl *ROWN* SO16 41 K4
Armada Dr *FAWY* SO45 91 G4
Arminers Cl *GPORT* PO12 132 E7
Armitage Av *FAWY* SO45 91 G5
Armory La *PSEA* PO1 17 M6
Armstrong Cl *WVILLE* PO7 81 J4 1
Armstrong Ct *ROWN* SO16 42 A6 1
Arnaud Cl *NEND* PO2 134 C1
Arnheim Cl *ROWN* SO16 42 D7
Arnheim Rd *ROWN* SO16 42 E7
Arnold Rd *ELGH* SO50 44 D3
PTSW SO17 55 K2
Arnside Rd *WVILLE* PO7 81 K5
Arnwood Av *FAWY* SO45 91 G6
Arragon Ct *WVILLE* PO7 82 B5
Arran Cl *CHAM* PO6 100 E5
Arreton *HLER* SO31 73 F7 1
Arrow Cl *ELGH* SO50 38 D6
ITCH SO19 10 B8
Arters Lawn *TOTT* SO40 69 G7
Arthur Rd *ELGH* SO50 38 D6
WINC SO23 2 E1
WSHM SO15 4 B5
Arthurs Gdns *HEND* SO30 58 A1 1
Arthur St *NEND* PO2 134 D1 1
Artillery Cl *CHAM* PO6 100 B6
Arundel Dr *FHAM/PORC* PO16 13 G4
Arundel Rd *ELGH* SO50 38 D4
GPORT PO12 132 C3
TOTT SO40 53 F4
Arundel St *PSEA* PO1 18 F3
Arun Rd *WEND* SO18 56 E2
Ascot Cl *FHAM/STUB* PO14 95 H4
Ascot Rd *ELGH* SO50 46 C4
HSEA PO3 135 F1
Ascupart St *SHAM* SO14 9 J1
Asford Gv *ELGH* SO50 39 G6
Ashbarn Crs *WINW* SO22 25 G3
Ashbridge Ri *CHFD* SO53 37 H1
Ashburnham Cl *ITCH* SO19 6 B9
Ashburton Cl *FAWY* SO45 90 E3 1
Ashburton Rd *GPORT* PO12 132 C6
SSEA PO5 18 C9
Ashby Rd *ITCH* SO19 11 K4
TOTT SO40 52 C5
Ash Cl *FAWY* SO45 91 H6
FHAM/STUB PO14 12 C7
GPORT PO12 16 A6
HLER SO31 73 J5 1
HORN PO8 81 K2
ITCH SO19 7 M7
NBAD SO52 36 A5
ROMY SO51 35 H4
RWIN SO21 39 J2
Ash Copse *HORN* PO8 64 A7
Ashdene *WSHM* SO15 54 C4 1
Ashdene Rd *TOTT* SO40 68 A3
Ashdown *FAWY* SO45 110 C4
LSOL/BMARY PO13 116 A6
Ashdown Cl *CHFD* SO53 31 K7
Ashdown Dr *CHFD* SO53 31 K7
Ashdown Rd *CHFD* SO53 37 K1
FAWY SO45 110 C5
Ashdown Wy *ROMY* SO51 35 G3
Ashen Cl *CHFD* SO53 37 K2
Ashe Rd *HAV* PO9 103 J1 1
Ashford Cl *CHAM* PO6 100 D5
Ashford Crs *FAWY* SO45 91 J3
Ash Gv *TOTT* SO40 68 B3
Ashington Cl *HORN* PO8 82 B2
Ashlea Cl *ELGH* SO50 46 C1
Ashleigh Cl *FAWY* SO45 91 H6
Ashlett Cl *FAWY* SO45 111 F4
Ashlett Rd *FAWY* SO45 111 F4
Ashley Cl *WINW* SO22 21 F4
HAV PO9 102 E2
HLER SO31 75 G6
HORN PO8 64 A7
Ashley Ct *HLER* SO31 73 K3 1
Ashley Crs *ITCH* SO19 11 L6
Ashleycross Cl *FAWY* SO45 110 A4 1
Ashley Gdns *BPWT* SO32 61 F1
CHFD SO53 38 B5
Ashley Mdw *ROMY* SO51 35 F2
Ashling Cl *WVILLE* PO7 80 E1
Ashling Gdns *WVILLE* PO7 80 E1
Ashling La *NEND* PO2 118 C7
Ashling Park Rd *WVILLE* PO7 80 E1
Ashlyn Cl *FHAM* PO15 96 C5
Ashmead Rd *ROWN* SO16 54 A1
Ashmore Rd *WINW* SO22 21 F6 1
Ashridge Cl *WSHM* SO15 4 D3
Ash Rd *TOTT* SO40 68 A3
Ashtead Cl *FHAM/PORC* PO16 98 D6
Ashton Cl *BPWT* SO32 48 B2
Ashton La *BPWT* SO32 48 B1
Ashton Wy *FHAM/STUB* PO14 114 E7
Ash Tree Rd *WEND* SO18 56 B3
Ashurst Bridge Rd *TOTT* SO40 52 B6
Ashurst Cl *WINW* SO22 21 G4
ITCH SO19 11 H8
TOTT SO40 68 A3
Ashurst Rd *CHAM* PO6 100 D6
Ashwood *FHAM* PO15 95 K1 1
HLER SO31 95 H4
Ashwood Cl *HAV* PO9 102 C3
HISD PO11 137 H5
Ashwood Gdns *ROWN* SO16 55 F1 2
TOTT SO40 52 B6 1
Aspen Av *HLER* SO31 94 C6
Aspen Cl *HEND* SO30 58 C5
RWIN SO21 39 K2
Aspengrove
LSOL/BMARY PO13 116 B6
Aspen Holt *ROWN* SO16 43 H6
Aspen Wk *TOTT* SO40 52 A4
Aspen Wy *HORN* PO8 64 B7
Aster Rd *ROWN* SO16 43 K7
Astley St *SSEA* PO5 18 C6
Aston Rd *ENEY* PO4 19 K7
WVILLE PO7 81 J5
Astra Ct *FAWY* SO45 91 H1
Astral Gdns *HLER* SO31 93 J3
Astrid Cl *HISD* PO11 137 K5
Asturias Wy *SHAM* SO14 9 L4
Asylum Rd *WSHM* SO15 5 G7
Atalanta Cl *ENEY* PO4 135 H3
Atheling Rd *FAWY* SO45 91 H2
Athelstan Rd *ITCH* SO19 6 C5
Athena Av *WVILLE* PO7 102 A3
Athena Cl *ELGH* SO50 39 K7
Atherfield Rd *ROWN* SO16 53 K1
Atherley Ct *WSHM* SO15 4 C3
Atherley Rd *HISD* PO11 137 F3
WSHM SO15 4 B6
Atkinson Cl *GPORT* PO12 132 D6 1
Atkins Pl *FHAM* PO15 96 D3
Atlantic Cl *SHAM* SO14 9 K6
Atlantic Park Vw *WEND* SO18 56 D2 1
Atlantis Av *WVILLE* PO7 102 A4
Attwoods Dro *RWIN* SO21 33 F1
Aubrey Cl *HISD* PO11 137 F4 1
Auckland Rd *WSHM* SO15 54 A5
Auckland Rd East *SSEA* PO5 134 B6
Auckland Rd West *SSEA* PO5 134 B6 1
Audret Cl *FHAM/PORC* PO16 116 E1
Augustine Rd *CHAM* PO6 101 H5
SHAM SO14 5 K7
Augustus Wy *CHFD* SO53 38 B3
Auriol Dr *CHAM* PO6 102 B6
Austen Av *WINW* SO22 25 F5
Austen Cl *TOTT* SO40 52 C6
WINC SO23 21 K5 2
Austen Gdns *HLER* SO31 75 H5
Austerberry Wy
LSOL/BMARY PO13 116 A7
Austin Ct *CHAM* PO6 100 A5
Australia Cl *PSEA* PO1 18 E3
Aust Rd *FHAM/STUB* PO14 12 A7
Autumn Rd *TOTT* SO40 70 B4
Avebury Gdns *CHFD* SO53 37 H1
Avenger Cl *CHFD* SO53 37 J5
Avens Cl *ELGH* SO50 46 B5
Avenue C *FAWY* SO45 92 B6
Avenue Ct *GPORT* PO12 132 D6
Avenue D *FAWY* SO45 92 B6
Avenue De Caen *SSEA* PO5 134 B7
Avenue E *FAWY* SO45 92 B6
Avenue Rd *FHAM/STUB* PO14 12 F6
WINW SO22 2 B3
GPORT PO12 16 C4
HISD PO11 121 G4
SHAM SO14 5 H3
The Avenue *BPWT* SO32 48 C3
FHAM PO15 12 E6
GPORT PO12 132 D5
PTSW SO17 5 G4
RWIN SO21 33 K3
Avery La *GPORT* PO12 132 C1
Avington Cl *ELGH* SO50 39 G5 1
Avington Ct *ROWN* SO16 43 G7
Avocet Quay *EMRTH* PO10 104 D7
Avocet Wk *LSOL/BMARY* PO13 115 H5
Avonborne Wy *CHFD* SO53 37 J2
Avon Cl *LSOL/BMARY* PO13 131 G3
Avon Crs *ROMY* SO51 35 H3
Avondale Rd *PSEA* PO1 19 J1
WVILLE PO7 82 A5
Avon Gn *CHFD* SO53 38 A5
Avon Rd *WEND* SO18 6 E1
Avon Wy *HEND* SO30 57 H2
Awbridge Rd *HAV* PO9 102 D2
Aylen Rd *HSEA* PO3 119 F5
Aylesbury Rd *NEND* PO2 118 E7
Ayling Cl *LSOL/BMARY* PO13 131 K1
Aylward St *PSEA* PO1 17 M3 1
Aysgarth Rd *WVILLE* PO7 81 K5

Azalea Cl HAV PO9 103 K2

B

Back La WHAM PO17 79 H7
Back of the Walls SHAM SO14 9 G3
Back St WINC SO23 25 J4
Bacon Cl ITCH SO19 10 F8
Bacon La HISD PO11 136 E5
Baddesley Cl NBAD SO52 36 A5
Baddesley Rd CHFD SO53 37 H1
Bader Cl HEND SO30 58 B4 1
Bader Wy FHAM PO15 95 K1
Badger Brow WVILLE PO7 82 B7
Badger Cl ELGH SO50 45 J1
FHAM PO15 12 A3
Badger Farm Rd WINW SO22 24 E3
Badgers Run HLER SO31 74 D7
The Badgers HLER SO31 73 F7 2
Badgers Wk FAWY SO45 91 G4 1
Badminston Dro FAWY SO45 111 F7
Badminston La FAWY SO45 111 F6
Baffins Rd HSEA PO3 19 L1
Bagber Rd TOTT SO40 52 E5
Baigent Cl WINC SO23 3 J4
Bailey Cl WINW SO22 25 G2
HEND SO30 58 E6
Bailey's Rd SSEA PO5 18 E5
Bakers Dro ROWN SO16 41 K6
Baker St NEND PO2 134 C1
Balaclava Rd WEND SO18 7 H4
Balderton Cl NEND PO2 118 E3 1
Balfour Cl
LSOL/BMARY PO13 132 A2 1
Balfour Rd ITCH SO19 7 K9
NEND PO2 118 D6
Ballard Cl ROWN SO16 53 H3
Balliol Cl FHAM/STUB PO14 95 H5
Balliol Rd NEND PO2 134 D1
Balmoral Cl CHFD SO53 37 J2 1
LSOL/BMARY PO13 116 A4
ROWN SO16 42 D6
Balmoral Dr WVILLE PO7 101 H2
Balmoral Rd FHAM PO15 12 D2
Balmoral Wy ROWN SO16 41 J5
Baltic Rd HEND SO30 57 H2
Banbury Av ITCH SO19 11 L1
Bangor Rd WSHM SO15 54 C6
Banister Gdns WSHM SO15 4 E5
Banister Rd WSHM SO15 4 F4
Bank Side WEND SO18 44 A7
Bank St BPWT SO32 48 E4
Banning St ROMY SO51 34 D4
Bapaume Rd HSEA PO3 118 E2
Barbe Baker Av HEND SO30 57 F2
Bardon Wy FHAM/STUB PO14 12 B8
Bar End Rd WINC SO23 3 G7
Barfield Cl WINC SO23 3 G7
Barfleur Cl FHAM PO15 12 A3
Barfleur Rd FHAM/STUB PO14 115 H2
Barford Cl CHFD SO53 37 J2 2
Bargate St SHAM SO14 8 F2
Barham Cl GPORT PO12 16 A2
Barham Wy NEND PO2 118 C3
Baring Rd WINC SO23 3 H6
Barker Mill Cl ROWN SO16 41 K5
Barle Cl WEND SO18 56 E3
Barley Down Dr WINW SO22 25 G4
Barlow Cl FHAM/STUB PO14 114 C5
Barnbrook Rd HLER SO31 94 D2
Barn Cl EMRTH PO10 104 A6
Barncroft Wy HAV PO9 102 E3
Barnes Cl HLER SO31 94 C2
ITCH SO19 7 L6
WINC SO23 2 B9
Barnes La HLER SO31 94 D2
Barnes Rd ITCH SO19 7 L6
PSEA PO1 19 H2
Barnes Wallis Rd FHAM PO15 95 J2 1
Barnes Wy HAV PO9 102 D3
Barney Evans Crs HORN PO8 81 J2
Barneyhayes La TOTT SO40 50 D4
Barnfield Cl EMRTH PO10 105 H4
ITCH SO19 10 D8
Barnfield Ct FHAM/STUB PO14 12 D8
ITCH SO19 10 E7
Barnfield Rd ITCH SO19 10 D7
Barnfield Wy ITCH SO19 10 E7
Barn Fold HORN PO8 82 C4
Barn Green Cl WVILLE PO7 80 E1
Barn Piece NBAD SO52 37 G4
Barnsfield Crs TOTT SO40 52 B5
Barnsland HEND SO30 57 F2
Baron Rd HLER SO31 93 J3
Barons Md ROWN SO16 53 K1
Barrie Cl HLER SO31 75 H5 1
Barrington Cl ELGH SO50 38 C5
Barrow Down Gdns ITCH SO19 73 H2
Barrow Hill Rd TOTT SO40 51 G1
Barry Rd ITCH SO19 7 L8
Barters Cl ROWN SO16 54 A3
Bartlett Cl FHAM PO15 12 C2
The Bartletts HLER SO31 93 K4
Bartley Av TOTT SO40 52 D6
Bartley Rd TOTT SO40 67 F2
Barton Cl ROMY SO51 35 G2 1
Barton Crs WEND SO18 6 F1
Barton Cross HORN PO8 64 C5
Barton Dr HEND SO30 58 C5
HLER SO31 93 J3
Barton Rd ELGH SO50 39 F7
Bartons Rd HAV PO9 103 H1
Bartram Rd TOTT SO40 53 F6
Barwell Gv EMRTH PO10 104 B3 1
Basing Rd HAV PO9 103 F1
Basingstoke Rd WINC SO23 22 C1
Basing Wy CHFD SO53 37 H6
Basingwell St BPWT SO32 48 D4
Basin St NEND PO2 118 C7
Bassett Av ROWN SO16 43 G6
Bassett Cl ROWN SO16 43 G7
Bassett Crs East ROWN SO16 43 G7
Bassett Crs West ROWN SO16 55 G1
Bassett Dl ROWN SO16 43 G5
Bassett Gdns ROWN SO16 43 F7
Bassett Gn ROWN SO16 43 J6
Bassett Green Cl ROWN SO16 43 J5
Bassett Green Dr ROWN SO16 43 H6
Bassett Green Rd ROWN SO16 43 H5
Bassett Heath Av ROWN SO16 43 G4
Bassett Meadow ROWN SO16 55 G1
Bassett Ms ROWN SO16 43 G6
Bassett Rw ROWN SO16 43 G5
Bassett Wood Dr ROWN SO16 43 G5
Bassett Wood Rd ROWN SO16 43 G5
Batchelor Gn HLER SO31 73 K5 1
Bath Cl ITCH SO19 7 J6
Bathing La PSEA PO1 17 K6
Bath La FHAM/PORC PO16 13 M6
Bath La (Lower)
FHAM/PORC PO16 13 M7
Bath Rd EMRTH PO10 104 C6
ENEY PO4 19 J8
ITCH SO19 7 J6
Bath Sq PSEA PO1 17 K6
Bath St SHAM SO14 5 H5
Bathurst Cl HISD PO11 137 F5
Battenburg Av NEND PO2 118 E5
Battenburg Rd GPORT PO12 16 C4 1
Battens Wy HAV PO9 103 G2
Battery Cl GPORT PO12 116 C7
Battery Hl BPWT SO32 48 C3
WINW SO22 25 F2
Battery Rw PSEA PO1 17 L8
Battle Cl HLER SO31 94 E2
B Av FAWY SO45 110 A2
Baxter Rd ITCH SO19 73 H1
Baybridge Rd HAV PO9 103 J1
Bay Cl ITCH SO19 11 H4
Bayly Av FHAM/PORC PO16 117 G1
Bay Rd GPORT PO12 132 C5
ITCH SO19 11 H3
Baythorn Cl NEND PO2 134 C1 1
Bay Trees ITCH SO19 57 H6
Beach Dr CHAM PO6 99 J6
Beach Rd EMRTH PO10 104 B6
HISD PO11 137 H5
LSOL/BMARY PO13 131 F3
SSEA PO5 134 C7
Beachway FHAM/PORC PO16 117 G1
Beacon Bottom HLER SO31 75 F7
Beacon Cl HLER SO31 75 F7
Beacon Mt HLER SO31 75 F7
Beacon Rd HEND SO30 57 G4
Beaconsfield Av CHAM PO6 101 F7
Beaconsfield Rd
FHAM/PORC PO16 13 J8
WVILLE PO7 81 K5 1
Beacon Sq EMRTH PO10 104 B7
Beacon Wy HLER SO31 95 F1
Bealing Cl ROWN SO16 43 J7
Bearslane Cl TOTT SO40 52 C3
Beatrice Rd ENEY PO4 19 H9
WSHM SO15 54 D5 1
Beattie Ri HEND SO30 58 B2 1
Beatty Cl HLER SO31 95 G2
Beatty Dr GPORT PO12 132 C6
Beauchamp Av
LSOL/BMARY PO13 115 K5
Beaucroft Rd BPWT SO32 61 F1
Beaufort Av FHAM/PORC PO16 12 E2
Beaufort Dr BPWT SO32 48 D3
Beaufort Rd HAV PO9 14 A3
SSEA PO5 134 C7 1
WINC SO23 2 C7
Beaulieu Av FHAM/PORC PO16 98 D6
HAV PO9 82 E7
Beaulieu Cl WINW SO22 21 G3 1
ROWN SO16 42 C6
Beaulieu Pl
LSOL/BMARY PO13 115 K5 1
Beaulieu Rd BROC SO42 88 E6
BROC SO42 108 D3
ELGH SO50 38 D6 1
FAWY SO45 91 F5
LYND SO43 86 E2
NEND PO2 118 D6
TOTT SO40 89 J1
Beaumaris Gdns FAWY SO45 91 G2
Beaumond Gn WINC SO23 2 D5
Beaumont Cl FHAM PO15 12 B1
ROWN SO16 55 F1 3
Beaumont Ct GPORT PO12 116 D7 1
Beaumont Ri FHAM PO15 96 E2 1
Beaumont Rd TOTT SO40 53 F5
Beauworth Av WEND SO18 7 M2
Beaver Dr ELGH SO50 45 K1
Beck Cl HLER SO31 94 D3
Beckford La WHAM PO17 79 H4
Beck St PSEA PO1 18 A3
Bedenham La
LSOL/BMARY PO13 116 B4
Bedfield La WINC SO23 22 A2
Bedford Av ITCH SO19 10 C6
Bedford Cl HAV PO9 15 J6
HEND SO30 58 C6 1
Bedford Pl WSHM SO15 4 F7
Bedford St GPORT PO12 132 D2
SSEA PO5 18 C5
Bedhampton Hl CHAM PO6 102 B5
Bedhampton Hill Rd
HAV PO9 102 C5 1
Bedhampton Rd HAV PO9 102 D4
NEND PO2 118 E6
Bedhampton Wy HAV PO9 103 G2
Bedwell Cl ROWN SO16 42 A6
Beecham Rd PSEA PO1 134 D1
Beech Av WEND SO18 6 D4
Beech Cl CHFD SO53 38 A2
WINW SO22 24 E3
HLER SO31 93 H4
HORN PO8 82 A3
ROMY SO51 35 H4
Beech Copse WINW SO22 21 F6
Beech Crs FAWY SO45 91 H6
Beechcroft Cl CHFD SO53 38 A5
FHAM PO15 96 C5
Beechcroft Rd GPORT PO12 132 D5
Beechcroft Wy CHFD SO53 38 A4 1
Beechdale Cl TOTT SO40 52 E4
Beechen La LYND SO43 86 E4
Beeches Hl BPWT SO32 48 E1
The Beeches ELGH SO50 46 C2 1
Beechfield Ct WSHM SO15 54 B4
Beech Gdns HLER SO31 93 H4
Beech Gv GPORT PO12 132 D5
HISD PO11 137 J4
Beechmount Rd ROWN SO16 43 G6
Beech Rd CHFD SO53 38 A2
FHAM PO15 12 D4
HEND SO30 58 C5
TOTT SO40 68 A3
WSHM SO15 54 C6
Beech Wy HORN PO8 64 C7
Beechwood Av WVILLE PO7 81 K7
Beechwood Cl CHFD SO53 37 H1
HLER SO31 94 C6 1
Beechwood Crs CHFD SO53 31 H7
Beechwood Gdns WEND SO18 6 D2
Beechwood Ri WEND SO18 7 L1
Beechwood Rd FAWY SO45 109 K4
NEND PO2 118 D3
TOTT SO40 50 C7
Beechwood Wy FAWY SO45 90 D4
Beechworth Rd HAV PO9 15 G4
Beehive Wk PSEA PO1 17 M6 1
Beggar's La WINC SO23 3 G4
Begonia Rd ROWN SO16 43 J7
Behrendt Cl GPORT PO12 132 D2
Belbins ROMY SO51 28 E5
Belfry Wk FHAM/STUB PO14 95 H4
Belgrave Rd PTSW SO17 55 K2
Belgravia Rd NEND PO2 118 E6
Bellair Rd HAV PO9 15 G5
Bell Crs WVILLE PO7 81 K7
Bell Davies Rd
FHAM/STUB PO14 114 C6
Bellemoor Rd WSHM SO15 54 E3
Bellevue La EMRTH PO10 104 C4
Bellevue Rd ELGH SO50 38 D7
WSHM SO15 5 G7
Bellevue Ter SSEA PO5 18 A8
Bellflower Wy NBAD SO52 37 G3
Bell Rd CHAM PO6 100 C6
Bells La FHAM/STUB PO14 114 D5
Bell St ROMY SO51 34 D3
SHAM SO14 9 H3
Belmont Cl FAWY SO45 91 H4
FHAM/STUB PO14 114 E4 1
HORN PO8 64 D2
Belmont Gv HAV PO9 102 D4 1
Belmont Pl SSEA PO5 18 D7
Belmont Rd CHFD SO53 38 A7
PTSW SO17 5 K2
Belmont St SSEA PO5 18 D7
Belmore Cl PSEA PO1 134 D1
Belney La WHAM PO17 80 D5
Belstone Rd TOTT SO40 52 D5
Belton Rd ITCH SO19 11 K4
Belvedere Rd FAWY SO45 91 H4
Belvidere Rd SHAM SO14 5 L9
Belvidere Ter SHAM SO14 5 L8
Belvoir Cl FHAM/PORC PO16 13 J7
Bembridge HLER SO31 73 F7
Bembridge Cl ROWN SO16 43 K6 1
Bembridge Crs ENEY PO4 134 D7
Bembridge Dr HISD PO11 137 K7
Benbow Cl HORN PO8 64 D5
Benbow Pl PSEA PO1 17 L3 1
Benedict Cl ROMY SO51 35 H3
Benedict Wy FHAM/PORC PO16 99 H4
Beneficial St PSEA PO1 17 L4 1
Benham Dr HSEA PO3 118 E3 2
Benham Gv FHAM/PORC PO16 117 G1
Benhams Farm Cl WEND SO18 7 G1
Benhams Rd WEND SO18 56 D2 2
Benmore Gdns CHFD SO53 37 J2
Benson Rd WSHM SO15 54 C4
Bentham Rd GPORT PO12 16 A8
Bentham Wy HLER SO31 74 C5
Bentley Cl HORN PO8 64 D4
WINC SO23 22 A1
Bentley Ct HAV PO9 103 J1 2
Bentley Crs FHAM/PORC PO16 12 F3
Bentley Gn WEND SO18 7 M2
Berber Cl FHAM PO15 75 H6
Bercote Cl WINW SO22 20 E2
Bere Cl CHFD SO53 37 H2
WINW SO22 21 G5
Bere Farm La WHAM PO17 78 C5
Bere Rd WVILLE PO7 80 E1
Beresford Cl CHFD SO53 38 B5 1
WVILLE PO7 81 K7
Beresford Gdns CHFD SO53 38 B5 2
Beresford Rd CHFD SO53 38 B5
FHAM/STUB PO14 114 E4
NEND PO2 118 D5
Bereweeke Av WINW SO22 21 H6
Bereweeke Cl WINW SO22 2 A1
Bereweeke Rd WINW SO22 2 A1
Bereweeke Wy WINW SO22 21 H5
Bergen Crs HEND SO30 58 B7
Berkeley Cl FHAM/STUB PO14 114 C5
WSHM SO15 4 D5
Berkeley Gdns HEND SO30 58 B7
Berkeley Rd WSHM SO15 4 D5
Berkeley Sq HAV PO9 15 J4
Berkshire Cl PSEA PO1 18 F4
Bernard Av CHAM PO6 101 F6
Bernard St SHAM SO14 9 G3
Berney Rd ENEY PO4 135 H4
Bernina Av WVILLE PO7 81 H3
Bernina Cl WVILLE PO7 81 H3
Bernwood Gv FAWY SO45 128 B1
Berry Cl HEND SO30 58 D6
Berrydown Rd HAV PO9 82 D6
Berry La FHAM/STUB PO14 114 B5
RWIN SO21 33 K2
Berrywood Gdns HEND SO30 58 A4 1
Bertie Rd ENEY PO4 135 G4
Beryl Av GPORT PO12 116 C7
Beryton Cl GPORT PO12 132 D2 2
Beryton Rd GPORT PO12 132 D2
Betteridge Dr ROWN SO16 41 J5
Bettesworth Rd PSEA PO1 134 D1
Betula Cl WVILLE PO7 82 B7 1
Beulah Rd ROWN SO16 54 B3
Bevan Cl ITCH SO19 10 D8
Bevan Rd HORN PO8 64 A7
Beverley Cl HLER SO31 95 H2
Beverley Gdns BPWT SO32 49 J6 1
HLER SO31 73 H4
ROMY SO51 35 H1 2
Beverley Hts WEND SO18 56 C1
Beverley Rd FAWY SO45 91 G6
FHAM/STUB PO14 114 D6
Beverly Cl LSOL/BMARY PO13 116 A5
Beverston Rd CHAM PO6 99 K5
Bevis Cl FAWY SO45 110 C5
HLER SO31 94 C6
Bevis Rd GPORT PO12 16 B4
NEND PO2 118 C6
Bevois Gdns SHAM SO14 5 G4
Bevois Hl PTSW SO17 5 J3
Bevois Valley Rd SHAM SO14 5 J5
Beyne Rd WINW SO22 24 E5
Bidbury La HAV PO9 102 D5
Biddenfield La WHAM PO17 76 E1
Biddlecombe Cl
LSOL/BMARY PO13 115 K7
Bideford Cl ROWN SO16 53 K3
Bilberry Cl HLER SO31 94 E4
Bilberry Dr TOTT SO40 69 K3
Billett Av WVILLE PO7 82 A4
Billing Cl ENEY PO4 135 G5 1
Billington Gdns HEND SO30 58 C3
Billy Lawn Av HAV PO9 103 G2
Bilton Wy HSEA PO3 119 H5
Bindon Cl ROWN SO16 54 B2
Bindon Rd ROWN SO16 54 B2
Binnacle Wy CHAM PO6 100 A6
Binness Wy CHAM PO6 101 K7
Binsey Cl ROWN SO16 53 K4
Binstead Cl ROWN SO16 43 K6
Binsteed Rd NEND PO2 118 D7
Birch Cl HORN PO8 81 K2
ROMY SO51 35 H4
ROWN SO16 54 B2
Birch Dl FAWY SO45 91 J4
Birchdale Cl HLER SO31 94 C6 2
Birch Dr LSOL/BMARY PO13 115 K3
Birchen Cl HLER SO31 95 H2 1
The Birches Cl NBAD SO52 36 A5
The Birches WEND SO18 7 K2
Birch Gv ELGH SO50 38 C4
Birchlands TOTT SO40 52 C7
Birchmore Cl
LSOL/BMARY PO13 115 K5 2
Birch Rd HEND SO30 58 C5
ROWN SO16 43 H3
ROWN SO16 54 B2
Birch Tree Cl EMRTH PO10 104 C2
Birch Tree Dr EMRTH PO10 104 C2
Birch Wd ITCH SO19 57 H7
Birchwood Gdns HEND SO30 58 B4 2
Birdham Rd HISD PO11 138 B6
Birdlip Cl HORN PO8 64 B6
Birdlip Rd CHAM PO6 100 A5
Birdwood Gv FHAM/PORC PO16 98 C6
Birinus Rd WINC SO23 2 F2
Birkdale Av CHAM PO6 101 H5
Biscay Cl FHAM/STUB PO14 114 C4 1
Bishops Cl TOTT SO40 52 D4
Bishops Ct ELGH SO50 39 G5
Bishops Crs ITCH SO19 10 E2
Bishopsfield Rd
FHAM/STUB PO14 12 D8
Bishops Ga FHAM/STUB PO14 95 H3
Bishop's La BPWT SO32 48 D4
BPWT SO32 61 J3
Bishops Rd ITCH SO19 10 D3
Bishopstoke La ELGH SO50 39 H4
Bishopstoke Rd ELGH SO50 39 F7
HAV PO9 103 F1
Bishop St PSEA PO1 17 M3
Bishop's Wood Rd BPWT SO32 61 J1
Bittern Cl GPORT PO12 132 E1
Bitterne Cl HAV PO9 83 G7
Bitterne Crs ITCH SO19 7 G7
Bitterne Pk Triangle WEND SO18 6 B1
Bitterne Rd East WEND SO18 7 J6
Bitterne Rd West WEND SO18 6 C4
Bitterne Wy ITCH SO19 6 E6
Blackberry Ter SHAM SO14 5 J5 1
Blackbird Cl HORN PO8 82 A1
Blackbird Rd ELGH SO50 44 A1
Blackbird Wy
LSOL/BMARY PO13 131 G1
Blackbrook House Dr
FHAM PO15 12 D5
Blackbrook Park Av
FHAM PO15 12 C5
Blackbrook Rd FHAM PO15 12 D5
Blackbushe Cl ROWN SO16 42 A6 2
Blackcap Cl HAV PO9 83 H4
Blackdown Cl FAWY SO45 90 E4 1
Blackdown Crs HAV PO9 103 F2
Blackfield Rd FAWY SO45 110 B6
Blackfriars Cl SSEA PO5 18 E5 2
Blackfriars Rd SSEA PO5 18 E4
Black Horse La BPWT SO32 61 F3
Blackhouse La WHAM PO17 78 D5
Blackthorn Cl ITCH SO19 6 F8 1
Blackthorn Dr GPORT PO12 116 D6
HISD PO11 137 K5
Blackthorn Gn RWIN SO21 39 K2
Blackthorn Rd HISD PO11 137 K5
ITCH SO19 6 E9
Blackwater Cl CHAM PO6 100 C6 1
Blackwater Dr TOTT SO40 52 C3
Blackwater Ms TOTT SO40 52 C3
Bladon Cl HAV PO9 15 L1
Bladon Rd ROWN SO16 54 D2
Blake Cl ROWN SO16 41 H6 1
Blakemere Crs CHAM PO6 100 B5
Blakeney Rd ROWN SO16 53 J2
Blake Rd CHAM PO6 101 J5
GPORT PO12 16 C4
Blakesley La HSEA PO3 119 H3
Blanchard Rd BPWT SO32 48 C3
Blankney Cl
FHAM/STUB PO14 114 C5 1
Blann Cl ROWN SO16 41 H6 2
Bleaklow Cl ROWN SO16 54 A4
Blechynden Ter WSHM SO15 4 D9
Blencowe Dr NBAD SO52 37 F5
Blendworth Crs HAV PO9 103 F3
Blendworth La HORN PO8 64 E5
WEND SO18 7 M4
Blendworth Rd ENEY PO4 135 G3 1
Blenheim Av PTSW SO17 5 G1
Blenheim Cl NBAD SO52 37 G6
TOTT SO40 52 C6
Blenheim Ct ENEY PO4 19 L8
Blenheim Gdns FAWY SO45 90 E4
GPORT PO12 116 E7
HAV PO9 15 L2
PTSW SO17 55 J2
Blenheim Rd ELGH SO50 44 D1
HORN PO8 64 B7
Bleriot Crs FHAM PO15 95 K1
Blighmont Crs WSHM SO15 54 C6
Blind La BPWT SO32 46 B6
BPWT SO32 59 K2
WHAM PO17 61 G7
Bliss Cl WVILLE PO7 101 K1
Blissford Cl HAV PO9 83 J7 1
Blossom Cl HEND SO30 58 D6
Blount Rd PSEA PO1 18 A7
Blue Ball Hl WINC SO23 3 G4
Bluebell Cl WVILLE PO7 82 A7
Bluebell Copse HLER SO31 94 E4
Bluebell Rd ROWN SO16 43 J7
Bluestar Gdns HEND SO30 58 B2
Blundell La HLER SO31 74 B3
Blyth Cl ROWN SO16 53 J2
Boakes Pl TOTT SO40 68 B3 1
Boarhunt Cl PSEA PO1 18 E3 1
Boarhunt Rd WHAM PO17 98 B3
Bodmin Rd CHAM PO6 99 K6 1
ELGH SO50 39 H7
Bodycoats Rd CHFD SO53 38 A4
Bolde Cl HSEA PO3 119 G4
Boldens Rd GPORT PO12 132 E7
Bolderwood Cl ELGH SO50 39 J7
Boldre Cl HAV PO9 102 D2 1
Boldrewood Rd ROWN SO16 43 F7
Bolhinton Av TOTT SO40 69 J4
The Boltons WVILLE PO7 101 K3 1
Bonchurch Cl ROWN SO16 43 K6 1
Bonchurch Rd ENEY PO4 19 M4
Bondfields Crs HAV PO9 83 G7
Bond Rd WEND SO18 6 B1
Bond St SHAM SO14 5 M7
Bonfire Cnr PSEA PO1 17 L2
Boniface Cl TOTT SO40 52 C4 1
Boniface Crs ROWN SO16 53 K1
Boothby Cl TOTT SO40 53 F6 1
Bordon Rd HAV PO9 103 G1
Borrowdale Rd ROWN SO16 53 K3
Boscobel Rd WINW SO22 2 C1
Bosham Rd NEND PO2 118 E7
Bosham Wk
LSOL/BMARY PO13 115 J5
Bosmere Gdns EMRTH PO10 104 B5
Bosmere Rd HISD PO11 138 B6
Bossington Cl ROWN SO16 41 K6 1
Bostock Cl RWIN SO21 20 A4
Boston Rd CHAM PO6 100 D5
Bosuns Cl FHAM/PORC PO16 115 J1
Bosville ELGH SO50 38 D4
Boswell Cl HEND SO30 58 E5
ITCH SO19 7 M7
Botany Bay Rd ITCH SO19 11 H5
Botley Dr HAV PO9 102 E1
Botley Gdns ITCH SO19 73 H2 2
Botley Rd BPWT SO32 48 B7
ELGH SO50 46 C3
HEND SO30 57 J3
HLER SO31 75 F5
ITCH SO19 11 M5
ITCH SO19 73 G2 1
NBAD SO52 36 D7
ROMY SO51 35 F3
Boulter La WHAM PO17 79 K6
Boulton Rd SSEA PO5 19 G8
Boundary Cl WSHM SO15 54 A6
Boundary Rd HLER SO31 73 J5
Boundary Wy CHAM PO6 101 G4
HAV PO9 14 D4
Bound La HISD PO11 137 H6
Boundstone FAWY SO45 91 G3 1
Bourne Av WSHM SO15 54 D3
Bourne Cl HORN PO8 64 C6
RWIN SO21 32 E5
Bourne La RWIN SO21 33 K2
TOTT SO40 51 G7
Bournemouth Av GPORT PO12 132 D1
Bournemouth Rd CHFD SO53 37 K5
LYND SO43 86 B1
ROWN SO16 43 H3
Bourne Rd CHAM PO6 100 A6
TOTT SO40 51 F7
WSHM SO15 4 B8
Bourne View Cl EMRTH PO10 105 G4
Bowater Cl TOTT SO40 52 B3
Bowater Wy TOTT SO40 52 B3
Bowcombe HLER SO31 73 F6
Bowden La PTSW SO17 55 K2
Bower Cl FAWY SO45 109 K4
ITCH SO19 10 F8
Bowers Cl HORN PO8 82 B1
Bowes Hl HAV PO9 83 K2
Bowland Ri CHFD SO53 37 H3
Bowland Wy FAWY SO45 128 B1 1
Bowler Av HSEA PO3 19 K1 1
Bowler Ct HSEA PO3 19 K1
Boxwood Cl
FHAM/PORC PO16 98 E5 1
WVILLE PO7 81 K7
Boyatt Crs ELGH SO50 38 D2
Boyatt La CHFD SO53 38 D1
ELGH SO50 38 D3
Boyd Cl FHAM/STUB PO14 114 C6 1
Boyd Rd LSOL/BMARY PO13 115 J4
Boyes La RWIN SO21 39 K1
Boyle Crs WVILLE PO7 101 J1
Boynton Cl CHFD SO53 37 J2
Brabant Cl HLER SO31 75 G6
Brabazon Rd FHAM PO15 95 J1
Bracken Cl NBAD SO52 36 B7
Bracken Crs ELGH SO50 45 J1
Bracken Heath HORN PO8 82 C4
Bracken La ROWN SO16 54 B3
Bracken Pl ELGH SO50 43 H4
Bracken Rd NBAD SO52 36 B7
The Brackens FAWY SO45 90 E3 2
HLER SO31 95 G4
Brackenway Rd CHFD SO53 37 K2
Bracklesham Cl ITCH SO19 10 F3
Bracklesham Rd HISD PO11 138 C7
LSOL/BMARY PO13 116 A7
Brackley Av ELGH SO50 46 A1
Brackley Wy TOTT SO40 52 C4
Bradford Rd SSEA PO5 18 F5
Brading Av ENEY PO4 135 F6
LSOL/BMARY PO13 115 K5
Brading Cl ROWN SO16 43 K6

Bradley Ct HAV PO9 103 J1
Bradley Gn ROWN SO16 42 C7
Bradley Peak WINW SO22 21 F6
Bradley Rd WINW SO22 21 F4
Bradly Rd FHAM PO15 96 D5
Bradshaw Cl ELGH SO50 46 D1 1
Braehead FAWY SO45 91 G4
Braemar Av CHAM PO6 101 G7
Braemar Cl FHAM PO15 12 D1
LSOL/BMARY PO13 116 A5
Braemar Rd
LSOL/BMARY PO13 116 A4
Braeside Cl WINW SO22 24 E4
ITCH SO19 6 C8
Braeside Crs ITCH SO19 6 D8
Braeside Rd ITCH SO19 6 C8
Braintree Rd CHAM PO6 100 C5
Brairwood Gdns HISD PO11 137 G5
Braishfield Cl ROWN SO16 54 A3
Braishfield Rd HAV PO9 103 H2
ROMY SO51 35 H1
Bramber Rd GPORT PO12 132 D1
Bramble Cl ELGH SO50 38 E5 2
FAWY SO45 109 K4
FHAM/STUB PO14 114 B6
Bramble Dr ROMY SO51 35 H1 3
Bramble Hl CHFD SO53 37 J4
Bramble La HLER SO31 94 D1
Bramble Ms WEND SO18 7 H2
Bramble Rd ENEY PO4 19 G6
Brambles Cl RWIN SO21 39 K2
Brambles Rd
LSOL/BMARY PO13 130 E1 1
Bramble Wy
LSOL/BMARY PO13 115 H5
Brambling Cl ROWN SO16 42 C5 1
Brambling Rd HAV PO9 83 J4
The Bramblings TOTT SO40 52 B4 2
Bramdean Dr HAV PO9 102 E1
Bramdean Rd WEND SO18 57 G5
Bramham Moor
FHAM/STUB PO14 114 C5 2
Bramley Cl WVILLE PO7 82 A5
Bramley Crs ITCH SO19 11 J6
Bramley Gdns EMRTH PO10 104 E6
GPORT PO12 132 D7
Brampton La HSEA PO3 119 H3
Bramshaw Cl WINW SO22 21 F4
Bramshaw Ct HAV PO9 103 J1 3
Bramshott Rd ENEY PO4 19 K6
ITCH SO19 10 F9
Bramston Rd WSHM SO15 54 D4
Brandon Rd SSEA PO5 134 C6
Branksome Av WSHM SO15 54 D3
Branksome Cl WINW SO22 24 E2
Bransbury Cl ROWN SO16 42 D7 1
Bransbury Rd ENEY PO4 135 G5
Bransgore Av HAV PO9 102 D2
Bransley Cl ROMY SO51 35 G1
Brasenose Cl FHAM/STUB PO14 95 H5
Brasher Cl ELGH SO50 45 K1
Brassey Rd WINW SO22 2 C1
Brasted Ct ENEY PO4 135 H3 1
Brazil Rd SHAM SO14 9 J6
Breach Av EMRTH PO10 105 G4
Breamore Cl ELGH SO50 38 D4 1
Breamore Rd WEND SO18 57 G5
Brean Cl ROWN SO16 53 K1
Brecon Av CHAM PO6 101 G5
Brecon Cl CHFD SO53 37 J7 1
FAWY SO45 91 F3
FHAM/STUB PO14 12 B7
Brecon Rd ITCH SO19 7 L8
Bredenbury Crs CHAM PO6 100 B5
Breech Cl HSEA PO3 118 E3 3
Brenchley Cl FHAM/PORC PO16 98 D7
Brendon Cl FAWY SO45 90 E4 2
Brendon Gn ROWN SO16 54 A4
Brendon Rd FHAM/STUB PO14 12 A8
Brent Ct EMRTH PO10 104 B6
Brentwood Crs WEND SO18 56 D3
Breton Cl FHAM PO15 75 G6
Brewer Cl HLER SO31 95 G2
Brewers La LSOL/BMARY PO13 115 K5
RWIN SO21 33 J4
Brewer St PSEA PO1 18 C2
Brewhouse Sq GPORT PO12 16 E3
Brewster Cl HORN PO8 82 B2
Briar Cl GPORT PO12 132 B5
HORN PO8 64 C7
Briardene Ct TOTT SO40 52 D5 1
Briarfield Gdns HORN PO8 64 C6
Briarswood ROWN SO16 54 C3
Briarswood Ri FAWY SO45 90 E4
Briar Wy ROMY SO51 35 H1
Briarwood Cl FHAM/PORC PO16 13 J7
Briarwood Rd TOTT SO40 52 B6
Brickfield La CHFD SO53 37 J5
Brickfield Rd PTSW SO17 55 K2
Brickmakers Rd RWIN SO21 39 J2
Brickwoods ROMY SO51 35 G2 2
Brickyard Rd BPWT SO32 61 G1
The Brickyard TOTT SO40 50 E4
Bridefield Cl HORN PO8 81 J2
Bridefield Crs HORN PO8 81 J2
Bridge Cl HLER SO31 74 A4
Bridgefoot Dr
FHAM/PORC PO16 13 M5
Bridgefoot Pth EMRTH PO10 104 C6
Bridgemary Av
LSOL/BMARY PO13 116 A4
Bridgemary Gv
LSOL/BMARY PO13 115 K3
Bridgemary Rd
LSOL/BMARY PO13 115 K2
Bridgemary Wy
LSOL/BMARY PO13 115 K2 1
Bridge Rd EMRTH PO10 104 C5
HLER SO31 74 D7
ITCH SO19 10 B3
ROMY SO51 34 E3
Bridgers Cl ROWN SO16 41 K6
Bridges Cl ELGH SO50 38 C7
Bridgeside Cl PSEA PO1 18 F3
Bridge St FHAM/STUB PO14 96 B6
WHAM PO17 77 H1
WHAM PO17 79 G7
WINC SO23 3 G5 1
Bridget Cl HORN PO8 64 D5
Bridgwater Ct WSHM SO15 4 A8

Bridlington Av WSHM SO15 4 A2
Bridport St PSEA PO1 18 D3
Brigantine Rd HLER SO31 94 D5
Brighstone Cl ROWN SO16 43 K6 3
Brighton Av GPORT PO12 116 C7
Brighton Rd WSHM SO15 4 F4
Brightside WVILLE PO7 81 J7
Brightside Rd ROWN SO16 54 A2
Brights La HISD PO11 137 G3
Brightstone Rd CHAM PO6 100 D7
Brindle Cl ROWN SO16 43 H6
Brinton La FAWY SO45 91 H1
Brinton's Rd SHAM SO14 5 H8
Brinton's Ter SHAM SO14 5 H7
Bristol Rd ENEY PO4 19 K9
Britain St PSEA PO1 17 M4
Britannia Gdns HEND SO30 58 A1 2
Britannia Rd SHAM SO14 5 K8
SSEA PO5 18 F6 1
Britannia Rd North SSEA PO5 18 F6
Briton St SHAM SO14 8 F4
Britten Rd LSOL/BMARY PO13 131 F2
Britten Wy WVILLE PO7 101 K2
Broadbent Cl ROWN SO16 41 J5
Broad Chalke Down WINW SO22 25 F4
Broad Cft HAV PO9 83 K3
Broadcut FHAM/PORC PO16 13 M3
Broad Gdns CHAM PO6 101 K6
Broad Gn SHAM SO14 5 H9
Broadlands Av ELGH SO50 38 D5
WVILLE PO7 81 K7
Broadlands Rd PTSW SO17 55 J1
Broad La BPWT SO32 49 H6
NBAD SO52 35 K5 1
WVILLE PO7 62 A6
Broadley Cl FAWY SO45 109 K3 1
Broadmeadow Cl TOTT SO40 52 D5
Broadmeadows La
WVILLE PO7 82 B6 1
Broadmead Rd ROWN SO16 41 J5
Broadmere Av HAV PO9 103 G1
Broad Oak HEND SO30 58 D5
Broadoak Cl FAWY SO45 109 K4
Broadsands Dr GPORT PO12 132 A5
Broad St PSEA PO1 17 K7
Broad View La WINW SO22 24 D5
Broadwater Rd ROMY SO51 34 D4
WEND SO18 56 C1
Broad Wy HLER SO31 93 H1
Broadway La HORN PO8 63 J6
The Broadway WINC SO23 2 F5
Brockenhurst Av HAV PO9 82 E7
Brockhampton La HAV PO9 14 D5
Brockhampton Rd HAV PO9 14 B5
Brockhurst Rd GPORT PO12 132 C1
Brockishill Rd LYND SO43 66 C1
TOTT SO40 50 D7
Brocklands HAV PO9 14 B4
Brocks Cl FAWY SO45 90 E4
Brodrick Av GPORT PO12 132 D5
Brokenford Av TOTT SO40 53 F5
Brokenford La TOTT SO40 52 E5
Bromley Rd WEND SO18 6 F1
Brompton Rd ENEY PO4 19 K9
Bromyard Crs CHAM PO6 100 B6
Bronte Cl TOTT SO40 52 C6
Bronte Gdns FHAM PO15 75 H5 2
Bronte Wy ITCH SO19 6 D7
Brook Av HLER SO31 94 B3
Brook Cl HLER SO31 94 C3 1
NBAD SO52 36 B7
Brookdale Cl WVILLE PO7 81 K5
Brookers La
LSOL/BMARY PO13 115 H4
Brook Farm Av FHAM PO15 12 E5
Brookfield Cl HAV PO9 14 D2
Brookfield Gdns HLER SO31 94 E2
Brookfield Rd ELGH SO50 46 A1
PSEA PO1 19 H2
Brook Gdns EMRTH PO10 104 A6
Brooklands Rd BPWT SO32 48 D3
HAV PO9 102 C4
Brook La HEND SO30 58 E6
HLER SO31 94 D3
Brooklyn Cl RWIN SO21 33 F6
Brooklyn Dr WVILLE PO7 82 A5 1
Brooklynn Cl BPWT SO32 61 F2
Brookmeadow FHAM PO15 12 E5
Brookmead Wy HAV PO9 14 E8
Brook Rd ELGH SO50 46 B1
WEND SO18 7 H4
Brookside LSOL/BMARY PO13 115 J2
TOTT SO40 52 E7
Brookside Av WSHM SO15 54 A5
Brookside Cl WVILLE PO7 80 E1
Brookside Rd HAV PO9 14 B6
Brookside Wy HEND SO30 57 H1 1
WEND SO18 44 B7
Brook St BPWT SO32 48 D4
Brookvale Rd PTSW SO17 55 H3
Brook Va ROWN SO16 54 B2
Brook Wy ROMY SO51 29 G7
Brookwood Av ELGH SO50 38 C7
Brookwood Rd ROWN SO16 53 J4
Broom Cl ENEY PO4 135 J4
WVILLE PO7 102 B1
Broomfield Crs
LSOL/BMARY PO13 131 J1
Broom Hill Wy ELGH SO50 38 C3
Brooms Gv ITCH SO19 73 G2
Broom Sq ENEY PO4 135 J4
Broom Wy LSOL/BMARY PO13 131 G1
Broomy Cl FAWY SO45 90 D2 1
Brougham La GPORT PO12 132 D2 3
Brougham Rd SSEA PO5 18 C6
Brougham St GPORT PO12 132 D2 4
Broughton Cl ROWN SO16 54 B3
Broughton Ct HSEA PO3 119 H3 2
Broughton Rd LYND SO43 66 B7
Browndown Rd
LSOL/BMARY PO13 131 K5
Brownhill Cl CHFD SO53 37 K3
Brownhill Ct ROWN SO16 53 K1
Brownhill Rd CHFD SO53 37 K3
NBAD SO52 36 C6
Brownhill Wy ROWN SO16 53 H1
Browning Av CHAM PO6 99 H5
ITCH SO19 57 G6
Browning Cl ELGH SO50 38 C7 1
HLER SO31 75 H5

TOTT SO40 52 C5
Browning Dr WINW SO22 21 G7
Brownlow Av ITCH SO19 7 G6
Brownlow Cl PSEA PO1 134 C1 2
Brownlow Gdns ITCH SO19 7 G7
Brownwich La
FHAM/STUB PO14 113 J2
The Brow WVILLE PO7 101 H4
Broxburn Cl CHFD SO53 38 B1
Broxhead Rd HAV PO9 83 H7 1
Bruce Cl FHAM/PORC PO16 13 H2
Bruce Rd ENEY PO4 134 E6
Brue Cl CHFD SO53 37 J3
Brune La LSOL/BMARY PO13 115 H6
Brunel Cl HEND SO30 58 C3 1
Brunel Rd NEND PO2 118 D4
TOTT SO40 52 C1
WSHM SO15 53 H5
Brunel Wy FHAM PO15 95 J1
Brunswick Gdns HAV PO9 14 A3
Brunswick Pl WSHM SO15 4 F7
Brunswick Sq SHAM SO14 9 G4
Brunswick St SSEA PO5 18 C6 1
Bryanston Rd ITCH SO19 10 B1
Bryher Island CHAM PO6 100 A7
Bryony Cl HLER SO31 94 E4 1
Bryony Gdns ELGH SO50 46 B5 1
Bryony Wy WVILLE PO7 82 B7
Bryson Rd CHAM PO6 100 C6 2
Bubb La BPWT SO32 46 B7
HEND SO30 58 A1
Buchanan Rd ROWN SO16 42 A6
Buchan Av FHAM PO15 75 H5
Buchan Ct FAWY SO45 90 D4
Buckby La HSEA PO3 119 H3
Bucketts Farm Cl BPWT SO32 49 J6
Buckingham Ga WSHM SO15 4 D3
Buckingham St PSEA PO1 18 D2
Buckland Cl ELGH SO50 38 D5
WVILLE PO7 81 J3
Buckland Gdns TOTT SO40 52 B2
Buckland St NEND PO2 134 D1 2
Bucklers Ct HAV PO9 82 E6
NEND PO2 118 C6 1
Bucklers Rd GPORT PO12 117 F7
Bucksey Rd
LSOL/BMARY PO13 115 K7
Buckthorn Cl TOTT SO40 51 K4
Buddens Rd WHAM PO17 77 H1
Budds La ROMY SO51 34 D1
Bude Cl CHAM PO6 99 J5
Bugle St SHAM SO14 8 F4
Bulbeck Rd HAV PO9 14 E5
Bullar Rd WEND SO18 6 C3
Bullar St SHAM SO14 5 J7
Bull Dro WINC SO23 26 A3
Bullfinch Cl TOTT SO40 52 B5 2
Bull Hl LYMN SO41 124 A7
Bull La BPWT SO32 60 E1
Bullrush Cl FAWY SO45 91 G5
Bulls Copse La HORN PO8 64 B6
Bunkers Hl WVILLE PO7 80 C2
Bunny La ROMY SO51 28 E3
Bunstead La RWIN SO21 32 A3
Bunting Gdns HORN PO8 82 A1
Burbidge Gv ENEY PO4 135 F6
Burbush Cl FAWY SO45 109 K4
Burcote Dr HSEA PO3 119 G3
Burdale Dr HISD PO11 138 A5
Burgate Cl HAV PO9 102 E3
Burgess Cl HISD PO11 138 A7
Burgess Gdns ROWN SO16 55 F1 4
Burgess Rd PTSW SO17 43 J7
WSHM SO15 54 E2
Burghclere Rd HAV PO9 83 J7
ITCH SO19 10 E9
Burgoyne Rd ITCH SO19 73 H1
SSEA PO5 134 C7
Burgundy Cl HLER SO31 94 E4 2
Buriton Cl FHAM/PORC PO16 99 G5
Buriton Rd WINW SO22 21 G3
Buriton St PSEA PO1 18 E2 1
Burke Dr ITCH SO19 7 M7
Burleigh Rd NEND PO2 118 E7
Burley Cl CHFD SO53 37 J6
HAV PO9 83 J7 2
Burley Down CHFD SO53 37 J6
Burley Rd WINW SO22 21 G3
Burlington Rd NEND PO2 118 D6
WSHM SO15 4 D6
Burmah Rd North FAWY SO45 111 F1
Burmah Rd South FAWY SO45 110 E2
Burma Wy TOTT SO40 70 A5
Burmese Cl FHAM PO15 75 H6
Burnaby Rd PSEA PO1 18 A4
Burnbank Gdns TOTT SO40 52 D5
Burnett Cl FAWY SO45 91 J4
WINW SO22 21 F5
WEND SO18 6 C1
Burnett Rd GPORT PO12 132 C2
Burnetts Flds ELGH SO50 46 B4
Burnetts Gdns ELGH SO50 46 C4
Burnetts La HEND SO30 46 A7
Burney Rd GPORT PO12 132 B5
Burnham Beeches CHFD SO53 37 J4
Burnham Cha WEND SO18 7 K4
Burnham Rd CHAM PO6 101 J5
Burnham Wd
FHAM/PORC PO16 13 G1
Burns Cl ELGH SO50 44 B2
Burnside LSOL/BMARY PO13 115 J2
WVILLE PO7 82 B4
Burns Pl ROWN SO16 54 B2
Burns Rd ELGH SO50 44 C2
ITCH SO19 57 G7
Burnt House La
FHAM/STUB PO14 114 E4
Burr Cl RWIN SO21 39 J2
Burrfields Rd HSEA PO3 119 F6
Burridge Rd HLER SO31 75 F3
Burrill Av CHAM PO6 101 F6
Burrows Cl HAV PO9 15 H1
Bursledon Hts HLER SO31 74 A4
Bursledon Pl WVILLE PO7 101 J1
Bursledon Rd HEND SO30 58 A7
ITCH SO19 7 H6
WVILLE PO7 101 J1
Burton Rd WSHM SO15 4 D5
Burwood Gv HISD PO11 137 H4
Bury Cl GPORT PO12 16 B6

Bury Crs GPORT PO12 16 A6
Bury Hall La GPORT PO12 132 C5
Bury La TOTT SO40 53 G7
Bury Rd GPORT PO12 16 A6
TOTT SO40 69 J2
Bush Saint West SSEA PO5 18 C7 1
Bush St East SSEA PO5 18 C7
Bushy Md WVILLE PO7 101 H3
Busket La WINC SO23 2 F5
Busketts Wy TOTT SO40 67 K3
Butcher St PSEA PO1 17 L4
Buttercup Cl FAWY SO45 91 H5 2
HEND SO30 57 K6 1
Buttercup Wy HLER SO31 94 D3
Butterfield Rd ROWN SO16 43 F7
Butterfly Dr CHAM PO6 99 K4
Buttermere Cl ROWN SO16 53 K2
Buttsash Av FAWY SO45 91 H6
Butts Ash Gdns FAWY SO45 91 H5
Butts Ash La FAWY SO45 91 H5 3
Butts Bridge Hl FAWY SO45 91 H4
Buttsbridge Rd FAWY SO45 91 H5
Butts Cl WINW SO22 21 G6
ITCH SO19 73 G1 1
Butt's Crs ITCH SO19 11 M2
Butts La BPWT SO32 48 E3
Butt's Rd ITCH SO19 73 G1 2
Butt's Sq ITCH SO19 11 M2
Byerley Cl EMRTH PO10 104 E1 1
Byerley Rd PSEA PO1 19 J2
Byeways FAWY SO45 91 G4 2
The Byeway SELS PO20 139 K7
By-pass Rd ROMY SO51 34 D4
Byrd Cl WVILLE PO7 101 K1
Byron Av WINW SO22 21 G7
Byron Cl BPWT SO32 49 F3
FHAM/PORC PO16 13 G3
Byron Rd ELGH SO50 38 E6
ITCH SO19 7 M8
NEND PO2 118 E7

C

Cable St SHAM SO14 5 L8
Cabot Dr FAWY SO45 90 D3
Cadgwith Pl CHAM PO6 100 A7
Cadland Rd FAWY SO45 92 A7
Cadlands Park Est FAWY SO45 109 K1
Cadnam La TOTT SO40 50 C1
Cadnam Rd ENEY PO4 135 G5
Cador Dr FHAM/PORC PO16 116 E1
Caerleon Av ITCH SO19 7 L7
Caerleon Dr ITCH SO19 7 L7
Caernarvon Gdns CHFD SO53 37 H6 1
Cains Cl FHAM/STUB PO14 114 D4
Cairo Ter NEND PO2 134 C1
Caistor Cl ROWN SO16 42 B7
Calabrese HLER SO31 75 G6
Calbourne HLER SO31 73 F6 1
Calcot Hl BPWT SO32 59 K1
Calcot La BPWT SO32 59 K2
Calder Cl ROWN SO16 53 K4
Calderwood Dr ITCH SO19 11 G1
Caledonia Dr FAWY SO45 90 E3
Calmore Crs TOTT SO40 52 A3
Calmore Dr TOTT SO40 52 B2
Calmore Gdns TOTT SO40 52 B5
Calmore Rd TOTT SO40 52 A3
Calpe Av LYND SO43 66 C7
Calshot Cl FAWY SO45 111 J7
Calshot Dr CHFD SO53 37 H6
Calshot Rd FAWY SO45 110 E4
HAV PO9 82 D6
Calshot Wy
LSOL/BMARY PO13 115 J6 2
Camargue Cl HLER SO31 75 G5
Camber Pl PSEA PO1 17 K7
Cambria Dr FAWY SO45 90 E3
Cambrian Cl HLER SO31 73 K3 2
Cambridge Dr CHFD SO53 37 K7
Cambridge Gn
FHAM/STUB PO14 95 H4
Cambridge Rd GPORT PO12 132 B2
LSOL/BMARY PO13 131 G3
PSEA PO1 18 A6
SHAM SO14 5 G3
Camcross Cl CHAM PO6 100 A5 1
Camden St GPORT PO12 132 D2
Camelia Cl HAV PO9 103 J3
NBAD SO52 36 B5
Camelia Gdns WEND SO18 56 D2 3
Camelia Gv ELGH SO50 46 D1
Camelot Crs FHAM/PORC PO16 98 E5
Cameron Cl
LSOL/BMARY PO13 115 K4 1
Camley Cl ITCH SO19 10 D8
Campbell Rd ELGH SO50 44 E2
SSEA PO5 18 F7
Campbell St SHAM SO14 5 L7
Campbell Wy ELGH SO50 46 B1
Campion Cl ELGH SO50 46 B5 2
HLER SO31 94 D5
WVILLE PO7 82 B7 2
Campion Dr ROMY SO51 35 H1
Campion Rd ITCH SO19 57 G7
Campion Wy WINC SO23 22 B1
Camp Rd LSOL/BMARY PO13 116 A4
Cams Bay Cl
FHAM/PORC PO16 98 C5 1
Cams Hl FHAM/PORC PO16 98 B5
WVILLE PO7 62 A3
Canada Rd ITCH SO19 10 D6
Canal Cl ROMY SO51 35 F1
Canal Wk ROMY SO51 34 E2
SHAM SO14 9 G3
SSEA PO5 18 E4
Canberra Cl GPORT PO12 132 C4 1
Canberra Rd EMRTH PO10 122 D4
ROWN SO16 41 G7
Candover Ct ITCH SO19 11 G9
Candy La WEND SO18 57 H5
Canford Cl BPWT SO32 61 F5
ROWN SO16 53 J2
Cannon St WSHM SO15 54 D4
Canoe Cl HLER SO31 94 E5
Canon's Barn Cl
FHAM/PORC PO16 99 F5 1
Canon St WINC SO23 2 D6

Canterbury Av ITCH SO19 11 L3
Canterbury Cl
LSOL/BMARY PO13 131 J4
Canterbury Dr FAWY SO45 90 D3
Canterbury Rd ENEY PO4 19 K7
FHAM/STUB PO14 114 D4
Canton St WSHM SO15 4 E6
Canute Rd SHAM SO14 9 K4
WINC SO23 3 H7
Capella Gdns FAWY SO45 90 E3 3
Capel Ley WVILLE PO7 101 K2
Capers End La BPWT SO32 59 K3
Captains Pl SHAM SO14 9 J4
Captains Rw PSEA PO1 17 K7
Carberry Dr FHAM/PORC PO16 98 E7
Carbery Ct HAV PO9 82 E6
Carbis Cl CHAM PO6 99 K7
Cardiff Rd NEND PO2 118 C5
Cardinal Dr WVILLE PO7 82 C4
Cardinal Wy HLER SO31 95 G3
Carey Rd ITCH SO19 7 M9
Carisbrooke HLER SO31 73 F6 2
Carisbrooke Av
FHAM/STUB PO14 114 B5
Carisbrooke Cl HAV PO9 15 J3
Carisbrooke Ct ROMY SO51 35 F1 1
Carisbrooke Crs CHFD SO53 38 B5
Carisbrooke Dr ITCH SO19 6 F7
Carisbrooke Rd ENEY PO4 19 L5 1
LSOL/BMARY PO13 115 J4
Carless Cl LSOL/BMARY PO13 132 A1
Carlisle Rd ROWN SO16 54 C4
SSEA PO5 18 F4
Carlton Crs WSHM SO15 4 F6
Carlton Pl WSHM SO15 4 F7
Carlton Rd FHAM/PORC PO16 99 G5
GPORT PO12 16 D5
WSHM SO15 4 F5
Carlton Wy GPORT PO12 16 D4
Carlyle Rd GPORT PO12 16 A3
Carlyn Dr CHFD SO53 38 A3
Carmans La RWIN SO21 33 G2
Carmarthen Av CHAM PO6 101 G5
Carnarvon Rd GPORT PO12 132 D4
NEND PO2 118 E7
Carnation Rd ROWN SO16 43 K7
Carne Cl CHFD SO53 37 K2
Caroline Pl GPORT PO12 16 B2
Carolyn Cl ITCH SO19 10 C6
Carpathia Cl WEND SO18 56 D2 4
Carpenter Cl ENEY PO4 19 M8 1
FAWY SO45 91 H2 2
Carraway FHAM PO15 75 J6
Carroll Cl ELGH SO50 46 C2 2
Carronade Wk HSEA PO3 118 E2
Carshalton Av CHAM PO6 101 G6
Carter's La TOTT SO40 89 K1
Carthage Cl CHFD SO53 38 C3
Cartwright Dr FHAM PO15 96 A4
Cascades Ap PSEA PO1 18 C2
Cask St PSEA PO1 18 D1 3
Caspar John Cl
FHAM/STUB PO14 114 C6
Caspian Cl HLER SO31 75 G6
Castle Av HAV PO9 15 K5
Castle Cl SSEA PO5 18 C7
Castle Ct WSHM SO15 54 B6
Castle Farm La WHAM PO17 77 J3
Castle Gv FHAM/PORC PO16 99 G7
Castle La CHFD SO53 37 H6
FAWY SO45 129 J1
NBAD SO52 36 E6
SHAM SO14 8 F2
Castlemans La HISD PO11 121 H6
Castle Rd HAV PO9 83 H3
HLER SO31 72 E7
SSEA PO5 18 B8
WEND SO18 56 B2
WHAM PO17 79 J7
Castleshaw Cl ROWN SO16 54 A5 1
Castle Sq SHAM SO14 8 F3
Castle St FHAM/PORC PO16 99 G7
FHAM/STUB PO14 96 A6
SHAM SO14 5 H5
Castle Vw GPORT PO12 116 E7
Castle View Rd
FHAM/PORC PO16 117 G1
Castleway HAV PO9 15 K5
Castle Wy SHAM SO14 8 F2
Catamaran Cl HLER SO31 94 E5
Cateran Cl ROWN SO16 54 A4 1
Cathay Gdns FAWY SO45 90 D3
Cathedral Vw WINC SO23 3 G7
Catherine Cl HEND SO30 57 H2
Catherine Gdns HEND SO30 57 H2
Catherington La HORN PO8 64 B3
Catherington Wy HAV PO9 103 G2
Catisfield La FHAM PO15 96 C5
Catisfield Rd ENEY PO4 135 G3
FHAM PO15 96 D5
Causeway Crs TOTT SO40 53 F4
Causeway Farm HORN PO8 64 C7
The Causeway
FHAM/PORC PO16 98 B5
Cavalier Cl FAWY SO45 90 D3
Cavanna Cl LSOL/BMARY PO13 115 J4
Cavell Dr CHAM PO6 100 D5
Cavendish Cl ROMY SO51 29 G7 1
WVILLE PO7 82 A5 2
Cavendish Dr WVILLE PO7 82 A6
Cavendish Gv WINC SO23 22 A4 1
WSHM SO15 4 F3
Cavendish Ms WSHM SO15 4 F3
Cavendish Rd SSEA PO5 18 E8
C Av FAWY SO45 110 A2
Caversham Cl HEND SO30 57 G3 1
ITCH SO19 11 H1
Cawte Rd WSHM SO15 4 A6
Caxton Av ITCH SO19 7 K6
Cecil Av ROWN SO16 54 C3
TOTT SO40 68 B3
Cecil Gv SSEA PO5 18 B8
Cecil Pl SSEA PO5 18 B8 1
Cecil Rd ITCH SO19 10 E4
Cedar Cl GPORT PO12 116 D6
HEND SO30 58 B5
HLER SO31 73 J5
WVILLE PO7 81 K7
Cedar Crs HORN PO8 64 D7
NBAD SO52 36 A5

Cedar Gdns HAV PO9 15 G2
Cedar Gv HSEA PO3 135 G1
Cedar Lawn ROMY SO51 35 H1
Cedarmount LYND SO43 86 C2
Cedar Rd ELGH SO50 44 B2
FAWY SO45 91 H7
SHAM SO14 5 H4
Cedar Wood Cl ELGH SO50 46 D1
TOTT SO40 52 B4 3
Cedric Cl FAWY SO45 110 C7
Celandine Av HLER SO31 94 E4
HORN PO8 82 D2
Celandine Cl NBAD SO52 37 G5 1
Celia Cl WVILLE PO7 82 C5
Cement Ter SHAM SO14 8 F3 1
Cemetery La EMRTH PO10 105 F3
WVILLE PO7 62 E7
Cemetery Rd WSHM SO15 4 D3
Centaur St NEND PO2 118 C7
Centaury Gdns ELGH SO50 46 B4 1
Central Br SHAM SO14 9 J3
Central Rd CHAM PO6 101 H7
FHAM/PORC PO16 98 E7
SHAM SO14 9 H5
Central Station Br WSHM SO15 4 C9
Central St PSEA PO1 18 E2
Centre Wy HLER SO31 95 F3
Cerdic Ms HLER SO31 93 K2
Cerne Cl NBAD SO52 35 K6
WEND SO18 56 E3
Chadderton Gdns PSEA PO1 18 A7
Chadwell Av ITCH SO19 11 K2
Chadwick Rd ELGH SO50 44 B1
Chafen Rd WEND SO18 6 A3
Chaffinch Cl TOTT SO40 52 B4 1
Chaffinch Gn HORN PO8 81 K1
Chaffinch Wy
FHAM/PORC PO16 98 C6
LSOL/BMARY PO13 131 G1 1
Chale Cl LSOL/BMARY PO13 115 K5
Chalewood Rd FAWY SO45 128 B1
Chalice Ct HEND SO30 58 A6 1
Chalk Hl WEND SO18 7 L1
Chalk La WHAM PO17 77 J6
Chalkpit Rd CHAM PO6 100 A4
Chalk Rdg HORN PO8 64 E1
WINC SO23 3 K6
Chalkridge Rd CHAM PO6 101 F5
Chalky La BPWT SO32 48 E3
Challenger Wy FAWY SO45 90 E2
Challis Ct SHAM SO14 9 H3
Chalmers Wy HLER SO31 93 H3
Chaloner Crs FAWY SO45 91 H5 1
Chalton Crs HAV PO9 102 E1
Chalvington Rd CHFD SO53 37 K5
Chalybeate Cl ROWN SO16 54 C2
Chamberlain Gv
FHAM/STUB PO14 13 G8
Chamberlain Rd PTSW SO17 55 H1
Chamberlayne Rd ELGH SO50 44 D2
HLER SO31 73 J5 2
Chambers Av ROMY SO51 35 G3
Chambers Cl ROWN SO16 41 H6
Chancellors La BPWT SO32 58 D1
Chancel Rd HLER SO31 95 G3
Chandlers Cl HISD PO11 137 K6 1
Chandlers Wy HLER SO31 75 G7
Chandos St SHAM SO14 9 H3
Channels Farm Rd ROWN SO16 44 A6
Channel Wy SHAM SO14 9 K4
Chantry Rd GPORT PO12 132 C1
HORN PO8 64 C5
SHAM SO14 9 K3
The Chantry FHAM/STUB PO14 95 H3
Chapel Crs ITCH SO19 11 H2
Chapel Dro ELGH SO50 46 B4
HEND SO30 58 A6
Chapel La BPWT SO32 59 K4
BROC SO42 125 H2
ELGH SO50 38 E1
FAWY SO45 110 B7
FAWY SO45 110 D4
LYND SO43 86 C2
ROMY SO51 28 C1
RWIN SO21 23 F5
TOTT SO40 52 D7
Chapel Rd BPWT SO32 49 J6
HEND SO30 57 H2
HLER SO31 74 D7
SHAM SO14 9 J2
Chapelside FHAM/STUB PO14 96 B6
Chapel St GPORT PO12 116 E7
NEND PO2 118 C7 1
SSEA PO5 18 B7 1
Chaplains Av HORN PO8 81 J2
Chaplains Cl HORN PO8 81 J1
Charden Rd ELGH SO50 45 K2
LSOL/BMARY PO13 116 A7
Charfield Cl FHAM/STUB PO14 12 A7
WINW SO22 25 H3
Chark La LSOL/BMARY PO13 115 G7
Charlecote Dr CHFD SO53 37 H2
Charlesbury Av GPORT PO12 132 C4 2
Charles Cl WINC SO23 21 K5
WVILLE PO7 81 J7
Charles Dickens St PSEA PO1 18 C4 1
Charles Knott Gdns
WSHM SO15 4 E4
Charles St PSEA PO1 18 E2
SHAM SO14 9 H3 1
Charleston Cl HISD PO11 137 F4
Charleston Rd FAWY SO45 92 A6
Charles Watts Wy HEND SO30 57 H5
Charlesworth Dr WVILLE PO7 81 J4
Charlesworth Gdns WVILLE PO7 81 J4
Charliejoy Gdns SHAM SO14 5 L7 1
Charlotte Pl SHAM SO14 5 H7 1
Charlotte St PSEA PO1 18 B1
Charlton Rd WSHM SO15 4 A4
Charminster Cl WVILLE PO7 81 K5
Charmus Rd TOTT SO40 52 A2
Charmwen Crs HEND SO30 57 F2
Charnwood
LSOL/BMARY PO13 116 A5
Charnwood Cl CHFD SO53 31 K7
TOTT SO40 52 C3
Charnwood Crs CHFD SO53 31 K7
Charnwood Gdns CHFD SO53 31 K7 1
Charnwood Wy FAWY SO45 128 A1
Charterhouse Wy HEND SO30 58 A3
Chartwell Cl ELGH SO50 38 E4
FHAM/STUB PO14 95 H5
Chartwell Dr HAV PO9 15 L1
Chase Farm Cl BPWT SO32 61 F1
Chase Gv BPWT SO32 61 F1
The Chase FHAM/STUB PO14 95 J4
GPORT PO12 132 C4
Chasewater Av HSEA PO3 135 F1
Chatburn Av HORN PO8 81 K2
Chatfield Av NEND PO2 117 K6
Chatfield Rd
LSOL/BMARY PO13 115 K3
Chatham Dr PSEA PO1 18 A7
Chatham Rd WINW SO22 25 F3
Chatsworth Av CHAM PO6 119 F1
Chatsworth Cl FHAM PO15 96 D5
Chatsworth Rd ELGH SO50 38 E4
ITCH SO19 7 H7
Chaucer Av CHAM PO6 99 H5
Chaucer Cl FHAM/PORC PO16 12 F4
WVILLE PO7 81 K3
Chaucer Rd ITCH SO19 57 G6
Chaundler Rd WINC SO23 21 K5
Chaveney Cl FAWY SO45 91 F5 1
FAWY SO45 91 G5 1
Chawton Cl WINW SO22 21 G3
WEND SO18 57 G4 1
Cheam Wy TOTT SO40 52 C3
Cheddar Cl ITCH SO19 10 C3
Chedworth Crs CHAM PO6 99 K5
Chelmsford Rd NEND PO2 118 E5
Chelsea Rd SSEA PO5 18 F8
Cheltenham Crs
LSOL/BMARY PO13 131 G2
Cheltenham Gdns HEND SO30 58 B1 1
Cheltenham Rd CHAM PO6 100 B6
Chelveston Crs ROWN SO16 42 A7
Cheping Gdns HEND SO30 59 F6
Chepstow Cl CHFD SO53 37 J4 1
TOTT SO40 52 B4 1
Chepstow Ct WVILLE PO7 82 C4
Cherbourg Rd ELGH SO50 44 C2
Cheriton Cl WINW SO22 21 G6
HAV PO9 102 E2 1
HORN PO8 64 B5
Cheriton Rd ELGH SO50 44 C1
WINW SO22 2 A2
GPORT PO12 132 C4
Cherque La LSOL/BMARY PO13 115 H7
Cherry Cl LSOL/BMARY PO13 131 G3
Cherry Dro ELGH SO50 46 B5
Cherry Gdns BPWT SO32 48 E4
Cherrygarth Rd FHAM PO15 96 D5
Cherryton Gdns FAWY SO45 109 J4 1
Cherry Tree Av
FHAM/STUB PO14 12 B8
HORN PO8 82 C3
Cherry Wk WSHM SO15 54 D4
Cherrywood HEND SO30 58 A6
Cherrywood Gdns TOTT SO40 52 B5 3
HISD PO11 137 G4
Chervil Cl HORN PO8 64 D3
Cherville St ROMY SO51 34 D2
Cherwell Crs ROWN SO16 53 K4
Cherwell Gdns CHFD SO53 38 A5
Cheshire Cl FHAM PO15 96 A1
Cheshire Wy EMRTH PO10 105 H4
Chesil St WINC SO23 3 G6
Cheslyn Rd HSEA PO3 135 G2
Chessel Av ITCH SO19 6 D6
Chessel Crs ITCH SO19 6 D5
Chester Crs LSOL/BMARY PO13 131 J4
Chesterfield Rd HSEA PO3 135 F1
Chester Pl SSEA PO5 18 E9
SSEA PO5 134 C6
Chester Rd WEND SO18 7 G1
WINC SO23 3 G5
Chesterton Gdns HORN PO8 81 K2
Chesterton Pl FHAM PO15 75 H5 3
Chestnut Av CHFD SO53 37 K7
ELGH SO50 43 K2
ENEY PO4 19 J5
WINW SO22 20 E3
HAV PO9 102 C3
HORN PO8 64 D7
RWIN SO21 39 J1
TOTT SO40 68 B2
Chestnut Cl CHFD SO53 43 K1
ROMY SO51 35 J4
WVILLE PO7 80 E1
Chestnut Ri ELGH SO50 44 A2 1
Chestnut Rd ROWN SO16 54 B2
The Chestnuts HLER SO31 95 F4
Chestnut Wk GPORT PO12 116 E6
Chestnut Wy FHAM/STUB PO14 95 J5
Chettle Rd ITCH SO19 57 H7
Chetwynd Dr ROWN SO16 43 G7
Chetwynd Rd ENEY PO4 19 G7
ROWN SO16 43 G7
Chevening Ct ENEY PO4 135 G3 2
Cheviot Dr FAWY SO45 90 E3
Cheviot Gn HLER SO31 94 C6 3
Cheviot Rd ROWN SO16 53 K4
Chewter Cl SSEA PO5 134 D7
Cheyne Wy
LSOL/BMARY PO13 131 G3 1
Chichester Av HISD PO11 137 G6
Chichester Cl HEND SO30 58 B3
HLER SO31 94 D3
LSOL/BMARY PO13 115 J5
Chichester Rd HISD PO11 121 K6
NEND PO2 118 D7
WEND SO18 7 G4
Chickenhall La ELGH SO50 45 F1
Chidden Holt CHFD SO53 37 H5
Chidham Cl HAV PO9 14 D2
Chidham Dr HAV PO9 14 C2
Chidham Rd CHAM PO6 101 F5
Chidham Sq HAV PO9 14 C3
Chilbolton Av WINW SO22 21 F7
Chilbolton Ct HAV PO9 83 J7 3
Chilcomb Cl
LSOL/BMARY PO13 131 G2 1
Chilcombe Cl HAV PO9 103 F3
Chilcomb La RWIN SO21 3 L9
WINC SO23 3 H9
Chilcomb Rd WEND SO18 7 L2
Chilcote Rd HSEA PO3 135 F1
Childe Sq NEND PO2 118 B5
Chilgrove Rd CHAM PO6 101 H6
Chilham Cl ELGH SO50 38 D3 1
Chilland La RWIN SO21 23 H1
Chillenden Ct TOTT SO40 52 B6 2
TOTT SO40 52 C6 1
Chillerton HLER SO31 73 F7
Chilling La HLER SO31 112 D2
Chillington Gdns CHFD SO53 37 J1 3
Chilsdown Wy WVILLE PO7 101 K1
Chiltern Cl TOTT SO40 52 C7 1
Chiltern Gn ROWN SO16 53 K4
Chilworth Cl ROWN SO16 42 E2
Chilworth Dro ROWN SO16 42 D3
Chilworth Gv GPORT PO12 132 D3
Chilworth Rd ROWN SO16 43 F2
Chine Av ITCH SO19 6 D7
Chine Cl HLER SO31 95 F2
The Chine
LSOL/BMARY PO13 116 B6 1
Chinham Rd TOTT SO40 50 E6
Chipstead Rd CHAM PO6 100 E6
Chisholm Cl ROWN SO16 42 A6
Chitty Rd ENEY PO4 19 M9
Chivers Cl SSEA PO5 18 D7 1
Christchurch Gdns
CHAM PO6 101 G4 1
WINC SO23 2 B9
Christchurch Rd WINC SO23 2 C9
Christie Av HLER SO31 75 H5
Christopher Wy EMRTH PO10 104 C4
Church Cl ELGH SO50 39 F6
HLER SO31 95 G3
NBAD SO52 36 B6
Churcher Cl GPORT PO12 132 A5
Churcher Rd EMRTH PO10 104 E2
Church Farm Cl FAWY SO45 70 C7
Churchfields FAWY SO45 110 E4 2
Churchfields Rd RWIN SO21 33 J3
Church Hl HEND SO30 57 F3
Churchill Av BPWT SO32 48 B2
Churchill Cl FHAM/STUB PO14 95 H5 1
Churchill Ct HORN PO8 64 B6 1
Churchill Dr EMRTH PO10 104 C2
Church La BPWT SO32 46 E5
BPWT SO32 49 K5
BPWT SO32 59 J4
BROC SO42 125 J3
ELGH SO50 39 H2
FAWY SO45 110 D4
WINW SO22 20 D1
HAV PO9 15 K7
HEND SO30 58 A7
HEND SO30 59 F7
HISD PO11 121 K4
HLER SO31 74 A5
LYND SO43 66 C7
PTSW SO17 55 J2
ROMY SO51 29 H2
ROMY SO51 34 D3
ROWN SO16 40 E6
RWIN SO21 22 E2
RWIN SO21 23 G1
RWIN SO21 33 K1
RWIN SO21 39 J2
WINC SO23 22 B1
WVILLE PO7 62 C1
Church Pth EMRTH PO10 104 C6
FHAM/PORC PO16 13 L5
GPORT PO12 16 F6
HORN PO8 64 E6
Church Pth North PSEA PO1 18 D2 1
Church Rd BPWT SO32 49 J5
BPWT SO32 60 E5
ELGH SO50 39 G5
EMRTH PO10 104 E3
EMRTH PO10 105 G7
EMRTH PO10 123 G6
FHAM/PORC PO16 117 H1
GPORT PO12 132 D6
HISD PO11 137 H3
HLER SO31 94 C6
HLER SO31 95 G3
ITCH SO19 10 B7
ROMY SO51 34 D3
Church St FHAM/STUB PO14 96 A6
PSEA PO1 18 E1
PSEA PO1 134 B1 1
ROMY SO51 34 D3
WSHM SO15 54 C4 2
WSHM SO15 54 D4
Church Street Rbt PSEA PO1 134 B1
Church Vw EMRTH PO10 104 E3 1
ENEY PO4 19 M5
Church View Cl ITCH SO19 11 G4
Churchward Gdns
HEND SO30 58 B2 2
Cinderford Cl CHAM PO6 100 B5 1
The Circle SSEA PO5 134 C6 1
WHAM PO17 77 G1
Circular Rd PSEA PO1 18 A2
The Circus WVILLE PO7 99 K4
Cirrus Gdns HLER SO31 93 J4
City Rd WINC SO23 2 D3
Civic Centre Rd HAV PO9 14 E2
SHAM SO14 4 F9
Civic Wy FHAM/PORC PO16 13 L5
Clacton Rd CHAM PO6 100 C6
Claire Gdns HORN PO8 64 D2
Clandon Dr ELGH SO50 38 C4
Clanfield Cl CHFD SO53 38 A4
Clanfield Dr CHFD SO53 38 A4
Clanfield Rd WEND SO18 7 M5
Clanfield Wy CHFD SO53 38 A4
Clanwilliam Rd
LSOL/BMARY PO13 131 F2
Clare Cl FHAM/STUB PO14 95 H5
Clare Gdns FAWY SO45 128 C1
Claremont Cl ELGH SO50 38 D4 2
Claremont Crs WSHM SO15 54 B5
Claremont Gdns WVILLE PO7 101 K2
Claremont Rd PSEA PO1 19 G4
WSHM SO15 54 B5
Clarence Esp SSEA PO5 18 A9
Clarence Pde SSEA PO5 18 B9
Clarence Rd GPORT PO12 16 F4
LYND SO43 86 C1 1
SSEA PO5 134 C7
Clarence St PSEA PO1 18 D1
Clarendon Cl ROMY SO51 35 G1 1
Clarendon Crs
FHAM/STUB PO14 95 G5
Clarendon Pl PSEA PO1 18 D3 1
Clarendon Rd HAV PO9 14 D5
ROWN SO16 54 B4
SSEA PO5 18 D9
Clarendon St PSEA PO1 18 F1
Clarendon Wy WINC SO23 2 E9
Clarkes Rd PSEA PO1 19 J2
Claude Ashby Cl WEND SO18 44 B7
Claudeen Cl WEND SO18 44 B6
Claudia Ct GPORT PO12 132 C2 1
Claudius Cl CHFD SO53 38 C3 1
Claudius Gdns CHFD SO53 38 C4
Clausentum Cl CHFD SO53 38 B3
Clausentum Rd SHAM SO14 5 H4
WINC SO23 25 J3
Claxton St PSEA PO1 18 E3
Claybank Sp HSEA PO3 119 F6
Claydon Av ENEY PO4 19 L5 2
Clayhall Rd GPORT PO12 132 D6
Clay Hl BROC SO42 86 D5
Clayhill Cl BPWT SO32 48 E7 1
Claylands Ct BPWT SO32 48 C3
Claylands Rd BPWT SO32 48 C3 1
Clay La LYND SO43 86 C2 1
Claypit Rd ROMY SO51 30 D2
Claypits La FAWY SO45 90 D2
Cleasby Cl ROWN SO16 53 K5
Clease Wy RWIN SO21 33 F2
Clee Av FHAM/STUB PO14 12 A7
Cleethorpes Rd ITCH SO19 11 K1
Cleeve Cl CHAM PO6 100 A5 2
The Cleeves TOTT SO40 52 B6
Clegg Rd ENEY PO4 19 L8
Clement Attlee Wy CHAM PO6 100 A6
Cleric Ct FHAM/STUB PO14 95 J3
Cleveland Ct WEND SO18 7 G1
Cleveland Dr FAWY SO45 90 E4
FHAM/STUB PO14 12 B7
Cleveland Rd GPORT PO12 16 B7 1
SSEA PO5 19 G6
WEND SO18 56 C2
Clevelands Cl CHFD SO53 31 J7 1
Clewers Hl BPWT SO32 48 E7
Clewers La BPWT SO32 48 E7
Cliffe Av HLER SO31 93 H3
Clifford Dibben Ms SHAM SO14 5 G3 1
Clifford Pl ELGH SO50 46 B1
Clifford St SHAM SO14 5 J9
Cliff Rd FHAM/STUB PO14 114 A6
WSHM SO15 4 A8
Cliff Wy RWIN SO21 33 G3
Clifton Crs WVILLE PO7 81 G1
Clifton Gdns WEND SO18 57 F3
Clifton Hl WINW SO22 2 C4
Clifton Rd WINW SO22 2 B3
LSOL/BMARY PO13 131 H4
SSEA PO5 134 B6
WSHM SO15 54 B4
Clifton St GPORT PO12 132 C2
PSEA PO1 19 G2
Clifton Ter WINW SO22 2 C4
Clinton Rd WVILLE PO7 81 H2
Clipper Cl HLER SO31 94 D5
Clive Gv FHAM/PORC PO16 99 F7
Clive Rd PSEA PO1 19 H2
Clock St PSEA PO1 17 L4
Clocktower Dr ENEY PO4 135 G6
The Cloisters FHAM PO15 96 D4
ROMY SO51 34 D2 1
ROWN SO16 43 H7
The Close Bellfield
FHAM/STUB PO14 96 A7
The Close CHAM PO6 101 F7 1
FAWY SO45 110 A4
FHAM/PORC PO16 99 F6
HEND SO30 58 A6
WEND SO18 57 G5
Closewood Rd WVILLE PO7 81 F4
Clovelly Rd EMRTH PO10 104 B6
ENEY PO4 19 M6
HISD PO11 121 K3
SHAM SO14 5 H7
Clover Cl HLER SO31 94 D4
LSOL/BMARY PO13 115 K5 3
Clover Wy HEND SO30 57 K6 2
ROMY SO51 35 H2
Club House La BPWT SO32 60 E1
Clydebank Rd NEND PO2 118 C7
Clyde Ct GPORT PO12 132 C2
Clyde Rd GPORT PO12 132 C2
Clydesdale Dr TOTT SO40 52 A4 1
Clydesdale Rd HLER SO31 75 G6
Clydesdale Wy TOTT SO40 52 A4
Coach Hl FHAM/STUB PO14 96 A6
Coach Hill Cl CHFD SO53 37 J3
Coachmans Copse WEND SO18 56 D2
Coach Rd HLER SO31 93 H4
Coal Park La HLER SO31 74 D4
Coalville Rd ITCH SO19 11 K1
Coastguard Cl GPORT PO12 132 C6
Coastguard La SELS PO20 139 H7
Coates Rd ITCH SO19 73 G1
Coates Wy WVILLE PO7 101 K1
Coat Gdns FAWY SO45 91 H3 2
Cobbett Cl WINW SO22 25 F3
Cobbett Rd WEND SO18 6 C4
Cobbett Wy HEND SO30 58 D5
Cobblewood EMRTH PO10 104 C3
Cobden Av HSEA PO3 119 F7
WEND SO18 6 C2
Cobden Crs WEND SO18 6 E3
Cobden Gdns WEND SO18 6 C1
Cobden St GPORT PO12 16 A3
Coblands Av TOTT SO40 52 C5
Coburg St PSEA PO1 18 F3
SHAM SO14 5 L7
Cochcrane Cl
LSOL/BMARY PO13 132 A2
Cockleshell Gdns ENEY PO4 135 H5
Cocklydown La TOTT SO40 52 D7
Coghlan Cl FHAM/PORC PO16 13 J3
Coker Cl WINW SO22 2 B3
Colburn Cl ROWN SO16 53 J2
Colbury Gv HAV PO9 102 D2
Colchester Av ELGH SO50 39 H6
Colchester Rd CHAM PO6 100 C5
Cold East Cl HLER SO31 94 D1
Coldeast Wy HLER SO31 94 E1
Cold Harbour Cl WHAM PO17 77 G1
Coldharbour Farm Rd
EMRTH PO10 104 C5
Coldharbour La ROWN SO16 41 F3
Coldhill La HORN PO8 63 K5
Colebrook Av HSEA PO3 135 G1
WSHM SO15 54 D3
Colebrook Pl WINC SO23 3 G6
Colebrook St WINC SO23 2 F6
Coleman St SHAM SO14 9 J1
Colemore Sq HAV PO9 103 G2 1
Colenso Rd FHAM/PORC PO16 13 H4
Coleridge Cl HLER SO31 94 C5
Coleridge Gdns HORN PO8 82 A1
Coleridge Rd CHAM PO6 99 J5
Colesbourne Rd CHAM PO6 100 A5
Coles Cl RWIN SO21 33 K2
Coles Mede RWIN SO21 32 E6
Coleson Rd WEND SO18 6 C3
Coleville Av FAWY SO45 110 E4
Colinton Av FHAM/PORC PO16 99 G5
College Cl HAV PO9 83 K4
HLER SO31 93 J4 1
College La PSEA PO1 17 L4 2
College Rd ITCH SO19 10 C6
PSEA PO1 17 L3
WVILLE PO7 101 K4
College St PSEA PO1 17 L4
SHAM SO14 9 H3
WINC SO23 2 E6
College Wk WINC SO23 2 F7
Collett Cl HEND SO30 58 A2
Colley Cl WINC SO23 21 K4
Collier Cl PTSW SO17 5 M2
Collingbourne Dr CHFD SO53 37 H4
Collington Crs CHAM PO6 100 A5
Collingwood Rd SSEA PO5 18 F9
Collingworth Cl HLER SO31 75 G7
Collins Cl NBAD SO52 37 G4 1
Collins La RWIN SO21 31 K2
Collins Rd ENEY PO4 19 L9
Collis Rd HSEA PO3 119 F7
Colne Av ROWN SO16 53 J1
Colpoy St SSEA PO5 18 B6
Colson Rd WINC SO23 3 H3
Colt Cl ROWN SO16 42 A6 3
Coltsfoot Cl HEND SO30 58 A5
Coltsfoot Dr HLER SO31 94 D4
WVILLE PO7 102 A1
Coltsfoot Wk ROMY SO51 35 H1 2
Coltsmead CHAM PO6 99 J6
Colts Rd ROWN SO16 41 K4
Colville Dr BPWT SO32 48 E3
Colville Rd CHAM PO6 101 F6
Colwell Cl ROWN SO16 53 J4
Colwell Rd CHAM PO6 100 E7
Comfrey Cl HORN PO8 64 D3 1
ROMY SO51 35 H1
Comines Wy HEND SO30 57 H6
Comley Hl HAV PO9 83 K6
Commercial Pl PSEA PO1 18 D2 2
Commercial Rd PSEA PO1 18 C3
PSEA PO1 18 D1 4
TOTT SO40 53 F5
WSHM SO15 4 F8
Commercial St WEND SO18 7 J5
Common Barn La
LSOL/BMARY PO13 131 G1 2
Common Cl CHFD SO53 37 K2
Common Gdns CHFD SO53 37 K2
Common Hill Rd ROMY SO51 29 J3
Common La FHAM/STUB PO14 95 J6
WHAM PO17 79 H7
Common Rd CHFD SO53 37 K2
EMRTH PO10 105 J1
Commonside EMRTH PO10 104 E1
Common St PSEA PO1 18 F2 1
Compass Cl
LSOL/BMARY PO13 132 A2 2
Compass Rd CHAM PO6 100 A6
Compton Cl ELGH SO50 38 C4
WINW SO22 24 E5
HAV PO9 14 E1
LSOL/BMARY PO13 131 H2
Compton Rd NEND PO2 118 E4
TOTT SO40 53 F4
WINC SO23 2 C6
Compton St RWIN SO21 33 F1
Compton Wk SHAM SO14 5 G8
Compton Wy WINW SO22 24 E5
Conan Rd NEND PO2 118 D3
Concorde Wy FHAM PO15 95 K1
Condor Av FHAM/PORC PO16 98 C6
Condor Cl ITCH SO19 10 A4
Conference Dr HLER SO31 95 G3 1
Conford Ct HAV PO9 82 E7
Conifer Cl FAWY SO45 91 G3 2
WINW SO22 2 B2
HORN PO8 82 B3
Conifer Gv LSOL/BMARY PO13 115 K3
Conifer Ms FHAM/PORC PO16 99 G5 1
Conifer Rd ROWN SO16 42 B7
Conigar Rd EMRTH PO10 104 C3
Coniston Av HSEA PO3 119 F7
Coniston Gdns HEND SO30 58 A7
Coniston Rd ELGH SO50 44 C1
ROWN SO16 53 H4
Connaught Rd HAV PO9 15 G4
NEND PO2 118 C5 1
Connemara Crs HLER SO31 75 G6
Connigar Cl
LSOL/BMARY PO13 131 K1 1
Conqueror Wy
FHAM/STUB PO14 114 E5
Conrad Gdns FHAM PO15 75 H5
Consort Rd ELGH SO50 38 E5
Constable Cl GPORT PO12 133 F7 1
ITCH SO19 11 L5
Constable's Ga WINC SO23 2 C5
Constantine Av CHFD SO53 38 B4
Constantine Cl CHFD SO53 38 C4 1
Convent La EMRTH PO10 104 C6
Conway Cl CHFD SO53 37 J7
Cooks La EMRTH PO10 105 H5
TOTT SO40 52 B2
Cook St SHAM SO14 9 H2
Coombedale HLER SO31 95 G4 1
Coombe Farm Av
FHAM/PORC PO16 13 H8
Coombe Rd GPORT PO12 132 E1
Coombs Cl HORN PO8 64 D3 2

Cooper Gv FHAM/PORC PO16 .... 117 G1
Cooper Rd HSEA PO3 .... 135 G1
TOTT SO40 .... 68 B2
Cooper's Cl WEND SO18 .... 57 F3
Cooper's La ITCH SO19 .... 10 B4
Copeland Rd ROWN SO16 .... 53 J3
Copinger Cl TOTT SO40 .... 52 B6
Copnor Rd NEND PO2 .... 118 E3
Copper Beech Dr CHAM PO6 .... 101 K6
Copperfield Rd ROWN SO16 .... 43 H6
Copperfields TOTT SO40 .... 52 A5
Copper St SSEA PO5 .... 18 B7
Coppice Cl WINW SO22 .... 21 F6
Coppice Hl BPWT SO32 .... 48 D4
Coppice Rd TOTT SO40 .... 52 B2
The Coppice HORN PO8 .... 64 B6
LSOL/BMARY PO13 .... 116 A5
Coppice Wy FHAM PO15 .... 12 A2
Coppins Gv FHAM/PORC PO16 .. 117 F1
Copse Cl NBAD SO52 .... 36 A6
RWIN SO21 .... 33 F5
TOTT SO40 .... 52 E6
WVILLE PO7 .... 101 J4
Copse La HISD PO11 .... 121 H7
HLER SO31 .... 93 J4
LSOL/BMARY PO13 .... 116 A6
ROWN SO16 .... 43 G2
Copse Rd WEND SO18 .... 56 C2
The Copse CHFD SO53 .... 38 B5
FHAM PO15 .... 96 E2
Copse Vw ITCH SO19 .... 57 H7
Copsewood Rd FAWY SO45 .... 91 G3
TOTT SO40 .... 68 B2
WEND SO18 .... 56 B2
Copsey Cl CHAM PO6 .... 101 J6
Copsey Gv CHAM PO6 .... 101 J7
Copthorne La FAWY SO45 .... 110 E4
Copythorne Crs TOTT SO40 .... 51 F2
Copythorn Rd NEND PO2 .... 118 E6
Coracle Cl HLER SO31 .... 94 E5
Coral Cl FHAM/PORC PO16 .... 117 F1
Coralin Gv WVILLE PO7 .... 82 C4
Coram Cl WINC SO23 .... 21 K5
Corbett Rd WVILLE PO7 .... 81 J7
Corbiere Cl ROWN SO16 .... 53 K1
Corbould Rd FAWY SO45 .... 91 G6
Corby Crs HSEA PO3 .... 119 G3
Cordelia Cl FAWY SO45 .... 90 E3
Corfe Cl FHAM/STUB PO14 .... 114 B5
Corhampton Crs HAV PO9 .... 102 E2
Coriander Dr TOTT SO40 .... 52 A5
Coriander Wy FHAM PO15 .... 75 J5
Corinna Gdns FAWY SO45 .... 90 E3
Corinthian Rd CHFD SO53 .... 38 B3
Cork La TOTT SO40 .... 70 A2
Cormorant Cl
FHAM/PORC PO16 .... 98 C6
Cormorant Dr FAWY SO45 .... 91 J4
Cornaway La FHAM/PORC PO16 .. 98 E7
Cornbrook Gv HORN PO8 .... 82 D1
Cornelius Dr WVILLE PO7 .... 82 C4
Cornel Rd ITCH SO19 .... 6 E9
Corner Md WVILLE PO7 .... 80 E1
Cornes Cl WINW SO22 .... 21 G7
Cornfield FHAM/PORC PO16 .... 97 J2
Cornfield Cl NBAD SO52 .... 37 G4
Cornfield Rd
LSOL/BMARY PO13 .... 131 G2
Cornflower Cl HLER SO31 .... 94 D4
Cornforth Rd TOTT SO40 .... 52 B3
Corn Market ROMY SO51 .... 34 D3
Cornmill St PSEA PO1 .... 18 D1
Cornwall Crs WEND SO18 .... 56 C2
Cornwallis Crs PSEA PO1 .... 18 D1
Cornwall Rd CHFD SO53 .... 37 K7
PSEA PO1 .... 19 G4
WEND SO18 .... 56 E2
Cornwell Cl LSOL/BMARY PO13 .. 132 A1
NEND PO2 .... 118 A5
Coronado Rd GPORT PO12 .... 16 A1
Coronation Pde HLER SO31 .... 93 H3
Coronation Rd BPWT SO32 .... 49 J6
HISD PO11 .... 138 B7
Corsair Dr FAWY SO45 .... 90 E2
Cortina Wy HEND SO30 .... 58 B7
Cort Wy FHAM PO15 .... 96 D2
Corvette Av HLER SO31 .... 94 E5
Cosford Cl ELGH SO50 .... 45 K1
Cosham Park Av CHAM PO6 .... 100 E7
Cossack Gn SHAM SO14 .... 9 H1
Cossack La WINC SO23 .... 2 F4
Cosworth Dr FAWY SO45 .... 90 E3
Cotsalls ELGH SO50 .... 46 B2
Cotswold Cl FAWY SO45 .... 90 E3
HAV PO9 .... 83 F7
Cotswold Rd ROWN SO16 .... 54 A4
Cottage Cl WVILLE PO7 .... 80 E2
Cottage Gv GPORT PO12 .... 16 A4
SSEA PO5 .... 18 D6
Cottage Vw PSEA PO1 .... 18 E3
Cottes Wy FHAM/STUB PO14 .... 114 B6
Cottesway East
FHAM/STUB PO14 .... 114 B6
Cotton Cl ELGH SO50 .... 39 H7
Cotton Dr EMRTH PO10 .... 104 B3
Cotwell Av HORN PO8 .... 82 C1
Coulmere Rd GPORT PO12 .... 132 D2
Coulsdon Rd HEND SO30 .... 58 B6
Coultas Rd CHFD SO53 .... 32 B7
Country Vw FHAM/STUB PO14 .. 114 C3
County Gdns FHAM/STUB PO14 .. 96 D6
Course Park Crs
FHAM/STUB PO14 .... 95 H4
Court Barn La
LSOL/BMARY PO13 .... 131 G1
Court Cl CHAM PO6 .... 101 G7
ITCH SO19 .... 7 J6
TOTT SO40 .... 52 B2
Courtenay Rd WINC SO23 .... 21 K5
Court House Cl FAWY SO45 .... 91 H2
Courtland Gdns ROWN SO16 .... 43 J6
Court La CHAM PO6 .... 101 G7
Court Md CHAM PO6 .... 101 G7
Courtmount Gv CHAM PO6 .... 101 F6
Court Rd LSOL/BMARY PO13 .... 131 F1
WINC SO23 .... 22 B2
WSHM SO15 .... 4 E4
Court Royal Ms WSHM SO15 .... 4 E2
Cousins Gv ENEY PO4 .... 135 F6
Coventry Rd WSHM SO15 .... 4 E6
Coverack Wy CHAM PO6 .... 100 A7
Covert Gv WVILLE PO7 .... 102 B1
The Covert ROMY SO51 .... 35 G4
Covington Rd EMRTH PO10 .... 104 E1
Cowan Rd WVILLE PO7 .... 101 J1
Coward Rd GPORT PO12 .... 132 C6
Cowdray Cl ELGH SO50 .... 45 J1
ROWN SO16 .... 42 C7
Cowdray Pk FHAM/STUB PO14 .. 114 B5
Cowes La HLER SO31 .... 112 C1
Cow La CHAM PO6 .... 100 C7
FHAM/PORC PO16 .... 99 H7
Cowley Cl ROWN SO16 .... 53 K2
Cowleys La BROC SO42 .... 109 F7
Cowper Rd ITCH SO19 .... 57 G6
PSEA PO1 .... 134 D1
Cowslip Cl HLER SO31 .... 94 D5
LSOL/BMARY PO13 .... 115 K5
Cox Dl FHAM/STUB PO14 .... 95 H5
Coxford Cl ROWN SO16 .... 54 B2
Coxford Dro ROWN SO16 .... 54 B1
Coxford Rd ROWN SO16 .... 54 A2
Cox Rw CHFD SO53 .... 38 A7
Cox's Dr ITCH SO19 .... 11 J6
Coxs Hl RWIN SO21 .... 33 K1
Cozens Cl ITCH SO19 .... 10 B8
Crabapple Cl TOTT SO40 .... 52 B5
Crabbe Ct SSEA PO5 .... 18 D6
Crabbs Wy TOTT SO40 .... 52 A5
Crabden La HORN PO8 .... 65 F4
Crableck La HLER SO31 .... 94 B1
Crabthorne Farm La
FHAM/STUB PO14 .... 114 C4
Crabtree ROWN SO16 .... 54 A3
Crabwood Cl ROWN SO16 .... 54 A3
Crabwood Ct HAV PO9 .... 82 E6
Crabwood Dr HEND SO30 .... 57 H3
Crabwood Rd ROWN SO16 .... 53 K2
Cracknore Hard TOTT SO40 .... 70 D3
Cracknore Hard La
TOTT SO40 .... 70 D3
Cracknore Rd WSHM SO15 .... 4 A9
Craigwell Rd WVILLE PO7 .... 101 J2
Crampmoor La ROMY SO51 .... 35 J1
Cranberry Cl TOTT SO40 .... 70 A4
Cranborne Gdns CHFD SO53 .... 37 J1
Cranborne Rd CHAM PO6 .... 101 F5
Cranbourne Cl WSHM SO15 .... 4 B1
Cranbourne Dr RWIN SO21 .... 32 E6
Cranbourne Rd GPORT PO12 .... 16 C7
Cranbury Av SHAM SO14 .... 5 H6
Cranbury Cl RWIN SO21 .... 32 E6
Cranbury Gdns HLER SO31 .... 73 J4
Cranbury Pl SHAM SO14 .... 5 G6
Cranbury Rd ELGH SO50 .... 44 D1
ITCH SO19 .... 10 F4
Cranbury Ter SHAM SO14 .... 5 H6
Craneswater Av ENEY PO4 .... 134 D6
Craneswater Ga ENEY PO4 .... 134 D7
Craneswater Pk ENEY PO4 .... 134 D6
Cranford Gdns CHFD SO53 .... 37 J2
Cranford Wy PTSW SO17 .... 55 H2
Cranleigh Av PSEA PO1 .... 19 H1
Cranleigh Rd FHAM/PORC PO16 .. 98 D7
HEND SO30 .... 58 B6
PSEA PO1 .... 19 H1
Cranmer Dr ROWN SO16 .... 41 H6
Cranmore HLER SO31 .... 73 F6
Cranworth Rd WINW SO22 .... 2 C2
Crasswell St PSEA PO1 .... 18 D2
Craven Ct FHAM PO15 .... 12 B2
Craven Rd CHFD SO53 .... 38 A4
Craven St SHAM SO14 .... 5 H9
Crawford Cl ROWN SO16 .... 41 J6
Crawford Dr FHAM/PORC PO16 .. 12 E1
Crawley Av HAV PO9 .... 83 H7
Crawte Av FAWY SO45 .... 110 A5
Credenhill Rd CHAM PO6 .... 100 B5
Creedy Gdns WEND SO18 .... 56 D1
Creek End EMRTH PO10 .... 104 C7
Creek Rd GPORT PO12 .... 16 E5
HISD PO11 .... 138 A6
Creighton Rd WSHM SO15 .... 54 A6
Cremyll Cl FHAM/STUB PO14 .... 114 D5
Crescent Cl WINW SO22 .... 24 E4
Crescent Rd FHAM/PORC PO16 .... 13 H6
GPORT PO12 .... 132 D7
HLER SO31 .... 94 E3
NBAD SO52 .... 36 A5
The Crescent BPWT SO32 .... 47 H1
ELGH SO50 .... 38 D6
EMRTH PO10 .... 105 G6
HLER SO31 .... 72 E7
ITCH SO19 .... 11 G5
ROMY SO51 .... 35 G2
RWIN SO21 .... 33 K3
TOTT SO40 .... 67 H2
TOTT SO40 .... 69 K4
WVILLE PO7 .... 101 H2
Cressey Rd ROMY SO51 .... 34 E3
Cressy Rd NEND PO2 .... 134 C1
Crest Cl FHAM/PORC PO16 .... 98 A5
Crestland Cl HORN PO8 .... 82 B2
The Crest WVILLE PO7 .... 101 H4
Crest Wy ITCH SO19 .... 11 M2
Crete La FAWY SO45 .... 91 G5
Crete Rd FAWY SO45 .... 91 G6
Cricket Dr HORN PO8 .... 64 B7
Cricklemede BPWT SO32 .... 48 E4
Cricklewood Cl BPWT SO32 .... 48 E4
Crigdon Cl ROWN SO16 .... 53 K4
Crinoline Gdns ENEY PO4 .... 135 F6
Cripple Gate La BROC SO42 .... 125 J3
Crispin Cl ELGH SO50 .... 46 B5
HLER SO31 .... 95 G2
Crispstead La WINC SO23 .... 25 J3
Crisspyn Cl HORN PO8 .... 64 C6
Crockford Br LYMN SO41 .... 124 C6
Crockford Rd EMRTH PO10 .... 104 E2
Croftlands Av
FHAM/STUB PO14 .... 114 D4
Croft La HISD PO11 .... 121 H6
Crofton Av LSOL/BMARY PO13 .. 114 D7
Crofton Cl PTSW SO17 .... 55 H3
WVILLE PO7 .... 101 H1
Crofton La FHAM/STUB PO14 .... 114 C6
Crofton Rd ENEY PO4 .... 135 G3
NEND PO2 .... 118 D5
Crofton Wy BPWT SO32 .... 49 H6
HLER SO31 .... 94 B5
Croft Rd NEND PO2 .... 118 C6
The Croft CHFD SO53 .... 37 K7
FHAM/STUB PO14 .... 114 D3
TOTT SO40 .... 52 B2
Cromarty Av ENEY PO4 .... 135 G4
Cromarty Cl FHAM/STUB PO14 .. 114 C4
Cromarty Rd ROWN SO16 .... 41 K6
Crombie Cl HORN PO8 .... 82 A1
Cromer Rd CHAM PO6 .... 100 C5
ROWN SO16 .... 53 J3
Cromhall Cl FHAM/STUB PO14 .. 96 D6
Crompton Wy FHAM PO15 .... 95 H1
Cromwell Rd ENEY PO4 .... 135 G6
WINW SO22 .... 25 G2
WSHM SO15 .... 4 E5
Crondall Av HAV PO9 .... 83 F7
Crooked Hays Cl TOTT SO40 .... 70 A4
Crooked Walk La WHAM PO17 .... 99 H3
Crookham Cl HAV PO9 .... 102 D2
Crookham Rd ITCH SO19 .... 10 F9
Crookhorn La WVILLE PO7 .... 101 K5
Crossbill Cl HORN PO8 .... 64 B5
Crosshouse Rd SHAM SO14 .... 9 L4
Cross Keys Pas WINC SO23 .... 2 F5
Crossland Cl GPORT PO12 .... 16 C8
Crossland Dr HAV PO9 .... 15 G1
Cross La HORN PO8 .... 64 B7
Cross Rd ITCH SO19 .... 6 C5
LSOL/BMARY PO13 .... 131 H4
Cross St BPWT SO32 .... 48 D3
PSEA PO1 .... 17 M3
SSEA PO5 .... 18 E5
WINC SO23 .... 2 D4
Cross Wy HAV PO9 .... 14 C3
RWIN SO21 .... 33 G4
The Crossways GPORT PO12 .... 16 A2
The Crossway
FHAM/PORC PO16 .... 99 F6
Crosswell Cl ITCH SO19 .... 7 L9
Croucher's Cft WINW SO22 .... 20 E6
Crouch La HORN PO8 .... 64 B5
Crowder Ter WINW SO22 .... 2 C5
Crown Cl WVILLE PO7 .... 101 K3
Crown St PSEA PO1 .... 18 F1
WSHM SO15 .... 54 C4
Crowsbury Cl EMRTH PO10 .... 104 B3
Crows Nest La BPWT SO32 .... 58 E3
Crowsport HLER SO31 .... 93 K3
Crowther Cl ITCH SO19 .... 11 M2
Croydon Cl ROWN SO16 .... 42 B7
Crummock Rd CHFD SO53 .... 37 H3
Crusader Rd HEND SO30 .... 58 C7
Crusaders Wy NBAD SO52 .... 37 G4
Crystal Wy WVILLE PO7 .... 82 C5
Cuckmere La ROWN SO16 .... 53 J4
Cuckoo Bushes La CHFD SO53 .... 37 J2
Cuckoo La FHAM/STUB PO14 .... 114 C3
Cudworth Md HEND SO30 .... 58 C3
Culford Av TOTT SO40 .... 52 E6
Culford Wy TOTT SO40 .... 52 E6
Culloden Cl FHAM PO15 .... 12 D1
Culloden Rd FHAM/STUB PO14 .. 115 G1
Culver HLER SO31 .... 73 F6
Culver Cl ROWN SO16 .... 53 J2
Culver Dr HISD PO11 .... 137 K7
Culver Rd ENEY PO4 .... 135 F6
WINC SO23 .... 2 D7
Culverwell Gdns WINC SO23 .... 2 D6
Culvery Gdns WEND SO18 .... 56 E2
Cumberland Av CHFD SO53 .... 38 B5
EMRTH PO10 .... 104 B2
Cumberland Pl WSHM SO15 .... 4 E8
Cumberland Rd SSEA PO5 .... 19 G4
Cumberland St PSEA PO1 .... 17 M2
SHAM SO14 .... 9 J1
Cumberland Wy FAWY SO45 .... 90 E3
Cumber Rd HLER SO31 .... 94 D3
Cumbrian Wy ROWN SO16 .... 53 K4
Cunard Av WSHM SO15 .... 54 D4
Cunard Rd SHAM SO14 .... 9 H6
Cunliffe Cl SELS PO20 .... 139 K6
Cunningham Av BPWT SO32 .... 48 B3
Cunningham Crs ITCH SO19 .... 11 H2
Cunningham Dr HLER SO31 .... 95 F2
LSOL/BMARY PO13 .... 116 A4
Cunningham Rd HORN PO8 .... 64 D5
WVILLE PO7 .... 101 J1
Cupernham Cl ROMY SO51 .... 35 F2
Cupernham La ROMY SO51 .... 29 F6
Curdridge Cl HAV PO9 .... 103 H1
Curdridge La BPWT SO32 .... 60 B2
Curlew Cl EMRTH PO10 .... 104 B6
ROWN SO16 .... 42 C6
Curlew Dr FAWY SO45 .... 91 J4
FHAM/PORC PO16 .... 98 C6
Curlew Gdns HORN PO8 .... 82 A1
Curtis Md NEND PO2 .... 118 E3
Curtiss Gdns GPORT PO12 .... 132 C4
The Curve HORN PO8 .... 64 A6
LSOL/BMARY PO13 .... 115 J5
Curzon Howe Rd PSEA PO1 .... 17 M3
Curzon Rd WVILLE PO7 .... 81 K6
Custards Rd LYND SO43 .... 66 C7
Cutbush La WEND SO18 .... 7 J2
Cuthbert Rd PSEA PO1 .... 19 J2
Cutlers La FHAM/STUB PO14 .... 114 D4
Cutter Av HLER SO31 .... 94 D5
Cut Throat La BPWT SO32 .... 49 K5
Cygnet Ct FHAM/PORC PO16 .... 98 C6
Cygnet Rd CHAM PO6 .... 102 A7
Cygnus Gdns FAWY SO45 .... 90 D3
Cypress Av ITCH SO19 .... 6 F8
Cypress Crs HORN PO8 .... 64 B7
Cypress Gdns HEND SO30 .... 59 F5
TOTT SO40 .... 52 B5
Cyprus Rd FHAM/STUB PO14 .... 95 H5
NEND PO2 .... 118 D7

D

Daffodil Rd ROWN SO16 .... 43 K7
Dahlia Rd ROWN SO16 .... 43 H7
Daintree Cl ITCH SO19 .... 73 G2
Dairy La ROWN SO16 .... 41 F7
Dairymoor WHAM PO17 .... 77 H1
Daisy La GPORT PO12 .... 132 D4
HLER SO31 .... 95 G3
Daisy Md WVILLE PO7 .... 82 B7
Daisy Rd ROWN SO16 .... 43 K7
Dale Cl WINW SO22 .... 20 D2
Dale Dr LSOL/BMARY PO13 .... 115 J2
Dale Rd FAWY SO45 .... 91 G3
FHAM/STUB PO14 .... 114 E4
ROWN SO16 .... 54 D2
Dales Wy TOTT SO40 .... 52 A4
The Dale WVILLE PO7 .... 101 H4
Dale Valley Cl ROWN SO16 .... 54 D2
Dale Valley Gdns ROWN SO16 .... 54 D2
Dale Valley Rd ROWN SO16 .... 54 D1
Dalewood Rd FHAM PO15 .... 12 B5
Dallington Cl
FHAM/STUB PO14 .... 114 D6
Dalmally Gdns WEND SO18 .... 6 D2
Damask Gdns WVILLE PO7 .... 82 C4
Damen Cl HEND SO30 .... 58 A7
Dampier Cl LSOL/BMARY PO13 .. 131 K1
Damson Hl BPWT SO32 .... 49 J3
Danbury Ct EMRTH PO10 .... 104 D4
Dances Wy HISD PO11 .... 137 F4
Dandelion Cl
LSOL/BMARY PO13 .... 115 J5
Dando Rd WVILLE PO7 .... 81 F1
Danebury Cl HAV PO9 .... 83 F7
Danebury Gdns CHFD SO53 .... 37 H6
Danebury Wy ROWN SO16 .... 53 J1
Dane Cl FAWY SO45 .... 110 C6
Danesbrook La WVILLE PO7 .... 82 B6
Danes Rd FHAM/PORC PO16 .... 98 E5
WINC SO23 .... 2 E1
Dapple Pl TOTT SO40 .... 70 B4
Dark La FAWY SO45 .... 110 C6
Darlington Gdns WSHM SO15 .... 4 A1
Darlington Rd ENEY PO4 .... 19 G7
Darren Cl FHAM/STUB PO14 .... 114 E3
Dartington Rd ELGH SO50 .... 39 G5
Dartmouth Rd HSEA PO3 .... 119 F5
Dart Rd WEND SO18 .... 56 E1
Darwin Rd ELGH SO50 .... 38 E6
WSHM SO15 .... 4 B5
Darwin Wy LSOL/BMARY PO13 .. 132 A2
Daulston Rd PSEA PO1 .... 134 D1
Davenport Cl
LSOL/BMARY PO13 .... 131 K2
Daventry La HSEA PO3 .... 119 H3
D Av FAWY SO45 .... 110 A1
Davis Cl LSOL/BMARY PO13 .... 115 K7
Daw La HISD PO11 .... 121 G7
Dawlish Av WSHM SO15 .... 4 A2
Dawnay Cl ROWN SO16 .... 44 A6
Dawn Gdns WINW SO22 .... 25 F2
Dawson Rd ITCH SO19 .... 11 L5
Day La HORN PO8 .... 63 J5
Dayrell Cl TOTT SO40 .... 52 A3
Dayshes Cl LSOL/BMARY PO13 .. 115 J4
Dayslondon Rd WVILLE PO7 .... 101 J1
Deacon Cl ITCH SO19 .... 7 G8
Deacon Crs ITCH SO19 .... 7 G7
Deacon Rd HLER SO31 .... 95 G3
ITCH SO19 .... 7 H8
Deal Cl FHAM/STUB PO14 .... 114 D3
Deal Rd CHAM PO6 .... 100 D5
Dean Cl WINW SO22 .... 21 F5
Dean Ct HEND SO30 .... 58 A5
Deane Ct HAV PO9 .... 103 J1
Deane Down Dro WINW SO22 .... 20 E3
The Deanery CHFD SO53 .... 37 J2
Deane's Park Rd
FHAM/PORC PO16 .... 98 A5
Deanfield Cl HLER SO31 .... 93 J4
Dean La RWIN SO21 .... 20 B4
Dean Rd CHAM PO6 .... 100 E7
ELGH SO50 .... 46 A2
WEND SO18 .... 7 H5
Deans Ga FHAM/STUB PO14 .... 114 D6
Dean St PSEA PO1 .... 17 M4
Deanswood Dr WVILLE PO7 .... 81 K4
Dearing Cl LYND SO43 .... 86 C1
Dee Cl CHFD SO53 .... 37 H5
Deeping Cl ITCH SO19 .... 10 F8
Deeping Ga WVILLE PO7 .... 82 B6
Deerhurst Cl TOTT SO40 .... 52 C6
Deerhurst Crs CHAM PO6 .... 99 K5
Deer Leap FHAM PO15 .... 96 E1
Deerleap La TOTT SO40 .... 68 C4
Deerleap Wy FAWY SO45 .... 91 H3
Defender Rd ITCH SO19 .... 10 B3
De Grouchy La PTSW SO17 .... 55 H3
Delamere Rd ENEY PO4 .... 19 H7
Delft Cl HLER SO31 .... 94 E3
Delft Gdns WVILLE PO7 .... 81 J3
De Lisle Cl NEND PO2 .... 118 E3
Delius Av ITCH SO19 .... 73 G2
Dell Cl CHAM PO6 .... 101 G4
ELGH SO50 .... 46 B2
Dellcrest Pth CHAM PO6 .... 101 G5
Dellfield Cl CHAM PO6 .... 99 K5
Dell Piece East HORN PO8 .... 64 E7
Dell Piece West HORN PO8 .... 64 D7
Dell Quay Cl FHAM/STUB PO14 .. 115 H5
Dell Rd WEND SO18 .... 56 C2
WINC SO23 .... 3 J7
The Dell FHAM/PORC PO16 .... 98 A5
HAV PO9 .... 102 C4
Delme Dr FHAM/PORC PO16 .... 98 A4
Delphi Wy WVILLE PO7 .... 102 A4
Dempsey Cl ITCH SO19 .... 11 J2
Denbigh Cl ELGH SO50 .... 38 C5
TOTT SO40 .... 52 C7
Denbigh Dr FHAM/PORC PO16 .... 12 F3
Denbigh Gdns ROWN SO16 .... 43 G7
Dene Cl HLER SO31 .... 94 D2
ROWN SO16 .... 43 G4
Dene Hollow CHAM PO6 .... 101 J6
Dene Rd TOTT SO40 .... 68 B3
Dene Wy TOTT SO40 .... 68 B2
Denewulf Cl BPWT SO32 .... 48 D3
Denham Cl FHAM/STUB PO14 .... 114 C5
WINC SO23 .... 21 J5
Denham Gdns HLER SO31 .... 92 E1
Denhill Cl HISD PO11 .... 137 F3
Denmead Rd WEND SO18 .... 7 L3
Denny Cl FAWY SO45 .... 110 E4
Denville Av FHAM/PORC PO16 .. 117 G1
Denville Cl CHAM PO6 .... 102 A6
Denvilles Cl HAV PO9 .... 15 J2
Denzil Av HLER SO31 .... 73 F7
SHAM SO14 .... 5 H6
Depedene Cl FAWY SO45 .... 109 J3
Derby Rd ELGH SO50 .... 44 C1
NEND PO2 .... 118 C6
SHAM SO14 .... 5 J8
Deridene Ct TOTT SO40 .... 52 C6
Derlyn Rd FHAM/PORC PO16 .... 13 H5
Derwent Cl
FHAM/STUB PO14 .... 114 E3
HORN PO8 .... 64 D2
WEND SO18 .... 56 E3
Derwent Dr TOTT SO40 .... 52 A4
Derwent Rd
LSOL/BMARY PO13 .... 131 G3
ROWN SO16 .... 53 K3
Desborough Cl CHAM PO6 .... 99 K5
Desborough Rd ELGH SO50 .... 44 D1
Devenish Rd WINW SO22 .... 21 G4
Deverell Pl WVILLE PO7 .... 101 H3
Devine Gdns ELGH SO50 .... 45 H1
Devon Dr CHFD SO53 .... 37 K7
Devon Rd HSEA PO3 .... 119 F4
Devonshire Av ENEY PO4 .... 19 J6
Devonshire Gdns FAWY SO45 .. 91 H6
HLER SO31 .... 73 J3
HLER SO31 .... 73 K3
Devonshire Rd WSHM SO15 .... 4 E6
Devonshire Sq ENEY PO4 .... 19 J6
Devonshire Wy
FHAM/STUB PO14 .... 96 D6
Dew La ELGH SO50 .... 38 C7
Diamond St SSEA PO5 .... 18 B7
Diana Cl EMRTH PO10 .... 104 B2
GPORT PO12 .... 132 B4
Dibble Dr NBAD SO52 .... 36 A7
Dibden Cl HAV PO9 .... 102 D2
Dibden Lodge Cl FAWY SO45 .... 91 G1
Dibles Rd HLER SO31 .... 94 C5
Dickens Cl NEND PO2 .... 134 C1
Dickens Dell TOTT SO40 .... 52 A5
Dickens Dr HLER SO31 .... 75 H5
Dickson Pl WHAM PO17 .... 77 H1
Didcot Rd WSHM SO15 .... 54 D3
Dieppe Crs NEND PO2 .... 118 D3
Dieppe Gdns GPORT PO12 .... 132 C4
Diligence Cl HLER SO31 .... 73 K4
Dimond Cl WEND SO18 .... 56 B3
Dimond Hl WEND SO18 .... 6 D1
Dimond Rd WEND SO18 .... 56 B2
Dingle Wy HLER SO31 .... 95 F2
Discovery Cl
FHAM/STUB PO14 .... 114 D2
Ditcham Crs HAV PO9 .... 103 F2
Ditton Cl FHAM/STUB PO14 .... 114 D4
Dockenfield Cl HAV PO9 .... 102 D2
Dock La BROC SO42 .... 108 D7
Dock Rd GPORT PO12 .... 16 D6
Dodds La BPWT SO32 .... 49 J6
Dodwell La HLER SO31 .... 74 A2
Dogkennel La WVILLE PO7 .... 63 G1
Dogwood Dell WVILLE PO7 .... 102 A1
Dolman Rd GPORT PO12 .... 16 D7
Dolphin Cl ELGH SO50 .... 45 J1
Dolphin Ct
FHAM/STUB PO14 .... 114 C3
Dolphin Crs GPORT PO12 .... 16 B7
Dolphin Hl RWIN SO21 .... 33 K4
Dolphin Wy GPORT PO12 .... 133 G7
Dolton Rd ROWN SO16 .... 54 A1
Dome Aly WINC SO23 .... 2 E6
Domum Rd NEND PO2 .... 118 E5
WINC SO23 .... 3 G7
Domvilles Ap NEND PO2 .... 118 A6
Donaldson Rd CHAM PO6 .... 118 E1
Doncaster Rd ELGH SO50 .... 44 D3
Donigers Dell BPWT SO32 .... 49 H5
Donnelly St GPORT PO12 .... 132 D2
Donnington Dr CHFD SO53 .... 37 H7
Donnington Gv PTSW SO17 .... 55 J2
Dorcas Cl WVILLE PO7 .... 82 B4
Dore Av FHAM/PORC PO16 .... 98 E6
Dores La ROMY SO51 .... 30 D1
Doric Cl CHFD SO53 .... 38 C3
Dorking Crs CHAM PO6 .... 100 E7
Dorland Gdns TOTT SO40 .... 52 C6
Dormington Rd CHAM PO6 .... 100 B5
Dormy Cl HLER SO31 .... 94 C3
Dormy Wy LSOL/BMARY PO13 .... 115 J6
Dornmere La WVILLE PO7 .... 82 B6
Dorothy Dymond St
PSEA PO1 .... 18 C4
Dorrien Rd GPORT PO12 .... 132 E1
Dorrita Av HORN PO8 .... 82 B1
Dorrita Cl ENEY PO4 .... 134 E6
The Dorrits TOTT SO40 .... 52 A5
Dorset Cl HORN PO8 .... 64 C6
Dorset Rd CHFD SO53 .... 37 K7
Dorset St SHAM SO14 .... 5 G6
Dorstone Rd CHAM PO6 .... 100 B5
Douglas Crs ITCH SO19 .... 7 M6
Douglas Gdns HAV PO9 .... 103 H2
Douglas Rd PSEA PO1 .... 134 E1
Douglas Wy FAWY SO45 .... 91 F2
Dove Cl HORN PO8 .... 82 A1
Dove Dl ELGH SO50 .... 44 A1
Dove Gdns HLER SO31 .... 95 G1
Dover Cl FHAM/STUB PO14 .... 114 C4
Dover Ct HISD PO11 .... 137 F3
Dovercourt Rd CHAM PO6 .... 119 F1
Dover Rd HSEA PO3 .... 119 F7
Dover St SHAM SO14 .... 5 H5
Dowds Cl HEND SO30 .... 58 A4
Down End CHAM PO6 .... 101 H5
Down End Rd CHAM PO6 .... 101 H5
Downend Rd FHAM/PORC PO16 .. 98 C5
Down Farm Pl HORN PO8 .... 64 D3
Downham Cl HORN PO8 .... 82 A2
Downland Cl HEND SO30 .... 58 E5
HLER SO31 .... 95 F2
Downland Pl HEND SO30 .... 74 A1
Downlands Rd WINW SO22 .... 24 E4
Downley Rd HAV PO9 .... 103 J2
Down Rd HORN PO8 .... 64 C3
Downs Cl WVILLE PO7 .... 102 A3
Downscroft Gdns HEND SO30 .... 58 A4
HEND SO30 .... 58 A5
Downside LSOL/BMARY PO13 .... 116 A5
Downside Av ITCH SO19 .... 7 G6
Downside Rd WINW SO22 .... 20 E5
WVILLE PO7 .... 101 H3
Down's Park Av TOTT SO40 .... 53 F6
Down's Park Crs TOTT SO40 .... 53 F6

Down's Park Rd *TOTT* SO40 .... 53 F6
The Downsway
FHAM/PORC PO16 .... 99 F6
Downton Rd *WEND* SO18 .... 56 C2
Downwood Cl *FAWY* SO45 .... 90 D4 1
Downwood Wy *HORN* PO8 .... 64 D3
Doyle Av *NEND* PO2 .... 118 D3
Doyle Cl *NEND* PO2 .... 118 D3
Doyle Ct *ITCH* SO19 .... 10 F8
Dragoon Cl *ITCH* SO19 .... 11 L2
Drake Cl *HLER* SO31 .... 95 G1
TOTT SO40 .... 70 A3
Drake Rd *ELGH* SO50 .... 39 H6
LSOL/BMARY PO13 .... 130 E1
Drakes Cl *FAWY* SO45 .... 91 G4 5
Draycote Rd *HORN* PO8 .... 64 D1
Drayton Cl *ITCH* SO19 .... 10 F9
Drayton La *CHAM* PO6 .... 101 G5
Drayton Pl *TOTT* SO40 .... 52 C5 1
Drayton Rd *NEND* PO2 .... 118 D6
Drayton St *WINW* SO22 .... 25 F2
Dreadnought Rd
FHAM/STUB PO14 .... 115 F2
Dresden Dr *HORN* PO8 .... 81 J3
Drift Rd *FHAM/PORC* PO16 .... 13 M3
The Drift *HAV* PO9 .... 83 J4
Driftwood Gdns *ENEY* PO4 .... 135 H6
TOTT SO40 .... 52 B6 4
Drill Shed Rd *NEND* PO2 .... 118 A6
Drinkwater Cl *ELGH* SO50 .... 38 C7
The Drive *EMRTH* PO10 .... 105 G6
FHAM/PORC PO16 .... 13 G5
HAV PO9 .... 14 E1
HEND SO30 .... 56 E1
LSOL/BMARY PO13 .... 115 H5
TOTT SO40 .... 52 E7
Drove Cl *RWIN* SO21 .... 33 J4
Drove Rd *ITCH* SO19 .... 11 K1
WHAM PO17 .... 99 K2
The Drove *BPWT* SO32 .... 47 J3
BPWT SO32 .... 49 J6
ELGH SO50 .... 46 C5
FAWY SO45 .... 110 B6
HEND SO30 .... 57 J1
RWIN SO21 .... 33 J4
TOTT SO40 .... 52 A3
WEND SO18 .... 7 H5
Droxford Cl *GPORT* PO12 .... 132 C4
Droxford Rd *BPWT* SO32 .... 49 K7
Drummond Cl *WINW* SO22 .... 25 H3 1
Drummond Rd *FAWY* SO45 .... 91 H2 4
HEND SO30 .... 58 B3
PSEA PO1 .... 18 E1
Drummond Wy *CHFD* SO53 .... 37 J2 3
Dryden Av *CHAM* PO6 .... 99 H5
Dryden Cl *FHAM/PORC* PO16 .... 12 F4
WVILLE PO7 .... 81 J3
Dryden Rd *ITCH* SO19 .... 57 H7
Drysdale Ms *ENEY* PO4 .... 135 G6 1
Duddon Cl *WEND* SO18 .... 56 E3
Dudleston Heath Dr *HORN* PO8 .. 82 C3
Dudley Rd *HSEA* PO3 .... 135 F1 1
Duffield La *EMRTH* PO10 .... 105 G3
Dugald Drummond St
PSEA PO1 .... 18 C4 3
Duisburg Wy *SSEA* PO5 .... 18 A8
Duke Crs *PSEA* PO1 .... 134 C1
Duke Rd *HEND* SO30 .... 58 C7
Dukes Rd *GPORT* PO12 .... 132 D2
PTSW SO17 .... 5 K3
SHAM SO14 .... 5 K3
Duke St *SHAM* SO14 .... 9 J3
Dukeswood Dr *FAWY* SO45 .... 91 G5
Dumbarton Cl *NEND* PO2 .... 118 C7 2
Dumbleton Cl *ITCH* SO19 .... 57 J7
Dummer Ct *HAV* PO9 .... 82 E7
Dummers Rd *ROMY* SO51 .... 29 J2
Dumpers Dro *ELGH* SO50 .... 46 C5
Dunbar Cl *ROWN* SO16 .... 42 A6
Dunbar Rd *ENEY* PO4 .... 135 G4
Duncan Cl *ITCH* SO19 .... 10 D8
Duncan Rd *HLER* SO31 .... 95 G1
SSEA PO5 .... 18 F9
Duncans Dr
FHAM/STUB PO14 .... 96 C6 1
Dundas Cl *HSEA* PO3 .... 119 G5
Dundas La *HSEA* PO3 .... 119 G6
Dundas Sp *HSEA* PO3 .... 119 G5
Dundee Cl *FHAM* PO15 .... 12 D2
Dundee Rd *PTSW* SO17 .... 5 M1
Dundonald Cl *HISD* PO11 .... 137 H3
ITCH SO19 .... 10 A8
Dundridge La *BPWT* SO32 .... 49 F2
Dundry Wy *HEND* SO30 .... 58 B5
Dunhurst Cl *HAV* PO9 .... 103 H3
Dunkeld Rd *GPORT* PO12 .... 132 C1
Dunkirk Cl *ROWN* SO16 .... 42 E7
Dunkirk Rd *ROWN* SO16 .... 42 E7
Dunlin Cl *ENEY* PO4 .... 135 J3
Dunn Cl *ENEY* PO4 .... 135 G5
Dunnings La *NBAD* SO52 .... 35 K5
Dunnock Cl *HAV* PO9 .... 83 J4
Dunsbury Wy *HAV* PO9 .... 103 F1
Dunsmore Cl *SSEA* PO5 .... 18 D6 2
Dunster Cl *ROWN* SO16 .... 42 D6
Dunvegan Dr *ROWN* SO16 .... 42 D6
Durban Cl *ROMY* SO51 .... 35 F1
Durban Rd *PSEA* PO1 .... 134 E1
Durford Ct *HAV* PO9 .... 82 E7 1
Durham Gdns *WVILLE* PO7 .... 102 A1
Durham St *GPORT* PO12 .... 132 D2
PSEA PO1 .... 18 D3
Durlands Rd *HORN* PO8 .... 64 D4 1
Durley Av *HORN* PO8 .... 82 A2
Durley Brook Rd *BPWT* SO32 .... 46 E5
Durley Crs *TOTT* SO40 .... 52 C7
Durley Hall La *BPWT* SO32 .... 47 G2
Durley Rd *ELGH* SO50 .... 46 D4
GPORT PO12 .... 132 C2
Durley St *BPWT* SO32 .... 47 J4
Durlston Rd *ROWN* SO16 .... 53 H3
Durnford Rd *SHAM* SO14 .... 5 J7
Durngate Pl *WINC* SO23 .... 3 G4
Durngate Ter *WINC* SO23 .... 3 G4
Durrants Gdns *HAV* PO9 .... 83 J5
Durrants Rd *HAV* PO9 .... 83 J6
Dursley Crs *CHAM* PO6 .... 100 B6
Dutton La *ELGH* SO50 .... 38 E7
Duttons Rd *ROMY* SO51 .... 34 D2
Dyer Rd *WSHM* SO15 .... 54 D5
Dymoke St *EMRTH* PO10 .... 104 B2
Dymott Cl *WSHM* SO15 .... 4 A8
Dyram Cl *ELGH* SO50 .... 38 C5
Dysart Av *CHAM* PO6 .... 101 G7
Dyserth Cl *ITCH* SO19 .... 11 J7
Dyson Dr *WINC* SO23 .... 21 K5

E

Eadens La *TOTT* SO40 .... 51 G5
Eagle Av *HORN* PO8 .... 81 J1
Eagle Cl *CHFD* SO53 .... 37 J6
FHAM/PORC PO16 .... 98 C6 3
Eagle Rd *LSOL/BMARY* PO13 .... 130 E1
Earls Cl *ELGH* SO50 .... 45 K1
Earlsdon St *SSEA* PO5 .... 18 C6 2
Earls Rd *FHAM/PORC* PO16 .... 13 J9
SHAM SO14 .... 5 H3
Earnley Rd *HISD* PO11 .... 138 C6
East Boldre Rd *BROC* SO42 .... 125 H1
Eastbourne Av *GPORT* PO12 .... 116 C7
WSHM SO15 .... 4 A2
Eastbourne Rd *HSEA* PO3 .... 119 F7 1
Eastbrook Cl *GPORT* PO12 .... 116 C7 1
HLER SO31 .... 95 F1
East Cams Cl
FHAM/PORC PO16 .... 98 C5 2
Eastchurch Cl *ROWN* SO16 .... 42 A7
Eastcliff Cl *LSOL/BMARY* PO13 .... 131 F1
East Cosham Rd *CHAM* PO6 .... 101 G6
Eastcot Cl *FAWY* SO45 .... 109 J4
East Ct *CHAM* PO6 .... 101 G6
Eastcroft Rd *GPORT* PO12 .... 132 D3
East Dr *ELGH* SO50 .... 39 G6
Eastern Av *HSEA* PO3 .... 135 G2
Eastern Pde *ENEY* PO4 .... 134 E7
FHAM/PORC PO16 .... 13 K9
Eastern Rd *CHAM* PO6 .... 119 J1
ENEY PO4 .... 135 G3
HAV PO9 .... 15 G3
HEND SO30 .... 57 G3
HSEA PO3 .... 135 G2
NEND PO2 .... 118 A5
Eastern Villas Rd *ENEY* PO4 .... 134 C7 2
Eastern Wy *FHAM/PORC* PO16 .... 13 L6
Eastfield Av *FHAM/STUB* PO14 .. 115 G1
East Field Cl *EMRTH* PO10 .... 105 H4
Eastfield Rd *CHAM* PO6 .... 100 A4
ENEY PO4 .... 19 L7
PTSW SO17 .... 5 M2
Eastgate St *SHAM* SO14 .... 9 G3
WINC SO23 .... 3 G5
East Hl *WINC* SO23 .... 3 G7
East Hill Cl *FHAM/PORC* PO16 .... 98 A4
East House Av
FHAM/STUB PO14 .... 114 E5
Eastleigh Rd *ELGH* SO50 .... 46 B2
East Leigh Rd *HAV* PO9 .... 103 K3
East Ldg *FHAM* PO15 .... 96 D5
East Lodge Pk *CHAM* PO6 .... 102 A6
Eastmeare Ct *TOTT* SO40 .... 52 B6
Eastney Farm Rd *ENEY* PO4 .... 135 H5 1
Eastney Rd *ENEY* PO4 .... 135 G5
Eastney St *ENEY* PO4 .... 135 G6 2
Eastoke Av *HISD* PO11 .... 138 A7
Easton La *RWIN* SO21 .... 22 C5
WINC SO23 .... 3 J3
Eastover Ct *HAV* PO9 .... 82 E7
East Park Ter *SHAM* SO14 .... 5 G8
East Rd *FAWY* SO45 .... 92 A6
WHAM PO17 .... 79 K7
East St *EMRTH* PO10 .... 104 E3
FHAM/PORC PO16 .... 13 M6
FHAM/STUB PO14 .... 96 A6
HAV PO9 .... 14 F5
PSEA PO1 .... 17 K6
SHAM SO14 .... 9 G2
WVILLE PO7 .... 62 C1
East Surrey St *PSEA* PO1 .... 18 D3 2
Eastville Rd *ELGH* SO50 .... 46 B2 2
Eastways *BPWT* SO32 .... 48 D4
Eastwood Cl *HISD* PO11 .... 137 J4
East Woodhay Rd *WINW* SO22 .... 21 G3 2
Eastwood Rd *NEND* PO2 .... 118 D3 1
E Av *FAWY* SO45 .... 110 B2
Ebden Rd *WINC* SO23 .... 3 H3
Ebery Gv *HSEA* PO3 .... 135 G2
Ecton La *HSEA* PO3 .... 119 H4
Edelvale Rd *WEND* SO18 .... 7 J1
Edenbridge Rd *ENEY* PO4 .... 135 G3
Eden Ri *FHAM/PORC* PO16 .... 13 J8
Eden Rd *WEND* SO18 .... 56 E2
Eden St *PSEA* PO1 .... 18 D2 2
Eden Wk *CHFD* SO53 .... 37 H5
Edgar Crs *FHAM/PORC* PO16 .... 117 G1
Edgar Rd *WINW* SO23 .... 2 C8
Edgecombe Crs
LSOL/BMARY PO13 .... 115 K7
Edgefield Gv *HORN* PO8 .... 82 D4
Edgehill Rd *WEND* SO18 .... 6 F1
Edgell Rd *EMRTH* PO10 .... 104 E2
Edgerly Gdns *CHAM* PO6 .... 118 E1
Edgeware Rd *ENEY* PO4 .... 19 M4
Edinburgh Rd *PSEA* PO1 .... 18 C3 1
Edington Cl *BPWT* SO32 .... 48 C3 2
Edington Rd *WINC* SO23 .... 21 K5
Edith Haisman Cl *WSHM* SO15 .... 4 B8
Edmund Rd *ENEY* PO4 .... 19 H7
Edmunds Cl *HEND* SO30 .... 58 C7
Edneys La *WVILLE* PO7 .... 63 F7
Edward Av *ELGH* SO50 .... 39 G6
Edward Cl *FAWY* SO45 .... 110 B6 1
Edward Gdns *HAV* PO9 .... 102 D5
Edward Gv *FHAM/PORC* PO16 .... 99 H5
Edward Rd *FAWY* SO45 .... 91 H2
WINC SO23 .... 25 H4
WSHM SO15 .... 54 C5
Edwards Cl *CHAM* PO6 .... 100 A5 3
WVILLE PO7 .... 82 A3
Edwina Cl *ITCH* SO19 .... 6 F7
NBAD SO52 .... 36 B6
Effingham Gdns *ITCH* SO19 .... 11 L1
Egan Cl *NEND* PO2 .... 118 E4
Egbert Rd *WINC* SO23 .... 2 E1
Eglantine Cl *HORN* PO8 .... 82 C1
Eglantine Wk *HORN* PO8 .... 82 C1
Eight Acres *ROMY* SO51 .... 35 G3 1
Elaine Gdns *HORN* PO8 .... 64 A7
Elan Cl *WEND* SO18 .... 56 E3
Elcombes Cl *LYND* SO43 .... 86 C1
Elderberry Wy *HORN* PO8 .... 82 C1
Elder Cl *WINW* SO22 .... 25 F4
HLER SO31 .... 94 E4 3
TOTT SO40 .... 70 B4
Elderfield Cl *EMRTH* PO10 .... 104 D3
Elderfield Rd *HAV* PO9 .... 82 E6
Elder Gn *RWIN* SO21 .... 39 K2
Elder Rd *HAV* PO9 .... 15 K1
Eldon St *SSEA* PO5 .... 18 C6
Eldridge Gdns *ROMY* SO51 .... 34 E2
Electron Wy *CHFD* SO53 .... 37 K4
Elettra Av *WVILLE* PO7 .... 81 H5
Elgar Cl *CHAM* PO6 .... 99 H6 1
GPORT PO12 .... 132 C6
ITCH SO19 .... 11 M4
Elgar Rd *ITCH* SO19 .... 11 M4
Elgar Wk *WVILLE* PO7 .... 102 A2 1
Elgin Cl *FAWY* SO45 .... 91 H3
FHAM PO15 .... 12 E3
Elgin Rd *CHAM* PO6 .... 118 E1
WSHM SO15 .... 4 A8
Eling Cl *WINW* SO22 .... 21 G4
Eling Ct *HAV* PO9 .... 82 E7
Eling Hl *TOTT* SO40 .... 53 G7
Eling La *TOTT* SO40 .... 53 F6
Elizabeth Cl *HEND* SO30 .... 57 G3
WHAM PO17 .... 77 G1 1
Elizabeth Ct
FHAM/STUB PO14 .... 97 G7 1
Elizabeth Gdns *ENEY* PO4 .... 134 E6
FAWY SO45 .... 91 H5
Elizabeth Rd
FHAM/STUB PO14 .... 114 E5
WHAM PO17 .... 77 H1
WVILLE PO7 .... 101 K1
Elizabeth Wy *BPWT* SO32 .... 48 C4
Elkstone Rd *CHAM* PO6 .... 100 A5
Ellachie Ms *GPORT* PO12 .... 132 E7
Ellachie Rd *GPORT* PO12 .... 132 E7
Elland Cl *ELGH* SO50 .... 46 B2
Ellanore La *SELS* PO20 .... 139 J5
Elldene Ct *TOTT* SO40 .... 52 D7 1
Ellen Gdns *CHFD* SO53 .... 37 H5
Ellerslie Cl *FHAM/STUB* PO14 .... 114 B6
Ellesmere Orch *EMRTH* PO10 .... 104 E2
Elliot Cl *TOTT* SO40 .... 52 C6
Elliot Ri *HEND* SO30 .... 58 B2
Ellisfield Rd *HAV* PO9 .... 103 F2
Ellis Rd *ITCH* SO19 .... 57 H7
Ellwood Av *ITCH* SO19 .... 57 H7
Ellwood Cl *ITCH* SO19 .... 57 H6
Elm Cl *HISD* PO11 .... 137 H5
Elm Crs *FAWY* SO45 .... 91 H7
Elmdale Cl *HLER* SO31 .... 94 C6
Elmes Dr *WSHM* SO15 .... 54 A5
Elmeswelle Rd *HORN* PO8 .... 64 B6
Elm Gdns *HEND* SO30 .... 57 G2
Elm Gv *ELGH* SO50 .... 44 C1
GPORT PO12 .... 16 B3
HISD PO11 .... 137 H5
SSEA PO5 .... 18 D7
Elmhurst Rd *FHAM/PORC* PO16 .... 13 J7
GPORT PO12 .... 16 C5
Elm La *HAV* PO9 .... 14 E4
Elmleigh Rd *HAV* PO9 .... 14 E2
Elmore Av *LSOL/BMARY* PO13 .... 131 G3
Elmore Cl *LSOL/BMARY* PO13 .... 131 G3
Elmore Rd *LSOL/BMARY* PO13 .... 131 G3
Elm Park Rd *HAV* PO9 .... 14 F3
Elm Rd *BPWT* SO32 .... 49 F3
WINW SO22 .... 2 B3
HAV PO9 .... 15 H6
Elms La *SELS* PO20 .... 139 K7
Elmsleigh Gdns *ROWN* SO16 .... 43 H7
Elmslie Gdns *HLER* SO31 .... 73 J4
Elms Ride *SELS* PO20 .... 139 K7
Elms Rd *FHAM/PORC* PO16 .... 13 J9
Elmstead Gdns *SELS* PO20 .... 139 K6
Elmstead Park Rd *SELS* PO20 .... 139 K6
Elm St *SHAM* SO14 .... 9 K2
SSEA PO5 .... 18 B7 3
Elms Wy *SELS* PO20 .... 139 K6
Elm Ter *SHAM* SO14 .... 9 K3
Elm Tree Cl *TOTT* SO40 .... 68 A3
Elmtree Gdns *ROMY* SO51 .... 35 H4
Elmtree Rd *CHAM* PO6 .... 101 K6 3
Elmwood Av *WVILLE* PO7 .... 81 K7
Elmwood Rd *NEND* PO2 .... 118 D3
Elphinstone Rd *SSEA* PO5 .... 18 C9
Elsfred Rd *FHAM/STUB* PO14 .... 114 B6
Elson La *GPORT* PO12 .... 116 D7
Elson Rd *GPORT* PO12 .... 116 C7
Elstead Gdns *WVILLE* PO7 .... 101 H2
Elstree Rd *ITCH* SO19 .... 6 D9
Elwell Gn *HISD* PO11 .... 137 G5
Emanuel St *NEND* PO2 .... 134 C1
Embley Cl *TOTT* SO40 .... 52 C2
Embsay Rd *HLER* SO31 .... 74 C5
Emerald Cl *ITCH* SO19 .... 7 J7
WVILLE PO7 .... 82 B6
Emer Cl *NBAD* SO52 .... 36 B5 1
Emmanuel Cl
FHAM/STUB PO14 .... 95 H4 1
Emmett Rd *ROWN* SO16 .... 42 A6
Emmons Cl *HLER* SO31 .... 93 J5
Empress Rd *LYND* SO43 .... 86 C1 2
SHAM SO14 .... 5 J4
SHAM SO14 .... 9 J7
Empshott Rd *ENEY* PO4 .... 19 K6
Empson Wk
LSOL/BMARY PO13 .... 131 G1 3
Emsbrook Dr *EMRTH* PO10 .... 104 C4 1
Emsworth Common Rd
EMRTH PO10 .... 104 A1
Emsworth House Cl
EMRTH PO10 .... 104 B5
Emsworth Rd *HAV* PO9 .... 15 K5
EMRTH PO10 .... 122 E3
HAV PO9 .... 15 G5
NEND PO2 .... 118 D6
WSHM SO15 .... 54 C4
Endeavour Cl *GPORT* PO12 .... 16 E6
WSHM SO15 .... 54 C5 2
Endeavour Wy *FAWY* SO45 .... 91 G1
Enderwood Cl *TOTT* SO40 .... 52 A4 2
Endle St *SHAM* SO14 .... 9 L3
Endofield Cl *FHAM/STUB* PO14 .. 115 G1
Enfield Gv *ITCH* SO19 .... 10 C4
Englefield Rd *WEND* SO18 .... 6 A4
English Rd *WSHM* SO15 .... 54 C5
Enmill La *WINW* SO22 .... 24 C3
Ennel Copse *NBAD* SO52 .... 36 B6
Ennerdale Cl *HORN* PO8 .... 64 D2 1
Ennerdale Gdns *WEND* SO18 .... 56 E3 1
Ennerdale Rd
FHAM/STUB PO14 .... 114 E3
ROWN SO16 .... 53 K2
Ensign Dr *LSOL/BMARY* PO13 .... 132 A2
Ensign Wy *HLER* SO31 .... 93 H4
Enterprise Cl *HLER* SO31 .... 94 D5 2
Enterprise Rd *ROWN* SO16 .... 42 D2
Enterprise Wy *SHAM* SO14 .... 9 J5
Epping Cl *WEND* SO18 .... 7 J1
Epsom Cl *ELGH* SO50 .... 46 C4 2
Epworth Rd *NEND* PO2 .... 118 E6
Erica Cl *HLER* SO31 .... 94 E3
HORN PO8 .... 82 C2
Erica Wy *HORN* PO8 .... 82 C1
Eric Rd *FHAM/STUB* PO14 .... 114 D5
Ernest Cl *EMRTH* PO10 .... 104 C5
Ernest Rd *HAV* PO9 .... 102 D2
PSEA PO1 .... 134 D1
Erskine Rd *WINW* SO22 .... 2 B6
Escombe Rd *ELGH* SO50 .... 39 G7
Escur Cl *NEND* PO2 .... 118 E3 4
Esher Gv *WVILLE* PO7 .... 81 H3
Eskdale Cl *HORN* PO8 .... 64 D2
Esmond Cl *EMRTH* PO10 .... 104 C6
Esmonde Cl
LSOL/BMARY PO13 .... 131 G2 2
Esplanade *ENEY* PO4 .... 134 D7
Esplanade Gdns *ENEY* PO4 .... 135 H6
The Esplanade *GPORT* PO12 .... 17 H6
Essex Rd *ENEY* PO4 .... 19 L6
Esslemont Rd *ENEY* PO4 .... 19 J7
Estella Rd *NEND* PO2 .... 118 C7
Estridge Cl *HLER* SO31 .... 73 K4 1
Ethelburt Av *ROWN* SO16 .... 43 K6
Ethelred Gdns *TOTT* SO40 .... 52 B6
Ethel Rd *PSEA* PO1 .... 19 G2
Eton Rd *SSEA* PO5 .... 19 G5
European Wy *SHAM* SO14 .... 9 J6
Euryalus Rd *FHAM/STUB* PO14 .. 115 G1
Euston Rd *ENEY* PO4 .... 135 G3
Evans Cl *NEND* PO2 .... 118 A5
Evans Rd *ENEY* PO4 .... 19 L6
Evans St *SHAM* SO14 .... 9 H2
Evelegh Rd *CHAM* PO6 .... 101 J6
Evelyn Cl *BPWT* SO32 .... 49 F7
Evelyn Crs *WSHM* SO15 .... 4 B3
Evenlode Rd *ROWN* SO16 .... 53 K3
Everdon La *HSEA* PO3 .... 119 H3 3
Everglades Av *HORN* PO8 .... 82 A2
Evergreen Cl *TOTT* SO40 .... 70 A4
WVILLE PO7 .... 81 J6 1
Eversley Crs *HAV* PO9 .... 102 E2
Eversley Pl *WINW* SO22 .... 25 G3
Evesham Cl *ROWN* SO16 .... 43 J6 1
Ewart Ct *FAWY* SO45 .... 91 H1
Ewart Rd *PSEA* PO1 .... 134 D1 4
Ewell Wy *TOTT* SO40 .... 52 C3
Ewhurst Cl *HAV* PO9 .... 102 E2
Exbury Cl *ELGH* SO50 .... 45 J1
Exbury Rd *FAWY* SO45 .... 110 B7
HAV PO9 .... 103 H1
Excellent Rd
FHAM/STUB PO14 .... 115 G2
Exchange Rd *PSEA* PO1 .... 18 B4 1
Exeter Cl *ELGH* SO50 .... 38 C5
EMRTH PO10 .... 104 C3
HLER SO31 .... 94 E3
WEND SO18 .... 7 H1
Exeter Rd *ENEY* PO4 .... 19 J9
WEND SO18 .... 7 H2
Exford Av *WEND* SO18 .... 7 L3
Exford Dr *WEND* SO18 .... 7 M4
Exleigh Cl *ITCH* SO19 .... 7 K6
Exmoor Rd *SHAM* SO14 .... 5 H7
Exmouth Gdns *ELGH* SO50 .... 46 B4 2
Exmouth Rd *GPORT* PO12 .... 116 D7
SSEA PO5 .... 18 F9
Exton Gdns *FHAM/PORC* PO16 .... 99 F5
Exton Rd *HAV* PO9 .... 103 J1
Eyebright Cl *ELGH* SO50 .... 46 B5 3
Eyeworth Wk *FAWY* SO45 .... 90 D2 2
Eynham Av *ITCH* SO19 .... 7 L6
Eynham Cl *ITCH* SO19 .... 7 K6
Eyre Cl *TOTT* SO40 .... 52 C6

F

Faber Cl *HAV* PO9 .... 103 H2
Fabian Cl *WVILLE* PO7 .... 82 B5 1
Factory Rd *ELGH* SO50 .... 44 D1
Fairacre Ri *FHAM/STUB* PO14 .... 96 C6
Fairbairn Wk *NBAD* SO52 .... 37 G4
Fairbourne Cl *HORN* PO8 .... 81 K3
Fairclose Dr *WINW* SO22 .... 20 E2
Faircross Cl *FAWY* SO45 .... 109 K4
Fairdown Cl *WINC* SO23 .... 3 J5
Fairfax Cl *WINW* SO22 .... 24 E3
Fairfax Ct *ITCH* SO19 .... 57 H7 1
Fairfax Ms *ITCH* SO19 .... 57 H6
Fair Fld *ROMY* SO51 .... 35 F1
Fairfield Av *FHAM/STUB* PO14 .... 12 D9
Fairfield Cl *EMRTH* PO10 .... 104 C4
FAWY SO45 .... 91 H2 5
Fairfield Rd *WINW* SO22 .... 2 B2
HAV PO9 .... 14 F4
RWIN SO21 .... 33 G4
Fairfield Sq *CHAM* PO6 .... 100 D6
Fair Gn *ITCH* SO19 .... 7 K8
Fairhome Cl *GPORT* PO12 .... 132 D1
Fair Isle Cl *FHAM/STUB* PO14 .... 114 C4
Fairisle Rd *ROWN* SO16 .... 41 K7
Fair La *RWIN* SO21 .... 23 F6
Fairlawn Cl *ROWN* SO16 .... 42 A5
Fairlead Dr
LSOL/BMARY PO13 .... 132 A2 3
Fairlea Rd *EMRTH* PO10 .... 104 C3
Fairlie Cl *HEND* SO30 .... 58 B1 2
Fairmead Wk *HORN* PO8 .... 82 C2
Fairmead Wy *TOTT* SO40 .... 52 D7
Fair Oak Rd *HAV* PO9 .... 14 E1
Fairoak Rd *ELGH* SO50 .... 45 G1
Fairthorne Gdns *GPORT* PO12 .... 132 D4
Fairview Cl *FAWY* SO45 .... 91 H3
ROMY SO51 .... 35 G1
Fairview Dr *FAWY* SO45 .... 91 G4
ROMY SO51 .... 35 G2
Fairview Pde *FAWY* SO45 .... 91 H4
Fairwater Cl
LSOL/BMARY PO13 .... 115 J6
Fairway Gdns *ROWN* SO16 .... 41 K6
Fairway Rd *FAWY* SO45 .... 91 G2
The Fairway *FHAM/PORC* PO16 .. 99 F6
HAV PO9 .... 83 K3
LSOL/BMARY PO13 .... 115 K6 2
Fairy Crossway *HORN* PO8 .... 82 C3
Falaise Cl *ROWN* SO16 .... 42 D7
Falcon Cl *FHAM/PORC* PO16 .... 98 C6 4
Falconer Ct *FAWY* SO45 .... 109 J1
Falcon Flds *FAWY* SO45 .... 110 E4
Falcon Rd *HORN* PO8 .... 64 B5
Falcon Sq *ELGH* SO50 .... 44 A2
Falcon Vw *WINW* SO22 .... 25 F4
Falcon Wy *BPWT* SO32 .... 59 F3
Falkland Rd *CHFD* SO53 .... 37 K7
WSHM SO15 .... 54 B5
Falklands Cl
LSOL/BMARY PO13 .... 131 G1
Falklands Rd *NEND* PO2 .... 118 D3 2
Fallow Fld *WINW* SO22 .... 25 F4
Falmouth Rd *CHAM* PO6 .... 99 J5
Falstaff Wy *TOTT* SO40 .... 52 D7 2
Fanshawe St *SHAM* SO14 .... 5 H6 1
Fareham Park Rd *FHAM* PO15 .... 96 D2
Fareham Rd
LSOL/BMARY PO13 .... 115 K2
WHAM PO17 .... 77 H2
WHAM PO17 .... 99 H1
Faringdon Rd *WEND* SO18 .... 57 G5
Farleigh Cl *HAV* PO9 .... 102 E1 1
Farley Cl *ELGH* SO50 .... 46 C2
WINW SO22 .... 24 E4
Farlington Av *CHAM* PO6 .... 101 H5
Farlington Rd *NEND* PO2 .... 118 D6
Far Meadow Wy *EMRTH* PO10 .. 104 A6
Farm Edge Rd
FHAM/STUB PO14 .... 114 D6
Farmery Cl *ELGH* SO50 .... 44 A7
Farm Gdns *HSEA* PO3 .... 118 E3
Farmhouse Wy *HORN* PO8 .... 64 B7
Farm La *RCCH* PO18 .... 105 J7
Farmlea Rd *CHAM* PO6 .... 99 J6
Farm Rd *FHAM/STUB* PO14 .... 95 K4
Farmside Gdns *HSEA* PO3 .... 118 E3
Farm Vw *EMRTH* PO10 .... 104 C3
Faroes Cl *FHAM/STUB* PO14 .... 114 C4 3
Farriers Wy *HORN* PO8 .... 82 D4
Farrier Wy
FHAM/PORC PO16 .... 115 J1 1
Farringdon Rd *HAV* PO9 .... 103 H2
Farringford Rd *ITCH* SO19 .... 57 G6
Farthings Ga *WVILLE* PO7 .... 101 K3
Fastnet Cl *ROWN* SO16 .... 41 K6 2
Fastnet Wy
FHAM/STUB PO14 .... 114 C4 4
Fathoms Reach *HISD* PO11 .... 137 F4
F Av *FAWY* SO45 .... 110 C1
Fawcett Rd *ENEY* PO4 .... 19 G5
Fawley By-pass *FAWY* SO45 .... 110 E4
Fawley Ct *HAV* PO9 .... 103 J1 3
Fawley Rd *FAWY* SO45 .... 91 J6
NEND PO2 .... 118 D2
WSHM SO15 .... 54 B6
Fay Cl *FHAM/STUB* PO14 .... 114 D5
Fayre Rd *FHAM/PORC* PO16 .... 13 H9
Fearon Rd *NEND* PO2 .... 118 D5
Felix Rd *GPORT* PO12 .... 132 E1
Fell Cl *HLER* SO31 .... 95 F2
Fell Dr *LSOL/BMARY* PO13 .... 131 G1
Feltham Cl *ROMY* SO51 .... 35 H2
Feltons Pl *HSEA* PO3 .... 118 E2
Fen Av *FHAM/PORC* PO16 .... 97 J7
Fennell Cl *WVILLE* PO7 .... 81 J4
Ferncroft Cl
FHAM/STUB PO14 .... 114 D6 2
Ferndale *HEND* SO30 .... 58 C7 1
WVILLE PO7 .... 82 A6
Ferndale Ms
LSOL/BMARY PO13 .... 115 J3
Ferndale Rd *TOTT* SO40 .... 70 A4
Ferndene Wy *WEND* SO18 .... 6 F2
Fern Dr *HAV* PO9 .... 15 G2
Ferneham Rd *FHAM* PO15 .... 96 D4
Fern Hill La *ROMY* SO51 .... 29 J1
Fernhills Rd *FAWY* SO45 .... 91 J5
Fernhurst Cl *HISD* PO11 .... 136 E5
Fernhurst Rd *ENEY* PO4 .... 19 J6
Fernie Cl *FHAM/STUB* PO14 .... 114 C5
Fernlea Gdns *ROWN* SO16 .... 55 F1 5
Fernlea Wy *FAWY* SO45 .... 90 E3
Fern Rd *FAWY* SO45 .... 91 G3
ITCH SO19 .... 10 E5
Fern Wy *FHAM* PO15 .... 95 J3
Fernwood Crs *WEND* SO18 .... 6 F2
Fernyhurst Av *ROWN* SO16 .... 42 A5
Ferrol Rd *GPORT* PO12 .... 16 C2
Ferry Rd *ENEY* PO4 .... 135 J5
FAWY SO45 .... 91 G3
HISD PO11 .... 136 B4
Festing Gv *ENEY* PO4 .... 134 E6
Festing Rd *ENEY* PO4 .... 19 J9
Fey Rd *GPORT* PO12 .... 16 C4
Field Cl *HLER* SO31 .... 95 G4
LSOL/BMARY PO13 .... 115 J2
ROMY SO51 .... 35 F3
ROWN SO16 .... 43 K6 4
RWIN SO21 .... 33 F3
Fielden Cl *NBAD* SO52 .... 36 A6
Fieldfare Ct *TOTT* SO40 .... 52 B4
Fieldhouse Dr
LSOL/BMARY PO13 .... 115 G7
Fieldmore Rd *GPORT* PO12 .... 132 E1
Fields Cl *FAWY* SO45 .... 110 B6 2
Field Vw *NBAD* SO52 .... 37 G4
Field Wy *RWIN* SO21 .... 33 F3
WVILLE PO7 .... 80 E1
Fifth Av *CHAM* PO6 .... 100 D6
HAV PO9 .... 15 K2
Fifth St *PSEA* PO1 .... 134 E1
Filmer Cl *LSOL/BMARY* PO13 .... 116 A7
Filton Cl *TOTT* SO40 .... 52 B4
Finchdean Rd *HAV* PO9 .... 83 K3
HAV PO9 .... 102 E2

Finch Rd ENEY PO4 135 J5
Finch's La RWIN SO21 33 J3
Findon Rd GPORT PO12 116 E7
Finisterre St FHAM/STUB PO14 114 C3
Finlay Cl ITCH SO19 11 M2
Finzi Cl ITCH SO19 11 M4
Fiona Cl WINC SO23 3 J3
Fir Cl LYND SO43 86 C2 2
Fir Copse Rd WVILLE PO7 101 J3
Fir Croft Dr CHFD SO53 38 A5
Firecrest Cl ROWN SO16 42 C6
Firgrove Cl NBAD SO52 36 A6
Firgrove Crs HSEA PO3 118 E2
Firgrove La WHAM PO17 78 C3
Firgrove Rd NBAD SO52 36 B5
WSHM SO15 54 D5
Firlands Ri CHAM PO6 102 B5
Firmstone Rd WINC SO23 3 J4
Fir Rd TOTT SO40 68 A3
Firs Av WVILLE PO7 82 A3
Firs Dr HEND SO30 57 K6
First Av CHAM PO6 100 E6
CHAM PO6 101 K6
EMRTH PO10 105 G6
HAV PO9 15 J3
HORN PO8 64 D1
WSHM SO15 53 J5
The Firs LSOL/BMARY PO13 116 A6
ROWN SO16 43 G7
First St FAWY SO45 92 B6
Fir Tree Cl ELGH SO50 46 B4
Firtree Gdns HORN PO8 64 D7
Fir Tree La ELGH SO50 46 A4
Fir Tree Rd HISD PO11 137 H5
TOTT SO40 50 D5
Firtree Wy ITCH SO19 7 K9
Firwood Cl CHFD SO53 37 K2
Fisgard Rd GPORT PO12 132 E1
Fisher Cl FHAM/STUB PO14 114 C4 5
The Fishermans
EMRTH PO10 104 D6 1
Fishermans Wk HISD PO11 138 B6
Fisher Rd LSOL/BMARY PO13 115 K4
Fishers Gv CHAM PO6 101 K7
Fishers Hl FHAM PO15 96 B4
Fisher's Rd TOTT SO40 53 F6
Fishery La HISD PO11 137 K6
Fishlake Mdw ROMY SO51 34 E1
Fitzgerald Cl HLER SO31 75 H5 4
Fitzherbert Rd CHAM PO6 101 J7
Fitzherbert Sp CHAM PO6 101 K7
Fitzherbert St PSEA PO1 134 B1 2
Fitzhugh Pl WSHM SO15 4 E5
Fitzhugh St SHAM SO14 4 E9 1
Fitzpatrick Ct CHAM PO6 100 C5 1
Fitzroy Cl ROWN SO16 43 G4
Fitzwilliam Av
FHAM/STUB PO14 114 B5 1
Fitzwygram Crs HAV PO9 14 E1
Five Bridges Rd WINC SO23 25 H5
Five Elms Dr ROMY SO51 35 G4
Fivefields Cl WINC SO23 3 J6
Fivefields Rd WINC SO23 3 K6
Five Heads Rd HORN PO8 64 B4
Five Post La GPORT PO12 16 A1
Flag Staff Gn GPORT PO12 16 E2
Flag Wk HORN PO8 64 A7
Flamborough Cl ROWN SO16 53 J2
Flamingo Ct FHAM/PORC PO16 98 C6
Flanders Rd HEND SO30 58 A4
Flathouse Rd PSEA PO1 134 B1
Fleet Cl LSOL/BMARY PO13 116 A6
Fleet End Bottom HLER SO31 94 E6
Fleetend Cl HAV PO9 83 F7 3
Fleet End Rd HLER SO31 94 E6
Fleming Av NBAD SO52 36 B6
Fleming Pl ROMY SO51 34 E3 1
RWIN SO21 39 J1
Fleming Rd WINW SO22 21 F4
ROWN SO16 44 A7
Fletcher Cl FAWY SO45 90 E3
Fletchwood La TOTT SO40 52 A6
Fletchwood Rd TOTT SO40 52 A6
Fleuret Cl FAWY SO45 91 H6
Flexford Cl CHFD SO53 37 H1
Flexford Rd NBAD SO52 36 D4
Flint Cl ITCH SO19 73 H1
Flint St SSEA PO5 18 B7
Floating Bridge Rd SHAM SO14 9 L4
Florence Rd ITCH SO19 10 B5
SSEA PO5 134 C7
Florentine Wy WVILLE PO7 82 B5 2
The Florins HLER SO31 95 F5
WVILLE PO7 101 K3 2
Flowerdown Cl TOTT SO40 52 B4
Flowers Cl HLER SO31 93 H3
Flume Rd FAWY SO45 111 F3
Foldsgate Cl LYND SO43 66 C7 1
Folkestone Rd HSEA PO3 135 F1
Folly Fld BPWT SO32 48 E4
Font Cl FHAM/STUB PO14 95 H3 1
Fontley Rd FHAM PO15 96 B3
Fontwell Cl TOTT SO40 52 B3
Fontwell Gdns ELGH SO50 46 C4 3
Fontwell Ms HORN PO8 82 C4
Fontwell Rd SSEA PO5 18 E9 1
Foord Rd HEND SO30 74 A1 1
Footner Cl ROMY SO51 29 H7
Forbes Cl ROWN SO16 42 A5
Forbury Rd SSEA PO5 18 E5 4
Ford Av CHFD SO53 38 A6
Fordingbridge Rd ENEY PO4 135 G5
Fordington Rd WINW SO22 2 A3
Ford Rd GPORT PO12 132 C2
Foreland Ct HISD PO11 137 K6
Foreshore North FAWY SO45 110 E1
Foreshore South FAWY SO45 110 E1
Forest Av HORN PO8 82 A2
Forest Cl BPWT SO32 61 F1
CHFD SO53 37 K2
HORN PO8 82 A2
NBAD SO52 35 K5
Forest Edge FAWY SO45 110 D4
Forest End WVILLE PO7 81 J6
Foresters Ga FAWY SO45 128 B1
Foresters Rd FAWY SO45 110 C5
Forest Front FAWY SO45 91 G6
Forest Gdns BPWT SO32 61 F1 1
LYND SO43 86 C1
Forest Ga FAWY SO45 128 C1
Forest Hills Dr WEND SO18 56 B1
Forest Hill Wy FAWY SO45 91 G4 4
Forest La FAWY SO45 109 J1 1
WHAM PO17 77 J5
Forest Md WVILLE PO7 80 E2
Forest Meadow FAWY SO45 91 H6
Forest Rd BPWT SO32 61 G1
CHFD SO53 38 A2
WVILLE PO7 79 K1
Forestside Av HAV PO9 103 H1
Forest Vw SHAM SO14 8 F3
Forest Wy LSOL/BMARY PO13 116 A5
TOTT SO40 51 K2
Forge Cl HLER SO31 73 K4
Forge Rd FAWY SO45 128 C1
Forneth Gdns FHAM PO15 96 C6 2
Forster Rd SHAM SO14 5 H4
Forsythia Cl HAV PO9 103 J2
HEND SO30 58 A4 3
Fort Cumberland Rd
ENEY PO4 135 J5
Fort Fareham Rd
FHAM/STUB PO14 115 G1
Forth Cl CHFD SO53 37 J5
FHAM/STUB PO14 114 C4 6
Forties Cl FHAM/STUB PO14 114 C3 2
Forton Rd GPORT PO12 16 A3
PSEA PO1 19 H1 2
Fort Rd GPORT PO12 132 D7
ITCH SO19 10 C4
Fortunes Wy CHAM PO6 102 A5
Foster Cl FHAM/STUB PO14 114 D3
Foster Rd GPORT PO12 16 A7
PSEA PO1 18 F1 1
Founders Wy
LSOL/BMARY PO13 116 A5
Foundry La WSHM SO15 54 C4
Fountain St PSEA PO1 18 C3 2
Four Acre HEND SO30 59 F6
Four Posts Hl WSHM SO15 4 C8
Fourshells Cl FAWY SO45 110 C5 1
Fourth Av CHAM PO6 100 D6
HAV PO9 15 J3
Fourth St PSEA PO1 19 J1
Fowey Cl CHFD SO53 37 J3
The Fowey FAWY SO45 110 B5
Fowlers Rd HEND SO30 58 A4
Fowler's Wk NBAD SO52 42 E1
Foxbury Cl FAWY SO45 91 H4
Foxbury Gv FHAM/PORC PO16 98 E7
Foxbury La EMRTH PO10 105 F2
LSOL/BMARY PO13 116 A3
Fox Cl ELGH SO50 45 J1
Foxcombe Cl BPWT SO32 49 H5
Foxcott Cl ITCH SO19 72 C5 3
Foxcott Gv HAV PO9 103 G1
Foxcroft Dr FAWY SO45 109 J4
Foxes Cl WVILLE PO7 81 K7
Foxglade FAWY SO45 128 C1 1
Foxgloves FHAM/PORC PO16 13 L1
The Foxgloves HEND SO30 58 C7 2
Foxhayes La FAWY SO45 128 C1
Foxhills TOTT SO40 68 B1
Foxhills Cl TOTT SO40 68 B2
Foxlands FAWY SO45 128 C1 2
Fox La WINW SO22 25 F3
Foxlea Gdns GPORT PO12 132 E1 1
Foxley Dr HSEA PO3 119 G3
Fox's Wk FAWY SO45 128 C1 3
Foxtail Dr FAWY SO45 91 G5
Foxy Paddock FAWY SO45 128 C1 4
Foy Gdns HLER SO31 94 B5
Foyle Rd CHFD SO53 37 J4
Frampton Cl RWIN SO21 39 J1
Frampton Wy TOTT SO40 52 E6
Frances Rd WVILLE PO7 101 J3
Francis Av ENEY PO4 19 J8
Francis Cl LSOL/BMARY PO13 131 H3
Francis Gdns WINC SO23 22 A5
Francis Pl FHAM/STUB PO14 114 E5
Francis Rd HORN PO8 64 D1
Frankland Ter EMRTH PO10 104 D6 2
Franklin Rd LSOL/BMARY PO13 131 K1
RWIN SO21 33 K2 1
Franklyn Av ITCH SO19 11 H1
Frarydene EMRTH PO10 105 G6
Fraser Cl ROWN SO16 42 A5
Fraser Gdns EMRTH PO10 105 H4
Fraser Rd HAV PO9 14 B2
LSOL/BMARY PO13 115 K3
NEND PO2 118 A5 1
SSEA PO5 18 E5
Frater La GPORT PO12 116 D6
Fratton Rd PSEA PO1 19 G2
Fratton Wy ELGH SO50 46 B2
Fraysea FAWY SO45 91 H4 1
Freda Routh Gdns ELGH SO50 46 C1 1
Frederick St PSEA PO1 18 D1 6
SHAM SO14 5 J6
Freedom Ct FAWY SO45 91 H3 3
Freegrounds Av HEND SO30 58 B6 1
Freegrounds Cl HEND SO30 58 B6
Freegrounds Rd HEND SO30 58 B6
Freemantle Cl ITCH SO19 6 E8
Freemantle Common Rd
ITCH SO19 6 E8
Freemantle Rd GPORT PO12 132 E1
Freestone Rd SSEA PO5 134 C6 2
Free St BPWT SO32 48 E3
Frenchies Vw WVILLE PO7 80 D1 1
French St PSEA PO1 17 L7 1
SHAM SO14 8 F4 1
Frendstaple Rd WVILLE PO7 102 B1
Frensham Cl HEND SO30 58 B6 2
Frensham Rd ENEY PO4 19 K6
Freshfield Gdns WVILLE PO7 81 K5
Freshfield Rd WSHM SO15 54 C5
Freshfield Sq WSHM SO15 54 C5
Freshwater Rd CHAM PO6 100 D7
Friarscroft HLER SO31 72 E6
Friars Cft TOTT SO40 52 A2
Friarsgate WINC SO23 2 F4
Friars Pond Rd FHAM PO15 96 D5 1
Friars Rd ELGH SO50 44 C2
Friars Wy WEND SO18 44 A7
Friary Cl SSEA PO5 134 B6 2
Fritham Cl TOTT SO40 52 B5
Fritham Rd WEND SO18 7 M2
Frith La WHAM PO17 61 H6
Frobisher Cl
LSOL/BMARY PO13 131 K2
Frobisher Gdns
EMRTH PO10 104 C6 1
ITCH SO19 11 M1
Frobisher Gv FHAM/PORC PO16 99 F7
Froddington Rd SSEA PO5 18 F5 1
Froghall FAWY SO45 91 G5
Frogmore FHAM/STUB PO14 96 D6
Frogmore La HORN PO8 64 B6
ROWN SO16 53 J1
Frogmore Rd ENEY PO4 19 K5
Frome Cl TOTT SO40 70 B3
Frome Rd WEND SO18 56 D1
Fromond Rd WINW SO22 21 F4
Frosthole Cl FHAM PO15 12 D1
Frosthole Crs FHAM PO15 12 C1
Frost La FAWY SO45 91 K4
Froxfield Cl WINW SO22 21 G3
Froxfield Gdns
FHAM/PORC PO16 99 F5
Froxfield Rd HAV PO9 103 J1
Froyle Ct HAV PO9 103 J1
Fry Cl FAWY SO45 110 C5
HLER SO31 93 K2
Fryern Cl CHFD SO53 38 B4
Fulflood Rd HAV PO9 103 F1
Fullerton Cl HAV PO9 103 J1 6
ITCH SO19 72 C5
Fulmar Cl ROWN SO16 42 C6
Fulmar Dr FAWY SO45 91 J4
Fulmer Wk HORN PO8 81 K1 1
HORN PO8 81 K1 2
Funtington Rd NEND PO2 118 E7
Funtley Hl FHAM/PORC PO16 97 F2
Funtley Rd FHAM PO15 96 E1
Furdies WVILLE PO7 80 D1 2
Furley Cl WINC SO23 3 H4
Furneaux Gdns
FHAM/PORC PO16 13 J1
Furness Rd SSEA PO5 134 C7 3
Furniss Wy HISD PO11 136 E4
Furnston Gv EMRTH PO10 105 H5
Fury Wy FHAM/STUB PO14 114 C4
Furzedale Gdns FAWY SO45 91 J5
Furzedale Pk FAWY SO45 91 J5
Furzedown Crs HAV PO9 103 H1
Furzedown Ms FAWY SO45 91 J5 1
Furzedown Rd PTSW SO17 55 H2
Furzehall Av FHAM/PORC PO16 13 L1
Furze La ENEY PO4 135 J3
Furzeley Rd WVILLE PO7 80 E3
Furze Rd ITCH SO19 7 H9
Furze Wy HORN PO8 82 C1
Furzey Cl FAWY SO45 110 C6
Furzey La BROC SO42 107 G6
Furzley Ct HAV PO9 82 D7
Fushia Cl HAV PO9 103 K2
Fushsia Gdns ROWN SO16 54 E2 1
Fyeford Cl ROWN SO16 42 A5
Fyfield Cl FHAM PO15 75 H5
Fyfield Wy WINW SO22 20 E2
Fyning St PSEA PO1 18 E2

G

Gables Ct ROWN SO16 43 G6 1
Gage Cl TOTT SO40 70 B3
Gainsborough Cl ITCH SO19 11 L5
Gainsborough Ms
FHAM/STUB PO14 96 A6 1
Gainsford Rd ITCH SO19 6 B9
Gain's Rd ENEY PO4 19 G9
Galaxie Rd HORN PO8 82 C1
Gale Moor Av GPORT PO12 132 A5
Galleon Cl HLER SO31 94 E5 1
The Gallops FHAM/STUB PO14 95 J4
Galsworthy Rd TOTT SO40 52 C5
Galt Rd CHAM PO6 101 J6
Gamble Cl ITCH SO19 10 F1
Gamblins La BPWT SO32 61 G4
Ganger Farm La ROMY SO51 29 H7
Ganger Rd ROMY SO51 29 H7 2
Gannet Cl FAWY SO45 91 J4
ROWN SO16 42 C6
The Gannets
FHAM/STUB PO14 114 C5
Garbett Rd WINC SO23 3 J4
Garden City FAWY SO45 70 B7
Garden Cl HISD PO11 137 G5
LYND SO43 86 B1
Garden La SSEA PO5 18 C8
WINC SO23 2 F4
Garden Ms HLER SO31 94 B5
The Gardens HAV PO9 15 K6
WVILLE PO7 62 C1
Gardiner Cl TOTT SO40 70 B3
Gardner Rd FHAM/STUB PO14 96 A7
Garfield Cl BPWT SO32 48 D3
Garfield Rd BPWT SO32 48 D3
HLER SO31 72 D7
ITCH SO19 6 C5
NEND PO2 118 C7
Garland Av EMRTH PO10 104 C3
Garnett Cl FHAM/STUB PO14 114 D3
Garnier Pk WHAM PO17 77 H1
Garnier Rd WINC SO23 2 D9
Garnier St PSEA PO1 18 F3
Garnock Rd ITCH SO19 10 B6
Garratt Cl HEND SO30 58 B2
Garrett Cl ITCH SO19 11 H8
Garrick Gdns ITCH SO19 11 H5
Garsons Rd EMRTH PO10 105 G6
Garstons Cl FHAM/STUB PO14 96 A6
Garstons Rd FHAM/STUB PO14 96 A6
Gar St WINC SO23 2 D5
Garton Rd ITCH SO19 10 B4
Gatcombe HLER SO31 73 F6
Gatcombe Av HSEA PO3 118 E5
Gatcombe Dr NEND PO2 118 E4
Gatcombe Gdns
FHAM/STUB PO14 96 C6
WEND SO18 56 D2 5
Gate House Rd
FHAM/PORC PO16 98 D7
Gate Hyde WINC SO23 2 E2 1
Gatekeeper Cl WINC SO23 3 K4
Gatwick Cl ROWN SO16 42 B7
Gaulter Cl HAV PO9 15 G1
Gavan St ITCH SO19 57 G7
G Av FAWY SO45 110 C1
Gaylyn Wy FHAM/STUB PO14 96 C6
Gaza Av BROC SO42 125 H2
Gemini Cl ROWN SO16 42 A7
Gento Cl HEND SO30 58 D6
Geoffrey Av WVILLE PO7 101 G4
Geoffrey Crs
FHAM/PORC PO16 115 J1
George Byng Wy NEND PO2 118 B7
George Curl Wy ELGH SO50 44 C5 1
George Eyston Dr WINW SO22 25 G2
George St ELGH SO50 38 D7
GPORT PO12 16 D4
PSEA PO1 134 D1
Gerard Crs ITCH SO19 57 G6
Gibbs Rd SHAM SO14 4 F9
Gibraltar Cl FHAM PO15 12 A3
Gibraltar Rd ENEY PO4 135 J5
FHAM/STUB PO14 115 G1
Gibson Cl FHAM PO15 75 K7
LSOL/BMARY PO13 131 G2 3
Gifford Cl FHAM PO15 12 C2
Gilbert Cl LSOL/BMARY PO13 116 A7 1
Gilbert Md HISD PO11 137 F4
Gilbert Wy WVILLE PO7 101 K1 1
Gilbury Cl WEND SO18 44 B7 2
Gilchrist Gdns HLER SO31 94 B7
Giles Cl FHAM/PORC PO16 13 K1
GPORT PO12 132 D2
HEND SO30 58 C3 2
Gilkicker Rd GPORT PO12 133 F7
Gillcrest FHAM PO15 95 H2
The Gillies FHAM/PORC PO16 13 H6
Gillman Rd CHAM PO6 101 K6
Gilpin Cl ITCH SO19 57 G7
Gins La BROC SO42 126 E7
Girton Cl FHAM/STUB PO14 95 H5
Gitsham Gdns WVILLE PO7 101 H3 2
The Glades HLER SO31 95 F2
The Glade CHFD SO53 38 C1
FAWY SO45 128 B1
FHAM PO15 96 E2
HISD PO11 137 K6
WVILLE PO7 82 B5
Gladstone Gdns
FHAM/PORC PO16 99 F7 1
Gladstone Rd GPORT PO12 132 D1
ITCH SO19 7 K9
Gladstone St WINC SO23 2 D3
Gladys Av HORN PO8 82 B1
NEND PO2 118 C5
Glamis Cl WVILLE PO7 82 B5
Glamorgan Rd HORN PO8 64 C2
Glasgow Rd ENEY PO4 135 G5
Glasslaw Rd WEND SO18 7 H2
Glasspool WVILLE PO7 62 D7
Glebe Cl HISD PO11 137 F3
Glebe Cnr WHAM PO17 77 J2
Glebe Ct ELGH SO50 46 C1
HEND SO30 59 F4 1
PTSW SO17 55 H2
Glebe Dr LSOL/BMARY PO13 115 K6
Glebefield Gdns CHAM PO6 100 D6 1
Glebe Park Av CHAM PO6 102 B5
The Glebe FHAM/STUB PO14 114 D6
Glenbrook Wk
FHAM/STUB PO14 96 D6
Glencarron Wy ROWN SO16 55 F1
Glencoe Rd PSEA PO1 134 E1
Glencoyne Gdns ROWN SO16 54 A2
Glenda Cl HLER SO31 94 C6 4
Glendale BPWT SO32 49 J7
Glen Dl HAV PO9 84 A4
Glendale HLER SO31 95 G4 2
Glendowan Rd CHFD SO53 37 H3
Gleneagles Dr HORN PO8 82 C3
Glenelg FHAM PO15 12 E3
Glenesha Gdns FHAM PO15 12 B3
Glen Eyre Dr ROWN SO16 43 H6
Glen Eyre Rd ROWN SO16 43 G6
Glen Eyre Wy ROWN SO16 43 H7
Glenfield Av WEND SO18 6 E4
Glenfield Crs WEND SO18 6 F4
Glenfield Wy WEND SO18 6 F4
Glenlea Cl HEND SO30 57 G3
Glenlea Dr HEND SO30 57 G3 2
Glenleigh Av CHAM PO6 100 E7 2
Glenleigh Pk HAV PO9 15 K3
Glenn Rd HEND SO30 57 G2
HLER SO31 74 D7
Glen Rd HLER SO31 74 D6
ITCH SO19 10 A7
Glenside FAWY SO45 91 G3
Glenside Av ITCH SO19 73 G1
The Glen LSOL/BMARY PO13 116 B6 2
Glenthorne Cl
FHAM/STUB PO14 114 E6
Glenthorne Rd HSEA PO3 119 F6
Glenwood Av ROWN SO16 43 H6
Glenwood Ct ELGH SO50 46 D1
Glenwood Gdns HORN PO8 82 A2
Glenwood Rd EMRTH PO10 105 G5
Glidden Cl PSEA PO1 18 E3
Glidden La WVILLE PO7 62 D1
Gloucester Rd PSEA PO1 17 M1
WVILLE PO7 82 A7
Gloucester Sq SHAM SO14 9 G4
Gloucester Ter SSEA PO5 18 C7 2
Gloucester Vw SSEA PO5 18 C7 3
Glyn Dr FHAM/STUB PO14 114 D5
Glyn Jones Cl FAWY SO45 110 C5
Glyn Wy FHAM/STUB PO14 114 D5
Godfrey Pink Wy BPWT SO32 48 E4 2
Godwin Cl EMRTH PO10 104 B3
WINW SO22 21 F4
Godwit Cl GPORT PO12 116 E7
Godwit Rd ENEY PO4 135 H2 1
Gofton Av CHAM PO6 101 G7
Goldcrest Cl
FHAM/PORC PO16 98 B6 1
HORN PO8 64 B5
Goldcrest Gdns ROWN SO16 42 B6
Goldcrest La TOTT SO40 52 B4
Golden Ct HEND SO30 57 J2
Golden Gv SHAM SO14 5 J9
Golden Hind Pk FAWY SO45 91 G4
Goldfinch La
LSOL/BMARY PO13 131 G1
Goldring Cl HISD PO11 137 H5
Goldsmith Av ENEY PO4 19 H4
Goldsmith Cl TOTT SO40 52 C5 2
Goldsmith Rd ELGH SO50 44 C2
Gold St SSEA PO5 18 B7 4
Golf Course Rd ROWN SO16 43 F5
Gomer La GPORT PO12 132 B4
Goodacre Dr NBAD SO52 37 G5
Goodison Cl ELGH SO50 46 A2 1
Goodlands V HEND SO30 57 K5 1
Goodsell Cl
FHAM/STUB PO14 114 C5 3
Goodwin Cl ROWN SO16 53 J2 1
Goodwood Cl
FHAM/STUB PO14 95 H4
GPORT PO12 116 E7
WVILLE PO7 82 C4
Goodwood Ct EMRTH PO10 105 H6
Goodwood Gdns TOTT SO40 52 B4
Goodwood Rd ELGH SO50 38 B5
SSEA PO5 19 G8
Gordon Av SHAM SO14 5 G2
WINC SO23 3 J7
Gordon Rd BPWT SO32 60 A3
CHFD SO53 38 A1
EMRTH PO10 104 E7
FHAM/PORC PO16 13 G5
GPORT PO12 132 D4
PSEA PO1 18 A8
WINC SO23 2 F2
WVILLE PO7 81 J7
Gordon Ter ITCH SO19 11 G5 1
Goring Fld WINW SO22 21 F6
Gorley Ct HAV PO9 82 D7
Gorran Av LSOL/BMARY PO13 115 K6
Gorse Cl HLER SO31 94 E4
Gorselands Rd WEND SO18 7 J1
Gorselands Wy
LSOL/BMARY PO13 116 A7
Gort Crs ITCH SO19 11 J1
Gosport La LYND SO43 86 D2
Gosport Rd FHAM/PORC PO16 13 K7
FHAM/STUB PO14 114 E5
LSOL/BMARY PO13 131 G3
Gover Rd ROWN SO16 53 H3
Grace Dieu Gdns HLER SO31 73 J4 1
Graddidge Wy TOTT SO40 52 C5
Grafton Gdns ROWN SO16 42 D6
Grafton Rd WINC SO23 2 C7
Grafton St NEND PO2 134 B1
Graham Rd ENEY PO4 19 H8
GPORT PO12 132 D2
SHAM SO14 5 H7
Graham St SHAM SO14 5 L7
Grainger Gdns ITCH SO19 11 M4
Granada Cl HORN PO8 82 B2
Granada Rd ENEY PO4 134 D7
HEND SO30 57 K7
Granby Gv PTSW SO17 55 J1
Grand Pde WINW SO22 21 F2
HISD PO11 137 H6
PSEA PO1 17 L8
Grange Cl GPORT PO12 132 C2
HAV PO9 15 J3
WEND SO18 44 B7 3
Grange Crs GPORT PO12 132 C2
Grange Dr HEND SO30 58 C4
Grange La LSOL/BMARY PO13 115 K7
Grange Ms ROMY SO51 35 H1
Grange Rd HEND SO30 58 B4
HLER SO31 72 E7
LSOL/BMARY PO13 132 A3
NEND PO2 118 C6
ROWN SO16 54 C3
WINC SO23 25 H5
Grangewood Gdns
ELGH SO50 46 A1 1
Grantham Av HLER SO31 93 H3
Grantham Rd ELGH SO50 44 C1
ITCH SO19 6 E6
Grant Rd CHAM PO6 101 J6
Granville Cl HAV PO9 15 H5
Granville St SHAM SO14 9 K2
Grasdean Cl WEND SO18 56 D3 3
Grasmere ELGH SO50 44 C1 1
Grasmere Cl WEND SO18 56 E3 2
Grasmere Wy
FHAM/STUB PO14 114 E3
Grassmere Wy HORN PO8 82 C3
Grassymead FHAM PO15 95 H2 2
Grateley Cl ITCH SO19 10 F9
Grateley Crs HAV PO9 102 D2
Gravel Hl BPWT SO32 61 J1
Gray Cl HLER SO31 94 E4
Grayland Cl HISD PO11 137 F4 2
Grayling Md ROMY SO51 34 E1
Grays Av FAWY SO45 91 J3
Grays Cl ELGH SO50 39 J2
GPORT PO12 132 B5
ROMY SO51 35 F3
Grays Ct PSEA PO1 17 M6
Grayshott Cl WINW SO22 21 G3
Grayshott Rd ENEY PO4 19 K5
GPORT PO12 132 C4
Great Br ROMY SO51 28 D7
Greatbridge Rd ROMY SO51 28 D6
Great Copse Dr HAV PO9 103 G1
Great Elms Cl FAWY SO45 109 J4
Great Field Rd WINW SO22 21 G4
Greatfield Wy HAV PO9 83 J3
Great Gays FHAM/STUB PO14 114 B6
Great Md LYND SO43 86 C2 3
WVILLE PO7 81 F2
Great Minster St WINC SO23 2 E5
Great Southsea St SSEA PO5 18 C7
Great Well Dr ROMY SO51 34 E2
Greatwood Cl FAWY SO45 91 H4 2
Grebe Cl FHAM/PORC PO16 98 C6 5
HORN PO8 81 K1
Greenacre Gdns WVILLE PO7 101 J2
Greenacres Dr RWIN SO21 33 F6
Greenaway La HLER SO31 94 C4
Greenbank Crs ROWN SO16 43 G6
Greenbanks Gdns
FHAM/PORC PO16 98 A4
Green Cl FAWY SO45 91 H2 6
TOTT SO40 67 J1
Green Crs LSOL/BMARY PO13 115 K6
Greendale Cl CHFD SO53 38 B4 1
The Greendale FHAM PO15 96 E2

Greenfield Crs HORN PO8 82 C2
Greenfield Ri HORN PO8 82 C2
Greenfields Av TOTT SO40 52 D3
Greenfinch Cl ELGH SO50 44 A2 2
Greenhill Av WINW SO22 2 A4
Greenhill Cl WINW SO22 2 A4
Greenhill La ROWN SO16 41 K3
Greenhill Rd WINW SO22 21 G7
Greenhill Ter WINW SO22 2 A4
Green Hollow Cl
FHAM/PORC PO16 12 D1
Green Jacket Cl WINW SO22 2 A9
Green La BPWT SO32 49 K4
FAWY SO45 110 C7
GPORT PO12 132 D5 1
GPORT PO12 133 F1
HISD PO11 137 F6
HLER SO31 73 H4
HLER SO31 74 C5
HLER SO31 75 F4
HLER SO31 93 K4
HLER SO31 94 E5
HSEA PO3 119 F4
ROMY SO51 35 K2
ROWN SO16 43 C2
ROWN SO16 53 K2
TOTT SO40 40 A7
WVILLE PO7 62 D7
Greenlea Cl CHAM PO6 101 G4
Greenlea Crs ROWN SO16 44 A6
Greenlea Rd GPORT PO12 132 C1 2
Green Park Cl WINC SO23 22 A5 1
Green Park Rd ROWN SO16 53 K5
Green Pond Cnr HAV PO9 15 J5
Green Pond La ROMY SO51 30 D6
Green Rd FHAM/STUB PO14 114 D3
GPORT PO12 132 D6
SSEA PO5 18 C7
Greens Cl BPWT SO32 48 C3
ELGH SO50 45 K2
The Green HLER SO31 74 C7
ROMY SO51 29 H7 3
Greenway Rd GPORT PO12 16 A2
Greenways BPWT SO32 49 J6
CHFD SO53 38 A4
ROWN SO16 44 A6
The Greenwich FAWY SO45 110 B5 1
Greenwood Av CHAM PO6 100 C6
ROWN SO16 41 J5
Greenwood Cl
FHAM/PORC PO16 97 H2
ROMY SO51 35 F2 1
Greenwood La BPWT SO32 47 F3
Greetham St SSEA PO5 18 D4
Gregory Gdns TOTT SO40 52 B3 1
Gregory La BPWT SO32 47 G6
Gregson Cl LSOL/BMARY PO13 115 K4
Grenadier Cl HLER SO31 95 G4
Grendon Cl ROWN SO16 43 J6 2
Grenville Gdns FAWY SO45 91 H5
Grenville Rd ENEY PO4 19 G7 1
Gresley Gdns HEND SO30 58 B2 3
Grevillea Av FHAM PO15 95 K3
Greville Gn EMRTH PO10 104 B3
Greville Rd WSHM SO15 4 B4
Greyfriars Rd FHAM PO15 96 D4
Greyhound Cl HEND SO30 58 A1 3
Greyshott Av FHAM/STUB PO14 96 D6
Greywell Av ROWN SO16 42 C7
Griffen Cl ELGH SO50 45 H1 2
Griffin Ct PTSW SO17 5 M2
Griffin Wk LSOL/BMARY PO13 131 K2
Griffon Cl HLER SO31 73 K4
Gritanwood Rd ENEY PO4 135 G5
Grosvenor Cl PTSW SO17 55 K2
Grosvenor Dr WINC SO23 22 A5
Grosvenor Gdns HEND SO30 57 G3
PTSW SO17 55 K2 1
Grosvenor Rd CHFD SO53 38 B1
PTSW SO17 55 K2
Grosvenor Sq WSHM SO15 4 F7
Grosvenor St SSEA PO5 18 D5
Grove Av FHAM/PORC PO16 117 F1
GPORT PO12 16 C4
Grove Gdns ITCH SO19 11 K7
Grovelands Rd WINW SO22 20 E6
Grovely Wy ROMY SO51 35 K1
Grove Pl ITCH SO19 11 K6
Grove Rd CHAM PO6 101 H7
FHAM/PORC PO16 13 G6
GPORT PO12 16 A1
HAV PO9 14 F5
LSOL/BMARY PO13 131 F2
RWIN SO21 33 G4
WSHM SO15 54 D5
Grove Rd North SSEA PO5 18 D7
Grove Rd South SSEA PO5 18 D8
The Grove EMRTH PO10 104 E3
FHAM/STUB PO14 114 C5
HLER SO31 73 G6
ITCH SO19 11 K7
Gruneisen Rd NEND PO2 118 B5
Guardhouse Rd PSEA PO1 134 A1
Guardroom Rd NEND PO2 118 A6
Gudge Heath La FHAM PO15 12 B2
Guernsey Cl ROWN SO16 53 K1
Guessens La FHAM/STUB PO14 96 A6
Guest Rd ELGH SO50 39 G7
Guildford Cl EMRTH PO10 105 G5
Guildford Dr CHFD SO53 37 J7
Guildford Rd PSEA PO1 19 H2
Guildford St SHAM SO14 5 K8 1
Guildhall Wk PSEA PO1 18 B5
Guillemot Cl FAWY SO45 91 J3
Guillemot Gdns
LSOL/BMARY PO13 115 J4
Gull Cl LSOL/BMARY PO13 115 J5
The Gulls TOTT SO40 70 A3
Gullycroft Md HEND SO30 58 A5
Gunners Pk BPWT SO32 49 F3
Gunners Rw ENEY PO4 135 G6
Gunners Wy GPORT PO12 116 C7
LSOL/BMARY PO13 116 D6
Gunwharf Rd PSEA PO1 17 L6
Gurnard Rd CHAM PO6 100 D7
Gurney Rd ENEY PO4 135 G4
WSHM SO15 54 D4
Gutner La HISD PO11 121 K6
Gwatkin Cl HAV PO9 102 D3 1
Gypsy La HORN PO8 64 A7

H

Hack Dr RWIN SO21 39 J2
Hackworth Gdns HEND SO30 58 B2
Haddon Cl FHAM PO15 12 D6
Haddon Dr ELGH SO50 38 D5
Hadleigh Gdns ELGH SO50 38 D5
Hadleigh Rd CHAM PO6 100 C6 3
Hadley Fld FAWY SO45 109 J2 1
Hadrians Cl CHFD SO53 38 B4
Hadrian Wy ROWN SO16 43 F4
Haflinger Dr HLER SO31 75 G5
Haig Rd ELGH SO50 45 K2
Haileybury Gdns HEND SO30 58 B3 1
Halden Cl ROMY SO51 35 G1
Hales Dr HEND SO30 57 K7
Hale St North PSEA PO1 18 F1 2
Hale St South PSEA PO1 18 F1
Halfpenny La PSEA PO1 17 M7 1
Halifax Ri WVILLE PO7 82 A6
Hall Cl BPWT SO32 48 C3
Hallet Cl WEND SO18 56 D2 3
Hallett Rd HAV PO9 15 K3
Halletts Cl FHAM/STUB PO14 114 D4
The Halliards FHAM/PORC PO16 97 J7
Halliday Cl GPORT PO12 16 B4
Halliday Crs ENEY PO4 135 H5
Hall Lands La ELGH SO50 46 C1
Halls Farm Cl WINW SO22 21 H4
The Hall Wy WINW SO22 20 E2
Halsey Cl GPORT PO12 132 C5
Halstead Rd CHAM PO6 100 C6
WEND SO18 56 C2
Halterworth Cl ROMY SO51 35 G3 2
Halterworth La ROMY SO51 35 H2
Haltons Cl TOTT SO40 52 C3
Halyard Cl LSOL/BMARY PO13 132 A1
Hambert Wy TOTT SO40 52 D7 3
Hamble Cl HLER SO31 94 B5
Hamble Ct CHFD SO53 38 A5 1
Hambledon Cl WINW SO22 21 G3
Hambledon Rd WVILLE PO7 62 C5 1
Hamble House Gdns
HLER SO31 93 K4 1
Hamble La HLER SO31 73 J3
WVILLE PO7 101 K1
Hamble Rd GPORT PO12 132 C4
Hamble Springs BPWT SO32 48 E4
Hamblewood HEND SO30 59 F6
Hambrook Rd GPORT PO12 132 D2
Hambrook St SSEA PO5 18 B8
Hameldon Cl ROWN SO16 54 A5 2
Hamfield Dr HISD PO11 137 F4
Hamilton Cl HAV PO9 14 F7
Hamilton Gv
LSOL/BMARY PO13 115 J6
Hamilton Ms FAWY SO45 91 J5 2
Hamilton Rd CHAM PO6 99 H6
ELGH SO50 39 G7
FAWY SO45 91 J6
SSEA PO5 18 E9
Ham La EMRTH PO10 105 G7
GPORT PO12 116 D6
HORN PO8 64 A4
Hamlet Wy GPORT PO12 116 D6
LSOL/BMARY PO13 116 C6
Hammond Cl FHAM PO15 12 B3
Hammond Rd FHAM PO15 12 C3
Hammonds Cl TOTT SO40 52 D4
Hammond's Gn TOTT SO40 52 C4
Hammonds La TOTT SO40 52 D4
Hammonds Wy TOTT SO40 52 D4
Hampshire St PSEA PO1 134 D1
Hampshire Ter PSEA PO1 18 B6
Hampton Cl FAWY SO45 110 B7
WVILLE PO7 82 B6 4
Hampton Gdns FAWY SO45 110 B7
Hampton Gv FHAM PO15 96 C5
Hampton Hl BPWT SO32 49 J5
Hampton La FAWY SO45 110 B5
WINW SO22 21 F6
Hamtun Crs TOTT SO40 52 D3 1
Hamtun Gdns TOTT SO40 52 D3
Hamtun Rd ITCH SO19 11 L5
Hamtun St SHAM SO14 8 F3
Hanbidge Crs
LSOL/BMARY PO13 116 A3
Handel Rd WSHM SO15 4 E8
Handel Ter WSHM SO15 4 D8
Handford Pl WSHM SO15 4 F6
Handley Rd GPORT PO12 132 C2 2
The Hangers BPWT SO32 48 E1
Hanley Rd WSHM SO15 4 B3
Hannah Gdns WVILLE PO7 82 A5 3
Hannay Ri ITCH SO19 57 G7
Hannington Rd HAV PO9 82 E6 2
Hann Rd ROWN SO16 41 K5
Hanns Wy ELGH SO50 44 D1
Hanover Buildings SHAM SO14 9 G2
Hanover Gdns
FHAM/PORC PO16 13 J1
Hanoverian Wy FHAM PO15 75 H6
Hanover St PSEA PO1 17 L3
Hanway Rd NEND PO2 118 C7
Ha'penny Dell WVILLE PO7 101 K3 3
Harborough Rd WSHM SO15 4 E6
Harbourne Gdns WEND SO18 56 E2
Harbour Pde SHAM SO14 8 E1
WSHM SO15 8 D1
Harbour Rd GPORT PO12 16 F4
HISD PO11 136 D4
Harbourside HAV PO9 121 G1
Harbour Vw
FHAM/PORC PO16 117 F1
Harbour Wy EMRTH PO10 104 D6 3
NEND PO2 118 B5
Harbridge Ct HAV PO9 82 E6
Harcourt Cl HORN PO8 82 B1
Harcourt Rd FHAM/STUB PO14 96 C7
GPORT PO12 132 D3
PSEA PO1 134 D1
WEND SO18 6 B2
Harding Rd GPORT PO12 132 C2
Hardley La FAWY SO45 91 J7
The Hard PSEA PO1 17 L3
Hardwicke Cl ROWN SO16 54 A2
Hardwicke Wy HLER SO31 93 H3 2
Hardwick Rd CHFD SO53 38 A4 2
Hardy Cl HLER SO31 95 G2
WSHM SO15 54 C6
Hardy Dr FAWY SO45 91 J5
Hardy Rd CHAM PO6 101 K7
ELGH SO50 44 C2
Harebell Cl FHAM/PORC PO16 13 L1
Harefield Ct ROMY SO51 35 G2 3
Harefield Rd PTSW SO17 55 K1
Hare La RWIN SO21 33 K5
Harestock Cl WINW SO22 21 G2
Harestock Rd WINW SO22 21 G3
HAV PO9 14 B1
Harewood Cl ELGH SO50 38 D5
Harkness Dr WVILLE PO7 82 C5
Harland Crs WSHM SO15 54 E3
Harlaxton Cl ELGH SO50 38 C5
Harlech Dr CHFD SO53 37 H6
Harlequin Gv FHAM PO15 12 D5
Harleston Rd CHAM PO6 100 C5
Harlyn Rd ROWN SO16 54 A3
Harold Cl TOTT SO40 52 C6
Harold Rd EMRTH PO10 104 E2
ENEY PO4 19 H8
FHAM/STUB PO14 114 E4
HISD PO11 137 J6
WSHM SO15 54 D5
The Harrage ROMY SO51 34 E3
Harrier Cl HORN PO8 64 B5
LSOL/BMARY PO13 131 G2 4
ROWN SO16 42 C5
Harrier Wy FAWY SO45 109 J1
Harriet Cl FHAM/STUB PO14 114 C5
Harris Av HEND SO30 58 B4 3
Harrison Rd FHAM/PORC PO16 13 J3
PTSW SO17 55 K1
Harris Rd LSOL/BMARY PO13 115 K4
Harrow Down WINW SO22 25 G4
Harrowgate La WVILLE PO7 62 E4
Harrow Rd SSEA PO5 19 G5
Hart Hl FAWY SO45 91 K5
Harting Gdns FHAM/PORC PO16 99 F5
Hartington Rd GPORT PO12 132 C2
SHAM SO14 5 K8
Hartland Ct EMRTH PO10 105 G5
Hartland's Rd
FHAM/PORC PO16 13 K6
Hartley Av PTSW SO17 55 J2
Hartley Cl ELGH SO50 45 K2
FAWY SO45 91 H5 3
Hartley Ct ROWN SO16 43 H7
Hartley Rd ELGH SO50 45 K1
NEND PO2 118 C4
Hartley Wk FAWY SO45 91 G5 2
Hart Plain Av HORN PO8 81 K3
Harts Farm Wy HAV PO9 102 D6
Hartsgrove Cl FAWY SO45 110 B7
Hartwell Rd HSEA PO3 119 G4 2
Hartwood Gdns HORN PO8 81 K3
Harvest Cl WINW SO22 25 G4
Harvester Dr FHAM PO15 96 C5
Harvest Rd NBAD SO52 37 G4
WVILLE PO7 80 D1
Harvey Ct FAWY SO45 110 B5 2
Harvey Crs HLER SO31 94 E4
Harvey Gdns FAWY SO45 91 J3
Harvey Rd ELGH SO50 39 H7
Harwich Rd CHAM PO6 100 C5
Harwood Cl
LSOL/BMARY PO13 115 K3 1
TOTT SO40 52 C4
Harwood Rd
LSOL/BMARY PO13 115 K4
Haselbury Rd TOTT SO40 52 E5
Haselfoot Gdns WEND SO18 57 H5 1
Haselworth Dr GPORT PO12 132 E7
Haskells Cl LYND SO43 86 B1 1
Haslar Crs WVILLE PO7 81 H3
Haslar Rd GPORT PO12 16 E9
Haslemere Gdns HISD PO11 138 C6
Haslemere Rd EMRTH PO10 105 G4
ENEY PO4 19 K8
The Hassocks WVILLE PO7 82 B6
Hastings Av GPORT PO12 116 C7
Hatch Ct HAV PO9 82 D6
Hatchet La BROC SO42 107 J7
Hatch Md HEND SO30 57 F2
Hatfield Rd ENEY PO4 19 L8
Hathaway Cl ELGH SO50 38 E6
Hathaway Gdns WVILLE PO7 82 C4
Hatherell Cl HEND SO30 57 G3
Hatherley Crs
FHAM/PORC PO16 98 E7
Hatherley Dr
FHAM/PORC PO16 98 E6 1
Hatherley Rd CHAM PO6 99 K5
WINW SO22 2 B2
Hatley Rd WEND SO18 7 H3
Havant Farm Cl HAV PO9 14 F1
Havant Rd CHAM PO6 101 K6
EMRTH PO10 15 M5
HAV PO9 15 J6
HISD PO11 121 G4
HORN PO8 64 E6
NEND PO2 118 C6
Havant St PSEA PO1 17 L4 3
Havelock Rd HLER SO31 94 B5
SHAM SO14 4 E8
SSEA PO5 18 F6
WSHM SO15 4 E8
Haven Crs FHAM/STUB PO14 114 A6
Havendale HEND SO30 58 C7 3
Haven Rd HISD PO11 138 B7
Havenstone Wy WEND SO18 44 A7 1
The Haven ELGH SO50 38 E5
ENEY PO4 135 G3
GPORT PO12 132 E6
H Av FAWY SO45 110 C1
Havisham Rd NEND PO2 134 C1 3
Hawfinch Cl ROWN SO16 42 C5
Hawk Cl FHAM/STUB PO14 114 C5
Hawke St PSEA PO1 17 L3
Hawkeswood Rd WEND SO18 5 M4
Hawkewood Av WVILLE PO7 81 J3
Hawkhill FAWY SO45 90 D2
Hawkhurst Cl ITCH SO19 11 H8
Hawkins Rd
LSOL/BMARY PO13 116 A5
Hawkley Cl HAV PO9 83 F7 4
Hawkley Gn ITCH SO19 10 E8
Hawkwell FHAM/PORC PO16 98 C6
Hawswater Cl ROWN SO16 54 A3 2
Hawthorn Cl ELGH SO50 46 B1 1
FHAM/PORC PO16 98 E5
HEND SO30 58 C6 2
RWIN SO21 39 K2
Hawthorn Crs CHAM PO6 119 F1
Hawthorne Gv HISD PO11 137 H4
Hawthorne Rd TOTT SO40 52 C4
Hawthorn La HLER SO31 94 D1
Hawthorn Rd FAWY SO45 91 G3 3
HORN PO8 64 D2
PTSW SO17 55 H2
WVILLE PO7 80 C1
The Hawthorns ELGH SO50 44 B2 1
TOTT SO40 70 B4
Hayburn Rd ROWN SO16 53 J2
Haydock Cl TOTT SO40 52 B4
Haydock Ms WVILLE PO7 82 C4
Hayes Md FAWY SO45 109 J2
Hayle Rd WEND SO18 56 E2
Hayley Cl FAWY SO45 91 G6
Hayling Av HSEA PO3 135 G1
Hayling Cl FHAM/STUB PO14 12 A8
Hay St PSEA PO1 18 A4
Hayter Gdns ROMY SO51 35 F2
Hayward Cl TOTT SO40 52 C5
Hayward Ct FAWY SO45 109 K3 2
Hazel Cl CHFD SO53 31 K7
RWIN SO21 39 K1
Hazeldean Dr HAV PO9 83 J4
Hazeldown Cl ROWN SO16 41 K6
Hazeleigh Av ITCH SO19 10 C5
Hazeley Rd RWIN SO21 33 K3
Hazel Farm Rd TOTT SO40 52 B5
Hazel Gv WINW SO22 25 G3
HLER SO31 95 G4
TOTT SO40 67 J2
Hazelholt Dr HAV PO9 14 A1
Hazel Rd ITCH SO19 10 A2
Hazelwood
FHAM/STUB PO14 114 C2 1
Hazelwood Av HAV PO9 102 C3
Hazelwood Rd WEND SO18 56 D3 4
Hazleton Wy HORN PO8 64 C7
Headland Dr HLER SO31 95 F2
Headley Cl
LSOL/BMARY PO13 131 G2 5
Hearne Gdns BPWT SO32 61 H3
Heath Cl ELGH SO50 46 C2
HORN PO8 64 C5
Heathcote Pl RWIN SO21 31 J2
Heathcote Rd CHFD SO53 38 A4
NEND PO2 118 E6
Heathen St BPWT SO32 47 G7
Heatherbrae Gdns
NBAD SO52 36 A6 1
Heather Cha ELGH SO50 45 K1 2
Heather Cl LSOL/BMARY PO13 115 J5
TOTT SO40 52 D5
WVILLE PO7 82 A7
Heatherdeane Rd PTSW SO17 55 H2
Heatherdene Rd CHFD SO53 38 B1
Heather Gdns FHAM PO15 12 B2
Heatherlands Rd ROWN SO16 43 G3
Heather Rd FAWY SO45 110 C5
Heatherstone Av FAWY SO45 91 G6
Heatherton Ms EMRTH PO10 104 C3
Heatherview Cl NBAD SO52 36 A5 1
Heathfield FAWY SO45 91 G4 5
Heathfield Av FHAM PO15 12 A6
Heathfield Cl ITCH SO19 11 L4 1
Heathfield Rd CHFD SO53 31 K7
ITCH SO19 11 K4
NEND PO2 118 C7
Heath Gdns HLER SO31 73 G6
Heath House Cl HEND SO30 74 A1
Heath House Gdns HEND SO30 74 A1
Heathhouse La HEND SO30 74 A1
Heathlands Cl CHFD SO53 37 K2
Heathlands Rd CHFD SO53 37 K2
Heath La BROC SO42 125 H1
Heath Lawns FHAM PO15 12 B6
Heath Rd HLER SO31 94 E3
ITCH SO19 7 G9
NBAD SO52 36 B7
Heath Rd North HLER SO31 94 E3
Heath Rd South HLER SO31 94 E3
The Heath WVILLE PO7 81 F1
Heaton Rd GPORT PO12 132 C1
Hebrides Cl
FHAM/STUB PO14 114 C4 7
Heckfield Cl HAV PO9 103 J1 7
Hector Cl WVILLE PO7 101 K4
Hector Rd FHAM/STUB PO14 115 H2
Hedera Rd HLER SO31 94 E3
Hedgerow Cl ROWN SO16 41 K5
Hedgerow Dr WEND SO18 7 K1 1
Hedgerow Gdns EMRTH PO10 104 C3
Hedley Cl FAWY SO45 110 C6
Hedley Gdns HEND SO30 58 A1 4
Heidelberg Rd ENEY PO4 19 J5
The Heights FHAM/PORC PO16 98 A4
HEND SO30 57 K6
Helena Rd ENEY PO4 134 E6
Helford Gdns WEND SO18 56 E2 1
Hellyer Rd ENEY PO4 19 L8
Helm Cl LSOL/BMARY PO13 132 A2
Helsted Cl GPORT PO12 132 B4
Helston Dr EMRTH PO10 104 B3
Helston Rd CHAM PO6 99 J5
Helvellyn Rd ROWN SO16 54 A4
Hemdean Gdns HEND SO30 57 G3
Hemlock Rd HORN PO8 81 K1
Hemlock Wy NBAD SO52 37 G5
Hemming Cl TOTT SO40 52 D6
Hemmingway Gdns
FHAM PO15 75 H5
Hempsted Rd CHAM PO6 100 A5
Hemsley Wk HORN PO8 82 B1
Henderson Rd ENEY PO4 135 G5
Hendy Cl SSEA PO5 18 E7 1
Henery St GPORT PO12 16 D5 1
Henley Gdns FHAM PO15 96 E2
Henley Rd ENEY PO4 19 J8 3
Henry Cl FAWY SO45 109 J1 2
Henry Rd ELGH SO50 39 G6 1
WSHM SO15 54 D5
Henry St WSHM SO15 4 E6 1
Henstead Rd WSHM SO15 4 E7
Henty Rd ROWN SO16 54 B4
Henville Cl LSOL/BMARY PO13 116 A7
Hepworth Cl ITCH SO19 11 L6 1
Herbert Rd ENEY PO4 134 D6 1
GPORT PO12 132 C3
Herbert St PSEA PO1 134 B1
Herbert Walker Av WSHM SO15 8 E3
Hercules St NEND PO2 118 C7 3
Hereford Rd SSEA PO5 18 E8
Hereward Cl ROMY SO51 35 G3 3
Hermes Rd LSOL/BMARY PO13 130 E1
Hermitage Cl BPWT SO32 48 B3 2
HAV PO9 103 F2
Herne Rd CHAM PO6 100 D6
Heron Cl ENEY PO4 135 G3
Heron La ROMY SO51 28 C3
Heron Quay EMRTH PO10 104 D7
Herons Cl FHAM/STUB PO14 114 D3
Heron Sq ELGH SO50 44 B2
Heron Wy LSOL/BMARY PO13 115 H4
Herrick Cl ITCH SO19 73 G1
Herriott Cl HORN PO8 64 B7
Hertford Pl PSEA PO1 134 C1
Hertsfield FHAM/STUB PO14 95 H2
Hester Rd ENEY PO4 135 G4 1
Hestia Cl ROMY SO51 35 H2
Hewett Cl FHAM/STUB PO14 96 A7
Hewett Rd FHAM/STUB PO14 96 A7
NEND PO2 118 D5
Hewetts Ri HLER SO31 94 B6
Hewitt Cl GPORT PO12 132 D2 5
Hewitt's Rd WSHM SO15 4 B9
Heyes Dr ITCH SO19 11 L4
Heysham Rd WSHM SO15 54 C4
Heyshott Rd ENEY PO4 19 K6
Heyward Rd ENEY PO4 19 G6
Heywood Gn ITCH SO19 57 H7
Hickory Dr WINW SO22 21 F3
Hickory Gdns HEND SO30 57 G1
Highbank Av WVILLE PO7 101 G3
Highbridge Rd ELGH SO50 39 G3
Highbury Cl ELGH SO50 46 B2
Highbury Gv CHAM PO6 119 F1
Highbury St PSEA PO1 17 M6
Highbury Wy CHAM PO6 118 E1
Highclere Av HAV PO9 102 E2
Highclere Rd ROWN SO16 54 E1
Highclere Wy CHFD SO53 37 H7
Highcliff Av SHAM SO14 5 H3
Highcliffe Dr ELGH SO50 38 D3
Highcliffe Rd GPORT PO12 132 C4
WINC SO23 3 G7
Highcroft La HORN PO8 64 D4
Highcrown St PTSW SO17 55 H2
High Dr LSOL/BMARY PO13 115 K6
Highfield RWIN SO21 33 K4
Highfield Av FHAM/STUB PO14 12 E8
PTSW SO17 55 G1
RWIN SO21 33 K4
WVILLE PO7 82 B5
Highfield Cl CHFD SO53 38 A4
PTSW SO17 55 H2 1
WVILLE PO7 82 A4
Highfield Crs PTSW SO17 55 J2
Highfield La PTSW SO17 55 H2
Highfield Rd CHFD SO53 38 B4
GPORT PO12 132 C2
PSEA PO1 18 F3
PTSW SO17 55 G3
High Firs Gdns ROMY SO51 35 H3
High Firs Rd ITCH SO19 7 K9
ROMY SO51 35 H2
Highgate Rd HSEA PO3 119 F6
Highgrove Cl TOTT SO40 52 C7 2
Highgrove Rd HSEA PO3 119 G7
Highland Cl EMRTH PO10 104 B6
Highland Rd EMRTH PO10 104 B5
ENEY PO4 19 K8
Highlands Cl FAWY SO45 91 H4
NBAD SO52 35 K5 2
Highlands Rd CHAM PO6 101 J6
FHAM PO15 12 A2
Highland St ENEY PO4 19 M9
Highlands Wy FAWY SO45 91 G4
High Lawn Wy HAV PO9 103 F1
High Md FHAM PO15 12 C1
High Meadow ITCH SO19 7 L7
Highmount Cl WINC SO23 3 H6
Highnam Gdns HLER SO31 94 E2
High Oaks Cl HLER SO31 95 F3
High Rd ELGH SO50 44 A6
ROWN SO16 56 A1
High St BPWT SO32 48 D4
BPWT SO32 61 F5
BROC SO42 108 A7
CHAM PO6 100 E7
ELGH SO50 44 D2
EMRTH PO10 104 C6
FAWY SO45 91 H1
FHAM/PORC PO16 13 L4
FHAM/STUB PO14 96 A6
GPORT PO12 16 F5
HEND SO30 57 H3 1
HEND SO30 59 F5
HLER SO31 74 A6
LSOL/BMARY PO13 131 F2
LYND SO43 86 C1
PSEA PO1 17 L7
RWIN SO21 33 K4
SHAM SO14 9 G4
TOTT SO40 53 F5
WHAM PO17 79 J7
WINC SO23 2 D4
WVILLE PO7 62 C1
High Trees ELGH SO50 46 D1
WVILLE PO7 82 A5
High Trees Dr WINW SO22 21 H5
High Vw FHAM/PORC PO16 99 F5
High View Wy WEND SO18 6 F2
Highways Rd RWIN SO21 33 F4
Highwood La ROMY SO51 35 J2
Highwood Rd
LSOL/BMARY PO13 131 K1
Higworth La HISD PO11 137 G3
Hilary Av CHAM PO6 101 F7
Hilda Gdns WVILLE PO7 81 F1
Hilden Wy WINW SO22 20 D2
Hillary Cl FHAM/PORC PO16 12 E3
LYND SO43 86 D3
Hillborough Crs SSEA PO5 18 E8 2
Hillbrow Cl FHAM PO15 12 B1

Hill Brow Cl HAV PO9 83 J4
Hillcrest Av CHFD SO53 38 A4
Hillcrest Cl NBAD SO52 36 A5
Hillcrest Dr CHFD SO53 38 A4 3
Hill Crest Gdns BPWT SO32 48 E7
Hill Cft FHAM PO15 95 J3
Hilldene Wy HEND SO30 57 H3 2
Hilldown Rd PTSW SO17 55 H1
Hilldowns Av NEND PO2 118 B5
Hill Farm Rd WSHM SO15 4 C6
Hillgrove Rd WEND SO18 56 C1 1
Hill Head Rd FHAM/STUB PO14 114 B6
Hillier Wy WINC SO23 21 K5
Hill La ROWN SO16 54 E1
RWIN SO21 39 J1
WSHM SO15 55 F3
Hillmead Gdns HAV PO9 102 C4
Hill Park Rd FHAM PO15 96 E2
GPORT PO12 132 C2
Hill Pl HLER SO31 74 A5
Hill Ri RWIN SO21 33 K3
Hill Rd FHAM/PORC PO16 99 G5
Hillside WINW SO22 21 F2
Hillside Av ROMY SO51 35 F3
WEND SO18 56 B3
WVILLE PO7 101 G4
Hillside Cl CHFD SO53 38 A4
WINW SO22 21 F5
Hillside Crs CHAM PO6 99 J5
Hillside Rd WINW SO22 21 F6
Hillsley Rd CHAM PO6 99 J4
Hillson Dr FHAM PO15 96 D3
Hill St ROMY SO51 40 B5
Hilltop WINW SO22 21 F2
Hilltop Crs CHAM PO6 101 G4
Hilltop Dr ITCH SO19 11 M1
Hilltop Gdns HORN PO8 64 E1
Hilltop Rd WVILLE PO7 99 K4
Hillview HORN PO8 64 D7
Hillview Rd FAWY SO45 91 G3
Hill View Rd FHAM/PORC PO16 99 F5
ROMY SO51 28 B1
ROMY SO51 29 H3
The Hillway CHFD SO53 38 A3
FHAM/PORC PO16 99 F6
Hillyfields ROWN SO16 41 H7
Hilsea Crs NEND PO2 118 D2
Hiltingbury Av HAV PO9 103 H1 2
Hiltingbury Cl CHFD SO53 38 A1
Hiltingbury Rd CHFD SO53 37 J1
Hilton Rd GPORT PO12 16 D8
Hinkler Rd ITCH SO19 7 M9
Hinton Cl HAV PO9 102 D2
Hinton Crs ITCH SO19 57 H7
Hinton Flds WINC SO23 22 B1
Hinton Manor La HORN PO8 63 K3
Hipley Rd HAV PO9 103 H3
Hirst Rd FAWY SO45 91 J3
Hispano Av FHAM PO15 75 H6
Hither Gn EMRTH PO10 105 H4
Hitherwood Cl HORN PO8 82 C4
Hoad's Hl WHAM PO17 77 J3
Hobart Dr FAWY SO45 91 J3
Hobb La HEND SO30 58 C6
Hobby Cl HSEA PO3 119 F3
Hobson Wy FAWY SO45 110 A4 2
Hockham Ct HAV PO9 82 D6
Hockley Cl CHAM PO6 100 C6 4
Hockley Link RWIN SO21 25 H6
Hocombe Dr CHFD SO53 31 J7
Hocombe Park Cl CHFD SO53 31 J7
Hocombe Rd CHFD SO53 31 J7
Hocombe Wood Rd CHFD SO53 31 H7
Hodder Cl CHFD SO53 37 J5 1
Hodges Cl HAV PO9 15 G1
Hoeford Cl FHAM/PORC PO16 115 J1
Hoe La ROMY SO51 41 H1
Hoe Rd BPWT SO32 49 F4
The Hoe LSOL/BMARY PO13 116 B6 3
Hogarth Cl ROMY SO51 35 G1
Hogwood La HEND SO30 45 H5
Holbrook Rd FHAM/PORC PO16 13 J7
PSEA PO1 18 F1
Holbury Ct HAV PO9 103 J1 3
Holbury Dro FAWY SO45 109 J3
Holcot La HSEA PO3 119 H3
Holcroft Rd ITCH SO19 57 H7
Holdenbury Ct HSEA PO3 119 H2
Holdenhurst Cl HORN PO8 64 D3 4
Hole La BPWT SO32 60 B3
Holkham Cl ROWN SO16 53 K1 1
Hollam Cl FHAM/STUB PO14 96 C6
Hollam Crs FHAM/STUB PO14 96 C6
Hollam Dr FHAM/STUB PO14 96 C6
Hollam Rd ENEY PO4 135 G3
Holland Pk HLER SO31 94 E3
Holland Pl
LSOL/BMARY PO13 116 A5 2
ROWN SO16 54 C3
Holland Rd ENEY PO4 19 G6
ITCH SO19 10 B6
TOTT SO40 52 B5
Hollingbourne Cl WEND SO18 6 B3
Hollman Dr ROMY SO51 34 C2
Hollow La HISD PO11 137 G5
Hollybank LSOL/BMARY PO13 131 G3
Holly Bank Cl HORN PO8 64 D7
Hollybank Crs FAWY SO45 91 G2
Hollybank La EMRTH PO10 104 C2
Hollybank Rd FAWY SO45 91 G3
Hollybrook Av ROWN SO16 54 D1
Hollybrook Cl ROWN SO16 54 C3
Hollybrook Gdns HLER SO31 95 F1
Hollybrook Rd ROWN SO16 54 D2
Holly Cl FAWY SO45 91 H7
HLER SO31 94 D3
Holly Dell ROWN SO16 43 F6
Holly Dr WVILLE PO7 82 B7
Holly Gdns HEND SO30 57 G1
Holly Gv FHAM/PORC PO16 97 F2
Holly Hatch Rd TOTT SO40 52 D6
Holly Hl ROWN SO16 43 F6
Holly Hill Cl ROWN SO16 43 F6
Holly Hill La HLER SO31 74 D7
Holly La LYMN SO41 124 A7
Holly Oak Rd ROWN SO16 54 B1
Holly Rd FAWY SO45 110 B7
TOTT SO40 68 A3
Holly St GPORT PO12 16 D5
Hollywell Dr CHAM PO6 100 A7
Hollywood Cl NBAD SO52 36 A6
Holman Cl HORN PO8 82 B3
Holmdale Rd GPORT PO12 132 C1
Holmefield Av
FHAM/STUB PO14 115 G1
Holmesland Dr HEND SO30 58 E5
Holmesland La HEND SO30 58 E5
Holmgrove FHAM/STUB PO14 95 H3 2
Holm Oak Cl WINW SO22 20 D2
Holmsley Cl WEND SO18 7 M5
Holne Ct ENEY PO4 135 H5
Holst Wy WVILLE PO7 102 A1
Holt Cl WHAM PO17 77 G1
Holt Ct ITCH SO19 10 D9
Holt Gdns HAV PO9 83 J2
Holt Rd WSHM SO15 4 E5
Holyborne Rd ROMY SO51 35 G3
Holybourne Rd HAV PO9 14 E1
Holyrood Av PTSW SO17 55 J2
Holyrood Cl WVILLE PO7 82 B6 3
Home Farm Cl FAWY SO45 91 J4
Homefield ROMY SO51 35 F1 2
Home Field Dr ROWN SO16 41 H6
Homefield Rd CHAM PO6 101 H7
EMRTH PO10 104 E2
Home Md WVILLE PO7 80 E2
Homer Cl HORN PO8 81 K3
LSOL/BMARY PO13 115 J7
Homer Farm La FAWY SO45 128 B2
Home Rule Rd HLER SO31 95 F2
Homewell HAV PO9 14 E5
Honey La FHAM PO15 96 E1
Honeysuckle Cl WINW SO22 25 G4
HLER SO31 95 F1
LSOL/BMARY PO13 115 J4 1
Honeysuckle Ct WVILLE PO7 102 A1 2
Honeysuckle Rd ROWN SO16 43 J7
Honeysuckle Wy NBAD SO52 37 H4
Honeywood Cl HSEA PO3 118 E3
TOTT SO40 52 C3
Hood Cl HLER SO31 95 G2
Hood Rd WEND SO18 7 H2
Hook Cl CHFD SO53 31 H7
Hook Crs CHFD SO53 31 H7
Hook La HLER SO31 95 F7
Hook Park Rd HLER SO31 112 D1
Hook Rd ROMY SO51 31 F6
Hook Water Rd CHFD SO53 31 H7
Hookwood La ROMY SO51 31 G7
Hook's Farm Wy HAV PO9 14 A1
Hook's La HAV PO9 14 A1
Hope Rd HEND SO30 57 H2
Hope St PSEA PO1 18 C1
Hopfield Cl WVILLE PO7 81 K7
Hopfield Ms WVILLE PO7 81 K7 1
Hopkins Cl CHAM PO6 99 H6 2
Hordle Rd HAV PO9 102 D2
Hornbeam Cl HEND SO30 58 C6 5
Hornbeam Gdns HEND SO30 57 G2 1
Hornbeam Rd HAV PO9 15 K1
NBAD SO52 37 F5
Hornby Cl HLER SO31 95 H5
Hornchurch Rd ROWN SO16 42 A6
Horndean Rd EMRTH PO10 104 A2
HORN PO8 65 F4
Hornet Cl FHAM PO15 12 A3
GPORT PO12 16 D8
Hornet Rd EMRTH PO10 122 D4
FHAM/STUB PO14 115 G2
Horns Dro ROWN SO16 41 K5
Horsea La NEND PO2 118 C3
Horsea Rd NEND PO2 118 D2
Horsebridge Rd HAV PO9 103 H2
Horsebridge Wy ROWN SO16 41 K6
Horsecroft ROMY SO51 34 E2 1
Horsefair Ct ROMY SO51 34 D3
Horsepost La WVILLE PO7 63 G2
Horse Sands Cl ENEY PO4 135 J5
Horseshoe Cl
FHAM/STUB PO14 95 J4 1
Horseshoe Ldg HLER SO31 94 D5
Horton Rd LSOL/BMARY PO13 115 K3
Horton Wy ELGH SO50 45 J2
Hospital La FHAM/PORC PO16 117 H1
Hospital Rd BPWT SO32 61 H3
Hotspur Cl FAWY SO45 91 G1
Houchin St BPWT SO32 48 D4
Houghton Cl HAV PO9 83 J7 1
Hound Cl HLER SO31 93 G1
Hound Rd HLER SO31 73 G7
Hound Road Gdns HLER SO31 93 G1
Hound Wy HLER SO31 73 G7
Houndwell Pl SHAM SO14 9 H2
Hounsdown Av TOTT SO40 52 E7
Hounsdown Cl TOTT SO40 52 E7
House Cl RWIN SO21 39 K1
House Farm Rd GPORT PO12 132 B4
Hoveton Gv CHFD SO53 37 J2
Howard Cl CHFD SO53 38 A6
ELGH SO50 46 B1
WEND SO18 44 B7 1
Howard Rd NEND PO2 118 D3
WSHM SO15 4 B6
Howard's Gv WSHM SO15 54 D4
Howe Rd LSOL/BMARY PO13 131 K2
Howerts Cl HLER SO31 94 C7
Hoylake Cl
LSOL/BMARY PO13 115 K6 1
Hoylake Rd CHAM PO6 101 H5
Hoylecroft Cl FHAM PO15 12 C1
Hubert Rd WINC SO23 25 H4
Hudson Cl
LSOL/BMARY PO13 131 K2 2
Hudson Ct TOTT SO40 52 C6 2
Hudson Rd SSEA PO5 18 E6
Hugh's Cl FAWY SO45 110 B6
Hulbert Rd HAV PO9 102 C1
WVILLE PO7 82 B6
Hulles Wy NBAD SO52 36 A6
Hulse Rd WSHM SO15 4 F3
Hulton Cl ITCH SO19 10 B8
Humber Cl
FHAM/STUB PO14 114 C4 3
Humber Gdns HLER SO31 73 K4 2
The Hummicks BROC SO42 108 C7 1
Hundred Acres Rd WHAM PO17 78 B2
The Hundred ROMY SO51 34 D3
WVILLE PO7 81 J4
Hungerford HLER SO31 73 J6
Hunt Av HLER SO31 73 F7
Hunter Cl FAWY SO45 109 J1 3
LSOL/BMARY PO13 132 A1
Hunter Rd EMRTH PO10 122 D3
ENEY PO4 19 K8
Hunters Cha BPWT SO32 61 K1 1
Hunters Crs ROMY SO51 29 H7
TOTT SO40 52 A6
Hunters Hl TOTT SO40 68 C2
Hunters Ldg FHAM PO15 96 C6
Hunters Ride WVILLE PO7 81 K6
Hunters Wy ELGH SO50 45 K1
Huntingdon Cl
FHAM/STUB PO14 95 H5 2
TOTT SO40 52 D3
Huntley Cl CHAM PO6 100 A5 4
Huntly Wy WEND SO18 6 E4
Hunton Cl ROWN SO16 54 E1
Hunts Pond Rd HLER SO31 95 G2
The Hurdles FHAM/STUB PO14 95 J4
Hurdle Wy RWIN SO21 33 F1
Hurlingham Gdns
ROWN SO16 43 H6 1
Hurn Ct HAV PO9 83 J7
Hurricane Dr ROWN SO16 41 K5
Hursley Dr FAWY SO45 128 B1
Hursley Rd CHFD SO53 31 J7
HAV PO9 102 E1
RWIN SO21 31 J5
Hurstbourne Cl HAV PO9 82 E7 2
Hurst Cl CHFD SO53 37 H6
FHAM/STUB PO14 114 B6
TOTT SO40 52 E4
Hurst Gn LSOL/BMARY PO13 115 J5
Hurst Green Cl HORN PO8 82 C3
ITCH SO19 11 H8
Hurstville Dr WVILLE PO7 82 A6
Hurstwood Av EMRTH PO10 105 H6
Hussey Cl WINC SO23 21 K5 4
Hutwood Rd ROWN SO16 43 H3
Huxley Cl HLER SO31 95 G4
Huxley Ct FAWY SO45 90 D4
Hyde Abbey Rd WINC SO23 2 E3
Hyde Church La WINC SO23 2 E2
Hyde Cl TOTT SO40 52 A5
WINC SO23 2 D2
WSHM SO15 54 D3
Hyde Park Rd SSEA PO5 18 D5
Hyde St SSEA PO5 18 C7 1
WINC SO23 2 E2
Hymans Wy TOTT SO40 52 D5
Hyssop Cl FHAM PO15 75 J6
Hythe By-pass FAWY SO45 90 C2
Hythe Rd CHAM PO6 100 D6
TOTT SO40 70 A5

I

Ibbotson Wy TOTT SO40 52 C7
Ibsen Cl HLER SO31 75 H5
Ibsley Gv HAV PO9 14 A1
Icarus Pl WVILLE PO7 102 A4
Idsworth Cl HORN PO8 64 E6
Idsworth Rd HORN PO8 82 C3
HSEA PO3 119 F7
Iford Ct HAV PO9 83 J7 5
Ilex Crs HLER SO31 94 E3
Ilex Wk HISD PO11 137 K5
Imber Cl ITCH SO19 11 L2
Imber Rd WINC SO23 3 J3
Imber Wy ITCH SO19 11 L2
Imperial Av WSHM SO15 54 C5
Imperial Rd SHAM SO14 5 J5
Implacable Rd
LSOL/BMARY PO13 130 E1
Ingersley Ri HEND SO30 57 G3
Ingledene Cl GPORT PO12 16 A6
HAV PO9 14 A3
Ingle Gln FAWY SO45 91 H5 2
Ingle Gn TOTT SO40 52 A3
Ingleside HLER SO31 73 F6
Ingleside Cl FHAM/STUB PO14 96 C6 3
Ingleton Rd ROWN SO16 53 K3
Inglis Rd SSEA PO5 19 G7
Inhams La WVILLE PO7 80 C1
Inhurst Av WVILLE PO7 82 B5
Inhurst Rd NEND PO2 118 D5
Inkerman Rd ITCH SO19 10 B4
Inlands Rd RCCH PO18 105 J5
International Wy ITCH SO19 10 D9
Invergordon Av CHAM PO6 101 G7
Inverkip Cl
LSOL/BMARY PO13 131 F1 1
Inverness Av FHAM PO15 12 C2
Inverness Rd GPORT PO12 132 D3
NEND PO2 134 D1
Ionic Cl CHFD SO53 38 C3
Iping Av HAV PO9 102 E1
Ipley Wy FAWY SO45 91 H4
Ireland Wy WVILLE PO7 101 K1
Iris Rd ROWN SO16 43 J7
Ironbridge Crs HLER SO31 75 F7
Ironbridge La ENEY PO4 135 H4
Iron Mill Cl FHAM PO15 12 A1
Ironmill La FHAM PO15 96 C1
Irvine Cl FHAM/PORC PO16 13 G2
Irving Rd ROWN SO16 54 A3
Irwell Cl CHFD SO53 37 H5
Isambard Brunel Rd PSEA PO1 18 C4
Isis Cl ROWN SO16 53 K4
Island Cl HISD PO11 121 H4
Island View Ter NEND PO2 118 B6
Islay Gdns CHAM PO6 100 E5
Itchen Av ELGH SO50 45 J1
Itchenor Rd HISD PO11 138 C6
Itchen Rd HAV PO9 83 J7
Itchenside Cl WEND SO18 44 C7
Itchen Wy ELGH SO50 38 E4
ITCH SO19 10 A2
RWIN SO21 22 C2
Itchin Cl TOTT SO40 52 C6
Ithica Cl HISD PO11 137 H4
Ivanhoe Rd WSHM SO15 54 E3
Ivor Cl FAWY SO45 109 K3
Ivy Cl WINW SO22 25 H3
TOTT SO40 52 D2
Ivy Ct WVILLE PO7 101 J2 1
Ivy Dene ITCH SO19 73 G1
Ivydene Gdns HORN PO8 82 B1
Ivy La HEND SO30 56 E2
Ivy Rd PTSW SO17 5 M2

J

Jacaranda Cl FHAM PO15 95 K3 1
Jack Cockerill Wy SSEA PO5 134 C7 4
Jackdaw Cl HORN PO8 81 K1
Jackdaw Ri ELGH SO50 44 A2 5
Jackie Wigg Gdns TOTT SO40 52 E5
Jackmans Cl ITCH SO19 10 A4 1
Jackson Cl CHAM PO6 119 H1
Jacobs Cl ROMY SO51 35 F3 1
Jacob's Gutter La TOTT SO40 52 E7
Jacob's St PSEA PO1 18 D2
Jacobs Wk TOTT SO40 68 D1
Jacomb Pl
LSOL/BMARY PO13 116 A5 3
Jacqueline Av WVILLE PO7 101 J2
Jago Rd PSEA PO1 17 K2
Jamaica Pl GPORT PO12 16 C6
Jamaica Pl GPORT PO12 16 C6
Jamaica Rd GPORT PO12 16 F3
James Callaghan Dr CHAM PO6 99 K4
James Cl HISD PO11 137 F5
LSOL/BMARY PO13 115 K3
James Copse Rd HORN PO8 64 A7
James Grieve Av HLER SO31 95 F4
Jameson Rd ITCH SO19 10 E4
James Rd HAV PO9 14 B2
LSOL/BMARY PO13 115 K3
James St SHAM SO14 9 J1
Janaway Gdns PTSW SO17 5 M2
Janes Cl FAWY SO45 110 B7
Janson Rd WSHM SO15 54 D5
Japonica Wy HAV PO9 103 K2
Jarvis Flds HLER SO31 74 A5
Jasmine Gv WVILLE PO7 82 B7
Jasmine Rd HEND SO30 58 A4
Jasmond Rd CHAM PO6 118 E1
Jason Pl WVILLE PO7 101 K4
Jason Wy GPORT PO12 116 C7 2
Java Dr FHAM PO15 75 H6
Java Rd SHAM SO14 9 K7
Javelin Rd EMRTH PO10 122 D4
J Av FAWY SO45 110 C1
Jay Cl FHAM/STUB PO14 114 C3
HORN PO8 64 B5
Jeffries Cl ROWN SO16 41 K6
Jellicoe Av GPORT PO12 132 C6
Jenkins Cl HEND SO30 59 F5
Jenkins Gv HSEA PO3 135 G1
Jenner Wy ROMY SO51 35 H2
Jennings Rd TOTT SO40 53 F4
Jermyns La ROMY SO51 29 H6
Jerome Ct ITCH SO19 57 G6
Jerram Cl GPORT PO12 132 C5
Jerrett's La ROWN SO16 53 J1
Jersey Cl FHAM/STUB PO14 114 E6
ROWN SO16 53 K1
Jersey Rd NEND PO2 118 D7
Jervis Court La BPWT SO32 49 H3
Jervis Dr GPORT PO12 16 A2
Jervis Rd NEND PO2 118 B5
Jesmond Gv HLER SO31 95 F5
Jessamine Rd ROWN SO16 54 C2
Jessica Cl WVILLE PO7 82 C4
Jessie Rd ENEY PO4 19 H6
GPORT PO12 132 D4
HAV PO9 102 D3
Jessop Cl FAWY SO45 91 G1
Jetty Rd FAWY SO45 110 E2
Jewry St WINC SO23 2 E4
Jex Blake Cl ROWN SO16 42 C7
Jinny La ROMY SO51 28 D4
Jockey La ELGH SO50 39 H5
Jodrell Cl HORN PO8 64 D5
John Bunyan Cl FHAM PO15 75 H5 3
Johnson St SHAM SO14 9 H1 3
Johnson Vw FHAM PO15 75 K7
Johns Rd FHAM/PORC PO16 13 J9
ITCH SO19 10 B5
John St SHAM SO14 9 H4
Jonathan Rd FHAM PO15 12 C5
Jones La FAWY SO45 91 G2
Jordans La LYMN SO41 124 A7
Joseph St GPORT PO12 16 D5 2
Jubilee Av CHAM PO6 99 H6
Jubilee Cl ELGH SO50 44 C2 1
Jubilee Ct FHAM/STUB PO14 97 H7
Jubilee Gdns WEND SO18 7 J5
Jubilee Pth HAV PO9 102 D5
Jubilee Rd ENEY PO4 19 J7
FHAM/PORC PO16 99 G6
GPORT PO12 16 A4
ROMY SO51 34 D2
WVILLE PO7 81 K5
Jubilee Ter SSEA PO5 18 B7 3
Julian Cl ROWN SO16 43 G5
Julian Rd ITCH SO19 11 K3
Julie Av FHAM PO15 12 C5
Juliet Ct WVILLE PO7 82 B5 3
Julius Cl CHFD SO53 38 B4
Jumar Cl HLER SO31 94 C7
Junction Rd TOTT SO40 53 F5
Juniper Cl WINW SO22 25 G3
NBAD SO52 36 A5
Juniper Rd HORN PO8 64 D3 3
WEND SO18 6 E5
Juniper Sq HAV PO9 14 F5
Jupiter Cl ROWN SO16 41 K7
Jura Cl CHAM PO6 100 E5
Jurds Lake Wy ITCH SO19 10 B8
Jurd Wy HLER SO31 73 J4
Justin Cl FHAM/STUB PO14 12 C6
Justinian Cl CHFD SO53 38 C3
Jute Cl FHAM/PORC PO16 98 E5
Jutland Cl FHAM PO15 75 G6

K

Kanes Hl ITCH SO19 57 J6
Karen Av CHAM PO6 119 H1
Kassassin St ENEY PO4 19 M9
Kassel Cl WVILLE PO7 82 C4
Kathleen Rd ITCH SO19 11 H3
Katrina Gdns HISD PO11 137 H3
Katrine Crs CHFD SO53 37 H3
Kayak Cl HLER SO31 94 D5
Kayleigh Cl TOTT SO40 52 C6
Kealy Rd GPORT PO12 132 D2
Kearsney Av NEND PO2 118 D4 1
Keats Av CHAM PO6 99 H5
Keats Cl WINW SO22 25 F4
HORN PO8 82 A1
Keats Rd ITCH SO19 7 L6
Keble Cl CHFD SO53 37 K6 1
Keble Rd CHFD SO53 37 K6
Keble St WINW SO22 25 F2
Keel Cl HSEA PO3 119 H4
LSOL/BMARY PO13 132 A1 1
Keepers Cl CHFD SO53 37 J4
The Keep FHAM/PORC PO16 99 H6
Kefford Cl HORN PO8 64 C6
Keith Cl GPORT PO12 16 A1
Kelburn Cl CHFD SO53 37 J3
Kellett Rd WSHM SO15 4 C2
Kelly Rd WVILLE PO7 101 K1
Kelmscott Gdns CHFD SO53 37 H1
Kelsey Av EMRTH PO10 105 H5
Kelsey Cl FHAM/STUB PO14 95 G5
Kelvin Cl FAWY SO45 91 H3
Kelvin Gv FHAM/PORC PO16 99 G6
HLER SO31 73 F7
Kelvin Rd ELGH SO50 44 C1
Kempton Pk WVILLE PO7 82 C4
Kemshott Ct HAV PO9 82 E7
Ken Berry Ct HAV PO9 83 J7
Kendal Av HSEA PO3 119 F6
ROWN SO16 53 K4
Kendal Cl CHFD SO53 38 B3
HORN PO8 82 B1
Kenilworth Cl
LSOL/BMARY PO13 131 G1 4
Kenilworth Dr ELGH SO50 38 D4
Kenilworth Gdns HEND SO30 57 H3
Kenilworth Rd SSEA PO5 134 C7 5
WSHM SO15 4 E7
Kenmore Cl TOTT SO40 52 C7
Kennedy Av FHAM PO15 97 F2
Kennedy Cl WVILLE PO7 101 K2
Kennedy Crs GPORT PO12 132 B6
Kennedy Rd ROWN SO16 54 A1
Kennel Rd WINW SO22 20 E3
Kennet Cl GPORT PO12 132 E7
WEND SO18 56 E1
Kennett Rd ROMY SO51 35 H2
Kennington La TOTT SO40 50 E5
Kensington Cl ELGH SO50 39 G5 2
Kensington Flds FAWY SO45 90 E4
Kensington Gdns
FHAM/STUB PO14 95 H4 2
Kensington Rd GPORT PO12 16 C7
NEND PO2 118 E5
Kenson Gdns ITCH SO19 11 G2
Kent Gv FHAM/PORC PO16 117 F1
Kentidge Rd WVILLE PO7 101 J1 3
Kentish Rd WSHM SO15 54 D5
Kent Rd CHFD SO53 37 K7
LSOL/BMARY PO13 115 J3
SSEA PO5 18 C8
Kent St PSEA PO1 17 M4
SHAM SO14 5 L8
Kenwood Rd
FHAM/PORC PO16 117 G2
Kenwyn Cl WEND SO18 56 E2
Kenya Rd FHAM/PORC PO16 98 E7
Kenyon Rd NEND PO2 118 E5
Kern Cl ROWN SO16 54 A1
Kerrfield WINW SO22 25 G1
Kerrfield Ms WINW SO22 25 G1
Kerry Cl CHFD SO53 37 K4
Kesteven Wy WEND SO18 7 H2
Kestrel Cl BPWT SO32 48 B3
BPWT SO32 59 F3
FHAM/STUB PO14 114 C3
WINW SO22 25 G4
ROWN SO16 42 C6
TOTT SO40 69 K4
Kestrel Pl CHAM PO6 102 A7
Kestrel Rd ELGH SO50 44 B1
Keswick Av HSEA PO3 119 F7
Keswick Rd ITCH SO19 10 A4
Kettering Ter NEND PO2 118 B7
Kevlyn Crs HLER SO31 73 J4 2
Kewlake La ROMY SO51 50 A2
Kew La HLER SO31 73 K6
Keydell Cl HORN PO8 64 B7
Keyes Cl LSOL/BMARY PO13 115 K3
Keyes Rd LSOL/BMARY PO13 115 K4
Keyhaven Cl
LSOL/BMARY PO13 115 H5 1
Keyhaven Dr HAV PO9 102 D1
Keynsham Rd ITCH SO19 7 J7
Khandala Gdns WVILLE PO7 102 A2 2
Khartoum Rd PTSW SO17 55 H2
Kidmore La WVILLE PO7 62 E6
Kielder Cl CHFD SO53 37 H3
Kielder Gv
LSOL/BMARY PO13 116 A5 4
Kilford Ct HEND SO30 59 F6
Kilham La WINW SO22 24 E2
Killarney Cl ITCH SO19 73 H2 3
Kilmiston Cl PSEA PO1 134 D1
Kilmiston Dr FHAM/PORC PO16 99 F5
Kiln Cl FAWY SO45 91 F3
Kiln La ROMY SO51 29 G3
RWIN SO21 32 E7
WVILLE PO7 79 G1
Kiln Rd FHAM/PORC PO16 97 G2
Kilnside WVILLE PO7 80 E2
Kilnyard Cl TOTT SO40 52 C3
Kilpatrick Cl NEND PO2 118 C7 1
Kilwich Wy FHAM/PORC PO16 116 E1
Kimberley Cl ELGH SO50 46 C1
Kimberley Rd ENEY PO4 19 L9
Kimbolton Rd HSEA PO3 19 L1
Kimbridge Crs HAV PO9 83 H7
Kimpton Cl
LSOL/BMARY PO13 131 G2 3
Kimpton Ct HAV PO9 83 J7 6
Kineton Rd WSHM SO15 4 C1
King Albert St PSEA PO1 18 F1 3
King Alfred Pl WINC SO23 2 E2
King Alfred Ter WINC SO23 2 E2
King Arthur's Ct CHAM PO6 101 J6 1

Kings Rd *WINW* SO22 .... 25 F2 1
King Charles St *PSEA* PO1 .... 17 L6
King Cup Av *HLER* SO31 .... 94 E4
King Edward Av *ROWN* SO16 .... 54 B4
King Edward's Crs
NEND PO2 .... 118 C5 2
Kingfisher Cl *HAV* PO9 .... 83 J4
HISD PO11 .... 137 K6
HLER SO31 .... 93 K2 1
HORN PO8 .... 81 K1 3
Kingfisher Copse *HLER* SO31 .... 95 G3
Kingfishers *FHAM/PORC* PO16 .... 98 C6
Kingfisher Wy *ROMY* SO51 .... 34 E2 2
TOTT SO40 .... 69 K4
King George Rd
FHAM/PORC PO16 .... 99 F7
King George's Av *WSHM* SO15 .... 54 A6
King Henry I St *PSEA* PO1 .... 18 B4
King John Av *FHAM/PORC* PO16 .... 98 E7
King Richard 1 Rd *PSEA* PO1 .... 18 B5 1
Kings Av *WINW* SO22 .... 2 A9
HLER SO31 .... 93 H3
Kingsbury Rd *SHAM* SO14 .... 5 J5
Kingsclere Av *HAV* PO9 .... 102 E1
ITCH SO19 .... 10 E8
Kingsclere Cl *ITCH* SO19 .... 10 E8
King's Cl *CHFD* SO53 .... 38 A3
HAV PO9 .... 83 H3
LYND SO43 .... 86 C1
RWIN SO21 .... 33 K2
Kings Copse Av *HEND* SO30 .... 58 C5
King's Copse Rd *FAWY* SO45 .... 109 K7
HEND SO30 .... 58 B7
Kingscote Rd *CHAM* PO6 .... 99 J4
HORN PO8 .... 81 J2
Kingscroft Ct *HAV* PO9 .... 14 B5
King's Croft La *HAV* PO9 .... 102 D5
Kingsdown Pl *PSEA* PO1 .... 19 G4 2
Kingsdown Rd *WVILLE* PO7 .... 81 H3
Kingsdown Wy *WEND* SO18 .... 56 C2
Kingsey Av *EMRTH* PO10 .... 104 B6
Kings Fld *HLER* SO31 .... 73 K4
Kings Field Gdns *HLER* SO31 .... 73 K4
Kingsfold Av *WEND* SO18 .... 56 C1
Kingsgate Rd *WINC* SO23 .... 2 D9
Kingsgate St *WINC* SO23 .... 2 E7
Kingsland Cl *CHAM* PO6 .... 100 B5
Kings La *RWIN* SO21 .... 26 E2
Kingsley Gdns *TOTT* SO40 .... 52 A5
Kingsley Pl *WINW* SO22 .... 2 B9
Kingsley Rd *ENEY* PO4 .... 135 G5
GPORT PO12 .... 132 C1
WSHM SO15 .... 54 C5
Kingsmead *WHAM* PO17 .... 61 K5
Kingsmead Av
FHAM/STUB PO14 .... 114 E6
Kings Mede *HORN* PO8 .... 64 C6
Kingsmill Cl *GPORT* PO12 .... 132 C4
Kings Park Rd *WSHM* SO15 .... 5 G7
Kings Ride *FAWY* SO45 .... 128 B1
King's Rd *CHFD* SO53 .... 37 K4
EMRTH PO10 .... 104 B6
FHAM/PORC PO16 .... 13 J6
GPORT PO12 .... 16 B5
HISD PO11 .... 137 H3
LSOL/BMARY PO13 .... 131 F1
PSEA PO1 .... 17 K2
SSEA PO5 .... 18 B7
King's Ter *EMRTH* PO10 .... 104 C6 2
PSEA PO1 .... 18 B7
Kingston *HLER* SO31 .... 73 F6 1
Kingston Crs *NEND* PO2 .... 118 C7
Kingston Gdns *FHAM* PO15 .... 96 E2
Kingston Rd *GPORT* PO12 .... 132 C3
NEND PO2 .... 118 D7
WSHM SO15 .... 4 A7
King St *EMRTH* PO10 .... 104 E3
GPORT PO12 .... 16 F4
SHAM SO14 .... 9 H3
SSEA PO5 .... 18 B6
King's Wy *FHAM/PORC* PO16 .... 98 C6
RWIN SO21 .... 23 K1
RWIN SO21 .... 27 J4
WHAM PO17 .... 79 J4
WINC SO23 .... 2 F1
Kingsway *CHFD* SO53 .... 38 A4
HISD PO11 .... 121 H4
Kingsway Gdns *CHFD* SO53 .... 38 B2
The Kingsway
FHAM/PORC PO16 .... 99 F6
Kingswell St *PSEA* PO1 .... 18 C3 3
Kingswood *TOTT* SO40 .... 70 B4
Kingsworthy Rd *HAV* PO9 .... 103 G3
King William St *PSEA* PO1 .... 17 M2
Kinnell Cl *EMRTH* PO10 .... 104 C6
Kinross Crs *CHAM* PO6 .... 101 G7
Kinross Rd *TOTT* SO40 .... 52 E5
Kinsbourne Cl *ITCH* SO19 .... 57 J6 1
Kinsbourne Ri *ITCH* SO19 .... 57 J7
Kinsbourne Wy *ITCH* SO19 .... 57 H7 2
Kintyre Rd *CHAM* PO6 .... 100 E5
Kinver Cl *ROMY* SO51 .... 35 G1
Kipling Ct *ITCH* SO19 .... 10 E8
Kipling Rd *ELGH* SO50 .... 38 C7
NEND PO2 .... 118 D4
Kirby Rd *NEND* PO2 .... 118 D5
Kirk Gdns *TOTT* SO40 .... 52 E7
Kirkstall Rd *ENEY* PO4 .... 134 D7 2
Kirtley Cl *CHAM* PO6 .... 119 H1
Kirton Rd *CHAM* PO6 .... 101 H7
Kitchener Rd *PTSW* SO17 .... 55 K1
Kite Cl *HORN* PO8 .... 81 K1
Kites Croft Cl *FHAM/STUB* PO14 .... 95 H5
Kitnocks Hl *BPWT* SO32 .... 59 K4
Kittiwake Cl
LSOL/BMARY PO13 .... 115 J5
Knapp La *ROMY* SO51 .... 30 E5
Knatchbull Cl *ROMY* SO51 .... 34 E3 2
Knellers La *TOTT* SO40 .... 68 C1
Knight Cl *WINC* SO23 .... 21 K5
Knighton Rd *ITCH* SO19 .... 10 E3
Knights Bank Rd
FHAM/STUB PO14 .... 114 A6
Knights Cl *HLER* SO31 .... 94 D5 3
Knightstone Gra *FAWY* SO45 .... 91 H4 3
Knightwood Av *HAV* PO9 .... 103 H1
LYND SO43 .... 86 C1
Knightwood Cl *LYND* SO43 .... 86 C1
TOTT SO40 .... 68 A3
Knightwood Rd *FAWY* SO45 .... 91 J4
NBAD SO52 .... 37 G2
Knottgrass Rd *HLER* SO31 .... 94 D4
Knowle Hl *ELGH* SO50 .... 38 E3
Knowle La *ELGH* SO50 .... 46 C4
Knowsley Crs *CHAM* PO6 .... 101 F7
Knowsley Rd *CHAM* PO6 .... 100 E7
Knox Rd *HAV* PO9 .... 14 B4
NEND PO2 .... 118 B6
Knyght Cl *ROMY* SO51 .... 35 F4
Kootenay Av *WEND* SO18 .... 57 H5
Kynegils Rd *WINW* SO22 .... 21 G5
Kynon Cl *GPORT* PO12 .... 117 F7 2
Kytes La *BPWT* SO32 .... 47 G6

L

Laburnum Av *CHAM* PO6 .... 101 H7
Laburnum Cl *NBAD* SO52 .... 36 B5
Laburnum Crs *FAWY* SO45 .... 91 J6 1
Laburnum Gv *ELGH* SO50 .... 38 D7 1
HISD PO11 .... 137 J4
NEND PO2 .... 118 D6
Laburnum Rd
FHAM/PORC PO16 .... 115 J1
HEND SO30 .... 58 C6
ROWN SO16 .... 43 K7
WVILLE PO7 .... 81 K7
Lackford Av *TOTT* SO40 .... 52 D6
Lacon Cl *WEND* SO18 .... 6 D2
Ladram Rd *GPORT* PO12 .... 132 B4
Lady Betty's Dr *FHAM* PO15 .... 75 K7
Ladybridge Rd *WVILLE* PO7 .... 101 H2
Ladycross Rd *FAWY* SO45 .... 91 H4
Ladywood *ELGH* SO50 .... 38 C4
Lainston Cl *WINW* SO22 .... 21 F5
Lake Farm Cl *HEND* SO30 .... 58 B4 4
Lakeland Gdns *TOTT* SO40 .... 69 K4 1
Lakelands Dr *WSHM* SO15 .... 54 D6 1
Lake Rd *BPWT* SO32 .... 60 A4
CHFD SO53 .... 38 B2
ITCH SO19 .... 10 A4
PSEA PO1 .... 18 D2 4
PSEA PO1 .... 18 E1
Lakeside *ELGH* SO50 .... 44 C3
LSOL/BMARY PO13 .... 131 G4
WHAM PO17 .... 97 F1
Lakeside Av *HSEA* PO3 .... 135 G2
ROWN SO16 .... 41 K6
Lakeside Gdns *HAV* PO9 .... 15 G2
Lakesmere Rd *HORN* PO8 .... 64 D6
The Lakes *BPWT* SO32 .... 49 H7
Lakewood Cl *CHFD* SO53 .... 38 A2
Lakewood Rd *CHFD* SO53 .... 38 A2
TOTT SO40 .... 68 B2
Lamberhurst Cl *ITCH* SO19 .... 72 D5
Lambert Cl *WVILLE* PO7 .... 101 K1
Lambourn Cl *FHAM/STUB* PO14 .... 12 B7
Lambourne Cl *FAWY* SO45 .... 91 G5 3
Lambourne Dr *HLER* SO31 .... 95 F3
Lambourne Rd *WEND* SO18 .... 56 E2
Lambourn Sq *CHFD* SO53 .... 37 H4
Lammas Rd *FAWY* SO45 .... 91 H4
Lampeter Av *CHAM* PO6 .... 101 G6
Lancaster Cl *FHAM/PORC* PO16 .... 98 E5
HLER SO31 .... 73 K4 3
LSOL/BMARY PO13 .... 131 J4
Lancaster Rd *ROWN* SO16 .... 54 A1
Lancaster Wy *WVILLE* PO7 .... 82 A7
Lance's Hl *ITCH* SO19 .... 6 F5
Landguard Rd *ENEY* PO4 .... 19 L7
WSHM SO15 .... 4 B7
Landon Rd *LSOL/BMARY* PO13 .... 116 A7
Landport St *PSEA* PO1 .... 18 E2 2
SSEA PO5 .... 18 B6 1
Landport Ter *PSEA* PO1 .... 18 B6
Landport Vw *PSEA* PO1 .... 18 D2 3
Landsdowne St *SSEA* PO5 .... 18 B6 2
Landseer Rd *ITCH* SO19 .... 11 L3
Lands End Rd *HLER* SO31 .... 74 A6
Lane End Dr *EMRTH* PO10 .... 104 C6
Lanehays Rd *FAWY* SO45 .... 91 G3
Lanesbridge Cl *TOTT* SO40 .... 51 J7
Lanes End *FHAM/STUB* PO14 .... 114 D5
The Lane *ENEY* PO4 .... 19 J9
FAWY SO45 .... 110 E4 4
GPORT PO12 .... 132 D7
Langbar Cl *ITCH* SO19 .... 6 D7
Langbrook Cl *HAV* PO9 .... 14 E7
Langdale Av *CHAM* PO6 .... 101 G7
Langdale Cl *ROWN* SO16 .... 54 A4 2
Langdown Lawn *FAWY* SO45 .... 91 H4
Langdown Lawn Cl
FAWY SO45 .... 91 H4 4
Langdown Rd *FAWY* SO45 .... 91 H3
Langford Rd *NEND* PO2 .... 134 E1
Langham Cl *NBAD* SO52 .... 36 A6
Langhorn Rd *ROWN* SO16 .... 43 K7
Langley Lodge Gdns
FAWY SO45 .... 128 C1 5
Langley Rd *NEND* PO2 .... 118 D7
WSHM SO15 .... 54 B6
Langrish Cl *HAV* PO9 .... 83 H7 2
Langrish Rd *ROWN* SO16 .... 42 C7
Langstone Av *HAV* PO9 .... 14 E8
Langstone High St *HAV* PO9 .... 121 G1
Langstone Rd *HAV* PO9 .... 14 E9
HSEA PO3 .... 19 L2
Langstone Wk
FHAM/STUB PO14 .... 96 D6
LSOL/BMARY PO13 .... 115 J5
Langton Cl *WINW* SO22 .... 2 A2
Langton Rd *BPWT* SO32 .... 48 C3
Lanham La *WINW* SO22 .... 20 C7
Lankhills Rd *WINC* SO23 .... 21 J5
Lansdown Av
FHAM/PORC PO16 .... 117 G1
Lansdowne Av *WINC* SO23 .... 2 C9
WVILLE PO7 .... 101 G3
Lansdowne Cl *ROMY* SO51 .... 34 D2 2
Lansdowne Hl *SHAM* SO14 .... 8 F3 2
Lansdowne Rd *WSHM* SO15 .... 54 B5
Lantana Cl *WVILLE* PO7 .... 82 A7 1
Lanyard Dr *LSOL/BMARY* PO13 .... 132 A2
Lapthorn Cl
LSOL/BMARY PO13 .... 115 J3
Lapwing Cl *GPORT* PO12 .... 132 E1 2
HORN PO8 .... 64 B5
Lapwing Dr *TOTT* SO40 .... 52 B4
Lapwing Gv
FHAM/PORC PO16 .... 98 C6 6
Larch Av *FAWY* SO45 .... 109 K2
Larch Cl *HEND* SO30 .... 57 G1
LSOL/BMARY PO13 .... 131 H3 1
Larchdale Cl *HLER* SO31 .... 94 C6 3
Larches Gdns *FHAM* PO15 .... 96 D5
Larchfield Wy *HORN* PO8 .... 64 D7
Larch Rd *ROWN* SO16 .... 54 B1
Larch Wy *HLER* SO31 .... 73 J5
Larchwood Av *HAV* PO9 .... 102 C2
Larchwood Rd *TOTT* SO40 .... 52 B6
Larg Dr *WINW* SO22 .... 21 F3
Lark Hill Ri *WINW* SO22 .... 25 G4
Larkhill Rd *HSEA* PO3 .... 118 E3
Larkspur Cha *ITCH* SO19 .... 57 H7
Larkspur Cl *BPWT* SO32 .... 49 H6
HLER SO31 .... 94 E4 4
Larkspur Dr *NBAD* SO52 .... 37 G4
TOTT SO40 .... 69 K5
Larkspur Gdns *FAWY* SO45 .... 109 J3
HEND SO30 .... 58 D6 3
Laser Cl *HLER* SO31 .... 94 D5
Lashly Meadow *WVILLE* PO7 .... 62 B1
Latchmore Dr *FAWY* SO45 .... 90 D2
Latchmore Forest Gv
HORN PO8 .... 82 A2
Latchmore Gdns *HORN* PO8 .... 81 K2
Latelie Cl *HLER* SO31 .... 93 F1 1
Latham Cl *ELGH* SO50 .... 46 A1
Latham Ct *WSHM* SO15 .... 54 C5
Latham Rd *ELGH* SO50 .... 46 A1
ROMY SO51 .... 35 F2 2
Latimer Ct *HSEA* PO3 .... 119 G3 1
Latimer St *ROMY* SO51 .... 34 D3
SHAM SO14 .... 9 H4
Lauder Cl *EMRTH* PO10 .... 105 G4
Launcelyn Cl *NBAD* SO52 .... 36 A7
Launceston Dr *ELGH* SO50 .... 38 C5 1
Laundry Rd *ROWN* SO16 .... 54 C2
Laurel Cl *FAWY* SO45 .... 91 F3
HLER SO31 .... 95 G2 1
ITCH SO19 .... 10 A4
Laurel Gdns *HLER* SO31 .... 95 G2
Laurel Rd *HLER* SO31 .... 95 G2
HORN PO8 .... 82 D1
Lauriston Dr *CHFD* SO53 .... 37 J1 3
Laurus Cl *WVILLE* PO7 .... 102 B1
Lavant Cl *HORN* PO8 .... 82 C4
Lavant Dr *HAV* PO9 .... 15 G1
Lavender Cl *ITCH* SO19 .... 6 E9 1
Lavender Rd *WVILLE* PO7 .... 82 B7
Laverock Lea
FHAM/PORC PO16 .... 99 F5
Laverstoke Cl *ROWN* SO16 .... 41 K5 1
Lavey's La *FHAM* PO15 .... 76 C7
Lavington Gdns *NBAD* SO52 .... 36 A7
Lavinia Rd *GPORT* PO12 .... 132 D3
Lawford Wy *TOTT* SO40 .... 52 D4
Lawn Cl *LSOL/BMARY* PO13 .... 116 A6 1
Lawn Dr *HLER* SO31 .... 95 F4
Lawn Rd *ELGH* SO50 .... 38 E5
WINW SO22 .... 21 F2
PTSW SO17 .... 5 J3
Lawn St *WINC* SO23 .... 2 F4
Lawnside Rd *WSHM* SO15 .... 54 B4
Lawnswood Cl *HORN* PO8 .... 82 A3
Lawrence Av *HORN* PO8 .... 81 K3
Lawrence Gv *ITCH* SO19 .... 10 E6
Lawrence Rd *FHAM* PO15 .... 12 E4
SSEA PO5 .... 19 G8
Lawson Cl *HLER* SO31 .... 74 C5 1
Lawson Rd *SSEA* PO5 .... 19 G6
Laxton Cl *HLER* SO31 .... 95 G3
ITCH SO19 .... 11 H6
Layton Rd *LSOL/BMARY* PO13 .... 115 K4
Lazy Acre *EMRTH* PO10 .... 105 G6
Leacock Cl *BPWT* SO32 .... 49 J7
Leafy La *FHAM* PO15 .... 75 K7
Lealand Gv *CHAM* PO6 .... 101 J6
Lealand Rd *CHAM* PO6 .... 101 J7
Leamington Crs
LSOL/BMARY PO13 .... 131 G2
Leander Cl *ELGH* SO50 .... 38 D5 1
Lea-oak Gdns *FHAM* PO15 .... 12 A2
Lea Rd *FAWY* SO45 .... 128 B1
Lear Rd *GPORT* PO12 .... 16 B4
Leaside Wy *ROWN* SO16 .... 43 K6
Leatherhead Gdns
HEND SO30 .... 58 C2 1
The Leaway *FHAM/PORC* PO16 .... 99 G6
Lebanon Rd *WSHM* SO15 .... 53 J5
Lechlade Gdns *FHAM* PO15 .... 96 E2
Leckford Cl *FHAM/PORC* PO16 .... 99 F5
WEND SO18 .... 57 G4 2
Leckford Rd *HAV* PO9 .... 83 J7
Ledbury Rd *CHAM* PO6 .... 100 B5
Lederle La *LSOL/BMARY* PO13 .... 115 K2
Lee Church La *ROMY* SO51 .... 40 E3
Lee Dro *ROMY* SO51 .... 41 F2
Lee La *ROMY* SO51 .... 35 F6
Leep La *GPORT* PO12 .... 132 E6
Lee Rd *GPORT* PO12 .... 132 D2
Leesland Rd *GPORT* PO12 .... 132 D3
Lees La *GPORT* PO12 .... 16 A3
Legion Rd *HISD* PO11 .... 137 H4
Leicester Rd *WSHM* SO15 .... 54 E2
Leicester Wy *WINC* SO23 .... 3 K1
Leigh Rd *CHFD* SO53 .... 37 K6
ELGH SO50 .... 38 E7 1
FHAM/PORC PO16 .... 13 G4
HAV PO9 .... 14 F2
PTSW SO17 .... 5 G1
Leighton Av *WSHM* SO15 .... 54 C4
Leighton Rd *ITCH* SO19 .... 10 D3
Leith Av *FHAM/PORC* PO16 .... 99 G5
Lemon Rd *WSHM* SO15 .... 54 C5
Lendorber Av *CHAM* PO6 .... 101 F7
Lennox Cl *CHFD* SO53 .... 38 B2
GPORT PO12 .... 132 E7
ROWN SO16 .... 42 A6
Lennox Rd North *SSEA* PO5 .... 18 E9 2
Lennox Rd South *SSEA* PO5 .... 134 C6
Lensyd Gdns *HORN* PO8 .... 64 A6
Leofric Ct *ENEY* PO4 .... 135 H5
Leominster Rd *CHAM* PO6 .... 100 A5
Leonard Rd *GPORT* PO12 .... 16 D4
Leopold Dr *BPWT* SO32 .... 48 C4
Leopold St *ENEY* PO4 .... 19 H9
Lepe Rd *FAWY* SO45 .... 128 C1
Lerryn Rd *LSOL/BMARY* PO13 .... 116 A5
Lester Av *HAV* PO9 .... 102 D4
Lester Rd *GPORT* PO12 .... 132 C3
Leven Cl *CHFD* SO53 .... 37 H2
Leventhorpe Ct *GPORT* PO12 .... 16 C6 1
Leveson Cl *GPORT* PO12 .... 132 C5
Leviathan Cl *FHAM/STUB* PO14 .... 114 E5
Lewes Cl *ELGH* SO50 .... 38 D4
Lewin Cl *RWIN* SO21 .... 39 K2
Lewis Cl *FAWY* SO45 .... 90 D4
Lewis Rd *EMRTH* PO10 .... 104 D3
Lewis Silkin Wy *ROWN* SO16 .... 42 B7
Lewry Cl *HEND* SO30 .... 58 B5
Lexby Rd *TOTT* SO40 .... 53 F6
Lexden Gdns *HISD* PO11 .... 137 F4 3
Leybourne Av *WEND* SO18 .... 6 F2
Leyland Cl *GPORT* PO12 .... 16 B8
Leyton Rd *SHAM* SO14 .... 5 L7
Liam Cl *HAV* PO9 .... 103 H2
The Liberty *WVILLE* PO7 .... 80 D2
Library Rd *TOTT* SO40 .... 53 F5
Lichen Wy *TOTT* SO40 .... 70 A5
Lichfield Rd *FHAM/STUB* PO14 .... 95 H3
HSEA PO3 .... 19 L1
Liddel Wy *CHFD* SO53 .... 37 H5
Liddiards Wy *WVILLE* PO7 .... 101 K3
Lidiard Gdns *ENEY* PO4 .... 135 G6
Lilac Cl *HAV* PO9 .... 103 K3
Lilac Rd *ROWN* SO16 .... 43 J7
Lily Av *WVILLE* PO7 .... 101 G4
Lime Av *ITCH* SO19 .... 7 H9
Lime Cl *FAWY* SO45 .... 91 F4
ITCH SO19 .... 7 H9
RWIN SO21 .... 39 K2
Lime Gdns *HEND* SO30 .... 57 G1
Lime Gv *CHAM* PO6 .... 100 A5
HISD PO11 .... 136 D5
Lime Kiln La *FAWY* SO45 .... 109 J3
The Limes *LSOL/BMARY* PO13 .... 116 A6
TOTT SO40 .... 70 B4 2
Lime St *SHAM* SO14 .... 9 H3
Limetree Wk *WINC* SO23 .... 3 K4
Lime Wk *FAWY* SO45 .... 91 F4
Linacre Rd *ITCH* SO19 .... 73 G1
Lincoln Cl *FHAM/STUB* PO14 .... 95 H3
Lincoln Ct *WSHM* SO15 .... 54 E2 2
Lincoln Ri *HORN* PO8 .... 82 B1
Lincoln Rd *PSEA* PO1 .... 19 H3
Lincolns Ri *ELGH* SO50 .... 38 E2
Linda Gv *HORN* PO8 .... 82 A2
Linda Rd *FAWY* SO45 .... 110 E4 5
Lindberg Ri *FHAM* PO15 .... 75 K7
Lind Cl *WVILLE* PO7 .... 102 A3
Linden Cl *BPWT* SO32 .... 61 F1
Linden Gdns *HEND* SO30 .... 58 C7
Linden Gv *CHFD* SO53 .... 37 K2
GPORT PO12 .... 16 A7
HISD PO11 .... 137 H5
Linden Lea *FHAM/PORC* PO16 .... 99 F5
Linden Rd *ROMY* SO51 .... 34 E3
ROWN SO16 .... 42 B7
Lindens Cl *EMRTH* PO10 .... 104 C3
Linden Wk *NBAD* SO52 .... 36 A5
Linden Wy *HAV* PO9 .... 103 G3 3
HORN PO8 .... 64 C7
Lindisfarne Cl *CHAM* PO6 .... 101 F7
Lindley Av *ENEY* PO4 .... 19 L9
Lind Rd *GPORT* PO12 .... 133 F7
Lindsay Rd *ITCH* SO19 .... 57 H6
Lindway *HLER* SO31 .... 75 F7
Linford Ct *HAV* PO9 .... 82 E6
Linford Crs *ROWN* SO16 .... 54 E1
Ling Dl *ROWN* SO16 .... 43 G4
Lingfield Gdns *WEND* SO18 .... 56 C2 1
Lingwood Cl *ROWN* SO16 .... 43 G4
Lingwood Wk *ROWN* SO16 .... 43 G4 1
Linkenholt Wy *HAV* PO9 .... 102 D1
Link Rd *CHAM* PO6 .... 100 A4
ROWN SO16 .... 54 A1
Links La *HAV* PO9 .... 83 J2
HISD PO11 .... 136 D5
Links Rd *WINW* SO22 .... 21 G6
The Links *LSOL/BMARY* PO13 .... 115 K6
Links View Wy *ROWN* SO16 .... 43 G5
The Link *WVILLE* PO7 .... 82 B4
Linkway *FHAM/STUB* PO14 .... 114 D6
Linnet Cl *HORN* PO8 .... 81 K1
Linnet Sq *ELGH* SO50 .... 44 A2
The Linnets
FHAM/PORC PO16 .... 98 C6 7
TOTT SO40 .... 52 B4 3
Linwood Cl *FAWY* SO45 .... 91 H4
Lionheart Wy *HLER* SO31 .... 73 J4
Lion St *PSEA* PO1 .... 18 A3
Lipizzaner Flds *HLER* SO31 .... 75 G5
Lisbon Rd *WSHM* SO15 .... 4 A6
Lisle Cl *WINW* SO22 .... 24 D5
Lisle Wy *EMRTH* PO10 .... 104 B3
Liss Rd *ENEY* PO4 .... 19 K6
Litchfield Crs *WEND* SO18 .... 56 C3
Litchfield Rd *WINW* SO22 .... 21 G3
WEND SO18 .... 56 C3
Lith Av *HORN* PO8 .... 64 D4
Lith La *HORN* PO8 .... 64 D3
Little Abshot Rd
FHAM/STUB PO14 .... 95 G6
Little Anglesey Rd
GPORT PO12 .... 132 D6
Little Arthur St *NEND* PO2 .... 134 D1 3
Little Bull La *BPWT* SO32 .... 60 E2
Little Cnr *WVILLE* PO7 .... 80 E2
Littlefield Crs *NBAD* SO52 .... 37 F4
Little Gays *FHAM/STUB* PO14 .... 114 A5
Little George St *PSEA* PO1 .... 134 D1 3
Little Gn *GPORT* PO12 .... 132 D6
Littlegreen Av *HAV* PO9 .... 103 H3
Little Hambrook St *SSEA* PO5 .... 18 B7 3
Little Lance's Hl *ITCH* SO19 .... 6 E5
Little La *GPORT* PO12 .... 132 D6 2
Little Md *WVILLE* PO7 .... 81 F2
Littlemeads *ROMY* SO51 .... 34 C3
Little Minster St *WINC* SO23 .... 2 E5
Little Oak Rd *ROWN* SO16 .... 43 G7
Littlepark Av *HAV* PO9 .... 102 C3
Little Park Cl *HEND* SO30 .... 58 A6 2
Little Park Farm Rd *FHAM* PO15 .... 95 H1
Little Quob La *HEND* SO30 .... 57 H2
Little Shore La *BPWT* SO32 .... 48 D4
Little Southsea St *SSEA* PO5 .... 18 B7 7
Littleton Gv *HAV* PO9 .... 103 G2
Littleton La *RWIN* SO21 .... 20 A5
Littlewood Gdns *HEND* SO30 .... 57 G3
HLER SO31 .... 94 D3 1
Little Woodham La
LSOL/BMARY PO13 .... 131 K3
Liverpool Rd
FHAM/STUB PO14 .... 115 G1
PSEA PO1 .... 19 H3
Liverpool St *SHAM* SO14 .... 5 G5
Livingstone Rd *SHAM* SO14 .... 5 H2
SSEA PO5 .... 18 F7
Lloyd Av *TOTT* SO40 .... 69 K4 2
Loane Rd *ITCH* SO19 .... 10 F3
Lobelia Rd *ROWN* SO16 .... 43 K7
Locarno Rd *HSEA* PO3 .... 118 E5
Lock Appoach *CHAM* PO6 .... 99 K7
Lockerley Crs *ROWN* SO16 .... 54 A2
Lockerley Rd *HAV* PO9 .... 103 H3
Locke Rd *HEND* SO30 .... 58 B4
Lockhams Rd *BPWT* SO32 .... 60 A4
Locksash Cl *SELS* PO20 .... 139 J6
Locksheath Cl *HAV* PO9 .... 82 E7 3
Locksheath Park Rd *HLER* SO31 .... 95 G5
Lock's La *RWIN* SO21 .... 20 A4
Locksley Rd *ELGH* SO50 .... 44 B2
Locks Rd *HLER* SO31 .... 95 F2
Locksway Rd *ENEY* PO4 .... 135 G4
Lockswood Rd *HLER* SO31 .... 94 E3
Lock Vw *CHAM* PO6 .... 99 K7
Lodge Av *CHAM* PO6 .... 101 F6
Lodgebury Cl *EMRTH* PO10 .... 105 H6
Lodge Dr *FAWY* SO45 .... 91 G5
Lodge Gdns *GPORT* PO12 .... 132 D4
Lodge La *BROC* SO42 .... 125 K2
Lodge Rd *HAV* PO9 .... 102 C5
HLER SO31 .... 95 G3
SHAM SO14 .... 5 G4
Lofting Cl *ELGH* SO50 .... 45 H1 3
Logan Cl *ROWN* SO16 .... 42 A6
Lomax Cl *HEND* SO30 .... 58 B3 2
Lombard St *PSEA* PO1 .... 17 L7 2
Lombardy Cl
LSOL/BMARY PO13 .... 116 B5 1
Lombardy Ri *WVILLE* PO7 .... 102 A1
Lomond Cl *NEND* PO2 .... 118 C7
Londesborough Rd *ENEY* PO4 .... 19 H7
London Av *NEND* PO2 .... 118 C5
London Rd *CHAM* PO6 .... 100 E6
HORN PO8 .... 64 E1
NEND PO2 .... 118 D5
WINC SO23 .... 22 A2
WSHM SO15 .... 4 F7
WVILLE PO7 .... 81 K5
WVILLE PO7 .... 101 H2
Lone Va *WVILLE* PO7 .... 101 H3
Longacres *FHAM/STUB* PO14 .... 95 H2
Long Beech Dr *TOTT* SO40 .... 52 C6
Longbridge Cl *TOTT* SO40 .... 52 C2
Longclose Rd *HEND* SO30 .... 58 C5
Long Copse *FAWY* SO45 .... 110 B4
Long Copse La *EMRTH* PO10 .... 104 C2
Long Curtain Rd *PSEA* PO1 .... 17 M8
Longdean Cl *CHAM* PO6 .... 99 K5
Long Dr *HEND* SO30 .... 57 H2
LSOL/BMARY PO13 .... 115 K6
Longfield Av *FHAM/STUB* PO14 .... 12 B9
Longfield Cl *ENEY* PO4 .... 135 H3 2
Longfield Rd *EMRTH* PO10 .... 104 B3
WINC SO23 .... 3 L4
Longhouse Gn *WINC* SO23 .... 3 K4
Longlands Rd *EMRTH* PO10 .... 105 G6
Long La *FAWY* SO45 .... 109 K2
HLER SO31 .... 73 K4
TOTT SO40 .... 69 J4
Long Lane Cl *FAWY* SO45 .... 110 A4
Longleat Gdns *ROWN* SO16 .... 42 C6
Longmead Av *ELGH* SO50 .... 39 G6
Longmead Gdns *HAV* PO9 .... 14 F8
Longmeadow Gdns *FAWY* SO45 .... 91 H2
Longmead Rd *WEND* SO18 .... 56 D3 2
Longmore Av *ITCH* SO19 .... 10 B6
Longmore Crs *ITCH* SO19 .... 10 B6
Longmynd Dr
FHAM/STUB PO14 .... 12 B8
Longridge Rd *HEND* SO30 .... 58 B6
Longshore Wy *ENEY* PO4 .... 135 J4
HSEA PO3 .... 135 J3
Longs La *FHAM/STUB* PO14 .... 114 D4
Longstaff Gdns
FHAM/PORC PO16 .... 12 F2
Longstock Cl *ITCH* SO19 .... 11 G9 1
Longstock Crs *TOTT* SO40 .... 52 C5
Longstock Rd *HAV* PO9 .... 83 J7
Long Wk *RWIN* SO21 .... 22 C3
Long Water Dr *GPORT* PO12 .... 133 F7
Longwood Av *HORN* PO8 .... 82 A2
Lonsdale Av *CHAM* PO6 .... 101 F7
FHAM/PORC PO16 .... 117 G1
Loperwood *TOTT* SO40 .... 51 J2
Loperwood La *TOTT* SO40 .... 52 A2
Lordington Cl *CHAM* PO6 .... 101 G6 1
Lord Montgomery Wy
SSEA PO5 .... 18 B5 2
Lord Mountbatten Cl
WEND SO18 .... 44 B7 5
Lord's Hl Centre East
ROWN SO16 .... 42 A6
Lord's Hl Centre West
ROWN SO16 .... 42 A7
Lord's Hill Wy *ROWN* SO16 .... 42 A6
Lords St *PSEA* PO1 .... 18 F1
Lordswood *ELGH* SO50 .... 39 H3
Lordswood Cl *ROWN* SO16 .... 54 E1 1
Lordswood Gdns *ROWN* SO16 .... 42 E7
Lordswood Rd *ROWN* SO16 .... 42 D7
Loreille Cl *ROWN* SO16 .... 41 K4
Lorne Rd *SSEA* PO5 .... 19 G6
Loughwood Cl *ELGH* SO50 .... 38 D4
Lovage Gdns *TOTT* SO40 .... 52 B5
Lovage Rd *FHAM* PO15 .... 75 J6
Lovage Wy *HORN* PO8 .... 64 D3
Lovedean La *HORN* PO8 .... 63 K4
Love La *ROMY* SO51 .... 34 D3
Lovett Rd *HSEA* PO3 .... 118 E4
Lowcay Rd *SSEA* PO5 .... 19 G9
Lowden Cl *WINW* SO22 .... 25 G4
Lower Alfred St *SHAM* SO14 .... 5 J6
Lower Banister St *WSHM* SO15 .... 4 F7
Lower Bellfield
FHAM/STUB PO14 .... 96 A7

Lower Bere Wd *WVILLE* PO7 82 A6
Lower Brookfield Rd
PSEA PO1 19 H2 5
Lower Brook St *WINC* SO23 2 F4
Lower Brownhill Rd
ROWN SO16 53 H2
Lower Canal Wk *SHAM* SO14 9 G5
Lower Chase Rd *BPWT* SO32 49 H6
Lower Church Pth *PSEA* PO1 18 D3 3
Lower Church Rd
FHAM/STUB PO14 95 H3
Lower Crabbick La *WVILLE* PO7 80 A1
Lower Derby Rd *NEND* PO2 118 B6
Lower Drayton La *CHAM* PO6 101 H7
Lower Duncan Rd *HLER* SO31 95 G1
Lower Farlington Rd
CHAM PO6 101 K6
Lower Forbury Rd *SSEA* PO5 18 E5 2
Lower Grove Rd *HAV* PO9 15 G6
Lower La *BPWT* SO32 48 E3
Lower Moors Rd *RWIN* SO21 39 J1
Lower Mortimer Rd *ITCH* SO19 10 B3
Lower Mullin's La *FAWY* SO45 91 F2
Lower New Rd *HEND* SO30 57 G3
Lower Northam Rd *HEND* SO30 58 B5
Lower Quay Cl
FHAM/PORC PO16 13 J8
Lower Quay Rd
FHAM/PORC PO16 13 K8
Lower Rd *HAV* PO9 102 C5
Lower St Helens Rd *HEND* SO30 58 B7
Lower Spinney *HLER* SO31 94 B7
Lower St *ROMY* SO51 29 G2
Lower Swanwick Rd
HLER SO31 74 C5 2
Lower Vicarage Rd *ITCH* SO19 10 A3
Lower William St *SHAM* SO14 6 A7
Lower Wingfield St *PSEA* PO1 18 E1 2
Lower York St *SHAM* SO14 5 M7
Lowestoft Rd *CHAM* PO6 100 C5
Lowford Hl *HLER* SO31 73 J4
Lowland Rd *WVILLE* PO7 80 D1
Lowry Gdns *ITCH* SO19 11 L6
Loxwood Rd *HORN* PO8 64 A6
Luard Ct *HAV* PO9 15 J5
Lucas Cl *ROWN* SO16 42 A6 1
Luccombe Pl *WSHM* SO15 54 E2
Luccombe Rd *WSHM* SO15 54 E2
Lucerne Av *WVILLE* PO7 81 J3
Lucerne Gdns *HEND* SO30 57 K6
Lucknow St *PSEA* PO1 19 G4
Ludcombe *WVILLE* PO7 62 E7
Ludlow Rd *CHAM* PO6 100 B5
ITCH SO19 10 D2
Ludwell's La *BPWT* SO32 49 G7
Lugano Cl *WVILLE* PO7 81 J4
Lukin Dr *ROWN* SO16 41 H6
Lulworth Cl *CHFD* SO53 37 J7
HISD PO11 137 H3
ROWN SO16 53 K2
Lulworth Gn *ROWN* SO16 53 K2
Lulworth Rd
LSOL/BMARY PO13 131 F2
Lumley Rd *EMRTH* PO10 104 D5
Lumsden Av *WSHM* SO15 54 E3
Lumsden Rd *ENEY* PO4 135 J5
Lundy Cl *ROWN* SO16 41 K6
Lunedale Rd *FAWY* SO45 91 F6
Lupin Rd *ROWN* SO16 43 K6
Lutman St *EMRTH* PO10 104 B2
Luton Rd *ITCH* SO19 11 K1
Luxton Cl *HEND* SO30 58 E4
Luzborough La *ROMY* SO51 35 G6
Lyburn Cl *ROWN* SO16 42 D7 2
Lychgate Dr *HORN* PO8 64 C5
Lychgate Gn *FHAM/STUB* PO14 114 D2
Lydgate *TOTT* SO40 52 C5 3
Lydgate Cl *ITCH* SO19 73 G1
Lydgate Gn *ITCH* SO19 73 G1
Lydgate Rd *ITCH* SO19 73 G1 1
Lydiard Cl *ELGH* SO50 38 D5
Lydlynch Rd *TOTT* SO40 52 D5
Lydney Cl *CHAM* PO6 100 B6
Lydney Rd *HLER* SO31 94 E4
Lymbourn Rd *HAV* PO9 15 G5
Lyme Cl *ELGH* SO50 38 C5 2
Lymer La *ROWN* SO16 41 H5
Lynch Cl *WINW* SO22 21 H5
Lyndale Rd *HLER* SO31 95 G2
Lynden Cl *FHAM/STUB* PO14 96 C6
Lynden Ga *ITCH* SO19 11 H3 1
Lyndhurst Cl *WINW* SO22 21 G3
HISD PO11 137 H6
Lyndhurst Rd *GPORT* PO12 132 D3
NEND PO2 118 E5
TOTT SO40 50 B5
TOTT SO40 68 B3
Lyndock Cl *ITCH* SO19 10 D5
Lyndock Pl *ITCH* SO19 10 D5
Lyne Pl *HORN* PO8 64 C6
Lynford Av *WINW* SO22 21 H5
Lynford Wy *WINW* SO22 21 H5
Lynn Rd *NEND* PO2 118 E7
Lynn Wy *WINC* SO23 22 B1
Lynton Ct *TOTT* SO40 52 D6
Lynton Gdns *FHAM/PORC* PO16 12 E1
Lynton Gv *HSEA* PO3 119 F7
Lynton Rd *HEND* SO30 58 B5
Lynwood Av *WVILLE* PO7 81 J2
Lynx Cl *ELGH* SO50 45 J1
Lyon St *SHAM* SO14 5 J6
Lysander Wy *WVILLE* PO7 82 B5
Lytham Rd *WEND* SO18 7 G2
Lytton Rd *FAWY* SO45 91 J4

M

Mabey Cl *GPORT* PO12 133 F6
Mablethorpe Rd *CHAM* PO6 100 D5
Macarthur Crs *WEND* SO18 7 G3
Macaulay Av *CHAM* PO6 99 J5
Macnaghten Rd *WEND* SO18 6 R4
Madden Cl *GPORT* PO12 132 C5
Maddison St *SHAM* SO14 8 F3 3
Maddoxford Wy *BPWT* SO32 58 E3
Madeira Rd *NEND* PO2 118 D4
Madison Cl
LSOL/BMARY PO13 116 B7 1
Mafeking Rd *ENEY* PO4 19 K7
Magazine La *TOTT* SO40 70 B2
Magdala Rd *CHAM* PO6 100 E7
HISD PO11 137 F5
Magdalene Wy
FHAM/STUB PO14 95 H5
Magdalen Hl *WINC* SO23 3 G5
Magdalen Rd *NEND* PO2 118 D4
Magennis Cl
LSOL/BMARY PO13 132 A1
Magnolia Cl *FAWY* SO45 90 D2 3
FHAM/STUB PO14 12 C7
Magnolia Gv *ELGH* SO50 46 D1
Magnolia Rd *ITCH* SO19 6 E9
Magnolia Wy *HORN* PO8 82 D1
Magpie Dr *TOTT* SO40 52 B5
Magpie Gdns *ITCH* SO19 11 L2
Magpie La *ELGH* SO50 44 B1
LSOL/BMARY PO13 131 G1 3
Magpie Rd *HORN* PO8 65 K7
Magpie Wk *HORN* PO8 81 J1
Maidford Gv *HSEA* PO3 119 H3 4
Maidstone Crs *CHAM* PO6 100 D5
Main Dr *FAWY* SO45 127 H2
WHAM PO17 79 K7
Main Rd *EMRTH* PO10 105 F6
FAWY SO45 70 B6
FAWY SO45 109 K1
WINW SO22 20 D1
LSOL/BMARY PO13 116 A3
PSEA PO1 17 K3
RWIN SO21 32 E7
TOTT SO40 68 D1
TOTT SO40 70 A4
Mainsail Dr *FHAM/PORC* PO16 13 J8
Mainstone *ROMY* SO51 34 C4
Mainstream Ct *ELGH* SO50 39 G7 1
Maisemore Gdns *EMRTH* PO10 104 A6
Maitland St *PSEA* PO1 134 C1
Majestic Rd *ROWN* SO16 41 G7
Malcolm Cl *CHFD* SO53 38 B1
HLER SO31 95 G3
Malcolm Rd *CHFD* SO53 38 B1
Malcroft Ms *TOTT* SO40 70 B4 3
Maldon Cl *ELGH* SO50 39 G7
Maldon Rd *CHAM* PO6 100 C6 5
ITCH SO19 10 D1
Malibres Rd *CHFD* SO53 38 C2
Malin Cl *FHAM/STUB* PO14 114 C4
ROWN SO16 41 K7
Malins Rd *NEND* PO2 134 C1
Mallard Cl *BPWT* SO32 48 B3
ROMY SO51 34 E2
Mallard Gdns *HEND* SO30 58 B2
LSOL/BMARY PO13 115 J5 2
Mallard Rd *ENEY* PO4 135 G3
HAV PO9 83 J4
Mallards Rd *HLER* SO31 73 J6
The Mallards *FHAM/PORC* PO16 13 H1
HAV PO9 14 D8
Mallett Cl *HEND* SO30 58 D2
Mallory Crs *FHAM/PORC* PO16 13 G2
Mallow Cl *CHAM* PO6 100 E6 1
WVILLE PO7 82 A7
Mallow Rd *HEND* SO30 57 K6
Malmesbury Cl *ELGH* SO50 46 B1 2
Malmesbury Gdns *WINW* SO22 21 G5 1
Malmesbury Pl *WSHM* SO15 4 A5
Malmesbury Rd *ROMY* SO51 34 D2
WSHM SO15 4 A5
Malory Cl *ITCH* SO19 57 G6
Malta Rd *NEND* PO2 118 D7
Malthouse Cl *ROMY* SO51 34 D2 3
RWIN SO21 22 E2
Malthouse Gdns *TOTT* SO40 70 A4
Malthouse La
FHAM/PORC PO16 13 J5
Malthouse Rd *NEND* PO2 118 C7
The Maltings
FHAM/PORC PO16 98 A4 1
WINC SO23 2 E5
Malt La *BPWT* SO32 48 D3
Malus Cl *FHAM/STUB* PO14 97 G7
Malvern Av *FHAM/STUB* PO14 12 C8
Malvern Cl *BPWT* SO32 48 E4
Malvern Dr *FAWY* SO45 90 E3
Malvern Gdns *HEND* SO30 58 C5
Malvern Ms *EMRTH* PO10 104 C5
Malvern Rd *GPORT* PO12 132 C3
ROWN SO16 54 D2
SSEA PO5 134 C7
Malwood Av *ROWN* SO16 54 E1
Malwood Cl *HAV* PO9 83 H7
Malwood Gdns *TOTT* SO40 52 B4
Malwood Rd *FAWY* SO45 91 G2
Malwood Rd West *FAWY* SO45 91 F2
Manchester Rd *PSEA* PO1 19 H3
Mancroft Av
FHAM/STUB PO14 114 D6
Mandela Wy *WSHM* SO15 4 C8
Manley Rd *HLER* SO31 73 J4
Manners La *ENEY* PO4 19 G5
Manners Rd *ENEY* PO4 19 H5
Manningford Cl *WINC* SO23 21 K4
Manns Cl *WEND* SO18 57 F2
Mannyngham Wy *ROMY* SO51 28 C2
Manor Cl *HLER* SO31 73 J4 3
TOTT SO40 52 D6
WHAM PO17 77 H3
WINC SO23 3 H3
Manor Crs *CHAM* PO6 101 G7
HLER SO31 73 J4
Manor Farm Gn *RWIN* SO21 33 J4
Manor Farm Gv *ELGH* SO50 45 H1 4
Manor Farm Rd *WEND* SO18 56 A3
Manor Gdns *EMRTH* PO10 105 G5
Manor House Av *WSHM* SO15 53 K6
Manor Lodge Rd *HAV* PO9 83 J5
Manor Ms *CHAM* PO6 101 H6
Manor Park Av *HSEA* PO3 119 F7
Manor Rd *BPWT* SO32 47 J4
ELGH SO50 45 H1
EMRTH PO10 105 G5
FAWY SO45 109 K3
HISD PO11 137 G2
PSEA PO1 134 D1
ROWN SO16 42 E2
RWIN SO21 33 J4
TOTT SO40 90 B1
Manor Rd North *ITCH* SO19 10 C2
Manor Rd South *ITCH* SO19 10 C4
Manor Wy *EMRTH* PO10 105 G5
HISD PO11 137 H6
LSOL/BMARY PO13 131 F2
Mans Br *WEND* SO18 44 C7
Mansbridge Rd *ELGH* SO50 44 D2
WEND SO18 44 C7
Mansel Ct *ROWN* SO16 53 K2
Mansell Cl *FAWY* SO45 91 F6
Mansel Rd East *ROWN* SO16 53 K3
Mansel Rd West *ROWN* SO16 53 J2
Mansfield La *WHAM* PO17 76 C1
Mansfield Rd
LSOL/BMARY PO13 115 K7
Mansion Rd *ENEY* PO4 134 D7
WSHM SO15 54 D6
Mansvid Av *CHAM* PO6 101 G7
Mantle Cl *LSOL/BMARY* PO13 132 A1
Mantle Sq *NEND* PO2 118 A5
Maple Cl *EMRTH* PO10 104 C4
FHAM PO15 96 D5
LSOL/BMARY PO13 131 G3 2
ROMY SO51 35 H4
Maple Dr *WVILLE* PO7 81 F2
Maple Gdns *TOTT* SO40 52 B6 5
Maple Rd *FAWY* SO45 91 J6 2
SSEA PO5 134 C6 2
WEND SO18 6 D4
Maple Sq *ELGH* SO50 44 B2 2
The Maples *CHFD* SO53 37 K2
Mapleton Rd *HEND* SO30 58 C6 5
Mapletree Av *HORN* PO8 64 D7
Maplewood Cl *TOTT* SO40 52 B6
Maplin Rd *ROWN* SO16 53 J2
Maralyn Av *WVILLE* PO7 81 K7
Marathon Pl *ELGH* SO50 46 A1
Marchwood By-pass *TOTT* SO40 52 E7
Marchwood Rd *HAV* PO9 83 F7
TOTT SO40 69 H1
WSHM SO15 54 C6
Marcus Cl *ELGH* SO50 46 A1
Mardale Rd *ROWN* SO16 53 J4
Mardon Cl *ELGH* SO50 44 B6
Margam Av *ITCH* SO19 6 F9
Margaret Cl *WVILLE* PO7 81 J4
Margarita Rd *FHAM* PO15 12 C4
Margate Rd *SSEA* PO5 18 E6
Margery's Ct *PSEA* PO1 17 M4 2
Marianne Cl *WSHM* SO15 54 A6 1
Marie Rd *ITCH* SO19 11 M3
Marigold Cl *FHAM* PO15 12 C4
Marina Cl *EMRTH* PO10 104 D6 3
Marina Gv *FHAM/PORC* PO16 117 F1
HSEA PO3 135 G2
Marina Keep *CHAM* PO6 99 K7
Marine Ct *ENEY* PO4 135 F6
Marine Pde *SHAM* SO14 9 K2
Marine Pde East
LSOL/BMARY PO13 131 F3
Marine Pde West
LSOL/BMARY PO13 130 E1
Mariner's Cl *HLER* SO31 93 K4
Mariners Ms *FAWY* SO45 91 H2 7
Mariners Wk *ENEY* PO4 135 G3
Mariners Wy *GPORT* PO12 16 E7
HLER SO31 94 B5
Marine Wk *HISD* PO11 138 A5
Marion Rd *ENEY* PO4 134 D6
Maritime Av *TOTT* SO40 70 B2
Maritime Wk *SHAM* SO14 9 J6
Maritime Wy *SHAM* SO14 9 H5
Marjoram Crs *HORN* PO8 82 C2
Marjoram Wy *FHAM* PO15 75 J6
Mark Cl *HSEA* PO3 118 E3
WSHM SO15 54 B5
Marken Cl *HLER* SO31 94 D3
Market La *WINC* SO23 2 E5
Market Pde *HAV* PO9 14 E4
Market Pl *SHAM* SO14 9 G4
Market St *ELGH* SO50 44 E2
WINC SO23 2 E5
Marketway *PSEA* PO1 18 C2
Mark's Rd *FHAM/STUB* PO14 115 F5
Marks Tey Rd
FHAM/STUB PO14 114 D2
Markway Cl *EMRTH* PO10 104 A5
Marlborough Cl *WVILLE* PO7 101 J1 2
Marlborough Ct *FAWY* SO45 91 F4 1
Marlborough Gdns
HEND SO30 58 B1 2
Marlborough Gv
FHAM/PORC PO16 99 F7
Marlborough Pk *HAV* PO9 15 K2
Marlborough Rd *CHFD* SO53 38 B1
GPORT PO12 132 C2
WSHM SO15 54 C4
Marlborough Rw *PSEA* PO1 17 M2
Marldell Cl *HAV* PO9 103 H1
Marles Cl *LSOL/BMARY* PO13 132 A1
Marlhill Cl *WEND* SO18 56 C2
Marlin Cl *LSOL/BMARY* PO13 132 A2
Marlow Cl *FHAM* PO15 97 F2
Marlowe Ct *WVILLE* PO7 81 J4
Marlow Rd *BPWT* SO32 48 B2
Marlpit La *EMRTH* PO10 105 K2
Marls Rd *HEND* SO30 58 C6 5
Marmion Av *SSEA* PO5 18 E9 3
Marmion Rd *SSEA* PO5 18 D9
Marne Rd *WEND* SO18 7 H4
Marples Wy *HAV* PO9 14 B5
Marrels Wd *WVILLE* PO7 101 H2
Marsden Rd *CHAM* PO6 100 A6
Marshall Rd *HISD* PO11 137 K6
Marsh Cl *CHAM* PO6 119 H1
Marshfield Cl *TOTT* SO40 69 J4
Marsh Gdns *HEND* SO30 58 B1 4
Marshlands Rd *CHAM* PO6 101 J7
Marsh La *FAWY* SO45 110 E3
RCCH PO18 123 K3
SHAM SO14 9 H3
The Marsh *FAWY* SO45 91 H1
Marshwood Av *WVILLE* PO7 82 B6
Marston La *HSEA* PO3 119 G3
Marston Rd *ITCH* SO19 57 G7
Martello Cl *GPORT* PO12 132 A5
Martin Av *FHAM/STUB* PO14 114 E5
WVILLE PO7 81 F1
Martin Cl *BPWT* SO32 49 J7
LSOL/BMARY PO13 131 G1 6
Martin Rd *FHAM/STUB* PO14 114 E5
HAV PO9 103 H2
HSEA PO3 119 F7
Martins Flds *RWIN* SO21 25 F7
The Martins *ELGH* SO50 46 C2 3
Martin St *BPWT* SO32 48 C4
Martley Gdns *HEND* SO30 58 C2
Marvic Ct *HAV* PO9 83 F7 3
Marvin Wy *HEND* SO30 58 C5 1
WEND SO18 7 M6
Marybridge Cl *TOTT* SO40 52 D6
Maryfield *SHAM* SO14 9 J2
Maryland Cl *WEND* SO18 56 C1
Mary Rose Cl *FHAM* PO15 12 C1
The Mary Rose St *PSEA* PO1 18 C4 4
Masefield Av *CHAM* PO6 99 J5
Masefield Cl *ELGH* SO50 38 C7 2
Masefield Crs *HORN* PO8 82 A2
Masefield Gn *ITCH* SO19 57 G6 1
Masseys La *BROC* SO42 125 H1
Masten Crs *LSOL/BMARY* PO13 115 K7
Matapan Rd *NEND* PO2 118 C3
Matheson Rd *ROWN* SO16 42 A5
Matley Gdns *TOTT* SO40 52 A5
Matthews Cl *HAV* PO9 102 D3
Matthews La *BROC* SO42 125 H2
Maunsell Wy *HEND* SO30 58 B1
Maurepas Wy *WVILLE* PO7 81 J6
Mauretania Rd *ROWN* SO16 41 G7
Maurice Rd *ENEY* PO4 135 H4
Mavis Crs *HAV* PO9 14 E3
Maxstoke Cl *SSEA* PO5 18 E4 1
Maxwell Rd *ENEY* PO4 19 L7
ITCH SO19 11 G3
Maybray King Wy *WEND* SO18 6 F5
Maybush Dr *RCCH* PO18 105 K7
Maybush Rd *ROWN* SO16 53 K2
May Cl *FAWY* SO45 110 A4
May Copse *FAWY* SO45 110 A4
May Crs *FAWY* SO45 110 A4
Maydman Sq *HSEA* PO3 19 M1
Mayfair Ct *HEND* SO30 59 F5
Mayfair Gdns *WSHM* SO15 4 E5
Mayfield Av *TOTT* SO40 52 D4
Mayfield Cl *FHAM/STUB* PO14 114 E4
Mayfield Rd *GPORT* PO12 16 B7
NEND PO2 118 D5
PTSW SO17 55 J1
Mayflower Cl *CHFD* SO53 37 J5
FHAM/STUB PO14 114 D6 3
Mayflower Rd *WSHM* SO15 54 D4 1
Mayflower Rbt *WSHM* SO15 8 E4
The Mayflowers *ROWN* SO16 43 H7
Mayhall Rd *HSEA* PO3 119 F6
Maylands Av *ENEY* PO4 19 M5
Maylands Rd *HAV* PO9 102 C4
Mayles Cl *WHAM* PO17 77 H2
Mayles La *WHAM* PO17 77 F4
Mayles Rd *ENEY* PO4 135 G3
Maylings Farm Rd
FHAM/PORC PO16 12 F2
Maynard Cl *LSOL/BMARY* PO13 115 K3
Maynard Pl *HORN* PO8 64 C5
Maynard Rd *TOTT* SO40 52 E5
Mayo Cl *PSEA* PO1 134 C1
Mayridge *FHAM/STUB* PO14 95 H3
May Rd *WSHM* SO15 54 D5 2
May's La *FHAM/STUB* PO14 114 E3
May Tree Cl *WINW* SO22 25 F4
Maytree Cl *HLER* SO31 95 F3
Maytree Gdns *HORN* PO8 81 K2
Maytree Rd *CHFD* SO53 31 K7
FHAM/PORC PO16 13 G6
HORN PO8 81 K2
Mayvale Cl *TOTT* SO40 70 A4
Meacher Cl *TOTT* SO40 52 D4 3
Meadbrook Gdns *CHFD* SO53 37 K4
Mead Cl *ROMY* SO51 35 G3
Mead Crs *WEND* SO18 56 A1
Meadcroft Cl *HLER* SO31 94 C6
Meadend Cl *HAV* PO9 103 J1 3
Mead End Rd *WVILLE* PO7 81 F2
Meadow Av *HLER* SO31 95 F2
Meadowbank Rd *FHAM* PO15 12 A5
Meadow Cl *BPWT* SO32 49 F7 1
HEND SO30 57 H2
HISD PO11 121 G4
NBAD SO52 36 B7
TOTT SO40 52 E7
Meadowcroft Cl *RWIN* SO21 33 F6 1
Meadow Edge *WVILLE* PO7 101 F4
Meadow Gdns *BPWT* SO32 49 F7
Meadowhead Rd *ROWN* SO16 55 G1 1
Meadowlands *HAV* PO9 15 H5
HAV PO9 83 K2
Meadow La *HLER* SO31 93 K4
Meadowmead Av *WSHM* SO15 54 B5
Meadow Ri *HORN* PO8 82 C2
Meadowside Cl *WEND* SO18 44 B7 5
The Meadows
FHAM/PORC PO16 13 M1
LYND SO43 86 D2 1
Meadow St *SSEA* PO5 18 B7 3
Meadowsweet *WVILLE* PO7 82 C4
Meadowsweet Wy *CHAM* PO6 100 C5
ELGH SO50 46 B5
The Meadow *ROMY* SO51 34 E1 1
WVILLE PO7 80 E1
Meadow Wk
LSOL/BMARY PO13 115 J2
Meadow Wy *FAWY* SO45 110 E4 6
WINW SO22 25 F4
Mead Rd *CHFD* SO53 37 K4
WINC SO23 25 H4
The Meads *CHFD* SO53 37 H5
ROMY SO51 34 C3
The Mead *FAWY* SO45 91 F3
LSOL/BMARY PO13 115 J4 2
Mead Wy *FHAM/PORC* PO16 13 J2
Meadway *WVILLE* PO7 82 B4
Mears Rd *ELGH* SO50 46 B1
Meath Cl *HISD* PO11 137 K7
Medina Cl *CHFD* SO53 38 B5 3
Medina Rd *CHAM* PO6 100 C6
WSHM SO15 54 C3
Medlar Cl *HEND* SO30 58 C6 6
Medlicott Wy *BPWT* SO32 49 J7
Medstead Rd *HAV* PO9 103 G3
Medwall Gn *ITCH* SO19 57 G7
Medway Dr *CHFD* SO53 37 H2
Megana Wy *ROMY* SO51 29 H4
Megan Rd *HEND* SO30 57 G2
Meggeson Av *WEND* SO18 56 D2
Melbourne Pl *SSEA* PO5 18 B5
Melbourne Rd *HEND* SO30 58 B6
Melbourne St *SHAM* SO14 9 K2
Melchet Rd *WEND* SO18 7 L2
Melick Cl *TOTT* SO40 70 A3
Mellor Cl *CHAM* PO6 100 C6 3
Melrose Cl *ENEY* PO4 135 G4 2
Melrose Ct *TOTT* SO40 52 B3
Melrose Gdns *GPORT* PO12 132 C1
Melrose Rd *WSHM* SO15 54 E2
Melville Cl *ROWN* SO16 42 D6
Melville Rd *ENEY* PO4 135 H6
GPORT PO12 132 D1
Mendip Gdns *FAWY* SO45 90 E4 3
Mendip Rd *ROWN* SO16 54 A4
Mendips Rd *FHAM/STUB* PO14 12 B8
Mendips Wk *FHAM/STUB* PO14 12 B8
Mengham Av *HISD* PO11 137 H6
Mengham La *HISD* PO11 137 H5
Mengham Rd *HISD* PO11 137 H5
Menslands La *WVILLE* PO7 62 A3
Menzies Cl *ROWN* SO16 42 A6
Meon Cl *LSOL/BMARY* PO13 115 J5
ROMY SO51 35 H3
Meon Ct *WEND* SO18 57 G4
Meon Crs *CHFD* SO53 38 A4
Meon Rd *ENEY* PO4 19 M5
ROMY SO51 35 H3
Mercer Wy *ROMY* SO51 34 E2 3
ROMY SO51 35 F2 3
Merchants Pl *WINC* SO23 2 F4
Merchistoun Rd *HORN* PO8 64 C6
Mercury Cl *ROWN* SO16 42 A7
Mercury Gdns *HLER* SO31 93 K2
Mercury Pl *WVILLE* PO7 101 K4
Merdon Av *CHFD* SO53 38 A2
Merdon Cl *CHFD* SO53 38 A2
Mere Cft *FHAM* PO15 95 J3 1
Meredith Gdns *TOTT* SO40 52 C6
Meredith Rd *NEND* PO2 118 D4
Meredun Cl *RWIN* SO21 31 J2
Merganser Cl *GPORT* PO12 132 E1
Meriden Rd *SSEA* PO5 18 B5 3
Merlin Cl *BPWT* SO32 48 C3
Merlin Dr *HSEA* PO3 118 E3
Merlin Gdns *FHAM/PORC* PO16 98 E5
HEND SO30 58 A5
Mermaid Rd *FHAM/STUB* PO14 115 G2
Mermaid Wy *SHAM* SO14 9 J5 1
Merrick Wy *CHFD* SO53 37 G2
Merridale Rd *ITCH* SO19 6 D8
Merrieleas Cl *CHFD* SO53 37 K3
Merrieleas Dr *CHFD* SO53 37 K3
Merriemeade Cl *FAWY* SO45 91 F5
Merrivale Cl *FAWY* SO45 91 F3
Merrivale Rd *NEND* PO2 118 D4
Merryfield *FHAM/STUB* PO14 95 H2
Merryfield Av *HAV* PO9 102 E1
Merry Gdns *NBAD* SO52 36 B5
Merryoak Gn *ITCH* SO19 6 F9
Merryoak Rd *ITCH* SO19 10 E1
Mersea Gdns *ITCH* SO19 11 G2
Mersham Gdns *WEND* SO18 6 F4
Merstone Rd
LSOL/BMARY PO13 115 K5
Merthyr Av *CHAM* PO6 101 G5
Merton Av *FHAM/PORC* PO16 117 G1
Merton Crs *FHAM/PORC* PO16 117 G1
Merton Rd *PTSW* SO17 55 J2
SSEA PO5 18 D9
Meryl Rd *ENEY* PO4 135 H4
Meteor Rd *EMRTH* PO10 122 D4
Methuen Rd *ENEY* PO4 19 L8
Methuen St *SHAM* SO14 5 G5
Metuchen Wy *HEND* SO30 74 B1
Mewsey Ct *HAV* PO9 82 E6
Mews La *WINW* SO22 2 B5
The Mews *FAWY* SO45 128 C1 1
HAV PO9 103 F2
ROWN SO16 42 A5
Mey Cl *WVILLE* PO7 82 A6
Meynell Cl *ELGH* SO50 38 C7
Meyrick Rd *HAV* PO9 14 B4
NEND PO2 118 B6
Michael Crook Cl *HAV* PO9 102 D3
Michaels Wy *ELGH* SO50 46 C1
FAWY SO45 91 G2
Michelmersh Cl *ROWN* SO16 41 K6 3
Michigan Wy *TOTT* SO40 52 A4
Midanbury Crs *WEND* SO18 6 E1
Midanbury La *WEND* SO18 6 D4
Middlebridge St *ROMY* SO51 34 D4
Middlebrook *BPWT* SO32 48 D3 2
Middle Brook St *WINC* SO23 2 F4
Middlecroft La *GPORT* PO12 132 C2
Middlefield *SELS* PO20 139 K7
Middle Md *FHAM/STUB* PO14 96 C6
Middle Park Wy *HAV* PO9 102 E2
Middle Rd *WINW* SO22 2 B3
HLER SO31 95 G1
ITCH SO19 11 G4
NBAD SO52 36 B5
Middlesex Rd *ENEY* PO4 19 M7
Middle St *SHAM* SO14 5 G5
SSEA PO5 18 C5
Middleton Cl *FHAM/STUB* PO14 12 C9
WEND SO18 56 D2
Midfield Cl *FHAM/STUB* PO14 97 G7
Midlands Est *HEND* SO30 57 F2
Midway *FAWY* SO45 91 G3 4
Midway Rd *NEND* PO2 118 D2 1
Midways *FHAM/STUB* PO14 114 D6
Milbeck Cl *HORN* PO8 82 B2
The Milburns *ROMY* SO51 28 C2 1
Milbury Crs *WEND* SO18 7 H6
Mildmay St *WINW* SO22 25 G3
Milebush Rd *ENEY* PO4 135 H3
Mile End Rd *PSEA* PO1 134 B1
Milford Cl *HAV* PO9 102 E3 1
Milford Gdns *CHFD* SO53 38 B4
Milford Rd *PSEA* PO1 18 E3
Military Rd *FHAM/PORC* PO16 98 B4
GPORT PO12 132 B4
GPORT PO12 133 F7
HSEA PO3 118 E2
PSEA PO1 18 B1
Milkwood Ct *TOTT* SO40 52 B5 3
Millais Rd *ITCH* SO19 10 D3
Milland Rd *WINC* SO23 3 H8

Millbank St *SHAM* SO14 .... 5 L8
Millbridge Gdns *ITCH* SO19 .... 11 J1
Millbrook Cl *CHFD* SO53 .... 37 J5
Millbrook Dr *HAV* PO9 .... 83 H7
Millbrook Point Rd *WSHM* SO15 .. 54 B6
Millbrook Rd East *WSHM* SO15 .... 54 D7
Millbrook Rd West *WSHM* SO15 .. 53 K5
Mill Cl *HISD* PO11 .... 121 G5
ROWN SO16 .... 41 J6
WVILLE PO7 .... 81 G1
Mill End *EMRTH* PO10 .... 104 E6
Miller Dr *FHAM/PORC* PO16 .... 12 F2
Millers La *WINW* SO22 .... 24 C5
Mill Hl *HEND* SO30 .... 59 F5
Milliken Cl *FAWY* SO45 .... 110 C5
Mill La *BPWT* SO32 .... 59 J1
BROC SO42 .... 106 A5
EMRTH PO10 .... 104 E4
FHAM PO15 .... 96 B5
GPORT PO12 .... 16 B2
HAV PO9 .... 102 D5
HAV PO9 .... 121 F1
LYND SO43 .... 66 B3
PSEA PO1 .... 134 B1
ROMY SO51 .... 34 C3
ROWN SO16 .... 40 D7
WHAM PO17 .... 61 H7
WVILLE PO7 .... 100 D2
Mill Pond Rd *GPORT* PO12 .... 16 A2
The Mill Pond *FAWY* SO45 .... 109 J1
Mill Quay *EMRTH* PO10 .... 104 D7
Mill Rd *EMRTH* PO10 .... 104 E2
FHAM/PORC PO16 .... 13 J8
GPORT PO12 .... 132 D2
TOTT SO40 .... 53 F5
WSHM SO15 .... 54 B5
WVILLE PO7 .... 81 F1
WVILLE PO7 .... 81 J7
Mill Rythe La *HISD* PO11 .... 137 H1
Mills Rd *NEND* PO2 .... 118 C7
Millstream Ri *ROMY* SO51 .... 34 C3
Mill St *FHAM/STUB* PO14 .... 96 B6
Millvina Cl *TOTT* SO40 .... 67 J1
Mill Wy *TOTT* SO40 .... 52 D7
Milne Cl *FAWY* SO45 .... 90 D4
Milner Ct *WSHM* SO15 .... 54 D4
Milner Pl *WINW* SO22 .... 2 B8
Milnthorpe La *WINW* SO22 .... 2 A6
Milton Gv *HLER* SO31 .... 95 G5
Milton Pde *WVILLE* PO7 .... 81 K3
Milton Park Av *ENEY* PO4 .... 135 G4 5
Milton Rd *ELGH* SO50 .... 38 E5 5
ENEY PO4 .... 19 M4
HSEA PO3 .... 19 L1
WSHM SO15 .... 4 D6
WVILLE PO7 .... 81 J4
Milverton Rd *WINW* SO22 .... 2 A3
TOTT SO40 .... 53 F6
Milvil Rd *LSOL/BMARY* PO13 .... 131 F3
Mimosa Dr *ELGH* SO50 .... 46 D1
Mincingfield La *BPWT* SO32 .... 47 J7
Minden Wy *WINW* SO22 .... 25 F3
Minerva Cl *WVILLE* PO7 .... 101 K4 1
Minley Ct *HAV* PO9 .... 103 J1
Minnitt Rd *GPORT* PO12 .... 17 G5
Minstead Cl *WINW* SO22 .... 21 G3 3
Minstead Rd *ENEY* PO4 .... 135 G5
Minster Cl *FHAM* PO15 .... 96 D5
Minster La *WINC* SO23 .... 2 E5
Mintern Cl *ELGH* SO50 .... 39 G5 3
Minters Lepe *WVILLE* PO7 .... 101 K3
Mirror Cl *HLER* SO31 .... 94 E5
Mislingford Rd *BPWT* SO32 .... 61 K1
Missenden Acres *HEND* SO30 .... 58 B4 5
Misslebrook La *NBAD* SO52 .... 36 E6
Mitchell Rd *ELGH* SO50 .... 44 E1
HAV PO9 .... 102 C3
Mitchells Cl *ROMY* SO51 .... 34 E3
Mitchell Wy *ELGH* SO50 .... 44 C4
HSEA PO3 .... 119 G4
Mitre Copse *ELGH* SO50 .... 45 J1
Mizen Wy
LSOL/BMARY PO13 .... 132 A2 4
Moat Cl *FAWY* SO45 .... 109 J4
Moat Dr *GPORT* PO12 .... 132 A5
Moat Hl *WEND* SO18 .... 56 C1
Mole Hl *WVILLE* PO7 .... 102 A1
Molesworth Rd *GPORT* PO12 .... 16 C6 2
Momford Rd *WINW* SO22 .... 24 E5
Monarch Cl *HLER* SO31 .... 95 F4
WVILLE PO7 .... 82 B6 6
Monarch's Wy *HAV* PO9 .... 84 C4
HORN PO8 .... 64 E7
ROMY SO51 .... 30 D5
Monarch Wy *WINW* SO22 .... 25 F2
HEND SO30 .... 57 H2 1
Monastery Rd *WEND* SO18 .... 6 D4
Monckton Rd *GPORT* PO12 .... 132 E7
HSEA PO3 .... 118 E5
Mon Crs *WEND* SO18 .... 7 L5
Moneyfield Av *HSEA* PO3 .... 119 F7
Moneyfield La *HSEA* PO3 .... 119 F7 2
Monks Brook Cl *ELGH* SO50 .... 44 B2
Monk's Hl *EMRTH* PO10 .... 84 D7
Monks Pl *TOTT* SO40 .... 52 C6
Monks Rd *HLER* SO31 .... 72 E7
WINC SO23 .... 2 E2
Monks Wk *FAWY* SO45 .... 91 F6
Monks Wy *ELGH* SO50 .... 44 C2
FHAM/STUB PO14 .... 114 C7
WEND SO18 .... 44 B7
Monks Wood Cl *ELGH* SO50 .... 43 J5
Monkton La *TOTT* SO40 .... 52 B6
Monkwood Cl *HAV* PO9 .... 102 E1 2
Monmouth Cl *CHFD* SO53 .... 37 J4
Monmouth Rd *NEND* PO2 .... 118 C5
Monmouth Sq *WINW* SO22 .... 24 E2 1
Monnow Gdns *WEND* SO18 .... 56 E3
Monroe Cl *GPORT* PO12 .... 132 B5
Montague Av *ITCH* SO19 .... 73 G2
Montague Cl *ITCH* SO19 .... 73 G2 2
Montague Rd *NEND* PO2 .... 118 D6
Monterey Dr *HAV* PO9 .... 103 H2
HLER SO31 .... 95 F4
Montfort Cl *ROMY* SO51 .... 35 H3
Montfort Hts *ROMY* SO51 .... 35 H3 1
Montfort Rd *ROMY* SO51 .... 35 H4
Montgomerie Rd *PSEA* PO5 .... 18 E5
Montgomery Av *TOTT* SO40 .... 52 C4
Montgomery Rd *HAV* PO9 .... 15 G4
LSOL/BMARY PO13 .... 115 K3
WEND SO18 .... 7 G3
Montgomery Wk *WVILLE* PO7 .... 101 H1
Montgomery Wy *CHFD* SO53 .... 37 J7
Montpelier Cl *HLER* SO31 .... 95 H3 3
Montrose Av *FHAM/PORC* PO16 .. 99 H5
Montrose Cl *HEND* SO30 .... 58 D6 1
Montserrat Rd
LSOL/BMARY PO13 .... 131 F2
Monument La *RCCH* PO18 .... 85 J6
WHAM PO17 .... 98 E2
Moody Rd *FHAM/STUB* PO14 .... 114 C6
Moonhills La *BROC* SO42 .... 108 C5
Moonscross Av *TOTT* SO40 .... 68 E1
Moore Crs *HLER* SO31 .... 72 E7
Moore Gdns *GPORT* PO12 .... 132 C4
Moorgreen Rd *HAV* PO9 .... 103 H1
HEND SO30 .... 57 H3
Moorhill Gdns *WEND* SO18 .... 57 H5
Moorhill Rd *HEND* SO30 .... 57 G4
The Moorings
FHAM/PORC PO16 .... 97 J7 1
Moorings Wy *ENEY* PO4 .... 135 H2
Moorland Cl *FAWY* SO45 .... 90 E3 3
HLER SO31 .... 95 F2
Moorland Rd *PSEA* PO1 .... 19 H2
Moorlands Crs *WEND* SO18 .... 7 H2
Moorlands Rd *BPWT* SO32 .... 49 H5
Moor Pk *HORN* PO8 .... 82 C4
Moors Cl *RWIN* SO21 .... 39 J1
Moorside Rd *WINC* SO23 .... 22 B5
Moortown Av *CHAM* PO6 .... 101 H5
Mopley *FAWY* SO45 .... 128 C1
Mopley Cl *FAWY* SO45 .... 128 C1
Moraunt Cl *GPORT* PO12 .... 116 E7 1
Moraunt Dr *FHAM/PORC* PO16 .. 116 E1
Mordaunt Rd *SHAM* SO14 .... 5 G5
Moreland Rd *GPORT* PO12 .... 16 A4
Morelands Rd *WVILLE* PO7 .... 101 K2
Morestead Rd *RWIN* SO21 .... 26 A3
RWIN SO21 .... 26 D6
Morgan Rd *ENEY* PO4 .... 135 H4
HEND SO30 .... 58 B7 1
Morgans Dr *FHAM/STUB* PO14 .. 114 D2
Morland Rd *WSHM* SO15 .... 54 D3
Morley Cl *ITCH* SO19 .... 6 E7
Morley Crs *HORN* PO8 .... 82 B2
Morley Dr *BPWT* SO32 .... 48 D3
Morley Rd *ENEY* PO4 .... 19 M9
Morningside Av
FHAM/PORC PO16 .... 99 G5
Mornington Dr *WINW* SO22 .... 21 F5
Morpeth Av *TOTT* SO40 .... 52 E4
Morris Cl *FAWY* SO45 .... 90 E2
LSOL/BMARY PO13 .... 115 K3
Morris Rd *WSHM* SO15 .... 4 D8
Morshead Crs
FHAM/PORC PO16 .... 12 F2
Mortimer Cl *HLER* SO31 .... 72 E7
TOTT SO40 .... 52 C3
WINC SO23 .... 22 A7
Mortimer Rd *CHAM* PO6 .... 100 B5
HEND SO30 .... 59 F6
ITCH SO19 .... 10 C2
Mortimers Dr *ELGH* SO50 .... 46 C1 2
Mortimers La *ELGH* SO50 .... 46 C1
Mortimer Wy *NBAD* SO52 .... 36 A7
Mortimore Rd *GPORT* PO12 .... 132 C2
Mosalc Cl *ITCH* SO19 .... 73 J1 1
Mosdell Rd *EMRTH* PO10 .... 105 G6
Moss Dr *TOTT* SO40 .... 70 A3
Mossleigh Av *ROWN* SO16 .... 42 A6
Moss Rd *WINC* SO23 .... 3 H4
Mottisfont Cl *WSHM* SO15 .... 54 B6 1
Mottisfont Rd *ELGH* SO50 .... 38 D6
Mound Cl *GPORT* PO12 .... 132 D5
Mountain Ash Cl *WEND* SO18 .... 7 M5
Mountbatten Av *ROMY* SO51 .... 34 E3
Mountbatten Cl
LSOL/BMARY PO13 .... 115 K3 2
Mountbatten Ct *WINW* SO22 .... 21 H4
Mountbatten Dr *WVILLE* PO7 .... 81 H7
Mountbatten Rd *ELGH* SO50 .... 38 D5 2
TOTT SO40 .... 52 C4
Mountbatten Sq *ENEY* PO4 .... 135 G6 3
Mount Cl *WINW* SO22 .... 21 H4
Mount Dr *CHFD* SO53 .... 38 B6
FHAM PO15 .... 96 C6
Mountfield *FAWY* SO45 .... 91 F2
Mount House Cl *FAWY* SO45 .... 91 H1 1
Mount Pleasant *WINC* SO23 .... 22 A1
Mount Pleasant Rd
GPORT PO12 .... 16 A9
SHAM SO14 .... 5 J5
The Mount
LSOL/BMARY PO13 .... 116 B6 4
ROWN SO16 .... 43 G7 1
ROWN SO16 .... 54 B3 1
Mount Vw *ELGH* SO50 .... 38 E6
Mountview Av
FHAM/PORC PO16 .... 99 H5
Mountwood Rd *EMRTH* PO10 .... 105 G5
Mousehole La *FAWY* SO45 .... 91 H3
WEND SO18 .... 6 F3
Mousehole Rd *CHAM* PO6 .... 99 J5
Mowbray Rd *ITCH* SO19 .... 11 K1
Muccleshell Cl *HAV* PO9 .... 103 H2 2
Mulberry Av *CHAM* PO6 .... 101 F7
FHAM/STUB PO14 .... 114 D6
Mulberry Cl *GPORT* PO12 .... 16 A6
Mulberry La *CHAM* PO6 .... 101 F7
Mulberry Rd *TOTT* SO40 .... 70 A4
Mulberry Wk *WSHM* SO15 .... 54 D4
Mullen Cl *ITCH* SO19 .... 10 C2
Mullin's La *FAWY* SO45 .... 91 G4
Mullion Cl *CHAM* PO6 .... 100 A7
Mumby Rd *GPORT* PO12 .... 16 F4
Mundays Rw *HORN* PO8 .... 64 D3 5
Munro Crs *WSHM* SO15 .... 54 A5
Munster Rd *NEND* PO2 .... 118 C5
Murefield Rd *PSEA* PO1 .... 18 F3 1
Muriel Rd *WVILLE* PO7 .... 81 K5
Murray Cl *FHAM* PO15 .... 12 D4
ITCH SO19 .... 57 H6
Murray Rd *HORN* PO8 .... 64 C6
Murray's La *PSEA* PO1 .... 17 K1
Muscliffe Ct *HAV* PO9 .... 103 J1 10
Museum Rd *PSEA* PO1 .... 18 A6
Mussett Cl *TOTT* SO40 .... 52 D5
Mustang Av *FHAM* PO15 .... 75 G6
Myers Cl *BPWT* SO32 .... 49 J6
My Lords La *HISD* PO11 .... 137 J5
Myrtle Av *FHAM/PORC* PO16 .... 99 G7
TOTT SO40 .... 52 C6
Myrtle Cl *LSOL/BMARY* PO13 .... 115 J4 3
Myrtle Gv *HSEA* PO3 .... 135 G2
Myrtle Rd *ROWN* SO16 .... 42 C7
Myvern Cl *FAWY* SO45 .... 109 K4

N

Nailsworth Rd *CHAM* PO6 .... 100 A5
Naish Ct *HAV* PO9 .... 82 D6
Naish Dr *GPORT* PO12 .... 116 D6
Napier Crs *FHAM* PO15 .... 96 D5
Napier Rd *HORN* PO8 .... 64 D6
ITCH SO19 .... 57 H7
SSEA PO5 .... 18 F9
Narrow La *ROMY* SO51 .... 34 D3 3
Narvik Rd *NEND* PO2 .... 110 C3
Nash Cl *FAWY* SO45 .... 90 E4
Nashe Cl *FHAM* PO15 .... 12 A2
Nashe Wy *FHAM* PO15 .... 96 D4
Nash Rd *FAWY* SO45 .... 90 E5
Nasmith Cl *LSOL/BMARY* PO13 .. 132 A4
Navigator's Wy *HEND* SO30 .... 58 B4
Navy Rd *PSEA* PO1 .... 17 L1
Neath Wy *CHFD* SO53 .... 37 H5
Neelands Gv *CHAM* PO6 .... 99 H6
Neilson Cl *CHFD* SO53 .... 37 K3
Nelson Av *FHAM/PORC* PO16 .... 98 E7
NEND PO2 .... 118 C5
Nelson Cl *FAWY* SO45 .... 109 K4
ROMY SO51 .... 34 E2 4
ROMY SO51 .... 35 F2 4
Nelson Ct *FHAM/STUB* PO14 .... 115 G1
Nelson Crs *HORN* PO8 .... 64 D5 2
Nelson La *WHAM* PO17 .... 99 F3
Nelson Rd *ELGH* SO50 .... 39 G6
GPORT PO12 .... 16 B6 1
PSEA PO1 .... 134 C1
SSEA PO5 .... 18 D8
WINC SO23 .... 3 J6
WSHM SO15 .... 54 D6
Nelsons Gdns *HEND* SO30 .... 58 B1
Nepean Cl *GPORT* PO12 .... 132 E7
Neptune Rd *FHAM* PO15 .... 96 D4
FHAM/STUB PO14 .... 115 G2
Neptune Wy *SHAM* SO14 .... 9 J5
Nerissa Cl *WVILLE* PO7 .... 82 C5
Nerquis Cl *ROMY* SO51 .... 35 G2 4
Nesbitt Cl *LSOL/BMARY* PO13 .. 115 J4 5
Nessus St *NEND* PO2 .... 118 C7
Netherfield Cl *HAV* PO9 .... 15 H6
Nether Hill La *BPWT* SO32 .... 59 G2
Netherton Rd *GPORT* PO12 .... 132 C1
Netley Cl *CHFD* SO53 .... 37 J7 2
Netley Firs Rd *ITCH* SO19 .... 73 J1
Netley Hill Est *ITCH* SO19 .... 73 J1
Netley Lodge Cl *HLER* SO31 .... 93 F1
Netley Rd *FHAM/STUB* PO14 .... 95 H5
SSEA PO5 .... 134 B6 3
Netley Ter *SSEA* PO5 .... 134 B6 4
Nettlecombe Av *ENEY* PO4 .... 134 D7 3
Nettlestone *HLER* SO31 .... 73 F6 3
Nettlestone Rd *ENEY* PO4 .... 135 F6 1
Neva Rd *WEND* SO18 .... 6 E2
Neville Av *FHAM/PORC* PO16 .... 117 G1
Neville Dr *ROMY* SO51 .... 34 E2 3
Neville Gdns *EMRTH* PO10 .... 104 B3
Neville Rd *HSEA* PO3 .... 135 F1
Neville Shute Rd *HSEA* PO3 .... 119 F4
Newbarn La *RCCH* PO18 .... 85 J5
Newbarn Rd *HAV* PO9 .... 102 D3
Newbolt Cl *HORN* PO8 .... 81 K2
Newbolt Rd *CHAM* PO6 .... 99 J5
Newbridge *HLER* SO31 .... 73 F7 3
Newbridge Rd *TOTT* SO40 .... 50 C1
New Brighton Rd
EMRTH PO10 .... 104 C4
Newbroke Rd
LSOL/BMARY PO13 .... 116 B7 2
Newburgh St *WINC* SO23 .... 2 D3 1
Newbury Cl *ELGH* SO50 .... 46 A1 2
Newbury Pl *HLER* SO31 .... 94 E4
Newbury Rd *WSHM* SO15 .... 54 D3 2
New Cliffe Gdns *HEND* SO30 .... 58 A7 1
Newcombe Rd *WSHM* SO15 .... 4 D6
Newcomen Rd *NEND* PO2 .... 118 B5
Newcome Rd *PSEA* PO1 .... 19 H2
New Cut *HISD* PO11 .... 121 G4
New Down La *WVILLE* PO7 .... 101 F4
Newgate La *FHAM/STUB* PO14 .. 115 H1
New Inn La *BROC* SO42 .... 125 H3
TOTT SO40 .... 50 E6
New Inn Rd *TOTT* SO40 .... 50 E6
Newland Av *GPORT* PO12 .... 132 D4
Newlands Av *WSHM* SO15 .... 54 D5
Newlands Cl *FAWY* SO45 .... 110 B7
NBAD SO52 .... 37 F5
Newlands Copse *FAWY* SO45 .... 110 C6
Newlands La *WVILLE* PO7 .... 80 E3
Newlands Rd *FAWY* SO45 .... 110 B5
WVILLE PO7 .... 101 J1
New La *HAV* PO9 .... 15 G3
Newlease Rd *WVILLE* PO7 .... 102 A1
Newlyn Wk *ROMY* SO51 .... 35 F1
Newlyn Wy *CHAM* PO6 .... 99 K7
Newmans Hl *WHAM* PO17 .... 61 K4
Newman St *ROWN* SO16 .... 54 C4 3
Newmarket Cl *ELGH* SO50 .... 46 C4 4
Newmer Ct *HAV* PO9 .... 82 D7
Newney Cl *NEND* PO2 .... 118 E3 5
Newnham Ct *HAV* PO9 .... 103 J1 11
Newport Cl *CHFD* SO53 .... 37 H6 3
Newport La *ROMY* SO51 .... 29 G3
Newport Rd *GPORT* PO12 .... 132 C3
New Rd *BPWT* SO32 .... 48 E1
BPWT SO32 .... 49 G7
ELGH SO50 .... 46 A1
EMRTH PO10 .... 104 E3
EMRTH PO10 .... 105 H6
FAWY SO45 .... 109 J1
FAWY SO45 .... 110 B6
FHAM/PORC PO16 .... 13 H5
WINW SO22 .... 20 E1
HAV PO9 .... 14 D2
HLER SO31 .... 72 E7
HLER SO31 .... 74 E5
HLER SO31 .... 94 E6
HORN PO8 .... 63 K6
NEND PO2 .... 134 D1
ROMY SO51 .... 28 C2
ROMY SO51 .... 35 F2
RWIN SO21 .... 39 J1
SHAM SO14 .... 5 G9
TOTT SO40 .... 68 B3
New Rd East *NEND* PO2 .... 118 E7
Newton Cl *FHAM/STUB* PO14 .... 114 D3
Newton La *ROMY* SO51 .... 34 D3
Newton Pl *LSOL/BMARY* PO13 .. 131 F1
Newton Rd *RWIN* SO21 .... 33 K2
WEND SO18 .... 56 B3
New Town *FHAM/PORC* PO16 .... 99 G6
Newtown La *HISD* PO11 .... 137 F4 4
Newtown Rd *ELGH* SO50 .... 38 D6
HLER SO31 .... 94 B6
ITCH SO19 .... 11 H6
Nicholas Crs *FHAM* PO15 .... 12 E4
Nicholas Rd *FAWY* SO45 .... 128 B1
Nicholl Pl *LSOL/BMARY* PO13 .. 115 K5 1
Nichol Rd *CHFD* SO53 .... 38 A1
Nicholson Wk *ROWN* SO16 .... 41 J5
Nicholson Wy *HAV* PO9 .... 14 D1
Nichols Rd *SHAM* SO14 .... 5 J8
Nickel Cl *WINC* SO23 .... 3 H3
Nickel St *SSEA* PO5 .... 18 B7 2
Nickleby Gdns *TOTT* SO40 .... 52 A5 1
Nickson Cl *CHFD* SO53 .... 37 J2
Nightingale Av *ELGH* SO50 .... 44 A1
Nightingale Cl *WINW* SO22 .... 24 E2
GPORT PO12 .... 132 C2 3
HAV PO9 .... 83 H4
ROMY SO51 .... 35 G3 4
Nightingale Crs *BPWT* SO32 .... 61 G4
Nightingale Dr *TOTT* SO40 .... 52 B4
Nightingale Gv *WSHM* SO15 .... 54 D5
Nightingale La *RCCH* PO18 .... 105 K3
Nightingale Pk *HAV* PO9 .... 15 J5
Nightingale Rd *HLER* SO31 .... 73 J5
SSEA PO5 .... 18 B9
Nightingale Wk *HLER* SO31 .... 93 F2
Nightjar Cl *HORN* PO8 .... 64 B6
Nile Rd *PTSW* SO17 .... 55 H2
Nile St *EMRTH* PO10 .... 104 C6
Nimrod Dr *LSOL/BMARY* PO13 .... 132 A2
Nine Elms La *WHAM* PO17 .... 98 B2
Ninian Cl *ELGH* SO50 .... 46 B2
Ninian Park Rd *HSEA* PO3 .... 119 F5
Niton Cl *LSOL/BMARY* PO13 .... 115 K5 3
Noads Cl *FAWY* SO45 .... 91 G4 3
Noads Wy *FAWY* SO45 .... 91 F5
Nobbs La *PSEA* PO1 .... 17 M6 2
Nobes Av *LSOL/BMARY* PO13 .... 115 K4
Nobes Cl *LSOL/BMARY* PO13 .... 116 A5
Noble Rd *HEND* SO30 .... 58 C6
Nob's Crook *RWIN* SO21 .... 39 K3
Nogarth Cl *ROMY* SO51 .... 35 G1 2
Nomad Cl *WEND* SO18 .... 7 J1
The Nook *ELGH* SO50 .... 38 E5
LSOL/BMARY PO13 .... 116 B6
Norbury Cl *CHFD* SO53 .... 37 J3
Norbury Gdns *HLER* SO31 .... 93 H4
Norcliffe Rd *PTSW* SO17 .... 5 G2
Nordik Gdns *HEND* SO30 .... 58 B7
Nore Crs *EMRTH* PO10 .... 104 A5
Nore Farm Av *EMRTH* PO10 .... 104 A5
Norfolk Rd *GPORT* PO12 .... 132 C1
WSHM SO15 .... 4 A3
Norfolk St *SSEA* PO5 .... 18 C7
Norgett Wy *FHAM/PORC* PO16 .. 116 E1
Norham Av *ROWN* SO16 .... 54 D2
Norham Cl *ROWN* SO16 .... 54 D2
Norland Rd *ENEY* PO4 .... 19 G7 2
Norlands Dr *RWIN* SO21 .... 33 F5
Norley Cl *HAV* PO9 .... 103 F1
Norleywood Rd *LYMN* SO41 .... 124 C7
Norman Cl *FHAM/PORC* PO16 .... 117 G1
Normandy Cl *ROWN* SO16 .... 41 J5
Normandy Gdns
GPORT PO12 .... 132 C4 4
Normandy Rd *NEND* PO2 .... 118 C3
Normandy Wy *TOTT* SO40 .... 70 A2
Norman Gdns *HEND* SO30 .... 57 K7 1
Norman Rd *ENEY* PO4 .... 19 G8
FAWY SO45 .... 110 C7
GPORT PO12 .... 132 D3
HISD PO11 .... 137 J6
WINC SO23 .... 2 C8
Norman Wy *HAV* PO9 .... 102 D4
Norris Cl *ROMY* SO51 .... 29 H7 4
Norris Gdns *HAV* PO9 .... 15 H6
Norris Hl *WEND* SO18 .... 6 D1
Norset Rd *FHAM* PO15 .... 96 D4
Northam Br *WSHM* SO15 .... 5 M6
Northam Ms *PSEA* PO1 .... 18 E3 2
Northampton La *FAWY* SO45 .... 110 B7
Northam Rd *SHAM* SO14 .... 5 K8
Northam St *PSEA* PO1 .... 18 F3 3
Northarbour Rd *CHAM* PO6 .... 100 C7
North Av *NEND* PO2 .... 118 D2
North Battery Rd *NEND* PO2 .... 118 A5
North Bay *EMRTH* PO10 .... 122 D4
Northbourne Cl *FAWY* SO45 .... 91 H5 7
Northbrook Av *WINC* SO23 .... 3 H5
Northbrook Cl *PSEA* PO1 .... 134 C1 3
WINC SO23 .... 3 J5
Northbrook Rd *SHAM* SO14 .... 5 J8
North Cl *GPORT* PO12 .... 132 C4
HAV PO9 .... 15 G6
ROMY SO51 .... 35 H1
Northcote Av *NEND* PO2 .... 118 E7 1
Northcote Rd *ENEY* PO4 .... 19 H8 1
PTSW SO17 .... 55 K2
North Crs *HISD* PO11 .... 137 J5
Northcroft Rd *GPORT* PO12 .... 132 C2
North Cross St *GPORT* PO12 .... 16 F5
Northdene Rd *CHFD* SO53 .... 37 K5
North Dr *WINW* SO22 .... 20 E2
North East Cl *ITCH* SO19 .... 7 K9
North East Rd *ITCH* SO19 .... 11 H2
North End Av *NEND* PO2 .... 118 C5
North End Cl *CHFD* SO53 .... 37 K6
North End Gv *NEND* PO2 .... 118 C5
Northern Access Rd
FAWY SO45 .... 111 G5
Northern Anchorage *ITCH* SO19 .... 9 M3
Northern Pde *NEND* PO2 .... 118 C4
Northern Rd *CHAM* PO6 .... 118 E1
Northerwood Av *LYND* SO43 .... 86 B1
Northerwood Cl *NBAD* SO52 .... 36 A6 2
Northfield Av *FHAM/STUB* PO14 .. 97 G7
Northfield Cl *BPWT* SO32 .... 48 B2
HORN PO8 .... 64 D2
Northfield Rd *WEND* SO18 .... 56 C1
Northfields Farm La
WHAM PO17 .... 61 H7
North Front *SHAM* SO14 .... 5 H9
North Hl *CHAM* PO6 .... 100 A4
FHAM/PORC PO16 .... 13 J1
North Hill Cl *WINW* SO22 .... 21 J5
Northlands Cl *TOTT* SO40 .... 52 C4
Northlands Dr *WINC* SO23 .... 21 K5
Northlands Gdns *WSHM* SO15 .... 4 C4
Northlands Rd *ELGH* SO50 .... 38 D7 2
ROMY SO51 .... 35 H4
TOTT SO40 .... 52 C4
WSHM SO15 .... 4 D5
North La *BROC* SO42 .... 107 K2
North Millers Dl *CHFD* SO53 .... 37 H1
Northmore Cl *HLER* SO31 .... 95 G1 2
Northmore Rd *HLER* SO31 .... 95 G1
Northney La *HISD* PO11 .... 121 K3
Northney Rd *HISD* PO11 .... 121 J3
Northolt Gdns *ROWN* SO16 .... 42 B7
Northover Rd *HSEA* PO3 .... 119 G7
North Rd *FAWY* SO45 .... 90 E4
HORN PO8 .... 64 D2
PTSW SO17 .... 5 M1
WVILLE PO7 .... 99 K4
North Rd East *WHAM* PO17 .... 79 K7
North Rd West *WHAM* PO17 .... 79 J7
North Shore Rd *HISD* PO11 .... 136 E3
North St *EMRTH* PO10 .... 104 C5
EMRTH PO10 .... 104 E2
HAV PO9 .... 14 A3
HAV PO9 .... 14 F4
PSEA PO1 .... 17 M3
PSEA PO1 .... 18 E1
North Town *RWIN* SO21 .... 33 K2
North Trestle Rd *FAWY* SO45 .... 110 E1
Northumberland Rd
SHAM SO14 .... 5 K6 1
SSEA PO5 .... 19 G4 3
North Wallington
FHAM/PORC PO16 .... 13 M3
North Walls *WINC* SO23 .... 2 F3
Northway *FHAM* PO15 .... 95 K3
North Wy *HAV* PO9 .... 14 D4
Northways *FHAM/STUB* PO14 .... 114 E5
Northwood Cl *ROWN* SO16 .... 43 H5 1
Northwood La *HISD* PO11 .... 121 H6
Northwood Rd *NEND* PO2 .... 118 D3
Norton Cl *ITCH* SO19 .... 10 C3
WHAM PO17 .... 79 J7
WVILLE PO7 .... 81 J6
Norton Dr *FHAM/PORC* PO16 .... 13 H3
Norton Rd *WHAM* PO17 .... 79 J7
Norton Welch Cl *NBAD* SO52 .... 36 C6
Norway Rd *HSEA* PO3 .... 118 E3
Norwich Cl *HLER* SO31 .... 94 D2
Norwich Pl *LSOL/BMARY* PO13 .. 131 F1
Norwich Rd *CHAM* PO6 .... 100 C5
WEND SO18 .... 56 C2
Nottingham Pl
LSOL/BMARY PO13 .... 131 F1 2
Novello Gdns *WVILLE* PO7 .... 101 K1
Noyce Dr *ELGH* SO50 .... 46 C2
Nuns Rd *WINC* SO23 .... 2 F1
Nuns Wk *WINC* SO23 .... 2 F1
WINC SO23 .... 22 A5
Nursery Cl *EMRTH* PO10 .... 104 C3
LSOL/BMARY PO13 .... 115 J4
Nursery Gdns *CHFD* SO53 .... 37 K7
WINW SO22 .... 21 G7
HORN PO8 .... 64 B7
ITCH SO19 .... 7 K6
ROMY SO51 .... 35 F3 2
Nursery Gv *HEND* SO30 .... 58 B7
Nursery La *FHAM/STUB* PO14 .... 114 D6
Nursery Rd *HAV* PO9 .... 102 D4
WEND SO18 .... 56 A3
Nursling Crs *HAV* PO9 .... 103 H1
Nursling St *ROWN* SO16 .... 41 H6
Nutash *FHAM* PO15 .... 95 H2
Nutbeem Rd *ELGH* SO50 .... 44 D1
Nutbourne Rd *CHAM* PO6 .... 101 J7
HISD PO11 .... 138 B7
Nutburn Rd *NBAD* SO52 .... 36 C5
Nutfield Ct *ROWN* SO16 .... 53 K1
Nutfield Pl *PSEA* PO1 .... 18 F1
Nutfield Rd *ROWN* SO16 .... 41 J5
Nuthatch Cl *HAV* PO9 .... 83 J4
Nutley Rd *HAV* PO9 .... 102 E1
Nutsey Av *TOTT* SO40 .... 52 C2
Nutsey La *TOTT* SO40 .... 52 D2
Nutshalling Av *ROWN* SO16 .... 41 K6
Nutshalling Cl *TOTT* SO40 .... 52 B3
Nutwick Rd *HAV* PO9 .... 15 K1
HAV PO9 .... 103 J2
Nutwood Wy *TOTT* SO40 .... 52 D2
Nyewood Av *FHAM/PORC* PO16 .. 99 G5
Nyria Wy *GPORT* PO12 .... 16 E6

O

Oakapple Gdns *CHAM* PO6 .... 101 K6 4
Oakbank Rd *ELGH* SO50 .... 39 F7
ITCH SO19 .... 10 A4
Oak Cl *FAWY* SO45 .... 91 F5
HORN PO8 .... 81 K3
LYND SO43 .... 86 C2 4
WSHM SO15 .... 53 H5
Oak Coppice Cl *ELGH* SO50 .... 45 K1
Oakcroft La *FHAM/STUB* PO14 .. 114 D2
Oakdene *LSOL/BMARY* PO13 .... 116 A6
TOTT SO40 .... 52 A5
Oakdown Rd
FHAM/STUB PO14 .... 114 E4
Oak Dr *ELGH* SO50 .... 46 B1
Oakenbrow *FAWY* SO45 .... 90 E4
The Oakes *FHAM/STUB* PO14 .... 114 C3
Oakfield Ct *HAV* PO9 .... 103 J1 12
Oakfield Rd *TOTT* SO40 .... 50 E5
TOTT SO40 .... 52 E5
Oakfields *ELGH* SO50 .... 38 D3

Oak Green Wy *WEND* SO18 7 G2
Oakgrove Rd *ELGH* SO50 45 H1
Oakhill *HLER* SO31 74 A4
Oakhill Cl *CHFD* SO53 38 B5
HLER SO31 74 A4
Oakhurst Cl *HLER* SO31 73 F7 4
Oakhurst Dr *WVILLE* PO7 82 B5
Oakhurst Gdns *CHAM* PO6 101 G4
Oakhurst Rd *PTSW* SO17 55 H1 1
Oakhurst Wy *HLER* SO31 73 F7
Oakland Dr *TOTT* SO40 70 A4
Oaklands Av *TOTT* SO40 52 E5
Oaklands Cl *WINW* SO22 24 E2
Oaklands Gdns
FHAM/STUB PO14 95 H5
Oaklands Gv *HORN* PO8 81 K2
Oaklands Rd *HAV* PO9 15 G4
The Oaklands *CHFD* SO53 37 K7 3
Oaklands Wy *FAWY* SO45 90 D4
FHAM/STUB PO14 95 H5
ROWN SO16 43 G7
Oakleigh Crs *TOTT* SO40 52 D6
Oakleigh Gdns *ROMY* SO51 35 F3 3
Oakley Cl *FAWY* SO45 109 K3
Oakley Rd *HAV* PO9 102 E1
ROWN SO16 54 A4
Oakmeadow Cl *EMRTH* PO10 104 D3
Oakmont Dr *WVILLE* PO7 82 A3
Oakmount Av *CHFD* SO53 38 A6
PTSW SO17 55 H3
TOTT SO40 52 E4
Oakmount Rd *CHFD* SO53 38 A6
Oak Park Dr *HAV* PO9 15 G1
Oakridge Rd *WSHM* SO15 53 J4
Oak Rd *BPWT* SO32 48 E3
FAWY SO45 91 F5
FHAM PO15 12 A4
HLER SO31 73 H5
ITCH SO19 10 B5
Oaks Coppice *HORN* PO8 64 B6
Oakshott Dr *HAV* PO9 103 H1
The Oaks *HLER* SO31 73 J5
ITCH SO19 6 E8
Oak St *GPORT* PO12 16 D5
Oakthorn Cl
LSOL/BMARY PO13 131 K2
Oak Tree Cl *RWIN* SO21 39 J2
Oak Tree Dr *EMRTH* PO10 104 B2
Oak Tree Gdns *HEND* SO30 58 A6 3
Oak Tree Rd *WEND* SO18 56 A3
Oak Tree Wy *ELGH* SO50 38 D5
Oak V *HEND* SO30 56 E1
Oakwood Av *HAV* PO9 102 C3
RWIN SO21 33 F6
Oakwood Cl *HLER* SO31 94 C6
ROMY SO51 35 H1
RWIN SO21 33 F5
Oakwood Ct *HEND* SO30 57 H2 2
Oakwood Dr *ROWN* SO16 42 C6
Oakwood Rd *CHFD* SO53 38 A2
HISD PO11 137 G5
NEND PO2 118 D3
Oakwood Wy *HLER* SO31 93 K3 1
Oatfield Gdns *TOTT* SO40 52 B3
Oatlands *ROMY* SO51 34 E2 6
Oatlands Cl *BPWT* SO32 58 E3
Oatlands Rd *BPWT* SO32 58 E3
Obelisk Rd *ITCH* SO19 10 B5
Oberon Cl *WVILLE* PO7 82 B5
Occupation La
FHAM/STUB PO14 95 K7
Ocean Cl *FHAM* PO15 12 B3
Ocean Rd *FHAM/STUB* PO14 115 G2
SHAM SO14 9 H8
Ocean Wy *SHAM* SO14 9 J6
Ockendon Cl *SSEA* PO5 18 D6 3
Ocknell Gv *FAWY* SO45 90 D3
O'connell Rd *ELGH* SO50 44 B1
Octavia Gdns *CHFD* SO53 38 C3
Octavia Hl *WINW* SO22 25 G2
Octavia Rd *WEND* SO18 44 B7
Octavius Ct *WVILLE* PO7 82 C4
Odell Cl *FHAM/PORC* PO16 12 E1
Odiham Cl *ROWN* SO16 42 A7
Oglander Rd *WINC* SO23 21 K5
Ogle Rd *SHAM* SO14 8 F1
Okement Cl *WEND* SO18 56 E2
Olave Cl *LSOL/BMARY* PO13 131 F2 1
Old Agwi Rd *FAWY* SO45 111 F2
Oldbarn Cl *TOTT* SO40 52 B2
Old Barn Crs *WVILLE* PO7 62 B2
Old Bridge House Rd
HLER SO31 74 A5
Old Bridge Rd *ENEY* PO4 134 D6
Oldbury Ct *ROWN* SO16 53 J2
Oldbury Wy *FHAM/STUB* PO14 96 D6
Old Canal *ENEY* PO4 135 G4 4
Old Commercial Rd
PSEA PO1 134 B1 3
Old Common *HLER* SO31 95 F2
Old Common Gdns *HLER* SO31 95 F3
Old Copse Rd *HAV* PO9 14 F2
Old Cracknore Cl *TOTT* SO40 70 A3
Oldenburg *HLER* SO31 75 G5
Old Farm Dr *WEND* SO18 56 C2
Old Farm La *EMRTH* PO10 104 E3
FHAM/STUB PO14 114 D6
Old Farm Wy *CHAM* PO6 101 K7
Old Garden Cl
FHAM/STUB PO14 95 H4
Old Gdns *WINW* SO22 21 J5
Oldgate Gdns *NEND* PO2 118 E3 6
Old Gosport Rd
FHAM/PORC PO16 13 K8
Old Hillside Rd *WINW* SO22 21 F6
Old Ivy La *WEND* SO18 56 E2
Old Kennels Cl *WINW* SO22 24 D5
Old Kennels La *RWIN* SO21 24 B7
Old Lyndhurst Rd *TOTT* SO40 50 C4
Old Magazine Cl *TOTT* SO40 70 A3
Old Manor Wy *CHAM* PO6 101 G7
Old Mill La *HORN* PO8 63 G4
Old Mill Wy *ROWN* SO16 54 B3
Old Parsonage Ct *RWIN* SO21 33 F6
Old Priory Cl *HLER* SO31 93 K4
Old Rectory Cl *EMRTH* PO10 104 E3 2
Old Rectory Gdns *WINC* SO23 22 C1 1
Old Rectory La *RWIN* SO21 33 K2
Old Rectory Rd *CHAM* PO6 101 K6
Old Redbridge Rd *WSHM* SO15 53 H4
Old Reservoir Rd *CHAM* PO6 101 J7
Old River *WVILLE* PO7 80 E2
Old Rd *GPORT* PO12 16 D7
ROMY SO51 35 F2
SHAM SO14 9 J5
The Old Rd *CHAM* PO6 118 E1
Old Romsey Rd *TOTT* SO40 50 B4
Old School Cl *FAWY* SO45 109 J1
HLER SO31 73 G6 1
Old School Dr *HISD* PO11 137 J6
Old School Gdns *HEND* SO30 57 H2
Old Shamblehurst La
HEND SO30 58 B2
Old Star *PSEA* PO1 17 L3
Old Station Ap *WINC* SO23 3 H5
Old St *FHAM/STUB* PO14 114 C4
Old Timbers *HISD* PO11 137 G5
Old Tpk *FHAM/PORC* PO16 13 J2
The Old Well Cl *ITCH* SO19 11 L4
Old Wymering La *CHAM* PO6 100 D6
Oleander Cl *HLER* SO31 95 F1
Olinda St *PSEA* PO1 19 H2
Olive Crs *FHAM/PORC* PO16 117 G1
Olive Rd *ROWN* SO16 42 B7
Oliver Rd *ENEY* PO4 19 L8
WEND SO18 56 A1
Oliver's Battery Crs *WINW* SO22 24 E4
Oliver's Battery Gdns
WINW SO22 24 E5
Oliver's Battery Rd North
WINW SO22 24 E3
Oliver's Battery Rd South
WINW SO22 24 E5
Olivers Cl *TOTT* SO40 52 A5
Olivia Cl *WVILLE* PO7 82 B4
Olympic Wy *ELGH* SO50 39 K7 1
Omdurman Rd *PTSW* SO17 55 H2
Omega St *SSEA* PO5 18 E4
Onibury Cl *WEND* SO18 56 D3
Onibury Rd *WEND* SO18 56 D3
Onslow Rd *SHAM* SO14 5 H6
SSEA PO5 134 C7 6
Ophir Rd *NEND* PO2 118 C5
Oracle Dr *WVILLE* PO7 101 K3
Orange Gv
LSOL/BMARY PO13 116 A6 2
Orange Rw *EMRTH* PO10 104 C6 3
Orchard Av *ELGH* SO50 45 J2
Orchard Cl *FAWY* SO45 110 E4
GPORT PO12 116 D6
HORN PO8 64 D6
NBAD SO52 36 A5
RWIN SO21 39 J1
TOTT SO40 52 E7
Orchard Ct *HEND* SO30 58 D5
Orchard Gv *FHAM/PORC* PO16 98 D7
HORN PO8 82 A2
Orchard La *EMRTH* PO10 104 D6
ROMY SO51 34 D3
SHAM SO14 9 H3
Orchardlea *BPWT* SO32 61 J1
Orchard Pl *SHAM* SO14 9 H4
Orchard Rd *ELGH* SO50 46 B1
ENEY PO4 19 H5
GPORT PO12 16 F2
HAV PO9 14 F6
HISD PO11 137 H6
HLER SO31 94 E4
Orchards Wy *HEND* SO30 57 G3 3
PTSW SO17 55 H2
The Orchard *CHAM* PO6 100 E7
ROWN SO16 43 F2
WVILLE PO7 80 E1
Orchard Wy *FAWY* SO45 91 F4
Ordnance Rd *GPORT* PO12 16 E5
WSHM SO15 5 G6
Ordnance Rw *PSEA* PO1 17 L4
Ordnance Wy *TOTT* SO40 70 B2
Oregon Cl *ITCH* SO19 11 G1
Oriel Dr *FHAM/STUB* PO14 95 H5
Oriel Rd *NEND* PO2 118 C5
Orient Dr *WINW* SO22 21 F4
Orion Cl *FHAM/STUB* PO14 114 E5 1
ROWN SO16 42 A7
Orkney Cl *ROWN* SO16 41 K7
Orkney Rd *CHAM* PO6 100 E5
Ormesby Dr *CHFD* SO53 37 J2
Ormsby Rd *SSEA* PO5 18 D8 6
Orpen Rd *ITCH* SO19 11 L3
Orsmond Cl *WVILLE* PO7 82 A7 2
Orwell Cl *ROWN* SO16 53 K3 1
Orwell Crs *FHAM/STUB* PO14 95 H4
Osborn Crs *LSOL/BMARY* PO13 115 J3
Osborne Cl *WVILLE* PO7 82 B6 7
Osborne Dr *CHFD* SO53 38 B5
Osborne Gdns *ELGH* SO50 46 C2 4
Osborne Rd *GPORT* PO12 16 E3
HLER SO31 94 B6
LSOL/BMARY PO13 131 F2 2
SSEA PO5 18 B9
TOTT SO40 53 F5
Osborne Rd North *PTSW* SO17 5 L1
Osborne Rd South *PTSW* SO17 5 L3
Osborne View Rd
FHAM/STUB PO14 114 B6
Osborn Rd *FHAM/PORC* PO16 13 K5
Osborn Rd South
FHAM/PORC PO16 13 J5
Osier Cl *NEND* PO2 118 B5
Oslands Dr *HLER* SO31 74 C6
Osprey Cl *ROWN* SO16 42 C6
TOTT SO40 69 K4
Osprey Dr *HISD* PO11 137 J5
Osprey Gdns
LSOL/BMARY PO13 131 G2 7
Osprey Quay *EMRTH* PO10 104 E7
Osterley Cl *HEND* SO30 58 D5
Osterly Rd *ITCH* SO19 6 C9
Othello Dr *WVILLE* PO7 82 B5
Otterbourne Crs *HAV* PO9 102 E1
Otterbourne Hl *CHFD* SO53 38 D1
Otterbourne Rd *RWIN* SO21 33 F5
Otter Cl *ELGH* SO50 45 K1
Ouse Cl *CHFD* SO53 37 H2
Outer Cir *ROWN* SO16 42 B7
Outlands La *HEND* SO30 59 J6
Outram Rd *SSEA* PO5 18 F7
Oval Gdns *GPORT* PO12 132 C5
Overbrook *FAWY* SO45 91 G4
Overbrook Wy *NBAD* SO52 35 K5 3
Overcliff Ri *ROWN* SO16 43 F7
Overton Crs *HAV* PO9 102 E1
Oviat Cl *TOTT* SO40 52 A5
Owen Cl *LSOL/BMARY* PO13 131 K1
Owen Rd *ELGH* SO50 44 C1
Owen's Rd *WINW* SO22 2 C1
Owen St *ENEY* PO4 19 M9
Owslebury Gv *HAV* PO9 103 G1
Oxburgh Cl *ELGH* SO50 38 C5
Oxford Av *SHAM* SO14 5 H8
Oxford Cl *FHAM/PORC* PO16 12 F3
Oxford Rd *GPORT* PO12 132 C3
SHAM SO14 5 G4
SSEA PO5 19 G8
Oxford St *SHAM* SO14 9 H4
Oxlease Cl *ROMY* SO51 35 F1
Oxleys Cl *FHAM/STUB* PO14 96 C6
Oxted Ct *ENEY* PO4 135 G3 3
Oyster Ms *PSEA* PO1 17 L7 3
Oyster Quay *CHAM* PO6 118 A1
Oyster St *PSEA* PO1 17 L7
Ozier Rd *WEND* SO18 56 D2

P

Pacific Cl *SHAM* SO14 9 K6
SHAM SO14 9 L6
Packridge La *ROMY* SO51 42 A2
Padbury Cl *NEND* PO2 118 E3 7
Paddington Rd *NEND* PO2 118 E6
Paddock End *WVILLE* PO7 80 E2
The Paddocks *FAWY* SO45 110 E4 7
The Paddock *ELGH* SO50 38 E4 1
FHAM/STUB PO14 114 D3 1
GPORT PO12 132 D5
TOTT SO40 52 B2
WINC SO23 22 B1
Padnell Av *HORN* PO8 82 B3
Padnell Rd *HORN* PO8 82 C2
Padwell Rd *SHAM* SO14 5 G4
Padwick Av *CHAM* PO6 101 F6
Paffard Cl *LSOL/BMARY* PO13 131 K1
Page Cl *FAWY* SO45 110 A5
Pages La *BROC* SO42 125 H2
Paget Rd *GPORT* PO12 132 D6
Paget St *SHAM* SO14 9 K3
Pagham Cl *EMRTH* PO10 104 D6
Pagham Gdns *HISD* PO11 138 C6
Paignton Av *HSEA* PO3 119 F7
Paignton Rd *ROWN* SO16 54 A4
Pain's Rd *SSEA* PO5 18 E6
Painswick Cl *CHAM* PO6 100 B6
HLER SO31 74 E7
Palace La *BROC* SO42 108 B6
Palk Rd *HAV* PO9 14 B4
Pallant Gdns *FHAM/PORC* PO16 98 A4
The Pallant *HAV* PO9 14 F4
Pallet Cl *RWIN* SO21 39 J2
Pallot Cl *HLER* SO31 73 J5
Palmers Cl *ELGH* SO50 46 C1 3
Palmer's Rd *EMRTH* PO10 104 C5
Palmerston Av
FHAM/PORC PO16 13 K5
Palmerston Dr
FHAM/STUB PO14 97 H7
Palmerston Rd *HISD* PO11 137 H4
SHAM SO14 5 G9
SSEA PO5 134 B6
Palmerston St *ROMY* SO51 34 D3 4
ROMY SO51 34 E3 3
Palmerston Wy *GPORT* PO12 132 B6
Palm Hall Cl *WINC* SO23 3 J5
Palm Rd *ROWN* SO16 54 A1
Palmyra Rd *GPORT* PO12 132 D1
Pamela Av *CHAM* PO6 99 J6
Pangbourne Av *CHAM* PO6 101 G7
Pangbourne Cl *ITCH* SO19 11 H1
Pannall Rd *GPORT* PO12 132 D1
Pan St *PSEA* PO1 18 D2 6
Pansy Rd *ROWN* SO16 43 H7
Pantheon Rd *CHFD* SO53 38 C3
Panton Cl *EMRTH* PO10 104 B3 2
Panwell Rd *WEND* SO18 7 G5
The Parade *PSEA* PO1 17 L1
Paradise La *BPWT* SO32 49 F5
EMRTH PO10 104 E2
FHAM/PORC PO16 98 B5
TOTT SO40 51 G6
Paradise St *PSEA* PO1 18 D3
Parchment St *WINC* SO23 2 E4
The Parchment *HAV* PO9 14 E5
Pardoe Cl *HEND* SO30 58 B7
Parham Dr *ELGH* SO50 38 C6
Parham Rd *GPORT* PO12 16 C2
Park Av *WINC* SO23 2 F3
WVILLE PO7 101 H3
Park Cl *FAWY* SO45 91 J2
GPORT PO12 132 C2
TOTT SO40 69 J4
WINC SO23 21 K5
Park Crs *EMRTH* PO10 104 A5
Parker Cl *GPORT* PO12 116 D6
Parker Gdns *WVILLE* PO7 101 H4
Park Farm Av *FHAM* PO15 96 D2
Park Farm Cl *FHAM* PO15 12 A1
Park Farm Rd *WVILLE* PO7 101 J2
Park Gln *FHAM* PO15 95 H2
Park Gv *CHAM* PO6 100 E7
Park Hill Cl *FAWY* SO45 109 K4
Park House Farm Wy *HAV* PO9 102 C1
Parklands *HLER* SO31 95 F2
WEND SO18 6 D1
Parklands Av *HORN* PO8 64 B7
Parklands Cl *CHFD* SO53 37 K3
GPORT PO12 16 A2 1
Park La *BPWT* SO32 49 K2
CHAM PO6 101 F7
ELGH SO50 38 E2
EMRTH PO10 84 E5
FAWY SO45 109 J3
FHAM/PORC PO16 13 H3
FHAM/STUB PO14 114 D4
HAV PO9 82 D5
HAV PO9 102 D3
HORN PO8 82 B3
RWIN SO21 22 C1
RWIN SO21 33 K4
TOTT SO40 69 H3
Park Pde *HAV* PO9 103 F2 3
Park Rd *BPWT* SO32 48 B3
CHFD SO53 37 K2
EMRTH PO10 105 G5
WINW SO22 21 J5
GPORT PO12 16 B9
HISD PO11 136 D4
PSEA PO1 17 M4
WSHM SO15 4 A6
WSHM SO15 54 D6
WVILLE PO7 62 E7
WVILLE PO7 101 H2
Park Rd North *HAV* PO9 14 D3
Park Rd South *HAV* PO9 14 E5
Parkside *HAV* PO9 102 D4
TOTT SO40 52 E7
Parkside Av *ROWN* SO16 53 J4
Parkside Gdns *WINW* SO22 21 F5
Parkstone Av *ENEY* PO4 134 D7
Park St *GPORT* PO12 16 B4
ROWN SO16 54 C4
SSEA PO5 18 B6
Park Vw *HEND* SO30 58 A5
HEND SO30 59 F5
Parkville Rd *ROWN* SO16 44 A7
Park Wk *SHAM* SO14 5 G9
Parkway *FHAM* PO15 75 K6
Park Wy *HAV* PO9 14 D4
Parkway Gdns *CHFD* SO53 37 K3
The Parkway
LSOL/BMARY PO13 115 J5
ROWN SO16 43 H6
Parliament Pl *WINW* SO22 25 F4
Parnell Rd *ELGH* SO50 44 C1
Parr Rd *CHAM* PO6 100 C6 7
Parry Cl *CHAM* PO6 99 H6
Parry Rd *ITCH* SO19 73 G1
Parsonage La *BPWT* SO32 47 G5
Parsonage Rd *SHAM* SO14 5 K7
Parsons Cl *HSEA* PO3 118 E3
Partridge Cl
FHAM/PORC PO16 98 B6 2
Partridge Down *WINW* SO22 24 E5
Partridge Gdns *HORN* PO8 81 J1
Partridge Rd *FAWY* SO45 91 G5
Partry Cl *CHFD* SO53 37 H2
Passage La *HLER* SO31 94 A5
Passfield Av *ELGH* SO50 44 B1
Passfield Cl *ELGH* SO50 44 B1 1
Passingham Wk *HORN* PO8 82 B1
The Pastures
FHAM/STUB PO14 95 H2 3
WVILLE PO7 80 D2 1
Pat Bear Cl *WSHM* SO15 53 H4
Patchway Dr *FHAM/STUB* PO14 96 D6
Paternoster Rw *WINC* SO23 2 F5
Patricia Cl *HEND* SO30 57 G2
Patricia Dr *HEND* SO30 58 C5
Paulet Cl *WEND* SO18 56 D3
Paulet Lacave Av *ROWN* SO16 41 J5
Paulet Pl *WINW* SO22 2 A9
Pauletts La *TOTT* SO40 52 A1
Paulsgrove Rd *NEND* PO2 118 E7
Paulson Cl *CHFD* SO53 37 K2
Pauncefoot Hl *ROMY* SO51 34 B5
Pavilion Cl *ELGH* SO50 46 B3
Pavilion Rd *HEND* SO30 58 C4
Paxton Cl *HEND* SO30 58 C7 4
Paxton Rd *FHAM/STUB* PO14 12 F6
Paynes Hay Rd *ROMY* SO51 29 G1
Payne's Rd *WSHM* SO15 54 C6
Peach Rd *ROWN* SO16 42 B7
Peacock Cl *FHAM/PORC* PO16 98 B6
Peacock La *PSEA* PO1 17 M7
Peacock Pl *WINC* SO23 3 K4
Peak Cl *ROWN* SO16 54 A4
Peak Dr *FHAM/STUB* PO14 12 A7
Peakfield *WVILLE* PO7 80 D1 3
Peak La *FHAM/STUB* PO14 96 E7
The Peak *HAV* PO9 83 K3
Pearce Ct *GPORT* PO12 16 D4
Peartree Av *ITCH* SO19 10 C1
Pear Tree Cl *BPWT* SO32 58 E2 1
Peartree Cl
FHAM/STUB PO14 114 E4 2
ITCH SO19 10 B2
Peartree Rd *FAWY* SO45 91 F4
ITCH SO19 10 B2
Pebble Cl *HISD* PO11 137 J6 1
Pebble Ct *TOTT* SO40 70 A3 1
Pebmarsh Rd *CHAM* PO6 100 C6 3
Pedam Cl *ENEY* PO4 19 L8
Pedula Wy *ELGH* SO50 39 H5
Peel Cl *ROMY* SO51 35 H1
Peel Pl *SSEA* PO5 18 C6
Peel Rd *GPORT* PO12 16 D4
Peel St *SHAM* SO14 5 L8
Peewit Hl *HLER* SO31 73 K2
Peewit Hill Cl *HLER* SO31 73 K2
Pegasus Cl *HLER* SO31 93 J4 2
ROWN SO16 42 A7
Pelham Rd *GPORT* PO12 16 A4
SSEA PO5 18 D8
Pelham Ter *EMRTH* PO10 104 D6 5
Pelican Cl *FHAM* PO15 12 A3
Pelican Rd *FHAM/STUB* PO14 115 G2
Pembers Cl *ELGH* SO50 46 C1
Pemberton Rd *LYND* SO43 86 D1
Pembrey Cl *ROWN* SO16 42 A6
Pembroke Cl *ELGH* SO50 38 C5
PSEA PO1 17 M8 3
ROMY SO51 34 E3 4
TOTT SO40 53 F4
Pembroke Crs
FHAM/STUB PO14 114 B5
Pembroke Rd *WINW* SO22 21 F2
ITCH SO19 11 J1
PSEA PO1 17 M7
Pembury Rd
FHAM/STUB PO14 114 E3
HAV PO9 15 H6
Pemerton Rd *WINW* SO22 21 G4
Penarth Av *CHAM* PO6 101 G6
Pendennis Rd *CHAM* PO6 99 J6
Pendle Cl *ROWN* SO16 54 A4
Pendleton Gdns *FAWY* SO45 110 B6 3
Penelope Gdns *HLER* SO31 73 J3
Penfords Paddock
BPWT SO32 48 E4 3
Penhale Gdns
FHAM/STUB PO14 95 G5
Penhale Rd *PSEA* PO1 19 H3
Penhale Wy *TOTT* SO40 52 D7
Penhurst Rd *HAV* PO9 102 C4
Peninsula Rd *WINW* SO22 2 B6
Penistone Cl *ITCH* SO19 11 J7
Penjar Av *WVILLE* PO7 101 H2
Penk Rdg *CHAM* PO6 102 A6
Pennant Hills *HAV* PO9 102 C4
Pennard Wy *CHFD* SO53 37 H6
Pennerly Ct *HAV* PO9 82 E6
Penner Rd *HAV* PO9 14 C8
Pennine Gdns *FAWY* SO45 90 E4
Pennine Rd *ROWN* SO16 54 A5
Pennine Wy *CHFD* SO53 38 A6
LSOL/BMARY PO13 131 H4
Pennington Cl *ELGH* SO50 39 J2
Pennington Wy *FHAM* PO15 12 B1
Penn Wy *GPORT* PO12 132 B5
Pennycress *HLER* SO31 94 D4
Penny La *EMRTH* PO10 104 E6
Penny Pl *WVILLE* PO7 101 K3 4
Penny St *PSEA* PO1 17 L8
Penrhyn Cl *ELGH* SO50 38 C5
Penrose Cl *NEND* PO2 118 C5 3
Penshurst Wy *ELGH* SO50 38 D4
The Pentagon *FAWY* SO45 110 D5
Pentere Rd *HORN* PO8 64 B6
Pentire Av *WSHM* SO15 54 E2
Pentire Wy *WSHM* SO15 54 E2
Pentland Cl *FAWY* SO45 90 E4 4
Pentland Ri *FHAM/PORC* PO16 99 G5
Penton Ct *HAV* PO9 83 J7
Penton Rd *RWIN* SO21 33 K2 2
Pentridge Wy *TOTT* SO40 52 C7
Peper Harow *HORN* PO8 64 C6
Peppard Cl *WEND* SO18 7 H5
Peppercorn Wy *HEND* SO30 58 A1
Pepys Av *ITCH* SO19 57 G7
Pepys Cl *ENEY* PO4 19 J8
GPORT PO12 132 E7
Percival Rd *NEND* PO2 118 E7
Percy Chandler St *PSEA* PO1 18 E2 3
Percy Cl *FAWY* SO45 91 G1
Percy Rd *ENEY* PO4 19 G6
GPORT PO12 16 C5
ROWN SO16 54 B4
Peregrine Cl *TOTT* SO40 52 B6 6
The Peregrines
FHAM/PORC PO16 98 C6
Pern Dr *HEND* SO30 59 F5
Peronne Cl *HSEA* PO3 118 E2
Peronne Rd *HSEA* PO3 118 E2
Perran Rd *ROWN* SO16 53 J3
Perryvale Rd *NBAD* SO52 37 G5
Perrywood Cl *FAWY* SO45 109 K4
Perrywood Gdns *TOTT* SO40 52 A4 3
Perseus Pl *WVILLE* PO7 102 A3
Pershore Cl *HLER* SO31 95 F3
Persian Dr *HLER* SO31 75 G6
Perth Rd *ENEY* PO4 135 G4
LSOL/BMARY PO13 116 A4
Pervin Rd *CHAM* PO6 100 E7
Peter Ashley Rd *CHAM* PO6 101 J5
Peterborough Rd *CHAM* PO6 100 D5
SHAM SO14 5 H5
Peters Cl *HLER* SO31 94 D3
Peterscroft Av *TOTT* SO40 67 K4
Petersfield Rd *HAV* PO9 14 F1
RWIN SO21 27 K1
WINC SO23 3 J6
Petersham Cl *WVILLE* PO7 81 J4
Peters Rd *HLER* SO31 94 D3
Petrel Wk *LSOL/BMARY* PO13 115 J5
Petrie Rd *LSOL/BMARY* PO13 131 G2
Pettinger Gdns *PTSW* SO17 6 A2
Petty Cl *ROMY* SO51 35 F4 1
Pettycot Crs
LSOL/BMARY PO13 115 J4
Petworth Gdns *ELGH* SO50 38 D5 3
ROWN SO16 42 D6
Petworth Rd *HSEA* PO3 135 G2
Pevensey Cl *ROWN* SO16 53 J3
Peverells Rd *CHFD* SO53 38 B4
Peverells Wood Av *CHFD* SO53 38 B3
Peverells Wood Cl *CHFD* SO53 38 C3
Peveril Rd *ITCH* SO19 10 D2
Pewsey Pl *WSHM* SO15 54 E2
Pheonix Wy
LSOL/BMARY PO13 115 K6
Philip Rd *WVILLE* PO7 102 A1
Phillimore Rd *ROWN* SO16 44 A7
Phillips Cl *ROWN* SO16 41 K5
Philpott Dr *TOTT* SO40 70 A4
Phoenix Cl *HLER* SO31 73 K4 4
Phoenix Sq *NEND* PO2 118 D3
Pickwick Cl *TOTT* SO40 52 A5
Pier Head Rd *NEND* PO2 118 A7
Pier Rd *PSEA* PO1 18 A9
SSEA PO5 18 A9
Pier St *LSOL/BMARY* PO13 131 F2
Pigeon House La *WVILLE* PO7 100 C3
Pikes Hl *LYND* SO43 66 B6
Pilands Wood Rd *HLER* SO31 73 J5 3
Pilgrim Pl *WEND* SO18 44 B7 7
Pilgrims Cl *NBAD* SO52 37 G5
Pilgrims Ga *WINW* SO22 2 A2
Pilgrims Wy *FHAM/STUB* PO14 114 C6
Pilning Cl *FHAM/STUB* PO14 96 D6 2
Pimpernel Cl *HLER* SO31 94 D4
Pine Cl *FAWY* SO45 91 G4
WINW SO22 24 E5
NBAD SO52 36 A5 2
TOTT SO40 68 B2
Pine Crs *CHFD* SO53 37 K2
Pine Dr *WEND* SO18 57 G5
Pine Dr East *WEND* SO18 57 H5
Pinefield Rd *WEND* SO18 56 C2
Pine Gv *HAV* PO9 15 H5
Pinegrove Rd *ITCH* SO19 10 F3
Pinehurst Cl *HORN* PO8 82 D3
Pinehurst Rd *ROWN* SO16 43 G4 2
Pinelands Rd *ROWN* SO16 43 G3
Pine Rd *BPWT* SO32 48 E3
CHFD SO53 37 K1
ROMY SO51 35 H4
The Pines *FHAM/PORC* PO16 98 D5
Pine Tree Gdns *HORN* PO8 82 B3
Pine Trees Cl *FHAM/STUB* PO14 12 B7

Pineview Cl *HLER* SO31 73 K4
Pine Wk *HLER* SO31 95 F1
ROWN SO16 43 G4
Pine Wy *ROWN* SO16 43 G4
Pinewood *LSOL/BMARY* PO13 116 B6
Pinewood Av *HAV* PO9 102 C3
Pinewood Cl
FHAM/STUB PO14 114 E3 2
ROMY SO51 35 H1
Pinewood Crs *FAWY* SO45 91 J4 1
Pinewood Dr *FAWY* SO45 91 J4
Pinewood Pk *ITCH* SO19 57 J7
Pinkney La *LYND* SO43 86 B4
Pink Rd *NEND* PO2 118 D7 1
Pinks Hl *FHAM/PORC* PO16 98 A4
Pinsley Dr *WHAM* PO17 79 K7
Pinto Cl *FHAM* PO15 75 G6
Pipers Cl *TOTT* SO40 52 C6
Piping Cl *RWIN* SO21 39 J2
Piping Rd *RWIN* SO21 39 J2
Pipit Cl *GPORT* PO12 132 E1
Pirelli St *SHAM* SO14 8 E1
WSHM SO15 8 E1
Pirrie Cl *WSHM* SO15 4 A1
Pitcairn Ms *ENEY* PO4 135 G6 4
Pitchponds Rd *HLER* SO31 94 B6
Pitcroft Rd *NEND* PO2 118 C6
Pitmore Cl *ELGH* SO50 38 E2
Pitmore Rd *ELGH* SO50 38 E2
Pitreavie Rd *CHAM* PO6 119 F1
Pitter Cl *WINW* SO22 20 E2
Pitt Hill La *WVILLE* PO7 62 D3
Pitt Rd *WSHM* SO15 54 D6
Pitymoor La *WHAM* PO17 100 A2
Place Crs *WVILLE* PO7 102 A1
Place House Cl *FHAM* PO15 96 D5
Place La *RWIN* SO21 33 G1
Plaitford Gv *HAV* PO9 102 D2
Plantation Dr *TOTT* SO40 69 K4
The Plantation *BPWT* SO32 59 K2
Platform Rd *SHAM* SO14 9 G5
Players Crs *TOTT* SO40 52 D7
Playfair Rd *SSEA* PO5 18 E6
Pleasant La *EMRTH* PO10 123 G6
Pleasant Rd *ENEY* PO4 135 G4
Plough Wy *WINW* SO22 25 G4
Plover Cl *FHAM/STUB* PO14 114 C5
ROWN SO16 42 C6
Plover Reach *ENEY* PO4 135 G3 4
Plover Rd *TOTT* SO40 52 B5
Plovers Down *WINW* SO22 24 E5
Plovers Rd *HORN* PO8 64 B6
P.l.p.h. Rd *FAWY* SO45 110 E2
Plumpton Gdns *HSEA* PO3 119 G4 1
Plumpton Gv *WVILLE* PO7 82 C4
Plymouth Dr
FHAM/STUB PO14 114 C5
Plymouth St *SSEA* PO5 18 D5 1
Poets Wy *WINW* SO22 21 G7
Pointout Cl *ROWN* SO16 55 F1
Pointout Rd *ROWN* SO16 55 F1
Polesden Cl *CHFD* SO53 37 J2 4
Poles La *RWIN* SO21 31 J3
Pollards Moor Rd *TOTT* SO40 50 D3
The Polygon *WSHM* SO15 4 E8
Pond Cl *TOTT* SO40 70 A3
Pondhead Cl *FAWY* SO45 109 K4 1
Pond Piece *WVILLE* PO7 80 E2
Pond Rd *HLER* SO31 74 E7
Pondside La *BPWT* SO32 48 D2
Pook La *HAV* PO9 15 J7
WHAM PO17 97 J2
Pooksgreen *TOTT* SO40 69 J3
Poole Rd *ITCH* SO19 10 C2
Popes La *TOTT* SO40 52 E5
Popham Ct *HAV* PO9 82 D7
Poplar Dr *FHAM/STUB* PO14 12 C8
TOTT SO40 69 J4
Poplar Gv *HISD* PO11 137 H4
Poplar Rd *ITCH* SO19 6 F7
The Poplars *BPWT* SO32 60 E1
Poplar Wy *HEND* SO30 58 C5 2
NBAD SO52 36 A5
Poppy Cl *HLER* SO31 94 E4
Poppyfields *NBAD* SO52 37 H4 1
Poppy Rd *ROWN* SO16 43 K6
Porchester Rd *ITCH* SO19 10 C4
Porlock Rd *ROWN* SO16 53 H3
Portal Rd *ELGH* SO50 39 G7
ITCH SO19 11 J2
LSOL/BMARY PO13 115 K4
TOTT SO40 52 C5
WINC SO23 3 H7
Portchester La *WHAM* PO17 99 G4
Portchester Ri *ELGH* SO50 38 D3
Portchester Rd
FHAM/PORC PO16 98 D6
NEND PO2 118 D7
Portelet Pl *HEND* SO30 58 B7
Porteous Crs *CHFD* SO53 38 C4
Portersbridge St *ROMY* SO51 34 D3
Porter's La *SHAM* SO14 8 F4
Portland Dr *GPORT* PO12 132 A5
Portland Rd *SSEA* PO5 18 D9
WVILLE PO7 81 K6
Portland St *FHAM/PORC* PO16 13 K6
PSEA PO1 18 A3
SHAM SO14 8 F1
Portland Ter *SHAM* SO14 8 F1
Port La *RWIN* SO21 31 J2
Portobello Gv
FHAM/PORC PO16 99 G5
Port Royal St *SSEA* PO5 18 F4 1
Portsdown Av *CHAM* PO6 101 H6
Portsdown Hill Rd *CHAM* PO6 100 E5
WHAM PO17 98 D4
Portsdown Rd *CHAM* PO6 99 H6
Portsmouth Rd *CHAM* PO6 118 E1
HLER SO31 73 J4
HORN PO8 64 C7
ITCH SO19 10 D4
LSOL/BMARY PO13 131 G4
Portsview Av
FHAM/PORC PO16 99 G6
Portsview Gdns
FHAM/PORC PO16 99 G5
Portswood Av *PTSW* SO17 5 J2
Portswood Pk *PTSW* SO17 5 J3
Portswood Rd *HAV* PO9 82 E7
NEND PO2 118 D2 2
PTSW SO17 5 J3
Portview Rd *WEND* SO18 56 C2
Port Wy *CHAM* PO6 99 K6
Portway Cl *WEND* SO18 7 K4
Posbrooke Rd *ENEY* PO4 19 M5
Posbrook La
FHAM/STUB PO14 113 K2
Postern Cl *FHAM/PORC* PO16 99 G6
Post Office Rd *WVILLE* PO7 101 H1 1
The Potteries
FHAM/PORC PO16 13 K2
Potters Av *FHAM/PORC* PO16 97 H2
Potters Heron Cl *ROMY* SO51 31 F6
Potters Heron La *ROMY* SO51 31 F6
Poulner Cl *ITCH* SO19 11 G8
Poulner Ct *HAV* PO9 82 D7
Pound Cl *LSOL/BMARY* PO13 116 A7
Pound Gate Dr
FHAM/STUB PO14 95 H5
Pound La *ROMY* SO51 30 C7
TOTT SO40 51 F2
TOTT SO40 68 D2
Pound Lea *HISD* PO11 137 H3
Pound Rd *CHAM* PO6 100 A4
HLER SO31 73 J5
SELS PO20 139 J7
Pound St *WEND* SO18 7 H4
Pound Tree Rd *SHAM* SO14 9 G1
Powell Crs *TOTT* SO40 52 E7
Power Rd *PSEA* PO1 19 H1 5
Powerscourt Rd *NEND* PO2 118 D7
Poyner Cl *FHAM/PORC* PO16 13 J3
Poynings Pl *PSEA* PO1 18 A7 1
Precosa Rd *HEND* SO30 58 D7
Prelate Wy *FHAM/STUB* PO14 95 H4
Preshaw Cl *ROWN* SO16 42 D7
Preston Rd *NEND* PO2 118 E6
Prestwood Rd *HEND* SO30 58 B6
Pretoria Rd *ENEY* PO4 19 K7
HEND SO30 58 A7
Pricketts Hl *BPWT* SO32 61 G5
Prideaux-Brune Av
LSOL/BMARY PO13 115 K3
Priest Croft Dr *FAWY* SO45 110 B5
Priestfields *FHAM/STUB* PO14 95 H4
Priestlands *ROMY* SO51 34 D2
Priestlands Cl *TOTT* SO40 51 K6
Priestley Cl *TOTT* SO40 52 C5 4
Priestwood Cl *WEND* SO18 57 G5
Primate Rd *FHAM/STUB* PO14 95 J4
Primrose Cl *HEND* SO30 58 B7 2
LSOL/BMARY PO13 115 K2
NBAD SO52 37 G6 1
Primrose Rd *ROWN* SO16 43 H7
Primrose Wy *HLER* SO31 94 E4
ROMY SO51 35 H1 5
Prince Albert Rd *ENEY* PO4 19 M8
Prince Alfred St *GPORT* PO12 16 A7
Prince George's St *HAV* PO9 14 F4
Prince George St *PSEA* PO1 17 L3
Prince of Wales Av *WSHM* SO15 54 B5
Prince of Wales Cl
WVILLE PO7 82 B6 8
Prince of Wales Rd
GPORT PO12 16 D5 5
Prince Rd *FHAM/STUB* PO14 115 G1
ROWN SO16 41 K4
Princes Cl *BPWT* SO32 48 C3 5
Princes Ct *SHAM* SO14 5 L7
Princes Crs *LYND* SO43 86 D1
Princes Dr *WVILLE* PO7 82 B4
Princes Pl *WINW* SO22 2 B9
Princes Rd *ROMY* SO51 34 D2
WSHM SO15 4 A7
Princess Cl *HEND* SO30 57 H2
Princess Gdns *HORN* PO8 64 C5
Princess Rd *TOTT* SO40 68 A3
Prince's St *PSEA* PO1 134 C1
SHAM SO14 5 M7
Prinstead Cl *WINC* SO23 3 G8
Prinsted Crs *CHAM* PO6 101 J7
Prinsted La *EMRTH* PO10 105 G7
Priors Barton *WINC* SO23 2 D9
Priors Cl *EMRTH* PO10 105 H5
Priorsdean Av *HSEA* PO3 19 L2
Priorsdean Crs *HAV* PO9 102 E2
Priors Dean Rd *WINW* SO22 21 G3
Priors Leaze La *RCCH* PO18 105 J5
Priors Wy *WINW* SO22 24 E5
Priory Av *PTSW* SO17 6 A1
Priory Cl *BPWT* SO32 48 C3
PTSW SO17 6 A1
Priory Crs *ENEY* PO4 19 L5
Priory Gdns *FHAM/PORC* PO16 99 F6
WVILLE PO7 81 K4
Priory Rd *ELGH* SO50 44 C2
ENEY PO4 19 M9
FHAM PO15 12 A4
HLER SO31 72 E7
PTSW SO17 5 L3
WHAM PO17 79 K7
The Priory *BPWT* SO32 48 C4
Privett Pl *GPORT* PO12 132 B3
Privett Rd *FHAM* PO15 96 D4
GPORT PO12 132 B4
LSOL/BMARY PO13 131 K5
WVILLE PO7 101 J3
Prochurch Rd *HORN* PO8 82 C1
Proctor Cl *ITCH* SO19 57 G7
Proctor Dr *NBAD* SO52 36 A7
Proctor La *ENEY* PO4 19 J3
The Promenade *EMRTH* PO10 104 C7
FAWY SO45 91 H1
Prospect La *HAV* PO9 103 J1
Prospect Pl *CHFD* SO53 37 K4 1
FAWY SO45 91 H1
Prospect Rd *NEND* PO2 134 B1
Provene Cl *BPWT* SO32 49 F7
Provene Gdns *BPWT* SO32 48 E7
Providence Hl *HLER* SO31 73 K3
Prunus Cl *ROWN* SO16 42 D6
Pudbrooke Gdns *HEND* SO30 58 A4 4
Pudding La *WINC* SO23 22 A3
Puffin Cl *ROWN* SO16 42 C6
Puffin Crs *FHAM/STUB* PO14 114 C3
Puffin Gdns
LSOL/BMARY PO13 115 J4 5
Puffin Wk *HORN* PO8 81 J1
Pump La *HORN* PO8 64 B7
LSOL/BMARY PO13 115 K6
Purbeck Dr *FHAM/STUB* PO14 12 A8
Purbeck St *PSEA* PO1 18 A4 1
Purbrook Cl *ROWN* SO16 42 D7 5
Purbrook Gdns *WVILLE* PO7 101 H1
Purbrook Heath Rd
WVILLE PO7 100 E1
Purbrook Rd *PSEA* PO1 19 H4
Purbrook Wy *HAV* PO9 102 E2
WVILLE PO7 102 A2
Purcell Cl *WVILLE* PO7 101 K1
Purcell Rd *ITCH* SO19 73 G2
Purkess Cl *CHFD* SO53 38 A3
Purkiss Cl *TOTT* SO40 51 F7
Purvis Gdns *ITCH* SO19 11 L5
Pycroft Cl *HISD* PO11 121 K4
ITCH SO19 7 G9
Pye St *PSEA* PO1 18 D1 7
Pyland's La *HLER* SO31 74 A2
Pyle Cl *HORN* PO8 82 B1
Pylewell Rd *FAWY* SO45 91 H2 8
Pyrford Cl *GPORT* PO12 132 B5
WVILLE PO7 01 J3
Pytchley Cl *FHAM/STUB* PO14 114 B5

Q

The Quadrangle *ELGH* SO50 38 D6 2
Quail Wy *HORN* PO8 64 B6
Quantock Rd *ROWN* SO16 53 K4
The Quantocks *FAWY* SO45 90 E4 5
Quarely Rd *HAV* PO9 82 D7
Quarry Rd *WINC* SO23 3 H6
Quarterdeck Av *NEND* PO2 118 A6
Quartremaine Rd *HSEA* PO3 119 G4
Quay Hvn *HLER* SO31 74 C5
Quay La *GPORT* PO12 116 E6
Quayside Rd *WEND* SO18 6 B5
Quayside Wk *TOTT* SO40 70 A2
Quay St *FHAM/PORC* PO16 13 L7
Quebec Gdns *HLER* SO31 73 J4 4
Queen Anne's Dr *HAV* PO9 102 D4
Queen Mary Rd
FHAM/PORC PO16 99 G7
Queen Rd *FHAM/STUB* PO14 115 G1
Queens Cl *FAWY* SO45 91 H3
LSOL/BMARY PO13 131 F2 5
Queens Crs *FHAM/STUB* PO14 114 E4
HORN PO8 64 C5
SSEA PO5 18 D8
Queen's Gv *SSEA* PO5 18 D9
WVILLE PO7 101 J1
Queens Md *WINW* SO22 25 F2 2
Queen's Pde *LYND* SO43 86 C1
Queen's Pl *SSEA* PO5 18 D8 7
Queens Ride *NBAD* SO52 35 K6
Queen's Rd *CHFD* SO53 38 A1
FHAM/PORC PO16 13 J6
GPORT PO12 16 C4
HLER SO31 94 B6
LSOL/BMARY PO13 131 G4
NEND PO2 118 D7
PSEA PO1 17 K1
WSHM SO15 54 D2
WVILLE PO7 81 K4
Queen's Ter *SHAM* SO14 9 H4
Queenstown Rd *WSHM* SO15 4 A7
Queen St *EMRTH* PO10 104 D6
PSEA PO1 17 L3
RWIN SO21 33 J4
Queens Vw *HLER* SO31 72 E7
Queensway *HISD* PO11 121 H4
Queen's Wy *SHAM* SO14 9 G4
SSEA PO5 18 D8 8
The Queensway
FHAM/PORC PO16 98 E6
Querida Cl *HLER* SO31 74 C5 5
Quilter Cl *ITCH* SO19 73 G1 4
Quinton Cl *SSEA* PO5 18 E5 6
Quintrell Av *FHAM/PORC* PO16 98 D6
Quob Farm Cl *HEND* SO30 57 H1
Quob La *HEND* SO30 57 H1

R

Racecourse Vw *LYND* SO43 66 C7 2
Rachel Cl *ELGH* SO50 46 A1
Racton Av *CHAM* PO6 101 G7
Racton Rd *EMRTH* PO10 104 C3
Radcliffe Rd *SHAM* SO14 5 K7
Radclyffe Rd *FHAM/PORC* PO16 13 M3
Radleigh Gdns *TOTT* SO40 52 A4
Radley Cl *HEND* SO30 58 B3 5
Radnor St *SSEA* PO5 18 D5
Radstock Rd *ITCH* SO19 10 C3
Radway Crs *WSHM* SO15 4 B2
Radway Rd *WSHM* SO15 4 B2
Raeburn Dr *HEND* SO30 58 B5
Raglan Cl *CHFD* SO53 37 G6
Raglan St *SSEA* PO5 18 E4
Rails La *HISD* PO11 137 J6
Railway Vw *PSEA* PO1 18 E3
Railway View Rd *PTSW* SO17 5 M2
Raley Rd *HLER* SO31 95 F4
Ramalley La *CHFD* SO53 37 J3
Rambler Dr *LSOL/BMARY* PO13 131 K2
Ramblers Wy *HORN* PO8 82 C4
Rampart Gdns *HSEA* PO3 118 E2
Rampart Rd *WEND* SO18 6 A4
Ramsay Pl
LSOL/BMARY PO13 115 K5 6
Ramsdale Av *HAV* PO9 102 D1
Ramsey Rd *HISD* PO11 137 H5
Randall Cl *TOTT* SO40 52 B2
Randall Rd *CHFD* SO53 32 A7
Randolph Rd *NEND* PO2 118 D4
Randolph St *WSHM* SO15 54 D5
Ranelagh Gdns *WSHM* SO15 4 D5
Ranelagh Rd *HAV* PO9 14 B4
NEND PO2 118 B6
WINC SO23 2 C8
Ranfurly Gdns *FAWY* SO45 91 F4
Range Gdns *ITCH* SO19 11 J4
Range Gn *NEND* PO2 118 B4
Rannoch Cl *FHAM* PO15 12 C2
Ransome Cl *FHAM/STUB* PO14 96 A7
Ranvilles La *FHAM/STUB* PO14 96 C7
Rapson Cl *CHAM* PO6 100 B5
Rareridge La *BPWT* SO32 49 F3
Ratcliffe Rd *FAWY* SO45 91 G5 4
HEND SO30 58 B5
Ratlake La *ROMY* SO51 31 G5
Rattigan Gdns *HLER* SO31 75 H5
Raven Cl *LSOL/BMARY* PO13 131 K2
Raven Rd *SHAM* SO14 5 J7
Ravens Cl *FHAM/STUB* PO14 114 E4
Ravenscroft Cl *HLER* SO31 73 J4
Ravenscroft Wy *BPWT* SO32 59 F3
Raven Sq *ELGH* SO50 44 A1 1
Ravenswood
FHAM/STUB PO14 95 H3 4
Raymond Cl *FAWY* SO45 110 A4
HEND SO30 57 J1
Raymond Rd *CHAM* PO6 99 H5
WSHM SO15 4 B4
Rayners Gdns *ROWN* SO16 44 A7 2
Raynes Rd *LSOL/BMARY* PO13 131 G4
Reading Room La *BPWT* SO32 59 J4
The Recess *ELGH* SO50 38 E5
Record Rd *EMRTH* PO10 104 B5
Rectory Av *CHAM* PO6 102 A5
Rectory Cl *FHAM/STUB* PO14 114 D4
GPORT PO12 132 D6
Rectory Ct *HEND* SO30 58 E5
Rectory Rd *HAV* PO9 14 E6
The Redan *GPORT* PO12 133 F7
Red Barn Av *FHAM/PORC* PO16 99 F5
Red Barn La *FHAM* PO15 97 F2
Redbridge Cswy *WSHM* SO15 53 G4
Redbridge Gv *HAV* PO9 102 E3
Redbridge Hl *ROWN* SO16 54 A3
Redbridge La *ROWN* SO16 53 G2
Redbridge Rd *WSHM* SO15 53 J4
Redcar Av *HSEA* PO3 119 F6
Redcote Cl *WEND* SO18 7 J4
Redcroft La *HLER* SO31 73 K4
The Redfords *TOTT* SO40 52 D3
Redhill *ROWN* SO16 43 F7
Redhill Cl *ROWN* SO16 43 F7
Red Hill Crs *ROWN* SO16 43 F7
Redhill Rd *HAV* PO9 83 J4
Red Hill Wy *ROWN* SO16 55 F1
Redhouse Park Gdns
LSOL/BMARY PO13 132 B1
Redlands Dr *ITCH* SO19 6 F6
Redlands Gv *ENEY* PO4 135 H4
Redlands La *EMRTH* PO10 104 C2
FHAM/STUB PO14 12 F6
Red Leaves *BPWT* SO32 61 F2
Red Ldg *CHFD* SO53 37 J7
Redlynch Cl *HAV* PO9 103 J2 1
Redmoor Cl *ITCH* SO19 6 E7
Red Oaks Dr *FHAM* PO15 95 G1
Redrise Cl *FAWY* SO45 109 J4
Redshank Rd *HORN* PO8 64 B5
Redward Rd *ROWN* SO16 42 A6
Redwing Ct *ENEY* PO4 135 H3 5
Redwing Gdns *TOTT* SO40 52 B4 7
Redwood Cl *FAWY* SO45 90 E3
HEND SO30 57 F2
Redwood Dr *FHAM/PORC* PO16 98 E6
Redwood Gdns *TOTT* SO40 52 B5
Redwood Gv *HAV* PO9 103 H2
Redwood Wy *ROWN* SO16 43 H5
Reed Dr *TOTT* SO40 70 A3
Reedmace Cl *WVILLE* PO7 82 B7 5
Reed's Pl *GPORT* PO12 16 A2 2
Reeds Rd *GPORT* PO12 132 E1
Reeves Wy *HLER* SO31 73 J4 5
Regal Cl *CHAM* PO6 100 E6
Regency Gdns *WVILLE* PO7 81 J7 1
Regency Pl *FHAM* PO15 12 C5
Regent Cl *RWIN* SO21 33 F5
Regent Pl *SSEA* PO5 18 B8 2
Regent Rd *CHFD* SO53 38 A4
Regents Ct *HAV* PO9 14 E7
Regents Ga *HLER* SO31 94 D1
Regent's Gv *WSHM* SO15 54 C4 4
Regent's Park Gdns
WSHM SO15 54 C5 1
Regent's Park Rd *WSHM* SO15 54 B5
Regent St *PSEA* PO1 134 B1
SHAM SO14 8 F1
Reginald Rd *ENEY* PO4 19 M8
Relay Rd *WVILLE* PO7 81 J5
Reliant Cl *CHFD* SO53 37 J6 1
Renda Rd *FAWY* SO45 109 K3
Renny Rd *PSEA* PO1 19 H4
Renown Cl *CHFD* SO53 37 J5
Renown Gdns *HORN* PO8 64 A7
Repton Cl *GPORT* PO12 132 B4
Reservoir La *HEND* SO30 57 K6
Rest-a-wyle Av *HISD* PO11 137 H3
The Retreat *ELGH* SO50 38 E6
SSEA PO5 18 D8
TOTT SO40 52 E7
Revenge Cl *ENEY* PO4 135 H2 2
Rewlands Dr *WINW* SO22 21 F3
Reynolds Dl *TOTT* SO40 52 C7
Reynolds Rd *ELGH* SO50 46 C2
WSHM SO15 54 D4
Rhinefield Cl *ELGH* SO50 45 J1 2
HAV PO9 102 D2 5
Rhyme Hall Ms *FAWY* SO45 110 E4 8
Ribble Cl *CHFD* SO53 38 A5
Ribble Ct *ROWN* SO16 53 K3
Richard Gv *GPORT* PO12 116 D6
Richards Cl *HLER* SO31 95 G3
Richlans Rd *HEND* SO30 58 B6
Richmond Cl *CHFD* SO53 37 J1
HISD PO11 137 F4
TOTT SO40 52 A3
Richmond Dr *HISD* PO11 136 E4
Richmond Gdns *PTSW* SO17 55 J3
Richmond La *ROMY* SO51 35 F1
Richmond Pk *RWIN* SO21 33 G5
Richmond Pl *PSEA* PO1 18 A4
SSEA PO5 18 D9 1
Richmond Ri *FHAM/PORC* PO16 99 F5
Richmond Rd *GPORT* PO12 132 D4
LSOL/BMARY PO13 130 E2
SSEA PO5 18 E9 4
WSHM SO15 54 D6
Richmond St *SHAM* SO14 9 H3
Richville Rd *ROWN* SO16 54 B4
Ridding Cl *WSHM* SO15 54 C4
Riders La *HAV* PO9 103 F2
Ridge La *HEND* SO30 75 J2
ROMY SO51 40 A2
Ridgemount Av *ROWN* SO16 43 G6
Ridgeway *WINW* SO22 25 F3
Ridgeway Cl *CHAM* PO6 99 J5 1
CHFD SO53 38 B5
The Ridgeway
FHAM/PORC PO16 98 B5
Ridgewood Cl *FAWY* SO45 90 D3 1
Ridgway *HAV* PO9 14 A5
The Ridings *BPWT* SO32 49 F7
ELGH SO50 45 K1
NEND PO2 118 E4
Ridley Cl *FAWY* SO45 109 K3 5
Rigby Rd *PTSW* SO17 5 J3
Rimington Rd *HORN* PO8 82 A2
Ringlet Wy *WINC* SO23 3 K4
The Ring *ROWN* SO16 43 F4
Ringwood Dr *NBAD* SO52 35 K5
Ringwood Rd *ENEY* PO4 135 G5
TOTT SO40 51 K5
Ripley Gv *HSEA* PO3 119 F7
Ripon Gdns *WVILLE* PO7 82 C4
Ripplewood *TOTT* SO40 70 B4 4
Ripstone Gdns *PTSW* SO17 55 J1
The Rise *WVILLE* PO7 101 J4
Ritchie Ct *ITCH* SO19 11 J1
Riverdale Av *WVILLE* PO7 82 B6
Riverdene Pl *WEND* SO18 6 B2
River Gn *HLER* SO31 93 K4
Riverhead Cl *ENEY* PO4 135 G3
River La *FHAM* PO15 76 D7
Rivermead Cl *ROMY* SO51 34 C3
Riversdale Cl *ITCH* SO19 10 D9
Riverside *ELGH* SO50 39 G7
Riverside Av *FHAM/PORC* PO16 98 A3
Riverside Cl *TOTT* SO40 51 F6
Riverside Gdns *ROMY* SO51 34 D4
River's St *SSEA* PO5 18 E5
River St *EMRTH* PO10 104 E2
Riverview *TOTT* SO40 52 E7
River View Rd *WEND* SO18 56 A2
River Wk *WEND* SO18 56 B1
River Wy *HAV* PO9 15 G1
Roads Hl *HORN* PO8 64 A3
Road Vw *NEND* PO2 118 B7
Robert Cecil Av *WEND* SO18 44 B7
Roberts Cl *WHAM* PO17 77 H1
Roberts Rd *FAWY* SO45 91 G2
GPORT PO12 132 C2 4
TOTT SO40 52 E7
WSHM SO15 4 B8
Robert Whitworth Dr
ROMY SO51 34 E1
Robina Cl *WVILLE* PO7 82 B6
Robin Gdns *HORN* PO8 81 J1
TOTT SO40 52 B4
Robinia Gn *ROWN* SO16 42 D6
Robins Cl *FHAM/STUB* PO14 114 D4
Robins Meadow
FHAM/STUB PO14 95 H5
Robinson Rd
FHAM/STUB PO14 114 C6
Robinson Wy *HSEA* PO3 119 H4
Robin Sq *ELGH* SO50 43 K2
Rochester Rd *ENEY* PO4 19 K7
Rochester St *SHAM* SO14 5 L9
Rochford Rd *CHAM* PO6 100 C6
Rockall Cl *ROWN* SO16 41 K6
Rockbourne Cl *HAV* PO9 102 D2 6
Rockbourne Rd *WINW* SO22 21 G3
Rockery Cl *FAWY* SO45 90 D2
Rockingham Wy
FHAM/PORC PO16 98 E6
Rockleigh Dr *TOTT* SO40 68 C1
Rockleigh Rd *ROWN* SO16 54 E1
Rockram Cl *TOTT* SO40 50 E5
Rockram Gdns *FAWY* SO45 90 D3 2
Rockrose Wy *CHAM* PO6 99 K4
Rockstone La *SHAM* SO14 5 H6
Rockstone Pl *WSHM* SO15 4 F6
Rockville Dr *WVILLE* PO7 81 K6
Rodney Cl *LSOL/BMARY* PO13 131 K2
Rodney Rd *ENEY* PO4 19 K3
Rodney Wy *HORN* PO8 64 C6
Roebuck Av *FHAM* PO15 96 E1
Roebuck Cl *CHAM* PO6 100 E7 5
Roewood Cl *FAWY* SO45 109 K4 2
Roewood Rd *FAWY* SO45 109 K4
Rogate Gdns *FHAM/PORC* PO16 99 F5
Rogers Cl *ELGH* SO50 39 H6
GPORT PO12 16 A1
Rogers Md *HISD* PO11 121 G4
Rogers Rd *ELGH* SO50 39 H6
Roker Wy *ELGH* SO50 46 A2
Roland Cl *HORN* PO8 64 C6
Rollestone Rd *FAWY* SO45 109 J4
Roman Cl *CHFD* SO53 38 B3
Roman Dr *ROWN* SO16 43 F4
Roman Gdns *FAWY* SO45 90 E5 1
Roman Gv *FHAM/PORC* PO16 117 G1
Roman Landing *SELS* PO20 139 J6
Roman Rd *FAWY* SO45 90 D4
FAWY SO45 109 J1
ROWN SO16 43 F2
RWIN SO21 33 K4
Romans' Rd *WINC* SO23 2 D7
Roman Wy *FAWY* SO45 90 E5
HAV PO9 102 D4
Romford Rd *HLER* SO31 94 C6
Romill Cl *WEND* SO18 56 E1
Romsey Av *FHAM/PORC* PO16 98 D6
HSEA PO3 135 G2
Romsey Cl *ELGH* SO50 38 D7
Romsey Rd *ELGH* SO50 38 D7
WINW SO22 2 A5
HORN PO8 64 D2
LYND SO43 66 C7
ROWN SO16 41 J6
TOTT SO40 50 C4
Romyns Ct *FHAM/STUB* PO14 12 E6
Rookery Av *FHAM* PO15 75 H6
HLER SO31 75 G6
The Rookery *EMRTH* PO10 104 D5
Rookes Cl *HORN* PO8 64 C6
Rookley *HLER* SO31 73 F6
Rooksbridge *FAWY* SO45 90 D3 5
Rooksbury Cft *HAV* PO9 103 H1 5
Rooks Down Rd *WINW* SO22 25 G3

Rooksway Gv
FHAM/PORC PO16 98 B6
Rookwood Cl ELGH SO50 38 E4 4
Rookwood La SELS PO20 139 K4
Rookwood Rd SELS PO20 139 K6
Rookwood Vw WVILLE PO7 62 E7
Ropley Cl ITCH SO19 11 G9
Ropley Rd HAV PO9 103 J1
Rosebank Cl ROWN SO16 41 K6
Rosebay Cl ELGH SO50 46 B5 4
Rosebay Ct WVILLE PO7 102 A1 3
Rosebery Av CHAM PO6 101 F7
Rosebery Crs ELGH SO50 38 E4
Rosebury Av FAWY SO45 91 H5
Rose Cl FAWY SO45 91 H4 5
HEND SO30 58 B4
Rosedale Av ROMY SO51 35 F3
Rosedale Cl FHAM/STUB PO14 96 A6
Rose Hl HORN PO8 64 B6
Roselands HEND SO30 57 G4 3
HORN PO8 64 B7
Roselands Gdns PTSW SO17 55 H2
Roseleigh Dr TOTT SO40 52 D6
Rosemary Gdns FHAM PO15 75 J5
HEND SO30 58 B7
Rosemary La PSEA PO1 17 L4 4
Rosemary Wy HORN PO8 82 C1
Rosemoor Gv CHFD SO53 37 J1
Rosendale Rd CHFD SO53 38 A6 1
Rose Rd SHAM SO14 5 G3
TOTT SO40 53 F6
The Rosery GPORT PO12 132 E7 1
Rosetta Rd ENEY PO4 135 G4
Rosewall Rd ROWN SO16 54 A1
Rosewarne Ct WINC SO23 2 D2
Rosewood LSOL/BMARY PO13 116 B6
Rosewood Gdns TOTT SO40 70 B4
Rosina Cl WVILLE PO7 82 C5
Rosoman Rd ITCH SO19 10 F2
Rossan Av HLER SO31 94 C7
Ross Gdns ROWN SO16 54 B2
Rossington Av WEND SO18 6 F4
Rossington Wy WEND SO18 6 F4
Rosslyn Cl NBAD SO52 36 B6
Ross Wy LSOL/BMARY PO13 131 G1
Rostron Cl WEND SO18 56 D1 2
Rosyth Rd WEND SO18 6 F4
Rotary Ct HLER SO31 72 E7
Rothbury Cl ITCH SO19 11 H2
TOTT SO40 52 C3
Rother Cl WEND SO18 56 E3
Rother Dl ITCH SO19 73 H2
Rotherwick Cl HAV PO9 103 J1
Rothesay Rd GPORT PO12 132 D1
Rothsbury Dr CHFD SO53 37 J4
Rothschild Cl ITCH SO19 10 C8
Rothville Pl CHFD SO53 31 J7 2
Rothwell Cl CHAM PO6 99 K5 3
Roughdown La FAWY SO45 109 K6
Roundcopse FAWY SO45 90 D3 4
Roundhill Cl WEND SO18 56 D3
Roundhouse Dr TOTT SO40 52 A6
Roundhouse Meadow
EMRTH PO10 104 D7
Roundhuts Ri WINC SO23 3 K4
Roundway WVILLE PO7 82 A5
Routs Wy ROWN SO16 41 K4
Rowallan Av
LSOL/BMARY PO13 115 J6
Rowan Av HORN PO8 82 C3
Rowan Cl BPWT SO32 49 J7 1
HLER SO31 73 J5
LSOL/BMARY PO13 131 G3
ROMY SO51 35 H4
ROWN SO16 54 A1
TOTT SO40 52 C6
Rowan Gdns HEND SO30 58 C6
Rowan Rd HAV PO9 103 J3
The Rowans TOTT SO40 70 A4
Rowan Wy FHAM/STUB PO14 96 D6
Rowborough Rd WEND SO18 6 F3
Rowbury Rd HAV PO9 82 E7
Rowe Ashe Wy HLER SO31 94 E3 1
Rowhill Dr FAWY SO45 90 D3
Rowin Cl HISD PO11 138 A6
Rowland Rd CHAM PO6 99 H5 1
FHAM PO15 12 E4
Rowlands Av WVILLE PO7 81 K4
Rowlands Castle Rd HORN PO8 65 G6
Rowlands Cl CHFD SO53 37 H6
Rowley Cl HEND SO30 58 E4 1
Rowley Dr HEND SO30 58 E4
Rowlings Rd WINW SO22 21 G4
Rowner Cl LSOL/BMARY PO13 115 K6
Rowner La LSOL/BMARY PO13 115 K7
Rowner Rd LSOL/BMARY PO13 115 J6
Rownhams Cl ROWN SO16 41 K5
Rownhams La NBAD SO52 36 A5
ROMY SO51 42 A2
ROWN SO16 42 A4
Rownhams Rd HAV PO9 102 E1
NBAD SO52 36 B7
ROWN SO16 54 A2
Rownhams Rd North
ROWN SO16 42 A6
Rownhams Wy ROWN SO16 41 K5
Rowse Cl ROMY SO51 34 E1 2
Row Wood La
LSOL/BMARY PO13 115 J6
Royal Crescent Rd SHAM SO14 9 J4
Royal Gdns HAV PO9 83 H4
Royal Ga ENEY PO4 135 G6
Royal Sovereign Av
FHAM/STUB PO14 115 G2
Royal Wy WVILLE PO7 82 B6
Royce Cl SELS PO20 139 K7
Royce Wy SELS PO20 139 K7
Roydon Cl WINW SO22 25 G3
Royston Av ELGH SO50 38 D5
Royston Cl PTSW SO17 55 J2
Rozelle Cl WINW SO22 20 D2
Ruby Rd ITCH SO19 7 H7
Rudd La ROMY SO51 28 C1
Rudgwick Cl
FHAM/PORC PO16 98 E6 2
Rudmore Sq NEND PO2 118 B7
Ruffield Cl WINW SO22 21 F5
Rufford Cl ELGH SO50 38 D4
Rufus Cl CHFD SO53 38 B2
ROWN SO16 41 J5
Rufus Gdns TOTT SO40 52 B5
Rugby Rd SSEA PO5 19 G5
Rumbridge Gdns TOTT SO40 53 F5 1
Rumbridge St TOTT SO40 52 E6
Runnymede FHAM PO15 96 E2
HEND SO30 57 G3 4
The Rushes TOTT SO40 70 A3
Rushington Av TOTT SO40 52 E6
Rushington La TOTT SO40 52 D7
Rushmere La WVILLE PO7 62 C5
Ruskin Rd ELGH SO50 38 D5
ENEY PO4 19 L5
Ruskin Wy HORN PO8 82 A1
Rusland Cl CHFD SO53 37 J3
Russell Cl LSOL/BMARY PO13 131 G2
Russell Pl FHAM/PORC PO16 13 J5
PTSW SO17 5 J1
Russell Rd HAV PO9 14 F1
LSOL/BMARY PO13 131 G3
WINC SO23 21 K5
Russell St GPORT PO12 132 D2
SHAM SO14 9 H3
Russet Gdns EMRTH PO10 104 E6
Russett Cl BPWT SO32 49 J7 2
Rustan Cl ELGH SO50 46 C1
HEND SO30 58 A6 1
Rutland Gdns HLER SO31 73 K4
Rutland Wy WEND SO18 7 H1
Ruxley Cl FAWY SO45 109 K3
Rydal Cl CHAM PO6 100 A5
Rydal Rd GPORT PO12 116 D7
Ryde Pl LSOL/BMARY PO13 131 H4
Ryde Ter SHAM SO14 9 K3
Rye Cl NBAD SO52 37 G4
Ryecroft FHAM/STUB PO14 95 H4 3
HAV PO9 15 K4
Rye Dl TOTT SO40 68 B2
Rye Paddock La FAWY SO45 110 E3
Rylandes Ct ROWN SO16 54 A1

S

Sabre Rd EMRTH PO10 122 D4
Sackville St SSEA PO5 18 C6
Saddlers Cl ELGH SO50 38 D4
Sadlers La FAWY SO45 91 H5
Sadlers Wk EMRTH PO10 104 D6
Saffron Wy FHAM PO15 75 J5
Sage Cl WVILLE PO7 82 B7
St Agatha's Rd HLER SO31 93 K2 2
St Alban's Rd HAV PO9 103 H2
SHAM SO14 5 J8
St Andrew Cl HORN PO8 64 D2
St Andrews Cl NBAD SO52 35 K5
ROMY SO51 28 C3
St Andrews Pk ELGH SO50 46 B5
St Andrews Rd SHAM SO14 5 H8
CHAM PO6 102 A6
GPORT PO12 16 B6
HISD PO11 137 J6
SSEA PO5 18 E7
St Annes Cl WINW SO22 25 F3
St Anne's Gdns ITCH SO19 10 D5
St Anne's Gv FHAM/STUB PO14 97 G7
St Annes La BPWT SO32 60 E5
St Anne's Rd ITCH SO19 10 D6
St Ann's Crs GPORT PO12 132 D2
St Ann's Rd ENEY PO4 19 K8 1
HORN PO8 64 D5
St Aubin's Av ITCH SO19 7 H8
St Aubin's Pk HISD PO11 136 E5
St Augustine Gdns PTSW SO17 6 A1
St Augustine Rd ENEY PO4 19 J8
St Austell Cl ELGH SO50 39 H7 1
St Barbara Wy NEND PO2 118 E3 3
St Barbe Cl ROMY SO51 35 F4 2
St Bartholomew's Gdns
SSEA PO5 18 F7 1
St Blaize Rd ROMY SO51 35 G2 3
St Bonnet Dr BPWT SO32 48 D3 3
St Catherine's Rd ELGH SO50 38 D5
HISD PO11 136 D5
WINC SO23 3 H7
St Catherine St SSEA PO5 134 C7
St Catherines Vw HEND SO30 57 K6 3
St Catherines Wy
FHAM/PORC PO16 98 B5
St Chad's Av NEND PO2 118 D5
St Christopher Av
FHAM/PORC PO16 13 K2
St Christophers Cl NBAD SO52 36 A6
St Christopher's Rd HAV PO9 102 D3
St Clares Av HAV PO9 82 E6
St Clements Cl ROMY SO51 34 D2 4
St Clement St WINC SO23 2 D5
St Colman's Av CHAM PO6 101 F6
St Cross Rd WINC SO23 25 H5
St Cuthberts Cl HLER SO31 95 G2 2
St Cuthberts La HLER SO31 95 G2
St David's Cl TOTT SO40 52 B3
St Davids Rd HLER SO31 94 E3
SSEA PO5 18 F6
St Denys' Rd PTSW SO17 5 M1
PTSW SO17 55 J3
PTSW SO17 55 J3
St Edmund Cl FHAM/STUB PO14 95 G5
St Edmund's Rd ROWN SO16 54 C4
St Edward's Rd GPORT PO12 16 B6
HLER SO31 72 E5
SSEA PO5 18 C8
St Elizabeth's Av WEND SO18 7 J5
St Evox Cl ROWN SO16 42 A6
St Faith's Cl GPORT PO12 132 D3
St Faith's Rd PSEA PO1 18 D2
WINC SO23 25 J3
St Francis Av WEND SO18 7 K2
St Francis Cl FAWY SO45 128 B1 2
St Francis Ct NEND PO2 118 D3 3
St Francis Pl HAV PO9 103 F3
St Francis Rd FAWY SO45 128 B1
GPORT PO12 133 F7
St Gabriel's Rd WEND SO18 7 J5
St George Cl HLER SO31 73 J4
St George's Av HAV PO9 15 K4
St Georges Rd HLER SO31 94 E3
CHAM PO6 100 E6
ENEY PO4 135 F6
HISD PO11 136 E5
PSEA PO1 17 L5
St Georges Sq PSEA PO1 17 M4 3
St Georges St SHAM SO14 9 G2
WINC SO23 2 E4
St George's Wy PSEA PO1 17 M4
St Giles Cl WINC SO23 3 H6
St Giles Wy HORN PO8 64 D2
St Helena Gdns WEND SO18 56 C1
St Helena Wy
FHAM/PORC PO16 99 F6
St Helen's Cl ENEY PO4 134 E6
St Helens Rd GPORT PO12 132 B5
HISD PO11 136 E5
St Hellen's Rd CHAM PO6 101 J6
St Hermans Rd HISD PO11 137 K6
St Hilda Av HORN PO8 64 D2
St Hubert Rd HORN PO8 64 D2
St James' La WINW SO22 2 B5
St James' Rd EMRTH PO10 104 C6
HEND SO30 57 G2
St James's Cl WSHM SO15 54 D3
St James's Park Rd ROWN SO16 54 D2
St James's Rd SSEA PO5 18 C6
WSHM SO15 54 D3
St James's St PSEA PO1 18 A3 1
St James' Ter WINW SO22 2 C5
St James' Vls WINC SO23 2 C6
St James Wy FHAM/PORC PO16 99 G6
St John's Av WVILLE PO7 101 K2
St John's Cl GPORT PO12 16 A3
HISD PO11 137 F5
ROWN SO16 41 K4
St Johns Ct TOTT SO40 70 A4 2
St Johns Dr TOTT SO40 69 K4
St Johns Gdns ROMY SO51 34 E2 7
St Johns Glebe ROWN SO16 42 A4
St John's Rd CHAM PO6 101 F6
ELGH SO50 38 E6
EMRTH PO10 105 F5
HAV PO9 102 D2
HEND SO30 73 K1
HLER SO31 95 G4
WINC SO23 3 H4
St John's St FAWY SO45 91 H2
WINC SO23 3 G5
St Lawrence Rd ELGH SO50 38 D6
SHAM SO14 9 J4
St Leonard's Av HISD PO11 137 H5
St Leonards Cl FHAM PO15 95 K3
St Leonard's Rd WINC SO23 3 J7
St Lukes Cl HEND SO30 58 B3 4
St Luke's Rd GPORT PO12 132 D2
St Margaret's Cl WEND SO18 7 K5
St Margarets La
FHAM/STUB PO14 95 K5
St Margarets Rd HISD PO11 137 H5
St Mark's Cl GPORT PO12 132 D7
St Mark's Rd GPORT PO12 132 D7
NEND PO2 118 C6 3
St Martin's Cl ROWN SO16 53 K1
WINC SO23 3 H4
St Mary's Av GPORT PO12 132 D6
St Marys Cl WINC SO23 22 B2
St Mary's Pl SHAM SO14 9 H1
St Mary's Rd ELGH SO50 39 G6
FHAM/STUB PO14 114 D3
HISD PO11 137 H4
HLER SO31 73 F7
PSEA PO1 19 H1
SHAM SO14 5 H7
St Mary's Ter RWIN SO21 33 K3 1
St Mary St WINW SO22 25 G3
SHAM SO14 9 J2
St Matthews Cl SHAM SO14 5 H8
St Matthew's Rd CHAM PO6 100 E6
WINW SO22 21 G5
St Michaels Cl FAWY SO45 110 B6
St Michaels Ct CHAM PO6 100 A5 3
St Michael's Gdns WINC SO23 2 D6
St Michael's Gv
FHAM/STUB PO14 12 F8
St Michaels Rd HLER SO31 94 E4
HAV PO9 102 D3
PSEA PO1 18 B5
TOTT SO40 52 E3
WINC SO23 2 D7
St Michael's St SHAM SO14 8 F3
St Michaels Wy HORN PO8 64 D2
St Monica Rd ITCH SO19 11 H4
St Nicholas WINC SO23 22 A1
St Nicholas Av
LSOL/BMARY PO13 131 K1
St Nicholas' Rd HAV PO9 102 D3 2
St Nicholas St PSEA PO1 17 M7
St Paul's Hl WINW SO22 2 C3
St Paul's Rd HLER SO31 74 D7
SSEA PO5 18 B5
St Paul's Sq SSEA PO5 18 B6 3
St Peter's Av HISD PO11 121 K5
St Peter's Gv SSEA PO5 18 E7
St Peter's Rd HISD PO11 121 K5
St Peter's Sq EMRTH PO10 104 C6
St Peter's St BPWT SO32 48 D3
St Peter St WINC SO23 2 E4
St Philip's Wy WEND SO18 7 J5
St Piran's Av HSEA PO3 135 F1
St Ronan's Av ENEY PO4 19 H9
St Ronan's Rd ENEY PO4 19 H9
St Sebastian Crs
FHAM/PORC PO16 13 K1
St Simon Cl HLER SO31 95 G3 2
St Simon's Rd SSEA PO5 134 C6
St Stephen's Rd WINW SO22 21 G5
NEND PO2 118 D7 2
St Swithun Cl BPWT SO32 48 C3 4
St Swithun's Cl ROMY SO51 35 J1 1
St Swithun's Rd NEND PO2 118 E5
St Swithun St WINC SO23 2 D6
St Theresas Cl HAV PO9 102 D3
St Thomas Av HISD PO11 136 E5
St Thomas Cl FHAM/PORC PO16 13 L3
St Thomas's Rd GPORT PO12 116 E7
St Thomas's St PSEA PO1 17 L7
St Thomas St WINC SO23 2 D6
St Tristan Cl HLER SO31 95 G3
St Ursula Gv SSEA PO5 18 E7 2
St Valerie Rd GPORT PO12 16 B8
St Vigor Wy RWIN SO21 39 J1
St Vincent Crs HORN PO8 64 C6
St Vincent Rd GPORT PO12 16 B1
SSEA PO5 18 E9
St Vincent St SSEA PO5 18 B5 4
St Winifred's Rd ROWN SO16 54 D2
Salcombe Av HSEA PO3 119 F6
Salcombe Cl CHFD SO53 37 J6
Salcombe Crs TOTT SO40 52 D6
Salcombe Rd TOTT SO40 52 D6
WSHM SO15 54 C5
Salcot Rd WINC SO23 21 K5
Salem St WSHM SO15 54 D3
Salerno Dr GPORT PO12 132 C4 5
Salerno Rd NEND PO2 118 C3
ROWN SO16 42 D7
Salet Wy WVILLE PO7 82 C4
Salisbury Cl ELGH SO50 38 E6 1
Salisbury Rd CHAM PO6 101 F7
ENEY PO4 134 E6
PTSW SO17 55 H1
TOTT SO40 40 A7
Salisbury St WSHM SO15 4 F7 1
Salisbury Ter
LSOL/BMARY PO13 131 G3
Salmon Dr ELGH SO50 45 J1
Salterns Av ENEY PO4 135 G3
Salterns Cl HISD PO11 137 K5
Salterns Est FHAM/PORC PO16 13 K9
Salterns La FAWY SO45 110 E3
FHAM/PORC PO16 97 J7
HISD PO11 137 J5
HLER SO31 73 K7
Salterns Rd FHAM/STUB PO14 114 C7
Salters Acres WINW SO22 21 F5
The Saltings CHAM PO6 101 K7
HAV PO9 121 G1
Saltmarsh La HISD PO11 137 F3
Saltmarsh Rd SHAM SO14 9 K4
Saltmead PTSW SO17 56 A3 2
Salt Meat La GPORT PO12 16 E2
Salvia Cl WVILLE PO7 82 B7 4
Salwey Rd HEND SO30 58 C7
Sampan Cl HLER SO31 94 D5
Sampson Rd
FHAM/STUB PO14 115 G1
PSEA PO1 17 K2
Samson Cl LSOL/BMARY PO13 132 A1
Samuel Rd PSEA PO1 19 J2
Sandcroft Cl GPORT PO12 132 B5 1
Sanderling Rd ENEY PO4 135 H3
The Sanderlings HISD PO11 137 H6 1
Sandford Av GPORT PO12 132 A4
Sandhill La LSOL/BMARY PO13 131 H1
Sandhurst Rd WSHM SO15 4 D7
San Diego Rd GPORT PO12 16 A1
Sandisplatt FHAM/STUB PO14 96 D6 3
Sandleford Rd HAV PO9 82 E6
Sandlewood Cl TOTT SO40 52 B4 1
Sandown Cl GPORT PO12 132 A5 1
Sandown Rd CHAM PO6 100 D7
WSHM SO15 54 C3
Sandpiper Cl HORN PO8 64 B5
TOTT SO40 69 K4
Sandpiper Rd ROWN SO16 42 B6
Sandport Gv FHAM/PORC PO16 98 E7
Sandringham Cl NBAD SO52 37 G6
Sandringham La PSEA PO1 19 G3 4
Sandringham Rd
FHAM/STUB PO14 96 C6
PSEA PO1 19 G3
WEND SO18 6 D1
Sandy Brow WVILLE PO7 101 J2
Sandycroft HLER SO31 94 C6
Sandy Field Crs HORN PO8 81 K2
Sandy La BPWT SO32 60 D3
ELGH SO50 46 A1
FHAM/STUB PO14 96 A6
LYND SO43 86 C2
NBAD SO52 36 C5 1
ROMY SO51 29 F6
Sandy Point Rd HISD PO11 138 B7
Sanross Cl FHAM/STUB PO14 114 B6
Sapphire Cl WVILLE PO7 82 B6 3
Sapphire Rdg WVILLE PO7 82 B6
Saracens Rd CHFD SO53 38 C3
Sarnia Ct ROWN SO16 53 K1
Sarum Cl WINW SO22 25 F1
Sarum Rd CHFD SO53 38 B4
WINW SO22 24 A1
Sarum Vw WINW SO22 24 E2
Satchell La HLER SO31 93 K3
Saturn Cl ROWN SO16 42 A7
Saunders Ms ENEY PO4 135 G6 3
Savernake Cl
LSOL/BMARY PO13 116 A5 3
ROMY SO51 35 G1 3
Saville Cl ELGH SO50 39 G5
GPORT PO12 132 C5
Saville Gdns FHAM/PORC PO16 12 F1
Sawyer Cl WINW SO22 21 F6 2
Saxholm Cl ROWN SO16 43 G5
Saxholm Dl ROWN SO16 43 G5
Saxholm Wy ROWN SO16 43 G5
Saxley Ct HAV PO9 82 D7
Saxon Cl FHAM/PORC PO16 98 E5
HLER SO31 94 D5
Saxon Gdns HEND SO30 57 K7
Saxon Rd FAWY SO45 110 C6
WINC SO23 2 E2
WSHM SO15 4 A9
Saxon Wy ROMY SO51 35 G3
Sayers Rd ELGH SO50 45 G1
Scafell Av FHAM/STUB PO14 12 B8
Scantabout Av CHFD SO53 38 B3
Scholars' Wk CHAM PO6 101 H7
School Cl CHFD SO53 37 J5
School La CHFD SO53 37 H6
EMRTH PO10 104 C6
EMRTH PO10 104 E1
HLER SO31 93 K5
RCCH PO18 105 J7
WINC SO23 22 A2
WVILLE PO7 62 C7
School Rd FAWY SO45 91 H2
FAWY SO45 110 D4
GPORT PO12 116 C6
HAV PO9 14 D5
HLER SO31 73 K5
ROMY SO51 35 H1
RWIN SO21 33 J3
TOTT SO40 53 F6
WHAM PO17 77 H2
Schooner Wy HLER SO31 94 D5
HSEA PO3 135 H2
The Scimitars
FHAM/STUB PO14 114 C4 3
Scivier's La BPWT SO32 47 H1
Scotland Cl ELGH SO50 46 D1
Scotney Ct HAV PO9 83 J7 2
Scott Cl FHAM/STUB PO14 114 D3
RWIN SO21 39 K2
Scotter Rd ELGH SO50 39 G7
Scott Rd ELGH SO50 44 C1
HSEA PO3 118 E2
ITCH SO19 10 F7
PSEA PO1 17 K2
Scratchface La HAV PO9 102 C4
WVILLE PO7 102 A2
Scullards La SHAM SO14 8 F1
Seabird Wy FHAM/PORC PO16 13 K9
Seacombe Gn ROWN SO16 53 J3
Sea Crest Rd
LSOL/BMARY PO13 131 G3
Seafield Park Rd
FHAM/STUB PO14 114 C6
Seafield Rd FHAM/PORC PO16 98 E7
HSEA PO3 119 F6
ROWN SO16 53 J2
Seafields EMRTH PO10 104 B6
Seaford Cl HLER SO31 73 J4 5
Sea Front HISD PO11 137 G6
Seagarth La ROWN SO16 54 E1
Seager's Ct PSEA PO1 17 K7 1
Sea Grove Av HISD PO11 137 H6
Seagrove Rd NEND PO2 118 C6
Seagull Cl ENEY PO4 135 H2 3
Seagull La EMRTH PO10 104 C5
The Seagulls
LSOL/BMARY PO13 131 H4 1
Sea Kings FHAM/STUB PO14 114 C5 4
Sea La LSOL/BMARY PO13 114 D7
Seamead FHAM/STUB PO14 114 D7
Searles Hl RWIN SO21 33 K3
Sea Rd ITCH SO19 10 B2
Seaton Av HSEA PO3 119 F7
Seaton Cl FHAM/STUB PO14 114 D5
WEND SO18 7 L1
Seaview Av FHAM/PORC PO16 99 H5
Sea View Rd CHAM PO6 101 H6
Seaview Rd HISD PO11 137 K5
Seaward Dr SELS PO20 139 K7
Seaward Rd FAWY SO45 91 J3
ITCH SO19 10 C1
Seaway Crs ENEY PO4 135 H4
Seaway Gv FHAM/PORC PO16 117 F1
Sebastian Gv WVILLE PO7 82 B5 4
Second Av CHAM PO6 100 D6
CHAM PO6 101 K7
EMRTH PO10 105 G6
HAV PO9 15 J3
WSHM SO15 53 J5
Second St FAWY SO45 92 B6
Sedbergh Rd ROWN SO16 53 J3
Sedgefield Cl CHAM PO6 99 J6
TOTT SO40 52 B4
Sedgeley Gv GPORT PO12 116 D7
Sedgemead HLER SO31 92 E1 1
Sedgewick Cl
LSOL/BMARY PO13 115 K7
Sedgewick Rd ELGH SO50 39 G7
ITCH SO19 7 L9
Sedgley Cl SSEA PO5 18 E6
Segars La RWIN SO21 33 J4
Segensworth Rd FHAM PO15 95 K3
Selangor Av EMRTH PO10 104 A5
Selborne Av HAV PO9 102 E1
WEND SO18 7 L2
Selborne Gdns GPORT PO12 132 D4
Selborne Pl WINW SO22 25 G3 1
Selbourne Dr ELGH SO50 38 D6
Selbourne Rd HAV PO9 14 D5
TOTT SO40 52 C4 2
Selbourne Ter PSEA PO1 19 H4
Seldon Cl WINW SO22 24 E4
Selhurst Wy ELGH SO50 46 B2
Sellwood Rd HLER SO31 73 F7
Selsdon Av ROMY SO51 35 G2
Selsey Av ENEY PO4 135 F6
GPORT PO12 116 C7
Selsey Cl HISD PO11 138 C6
ROWN SO16 53 K2
Selsmore Av HISD PO11 137 K6
Selsmore Rd HISD PO11 137 H5
Selwyn Gdns ELGH SO50 38 D5
Sengana Cl HEND SO30 58 C6 2
Senlac Rd ROMY SO51 35 G3
Sennen Pl WHAM PO17 99 K7
Sentinel Cl WVILLE PO7 82 C4
Seps 4 Rd FAWY SO45 110 E3
September Cl HEND SO30 57 G3
Serle Cl TOTT SO40 52 A5
Serle Gdns TOTT SO40 52 C6
Sermon Rd WINW SO22 20 E6
Serpentine Rd
FHAM/PORC PO16 13 J2
SSEA PO5 18 C9 2
WVILLE PO7 101 H3
Setters Cl RWIN SO21 39 J2
Settle Cl ROWN SO16 54 C4 5
Settlers Cl PSEA PO1 18 E2 5
Sevenoaks Rd CHAM PO6 100 D6
Severn Cl CHAM PO6 100 A5
FHAM/PORC PO16 98 D6 1
Severn Rd ROWN SO16 53 K4
Severn Wy HEND SO30 57 G3 3
Seward Ri ROMY SO51 35 H2 1
Seymour Cl CHFD SO53 38 B5
NEND PO2 134 C1
TOTT SO40 52 B3
Seymour La NBAD SO52 36 A6
Seymour Rd
LSOL/BMARY PO13 131 G4
ROWN SO16 54 D1
Shackleton Rd
LSOL/BMARY PO13 116 A7
Shadwell Rd NEND PO2 118 D5
Shaftesbury Av CHFD SO53 37 K6
PTSW SO17 55 J3
WVILLE PO7 101 J2
Shaftesbury Rd SSEA PO5 18 C9
Shaftsbury Rd GPORT PO12 16 C6 3
Shaggs Meadow LYND SO43 86 C1

Shakespeare Av PTSW SO17 5 J2
Shakespeare Dr TOTT SO40 52 C2
Shakespeare Gdns HORN PO8 81 K2
Shakespeare Rd ELGH SO50 38 C5
PSEA PO1 19 H1
Shalbourne Rd GPORT PO12 132 D1
Shalcombe HLER SO31 73 F6
Shaldon Cl ROWN SO16 42 C7
Shaldon Rd HAV PO9 83 J7 8
Shales Rd WEND SO18 7 J4
Shamblehurst La HEND SO30 58 B3
Shamblehurst La North
BPWT SO32 58 C1
Shamblehurst La South
HEND SO30 58 B4
Shamrock Cl GPORT PO12 16 E6
Shamrock Rd ITCH SO19 10 B3
Shamrock Wy FAWY SO45 91 H1
Shanklin Crs WSHM SO15 54 E3
Shanklin Rd ENEY PO4 19 H6 1
WSHM SO15 54 E2
Shannon Cl FHAM PO15 12 A3
Shannon Rd
FHAM/STUB PO14 114 C3 3
FHAM/STUB PO14 115 G2
Shannon Wy CHFD SO53 37 J4
Shapton Cl FAWY SO45 109 J3 1
Sharon Rd HEND SO30 57 F2
Sharpness Cl
FHAM/STUB PO14 96 D6 4
Sharps Cl HSEA PO3 119 G4
Sharps Rd HAV PO9 103 J1
Shaw Cl TOTT SO40 52 C5 5
WEND SO18 56 D2
Shawfield Rd HAV PO9 15 H6
Shawford Cl ROWN SO16 43 F7 1
TOTT SO40 52 A5 2
Shawford Gv HAV PO9 102 D1
Shawford Rd RWIN SO21 33 J3
Shearer Rd PSEA PO1 19 H1
Shears Rd ELGH SO50 39 H7
Shearwater Av
FHAM/PORC PO16 98 B6
Shearwater Cl
LSOL/BMARY PO13 115 J5
Shearwater Dr CHAM PO6 102 A7
Sheepwash La WVILLE PO7 80 E5
Sheffield Cl ELGH SO50 39 G5
Sheffield Rd PSEA PO1 19 G3
Sheldrake Gdns ROWN SO16 42 C6
Shelford Rd ENEY PO4 135 G3
Shellcroft HLER SO31 94 C6 6
Shelley Av CHAM PO6 99 H5
Shelley Cl WINW SO22 21 G7
RWIN SO21 23 K1
Shelley Gdns HORN PO8 81 K2
Shelley Rd ELGH SO50 44 C2
ITCH SO19 57 G6
TOTT SO40 52 C2
Shenley Cl FHAM PO15 96 D4
Shepards Cl FHAM/STUB PO14 96 D6
Shepherds Cl WINW SO22 24 E4
TOTT SO40 50 E6
Shepherds Hey Rd TOTT SO40 52 A3
Shepherds La RWIN SO21 32 C3
Shepherds Purse Cl
HLER SO31 94 E4 5
Shepherds Rd TOTT SO40 50 E6
WINC SO23 3 K4
Shepherds Wy ROWN SO16 41 H6
Sheppard Cl HORN PO8 64 B6
Shepton Br BROC SO42 107 G2
Sherborne Ct ELGH SO50 38 C4
Sherborne Rd PTSW SO17 55 J2
Sherborne Wy HEND SO30 58 B6
Sherfield Av HAV PO9 103 H1
Sheridan Cl WINW SO22 25 F3
ITCH SO19 7 M8
Sheridan Gdns HLER SO31 75 H5
TOTT SO40 52 C5
Sheringham Rd CHAM PO6 100 C5 2
Sherringham Cl FAWY SO45 110 E4
Sherwood Av HEND SO30 74 B1
Sherwood Cl ROWN SO16 55 F1 6
Sherwood Gdns HLER SO31 94 D2
Sherwood Rd CHFD SO53 38 B1
GPORT PO12 132 D4
Sherwood Wy FAWY SO45 128 B1
Shetland Cl CHAM PO6 100 E5
TOTT SO40 52 A4
Shetland Ri HLER SO31 75 G7
Shillinglee WVILLE PO7 101 K3
Shipbuilding Rd PSEA PO1 133 J1
Shipcote La BPWT SO32 48 D1
Ship Leopard St PSEA PO1 17 L4 5
Shipley Rd RWIN SO21 33 K2
Shire Cl HLER SO31 75 G6
HORN PO8 82 C4
The Shires HEND SO30 57 K6
Shirley Av ENEY PO4 135 H4
WSHM SO15 54 D4
Shirley High St ROWN SO16 54 C4
Shirley Park Rd ROWN SO16 54 C4
Shirley Rd SSEA PO5 134 D6
WSHM SO15 54 D4
Sholing Ct HAV PO9 82 E7
Sholing Rd ITCH SO19 10 C1
Shooters Hill Cl ITCH SO19 11 J4
Shoot Hl WHAM PO17 79 G2
Shoot La LSOL/BMARY PO13 115 H7
Shop La HLER SO31 73 H2
Shore Av HSEA PO3 135 G2
Shore Crs BPWT SO32 48 E4 4
Shorefield Rd TOTT SO40 70 A3
Shorehaven CHAM PO6 99 J6
Shore La BPWT SO32 48 E4
Shore Rd FAWY SO45 91 J2
Shorewell HLER SO31 73 F6 6
Shorewood Cl HLER SO31 95 F5
Short Hl ROMY SO51 35 H1
Short Rd FHAM/STUB PO14 114 B5
Short Rw PSEA PO1 17 M2
Shorts Rd ELGH SO50 46 A1
Shraveshill Cl TOTT SO40 52 C3
Shrubbery Cl FHAM/PORC PO16 99 F7
The Shrubbery GPORT PO12 132 C1
Shrubbs Hill Gdns LYND SO43 86 C2 5
Shrubbs Hill Rd LYND SO43 86 C2
Shrubland Cl WEND SO18 7 J2
Sibland Cl FHAM/STUB PO14 12 A8
The Sidings HLER SO31 93 G1
Sidlesham Cl HISD PO11 138 C6
Sidmouth Av HSEA PO3 119 F7
Silchester Rd HSEA PO3 135 G1
Silkin Gdns TOTT SO40 52 C6
Silkstead Av HAV PO9 83 G7
Silkstead La RWIN SO21 32 C4
Silver Birch Av
FHAM/STUB PO14 12 C7
Silver Birch Cl ITCH SO19 11 K2
Silver Birches HLER SO31 73 J5
Silverdale Dr WVILLE PO7 81 H3
Silverdale Rd WSHM SO15 4 D5
Silver Hl WINC SO23 2 F5
Silverlock Cl NEND PO2 118 C7 5
Silversands Gdns HISD PO11 137 J6
Silvers End FAWY SO45 91 H5 8
Silver St LYND SO43 86 A1
SSEA PO5 18 B7
Silvers Wd TOTT SO40 52 B3
Silverthorne Wy WVILLE PO7 81 J5
Silvertrees EMRTH PO10 104 C4
Silverwood Cl WINW SO22 25 G3
Silvester Rd HORN PO8 81 K3
Silwood Cl WINW SO22 21 G6
Simmons Cl HEND SO30 58 B4
Simmons Gn HISD PO11 137 K5
Simnel St SHAM SO14 8 F3 4
Simon Wy WEND SO18 57 H5
Simpson Cl FHAM/PORC PO16 99 F6
Simpson Rd NEND PO2 118 B6
Sinah La HISD PO11 136 D5
Sinclair Rd ROWN SO16 42 B6
Singleton Wy TOTT SO40 52 A4
Sir Christopher Cl FAWY SO45 91 J2 1
Sirdar Rd PTSW SO17 55 K1
Sir Galahad Rd NBAD SO52 37 G4 2
Sir George's Rd WSHM SO15 4 A7
Sir Lancelot Cl NBAD SO52 37 G4
Siskin Cl BPWT SO32 48 B3
ROWN SO16 42 B6
Siskin Gv WVILLE PO7 82 B7
Sissinghurst Cl ITCH SO19 11 H8
Sissinghurst Rd
FHAM/PORC PO16 98 E7 1
Six Oaks Rd NBAD SO52 36 B5
Sixpenny Cl HLER SO31 95 F5
Sixth Av CHAM PO6 100 D6
Sizer Wy FAWY SO45 90 D2
Skew Rd WHAM PO17 99 F4
Skipper Wy LSOL/BMARY PO13 131 G3
Skipton Rd CHFD SO53 38 A6
Skylark Mdw FHAM PO15 96 A1
Skys Wood Rd NBAD SO52 37 G3
Slades Hl FAWY SO45 110 C5
Slater Cl TOTT SO40 52 A4
Sleepers Delle Gdns WINW SO22 2 A7
Sleepers Hl WINW SO22 25 G2
WINW SO22 25 G2
Sleepers Hill Gdns WINW SO22 25 G2 1
Slindon St PSEA PO1 18 D3 4
Slingsby Cl PSEA PO1 18 B7 10
Slipper Rd EMRTH PO10 104 D7
Sloane Av FAWY SO45 110 A3 1
Sloane Ct FAWY SO45 110 A3 2
Sloane Pk BPWT SO32 60 E5
Sloe Tree Cl HLER SO31 95 H4 4
Smallcutts Av EMRTH PO10 105 G5
Smeeton Rd
LSOL/BMARY PO13 131 G2
Smith Cl FAWY SO45 110 C5
Smithe Cl ELGH SO50 38 D7 3
Smith Gv HEND SO30 58 B7
Smith La EMRTH PO10 123 F6
Smith's Fld ROMY SO51 35 F1 3
Smiths La BPWT SO32 61 G4
Smith St GPORT PO12 132 C3
The Smithy WVILLE PO7 80 D1
Smythe Rd ITCH SO19 73 G2
Snakemoor La BPWT SO32 46 D6
Snapdragon Cl HLER SO31 94 E4 6
Snape Cl LSOL/BMARY PO13 115 K7 2
Snellgrove Cl TOTT SO40 52 B2
Snellgrove Pl TOTT SO40 52 B2 1
Snowberry Crs HAV PO9 103 J3
Snowdon Dr FHAM/STUB PO14 12 C8
Soake Rd WVILLE PO7 81 G2
Soberton Rd HAV PO9 103 F3
Soldridge Cl HAV PO9 83 J7 9
Solent Av ITCH SO19 57 H6
Solent Cl CHFD SO53 38 B4
Solent Dr FAWY SO45 91 G2
HISD PO11 137 G6
HLER SO31 112 C1
Solent Mdw HLER SO31 93 K5
Solent Rd CHAM PO6 101 H6
FAWY SO45 91 F6
FHAM/STUB PO14 114 B6
HAV PO9 14 C5
Solent Vw FHAM/PORC PO16 98 E5
Solent Wy BROC SO42 108 D2
BROC SO42 126 C1
FHAM/STUB PO14 114 B6
GPORT PO12 16 E9
GPORT PO12 132 B5
HAV PO9 14 A7
HSEA PO3 135 J2
LSOL/BMARY PO13 131 H5
PSEA PO1 17 M4 4
SHAM SO14 9 G5
Solomons La BPWT SO32 61 G2
Solona Cl CHFD SO53 38 C3 2
Somborne Dr HAV PO9 103 G1
Somerford Cl ITCH SO19 7 G8
Somers Cl WINW SO22 25 G3
Somerset Av WEND SO18 7 L5
Somerset Crs CHFD SO53 37 K7
Somerset Rd PTSW SO17 55 K2
SSEA PO5 134 C7
Somerset Ter WSHM SO15 54 C6
Somers Rd SSEA PO5 18 F5
Somers Rd North PSEA PO1 18 F4
Somerton Av WEND SO18 7 K4
Somervell Cl GPORT PO12 132 D6
Somervell Dr FHAM/PORC PO16 13 G2
Sonnet Wy WVILLE PO7 82 C5 1
Sopley Ct HAV PO9 83 J7 10
Sopwith Wy HLER SO31 74 D5
Sorrel Cl ROMY SO51 35 H1
WVILLE PO7 82 B7
Sorrel Dr FHAM PO15 75 J6
Sorrell Cl HLER SO31 94 E4
Southampton Hl
FHAM/STUB PO14 96 A5
Southampton Rd CHAM PO6 99 J6
ELGH SO50 44 E1
FAWY SO45 91 H3
FHAM PO15 95 H1
FHAM/PORC PO16 13 J4
FHAM/STUB PO14 95 J4
LYND SO43 67 F7
ROMY SO51 35 F4
TOTT SO40 50 E5
Southampton St WSHM SO15 4 F6 1
South Av FAWY SO45 110 B4
NEND PO2 118 D3
South Bay EMRTH PO10 122 D4
Southbourne Av CHAM PO6 101 G7
EMRTH PO10 104 E6
FAWY SO45 109 K3
Southbrook Cl HAV PO9 14 E7
Southbrook Rd HAV PO9 14 E8
Southcliff
LSOL/BMARY PO13 131 F1 3
Southcliff Rd SHAM SO14 5 H5
South Cl GPORT PO12 132 C6
HAV PO9 15 G6
ROMY SO51 35 H1 6
South Ct HLER SO31 93 H4
Southcroft Rd GPORT PO12 132 C3
South Cross St GPORT PO12 16 F5
Southdene Rd CHFD SO53 37 K5
Southdown Rd CHAM PO6 101 F6
HORN PO8 64 D1
RWIN SO21 33 G3
South Downs Wy WINC SO23 3 H7
Southdown Vw WVILLE PO7 81 H3
South Dr WINW SO22 20 D3
ROMY SO51 28 A6
South East Crs ITCH SO19 11 G2
South East Rd ITCH SO19 11 G1
South End Cl RWIN SO21 31 J3
Southern Gdns TOTT SO40 52 D5
Southern Rd HEND SO30 57 G4
WSHM SO15 8 C1
Southfields Cl BPWT SO32 48 D3
South Front SHAM SO14 9 H1
Southgate St WINC SO23 2 D5
South La EMRTH PO10 105 H3
HORN PO8 65 J1
Southleigh Gv HISD PO11 137 G4
Southleigh Rd EMRTH PO10 104 C3
HAV PO9 15 J5
South Ldg FHAM PO15 96 C5
Southmead Rd FHAM PO15 12 B5
South Millers Dl CHFD SO53 37 J3
South Mill Rd WSHM SO15 54 A5
Southmoor La HAV PO9 14 B8
South Pde ENEY PO4 134 C7
South Pl LSOL/BMARY PO13 131 H4
South Rd CHAM PO6 99 K4
CHAM PO6 101 J7
HISD PO11 137 G5
HORN PO8 64 D3
PSEA PO1 134 D1
PTSW SO17 5 L2
WHAM PO17 79 K7
Southsea Ter SSEA PO5 18 B8
South Sp CHAM PO6 100 A4
South St ELGH SO50 44 D3
EMRTH PO10 104 C6
FAWY SO45 91 H3
FHAM/STUB PO14 96 A6
GPORT PO12 16 E6
HAV PO9 14 F6
SSEA PO5 18 B7 11
South Ter PSEA PO1 17 L3 2
South Trestle Rd FAWY SO45 111 F2
South Vw WINW SO22 2 B4
South View Rd WINW SO22 24 E5
WSHM SO15 4 B3
Southway FHAM PO15 95 K3
Southways FHAM/STUB PO14 114 E5
Southwick Av
FHAM/PORC PO16 99 H5
Southwick Cl WINW SO22 21 G3 4
Southwick Ct
FHAM/STUB PO14 115 H1 1
Southwick Hill Rd CHAM PO6 100 D5
Southwick Rd CHAM PO6 100 B4
WHAM PO17 77 K2
WVILLE PO7 80 D1
South Wood Gdns HLER SO31 94 E3
Southwood Rd HISD PO11 137 K6
NEND PO2 118 D3
Sovereign Crs
FHAM/STUB PO14 95 F5
Sovereign Dr ENEY PO4 135 J3 1
HEND SO30 58 C6
Sovereign La WVILLE PO7 101 K3
Sovereign Wy ELGH SO50 38 C4
Sowden Cl HEND SO30 58 A5
Spalding Rd ITCH SO19 57 G7
Spaniard's La ROMY SO51 34 E7
Sparkford Cl WINW SO22 2 B7
Sparkford Rd WINW SO22 2 B7
Spa Rd SHAM SO14 8 F2
Sparrow Cl HORN PO8 82 A1
Sparrow Ct
LSOL/BMARY PO13 131 G1 7
Sparrowgrove RWIN SO21 33 F5
Sparrow Sq ELGH SO50 44 A1
Sparsholt Cl HAV PO9 102 D1
Sparsholt Rd ITCH SO19 10 E9
Spartan Cl EMRTH PO10 122 D3
FHAM/STUB PO14 114 D2
Speakers Corner Rbt SHAM SO14 9 G2
Spear Rd SHAM SO14 5 H3
Specks La ENEY PO4 19 L5
Speedwell Cl HLER SO31 94 E4 7
Speggs Wk HEND SO30 58 B6
Speltham Hl WVILLE PO7 62 C2
Spencer Cl HISD PO11 137 H5 1
Spencer Ct FHAM/STUB PO14 115 F5
Spencer Dr LSOL/BMARY PO13 131 G3
Spencer Gdns HORN PO8 81 K2
Spencer Rd ELGH SO50 44 B1
EMRTH PO10 104 B2
ENEY PO4 134 E6
ITCH SO19 57 G6
Spenlow Cl NEND PO2 118 C7 6
Spenser Cl HLER SO31 94 C6 7
Spicer's Hl TOTT SO40 52 E7
Spicer St PSEA PO1 18 D2 7
Spicer's Wy TOTT SO40 52 D6
Spicewood FHAM PO15 12 C4
Spindle Cl HAV PO9 15 L1
Spindle Warren HAV PO9 15 L1
Spindlewood Cl ROWN SO16 43 H5
Spindlewood Wy TOTT SO40 70 A5
Spinnaker Cl HISD PO11 137 F4 5
LSOL/BMARY PO13 132 A1 2
Spinnaker Dr NEND PO2 118 C3
Spinnaker Gra HISD PO11 121 K3
Spinnaker Vw CHAM PO6 102 B5
Spinney Cl HORN PO8 81 K2
Spinney Dl FAWY SO45 91 J4
Spinney Gdns FAWY SO45 91 J4 2
The Spinney ELGH SO50 45 K1
FHAM/PORC PO16 98 C5
HORN PO8 64 B6
LSOL/BMARY PO13 116 A6 3
ROWN SO16 43 G5
RWIN SO21 33 F2
TOTT SO40 52 B3
WVILLE PO7 80 E2
Spinney Wk WEND SO18 56 C1
Spitfire End WINC SO23 3 L4
Spitfire Loop ELGH SO50 44 C4
Spitfire Wy HLER SO31 93 J4
Spithead Av GPORT PO12 133 F7
Spring Cl ELGH SO50 46 B1
ITCH SO19 10 F1
Spring Crs PTSW SO17 5 J3
Springcroft
LSOL/BMARY PO13 115 J2
Springfield Av FAWY SO45 110 A3
Springfield Cl HAV PO9 102 C4
Springfield Dr TOTT SO40 52 D6 1
Springfield Gv FAWY SO45 110 A3
Springfields Cl RWIN SO21 39 J1
Springfield Wy
FHAM/STUB PO14 114 D6
Springford Cl ROWN SO16 42 C7
Springford Crs ROWN SO16 54 C1
Springford Gdns ROWN SO16 42 C7
Springford Rd ROWN SO16 54 C1
Spring Garden La GPORT PO12 16 D4
Spring Gdns EMRTH PO10 104 C6
NBAD SO52 36 A5
PSEA PO1 18 B4 2
Spring Gv HLER SO31 73 K4
Springhill Rd CHFD SO53 37 K4
Spring Hills ITCH SO19 11 M1
Spring La BPWT SO32 49 J6
ELGH SO50 39 G7
RWIN SO21 39 J1
Springles La FHAM PO15 96 B1
Spring Pl ROMY SO51 34 D3 5
Spring Rd FAWY SO45 91 H2
HLER SO31 74 E7
ITCH SO19 6 F7
Spring St PSEA PO1 18 C3
The Spring WVILLE PO7 80 E2
Spring V BPWT SO32 49 H7
HORN PO8 82 C1
Springvale Av WINC SO23 22 A1
Springvale Rd WINC SO23 22 A2
Springwood Av WVILLE PO7 82 A7
Spruce Av WVILLE PO7 82 B6
Spruce Cl HLER SO31 94 C6
Spruce Dr ITCH SO19 57 H7
TOTT SO40 52 A4
Spurlings Rd WHAM PO17 98 A2
Spur Rd CHAM PO6 100 E6
WVILLE PO7 81 K6
The Spur GPORT PO12 132 C6
WHAM PO17 77 H1
The Square EMRTH PO10 104 E3 3
FAWY SO45 110 E4 9
GPORT PO12 116 E7
WHAM PO17 77 H2
WINC SO23 2 E5
Squires Wk ITCH SO19 10 D8
Squirrel Cl ELGH SO50 45 J1 3
Squirrel Dr ITCH SO19 11 G4
Squirrels Wk FAWY SO45 91 G4
Stable Cl FHAM/STUB PO14 95 J4
Stacey Ct HAV PO9 82 E6
Stafford Rd SSEA PO5 18 E8
WSHM SO15 4 A5
Staff Rd ROMY SO51 28 A1
Stagbrake Cl FAWY SO45 109 J4 2
Stag Cl ELGH SO50 45 J1
Stagshorn Rd HORN PO8 64 D5 3
Stag Wy FHAM PO15 96 E1
Stainer Cl ITCH SO19 73 G2
Staith Cl ITCH SO19 7 L8
Stakes Hill Rd WVILLE PO7 102 A2
Stakes La BPWT SO32 47 K1
Stakes Rd WVILLE PO7 101 J2
Stallard Cl EMRTH PO10 104 B5
Stalybridge Cl HLER SO31 75 F7
Stamford Av HISD PO11 137 F5
Stamford St PSEA PO1 18 F2
Stamford Wy ELGH SO50 46 B2 2
Stamshaw Rd NEND PO2 118 C6
Stanbridge La ROMY SO51 28 A6
Stanbridge Rd HAV PO9 103 J2
Standard Wy FHAM/PORC PO16 13 M1
Standen Rd ROWN SO16 41 H6
Standford St SHAM SO14 9 K2 1
Stanford Cl CHAM PO6 100 C6
Stanford Ct HAV PO9 103 J1 13
Stanhope Rd PSEA PO1 18 C3
Stanier Wy HEND SO30 58 B2
Stanley Av HSEA PO3 119 G7
Stanley Cl FHAM PO15 12 C5
GPORT PO12 116 D6
Stanley La SSEA PO5 18 D9
Stanley Rd EMRTH PO10 104 D6
FAWY SO45 110 A3
NEND PO2 118 B6
PTSW SO17 5 M1
TOTT SO40 52 C3
Stanley St SSEA PO5 18 D9
Stanmore La WINW SO22 25 F2
Stannington Crs TOTT SO40 52 E4
Stannington Wy TOTT SO40 52 E4
Stanstead Cl HAV PO9 83 K3
Stanstead Rd ELGH SO50 38 C6
Stansted Crs HAV PO9 83 J7
Stansted Rd SSEA PO5 18 F6
Stanswood Rd FAWY SO45 128 E4
HAV PO9 82 E7
Stanton Rd WSHM SO15 54 A5
Staple Cl WVILLE PO7 81 J4
Stapleford Cl ROMY SO51 29 G7
Stapleford La BPWT SO32 46 E6
Staple Gdns WINC SO23 2 D4
Staplehurst Cl ITCH SO19 11 J9
Staplers Reach
LSOL/BMARY PO13 115 J6
Stapleton Rd HSEA PO3 119 F7 3
Staplewood La TOTT SO40 69 H4
Stares Cl LSOL/BMARY PO13 131 K1
Starina Gdns WVILLE PO7 82 C5
Starling Sq ELGH SO50 44 A1 2
Station Ap PSEA PO1 17 L4
Station Cl RWIN SO21 23 K1
WHAM PO17 77 H1
Station Hl ELGH SO50 38 E7
HEND SO30 59 H5
HLER SO31 74 A6
RWIN SO21 23 K1
WINC SO23 2 D3 2
Station La CHFD SO53 37 K4
Station Rd BPWT SO32 48 D4
CHAM PO6 119 H1
FHAM/PORC PO16 99 G6
GPORT PO12 132 C1
HISD PO11 137 F4
HLER SO31 74 A5
HLER SO31 92 E1
HLER SO31 95 F1
HSEA PO3 119 F7
ITCH SO19 10 F4
ROMY SO51 34 E2
ROWN SO16 41 F6
WHAM PO17 77 H1
WINC SO23 2 C3
WSHM SO15 53 H4
Station Rd North TOTT SO40 53 F5 2
Station Rd South TOTT SO40 53 G5 1
Station St PSEA PO1 18 C3
Staunton Av HISD PO11 136 E5
Staunton Rd HAV PO9 14 C3
Staunton St PSEA PO1 18 D1
Staunton Wy HAV PO9 14 C2
HAV PO9 102 D6
Stead Cl HISD PO11 137 J5
Steele Cl CHFD SO53 38 A6
Steel St SSEA PO5 18 B7
Steep Cl FHAM/PORC PO16 99 F5 2
WEND SO18 7 M3
Steeple Wy FHAM/STUB PO14 95 J3
Steerforth Cl NEND PO2 134 C1
Steinbeck Cl FHAM PO15 75 H5
Stein Rd EMRTH PO10 105 G4
Stenbury Wy HLER SO31 73 F6
Stephen Cl HORN PO8 82 C3
Stephen Rd FHAM PO15 12 F5
Stephenson Cl GPORT PO12 132 D6 3
Stephenson Rd TOTT SO40 52 C2
Stephenson Wy HEND SO30 58 A1
Step Ter WINW SO22 2 B4
Steuart Rd WEND SO18 6 A4
Steventon Rd WEND SO18 7 M5
Stewarts Gn WVILLE PO7 62 B1
Stinchar Dr CHFD SO53 37 H5
Stirling Av WVILLE PO7 82 A6
Stirling Cl TOTT SO40 53 F4
Stirling Crs HEND SO30 58 B3
TOTT SO40 53 F4
Stirling St NEND PO2 118 C7
Stockbridge Cl HAV PO9 103 J1 14
Stockbridge Rd WINW SO22 2 A2
WINW SO22 21 G6
ROMY SO51 28 B2
Stocker Pl
LSOL/BMARY PO13 116 A5 6
Stockers Av WINW SO22 21 G6
Stockheath La HAV PO9 14 C2
Stockheath Rd HAV PO9 103 G2
Stockheath Wy HAV PO9 103 G3
Stockholm Dr HEND SO30 58 B7 3
Stockley Cl FAWY SO45 109 K4 3
Stockton Cl HEND SO30 58 C5 3
Stoddart Av ITCH SO19 6 E7
Stoke Common Rd ELGH SO50 39 H5
Stoke Gdns GPORT PO12 16 B6
Stoke Park Rd ELGH SO50 39 G6
Stoke Rd GPORT PO12 16 B6
ROWN SO16 54 B3
WINC SO23 21 K4
Stokesay Cl FAWY SO45 91 H6 2
Stokes Bay Rd GPORT PO12 132 A6
Stoke Wood Cl ELGH SO50 46 A1 3
Stonechat Dr TOTT SO40 52 A4
Stonechat Rd HORN PO8 64 B6
Stone Crop Cl HLER SO31 94 D5
Stoneham Cemetery Rd
WEND SO18 44 C7
Stoneham Cl ROWN SO16 44 A6 1
Stoneham La ELGH SO50 44 B3
ROWN SO16 44 A6
Stoneham Wy ELGH SO50 44 B6
Stonehills FAWY SO45 111 F5
Stone La GPORT PO12 16 B6 2
GPORT PO12 16 B7 2
Stoneleigh Cl
FHAM/PORC PO16 98 E6 3
Stoners Cl LSOL/BMARY PO13 115 J4
Stone Sq HAV PO9 103 G2
Stone St SSEA PO5 18 B7
Stoney La WINW SO22 21 G5
Stony La PSEA PO1 17 L2
Stonymoor Cl FAWY SO45 109 K4
Stour Cl WEND SO18 56 D1
Stourvale Gdns CHFD SO53 38 A5
Stowe Cl HEND SO30 58 C3
Stowe Rd ENEY PO4 135 G4
Stradbrook LSOL/BMARY PO13 115 J6
The Straight Mile ROMY SO51 35 K1
Strand SHAM SO14 9 G2
The Strand HISD PO11 137 K7
Stratfield Dr CHFD SO53 37 J1 5
Stratford Pl ELGH SO50 38 E6 2
Stratford Rd WVILLE PO7 82 B5
Strathmore Rd GPORT PO12 16 D5

Stratton Cl CHAM PO6 .... 100 B6
Stratton Rd WINC SO23 .... 3 H6
WSHM SO15.................................. 54 D3
Strawberry Hl HLER SO31 .... 94 E3
Streamleaze FHAM/STUB PO14 .. 95 H5
Street End NBAD SO52 .... 36 C5
Stride Av HSEA PO3........................ 19 M1
Strides Wy TOTT SO40 .... 52 A5
Strode Rd NEND PO2 .... 118 B5
Strongs Cl ROMY SO51 .... 35 G2 8
Strouden Ct HAV PO9 .... 82 E6
Stroud Green La
FHAM/STUB PO14...................... 114 E2
Stroudley Av CHAM PO6 .... 119 H1
Stroudley Wy HEND SO30 .... 58 C2
Stroudwood Rd HAV PO9 .... 103 H3
Stuart Cl FHAM/STUB PO14 .... 114 D5
Stuart Crs WINW SO22 .... 2 A9
Stubbington Av NEND PO2 .... 118 D6
Stubbington Gn
FHAM/STUB PO14....................... 114 D4
Stubbington La
FHAM/STUB PO14....................... 114 D7
Stubbington Wy ELGH SO50 .... 46 C2
Stubbs Dro HEND SO30 .... 58 C5
Stubbs Rd ITCH SO19 .... 11 M6
Studland Cl ROWN SO16................ 53 J3
Studland Rd
LSOL/BMARY PO13..................... 131 F2
ROWN SO16 .... 53 J3
Studley Av FAWY SO45 .... 109 K4
Sudbury Rd CHAM PO6 .... 100 C6
Suetts La BPWT SO32 .... 49 G4
Suffolk Av WSHM SO15 .... 4 B6
Suffolk Cl CHFD SO53 .... 43 K1
Suffolk Dr CHFD SO53.................... 43 K1
FHAM PO15 .... 75 G6
HLER SO31.................................... 75 G6
Suffolk Rd ENEY PO4 .... 19 M7
Sullivan Cl CHAM PO6 .... 99 H6
Sullivan Rd ITCH SO19 .... 73 G2 8
Sullivan Wy WVILLE PO7............. 101 K1
Sultan Rd EMRTH PO10 .... 104 C5
NEND PO2 .... 134 B1
Sumar Cl FHAM/STUB PO14......... 114 E2
Summerfield Gdns
ROWN SO16 .... 44 A6 2
Summerfield Rd SELS PO20......... 139 K6
Summerfields
FHAM/STUB PO14........................ 95 G5
Summerhill Rd HORN PO8............ 82 A2
Summerlands Rd ELGH SO50 .... 46 B1
Summer La BROC SO42 .... 109 F6
Summerleigh Wk
FHAM/STUB PO14 .... 114 E2 1
Summers St SHAM SO14 .... 5 K6
Summit Wy WEND SO18................. 6 E1
Sunbeam Wy GPORT PO12 .... 16 B8
Sunbury Ct FHAM PO15 .... 97 F2
Sundridge Cl CHAM PO6.............. 100 D6
Sunningdale FAWY SO45 .... 91 G4
Sunningdale Cl ELGH SO50 .... 45 J1 4
LSOL/BMARY PO13 .... 115 K6 5
Sunningdale Gdns WEND SO18...... 7 K5
Sunningdale Rd
FHAM/PORC PO16 .... 99 G7
HSEA PO3 .... 19 M1 1
Sunnydown Rd WINW SO22 .... 24 D5
Sunnyfield Ri HLER SO31 .... 73 K4 5
Sunnyheath HAV PO9................... 103 F2
Sunnymead Dr WVILLE PO7........... 81 H3
Sunny Wk PSEA PO1...................... 17 K3
Sunny Wy TOTT SO40 .... 52 E5 1
Sunset Av TOTT SO40 .... 52 D4
Sunset Rd TOTT SO40 .... 52 D4
Sunshine Av HISD PO11 .... 137 J6 2
Sun St PSEA PO1 .... 17 M4 5
Sunvale Cl ITCH SO19 .... 11 J4
Sunwood Rd HAV PO9 .... 102 E1
Surbiton Rd ELGH SO50 .... 38 E5
Surrey Cl TOTT SO40 .... 52 C7
Surrey Rd CHFD SO53.................... 37 K7
ITCH SO19 .... 10 B6
Surrey St PSEA PO1........................ 18 C3
Sussex Border Pth
EMRTH PO10.................................. 84 C7
HAV PO9... 84 A1
Sussex Pl SSEA PO5 .... 18 C8 5
Sussex Rd CHFD SO53................... 38 A7
SHAM SO14 .... 9 G1
SSEA PO5 .... 18 C8
Sussex St WINC SO23 .... 2 D4
Sutherland Cl ROMY SO51 .... 35 G1 4
Sutherland Rd ENEY PO4.............. 19 H7
ROWN SO16.................................... 42 A6
Sutherlands Ct CHFD SO53 ...... 37 K4 2
Sutherlands Wy CHFD SO53 .... 37 J3
Sutton Cl HORN PO8 .... 81 J2
HSEA PO3...................................... 119 G3
Sutton Gdns WINC SO23................. 2 E4
Sutton Rd HORN PO8 .... 81 J2
TOTT SO40 .... 52 C3
Swale Dr CHFD SO53...................... 37 H3
Swallow Cl HAV PO9 .... 15 J1
TOTT SO40 .... 52 A6
Swallow Ct
LSOL/BMARY PO13 .... 131 G1 5
Swallow Sq ELGH SO50 .... 44 A1 5
Swanage Cl ITCH SO19 .... 10 C2
Swanage Rd
LSOL/BMARY PO13........................ 131 F2
Swan Cl EMRTH PO10.................. 104 D6
HLER SO31...................................... 74 C6
Swancote FHAM/PORC PO16 ...... 98 C6
Swan La WINC SO23 .... 2 D3
Swanley Cl ELGH SO50 .... 38 D5
Swanmore Av ITCH SO19................ 11 K3
Swanmore Cl WINW SO22 .... 21 G3
Swanmore Rd BPWT SO32............. 49 G4
HAV PO9... 82 E6
Swanton Gdns CHFD SO53............ 37 J3
Swanwick La HLER SO31 .... 74 C5
Swanwick Shore Rd
HLER SO31 .... 74 C6 1
Swarraton Rd HAV PO9 .... 103 H2
Sway Ct HAV PO9 .... 103 J1 15
Swaythling Rd HAV PO9.............. 82 E7
HEND SO30 .... 56 E2
Sweetbriar Gdns
WVILLE PO7 .... 102 A1 4
Sweethills Crs HLER SO31 .... 75 G5
Sweyns Lease BROC SO42 .... 125 H2
Swift Cl ELGH SO50 .... 44 A1
WINW SO22 .... 25 G3
HORN PO8 .... 64 B5
LSOL/BMARY PO13 .... 131 G1 8
Swift Gdns ITCH SO19.................... 10 B7
Swift Hollow ITCH SO19................. 10 A7
Swift Rd EMRTH PO10 .... 122 D4
ITCH SO19 .... 10 A7
Swinburn Gdns HORN PO8 .... 82 A1
Swincombe Ri WEND SO18 .... 7 K1
Swiss Rd WVILLE PO7 .... 81 K6
Swivelton La WHAM PO17.............. 98 D3
Sword Cl GPORT PO12 .... 132 B6
Sword Sands Rd HSEA PO3 .... 135 H1
Sycamore Av CHFD SO53 .... 37 K1
Sycamore Cl
FHAM/STUB PO14 .... 95 H5 5
HLER SO31...................................... 73 J5
HORN PO8 .... 81 K2
LSOL/BMARY PO13 .... 116 B6 5
NBAD SO52 .... 36 A5
ROMY SO51 .... 35 H4
Sycamore Dr FAWY SO45 .... 109 J2
HISD PO11 .... 137 F4
Sycamore Rd BPWT SO32 .... 49 F3
FAWY SO45 .... 91 G3
ROWN SO16..................................... 54 B2
Sydenham Ter PSEA PO1 .... 18 F4
Sydmanton Cl ROMY SO51 .... 35 F4 5
Sydmonton Ct HAV PO9 .... 83 J7 11
Sydney Av HLER SO31 .... 93 H3
Sydney Rd ELGH SO50 .... 39 G6
GPORT PO12 .... 16 B5
WSHM SO15..................................... 54 C3
Sylvan Av ITCH SO19....................... 7 L7
Sylvan Dr NBAD SO52 .... 36 A6
Sylvan La HLER SO31 .... 93 K4
The Sylvans FAWY SO45 .... 90 E3 5
Sylvan Vw WVILLE PO7.................. 82 A7
Sylvia Crs TOTT SO40..................... 52 D3
Symes Rd ROMY SO51 .... 35 G3
Symonds Cl CHFD SO53 .... 38 A6
Symonds St WINC SO23 .... 2 E6
Sywell Crs HSEA PO3.................... 119 G3

T

Tadburn Cl CHFD SO53 .... 38 A5
ROMY SO51 .... 35 F3 4
Tadburn Rd ROMY SO51.................. 35 F4
Tadfield Rd ROMY SO51 .... 35 F3
Tagdell La HORN PO8 .... 64 A4
Tait Pl LSOL/BMARY PO13 .... 116 A6
Talbot Cl HAV PO9 .... 102 D3
ROWN SO16..................................... 54 A1
Talbot Rd ENEY PO4 .... 19 H6
FAWY SO45 .... 90 E5
HAV PO9.. 14 A1
Talland Rd FHAM/STUB PO14 .... 95 G5
Tamar Cl FHAM/PORC PO16........... 98 D5
Tamar Down WVILLE PO7 .... 82 B6
Tamar Gv FAWY SO45 .... 91 F3
Tamarisk Cl ENEY PO4 .... 135 H5
FHAM/STUB PO14 .... 114 D6 4
WVILLE PO7 .... 102 B1 1
Tamarisk Gdns WEND SO18............ 6 D3
Tamarisk Rd HEND SO30 .... 58 A5
Tamella Rd HEND SO30.................. 58 D6
Tammys Turn
FHAM/STUB PO14 .... 96 C6 4
Tamorisk Dr TOTT SO40 .... 52 B6
Tamworth Rd HSEA PO3 .... 19 M1
Tanfield La WHAM PO17.................. 77 G2
Tanfield Pk WHAM PO17 .... 77 G2
Tangier La BPWT SO32 .... 48 A4
Tangier Rd HSEA PO3 .... 135 F1
Tanglewood
FHAM/PORC PO16 .... 13 G1
TOTT SO40 .... 70 B4 5
Tanglewood Cl WVILLE PO7 .... 101 H2 5
Tangmere Dr ROWN SO16 .... 42 A7
Tangyes Cl FHAM/STUB PO14 .... 114 E4
Tanhouse Cl HEND SO30................. 58 B7
Tanhouse La HEND SO30 .... 58 C7
Tankerton Cl CHAM PO6 .... 100 D6 2
Tankerville Rd ITCH SO19............. 10 B3
Tanner's Brook Wy WSHM SO15.. 54 A6
Tanners La FHAM/STUB PO14 ...... 115 F1
WVILLE PO7 .... 62 E7
Tanner's Rdg WVILLE PO7 .... 101 K3
Tanners Rd NBAD SO52 .... 36 B6
The Tanners
FHAM/STUB PO14 .... 95 H5 4
Tanner St WINC SO23 .... 2 F5
Tansy Cl WVILLE PO7 .... 82 B7
Tansy Meadow NBAD SO52 .... 37 G6 2
The Tanyards CHFD SO53 .... 37 J1 5
Taplin Dr HEND SO30 .... 58 B4
Taplings Cl WINW SO22 .... 21 G4
Taplings Rd WINW SO22 .... 21 G4
Taranto Rd ROWN SO16 .... 42 D7
Tarbery Crs HORN PO8 .... 64 D5
Target Rd NEND PO2 .... 118 B4
Tarius Cl LSOL/BMARY PO13 .... 116 A5
Tarleton Rd CHAM PO6................. 100 A5
Tarn Ri HORN PO8 .... 64 D2
Tarrant Gdns HAV PO9 .... 14 B1
Tasman Cl SHAM SO14 .... 9 K6
Taswell Rd SSEA PO5 .... 134 C6 5
Tatchbury La TOTT SO40 .... 51 J3
Tate Rd WSHM SO15 .... 53 H4
Tates Rd FAWY SO45 .... 91 J3 1
FAWY SO45 .... 91 J4 5
Tattershall Crs
FHAM/PORC PO16 .... 98 E7
Tatwin Cl ITCH SO19 .... 57 G7
Tatwin Crs ITCH SO19..................... 57 G7
Taunton Dr WEND SO18 .... 7 K4
Tavells Cl TOTT SO40 .... 69 K4
Tavell's La TOTT SO40 .... 69 K4
Taverners Cl ITCH SO19 .... 73 G2
Tavistock Cl ROMY SO51 .... 35 G1 5
Tavistock Gdns HAV PO9 .... 15 J5
Tavy Cl CHFD SO53 .... 37 J4
Taw Dr CHFD SO53 .... 37 J3
Tawny Owl Cl
FHAM/STUB PO14 .... 114 C3 4
Taylor Cl ITCH SO19 .... 10 B8
Teachers Wy FAWY SO45 .... 109 J3 2
Teal Cl FHAM/PORC PO16............... 98 C6
HISD PO11 .... 137 J5
TOTT SO40 .... 52 B5 7
Tebourba Dr GPORT PO12 .... 132 D5
Tebourba Wy WSHM SO15............... 54 A5
Tedder Rd LSOL/BMARY PO13.... 116 A4
WEND SO18 .... 7 G3
Tedder Wy TOTT SO40 .... 52 C5
Teddington Rd ENEY PO4 .... 19 M6
Tees Cl CHFD SO53.......................... 37 H3
Teg Down Meads WINW SO22...... 20 E6
Teignmouth Rd GPORT PO12 ...... 132 C1
HSEA PO3....................................... 119 F7
Telegraph Rd HEND SO30 .... 57 H4
Telephone Rd ENEY PO4 .... 19 H5
Telford Gdns HEND SO30 .... 58 C2 2
Telford Rd NEND PO2 .... 118 D4
Teme Crs ROWN SO16..................... 53 K4
Teme Rd ROWN SO16 .... 53 K4 1
Tempest Av WVILLE PO7................ 82 B5
Templars Mede CHFD SO53 .... 37 J7
Templars Wy NBAD SO52 .... 37 G6
Templecombe Rd ELGH SO50 .... 45 J2
Temple Gdns ITCH SO19 .... 10 E5
Templemere FHAM/STUB PO14 .. 96 D7
Temple Rd ITCH SO19 .... 10 E5
Temple St PSEA PO1 .... 18 D2
Templeton Cl NEND PO2 .... 118 D4 2
Tenby Cl WEND SO18 .... 7 H3
Tenby Dr CHFD SO53....................... 37 H6
Tench Wy ROMY SO51 .... 34 E2
Tennyson Cl BPWT SO32 .... 49 F3
FAWY SO45 .... 109 J2 2
Tennyson Crs WVILLE PO7 .... 81 J4
Tennyson Gdns
FHAM/PORC PO16 .... 13 G4
Tennyson Rd ELGH SO50 .... 44 C1
NEND PO2 .... 118 E7
PTSW SO17 .... 5 K2
TOTT SO40 .... 52 C2
Tensing Cl FHAM/PORC PO16 .... 13 G1
Tenterton Av ITCH SO19.................. 11 J8
Terminus Ter SHAM SO14................. 9 J4
Tern Cl FAWY SO45.......................... 91 J4
Terrier Cl HEND SO30 .... 58 B1
Terriote Cl CHFD SO53 .... 37 K3
Testbourne Av TOTT SO40 .... 52 C5
Testbourne Cl TOTT SO40................ 52 C5
Testbourne Rd TOTT SO40 .... 52 C5
Testcombe Rd GPORT PO12 .... 132 D5
Testlands Av ROWN SO16................ 41 J5
Test La ROWN SO16......................... 53 G3
Test Rd SHAM SO14.......................... 9 J9
Test Wy TOTT SO40 .... 53 F3
Testwood Av TOTT SO40 .... 52 D2
Testwood Crs TOTT SO40................. 52 C2
Testwood La TOTT SO40.................. 52 E3
Testwood Pl TOTT SO40 .... 53 F4
Testwood Rd HAV PO9 .... 102 E1 5
WSHM SO15...................................... 54 C6
Tetney Cl ROWN SO16....................... 53 K1
Teviot Rd CHFD SO53 .... 37 H5
Tewkesbury Av FHAM PO15 .... 96 D3
GPORT PO12 .... 132 D1
Tewkesbury Cl CHAM PO6 .... 100 C6
Texas Dr WINW SO22......................... 24 E6
Thackeray Rd PTSW SO17 .... 5 K2
Thames Cl WEND SO18 .... 56 E2
Thames Dr FHAM PO15 .... 96 E2
Thamesmead Cl
GPORT PO12 .... 132 C1 5
Theatre Ms SSEA PO5 .... 18 F9 5
The Itchen Br SHAM SO14 .... 9 M4
Theseus Rd LSOL/BMARY PO13.. 130 E1
Thetford Gdns CHFD SO53............... 37 H3
The Thicket FHAM/PORC PO16 ...... 98 C5
LSOL/BMARY PO13 .... 116 B6 5
ROMY SO51 .... 35 H4 1
SSEA PO5 .... 18 E8 5
WVILLE PO7 .... 101 J4
Third Av CHAM PO6........................ 100 D6
HAV PO9.. 15 H3
WSHM SO15..................................... 54 A6
Thirlmere ELGH SO50 .... 44 C1 2
Thirlmere Cl
FHAM/STUB PO14 .... 114 E3 5
Thirlmere Rd ROWN SO16 .... 53 K2
Thirlstane Firs CHFD SO53 .... 37 J6 2
Thistledown HORN PO8 .... 64 C7
Thistledowne Gdns
EMRTH PO10.................................. 104 E6
Thistle Rd HEND SO30....................... 58 A6
NBAD SO52 .... 37 G5
Thomas Cl TOTT SO40 .... 52 C6 5
Thomas Lewis Wy PTSW SO17 ...... 55 K2
Thomas Rd NBAD SO52 .... 36 B6
Thompsons La WVILLE PO7 .... 62 B7
Thornbrake Rd GPORT PO12 ...... 16 D7 1
Thornbury Av FAWY SO45 .... 110 B7
WSHM SO15....................................... 4 C4
Thornbury Cl
FHAM/STUB PO14 .... 96 D6 5
Thornbury Hts CHFD SO53............ 38 C1
Thornbury Wd CHFD SO53.............. 38 C1
Thorncliffe Cl NEND PO2 .... 118 E3 5
Thorn Cl ELGH SO50 .... 38 D5 4
Thorncroft Rd PSEA PO1 .... 19 H4
Thorndike Cl ROWN SO16................ 54 B2
Thorness Cl ROWN SO16.................. 53 H3
Thorney Cl FHAM/STUB PO14 .... 12 A8
Thorney Old Pk EMRTH PO10 .... 123 G6
Thorney Rd EMRTH PO10 .... 122 E2
Thorngate Wy GPORT PO12 ...... 16 F5 1
Thornham La EMRTH PO10 .... 122 E1
Thornhill Av ITCH SO19.................. 57 G6
Thornhill Cl FAWY SO45 .... 110 C5 2
Thornhill Park Rd WEND SO18 ..... 57 G5
Thornhill Rd FAWY SO45............... 110 C5
ROWN SO16 .... 42 E7
Thorni Av FHAM PO15 .... 96 D3
Thornleigh Rd ITCH SO19................ 10 C5
Thornton Av HLER SO31.................. 94 B5
Thornton Cl CHAM PO6 .... 101 G4 2
Thornton Rd GPORT PO12.............. 116 E7
Thornycroft Av ITCH SO19.............. 10 A5
Thorold Rd CHFD SO53.................... 38 B1
WEND SO18 .... 6 C1
Three Acres WVILLE PO7 .... 81 F2
Three Castles Pth RWIN SO21 .... 22 B3
Threefield La SHAM SO14................. 9 H3
Three Oaks ITCH SO19 .... 57 H7
Three Tun Cl PSEA PO1.................... 17 M4
Thresher Cl HORN PO8 .... 82 D4 1
Thrush Wk HORN PO8 .... 81 K1 2
Thruxton Rd HAV PO9 .... 102 D1
Thurbern Rd NEND PO2 .... 118 D5
Thurmell Cl HEND SO30 .... 74 B1
Thurmond Crs WINW SO22 .... 25 F2
Thurmond Rd WINW SO22............... 25 F2
Thurston Cl CHFD SO53 .... 38 A3
Thyme Av FHAM PO15 .... 75 J5
Tichborne Gv HAV PO9 .... 102 E1 4
Tichborne Rd ELGH SO50 .... 44 C3
WEND SO18 .... 57 G4
Tichborne Wy
LSOL/BMARY PO13...................... 116 A6
Tickleford Dr ITCH SO19.................. 11 H8
Tickner Cl HEND SO30 .... 58 C7 5
Ticonderoga Gdns ITCH SO19 ..... 10 C8
Tides Reach WEND SO18 .... 6 A3
Tides Wy TOTT SO40 .... 70 A3
Tideway Gdns ENEY PO4 .... 135 H4
Tidworth Rd HAV PO9 .... 103 G2
Tiffield Cl HSEA PO3 .... 119 H3
Tilbrook Rd WSHM SO15 .... 54 B4
Tilden Rd RWIN SO21 .... 33 F4
Tilford Rd HORN PO8 .... 64 A6
Timberlane WVILLE PO7................. 101 J2
Timberly Cl FAWY SO45 .... 109 K3
The Timbers FHAM PO15 .... 96 D5
Timor Cl HLER SO31........................ 75 G5
Timpson Rd PSEA PO1 .... 18 F1
Timsbury Crs HAV PO9 .... 14 C1
Timsbury Dr ROWN SO16................ 54 A2
Timson Cl TOTT SO40 .... 52 B6 7
Tindale Rd ROWN SO16.................... 53 K2
Tinker Aly ELGH SO50 .... 44 D4
Tintagel Wy CHAM PO6 .... 100 A7
Tintern Cl CHAM PO6 .... 99 J5
Tintern Gv WSHM SO15 .... 4 C8
Tintern Rd GPORT PO12................. 132 D4
Tipner Gn NEND PO2 .... 118 B5 1
Tipner La NEND PO2 .... 118 B4
Tipner Rd NEND PO2..................... 118 B5
Tiptree Cl ELGH SO50 .... 38 D5
Tisted Ct HAV PO9 .... 103 J1 16
Titchfield Hl FHAM/STUB PO14.... 96 B6
Titchfield La FHAM PO15 .... 76 D5
WHAM PO17 .... 76 D4
Titchfield Park Rd FHAM PO15 .... 95 J3
Titchfield Rd
FHAM/STUB PO14........................ 114 D3
The Tithe WVILLE PO7 .... 80 E2 1
Tithewood Cl CHFD SO53 .... 31 J7 5
Titus Gdns WVILLE PO7................... 82 B5
Tivoli Cl CHFD SO53......................... 38 C3
Toby St PSEA PO1 .... 18 C2
Tokar St ENEY PO4 .... 19 M9
Tokio Rd HSEA PO3 .... 119 F6
Tolefrey Gdns NBAD SO52 .... 37 G4 5
Tollbar Wy HEND SO30.................... 57 K3
Tollgate CHFD SO53 .... 43 K1
Tollgate Rd HLER SO31 .... 74 C5
Tonbridge St SSEA PO5 .... 18 D9
Tonnant Cl
FHAM/STUB PO14 .... 114 E6 1
Toogoods Wy ROWN SO16............. 41 J6
Toomer Cl FAWY SO45................... 110 C5
Toothill Rd ROMY SO51 .... 41 H2
Topaz Gv WVILLE PO7..................... 82 C5
Topiary Gdns HLER SO31 .... 95 G2
Torch Cl ELGH SO50 .... 46 A1 4
Tor Cl FHAM/PORC PO16 .... 98 B5
Torcross Cl ITCH SO19..................... 10 D6
Torfrida Ct ENEY PO4 .... 135 H5
Tormead FAWY SO45 .... 91 G3 5
Tornay Gv NBAD SO52 .... 36 A6
Toronto Pl GPORT PO12 .... 16 B4
Toronto Rd NEND PO2 .... 134 D1
Torquay Av GPORT PO12 .... 116 D7
WSHM SO15..................................... 54 D4
Torque Cl ITCH SO19 .... 73 H1
Torre Cl ELGH SO50 .... 38 D4
Torridge Gdns WEND SO18 .... 56 E1 1
Torrington Cl ITCH SO19................. 11 H2
Torrington Rd NEND PO2.............. 118 D4
Tortworth Cl FHAM/STUB PO14 .. 12 A8
Torwood Gdns ELGH SO50.............. 45 J1
Tosson Cl ROWN SO16 .... 53 K4 2
Totland Cl ROWN SO16.................... 53 K4
Totland Rd CHAM PO6 .... 100 D7
LSOL/BMARY PO13 .... 115 K5
Totnes Cl ELGH SO50....................... 38 C5
Tottehale Cl NBAD SO52.................. 36 A7
Tottenham Rd PSEA PO1 .... 19 G1
Totton By-pass TOTT SO40 .... 53 F6
Tournerbury La HISD PO11 .... 137 H4
Tower Cl GPORT PO12................... 132 A5
Tower Gdns HAV PO9 .... 121 G1
Tower La ELGH SO50 .... 45 F1
Tower Pl HEND SO30......................... 57 G3
Tower Rd ENEY PO4 .... 19 K8
WINC SO23....................................... 2 D3
Tower St EMRTH PO10 .... 104 D6
PSEA PO1.. 17 K7
WINC SO23.. 2 D4
Town Hall Rd HAV PO9 .... 14 F5
Townhill Wy WEND SO18 .... 7 H2
Town Quay SHAM SO14 .... 8 F5
Towpath Md ENEY PO4 .... 135 H4 1
Toynbee Cl ELGH SO50 .... 38 D7
Toynbee Rd ELGH SO50 .... 38 D7
Trafalgar Cl CHFD SO53 .... 37 J5
Trafalgar Ct FHAM/STUB PO14 .... 97 G7
Trafalgar Pl PSEA PO1 .... 19 G2 5
Trafalgar Rd WSHM SO15................ 54 D6
Trafalgar Sq GPORT PO12 .... 16 A3
Trafalgar St WINC SO23 .... 2 D5
Trafalgar Wy FAWY SO45 .... 91 J5
Trafford Wy ELGH SO50 .... 46 A2
Trampers La WHAM PO17 .... 78 D4
Tranby Rd ITCH SO19 .... 10 C2
Tranmere Rd ENEY PO4 .... 135 G5 2
Treadwheel Rd HORN PO8.............. 65 H6
Treagore Rd TOTT SO40 .... 52 B3 2
Trearnan Cl ROWN SO16.................. 54 A4
Treble Cl WINW SO22...................... 24 E4
Tredegar Rd ENEY PO4.................... 19 K7
Treeside Av TOTT SO40 .... 53 F5
Treeside Rd WSHM SO15 .... 54 D4
Tree Side Wy WVILLE PO7 .... 81 K4
Trefoil Cl WVILLE PO7 .... 82 A6
Tregaron Av CHAM PO6 .... 101 G7
Treloar Rd HISD PO11 .... 138 B7
Treloyhan Cl CHFD SO53................. 38 A6
Tremona Rd ROWN SO16 .... 54 C1
Trenley Cl FAWY SO45 .... 109 K4
Trent Rd WEND SO18 .... 6 E1
Trent Wy LSOL/BMARY PO13 .. 131 G2 8
Tresillian Gdns WEND SO18 ...... 56 E2 2
Trevis Rd ENEY PO4 .... 135 H4
Trevone Cl TOTT SO40 .... 52 D7 4
Trevor Rd ENEY PO4........................ 19 H8
Trevose Cl CHFD SO53 .... 38 A6 2
LSOL/BMARY PO13....................... 115 K6
Trevose Crs CHFD SO53 .... 38 A5
Trevose Wy FHAM/STUB PO14 ..... 95 G5
Triangle La FHAM/STUB PO14 .... 113 K3
Tribe Rd GPORT PO12 .... 132 D3
Trimaran Cl HLER SO31 .... 94 D5
Trimaran Rd HLER SO31 .... 94 D5 4
Trinity Cl GPORT PO12 .... 16 F6
Trinity Gn GPORT PO12................... 17 G6
Trinity Rd SHAM SO14....................... 5 H8
Trinity St FHAM/PORC PO16 .... 13 J5
Tristan Cl FAWY SO45 .... 129 H1
Triumph Cl FHAM PO15 .... 12 B3
Triumph Rd FHAM/STUB PO14 .. 115 G2
Trojan Wy WVILLE PO7 .... 102 A3
Troon Crs CHAM PO6 .... 101 H5
Trosnant Rd HAV PO9 .... 14 C2
Trotts La TOTT SO40 .... 69 H1
Trowbridge Cl ROWN SO16 .... 41 K5
Truro Ri ELGH SO50......................... 39 H7
Truro Rd CHAM PO6 .... 99 J6
Trussell Cl WINW SO22 .... 21 G4
Trussell Crs WINW SO22 .... 21 G4
Tudor Av EMRTH PO10 .... 104 B2
Tudor Cl FHAM/PORC PO16 .... 98 E5 2
HISD PO11 .... 137 G6
LSOL/BMARY PO13 .... 116 A7 2
TOTT SO40 .... 52 B4
Tudor Ct FHAM/STUB PO14 ...... 97 G7 2
Tudor Crs CHAM PO6 .... 118 E1
Tudor Gdns HEND SO30 .... 57 K7
Tudor Wood Cl ROWN SO16 ...... 43 G7 2
Tuffin Cl ROWN SO16 .... 41 H6 5
Tukes Av LSOL/BMARY PO13 .... 115 J3
Tulip Gdns HAV PO9 .... 102 D4
HLER SO31...................................... 94 E3
Tulip Rd ROWN SO16 .... 43 K7 1
Tumulus Cl ITCH SO19 .... 73 J1 2
Tunstall Rd CHAM PO6 .... 100 C5
ITCH SO19 .... 73 H1
Tunworth Ct HAV PO9 .... 103 J1 17
Tuppenny La EMRTH PO10 .... 105 F6
Turner Av LSOL/BMARY PO13 .... 116 B6
Turnpike Down WINC SO23 .... 3 K4
Turnpike Wy HEND SO30 .... 57 K6
Turnstone Gdns ROWN SO16......... 42 C6
Turtle Cl FHAM/STUB PO14 .... 114 C3
Tuscan Wk CHFD SO53 .... 38 B4
Tuscany Wy WVILLE PO7 .... 82 C5
The Tussocks TOTT SO40 .... 70 A3
Tutland Rd NBAD SO52 .... 36 A6 5
Tutor Cl HLER SO31 .... 93 J3
Tweed Cl CHFD SO53....................... 37 H3
Twiggs End Cl HLER SO31 .... 94 E2
Twiggs La TOTT SO40 .... 69 J7
Twiggs Lane End TOTT SO40 .... 89 H1
Twyford Av NEND PO2 .... 118 C6
WSHM SO15...................................... 54 D3
Twyford Rd ELGH SO50 .... 38 E4
Twynhams Hl BPWT SO32 .... 61 H4
The Tyleshades ROMY SO51 ...... 35 F4 4
Tyne Cl CHFD SO53 .... 37 H5
Tynedale Cl GPORT PO12 .... 116 C7 5
Tyne Wy HEND SO30 .... 57 H2
Tyrell Rd CHFD SO53 .... 37 K3
Tyseley Rd SSEA PO5 .... 18 D5
Tytherley Rd WEND SO18.................. 7 L3

U

Ullswater Av WEND SO18................ 56 E3
Ullswater Rd ROWN SO16 .... 53 K3
Underdown Av WVILLE PO7 .... 101 J4
Underwood Cl ROWN SO16 .... 43 F7 2
Underwood Rd ELGH SO50 .... 39 G6
ROWN SO16...................................... 43 F7
Unicorn Rd LSOL/BMARY PO13 .. 130 E1
PSEA PO1.. 18 C2
Union Pl PSEA PO1 .... 18 F2
Union Rd HAV PO9 .... 14 D4
SHAM SO14 .... 5 K7
Union St FHAM/PORC PO16............. 13 M6
PSEA PO1.. 17 M3
WINC SO23... 3 G4
University Crs PTSW SO17 .... 55 J1
University Pkwy ROWN SO16 .... 42 D2
University Rd PTSW SO17 .... 55 H1
Unwin Cl ITCH SO19......................... 10 A8
Uphill Rd WINW SO22 .... 20 E2
Uplands Crs FHAM/PORC PO16....... 13 J3
Uplands Rd CHAM PO6................... 101 H5
WINW SO22 .... 21 H4
HAV PO9.. 83 K3
WVILLE PO7...................................... 62 A6
Uplands Wy PTSW SO17 .... 55 H2
Upper Arundel St PSEA PO1 .... 18 D3
Upper Banister St WSHM SO15 .... 4 F6 2
Upper Bere Wd WVILLE PO7 .... 82 A7
Upper Brook Dr HLER SO31............. 94 D4
Upper Brook St WINC SO23 .... 2 E4
Upper Brownhill Rd
ROWN SO16...................................... 54 A1
Upper Bugle St SHAM SO14.............. 8 F3
Upper Church Rd BPWT SO32 .... 61 F5
Upper Cornaway La
FHAM/PORC PO16 .... 98 E6
Upper Crabbick La WVILLE PO7 .. 62 B7
Upper Crescent Rd NBAD SO52 .. 36 A6
Upper Deacon Rd ITCH SO19........... 7 K7
Upper High St WINW SO22............... 2 C3

Upper House Ct WHAM PO17 77 H2
Upper Market St ELGH SO50 38 E7
Upper Mead Cl ELGH SO50 46 C1 4
Upper Moors Rd ELGH SO50 39 J1
RWIN SO21 39 J2
Upper Mullin's La FAWY SO45 91 F3
Upper New Rd HEND SO30 57 G3
Upper Northam Cl HEND SO30 57 K6
Upper Northam Dr HEND SO30 57 H6
Upper Northam Rd HEND SO30 57 K5
Upper Old St
FHAM/STUB PO14 114 C3
Upper Piece WVILLE PO7 81 F2
Upper St Helens Rd HEND SO30 74 A1
Upper Shaftesbury Av
PTSW SO17 55 J2
Upper Shirley Av WSHM SO15 54 D3
Upper Spinney HLER SO31 94 B6
Upper Toothill Rd ROWN SO16 41 K2
Upper Weston La ITCH SO19 11 H6
Upper Whf FHAM/PORC PO16 13 L7
Upton Cl HAV PO9 82 E6
Upton Crs ROWN SO16 41 H4
Upton Grey Cl WINW SO22 21 G4
Upton La ROWN SO16 41 G6

V

Vadne Gdns GPORT PO12 16 A1 1
Vale Dr WEND SO18 6 F1
Vale Gv GPORT PO12 132 D1
Valentine Av ITCH SO19 11 M4
Valentine Cl FHAM PO15 96 D3
Valentine Ct WVILLE PO7 82 B5 3
Valerian Cl ELGH SO50 46 B5 3
Valerian Rd HEND SO30 58 B6
Vale Rd WINC SO23 3 J7
The Vale FAWY SO45 91 G3
HLER SO31 95 G4
HORN PO8 64 D3
SSEA PO5 134 B6 7
Valetta Pk EMRTH PO10 104 B6
Valetta Rd EMRTH PO10 123 G6
Valiant Gdns NEND PO2 118 C3
Valiant Rd EMRTH PO10 123 G6
Valley Cl FAWY SO45 110 C6 1
RWIN SO21 39 J2
WVILLE PO7 101 H3
Valleydene FAWY SO45 91 G4
Valley Hl WINW SO22 21 F2
Valley Park Dr HORN PO8 64 E1
Valley Ri HLER SO31 94 D2
Valley Rd CHFD SO53 37 K3
WINW SO22 20 E2
TOTT SO40 52 E7
The Valley WINW SO22 25 G2
Valsheba Dr FHAM/STUB PO14 114 C6
Vanburgh Wy CHFD SO53 37 J1 7
Vanguard Hl WINW SO22 21 F1
Vanguard Rd WEND SO18 7 H3
Vanstone Rd
LSOL/BMARY PO13 116 A7
Vardy Cl ITCH SO19 73 G2 4
Varna Rd WSHM SO15 54 D7
Varos Cl GPORT PO12 132 D2
Varsity Rd EMRTH PO10 123 G6
Vaudrey Cl WSHM SO15 54 D3 3
Vaughan Cl ITCH SO19 57 H7
Vaughan Rd FAWY SO45 90 D2 4
Veal's La TOTT SO40 70 C6
Vear's La RWIN SO21 39 K2
Vectis Rd GPORT PO12 132 B5
Vectis Wy CHAM PO6 100 E7
Velder Av ENEY PO4 19 M4
Vellan Ct ROWN SO16 53 H3
Velmore Rd CHFD SO53 37 J6
Velsheda Ct FAWY SO45 91 H1
Venerable Rd
FHAM/STUB PO14 115 H2
Vengeance Rd
LSOL/BMARY PO13 131 F1
Venice Cl WVILLE PO7 82 B5
Ventnor Rd ENEY PO4 19 H6 2
LSOL/BMARY PO13 115 J4
Ventnor Wy FHAM/PORC PO16 98 B5
Venture Rd ROWN SO16 42 E2
Verbena Crs HORN PO8 82 C1
Verbena Wy HEND SO30 58 C6 3
Verdon Av HLER SO31 93 H3
Verger Cl FHAM/STUB PO14 95 H3 5
Vermont Cl ROWN SO16 43 G7
Vernham Rd WINW SO22 21 G5
Vernon Av ENEY PO4 19 L4
Vernon Cl GPORT PO12 132 D3
Vernon Hl BPWT SO32 48 D1
Vernon Rd GPORT PO12 132 D3
HSEA PO3 119 F5
Verona Rd CHFD SO53 38 B3
Verulam Rd SHAM SO14 5 J4
Verwood Rd HAV PO9 83 J7 12
Veryan FHAM PO15 12 C6
Vespasian Rd WEND SO18 6 A4
Vespasian Wy CHFD SO53 38 B4
Vesta Wy CHFD SO53 38 B3
Vian Cl LSOL/BMARY PO13 115 K3
Vian Rd WVILLE PO7 81 J7
Vicarage Dr HEND SO30 58 A7
Vicarage La BPWT SO32 49 K5
BPWT SO32 59 H4
FHAM/STUB PO14 114 D4
TOTT SO40 50 E3
WVILLE PO7 62 C1
Vicarage Rd TOTT SO40 70 A4
Viceroy Rd ITCH SO19 11 H4
Victena Rd ELGH SO50 46 B1
Victoria Av HISD PO11 137 G5
WVILLE PO7 101 G3
Victoria Cl HLER SO31 95 F5
Victoria Gld HLER SO31 93 F1
Victoria Gv SSEA PO5 18 F8
Victoria Pl GPORT PO12 16 B6 3
Victoria Rd BPWT SO32 48 C3
ELGH SO50 38 E5
EMRTH PO10 104 B5
HISD PO11 121 G5
HLER SO31 72 D7
ITCH SO19 10 A5
PSEA PO1 17 L1
WINC SO23 2 D2
WVILLE PO7 81 K6 1
Victoria Rd North SSEA PO5 18 F6
Victoria Sq LSOL/BMARY PO13 131 F2
Victoria St GPORT PO12 16 C4
PSEA PO1 134 B1
SHAM SO14 5 L9
Victor Rd EMRTH PO10 123 G6
HSEA PO3 134 E1 1
Victor St WSHM SO15 54 D4 2
Victory Av HORN PO8 64 B6
Victory Cl CHFD SO53 37 J5
Victory Crs WSHM SO15 54 C6 1
Victory Gn NEND PO2 118 B5 2
Victory Rd FHAM/STUB PO14 114 E5
PSEA PO1 17 L4 6
WSHM SO15 54 C6
Victory Sq WSHM SO15 54 C6 2
Viking Cl FAWY SO45 110 C7
FHAM/STUB PO14 114 C4
ROWN SO16 41 K6
The Vikings ROMY SO51 35 G3 5
Viking Wy HORN PO8 64 D1
Villa Gdns WVILLE PO7 81 K5
Village Cl FHAM/STUB PO14 114 D5
Village Rd GPORT PO12 132 C6
Ville De Paris Rd
FHAM/STUB PO14 115 H2
Villiers Rd FAWY SO45 91 G6
SSEA PO5 134 C7 7
WSHM SO15 54 D5
Vincent Av ROWN SO16 54 D2
Vincent Gv FHAM/PORC PO16 99 F7
Vincent Rd WSHM SO15 54 D4
Vincent's Gv WSHM SO15 54 D4 3
Vincent St WSHM SO15 54 C4
Vincent's Wk SHAM SO14 9 G2
Vine Bank WEND SO18 7 K2
Vine Cl HLER SO31 94 C3
Vine Coppice WVILLE PO7 101 K2
Vine Rd ROWN SO16 54 B1
Vinery Gdns ROWN SO16 54 C2
Vinery Rd ROWN SO16 54 D2 1
Vineside LSOL/BMARY PO13 116 B6
Vineyard Cl ITCH SO19 10 B3
The Vineyards NBAD SO52 36 B6
Viney Av ROMY SO51 35 G2
Violet Av FHAM/STUB PO14 114 C5
Violet Cl NBAD SO52 37 H4
Violet Rd ROWN SO16 43 H7
Virginia Park Rd GPORT PO12 132 C2
Vita Rd NEND PO2 118 D4
Vivash Rd PSEA PO1 19 G4 5
Vixen Cl FHAM/STUB PO14 114 C5
Vokes Cl ITCH SO19 7 J9
Vulcan Cl WSHM SO15 54 A6
Vulcan Rd EMRTH PO10 123 G6
WSHM SO15 54 A6
Vyse La SHAM SO14 8 F4 2

W

Wade Court Rd HAV PO9 15 G6
Wade La HAV PO9 15 G8
Wadham Rd NEND PO2 118 C5
Wadhurst Gdns ITCH SO19 11 H9
Wadhurst Rd HEND SO30 58 B6
The Wad SELS PO20 139 J7
Wagtail Rd HORN PO8 64 B6
Wagtail Wy FHAM/PORC PO16 99 G6
Wainscott Rd ENEY PO4 19 L9
Wainwright Cl CHAM PO6 119 H1
Wait End Rd WVILLE PO7 81 K7
Wakefield Av FHAM/PORC PO16 12 F1
Wakefield Ct WEND SO18 7 G1
Wakefield Rd WEND SO18 7 G1
Wakefords Wy HAV PO9 83 J7
Walberton Av CHAM PO6 101 F6
Waldegrave Cl ITCH SO19 10 A8
Walden Gdns HORN PO8 64 C5
Walden Rd NEND PO2 118 B5
Waldon Gdns WEND SO18 56 E2 3
Wales St WINC SO23 3 G4
Walford Rd CHAM PO6 100 B6
Walker Pl LSOL/BMARY PO13 116 A6 4
Walker Rd NEND PO2 118 B5
Walkers Cl ELGH SO50 46 C1 5
Walkers La North FAWY SO45 110 C6
Walker's La South FAWY SO45 128 C1
Wallace La BROC SO42 125 H2
Wallace Rd ITCH SO19 10 E8
NEND PO2 118 E7
Wallington Ct
FHAM/STUB PO14 115 G1 1
Wallington Dr CHFD SO53 37 H2
Wallington Hl
FHAM/PORC PO16 13 L4
Wallington Rd NEND PO2 118 E6
Wallington Shore Rd
FHAM/PORC PO16 13 M4
Wallington Wy
FHAM/PORC PO16 13 L4
Wallisdean Av
FHAM/STUB PO14 12 E8
HSEA PO3 135 G1
Wallis Gdns WVILLE PO7 81 K4
Wallis Rd WVILLE PO7 81 K4
Walmer Cl ELGH SO50 38 D3
Walmer Rd PSEA PO1 19 H4
Walnut Av WEND SO18 44 B6
Walnut Cl CHFD SO53 31 K7
ROWN SO16 54 A3
Walnut Dr FHAM/STUB PO14 114 C5
Walnut Gv WINW SO22 21 G6
ROWN SO16 54 A4
Walnut Tree Cl HISD PO11 137 G5 1
Walnut Tree Dr EMRTH PO10 105 H3
Wainwright Gdns HEND SO30 58 B1
Walpole La HLER SO31 74 D6
Walpole Rd WINW SO22 25 F3
GPORT PO12 16 D5
Walsall Rd HSEA PO3 19 M1
Walsingham Cl CHAM PO6 100 C5 3
Walsingham Gdns WEND SO18 56 B1
Waltham Cl FHAM/PORC PO16 99 F4
Waltham Crs ROWN SO16 42 C7
Waltham St SSEA PO5 18 B5 3
Walton Cl GPORT PO12 132 D4
WVILLE PO7 101 K1
Walton Ct FHAM PO15 96 E2
Walton Pl WINW SO22 25 G3
Walton Rd CHAM PO6 119 H1
GPORT PO12 132 D4
ITCH SO19 73 G1 5
Waltons Av FAWY SO45 110 A3
Wandesford Pl GPORT PO12 116 D6
Wangfield La BPWT SO32 59 H3
Wansbeck Cl CHFD SO53 37 J5 2
Warbler Cl HORN PO8 64 B5
ROWN SO16 42 C5
Warblington Av HAV PO9 15 K5
Warblington Cl CHFD SO53 37 J7 3
Warblington Rd EMRTH PO10 104 B7
Warblington St PSEA PO1 17 M6
Warbrook Ct HAV PO9 103 J1 18
Warburton Cl ITCH SO19 73 H1 1
Warburton Rd ITCH SO19 57 G7
Ward Crs EMRTH PO10 104 D3
Warden Cl HEND SO30 57 G3 6
Wardens Cl HISD PO11 137 G3
Wardle Rd ELGH SO50 39 G3
Ward Rd ENEY PO4 19 L9
Wardroom Rd NEND PO2 118 A6
Warfield Av WVILLE PO7 81 K6
Warfield Crs WVILLE PO7 81 K6
Warlock Cl ITCH SO19 73 G2 5
Warnford Cl GPORT PO12 132 C4 6
Warnford Crs HAV PO9 102 E1
Warren Av CHFD SO53 38 B5
ENEY PO4 19 M4
HSEA PO3 119 F3
ROWN SO16 54 C3
Warren Cl CHFD SO53 38 B5
HISD PO11 136 D4
ROWN SO16 54 B2
Warren Crs ROWN SO16 54 B2
Warren Pl TOTT SO40 52 B2
Warren Rd WINC SO23 3 K3
The Warren FAWY SO45 109 J2
Warrior Cl CHFD SO53 37 J6
Warrys Cl FAWY SO45 91 H6
Warsash Cl HAV PO9 83 F7 6
Warsash Gv
LSOL/BMARY PO13 115 K5 7
Warsash Rd FHAM/STUB PO14 95 K5
HLER SO31 94 C5
Warspite Cl NEND PO2 118 C3
Warton Cl BROC SO42 125 H2
Warwick Cl CHFD SO53 37 H6 4
LSOL/BMARY PO13 131 H4
Warwick Crs SSEA PO5 18 D6
Warwick Rd TOTT SO40 52 E4 1
WSHM SO15 54 E2
Wasdale Cl HORN PO8 64 D2
Washbrook Rd CHAM PO6 100 C6
Washington Rd EMRTH PO10 104 C5
NEND PO2 118 C7
Waterbeech Dr HEND SO30 58 B4 6
Waterberry Dr WVILLE PO7 81 H4
Waterhouse La WSHM SO15 54 C6 3
Waterhouse Wy WSHM SO15 54 C5
Water La FAWY SO45 91 F4
TOTT SO40 52 C4
WINC SO23 3 G4
Waterlock Gdns ENEY PO4 135 J4
Waterloo Cl HORN PO8 81 J2
Waterloo Rd GPORT PO12 133 F7
HAV PO9 14 F3
WSHM SO15 54 D6
Waterloo St SSEA PO5 18 D5
Waterloo Ter WSHM SO15 4 F7
Watermans La FAWY SO45 91 F5
Watermead Rd CHAM PO6 101 K7 1
Water's Edge HEND SO30 58 A6
Waters Edge Gdns
EMRTH PO10 104 C6
Watersedge Rd CHAM PO6 99 K6 2
Waterside FAWY SO45 91 G1
Waterside Gdns
FHAM/PORC PO16 98 A5 1
Waterside La
FHAM/PORC PO16 117 H1
Waterside Rd ROMY SO51 35 F1 4
Watersmeet
FHAM/PORC PO16 115 J1
The Waters WHAM PO17 97 F1
Waterworks Rd CHAM PO6 101 J6
RWIN SO21 33 F5
Watkin Rd HEND SO30 58 D2 1
Watley Cl ROWN SO16 41 J6
Watley La RWIN SO21 20 A3
Watson Wk TOTT SO40 52 B5 3
Watton Rd FAWY SO45 109 K4
Watts Cl ROWN SO16 53 K2
Watts Rd HEND SO30 58 B5
PSEA PO1 134 C1
Wavell Rd LSOL/BMARY PO13 116 A4
WEND SO18 7 G4
Wavell Wy WINW SO22 25 F3
Waveney Cl
LSOL/BMARY PO13 131 G2 3
Waveney Gn ROWN SO16 53 K3
Waverley Av HLER SO31 73 F7
Waverley Cl ROMY SO51 35 G1 6
Waverley Ct HLER SO31 93 F1 2
Waverley Gv ENEY PO4 134 D6 2
Waverley Rd CHAM PO6 101 H6
ENEY PO4 134 D6
SSEA PO5 19 G9
WSHM SO15 4 A8
Wayfarer Cl ENEY PO4 135 H3 4
HLER SO31 94 E5
Wayfarers LSOL/BMARY PO13 132 A1
Wayfarer's Wk HAV PO9 102 D4
WVILLE PO7 80 E5
Waylands Pl HEND SO30 73 K1
Waynflete Cl BPWT SO32 48 D3
Waynflete Pl WINW SO22 25 G2 2
Wayside HLER SO31 74 C5
Wayte St CHAM PO6 100 E7
Weald Cl HLER SO31 95 F2
Weardale Rd CHFD SO53 38 A6
Weavers Gn HAV PO9 15 L1
Weavers Pl CHFD SO53 37 J2
Weavills Rd ELGH SO50 45 K1
Webb Cl HISD PO11 137 H6
Webb La HISD PO11 137 H6
Webb Rd FHAM/PORC PO16 117 G1
Webburn Gdns WEND SO18 56 D1 3
Webster Rd WINW SO22 20 E6
Wedgewood Cl FAWY SO45 109 K3
FHAM/STUB PO14 114 D5 1
Wedgewood Wy WVILLE PO7 81 K3
Wedmore Cl WINW SO22 24 D5
Weeke Manor Cl WINW SO22 21 G5
Weevil La GPORT PO12 16 E2
Welbeck Av PTSW SO17 55 J2
Welch Rd ENEY PO4 134 D6
GPORT PO12 132 D1
Welch Wy ROWN SO16 41 K6
Welchwood Cl HORN PO8 64 A6
Welland Gdns WEND SO18 56 E2
Welland Gn ROWN SO16 53 K4
Wellands Rd LYND SO43 86 C1 3
Wellbrooke Gdns CHFD SO53 37 J3
Well Copse Cl HORN PO8 64 D3
Wellers Cl TOTT SO40 52 A5
Wellesley Cl WVILLE PO7 81 K6
Welles Rd CHFD SO53 38 A4
Well House La WINW SO22 21 H2
Wellington Av WEND SO18 7 K4
Wellington Cl FAWY SO45 90 E5
HORN PO8 64 E6
Wellington Gv
FHAM/PORC PO16 99 F7
Wellington Pk HEND SO30 57 K3
Wellington Rd WEND SO18 56 A2
Wellington St SSEA PO5 18 C5
Wellington Wy WVILLE PO7 81 K6 2
Well La BPWT SO32 49 J4
HLER SO31 93 K4
Well Meadow HAV PO9 83 F7
Wellowbrook Cl CHFD SO53 37 H4 2
Wellow Cl HAV PO9 14 B1
WEND SO18 7 L5
Wellow Gdns FHAM/STUB PO14 95 H4
Wellsfield SELS PO20 139 K7
Wellsmoor FHAM/STUB PO14 95 H3
Wells Pl ELGH SO50 44 E1
Wellswood Gdns HAV PO9 83 K2
Wellsworth La HAV PO9 83 K2
Wembley Gv CHAM PO6 119 F1 1
Wendover Rd HAV PO9 14 C3
Wensley Gdns EMRTH PO10 104 C3
Wentworth Dr HORN PO8 64 C5
Wentworth Gdns
FAWY SO45 110 A5 1
ITCH SO19 11 J8
Wentworth Gra WINW SO22 2 B7
Wentworth Gv FAWY SO45 110 A4
Wesermarsch Rd HORN PO8 82 B1
Wesley Cl ITCH SO19 73 G1
Wesley Gv HSEA PO3 118 E4
Wessex Cl FAWY SO45 110 C6
Wessex Dr WINW SO22 21 H5
Wessex Gdns
FHAM/PORC PO16 98 E7
ROMY SO51 35 G3
Wessex La WEND SO18 44 A7
Wessex Rd HORN PO8 64 D1
Wessex Wy RWIN SO21 39 K2
West Bargate SHAM SO14 8 F2 1
West Battery Rd NEND PO2 118 A6
Westborn Rd FHAM/PORC PO16 13 K5
Westbourne Av EMRTH PO10 104 D4
FAWY SO45 109 K3
Westbourne Cl EMRTH PO10 104 D4 1
Westbourne Crs PTSW SO17 55 G3
Westbourne Rd EMRTH PO10 104 D3
NEND PO2 118 E7
Westbroke Gdns ROMY SO51 34 E1 3
Westbrook Cl HLER SO31 95 F1
Westbrooke Cl HORN PO8 64 B6
Westbrook Gv WVILLE PO7 101 J1
Westbrook Rd
FHAM/PORC PO16 117 G1
Westbrook Wy WEND SO18 44 B7 3
Westbury Cl CHAM PO6 100 A5 6
Westbury Ct HEND SO30 58 B7
Westbury Rd WSHM SO15 54 A5
Westcliff Cl LSOL/BMARY PO13 131 F1
West Common FAWY SO45 128 A1
Westcot Rd FAWY SO45 109 J4 3
Westcroft Rd GPORT PO12 132 C3
West Downs Cl
FHAM/PORC PO16 97 H2
West Dr ELGH SO50 39 G6
West End Cl WINW SO22 2 B4
West End Rd HEND SO30 57 G3
HEND SO30 73 J1
Westend Rd WEND SO18 7 G5
West End Rd WEND SO18 7 H3
West End Ter WINW SO22 2 B4
Westerham Cl CHAM PO6 100 D6
Westering ROMY SO51 35 H1 2
ROMY SO51 35 H2 3
Westerley Cl HLER SO31 94 D5 5
Western Av EMRTH PO10 104 A6
Western District Cut
WSHM SO15 4 A5
Western Esp SHAM SO14 4 D9
Western Pde EMRTH PO10 104 B7
SSEA PO5 18 B8
Western Rd CHAM PO6 100 C7
CHFD SO53 38 B1
FHAM/PORC PO16 13 J6
WINW SO22 2 B3
HAV PO9 14 C3
HEND SO30 57 G3
Western Wy FHAM/PORC PO16 13 H6
GPORT PO12 132 B5
Westfield Av FHAM/STUB PO14 12 F8
HISD PO11 137 F5
Westfield Cl ELGH SO50 46 B4
HLER SO31 93 H4
Westfield Common
HLER SO31 93 G4 1
Westfield Crs CHFD SO53 37 K7
Westfield Rd CHFD SO53 37 K7
ENEY PO4 19 L7
WINW SO22 20 E2
GPORT PO12 132 C3
TOTT SO40 52 E4
WSHM SO15 54 B5
Westgate FHAM/STUB PO14 114 D6
Westgate St SHAM SO14 8 F4
West Haye Rd HISD PO11 138 A7
West Hill Dr FAWY SO45 91 G1
WINW SO22 2 A4
West Hill Pk WINW SO22 21 G7
West Hoe La BPWT SO32 49 G3
West Horton La ELGH SO50 45 J2
Westland Dr WVILLE PO7 101 K2
Westland Gdns GPORT PO12 132 D5
Westlands Gv
FHAM/PORC PO16 99 F7
West La HISD PO11 137 F3
NBAD SO52 35 K5
Westley Cl WINW SO22 21 G6
Westley Gv FHAM/STUB PO14 12 E7
Westman Rd WINW SO22 21 G5
West Marlands Rd SHAM SO14 4 F9
Westmead Cl HISD PO11 136 E5
Westminster Gdns
FHAM/STUB PO14 95 H3 6
Westminster Ga WINW SO22 24 E3
Westmorland Wy CHFD SO53 38 B5
Weston Av ENEY PO4 135 G4
Weston Cl ITCH SO19 10 E8
Weston Crs WEND SO18 7 L4
Weston Grove Rd ITCH SO19 10 A6
Weston La ITCH SO19 10 C9
ROWN SO16 41 F7
Weston Pde ITCH SO19 10 D9
Weston Rd ELGH SO50 38 D7
Westover Rd HSEA PO3 119 G7
ROWN SO16 53 G4
West Park Rd WSHM SO15 4 E9
West Quay Rd WSHM SO15 8 E3
Westridge Rd PTSW SO17 5 K2
West Rd EMRTH PO10 104 B6
FAWY SO45 90 E5
FAWY SO45 92 A5
HEND SO30 57 J6
ITCH SO19 10 C5
SHAM SO14 9 G5
WHAM PO17 79 K7
Westrow Gdns WSHM SO15 4 D4
Westrow Rd WSHM SO15 4 D4
West St EMRTH PO10 104 C6
FAWY SO45 91 G1
FHAM/PORC PO16 13 H6
FHAM/STUB PO14 96 A6
HAV PO9 14 B4
PSEA PO1 17 K7
SHAM SO14 8 F3
WHAM PO17 79 H7
WVILLE PO7 62 B3
Westview Rd WINW SO22 20 D5
Westward Rd HEND SO30 58 B4
Westway FHAM PO15 95 K3
Westway Cl ROWN SO16 41 J5
Westways CHAM PO6 102 A6
FHAM/STUB PO14 114 E5
Westways Cl ROWN SO16 41 J6 1
Westwood Cl EMRTH PO10 104 D3
Westwood Gdns CHFD SO53 38 B2
Westwood Rd HLER SO31 72 E6
LYND SO43 66 C7
NEND PO2 118 D3
PTSW SO17 5 G2
Wetherby Gdns TOTT SO40 52 B4
Weyhill Cl FHAM/PORC PO16 99 F5
HAV PO9 102 E1 5
Weymouth Av GPORT PO12 116 C7
Whaddon Cha
FHAM/STUB PO14 114 C5
Whaddon Ct HAV PO9 82 D7
Whale Island Wy NEND PO2 118 B6
Whalesmead Cl ELGH SO50 45 J2
Whalesmead Rd ELGH SO50 45 J2
Whaley Rd NEND PO2 118 A6
Wharf Hl WINC SO23 3 G7
Wharf Rd ITCH SO19 10 A4
NEND PO2 118 B7
Wharncliffe Rd ITCH SO19 10 A3
Whartons La TOTT SO40 68 B1
Wheat Cl NBAD SO52 37 G4
Wheatcroft Dr WEND SO18 56 E3 5
WEND SO18 7 K1 2
Wheatcroft Rd
LSOL/BMARY PO13 131 G2
Wheatland Cl WINW SO22 25 G3
Wheatlands FHAM/STUB PO14 95 H2
Wheatlands Av HISD PO11 138 B7
Wheatlands Crs HISD PO11 138 B7 1
Wheatsheaf Ct HEND SO30 58 A6 5
Wheatsheaf Dr HORN PO8 81 J2
Wheatstone Rd ENEY PO4 19 H8
Wheeler Cl GPORT PO12 16 A1
Wheelers Wk FAWY SO45 110 B7
Whernside Cl ROWN SO16 54 A4 5
Wherwell Ct HAV PO9 103 J1 19
Whichers Cl HAV PO9 83 J5
Whichers Gate Rd HAV PO9 83 J5
Whimbrel Cl ENEY PO4 135 H3
Whinchat Cl FHAM PO15 96 D2
ROWN SO16 42 C5
Whinfield Rd FAWY SO45 91 F5
Whippingham Cl CHAM PO6 100 C6
Whistler Cl ITCH SO19 11 L4
Whistler Rd ITCH SO19 11 L4
Whitcombe Cl TOTT SO40 52 D5 2
Whitcombe Gdns HSEA PO3 19 K2
Whitebeam Cl
FHAM/STUB PO14 12 C7
HORN PO8 64 D7 1
RWIN SO21 39 K2
Whitebeam Rd HEND SO30 58 C6
Whitebeam Wy NBAD SO52 36 B5
Whitechimney Rw
EMRTH PO10 104 E3
Whitecliffe Av HSEA PO3 135 F1
White Cloud Pk ENEY PO4 19 K8
Whitecross Gdns NEND PO2 118 E4
Whitedell La WHAM PO17 98 A2
White Dirt La HORN PO8 64 C2
Whitefield Rd FAWY SO45 109 K4
White Gates BPWT SO32 47 G6
White Hart La
FHAM/PORC PO16 98 E7
TOTT SO40 50 C4
White Hart Rd ELGH SO50 46 B2
GPORT PO12 16 B6 4
PSEA PO1 17 L7
Whitehaven FHAM/PORC PO16 98 E7
HORN PO8 64 E6
White Heather Ct FAWY SO45 91 H1

Whitehill Cl WEND SO18 ... 7 L4 10
White Horse La WVILLE PO7 ... 63 F6
White House Gdns WSHM SO15 .. 54 B6
White Ladies Cl HAV PO9 ... 15 G5
White La RWIN SO21 ... 33 K1
Whitelaw Rd WSHM SO15 ... 54 C5
Whiteley La FHAM PO15 ... 75 J4
FHAM PO15 ... 96 A2
HLER SO31 ... 75 H4
Whiteley Wy FHAM PO15 ... 75 J7
Whitenap Cl ROMY SO51 ... 35 G4
Whitenap La ROMY SO51 ... 35 H4
White Rd ELGH SO50 ... 39 G6
Whiteshute La WINC SO23 ... 25 H4
Whites La FAWY SO45 ... 110 E4 10
White's Rd ITCH SO19 ... 7 H7
Whitestone Cl ROWN SO16 ... 54 A4 4
White Swan Rd PSEA PO1 ... 18 B4
Whitethorn Rd HISD PO11 ... 137 J5 1
Whitewater Ri FAWY SO45 ... 91 G4
Whithedwood Av WSHM SO15 ... 4 A2
Whithers La BROC SO42 ... 125 H2
Whitley Cl EMRTH PO10 ... 104 E1
Whitley Rd HORN PO8 ... 64 A6
Whitsbury Rd HAV PO9 ... 103 H1
Whitstable Rd CHAM PO6 ... 100 D6
Whittington Cl FAWY SO45 ... 91 G4
Whittington Ct EMRTH PO10 ... 104 C6
Whittle Av FHAM PO15 ... 95 H1
Whitwell HLER SO31 ... 73 F6 7
Whitwell Rd ENEY PO4 ... 134 D7
Whitworth Cl GPORT PO12 ... 132 D4
Whitworth Crs WEND SO18 ... 6 B3
Whitworth Rd GPORT PO12 ... 132 D3
NEND PO2 ... 118 E7
WEND SO18 ... 6 B3
Whyte Cl FAWY SO45 ... 109 J4
Whyteways ELGH SO50 ... 38 C6
The Wicket FAWY SO45 ... 91 G4
Wickham Rd FHAM/PORC PO16 .. 13 J1
WHAM PO17 ... 97 J2
Wickham St PSEA PO1 ... 17 L3
Wicklow Dr CHFD SO53 ... 37 H5
Wickor Cl EMRTH PO10 ... 104 D4
Wickor Wy EMRTH PO10 ... 104 C3
Wicor Mill La
FHAM/PORC PO16 ... 116 E1
Wicor Pth FHAM/PORC PO16 ... 117 H1
Widecombe Dr FAWY SO45 ... 91 F2
Wide La ELGH SO50 ... 44 C4
WEND SO18 ... 44 B6
Widgeon Cl GPORT PO12 ... 132 E1
ROWN SO16 ... 42 C5
Widley Ct FHAM/STUB PO14 ... 115 G1
Widley Court Dr CHAM PO6 ... 101 F7
Widley Gdns WVILLE PO7 ... 101 J3
Widley Rd CHAM PO6 ... 101 F6
NEND PO2 ... 118 B5
Widley Wk CHAM PO6 ... 100 E4
Wield Cl HAV PO9 ... 102 D2
Wigan Crs HAV PO9 ... 102 C4
Wilberforce Cl WINW SO22 ... 25 F2 3
Wilberforce Rd GPORT PO12 .. 133 F7 2
SSEA PO5 ... 18 C7 5
Wild Arum Wy NBAD SO52 ... 37 G5
Wildburn Cl TOTT SO40 ... 52 B2
Wild Cherry Wy NBAD SO52 ... 37 H4 3
Wilde Cl TOTT SO40 ... 52 C5 6
Wildern Cl HLER SO31 ... 94 E3 2
Wilderness Hts WEND SO18 ... 7 M1
Wildern La HEND SO30 ... 58 A4
Wild Ridings FHAM/STUB PO14 ... 96 C6
Wild Rose Crs HLER SO31 ... 94 D4
Wilks Cl ROWN SO16 ... 41 H6
Willersley Cl CHAM PO6 ... 100 B5
William Cl FHAM/STUB PO14 ... 114 E6
William Macleod Wy
ROWN SO16 ... 54 B4
William Price Gdns
FHAM/PORC PO16 ... 13 J3
Williams Cl FAWY SO45 ... 110 A4
LSOL/BMARY PO13 ... 132 A1
Williams Rd HSEA PO3 ... 119 G4
William St SHAM SO14 ... 5 M8
Willis Av NBAD SO52 ... 36 C6
Willis Rd GPORT PO12 ... 16 D5
PSEA PO1 ... 18 C3
ROWN SO16 ... 44 A6
Willis Waye WINC SO23 ... 22 B2
Willow Cl HAV PO9 ... 15 G5
HEND SO30 ... 57 H2 3
HEND SO30 ... 58 C6
Willow Ct ROWN SO16 ... 54 B1
Willowdene Cl HAV PO9 ... 102 C2
Willow Dr TOTT SO40 ... 70 A5
Willow Gdns EMRTH PO10 ... 104 E2
NBAD SO52 ... 36 A5
Willow Gn RWIN SO21 ... 39 K2
Willow Gv ELGH SO50 ... 46 C1
Willow Herb Cl HLER SO31 ... 94 D4
Willow Pl GPORT PO12 ... 16 B3
Willow Rd BPWT SO32 ... 49 F4
The Willows WVILLE PO7 ... 80 D1
Willow Tree Av HORN PO8 ... 82 C3
Willow Tree Gdns
FHAM/STUB PO14 ... 12 C7
Willow Tree Wk ITCH SO19 ... 11 K3
Willow Wood Rd HISD PO11 ... 137 H5 2
Wills Wy ROMY SO51 ... 35 F4
Wilmer Rd ELGH SO50 ... 44 D1
Wilmington Cl WEND SO18 ... 56 C1
Wilmot Cl ELGH SO50 ... 39 H5
Wilmott Cl GPORT PO12 ... 132 C3
Wilmott La GPORT PO12 ... 132 C3
Wilson Gv SSEA PO5 ... 18 F7
Wilson Rd NEND PO2 ... 118 B5
Wilson St SHAM SO14 ... 5 L8
Wilton Av WSHM SO15 ... 4 D6
Wilton Crs WSHM SO15 ... 54 E3
Wilton Dr HORN PO8 ... 64 B7
Wilton Gdns WSHM SO15 ... 54 E3
Wilton Pl SSEA PO5 ... 18 D9
Wilton Rd WSHM SO15 ... 54 E3
Wilton Ter SSEA PO5 ... 18 E9 6
Wiltshire Rd CHFD SO53 ... 38 A7
Wiltshire St SSEA PO5 ... 18 B5
Wilverley Av HAV PO9 ... 103 H2
Wilverley Pl FAWY SO45 ... 110 B6
Wimbledon Park Rd
SSEA PO5 ... 134 C6 7
Wimborne Rd ENEY PO4 ... 19 L6
Wimpole St PSEA PO1 ... 18 F2
Wimpson Gdns ROWN SO16 ... 54 A3
Wimpson La ROWN SO16 ... 53 K4
Wincanton Wy WVILLE PO7 ... 82 C4
Winchcombe Rd CHAM PO6 ... 100 A5
Winchester By-pass WINC SO23 .. 22 C1
Winchester Hl ROMY SO51 ... 35 G2
Winchester Rd BPWT SO32 ... 58 D1
BPWT SO32 ... 61 F4
CHFD SO53 ... 38 A4
NEND PO2 ... 118 D7
ROMY SO51 ... 35 F3
ROMY SO51 ... 35 J1 2
ROWN SO16 ... 54 B3
RWIN SO21 ... 33 G2
WHAM PO17 ... 61 G7
Winchester St HEND SO30 ... 59 F4
WSHM SO15 ... 4 F7
Winchester Wy TOTT SO40 ... 52 B5 9
Winchfield Cl ITCH SO19 ... 11 G9
Winchfield Crs HAV PO9 ... 102 D2
Windbury Rd ROWN SO16 ... 53 K2
Windermere Av
FHAM/STUB PO14 ... 114 E3
ROWN SO16 ... 53 J2
Windermere Gdns TOTT SO40 ... 52 D4
Windermere Rd NEND PO2 ... 118 E4
WEND SO18 ... 56 E3
Windfield Dr ROMY SO51 ... 35 G2 7
Windmill Copse FAWY SO45 ... 91 G5 3
Windmill Fld WVILLE PO7 ... 81 F1
Windmill Gv FHAM/PORC PO16 .. 116 E1
Windmill La HLER SO31 ... 73 K3
Windover Cl ITCH SO19 ... 7 M6
Windrush Gdns WVILLE PO7 ... 81 J6
Windrush Rd ROWN SO16 ... 53 K3
Windrush Wy FAWY SO45 ... 91 H3
Windsor Ct ELGH SO50 ... 39 G6 2
Windsor Ga ELGH SO50 ... 38 D4
Windsor Rd CHAM PO6 ... 100 E7
FHAM/PORC PO16 ... 99 G7
GPORT PO12 ... 132 D4
WVILLE PO7 ... 81 J3
Winfield Wy EMRTH PO10 ... 104 C2 1
Winfrith Wy ROWN SO16 ... 41 J6
Wingate Dr ITCH SO19 ... 7 J9
Wingate Rd TOTT SO40 ... 52 C4
Wingfield St PSEA PO1 ... 134 C1
Wingrove Rd TOTT SO40 ... 68 B2 1
Winifred Rd WVILLE PO7 ... 81 K5
Winkfield Rw HORN PO8 ... 64 C7
Winkle St SHAM SO14 ... 8 F5
Winkton Cl HAV PO9 ... 14 B1
Winnall Cl WINC SO23 ... 3 K2
Winnall Manor Rd WINC SO23 ... 3 K4
Winnall Valley Rd WINC SO23 ... 3 J3
Winnards Pk HLER SO31 ... 94 C3
Winnham Dr FHAM/PORC PO16 .. 98 D6
Winnington FHAM PO15 ... 96 E2
Winn Rd PTSW SO17 ... 5 G2
Winscombe Av HORN PO8 ... 82 B3
Winsford Av ELGH SO50 ... 45 K2
Winsford Cl ELGH SO50 ... 45 K2 1
Winsford Gdns ELGH SO50 ... 45 K2 2
Winslade Rd WINW SO22 ... 21 F3
HAV PO9 ... 102 E1 6
Winsor Cl HISD PO11 ... 138 A7
Winsor La TOTT SO40 ... 51 G4
Winsor Rd TOTT SO40 ... 50 E5
TOTT SO40 ... 53 F6
Winstanley Rd NEND PO2 ... 118 B6
ROWN SO16 ... 41 H6
Winston Churchill Av SSEA PO5 .. 18 D5
Winston Cl ELGH SO50 ... 38 D6
HISD PO11 ... 137 F5
ROWN SO16 ... 54 A2
Winstone Crs NBAD SO52 ... 36 B7
Winterbourne Rd CHAM PO6 ... 99 J5 2
ROMY SO51 ... 35 H1 5
Winterhill Rd CHAM PO6 ... 100 C6
Winter Rd ENEY PO4 ... 19 L8
Winters Cl FAWY SO45 ... 110 A4
Winters Hl BPWT SO32 ... 47 K3
Winterslow Dr HAV PO9 ... 83 F7 2
Wintoun Rd BPWT SO32 ... 61 H4
Winton Rd NEND PO2 ... 118 E5
Winton St SHAM SO14 ... 5 H9 2
Wisborough Rd SSEA PO5 ... 18 F9
Wish Pl SSEA PO5 ... 19 G9
Wisteria Gdns HAV PO9 ... 103 J2
Witchampton Cl HAV PO9 ... 103 H1 6
Witham Cl CHFD SO53 ... 37 H4
Witherbed La FHAM PO15 ... 95 J2
Withies Rd LSOL/BMARY PO13 .. 116 A7
Withy Cl ROMY SO51 ... 34 E2 3
Wittering Rd HISD PO11 ... 138 C6
ROWN SO16 ... 42 A6
Witt Rd ELGH SO50 ... 46 B1
Witts Hl WEND SO18 ... 6 F1
Winton Cl WINW SO22 ... 21 J5
Woburn Cl ELGH SO50 ... 38 D4
Woburn Rd ROWN SO16 ... 42 C6
Wode Cl HORN PO8 ... 64 D1
Wodehouse Rd ITCH SO19 ... 10 D2
Wolfe Cl WINW SO22 ... 25 F3
Wolseley Rd WSHM SO15 ... 54 D5
Wolverley Ct ROWN SO16 ... 54 E1 2
Wolverton Rd HAV PO9 ... 103 F1
SHAM SO14 ... 5 K8 2
Wolverton Wy SHAM SO14 ... 5 J8
Wolvesey Pl CHFD SO53 ... 37 H6 5
Wonston Ct HAV PO9 ... 83 J7 13
Wonston Rd ROWN SO16 ... 42 C7
Wood Barn Rd FHAM PO15 ... 12 A5
Woodberry La EMRTH PO10 ... 84 C6
HAV PO9 ... 84 A4
Woodbourne Cl FHAM PO15 ... 12 A4
Woodbury Av HAV PO9 ... 14 E7
Woodbury Gv HORN PO8 ... 64 A7
Wood Cl ITCH SO19 ... 11 M3
Woodcot Crs HAV PO9 ... 83 H7
Woodcote La
FHAM/STUB PO14 ... 115 H5
Woodcote Rd PTSW SO17 ... 55 K1 1
Woodcroft La HORN PO8 ... 63 K7
Wood End Wy NBAD SO52 ... 37 H3
Wooden House La LYMN SO41 .. 124 A6
Woodfield Av CHAM PO6 ... 101 K5
Woodfield Dr WINW SO22 ... 24 E2
Woodfield Park Rd
EMRTH PO10 ... 104 E5
Woodgason La HISD PO11 ... 121 K6
Wood Glade Cl TOTT SO40 ... 70 A4
Woodgreen Av HAV PO9 ... 14 B2
Woodgreen Rd WINW SO22 ... 21 G3
Woodhall Wy FHAM PO15 ... 12 D1
Woodhouse La HAV PO9 ... 83 K1
HEND SO30 ... 58 D4
HORN PO8 ... 65 H6
Woodhouse Rd HORN PO8 ... 65 G5
Woodington Cl HAV PO9 ... 83 H7 3
Woodland Cl WEND SO18 ... 57 G5
Woodland Dro RWIN SO21 ... 33 K6
Woodland Ms HEND SO30 ... 57 G3
Woodlands FHAM/PORC PO16 ... 98 A6
Woodlands Av EMRTH PO10 ... 104 B3
Woodlands Cl CHFD SO53 ... 32 A7
FAWY SO45 ... 91 F5
HLER SO31 ... 74 E7
LSOL/BMARY PO13 ... 131 K2
Woodlands Ct FAWY SO45 ... 91 F5 2
Woodlands Dr HLER SO31 ... 73 G7
Woodlands Dro TOTT SO40 ... 67 J2
Woodlands Gv WVILLE PO7 ... 101 J1
Woodlands La HISD PO11 ... 137 F3
RCCH PO18 ... 85 H3
Woodlands Rd TOTT SO40 ... 67 H1
The Woodlands WINC SO23 ... 22 B1
Woodland St PSEA PO1 ... 19 G1
Woodlands Wy HAV PO9 ... 103 G2 2
HLER SO31 ... 73 J5
NBAD SO52 ... 35 K6
WSHM SO15 ... 4 E2
Woodland Vw HLER SO31 ... 73 J5
HORN PO8 ... 64 A6
Wood La WHAM PO17 ... 79 K6
Woodlea Cl WINW SO22 ... 21 H5
Woodlea Gdns HEND SO30 ... 57 H3
Woodlea Wy ROMY SO51 ... 31 G7
Woodleigh Cl HAV PO9 ... 103 K3
Woodley Cl ROMY SO51 ... 29 H7
Woodley La ROMY SO51 ... 35 F1
Woodley Rd GPORT PO12 ... 16 C6 4
ITCH SO19 ... 10 A4
Woodley Wy ROMY SO51 ... 29 H7 3
Wood Ldg TOTT SO40 ... 52 A3
Woodman Cl RWIN SO21 ... 20 A5
Woodmancote La
EMRTH PO10 ... 105 H2
Woodmancote Rd ENEY PO4 ... 19 M6
Woodman La RWIN SO21 ... 20 B4
Woodmill La WEND SO18 ... 56 A1
Woodmoor Cl TOTT SO40 ... 70 B4 5
Woodpath SSEA PO5 ... 18 D8
Woodpecker Cl HAV PO9 ... 15 J4
Woodpecker Copse HLER SO31 .. 95 G3
Woodpecker Dr WINW SO22 ... 21 F5
TOTT SO40 ... 69 K4
Woodpecker Wy ELGH SO50 ... 44 A1
Wood Rd TOTT SO40 ... 68 A3
Woodrow WVILLE PO7 ... 80 D1
Woodrush Crs HLER SO31 ... 94 D4
Woodsedge WVILLE PO7 ... 82 B7
Woodside LSOL/BMARY PO13 ... 115 J2
ROWN SO16 ... 43 F1
Woodside Av ELGH SO50 ... 38 B7
Woodside Cl TOTT SO40 ... 69 K4
Woodside Crs ROWN SO16 ... 42 E1 1
Woodside Gdns TOTT SO40 ... 68 B3
Woodside Rd ELGH SO50 ... 38 B6
NBAD SO52 ... 36 A6 4
PTSW SO17 ... 5 K3
Woodside Wy HEND SO30 ... 57 K7
Woodstock Av HORN PO8 ... 64 B7
Woodstock Cl FHAM PO15 ... 12 C5
HEND SO30 ... 58 C7 6
Woodstock Dr PTSW SO17 ... 55 H3 2
Woodstock Rd GPORT PO12 ... 16 C6
HAV PO9 ... 102 D4
Woodthorpe Gdns HLER SO31 ... 74 E7
Woodvale FHAM PO15 ... 12 A4
Woodview Cl ROWN SO16 ... 43 H5
Woodville Dr PSEA PO1 ... 18 A7
Woodville Rd FAWY SO45 ... 110 E4
HAV PO9 ... 102 C4
Woodward Cl GPORT PO12 ... 132 C4
Woofferton Rd CHAM PO6 ... 99 K5
Woolford Cl WINW SO22 ... 25 F2 4
Woolmer Ct HAV PO9 ... 103 J1 10
Woolmer St EMRTH PO10 ... 104 B2
Woolner Av CHAM PO6 ... 101 F6
Woolston Rd HAV PO9 ... 82 D7
HLER SO31 ... 11 K9
Woolwich Cl HLER SO31 ... 73 J3
Wooton Rd LSOL/BMARY PO13 .. 131 H4
Wootton HLER SO31 ... 73 F6 8
Wootton St CHAM PO6 ... 100 E7
Worcester Pl ITCH SO19 ... 11 J6
Wordsworth Av CHAM PO6 ... 99 H5
Wordsworth Cl BPWT SO32 ... 49 F3
WINW SO22 ... 21 G7 1
Wordsworth Pl HLER SO31 ... 75 G4
Wordsworth Rd ROWN SO16 ... 54 D3
Workman's La HLER SO31 ... 112 D2
Workshop Rd WVILLE PO7 ... 99 K4
Worldham Rd HAV PO9 ... 83 J7
Worsley Rd SSEA PO5 ... 18 D8 11
Worsley St ENEY PO4 ... 135 F6 2
Worthing Av GPORT PO12 ... 116 C7
Worthing Rd SSEA PO5 ... 134 C6
Worthy Ct HAV PO9 ... 103 J1 21
Worthy La WINC SO23 ... 2 D2
Worthy Rd WINC SO23 ... 21 K5
Wraysbury Park Dr
EMRTH PO10 ... 104 C2
Wren Cl WINW SO22 ... 25 G3
Wren Rd ELGH SO50 ... 44 B2
Wren Wy FHAM/PORC PO16 ... 98 C6 8
Wrexham Gv HORN PO8 ... 64 C2 1
Wright's Hl ITCH SO19 ... 11 G5
Wryneck Cl ROWN SO16 ... 42 C5
Wyborn Cl HISD PO11 ... 137 H6
Wych La LSOL/BMARY PO13 ... 115 J2
Wychwood Dr FAWY SO45 ... 128 B1
Wychwood Gv CHFD SO53 ... 38 B2
Wycote Rd LSOL/BMARY PO13 .. 115 J3
Wyeford Cl HAV PO9 ... 83 J7 14
Wykeham Cl ROWN SO16 ... 43 F7 5
Wykeham Fld WHAM PO17 ... 77 H2
Wykeham Pl WINW SO22 ... 25 G3
Wykeham Rd HLER SO31 ... 72 E7
NEND PO2 ... 118 D6
Wyllie Rd NEND PO2 ... 118 D3
Wylye Cl WEND SO18 ... 56 E1
Wymering La CHAM PO6 ... 100 D6
Wymering Manor Cl
CHAM PO6 ... 100 D6 3
Wymering Rd NEND PO2 ... 118 D7
Wyndcliffe Rd ENEY PO4 ... 19 H8
Wyndham Cl HORN PO8 ... 82 C1
Wyndham Ms PSEA PO1 ... 17 M7 2
Wyndham Pl WSHM SO15 ... 4 D8
Wynter Rd WEND SO18 ... 7 J3
Wynton Wy FHAM PO15 ... 96 D3
Wynyards Gap NBAD SO52 ... 36 A6
Wyre Cl CHFD SO53 ... 37 J4
Wyvern Cl CHFD SO53 ... 38 A4

Y

Yaldhurst Ct HAV PO9 ... 83 J7 15
Yapton St PSEA PO1 ... 18 C3
Yarborough Rd SSEA PO5 ... 18 C8
Yardlea Cl HAV PO9 ... 83 J4
Yardley Cl HSEA PO3 ... 119 H3
Yardley Rd HEND SO30 ... 58 A7
Yarmouth Gdns WSHM SO15 ... 54 C3
Yarrow Wy HLER SO31 ... 94 D4
Yateley Cl HAV PO9 ... 102 D1
Yaverland HLER SO31 ... 73 F7
Yelverton Av FAWY SO45 ... 91 H5
Yeo Ct ENEY PO4 ... 135 H5
Yeomans Wy TOTT SO40 ... 52 E4
Yeovil Cha WEND SO18 ... 7 K3
Yew Rd WEND SO18 ... 7 H3
Yewside LSOL/BMARY PO13 ... 116 B6 7
The Yews HORN PO8 ... 64 E5
Yewtree Cl FAWY SO45 ... 91 H6
Yew Tree Cl HEND SO30 ... 58 A6 6
Yew Tree Dr FHAM PO15 ... 75 H5
HLER SO31 ... 75 G6
Yew Tree Gdns WVILLE PO7 ... 80 D1
Yewtree La ROWN SO16 ... 53 H1
Yew Tree Rd HISD PO11 ... 121 H7
Yoells Crs HORN PO8 ... 64 A6
Yoells La HORN PO8 ... 64 A6
Yokesford Hl ROMY SO51 ... 28 D4
Yonge Cl ELGH SO50 ... 38 E7
York Buildings SHAM SO14 ... 9 G2 1
York Cl ELGH SO50 ... 46 C4
NBAD SO52 ... 37 G6
SHAM SO14 ... 5 M7
TOTT SO40 ... 53 F4
York Crs LSOL/BMARY PO13 ... 131 H4
York Dro WEND SO18 ... 7 J5
Yorke St SSEA PO5 ... 18 B6
Yorke Wy HLER SO31 ... 93 H3
York Gdns FHAM/PORC PO16 ... 117 G1
York Pl PSEA PO1 ... 18 A2
York Rd ELGH SO50 ... 44 D2
WSHM SO15 ... 54 D5
Yves Ms SSEA PO5 ... 18 E9 8

Z

Zetland Rd CHAM PO6 ... 101 J7
GPORT PO12 ... 16 A4
Zeus La WVILLE PO7 ... 102 A3

Index - featured places

Abbey Chiropractic Clinic
ROMY SO51 ... 34 D3
Abbey Mead Surgery
ROMY SO51 ... 34 C3
Abbotswood Junior School
TOTT SO40 ... 52 C5
Abraham Gallery
SSEA PO5 ... 18 D8
Acorn Business Centre
CHAM PO6 ... 100 C6
Admiral Lord Nelson School
HSEA PO3 ... 119 G6
Albany Business Centre
WHAM PO17 ... 77 J6
Alderman Quilley
Secondary School
ELGH SO50 ... 44 C2
Aldermoor Health Centre
ROWN SO16 ... 42 D7
Allington Manor
Business Centre
ELGH SO50 ... 45 H4
All Saints Community
Primary School
WINC SO23 ... 3 H7
Alma Road Surgery
PTSW SO17 ... 5 G2
Alma Road Surgery
ROMY SO51 ... 34 E3
The Alpha Business Park
SHAM SO14 ... 5 L5
Alverstoke C of E
Junior School
GPORT PO12 ... 132 D5
Alverstoke County
Infant School
GPORT PO12 ... 132 D6
A M F Bowling
ITCH SO19 ... 7 G5
A M F Bowling
PSEA PO1 ... 18 D3
Ampfield Primary School
ROMY SO51 ... 30 D5
Anchor Business Centre
CHFD SO53 ... 37 J4
Andover Road Retail Park
WINW SO22 ... 2 C2
Anne Dale County
Junior & Infant School
FHAM/STUB PO14 ... 114 D5
Apple Industrial Estate
FHAM PO15 ... 95 H1
Applemore College
FAWY SO45 ... 90 D4
Applemore Recreation
Centre
FAWY SO45 ... 90 D3
The Art Gallery
EMRTH PO10 ... 104 E2
Art Space School
PSEA PO1 ... 134 B1
Arundel Court Junior &
Infant School
PSEA PO1 ... 18 E2
Ashurst Hospital
TOTT SO40 ... 68 A4
Associated Football Club
TOTT SO40 ... 53 F4
Atherley House Surgery
WSHM SO15 ... 4 B6
The Atherley School
ROWN SO16 ... 41 G5
Avington Park
RWIN SO21 ... 23 K2
Baddesley Park
Industrial Estate
NBAD SO52 ... 36 C6
Badger Farm Surgery
WINW SO22 ... 25 F4
Banister School
WSHM SO15 ... 4 E5
Bargate Museum
SHAM SO14 ... 9 G2
Bargate Shopping Centre
SHAM SO14 ... 9 G2
Barncroft Infant School
HAV PO9 ... 102 E2
Barncroft Junior School
HAV PO9 ... 102 D2
Barratt Industrial Park
FHAM PO15 ... 95 H1
Bartley C of E Middle School
TOTT SO40 ... 50 E5
Barton Peveril College
ELGH SO50 ... 44 C2
Bassett Green Junior School
ROWN SO16 ... 43 J7
Baycroft School
FHAM/STUB PO14 ... 114 E5
Bay House School
GPORT PO12 ... 132 B6
BBC South TV & Radio Solent
WSHM SO15 ... 4 E8
Beaulieu CP School
BROC SO42 ... 108 A6
Bedenham County
Junior & Infant School
LSOL/BMARY PO13 ... 116 A4
Beechwood Middle School
WEND SO18 ... 6 E4
Belbins Business Park
ROMY SO51 ... 29 F6
Belgrave Industrial Estate
PTSW SO17 ... 55 K2
Bellemoor Secondary School
ROWN SO16 ... 54 E2
Berrywood Primary School
HEND SO30 ... 58 C3
Bevois Town Primary School
SHAM SO14 ... 5 H4
Bidbury Junior & Infant School
HAV PO9 ... 14 A2
Bishops Waltham
County Infant School
BPWT SO32 ... 48 E3
Bitterne C of E First School
ITCH SO19 ... 6 F6
Bitterne C of E Infant School
ITCH SO19 ... 6 F6
Bitterne Health Centre
WEND SO18 ... 7 H5
Bitterne Leisure Centre
WEND SO18 ... 7 G5
Bitterne Manor Primary School
ITCH SO19 ... 6 B4
Bitterne Middle School
ITCH SO19 ... 6 F6
Bitterne Park Clinic
WEND SO18 ... 6 C2
Bitterne Park Junior &
Infant School
WEND SO18 ... 56 A2
Bitterne Park
Secondary School
WEND SO18 ... 56 B2
Bitterne Park Surgery
WEND SO18 ... 6 C2

Blackbrook Business Park *FHAM* PO15 12 C5
Blackfield Health Centre *FAWY* SO45 110 A5
Blackfield Junior & Infant School *FAWY* SO45 110 B6
The Boatyard Industrial Estate *FHAM/PORC* PO16 13 H8
Bosmere Junior School *HAV* PO9 14 E5
Botley Junior & Infant School *HEND* SO30 59 F5
Botley Park Hotel & Country Club *BPWT* SO32 58 E2
Boundary Oak School *WHAM* PO17 97 J1
The Bourne Community College *EMRTH* PO10 105 F5
Boyatt Shopping Centre *ELGH* SO50 38 D5
Boyatt Wood Surgery *ELGH* SO50 38 C5
Braishfield CP School *ROMY* SO51 29 J3
Brickfield Trading Estate *CHFD* SO53 37 J5
Bridge Gallery *WSHM* SO15 4 F6
Bridgemary Community School *LSOL/BMARY* PO13 115 K5
The Bridge Shopping Centre *PSEA* PO1 18 F3
Broadlands House *ROMY* SO51 34 D5
Brockhurst County Infant School *GPORT* PO12 132 C1
Brockhurst County Junior School *GPORT* PO12 132 D2
Brockhurst Medical Centre *GPORT* PO12 132 C1
Brompton Gallery *SHAM* SO14 5 H9
Brookes Hill Industrial Estate *TOTT* SO40 40 A7
Brookfield Secondary School *HLER* SO31 94 D2
Brookwood Industrial Estate *ELGH* SO50 38 C7
The Brownhill Surgery *CHFD* SO53 38 A3
Brune Park Community School *LSOL/BMARY* PO13 116 B7
Buckland Medical Centre *NEND* PO2 118 C7
Burgess Road Surgery *ROWN* SO16 43 K7
Burrfields Retail Park *HSEA* PO3 119 G6
Burridge Social & Sports Club *HLER* SO31 75 G3
Bursledon C of E Junior & Infant School *HLER* SO31 73 K5
Bursledon Windmill Museum *HLER* SO31 73 K3
Business Centre *SHAM* SO14 9 J5
Byngs Business Park *WVILLE* PO7 81 G3
By Pass Football Club *ROMY* SO51 34 E4
Cadnam Surgery *TOTT* SO40 50 D5
Calmore County Junior & Infant School *TOTT* SO40 52 B2
Calmore Industrial Estate *TOTT* SO40 52 D2
Calmore Sports Club *TOTT* SO40 51 K2
Calshot Castle *FAWY* SO45 112 A6
Cameleon Theatre *WSHM* SO15 4 A6
Campbell Surgery *SSEA* PO5 18 F7
Cams Hill School *FHAM/PORC* PO16 98 B6
Cantell Secondary School *ROWN* SO16 43 H7
The Canute Surgery *ITCH* SO19 10 C4
Castle County Primary School *FHAM/PORC* PO16 99 G7
Catherine Corbett Clinic *HAV* PO9 14 F3
Catherington C of E Controlled Infant School *HORN* PO8 64 C3
The Cedar School *ROWN* SO16 41 K7
Central Trading Estate *SHAM* SO14 9 L1
Centurion Industrial Park *SHAM* SO14 5 L5
Chamberlayne Park School *ITCH* SO19 11 G8
Chandlers Ford Infant School *CHFD* SO53 38 A3
Chesil Theatre *WINC* SO23 3 G6
Chevron Business Park *FAWY* SO45 109 J1
Christchurch Medical Centre *HAV* PO9 103 K3
Churchill Yard Industrial Estate *WVILLE* PO7 81 K4
City Business Centre *WINC* SO23 2 E2
City Grove Trading Estate *ELGH* SO50 38 B6
City Industrial Park *WSHM* SO15 8 C2
City Museum *PSEA* PO1 18 A7
City Museum & Art Gallery *PSEA* PO1 18 A7
City Offices *WINC* SO23 2 F5
The City of Portsmouth Boys School *NEND* PO2 118 D3
The City of Portsmouth Girls School *PSEA* PO1 19 G1
City of Portsmouth Sports Club *NEND* PO2 118 C4
Civic Centre *SHAM* SO14 4 F9
Civic Centre *TOTT* SO40 53 F4
Civil Service Sports Ground *HSEA* PO3 119 F4
Clayfields Sports Centre *FAWY* SO45 90 E2
Cliffdale Primary School *NEND* PO2 118 E5
Cluster Industrial Estate *HSEA* PO3 19 L3
The Coast Clinic *FAWY* SO45 110 E4
Colden Common Primary School *RWIN* SO21 39 J1
College Art School *WINC* SO23 2 D8
College Park Infant School *NEND* PO2 118 E5
Collingwood Business Park *FHAM/STUB* PO14 115 J1
Commercial Business Centre *CHFD* SO53 37 K4
Compton All Saints C of E Primary School *RWIN* SO21 33 G1
Continental Ferry Port *NEND* PO2 118 B7
Copnor Infant School *HSEA* PO3 119 F6
Copnor Junior School *NEND* PO2 118 E6
Copythorne First School *TOTT* SO40 50 E2
Corpus Christi RC Primary School *NEND* PO2 118 C6
Cosham Health Centre *CHAM* PO6 100 E7
Cottage Grove Primary School *SSEA* PO5 18 D7
County and Magistrates Court *PSEA* PO1 18 C5
Court Lane Junior & Infant School *CHAM* PO6 101 F7
Cowplain School *HORN* PO8 81 K3
Craneswater Junior School *ENEY* PO4 19 H9
Crescent Primary School *ELGH* SO50 38 D7
The Crestwood Community School *ELGH* SO50 38 C5
Crofton School *FHAM/STUB* PO14 115 F5
The Crookhorn Community School *WVILLE* PO7 102 A2
Cumberland Business Centre *SSEA* PO5 18 F4
Cumberland Infant School *ENEY* PO4 19 L8
Cupernham County Junior & Infants School *ROMY* SO51 35 G1
Curdridge Primary School *BPWT* SO32 59 J3
D Day Museum *SSEA* PO5 134 B7
Deacon Trading Estate *ELGH* SO50 45 F1
Deanery Campus *SHAM* SO14 9 J3
Dean Farm Estate *WHAM* PO17 97 H1
Delta Business Park *FHAM/PORC* PO16 97 J7
Denmead Health Centre *WVILLE* PO7 62 D7
Denmead Infant School *WVILLE* PO7 81 F1
Denmead Junior School *WVILLE* PO7 80 E1
Derby Road Surgery *NEND* PO2 118 C6
Devonshire Infant School *ENEY* PO4 19 H6
Devonshire Practice *ENEY* PO4 135 G5
Discover Bible School *WSHM* SO15 54 D6
Dockyard Apprentice Exhibition *PSEA* PO1 17 K3
Dorset Healthcare NHS Trust *WEND* SO18 7 L4
Dorset Medical Centre *SHAM* SO14 5 G9
Dr Munroe & Partners *TOTT* SO40 52 E4
Durley Primary School *BPWT* SO32 47 F5
Eastern Industrial Centre *CHAM* PO6 119 H1
Eastleigh Borough Council *ELGH* SO50 38 C7
Eastleigh College of Further Education *ELGH* SO50 44 D1
Eastleigh Football Club *ELGH* SO50 44 B4
Eastleigh Health Centre *ELGH* SO50 38 D7
Eastleigh Museum *ELGH* SO50 44 D1
Eastleigh Rugby Club *ELGH* SO50 39 F7
Eastney Health Centre *ENEY* PO4 19 M8
Eastney Swimming Baths *ENEY* PO4 135 H6
Easton Lane Business Park *WINC* SO23 3 J3
East Shore School *HSEA* PO3 135 G2
East Street Shopping Centre *SHAM* SO14 9 H2
Eling County Infant School *TOTT* SO40 53 F6
Elmhurst Business Park *GPORT* PO12 16 B5
Elson County Infant School *GPORT* PO12 116 D7
Elson County Junior School *GPORT* PO12 116 D7
Emsworth Museum *EMRTH* PO10 104 C5
Emsworth Primary School *EMRTH* PO10 104 B5
Emsworth Surgery *EMRTH* PO10 104 C6
English Gallery *HAV* PO9 83 K3
Enterprise Industrial Estate *HORN* PO8 64 D4
Fairfield Infant School *HAV* PO9 15 G4
Fairisle Junior & Infant School *ROWN* SO16 41 K7
Fairlands Montessori School *BPWT* SO32 61 F5
Fair Oak Junior & Infant School *ELGH* SO50 46 C2
Fairway Business Centre *HSEA* PO3 119 H4
Fareham Borough Council *FHAM* PO15 95 J1
Fareham Borough Council *FHAM/PORC* PO16 13 K5
Fareham Borough Council *FHAM/PORC* PO16 98 D7
Fareham College *FHAM/STUB* PO14 12 D6
The Fareham Gallery *FHAM/PORC* PO16 13 J6
Fareham Leisure Centre *FHAM/PORC* PO16 13 H4
Fareham Megabowl *FHAM/STUB* PO14 115 J2
Fareham Park C of E Controlled Junior School *FHAM* PO15 96 D3
Fareham Park Infant School *FHAM* PO15 96 D3
Fawley Business Centre *FAWY* SO45 110 D4
Fawley County First School *FAWY* SO45 110 D4
Fenwick Hospital *LYND* SO43 66 B7
Fernhurst Junior School *ENEY* PO4 19 J6
Flanders Industrial Park *HEND* SO30 58 A4
Fleming Park Leisure Centre *ELGH* SO50 38 B7
Flying Bull Junior & Infant School *NEND* PO2 118 C7
Forest Edge School *TOTT* SO40 52 D5
Forest End Surgery *WVILLE* PO7 81 J6
Forest Gate Surgery *TOTT* SO40 52 B5
Forestside Medical Practice *FAWY* SO45 91 F6
Fort Brockhurst *LSOL/BMARY* PO13 116 C6
Fort Cumberland *ENEY* PO4 135 K5
Forton Road Surgery *GPORT* PO12 16 A2
Fort Wallington Industrial Estate *FHAM/PORC* PO16 98 A4
Foundry Lane Middle & Primary School *WSHM* SO15 54 C4
Foxhills County First School *TOTT* SO40 68 C1
Freeground Junior & Infant School *HEND* SO30 58 C6
Freemantle Business Centre *WSHM* SO15 54 D7
Friarsgate Medical Centre *WINC* SO23 2 F5
Frobisher Industrial Centre *ROMY* SO51 34 C1
Front Lawn GM Junior School *HAV* PO9 83 G7
Front Lawn Infant School *HAV* PO9 103 G1
Fryern Junior & Infant School *CHFD* SO53 38 B4
The Fryern Surgery *CHFD* SO53 38 B3
The Futcher School *CHAM* PO6 101 H6
The Gallery *SSEA* PO5 18 D9
Gasholders *SHAM* SO14 5 K9
Gatcombe Park Infant School *NEND* PO2 118 E3
George & Dragon Surgery *EMRTH* PO10 104 E3
George Street School Branch Clinic *PSEA* PO1 134 E1
Glenfield Infant School *WEND* SO18 6 F4
Glenhurst School *HAV* PO9 15 G4
Glenwood School *EMRTH* PO10 104 B5
Goldfield Gallery *PSEA* PO1 17 M7
Goldsmith Infant School *ENEY* PO4 19 H7
Gomer County Junior & Infant School *GPORT* PO12 132 B5
Goodway Sea School *GPORT* PO12 116 D7
Goodwyn Gallery *PSEA* PO1 19 G3
Gosport Health Centre *GPORT* PO12 132 D4
Gosport Ice Rink *LSOL/BMARY* PO13 116 B6
Gosport Museum *GPORT* PO12 16 F5
Gosport War Memorial Hospital *GPORT* PO12 132 D4
Grange County Junior & Infant School *LSOL/BMARY* PO13 131 K1
Grange Farm Business Park *BPWT* SO32 60 D4
Gravatom Business Centre *BPWT* SO32 48 C3
Greatbridge Business Park *ROMY* SO51 34 C1
Greenacres School *WINW* SO22 21 H5
The Gregg School *WEND* SO18 56 D1
Greggs School *PTSW* SO17 5 G1
Grey Welles Surgery *HAV* PO9 103 G2
Group Surgery *ROWN* SO16 44 A7
Grove Medical Practice *WSHM* SO15 54 D5
Gudge Heath Surgery *FHAM* PO15 12 B2
Gurdwara Sikh Temple *SHAM* SO14 5 H6
Hall of Aviation *SHAM* SO14 9 K4
Halterworth CP School *ROMY* SO51 35 H3
Hamble County Primary School *HLER* SO31 93 H2
Hamble County Secondary School *HLER* SO31 93 H1
Hambledon Infant School *WVILLE* PO7 62 C1
Hammond County Junior & Infant School *FHAM/STUB* PO14 114 D5
Hammond Industrial Estate *FHAM/STUB* PO14 114 E6
Hampshire County Council *ELGH* SO50 38 B7
Hampshire County Council *ELGH* SO50 38 E7
Hampshire County Council *FHAM/PORC* PO16 13 K5
Hampshire County Council *GPORT* PO12 16 C6
Hampshire County Council *HAV* PO9 15 G5
Hampshire County Council *TOTT* SO40 68 E1
Hampshire County Council *WINC* SO23 2 C4
Hampshire County Cricket Club *WSHM* SO15 4 E3
Hamwic College *SHAM* SO14 9 H2
Hanway Group Practice *NEND* PO2 118 D6
Hanway Surgery *PSEA* PO1 134 C1
Hardley School *FAWY* SO45 109 K2
Harefield Clinic *WEND* SO18 7 H5
Harefield Junior & Infant School *WEND* SO18 7 K3
Harestock Infant School *WINW* SO22 21 G4
Harrison County Primary School *FHAM/PORC* PO16 13 K4
Hart Plain Infant School *HORN* PO8 81 K3
Hart Plain Junior School *WVILLE* PO7 81 K3
Haselworth County Primary School *GPORT* PO12 16 B7
Havant Business Centre *HAV* PO9 14 A6
Havant College *HAV* PO9 14 D1
Havant Leisure Centre *HAV* PO9 14 E2
Havant Museum *HAV* PO9 14 F5
Havant Retail Park *HAV* PO9 102 C5
Havant Rugby Football Club *HAV* PO9 14 A2
Havant Sports Club *HAV* PO9 14 E3
Havant Town Football Club *HAV* PO9 103 H1
Havant War Memorial Hospital *HAV* PO9 14 D3
Hayling Billy Business Centre *HISD* PO11 136 E4
Hayling Island Health Centre *HISD* PO11 137 H5
Hayward Business Centre *HAV* PO9 103 J3
Hazel Wood 1st School *TOTT* SO40 52 B5
Heathfield Infant & Middle School *ITCH* SO19 11 M4
Heathfield School *FHAM/STUB* PO14 96 D6
Hedge End Business Centre *HEND* SO30 58 A4
Hedge End Retail Park *HEND* SO30 57 K5
Hedge End Town Council *HEND* SO30 58 A6
Henry Beaufort School *WINW* SO22 21 H4
Henry Cort Community School *FHAM* PO15 96 C3
The Heritage Centre & Museum *TOTT* SO40 53 G6
Highbury College *CHAM* PO6 119 F2
Highbury College *PSEA* PO1 18 D3
Highbury College of Technology *PSEA* PO1 18 B1
Highbury Primary School *CHAM* PO6 119 F1
Highcroft Industrial Estate *HORN* PO8 64 D4
Highfield C of E (a) Primary School *PTSW* SO17 55 H2
Highgrove Industrial Park *HSEA* PO3 119 G4
Highlands Medical Centre *FHAM* PO15 12 A2
Highlands Medical Centre *FHAM* PO15 96 D3
Hightown Primary School *ITCH* SO19 73 H1
Hill Lane Surgery *WSHM* SO15 4 C5
Hill Park Clinic *FHAM* PO15 12 D1
Hillside Industrial Estate *HORN* PO8 64 D4
Hiltingbury County Junior & Infant School *CHFD* SO53 37 K1
Hindu Temple *SHAM* SO14 5 K7
Hiscock Gallery *SSEA* PO5 18 D9
Holbrook County Junior & Infant School *LSOL/BMARY* PO13 115 K4
Holbrook Recreation Centre *LSOL/BMARY* PO13 116 B6
Holbury County JMI School *FAWY* SO45 109 K4
Hollybrook First School *ROWN* SO16 54 E1
Hollybrook Middle School *ROWN* SO16 54 E1
Holy Family RC Primary School *ROWN* SO16 53 H2
Homewood Chiropractic Health Centre *FHAM/PORC* PO16 13 K4
Hook with Warsash Primary School *HLER* SO31 94 C6
Horndean C of E Junior School *HORN* PO8 64 D5
Horndean Community School *HORN* PO8 64 C5
Horndean Football Club *HORN* PO8 64 C5
Horndean Health Centre *HORN* PO8 64 E5
Horndean Infant School *HORN* PO8 64 D5
Hounsdown School *TOTT* SO40 68 E1
Hovercraft Terminal *SSEA* PO5 133 K6
Hulbert Junior School *WVILLE* PO7 82 A7
Hythe CP School *FAWY* SO45 91 H2
Hythe Medical Centre *FAWY* SO45 91 G4
Isambard Brunel Junior School *NEND* PO2 118 D7
Isle of Wight Car Ferry Terminal *PSEA* PO1 17 L6
Itchen College *ITCH* SO19 7 H8

J M L Trading Estate *WSHM* SO15 4 C9
Jubilee Business Centre *WVILLE* PO7 81 K5
Jubilee Surgery *FHAM/STUB* PO14 96 A6
Just Ahead Business School *PSEA* PO1 18 D1
Kanes Hill Primary School *ITCH* SO19 57 H6
Keble Memorial Primary School *RWIN* SO21 31 J3
King Alfred's College *WINW* SO22 21 G7
King Alfreds College of Higher Education *WINW* SO22 2 A6
King Edward VI School *WSHM* SO15 4 C2
King Richard School *CHAM* PO6 99 J6
Kings Copse Primary School *HEND* SO30 58 B7
Kingsland Market *SHAM* SO14 9 H1
The Kings Primary School *HEND* SO30 57 G1
Kings School *ELGH* SO50 46 A2
Kings School *WINW* SO22 24 E2
Kings Theatre *SSEA* PO5 18 F8
Kingsworthy Primary School *WINC* SO23 22 B1
Kin Hon Clinic *SSEA* PO5 18 B5
Knightwood Primary School *NBAD* SO52 37 G3
Lacey Lodge School *HSEA* PO3 135 G2
Langdown County Infants School *FAWY* SO45 91 J4
Langdown County Junior School *FAWY* SO45 91 J3
Langstone Junior School *HSEA* PO3 135 F1
Lankhills School *WINC* SO23 2 D1
Lee on Solent Health Centre *LSOL/BMARY* PO13 131 F2
Lee-on-the-solent Infant School *LSOL/BMARY* PO13 131 G3
Lee-on-the-solent Junior School *LSOL/BMARY* PO13 131 G3
Leesland C of E Infant School *GPORT* PO12 16 A5
Leesland C of E Junior School *GPORT* PO12 16 A5
Leigh House Hospital *CHFD* SO53 37 J2
Lido Sports Club *WINC* SO23 2 E2
Liner Industrial Estate *WSHM* SO15 54 D6
Locksheath County Infants & Primary School *HLER* SO31 95 F5
Locks Road Surgery *HLER* SO31 95 F4
Lockswood Surgery *HLER* SO31 95 F3
Longbridge Industrial Park *SHAM* SO14 9 K4
Longdown Estates *TOTT* SO40 68 D5
Lordshill Health Centre *ROWN* SO16 42 A7
LSU College of Higher Education *WSHM* SO15 4 F5
Lucia Foster Welch College *SHAM* SO14 9 J4
Ludlow Infant School *ITCH* SO19 10 C3
Ludlow Middle School *ITCH* SO19 10 D2
Lulworth Business Centre *TOTT* SO40 52 D2
Lydlynch County First School *TOTT* SO40 52 D5
Lyndhurst Infant School *LYND* SO43 86 C1
Lyndhurst Junior School *NEND* PO2 118 E6
Lyndhurst Surgery *LYND* SO43 86 C1
Malvern Business Centre *ROWN* SO16 54 E2
Manor Infant School *FAWY* SO45 109 K2
Manor Infant School *PSEA* PO1 134 D1
Mansbridge Primary School *WEND* SO18 44 B7
Mansel Infant & Junior Schools *ROWN* SO16 53 J2
Marchwood C of E Infant School *TOTT* SO40 69 K5
Marchwood Junior School *TOTT* SO40 70 A4
Marchwood Priory Hospital *TOTT* SO40 70 B6
Maritime Museum *BROC* SO42 126 E4
Marlands Shopping Centre *SHAM* SO14 8 F1
Marycourt Co-educational School *GPORT* PO12 132 D7
Mary Rose Exhibition *PSEA* PO1 17 K3
Mary Rose Ship Hall *PSEA* PO1 17 K2
Mason Manor Primary School *ROWN* SO16 54 A4
Mayflower Theatre *WSHM* SO15 4 D8
Mayville High School *SSEA* PO5 134 D6
Meadowlands Infant School *HORN* PO8 63 K7
Meadowlands Junior School *HORN* PO8 63 K7
Medina Primary School *CHAM* PO6 100 D7
Mengham Infant School *HISD* PO11 137 H4
Mengham Junior School *HISD* PO11 137 H4
Meoncross School *FHAM/STUB* PO14 114 E3
Meon Infant School *ENEY* PO4 135 G4
Meon Junior School *ENEY* PO4 135 G3
Meon Valley Golf & Country Club *BPWT* SO32 60 E4
Meon Valley Police Station *BPWT* SO32 48 E3
Merdon Junior School *CHFD* SO53 38 A3
Meredith Infant School *NEND* PO2 118 D7
Meridian TV Studios *SHAM* SO14 5 L6
Middle Park Medical Centre *HAV* PO9 102 D2
Millbrook Clinic *ROWN* SO16 53 K4
Millbrook Community School *ROWN* SO16 53 K1
Millbrook Secondary School *ROWN* SO16 53 K1
Millbrook Trading Estate *WSHM* SO15 53 K5
Millers Dale Surgery *CHFD* SO53 37 J2
Millhouse Business Centre *ITCH* SO19 10 A1
Milton Park Infant School *ENEY* PO4 135 G4
Milton Park Junior School *ENEY* PO4 135 G4
Monks Brook Industrial Park *CHFD* SO53 37 J5
Moorgreen Hospital *HEND* SO30 57 J2
Moorings Way Infant School *ENEY* PO4 135 H2
Moorlands Infant School *WEND* SO18 7 J1
Morelands Primary School *WVILLE* PO7 101 K4
Mountbatten Business Centre *WSHM* SO15 4 B8
Mountbatten Secondary School *ROMY* SO51 35 H4
The Mount Hospital *ELGH* SO50 39 G5
Mount Pleasant Industrial Estate *SHAM* SO14 5 K5
Mount Pleasant Junior School *SHAM* SO14 5 J5
National Motor Museum *BROC* SO42 108 A5
National Museum of Artillery *WHAM* PO17 98 E3
Natural Sciences Museum *ENEY* PO4 134 E7
Nelson Industrial Park *HEND* SO30 58 A3
Nethercliffe School *WINW* SO22 2 B2
Netley Abbey Infant School *HLER* SO31 72 E6
Netley Court School *HLER* SO31 92 E1
Netley Marsh C of E Controlled Infant School *TOTT* SO40 51 K5
Neville Lovett Community School *FHAM/STUB* PO14 12 E8
Newbridge Junior School *NEND* PO2 134 E1
New Forest Golf Club *LYND* SO43 66 E7
New Forest Museum & Visitors Centre *LYND* SO43 86 D1
Newlands Infant & Middle School *ROWN* SO16 53 K3
New Theatre Royal *PSEA* PO1 18 B4
The Newton Health Clinic *SHAM* SO14 5 H6
Nightingale County Junior & Infant School *ELGH* SO50 44 A2
Nightingale Surgery *ROMY* SO51 35 F2
Northam Business Centre *SHAM* SO14 5 L6
Northam Primary School *SHAM* SO14 5 L8
North Baddesley County Infants School *NBAD* SO52 36 C6
North Baddesley Junior School *NBAD* SO52 36 C6
Northbrook Industrial Estate *ROWN* SO16 54 D2
Northern County Junior & Infant School *FHAM/PORC* PO16 99 F5
Northern Parade Clinic *NEND* PO2 118 D3
Northern Parade Infant School *NEND* PO2 118 D4
Northern Parade Junior School *NEND* PO2 118 D4
Northview Gallery *HLER* SO31 74 B5
Norwood CP School *ELGH* SO50 38 D7
Nuffield Theatre *PTSW* SO17 55 H1
Nursling C of E Primary School *ROWN* SO16 41 J6
Nursling Industrial Estate *ROWN* SO16 41 G7
Nursling Industrial Estate *ROWN* SO16 53 G1
Oakfield Primary School *TOTT* SO40 52 D4
Oaklands Community School *ROWN* SO16 42 A6
Oaklands RC School *WVILLE* PO7 102 A1
Oak Lodge School *FAWY* SO45 90 D3
Oakwood First School *ROWN* SO16 42 C6
Oakwood Junior School *ROWN* SO16 42 C6
Oatlands House Health Clinic *ROWN* SO16 54 D2
Oceanographic Centre *SHAM* SO14 9 K6
Odeon Cinema *NEND* PO2 118 C6
Odeon Cinema *WSHM* SO15 8 D2
Oil Refinery *FAWY* SO45 110 C3
O Jays Industrial Park *HSEA* PO3 119 F5
Old Anchor Inn Surgery *ELGH* SO50 39 F7
Oldfield Gallery *SSEA* PO5 18 D7
The Old Fire Station Surgery *ITCH* SO19 10 D5
Olivers Battery Primary School *WINW* SO22 25 F5
On Line Gallery *WSHM* SO15 4 F7
Orchard County Infant & Junior School *FAWY* SO45 91 F4
Orchard Lea Junior & Infant Schools *FHAM* PO15 97 F2
Orion Business Centre *WEND* SO18 44 B6
The Osborn Clinic *FHAM/PORC* PO16 13 L5
Osborne Practice Surgery *SSEA* PO5 18 C9
Otterbourne Primary School *RWIN* SO21 32 E7
Padnell Infant School *HORN* PO8 82 B3
Padnell Junior School *HORN* PO8 82 C2
Palace House *BROC* SO42 107 K6
Palmerston Business Park *FHAM/STUB* PO14 97 H7
Park Community School *HAV* PO9 102 D1
Park Gate Business Centre *HLER* SO31 75 G7
Park Gate Junior School *HLER* SO31 95 G1
Park House Primary School *HAV* PO9 102 D1
Parklands Business Park *WVILLE* PO7 80 E2
Park Lane Medical Centre *HAV* PO9 102 E3
The Pascoe Practice *PSEA* PO1 18 A6
Paulsgrove Industrial Centre *CHAM* PO6 100 A6
Paulsgrove Primary School *CHAM* PO6 100 A6
Peacock Trading Estate *ELGH* SO50 38 B6
Peacock Trading Estate *ELGH* SO50 38 C5
Peel Common County Junior & Infant School *LSOL/BMARY* PO13 115 H5
Pegham Industrial Park *FHAM* PO15 76 C7
Penhale Infant School *PSEA* PO1 19 H3
Peter Dyer Gallery *SSEA* PO5 18 D9
Peter Dyer Gallery *SSEA* PO5 134 B6
Peter Symonds College *WINW* SO22 2 C1
Phoenix Industrial Park *ELGH* SO50 45 F1
Pilgrims School *WINC* SO23 2 F6
Pipers Wood Industrial Park *WVILLE* PO7 81 H5
Pitmore School *CHFD* SO53 38 C2
Plaza Theatre *ROMY* SO51 34 E3
Police Station & Courts *SHAM* SO14 4 F8
The Polygon School *WSHM* SO15 4 D7
Portchester Castle *FHAM/PORC* PO16 117 H2
Portchester Community School *FHAM/PORC* PO16 99 F7
Portchester Health Centre *FHAM/PORC* PO16 99 F6
Portsdown Group Practice *WVILLE* PO7 101 K3
Portsmouth City Council *CHAM* PO6 100 A5
Portsmouth City Council *CHAM* PO6 100 D7
Portsmouth City Council *CHAM* PO6 100 E6
Portsmouth City Council *HAV* PO9 103 G2
Portsmouth City Council *PSEA* PO1 17 M7
Portsmouth City Council *PSEA* PO1 19 G1
Portsmouth City Council *PSEA* PO1 134 D1
Portsmouth City Council *SSEA* PO5 18 C8
Portsmouth City Council *SSEA* PO5 18 D4
Portsmouth City Council *SSEA* PO5 18 E7
Portsmouth County Court *PSEA* PO1 18 C4
Portsmouth Crown Court *PSEA* PO1 18 C5
Portsmouth Grammar School *PSEA* PO1 18 A6
Portsmouth High School *SSEA* PO5 18 B8
Portsmouth Natural Health Centre *SSEA* PO5 18 B6
Portsmouth Rugby Football Club *HSEA* PO3 119 F3
Portsmouth Sixth Form College *HSEA* PO3 135 H1
Portswood Primary School *PTSW* SO17 55 K2
The Practice Doctors Surgery *FHAM/PORC* PO16 13 H5
Premier Business Park *FHAM/STUB* PO14 12 C7
Princes Mead School *RWIN* SO21 22 D1
Princess Anne Hospital *ROWN* SO16 54 C1
Priory School *SSEA* PO5 19 G5
Purbrook Cricket Club *WVILLE* PO7 101 G2
Purbrook Junior & Infant School *WVILLE* PO7 101 J1
Purbrook Park School *WVILLE* PO7 101 J3
Queen Alexandra Hospital *CHAM* PO6 100 D5
Queens Enclosure Primary School *WVILLE* PO7 82 B4
Queens Road Surgery *NEND* PO2 118 D7
Rachel Madocks School *HORN* PO8 81 J1
Ranvilles Junior & Infant School *FHAM/STUB* PO14 96 D6
Red Barn County Primary School *FHAM/PORC* PO16 98 E6
Redbridge Community School *ROWN* SO16 53 J4
Redbridge Primary School *ROWN* SO16 53 J4
Red Funnel Ferry Terminal *SHAM* SO14 8 F5
Red Gallery *SSEA* PO5 18 E9
Redlands County Primary School *FHAM/PORC* PO16 13 H9
Red Lodge School *ROWN* SO16 43 F7
Redwood Park School *CHAM* PO6 119 G1
Regents Park Girls School *ROWN* SO16 54 B4
Regents Park Surgery *WSHM* SO15 54 C4
Regional Film Theatre *SHAM* SO14 9 J6
Rex Industrial Estate *CHFD* SO53 37 K5
Richard Martin Gallery & Bookshop *GPORT* PO12 16 D6
Riders Junior & Infant School *HAV* PO9 102 E1
Ridgemede Junior School *BPWT* SO32 48 E3
Ridgeway House Special School *ITCH* SO19 6 E8
River Park Leisure Centre *WINC* SO23 2 F2
Riverside School *WVILLE* PO7 102 A3
Romsey Abbey C of E Primary School *ROMY* SO51 34 C3
Romsey County Junior School *ROMY* SO51 35 F2
Romsey Cricket Club *ROMY* SO51 34 E4
Romsey Hospital *ROMY* SO51 35 F3
Romsey Industrial Estate *ROMY* SO51 34 D1
Romsey Infant School *ROMY* SO51 34 E3
Romsey Rugby Football Club *ROMY* SO51 34 E4
The Romsey School *ROMY* SO51 34 D2
Romsey Sports Centre *ROMY* SO51 34 E4
Rookesbury Park School *WHAM* PO17 78 A1
Rowmans House Industrial Estate *ROWN* SO16 41 K5
Rowner County Infant School *LSOL/BMARY* PO13 116 A6
Rowner County Junior School *LSOL/BMARY* PO13 116 A6
Rowner Health Centre *LSOL/BMARY* PO13 115 K7
Rowner Swimming Centre *LSOL/BMARY* PO13 131 K2
Royal Hampshire County Hospital *WINW* SO22 2 B5
Royal Hampshire County Hospital *WINW* SO22 25 G1
Royal Hampshire Regiment Museum *WINC* SO23 2 D5
Royal Hospital Haslar *GPORT* PO12 16 F9
Royal Hospital Haslar *GPORT* PO12 133 G6
Royal Marines Museum *ENEY* PO4 135 G6
Royal Naval Museum *PSEA* PO1 17 J3
Royal Navy Submarine Museum Offices *GPORT* PO12 17 G8
Royal South Hants Hospital *SHAM* SO14 5 H6
Royal Winchester Golf Club *WINW* SO22 24 E1
Rushington Business Park *TOTT* SO40 52 D7
Russell Hicks & Temple *ROMY* SO51 34 D3
St Albans C of E Primary School *HAV* PO9 103 H3
St Andrews Surgery *ELGH* SO50 44 D1
St Annes School *LSOL/BMARY* PO13 131 F1
St Anthonys RC Primary School *FHAM/STUB* PO14 95 J4
St Bedes C of E Primary School *WINC* SO23 2 F3
St Catherines Road Junior School *ELGH* SO50 38 D5
St Christophers Hospital *FHAM/PORC* PO16 13 L2
St Christophers School *WEND* SO18 6 D3
St Denys Primary School *PTSW* SO17 5 M1
St Edmunds Catholic School *PSEA* PO1 18 E3
St Faiths Primary School *WINC* SO23 25 J3
St Francis Primary School *NBAD* SO52 37 G5
St Francis School *FHAM/STUB* PO14 96 D5
St Georges Beneficial C of E Primary School *PSEA* PO1 17 M4
St Georges Business Centre *PSEA* PO1 17 M4
St Georges Catholic Boys School *ELGH* SO50 43 K5
St Georges Industrial Estate *ENEY* PO4 19 L4
St Georges University School of Medicine *WINC* SO23 2 E4
St James C of E Primary School *EMRTH* PO10 104 B4
St James Hospital *ENEY* PO4 135 G3
St James Primary School *HEND* SO30 57 J2
St Johns Cathedral Primary School *PSEA* PO1 18 F3
St Johns C of E Infant School *HLER* SO31 95 H4
St Johns C of E Primary School *GPORT* PO12 132 E1
St Johns C of E Primary School *HAV* PO9 83 J5
St Johns College *SSEA* PO5 18 E8
St Johns RC Cathedral *PSEA* PO1 18 B2
St John the Baptist School *BPWT* SO32 61 F2

St Judes Catholic Primary School *FHAM/STUB* PO14 12 C6
St Judes C of E Primary School *PSEA* PO1 18 A7
St Lukes C of E School *SSEA* PO5 18 D4
St Lukes Surgery *HEND* SO30 58 A3
St Marks C of E Junior School *WSHM* SO15 4 A5
St Marys C of E Primary School *SHAM* SO14 5 J9
St Marys C of E Primary School *SHAM* SO14 5 K9
St Marys College *WEND* SO18 6 D3
St Marys Hospital *HSEA* PO3 19 M2
St Marys RC Primary School *GPORT* PO12 132 D3
St Marys Surgery *SHAM* SO14 9 J1
St Monica Infant School *ITCH* SO19 11 H4
St Monica Middle School *ITCH* SO19 11 G3
St Patricks RC Primary School *ITCH* SO19 10 C4
St Pauls Hospital *WINW* SO22 2 C3
St Pauls RC Primary School *CHAM* PO6 100 A6
St Peters School *WINW* SO22 24 E3
St Swithuns RC Primary School *SSEA* PO5 134 C6
St Swithuns School *RWIN* SO21 3 M4
St Swithun Wells RC Primary School *CHFD* SO53 38 A5
St Thomas Mores RC Primary School *HAV* PO9 14 A1
St Vincent College *GPORT* PO12 16 B3
Salterns School *TOTT* SO40 53 F4
Sarisbury Green C of E Primary School *HLER* SO31 94 D1
Sarisbury Infant School *HLER* SO31 94 D2
Sarum Road Hospital *WINW* SO22 25 F1
Saxon Shore Infant School *CHAM* PO6 99 H6
Scantabout Primary School *CHFD* SO53 38 C3
School *SHAM* SO14 8 F4
Shakespeare Business Centre *ELGH* SO50 38 E6
Shakespeare County Infant School *ELGH* SO50 38 D6
Shamblehurst CP School *HEND* SO30 58 B4
Sharps Copse Junior & Infant School *HAV* PO9 103 J1
Shawcross Industrial Park *HSEA* PO3 119 F2
Shepherds Down School *RWIN* SO21 33 F3
Sherborne House School *CHFD* SO53 38 A2
Shirley Business Park *WSHM* SO15 4 A6
Shirley Business Park *WSHM* SO15 54 D5
Shirley First & Middle School *WSHM* SO15 54 D3
The Shirley Health Centre *WSHM* SO15 54 D5
Shirley Swimming Pool *WSHM* SO15 54 D5
Shirley Warren Primary School *ROWN* SO16 54 B2
Sholing First School *ITCH* SO19 7 G9
Sholing Girls School *ITCH* SO19 10 F1
Sholing Infants School *ITCH* SO19 7 G9
Sholing Middle School *ITCH* SO19 7 G9
Sidings Industrial Estate *HLER* SO31 93 G1
Sikh Temple *SSEA* PO5 18 E6
Simcoe Clinic *WSHM* SO15 4 D5
Sinclair First & Junior School *ROWN* SO16 42 B6
Siskin County Junior & Infant School *LSOL/BMARY* PO13 132 A2
Solent Business Centre *WSHM* SO15 54 C6
Solent Industrial Centre *WSHM* SO15 54 D5
Solent Industrial Estate *HEND* SO30 58 A3
Solent Infant School *CHAM* PO6 101 J6
Solent Junior School *CHAM* PO6 101 J6
Solent Peoples Theatre *ITCH* SO19 11 L4
Somers Park Primary School *SSEA* PO5 18 E4
Somers Town Health Centre *SSEA* PO5 18 E5
Southampton Airport Parkway Station *ELGH* SO50 44 C5
Southampton Central Mosque *SHAM* SO14 5 K6
Southampton City College *SHAM* SO14 9 J2
Southampton City Council *PTSW* SO17 55 K2
Southampton City Council *ROWN* SO16 42 E6
Southampton City Council *ROWN* SO16 53 H2
Southampton City Council *ROWN* SO16 54 C3
Southampton City Council *SHAM* SO14 5 J9
Southampton City Council *SHAM* SO14 8 F3
Southampton City Council *SHAM* SO14 8 F4
Southampton City Council *SHAM* SO14 9 K1
Southampton City Council *WEND* SO18 7 L4
Southampton City Council *WSHM* SO15 4 C9
Southampton City Council *WSHM* SO15 4 F7
Southampton Football Club *WSHM* SO15 4 D6
Southampton General Hospital *ROWN* SO16 54 C1
Southampton Institute & Millais Gallery *WSHM* SO15 5 G8
Southampton Magistrates Court *WSHM* SO15 4 F6
Southampton & New Forest Magistrates Courts *WSHM* SO15 4 D8
Southampton Sports Centre *ROWN* SO16 42 E7
Southampton Sports Club *ROWN* SO16 53 H2
Southampton Technical College *SHAM* SO14 9 M3
Southampton University *ROWN* SO16 42 D2
Southbourne County Junior & Infant School *EMRTH* PO10 105 H6
Southbourne Surgery *EMRTH* PO10 105 H6
Southdown School *RWIN* SO21 33 F3
The South Downs College *WVILLE* PO7 102 B3
South Hants Country Club *WHAM* PO17 78 D4
South Parade Pier *SSEA* PO5 134 D7
Southsea Castle Museum *SSEA* PO5 134 B7
Southsea Infant School *SSEA* PO5 19 G9
South West Health Authority *HEND* SO30 74 A1
Southwick Park Naval Recreation Centre *WHAM* PO17 99 K1
Sparsholt Primary School *RWIN* SO21 20 A4
Spitfire Court Surgery *SHAM* SO14 9 M4
Springfield School *CHAM* PO6 101 H7
Springhill RC Primary School *WSHM* SO15 4 D6
Stakes Hill Infant School *WVILLE* PO7 82 A7
Stakes Lodge Surgery *WVILLE* PO7 82 B7
Stamshaw Infant School *NEND* PO2 118 C5
Stamshaw Junior School *NEND* PO2 118 B4
Stamshaw & Tipner Leisure Centre *NEND* PO2 118 B5
Stanbridge Earls School *ROMY* SO51 28 A6
Stanmore Primary School *WINW* SO22 25 H3
Stanton Industrial Estate *WSHM* SO15 54 B5
Station Theatre *HISD* PO11 136 E4
Staunton Park Community School *HAV* PO9 83 J6
Stoke Gallery *GPORT* PO12 16 B7
Stoke Park County Junior School *ELGH* SO50 39 H7
Stoke Park Infant School *ELGH* SO50 45 H1
Stokewood Surgery *ELGH* SO50 45 K1
Stroud School *ROMY* SO51 35 K2
Sunnyside Doctors Surgery *PSEA* PO1 19 G3
Sun Valley Business Park *WINC* SO23 3 K2
Super Bowl *WSHM* SO15 54 A5
Superstore *SHAM* SO14 4 E9
Superstore *SHAM* SO14 8 E1
Surrey House First School *ITCH* SO19 11 M3
Surrey House Health Centre *ITCH* SO19 11 M3
Swanmore Business Park *BPWT* SO32 49 G6
Swanmore C of E School *BPWT* SO32 49 J5
Swanmore County Secondary School *BPWT* SO32 49 H6
Swanwick Business Park *HLER* SO31 74 C6
Swaythling Clinic *PTSW* SO17 55 K1
Swaythling Primary School *PTSW* SO17 55 J1
The Synagogue *SHAM* SO14 5 G5
Talisman Business Centre *HLER* SO31 75 G7
Tankerville School *ELGH* SO50 38 E7
Tanners Brook Infant School *WSHM* SO15 54 A5
Tanners Brook Junior School *ROWN* SO16 54 A5
Tatchbury Manor House *TOTT* SO40 51 J3
Tatchbury Mount Hospital *TOTT* SO40 51 K2
Terminus Industrial Estate *PSEA* PO1 18 E4
Test Vale Surgery *TOTT* SO40 52 E4
Test Valley Business Centre *TOTT* SO40 53 G2
Testwood School *TOTT* SO40 52 E3
Thornden School *CHFD* SO53 38 C2
Thorney County Primary School *EMRTH* PO10 122 D4
Thornhill Clinic *ITCH* SO19 57 G7
Thornhill First School *ITCH* SO19 7 M7
Thornhill Junior School *ITCH* SO19 7 L8
Thornhill Park Surgery *ITCH* SO19 57 G6
Titchfield County Primary School *FHAM/STUB* PO14 96 A5
Totton College *TOTT* SO40 52 C4
Totton College *TOTT* SO40 52 D7
Totton Recreation Centre *TOTT* SO40 52 C4
Tower Industrial Estate *ELGH* SO50 45 F1
Town Hall *GPORT* PO12 16 E5
Townhill Infant School *WEND* SO18 56 D2
Townhill Middle School *WEND* SO18 56 D2
Townhill Park Health Clinic *WEND* SO18 56 D2
Townhill Surgery *WEND* SO18 56 E1
The Toynbee School *CHFD* SO53 38 A5
Treadgold Museum *PSEA* PO1 17 M3
Trinity Business Centre *TOTT* SO40 52 D2
Trinity Industrial Estate *WSHM* SO15 54 A5
Trojans Sports Club *ELGH* SO50 43 K4
Tudor House Museum *SHAM* SO14 8 F3
Turnpike Business Park *FHAM/PORC* PO16 13 K3
Twyford C of E Primary School *RWIN* SO21 33 J3
Twyford School *RWIN* SO21 33 K3
Twyford Surgery *RWIN* SO21 39 J1
United Services Cricket Ground *PSEA* PO1 17 M5
United Services Rugby Club *PSEA* PO1 18 A4
University of Portsmouth *ENEY* PO4 19 J9
University of Portsmouth *ENEY* PO4 135 G4
University of Portsmouth *HISD* PO11 136 A4
University of Portsmouth *PSEA* PO1 17 M3
University of Portsmouth *PSEA* PO1 17 M6
University of Portsmouth *PSEA* PO1 18 A4
University of Portsmouth *PSEA* PO1 18 A5
University of Portsmouth *PSEA* PO1 18 C2
University of Portsmouth *PSEA* PO1 18 F4
University of Portsmouth *SSEA* PO5 18 B8
University of Portsmouth *SSEA* PO5 18 C5
University of Portsmouth *SSEA* PO5 18 D6
University of Southampton *PTSW* SO17 55 J1
University of Southampton *ROWN* SO16 55 G1
University of Southampton *WSHM* SO15 4 F5
University Practice *SSEA* PO5 18 B6
Uplands County Primary School *FHAM/PORC* PO16 13 G2
Venture Industrial Park *LSOL/BMARY* PO13 116 A4
Vermont School *ROWN* SO16 43 F7
Victoria Cottage Hospital *EMRTH* PO10 104 C6
Victoria Park Swimming Centre *PSEA* PO1 18 B3
Victor Street Surgery *WSHM* SO15 54 C3
Victory Business Centre *PSEA* PO1 19 G4
Victory Retail Park *PSEA* PO1 134 B1
Victory Trading Estate *HSEA* PO3 119 G5
The Vine School *BPWT* SO32 59 J4
Virgin Cinemas *SHAM* SO14 9 J5
Wallisdean County Infant School *FHAM/STUB* PO14 12 D7
Wallisdean County Junior School *FHAM/STUB* PO14 12 E7
Waltham Business Park *BPWT* SO32 49 H7
Warblington School *HAV* PO9 15 J4
Warren Avenue Industrial Estate *ENEY* PO4 135 G3
Warren Park Primary School *HAV* PO9 82 E6
Warrior Business Centre *CHAM* PO6 101 K7
Waterfront Garden Surgery *FAWY* SO45 91 H1
Waterloo Industrial Estate *HEND* SO30 58 A3
The Waterloo School *WVILLE* PO7 81 K6
Waterlooville Football Club *WVILLE* PO7 81 K5
Waterlooville Health Centre *WVILLE* PO7 81 J3
The Waterside Health Centre *FAWY* SO45 91 H4
Waterside School *NEND* PO2 118 A4
Weeke CP School *WINW* SO22 21 G5
Wellington Sports Club *ELGH* SO50 44 A4
Wessex Nuffield Hospital *CHFD* SO53 38 C1
Wessex Nuffield Hospital *ELGH* SO50 38 E7
Wessex Regional Health Authority *HEND* SO30 58 A3
Wessex Superbowl *CHAM* PO6 102 B5
Westbourne County Primary School *EMRTH* PO10 104 E2
Westbourne Surgery *EMRTH* PO10 104 E3
West End Surgery *HEND* SO30 57 H2
Western Community Hospital *ROWN* SO16 54 B3
Western Primary School *WINW* SO22 21 G7
Westfield Junior School *CHAM* PO6 99 H6
The Westgate School *WINW* SO22 2 A2
The Westgate School *WINW* SO22 21 G6
West Hill Park School *FHAM/STUB* PO14 95 K6
Westlands Medical Centre *FHAM/PORC* PO16 99 F7
Weston Park Boys School *ITCH* SO19 11 L7
Weston Park First School *ITCH* SO19 11 H6
Weston Park Junior School *ITCH* SO19 11 G7
Weston Shore First School *ITCH* SO19 72 C5
Westover Primary School *HSEA* PO3 119 G7
West Quay Retail Park *WSHM* SO15 8 D1
West Quay Shopping Centre *SHAM* SO14 8 E1
West Wittering Parochial School *SELS* PO20 139 J7
Westwood Business Park *TOTT* SO40 52 E2
Whiteley County Primary School *FHAM* PO15 75 H6
The Whiteley Surgery *HLER* SO31 75 G5
Wickham C of E Controlled Primary School *WHAM* PO17 61 G7
Wickham Park Golf Club *WHAM* PO17 77 F1
Wickham Riding School *WHAM* PO17 78 B3
Wickham Surgery *WHAM* PO17 77 H1
Wicor County Primary School *FHAM/PORC* PO16 98 D6
Wildern Clinic *HEND* SO30 58 B5
The Wildern School *HEND* SO30 58 B5
Wildground County Infant School *FAWY* SO45 91 G5
Wildground County Junior School *FAWY* SO45 91 G5
Willments Industrial Estate *ITCH* SO19 6 B8
Wimbledon Park Sports Centre *SSEA* PO5 134 C6
Wimborne Junior & Infant School *ENEY* PO4 19 L6
Winchester Agricultural Museum *WINC* SO23 2 E2
Winchester City Museum *WINC* SO23 2 E5
Winchester College *WINC* SO23 2 E7
The Winchester Gallery *ROWN* SO16 55 F1
Winchester Lawn Tennis Club *WINW* SO22 21 G5
Winchester Rugby Football Club *WINC* SO23 3 G1
Winchester School of Art *WINC* SO23 3 G3
Winnall CP School *WINC* SO23 3 J4
Winnall Farm Industrial Estate *WINC* SO23 3 H3
Wolvesey Palace *WINC* SO23 2 F6
Woodhill Preparatory School *CHFD* SO53 38 A3
Woodhills School *HEND* SO30 58 E5
Woodlands Community School *WEND* SO18 57 G4
Wool House Maritime Museum *SHAM* SO14 8 F4
Woolston First School *ITCH* SO19 10 C5
Woolston School *ITCH* SO19 10 D4
Wordsworth Infant School *WSHM* SO15 54 D3
Wykeham House School *FHAM/PORC* PO16 13 M5
Wykeham Industrial Estate *WINC* SO23 3 J1
Wynford Farm Industrial Estate *ROMY* SO51 28 E5
The Wyvern Community Secondary School *ELGH* SO50 46 B2
Yeoman Industrial Park *TOTT* SO40 53 G2

Notes

Notes